COMPUTER-AIDED ARCHITECTURAL DESIGN FUTURES 2007

Computer-Aided Architectural Design Futures (CAADFutures) 2007

Proceedings of the 12th International CAADFutures Conference

Edited by

ANDY DONG
Key Centre of Design Computing and Cognition
University of Sydney
Sydney, NSW
Australia

ANDREW VANDE MOERE
Key Centre of Design Computing and Cognition
University of Sydney
Sydney, NSW
Australia

and

JOHN S. GERO
Krasnow Institute for Advanced Study
George Mason University
Fairfax, Virginia
USA

Springer

A C.I.P. Catalogue record for this book is available from the Library of Congress.

ISBN 978-94-017-8076-6
ISBN 978-1-4020-6528-6 (eBook)

Published by Springer,
P.O. Box 17, 3300 AA Dordrecht, The Netherlands.

www.springer.com

Printed on acid-free paper

Softcover re-print of the Hardcover 1st edition 2007

TABLE OF CONTENTS

PREFACE

Computer-aided architectural design has a very long history going back to the late 1950s and early 1960s when computers were used in the design and construction of the Sydney Opera House roof. For the first decades after then the use of computers remained peripheral to the primary activities of architecture although research continued apace. Over the last two decades the impact of computers on society had been matched by their impact on architecture. Initially in terms of documentation which soon morphed into the ability to model forms that would otherwise be difficult to represent through to novel concepts associated with virtuality. Architectural education embraced computers although the pedagogy that involves them varies very widely.

The early debates as to whether computational support would inhibit architectural creativity have now been resolved firmly in the negative. Much of today's architectural creativity is supported by computers. New areas have opened up, areas that would not have existed without computational support. New materials, novel forms, kinetic facades, kinetic forms and the various aspects of virtuality are all a function of the availability of computers and the research that has extended the range of computational support for design. Much of this is in evidence in these proceedings.

The *12th Computer-Aided Architectural Design Futures Conference*, held in Sydney, Australia in 2007, provided a forum for the presentation and discussion of a cross-section of the international research and development in computer-aided architectural design.

In these proceedings the 43 paper from 19 countries are grouped under the following eleven headings, inspired by Deleuze, describing both advances in theory and application and demonstrating the depth and breadth of the research in computer-aided architectural design. It is the nature of design to have no fixed nature, not to *be* in a static state but always in a state of *becoming* something other. Technology is our line of flight opening design to multiple becomings and multiple beings.

Becoming Virtual
Becoming Educated
Becoming Designed
Becoming Kinæsthetic
Becoming Logical
Being Supportive
Being Virtual
Becoming Tools
Becoming Futuristic
Becoming Determinable
Being Creative

Each submitted paper was reviewed by three referees drawn from the international panel of the referees listed. The reviewers' recommendations were then assessed before the final decision on each paper was taken. Thanks go to them, for the quality of these papers depends on their efforts.

Additional thanks to Mercèdes Paulini who assisted in the proofreading of the proceedings.

Andy Dong
Andrew Vande Moere
John S Gero
May 2007

LIST OF REFEREES

Henri Achten, Czech Technical University of Prague, Czech Republic
Francisco Santos Agostinho, Universidade Técnica de Lisboa, Portugal
Omer Akin, Carnegie Mellon University, USA
Zafer Bilda, University of Technology, Sydney, Australia
Dave Brown, Worcester Polytechnic University, USA
Carlos Calderon, Newcastle University, UK
Gabriela Celani, Unicamp, Brazil
Chiu Shui Chan, Iowa State University, USA
Chiung-Hui Chen, National Taiwan University, Taiwan
Mao-Lin Chiu, National Cheng-Kung University, Taiwan
Birgul Colakoglu, Yildiz Technical University, Turkey
Giovanni De Paoli, University of Montreal, Canada
Bauke de Vries, Eindhoven University of Technology, Netherlands
Lan Ding, CSIRO, Australia
Ellen Do, Georgia Institute of Technology, USA
Dirk Donath, Universität Weimar, Germany
Andy Dong, University of Sydney, Australia
Robin Drogemuller, CSIRO, Australia
Jose Duarte, Instituto Superior Técnico, Portugal
Haruyuki Fujii, Tokyo Institute of Technology, Japan
Thayaparan Gajendran, University of Newcastle, Australia
Petra Gemeinboeck, University of Sydney, Australia
John Gero, University of Sydney, Australia
Ewa Grabska, Jagiellonian University, Poland
Mark Gross, Carnegie Mellon University, USA
Ning Gu, University of Newcastle, Australia
Figen Gul, University of Sydney, Australia
Sean Hanna, University College London, UK
Christiane Margerita Herr, Hong Kong University, Hong Kong
Ann Heylighen, Catholic University of Leuven, Belgium
Urs Hirschberg, Graz University of Technology, Austria
Grazyna Hliniak, Jagiellonian University, Poland
Hans Hubers, Delft University of Technology, Netherlands
Tay-Sheng Jeng, National Cheng-Kung University, Taiwan

Nikolaos Kaimakamis, University of Athens, Greece
Axel Kilian, Massachusetts Institute of Technology, USA
Branko Kolarevic, University of Pennsylvania
Sotirios Kotsopoulos, Boston Architectural College, USA
Alexander Koutamanis, Delft University of Technology, Netherlands
Ramesh Krishnamurti, Carnegie Mellon University, USA
Pierre Leclerq, University of Liège, Belgium
Alpha Lee, Auckland University of Technology, New Zealand
Jackie Chia-Hsun Lee, Massachusetts Institute of Technology, USA
Robin Liggett, UCLA, USA
Ade Mabogunje, Stanford, USA
Mary Lou Maher, University of Sydney, Australia
Bob Martens, Vienna University of Technology, Austria
Elena Masala, Politecnico di Torino, Italy
Peter Matthews, Durham University, UK
Ali Mazalek, Georgia Institute of Technology, USA
Yukari Nagai, Japan Advanced Institute of Science and Technology, Japan
Herman Neuckermans, Catholic University of Leuven, Belgium
Rivka Oxman, Technion Israel Institute of Technology, Israel
Wei Peng, CSIRO, Australia
Frank Petzold, Universität Weimar, Germany
Jim Plume, University of New South Wales, Australia
Mike Rosenman, University of Sydney, Australia
Carmina Sanchez-del-Valle, Hampton University, USA
Larry Sass, Massachusetts Institute of Technology, USA
Rob Saunders, University of Sydney, Australia
Marc Aurel Schnabel, University of Sydney, Australia
Hartmut Seichter, University of Canterbury, New Zealand
Gregory Smith, University of Sydney, Australia
Masahiro Takatsuka, University of Sydney, Australia
Harry Timmermans, Eindhoven University of Technology, Netherlands
Zoopigi N. Touvra, National and Kapodistrian University of Athens, Greece
Andrew Vande Moere, University of Sydney, Australia
Aloys W J Borgers, Eindhoven University of Technology, Netherlands
Xiangyu Wang, University of Sydney, Australia
Madalina Wierzbicki-Neagu, University of British Columbia, Canada
Rob Woodbury, Simon Fraser University, Canada
Wei Yan, Texas A& M University, USA
Jadwiga Zarnowiecka, Politechnika Białostocka, Poland

BECOMING VIRTUAL

AUGMENTED REALITY AND TANGIBLE INTERFACES IN COLLABORATIVE URBAN DESIGN

A user study of augmented reality in an urban design studio

HARTMUT SEICHTER
University of Canterbury, New Zealand

Abstract. This paper outlines the design, execution and analysis of a user evaluation experiment using Augmented Reality (AR) in an urban design studio. The aim of the experiment was to gauge the differences between two interfaces in regard to their impact on the design process. The two conditions of the experiment were a direct manipulating tangible user interface and a pen-like 3D manipulation interface. Findings include differences in perceived object presence, performance measures, perceived performance and variations in the communication patterns. These findings have implications for the integration of this technology in a praxis relevant design work flow.

1. Introduction

Architectural design activity is, in large part, a joint effort of various parties. Supporting technologies have been subject of research in relation to distant collaborative work. Collaboration in the design process can, for instance, help to negotiate a consensus with the stakeholders involved. Collaboration can be conducted in various forms, through different media. However, some initial stages in the design process do not require a discussion with remote involvement.

Design collaboration in the early stages is similar to a brainstorming process, thus it requires free elaboration on a local platform for the purpose of presentation and manipulation. Usually the discussion takes place in a collocated setting. That means, the involved parties (e.g. designers, customers and consultants) gather in a local setting, allowing them to share information. To date this kind of communication in combination with digital design tools has not been investigated in detail. Emphasis in this research is given to the use of a localised table-top Augmented Reality (AR) setting as a

A Dong, A Vande Moere & JS Gero (eds), CAADFutures'07, 3–16.

discussion platform for spatial content for design. This study evaluates a multilayered communication system that tries to enhance collocated design through an AR environment with Tangible User Interfaces (TUIs). Objective is to foster these technologies for an externalised thought process for spatial content. This parallels conventional non-digital design tools, like the one in architectural design, which are functional as an external entity to provide a meaningful reference within the process of work and consideration.

AR provides new possibilities of three-dimensional input for the access of spatial content. But due to a lack of established methodologies no evaluation has been attempted in this area. This study will outline important issues of using augmented spatial representation for urban design.

Figure 1. Left (a): The BenchWorks table showing the virtual scenario with a massing model, initial developer proposal and a student design. Right (b): An earlier prototype with a pen-like 3D input device

Due to its status as an enabling technology AR can be applied in a diversity of user domain tasks. Naturally, existing studies are specifically tailored to task. Architectural design spans across various domains and inherently deals with spatial content. This overlaps with AR, where virtual and real spatial content converge. User evaluations in AR can utilise this breadth in order to outline a methodological framework. This study uses subjective and objective metrics to provide an insight in the practical usage of immersive AR technologies in the design process.

2. Context and Previous Work

This study is embedded in a wider body of work and extends the notion of other research projects. This section will shortly introduce the direct context of the research conducted and covers relevant earlier work.

Architectural design and the design process are influenced by the choice of tools and their application for the purpose of creating an architectural proposal. A series of studies in the Department of Architecture at the University of Hong Kong (Bradford, Cheng and Kvan 1994; Gao and Kvan

2004; Kuan and Kvan 2005; Kvan, Yip and Vera 1999; Schnabel and Kvan 2002) investigated the influence of digital media on the design process. The connecting theme of these research projects is to illuminate the impact of digital media, interfaces or settings on the design process and its outcome. Bradford et al. (1994) coined the term of the Virtual Design Studio and identified means of communication as a key factor for design within new media. Hirschberg et al. (1999) looked at the utilisation of time zones for a virtual design process and investigated the impact of the time shifts on the design process. Schnabel and Kvan (2002) extended this work by observing the quality of design and analysed communication across different settings, like Immersive Virtual Environment (IVE) and Desktop Virtual Environment (DVE). Gao and Kvan (2004) measured the influence of a communication medium in dyadic settings based on protocol analysis. Another study by Kuan and Kvan (2005) investigated the influence of voxel-based 3D modelling between two different technical implementations.

This study extends the aforementioned body of work into the domain of Augmented Reality (AR) and Tangible User Interface (TUI). This research is using a user evaluation to investigate TUI in a design aiding AR setting. It contributes new knowledge regarding the impact of different affordances of creation interfaces within the design process.

Only few studies brought forward methodologies for usability evaluation in AR by providing guidelines and a framework for simulation environments. A prominent body of research is the work at Virginia Tech (Gabbard, Swartz, Richey et al. 1999; Hinckley, Pausch, Proffitt et al. 1997) which provides taxonomies for usability evaluation of VEs. As Bowman et al. (2002) point out; these frameworks originate and are targeted at specific user groups with a 'problem' to solve. Therefore, each usability evaluation is tailored to a specific task.

For instance Tang et al. (2003) presented an AR system with the aim of assessing the feasibility of augmented assembly. However, it did not take into account the actual communication issues, which are important in a design setting where designers and their peers collaborate. Billinghurst et al. (2003) introduced a methodology for this problem covering a wider angle of aspects, like display technology and visual fidelity in regard to AR and communication. However, their experiment did not assess presence, which is an important metric for immersive systems (Sheridan 1992).

Designing with and within AR was investigated by few research projects. Aspects of collaboration between co-located parties have been covered by Regenbrecht et al. (2004) with a focus on social components of the collaboration process in AR. Klinker et al. (2002) identified visual fidelity and communication as important usability issues for AR through a system for design review and interactive collaboration. They highlighted the problem of feasibility in the visual representation within an immersive augmented display. ARTHUR (Broll, Lindt, Ohlenburg et al. 2004) is a system for collaborative urban design using AR for presentation. It allows designers a direct access to geometrical data and provides a tabletop immersive environment. Additionally it uses more advanced technology like see-through HMD and utilises a computer vision based tracking system for view and input registration. However, it attempts to incorporate manipulation techniques of CAD directly through spatialised 2D menus and does not provide an evaluation of this approach. Despite this, ARTHUR is in various ways similar to the system used here in this study. Tabletop AR has ben demonstrated as a viable technique to share information like plans, models and analytical data (Underkoffler and Ishii 1999).

This study looks into the usage and impact of TUIs for direct spatial manipulations in AR in a design environment. Earlier research implemented various ways to gain advantage from AR for tasks but evaluations were limited and did not cover variances in input devices for spatial content.

3. User Study

A usability evaluation allows an insight in how users perceive and interact with a system in a praxis relevant setting. It permits to create a hypothesis about the relation of interface, communication and the design task and the impact of human factors.

The aim of this study was to investigate TUIs, which lend themselves as a common ground for discussion in comparison to digitizer pens, which are inherently single user interfaces and have been adapted from 2D for the use in 3D. An urban design project in a Masters Degree course in architectural design was used as the context for the experimental setup. It provided a viable scenario for research of a collaborative AR system as it usually involves large virtual models, which need to be accessed by multiple users. Physical urban design models can be large in size and therefore difficult to handle easily. These physical properties also limit the ability of the model to present morphological information within its spatial context. For an assessment of the communication pattern the chosen scenario is valuable because urban design models are shared with several parties in order to discuss, analyse and re-represent design. These actions require the ability to change parts in-situ and visualise and discuss their impact. The experiment utilised a formal investigation task in order to evaluate the user input devices. This was preferential over using urban morphology methods, because methodological preferences would have masked the actual impact of the user interface.

3.1. INTERFACE CONDITIONS

The experiment design comprised of an observation phase and a creation phase. The observation phase utilised direct manipulated interfaces (i.e. AR Toolkit Markers) to view design proposals (see Figure 3). In the creative phase, users were asked to extend the design proposal. The independent variable in this experiment was the input interfaces for the creation phase of the design task. One condition implemented this through directly manipulated cubes (i.e. AR superimposed styro-foam cubes) (see Figure 2(b)), the other through a tool-object metaphor with a 3D pen based interface (i.e. Polhemus Isotrak with a 'Stylus') (see Figure 2(a)). In both conditions the users built an abstract massing model representing the extension of the existing proposal, which consisted of a fixed amount of cubes (see also Figure 1(a)).

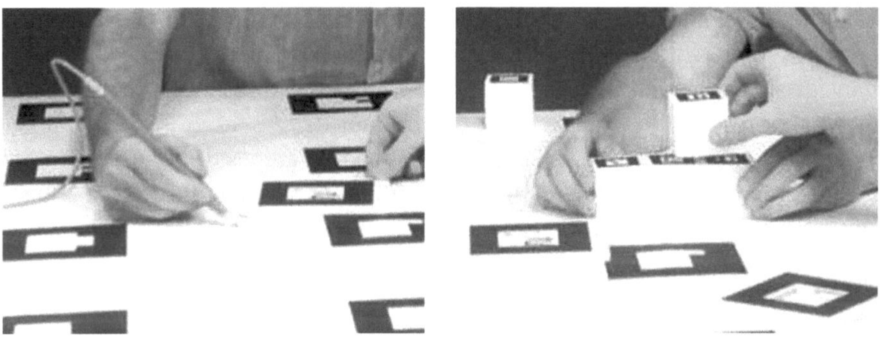

Figure 2. Left (a): Pen-shape interface for manipulation. Right (b): Tangible cube interface

3.2. PARTICIPANTS

Overall 28 students and staff from The University of Hong Kong (HKU) participated in the experiment. The age ranged between 22 and 40 years. The sample consisted of 9 female and 19 male participants. Overall, fourteen users used the pen setting, five female and nine male. The cube setting had the same amount of users, with four female and ten male. 21 were of Chinese origin, only 7 were of Caucasian origin. None of the users had encountered the system before. Four users identified themselves as practitioners, the rest as students. Six used Immersive Technology before, three of whom had more than five years of experience.

3.3. EXPERIMENT DESIGN

The experiment used a questionnaire for user survey and a video account of the trials with a subsequent coding analysis.

In order to get subjective data from the users a presence questionnaire developed by Gerhard et al. (2001) was choosen. Sheridan (1992) elaborates that presence is an essential metric for simulation environments and direct influences the performance 'within'.

The original design for the questionnaire anchored in a study about presence with an avatar aided VE. It was chosen as the most appropriate questionnaire for this experiment as it included aspects of direct collaboration, the presence of another person, the involvement in the task and satisfaction with the system. Original items related to avatars were replaced by questions about the other participant. Other minor adjustments were made in order to address AR specific issues and to reflect the architectural task in the brief. Conole and Dyke (2004) argue that an object providing an appropriate affordance, perceived or actual, contributes to the sense of presence. The questionnaire by Gerhard et al. (2001) originated from the 'Presence Questionnaire' (PQ) by Witmer and Singer (1998) which measures items like sensorial factors, distraction and realism. These are relevant in this experiment and were kept in the questionnaire. Presence questionnaires are a viable source of measuring the involvement with a simulation system. Gerhard et al. argue that awareness and involvement are essential for a sense of presence. This questionnaire also allows subcategories like 'spatial presence' important to understand for collaborative work with large datasets in collocated settings like the one in urban design.

Post-rationalisation of communication related items in a questionnaire is an apparent problem. A more reliable communication analysis can be achieved through post-experimental coding methods like the one proposed by Kraut et al. (2002). This coding schema analyses the videos taken during the experiment for instances where users *refer* to objects, name their *position* or *agree*. These three items are further divided in sub-items specifying the context. Thus, one can distinguish the frequency of references to an object directly or through the spatial context. Similarly, utterances regarding the position or the position context, agreement on general ideas or agreements on actions (i.e. behaviours) are coded.

3.4. DESIGN BRIEF

The design brief was tailored to the design studio the students were enrolled in at the time of the experiment. For the practitioners attending the experiment, the design problem was known as well. The task revolved around a publicly discussed large scale development project in Hong Kong. In a high density area, called Mong Kok, a development plan proposed to redevelop an area of low-rise buildings with high-rise buildings. Part of the research in the design studio was to prepare a design proposal for the area to be used for internal and public discussion. Hence, a key factor in the design brief was discussion. In the first phase both users had to discuss and choose between two design proposals on purely aesthetic grounds. These proposals were introduced to the users as suggestions by a fictitious developer. Both users were given AR ToolKit markers showing the virtual proposals as massing models; one L-Shape and a U-Shape high-rise building of the same height (see Figure 3). This phase of the experiment served as the initial encounter for the users with a tangible user interface. As result of their decision the users were asked to remove the rejected variant from the virtual building site.

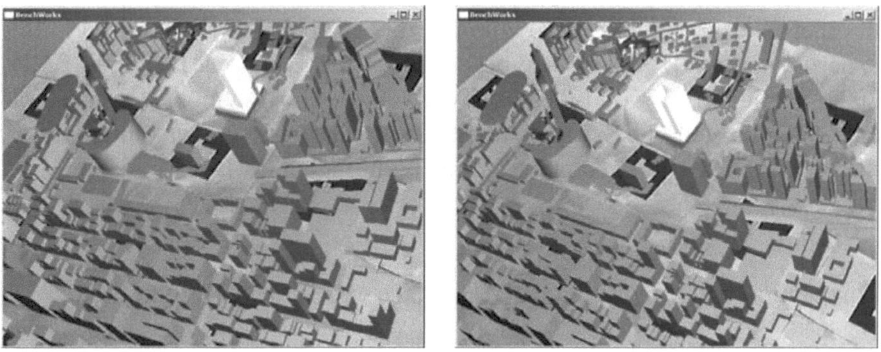

Figure 3. Left (a): L-shape proposal. Right (b): U-shape proposal

In the second phase, the users were asked to create an extension to the chosen proposal. The brief introduced some constraints regarding the extension. The users were made aware that the two phases were consecutive. Two spatial attributes within the brief for the experiment design were adjusted in order to make the task ambiguous. Ambiguity is needed to force the users to reinterpret the actual problem. The intention was to induce a discussion through an artificial wicked problem (Rittel and Weber 1984). This decision originated from pilot tests where it became clear that users went straight ahead to solve the task without any discussion of the actual task given. As the experimental set-up was ideal to review spatial content, factors related to the size of the massing models were made ambiguous. The virtual models of the proposals were skewed in their actual size.

3.5. APPARATUS

To capture data for this experiment a consistent experimental set-up was needed to let the users have an undisturbed experience. A software and hardware platform for this experiment called 'Benchworks' (Seichter 2004) was used.

'BenchWorks' utilised standard PCs for compatibility and maintainability reasons. The client systems consisted of two identical Dell Optiplex GX260 systems with 2.8GHz Intel Pentium 4 HT CPU, 512 MB of RAM, Western Digital 80 GB hard drives, Intel Pro/1000 MT Adapter and nVIDIA Geforce FX 5200 graphics adapter with 128 MB of DDR2 VRAM with AGP 8x enabled. The video capturing was supported through two identical Philips ToUCam Pro II with USB 2.0 HighSpeed interface. The server for connecting the client systems and handling the start-up sequence was a generic 1.5GHz Pentium 4 system with 512 MB RAM and an Intel Pro 10/100 Ethernet Adapter. All systems were connected with the local LAN at The University of Hong Kong through a separate SMC 4-port switch in order to reduce interference with network traffic. The HMDs used in this experiment were of different types. One was an Olympus Eye-Trek FMD-700, the other was an i-glasses SVGA Pro. The Olympus Eyetrak was connected through the S-Video interface with an AVERmedia Video splitter, the i-glasses HMD was connected directly through a DVI-VGA adapter.

4. Results

This section will provide an overview of the experimental results.

4.1. TIME MEASUREMENT

The users were asked to finish both phases of the brief in 20 min. They were allowed stop earlier if they fulfilled the brief. Expectantly the time to completion did not vary between the pen and the cube conditions. The users spent a mean time of 16 min. The difference between the two conditions was insignificant. However the time taken for the design phase was statistically different (t-value: 2.27, p-value: 0.04) (see Table 1).

TABLE 1. Time Measurements in min (values in brackets with removed outliers)

Condition	**Mean**	**σ**
Pen (Design)	5.8 (5.1)	4.1 (1.8)
Cube (Design)	10.1 (9.5)	3.9 (2.4)
Pen (Complete)	16.1	4.3
Cube (Complete)	16.2	3.6

4.2. PERCEIVED PERFORMANCE

Two items in the questionnaire assessed the impact of the tool on their perceived performance. The users judged the overall performance of the tool in regard to finalising the task. The data (see Table 2) show that these items were quite reliably reported. For the creation phase the data reported a significant difference between the conditions. The cube interface performed slightly better with statistical significant difference (t-value:-1.712, p-value: 0.01).

TABLE 2. Perceived performance for interfaces.
Range for means from 1–5 (1=agree, 5=disagree)

Relation	**Mean**	**σ**
Pen (Observation Interface)	2.8	0.95
Cube (Observation Interface)	2.5	1.40
Pen (Creation Interface)	4	0.78
Cube (Creation Interface)	3.2	1.53
Observation Interface (both)	3	0

4.3. PRESENCE

Presence is a key measurement factor for simulation environments. It measures the perceived level of the users being immersed within a system. Presence goes beyond the concept of immersion which is purely technical. There are various categories of presence. Spatial presence describes the 'being with' of a user in regard of the space of the simulated environment. Social presence reports in regard of a user 'being with' avatars, synthetic entities or real persons. Object presence is the state of 'being with' an object in the same space and shared with others (Witmer and Singer, 1998). Presence is important for this experiment as it is closely coupled with the concept of affordance and the performance within the simulated environment (Sheridan 1992). One item explicitly addressing the presence in regard to virtual objects within the same environment showed a statistically significant difference toward a preference for the cubes (see also Table 3).

TABLE 3. Comparing Means and Standard Deviation, t-test for all items

Item	**Mean (σ)**		**p-value**
	Pen	**Cube**	
The feeling of presence inside the simulation was compelling.	2.7 (0.83)	2.4 (1.09)	0.44
The other participant was naturally within my world.	2.4 (1.01)	2.7 (1.33)	0.43
I was so involved into communication and the assigned task that I lost track of time.	3.1 (1.03)	2.7 (1.33)	0.35
Events occurring outside of the simulation distracted me.	4.1 (1.10)	3.7 (1.27)	0.34
My senses were completely engaged during the experience.	2.6 (0.84)	2.6 (1.15)	1.00
Objects on the augmented urban design table seem to be part of my world.	3 (1.04)	2.1 (1.07)	**0.03**

4.4. COMMUNICATION PATTERN

There was no significant difference in the amount of utterances between the pen group (545 or 2.4 utterances/min per person) and the cube group (521 or 2.3 utterances/min per person) (see also Table 4). Nevertheless the communication showed different properties through the frequencies of utterances (see Figure 4). To investigate the communication patterns in more detail the sub items were measured regarding their density.

The absolute references (i.e. directly addressing objects in the simulation) showed a distinctive pattern for both settings with two peaks and a trough in between. The first peek accounts for the groups deciding for one of the proposals. The trough denotes the users changing the interface. And the second peak the discussion about the extension. Therefore the pen users used considerably more bandwidth in their conversation to discuss the design proposal.

TABLE 4. Utterances Data. Mean bandwidth in utterances/min per person

Category	Pen	Cube
References (R)	0.39	0.61
References in Context (CR)	0.40	0.32
Position (P)	0.53	0.34
Position in Context (PC)	0.32	0.31
Agreement for Understanding (AU)	0.64	0.59
Agreement for Behaviour (AB)	0.21	0.22

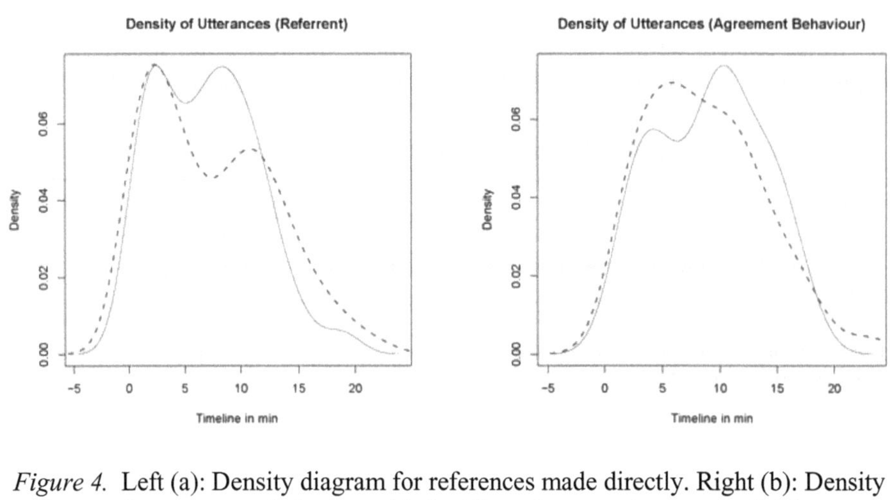

Figure 4. Left (a): Density diagram for references made directly. Right (b): Density diagram for agreement behaviour. (dashed lines denote cube-users, solid line pen users.)

5. Discussion

This user study used an explorative approach in order to gauge tendencies towards improvement or degradation between two interfaces. Furthermore, a user assessment regarding a design creation tool is not free from contextual influences. Therefore the data collected in this study might be only valid within the user population the experiment was conducted in. As reported there were a high number of 'early adopters' which is due to the specific curriculum at the undergraduate level at the HKU were students get exposure to various Virtual Reality systems and been taught to use them for design presentation.

In both conditions the participants finished earlier, however few groups took significantly longer to complete. The time frame for the design phase differed significantly. The cube users were using about double the time for design than the pen users. From the videos one can observe that the users in the cube condition spent more time on quickly discussing different (see Figure 5(b)) approaches, whereas the pen users were cautiously placing and moving cubes in the site (see Figure 5(a)). This difference can partly be accounted to the different affordances of the tools. The users with the pen needed to change to a different device. This change resulted in an adaptation to a different affordance of the tool in order to create objects. For the cube condition the users could perform the creation phase of the brief with the same learned knowledge of the first phase.

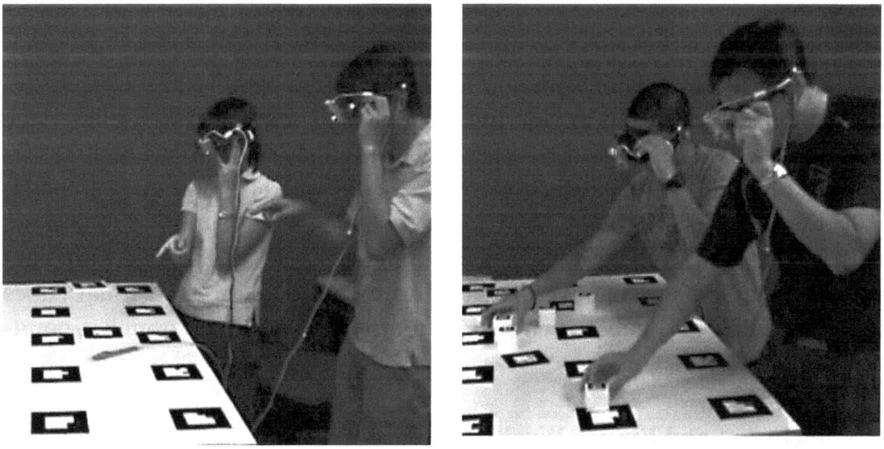

Figure 5. Left (a): Users in the pen condition planning ahead for the next move. Right (b): Cube condition users working in parallel on a solution

Gerhard, M, Moore, DJ and Hobbs, DJ: 2001, Continuous Presence in Collaborative Virtual Environments: Towards the Evaluation of a Hybrid Avatar-Agent Model for User Representation, *in International Conference on Intelligent Virtual Agents (IVA 2001)*, pp. 137-155.

Hinckley, K, Pausch, R, Proffitt, D, Patten, J and Kassell, N: 1997, Cooperative Bimanual Action, *SIGCHI conference on Human factors in computing systems (CHI '97)*, ACM Press, Atlanta, Georgia, USA, pp. 27-34.

Hirschberg, U, Schmitt, G, Kurmann, D, Kolarevic, B, Johnson, B and Donath, D: 1999, The 24 Hour Design Cycle: An Experiment in Design Collaboration over the Internet, *Proceedings of The Fourth Conference on Computer Aided Architectural Design Research in Asia*, Shanghai, pp. 181-190.

Klinker, G, Dutoit, AH, Bauer, M, Bayer, J, Novak, V and Matzke, D: 2002, Fata Morgana: A Presentation System for Product Design, *ISMAR '02: Proceedings of the International Symposium on Mixed and Augmented Reality (ISMAR '02)*, IEEE Computer Society, pp. 76.

Kraut, RE, Gergle, D and Fussel, SR: 2002, The Use of Visual Information in Shared Visual Spaces: Informing the Development of Virtual Co-Presence, *CSCW '02*, ACM Press, New Orleans, Louisiana, USA, pp. 31-40.

Kuan, S and Kvan, T: 2005, Supporting Objects in Voxel-based Design Environments, *in 10th International Conference on Computer Aided Architectural Design Research in Asia (CAADRIA 2005)*, New Delhi, India, pp. 105-113.

Kvan, T, Yip, WH and Vera, A: 1999, Supporting Design Studio Learning: An investigation into design communication in computer-supported collaboration, *in* CM Hoadley and J Roschell (eds), *Computer Support for Collaborative Learning (CSCL)*, Lawrence Erlbaum Associates, Palo Alto, Stanford University, California, pp. 328-332.

Regenbrecht, H and Schubert, T: 2002, Real and Illusory Interactions Enhance Presence in Virtual Environments, *Presence: Teleoperators and virtual environments* **11**(4): 425-434.

Regenbrecht, H, Wagner, M and Baratoff, G: 2004, MagicMeeting: A Collaborative Tangible Augmented Reality System, *Virtual Reality* **6**(3): 151-166.

Rittel, H and Weber, M: 1984, Planning Problems are Wicked Problems, *in* N Cross (ed), *Developments in Design Methodology*, Wiley, Chichester, pp. 135-144.

Schnabel, MA and Kvan, T: 2002, Design, Communication & Collaboration in Immersive Virtual Environments, *International Journal of Design Computing* **4**.

Seichter, H: 2004, BenchWorks - Augmented Reality Urban Design, *in* HS Lee and JW Choi (eds), *Computer Aided Architectural Design Research in Asia (CAADRIA 2004)*, Seoul, Korea, pp. 937-946.

Sheridan, TB: 1992, Musings on Telepresence and Virtual Presence, *Presence: Teleoperators and Virtual Environments* **1**(1): 120-125.

Tang, A, Owen, C, Biocca, F and Mou, W: 2003, Comparative Effectiveness of Augmented Reality in Object Assembly, *in* G Cockton and P Korhonen (eds), *CHI 2003*, ACM Press, New York, Ft. Lauderdale, Florida, pp. 73-80.

Underkoffler, J and Ishii, H: 1999, Urp: A luminous-tangible workbench for urban planning and design, in *Proceedings of the SIGCHI conference on Human factors in computing systems*, ACM Press, Pittsburgh, Pennsylvania, United States, pp. 386-393.

Vera, A, Kvan, T, West, RL and Lai, S: 1998, Expertise, collaboration and bandwidth, *CHI '98: SIGCHI conference on Human factors in computing systems*, ACM Press/Addison-Wesley Publishing Co., Los Angeles, California, USA, pp. 503-510.

Witmer, BG and Singer, MJ: 1998, Measuring Presence in Virtual Environments: A Presence Questionnaire, *Presence: Teleoperators and Virtual Environments* **7**(3): 225-240.

MUTUALLY AUGMENTED VIRTUAL ENVIRONMENTS FOR ARCHITECURAL DESIGN AND COLLABORATION

XIANGYU WANG
University of Sydney, Australia

Abstract. Augmented Reality (AR) augments real environment by means of virtual objects and Augmented Virtuality (AV) augments virtual environment with the insertion of real entities. Current AR and AV systems exist independently. This paper proposes a novel concept – Mutual Augmentation (MA) where AR and AV co-exist to form a seamlessly integrated mega-space by sharing certain real/virtual entity. This paper presents a systematic framework of exploring MA for supporting collaboration, communication, and coordination in architectural design beyond traditional single real/virtual space. It also opens up a key direction for future research into Collaborative Virtual Environments, AR and AV.

1. Introduction

Over the past decade, there has been a growing research interest and efforts in investigating techniques to combine real and virtual spaces. Various techniques have been investigated including Augmented Reality, Augmented Virtuality, Mixed Reality boundaries, etc. Milgram et al. (1999) presented a Reality-Virtuality (RV) continuum as shown in Figure 1 to describe the distinctions of those techniques. As a more enveloping term, Mixed Reality (MR) could create spatial environments where participants can interact with real and virtual entities in an integrated way (Milgram and Kishino 1994). Mixed Reality may also be shared and enable distributed people across multiple physical and virtual spaces to communicate with one another (Benford et al. 1998).

As a major sub-mode of Mixed Reality, Augmented Reality (AR) overlays virtual information onto a real world scene as if the virtual information is attached to physical objects (see the left example in Figure 2). In contrast, Augmented Virtuality (AV) (Milgram and Kishino 1994) takes a

A Dong, A Vande Moere & JS Gero (eds), CAADFutures'07, 17–29.

virtual world as its starting point and then embeds representations of real objects within this (see the right example in Figure 2). It is imperative to clarify the terms "real" and "virtual" entities/spaces. The real entity, either the augmented real environment in AR or augmenting real content in AV, refers to ones which the computer does not possess, or does not attribute meaning (Milgram et al. 1999). Real entity therefore could encompass any kind of sampled image data, and include photographic images (visible or infrared), image of real documents, real-time video, telemetry data, radar, X-ray and ultrasound, as well as laser scanned data (2D and 3D both range and light intensity data). In Augmented Reality, for instance, the real world scene could be either the local environment with the virtual information overlaid via an optical see-through head-mounted display, or a remote video scene augmented with virtual information. Likewise, the real entities in Augmented Virtuality might take the form of textured video views, such as real video views of human's face on his/her virtual avatar (Nakanishi et al. 1996), or views of remote physical locations (Reynard et al. 1998). Alternatively, telemetry data captured by remote physical sensors should also regarded as real entities, which could be visualized using graphics, text and audio, considering that computer does not hold any knowledge about the data. Likewise, the virtual entity, either the augmented virtual environment in AV or augmenting virtual content in AR, refers to ones which the computer does possess, or does attribute meaning. Virtual environments must consist of virtual entities in order to be rendered, and real environments must be representations of a real world, or region, involving only real entities.

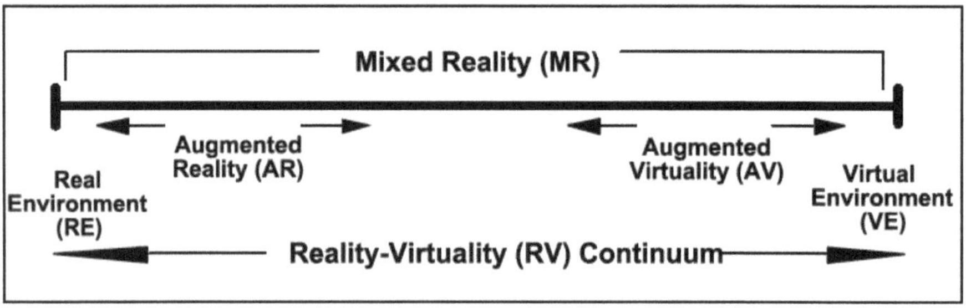

Figure 1. Definition of Mixed Reality within the context of Reality-Virtuality (RV) continuum (Milgram et al. 1999)

There are only two illustrations (Augmented Reality and Augmented Virtuality) which purposely emphasise the major distinctions between fundamentally opposing RV mixtures (Milgram et al. 1999), because it is obvious in these two terms whether the primary environment or substratum is real or virtual. There could be many other modes apart from distinct AR and AV along the RV continuum. A thorough observation of AR and AV systems reveals that either AR or AV exists individually. It is possible that the very real environment which is augmented in an AR space could meanwhile augment another virtual environment to create a resulting AV space. Likewise, the very virtual environment that is augmented in an AV space could augment a real environment and thus create an AR space. Thus, more modes along RV continuum might be possible and feasible. It is therefore argued that a more enveloping term becomes necessary, to encompass all modes between the extremes of the RV continuum. This paper develops a novel concept — *Mutual Augmentation* (MA) where real and virtual entities mutually augment each other, forming different augmented cells/spaces. In Mutual Augmentation, AR and AV could actually co-exist together to form a seamlessly integrated *mega-space* by sharing certain real/virtual entity. Mega-space is actually an environment formed by interweaving/inter-augmenting real and virtual spaces together. This concept puts equal weight onto real and virtual environments, considering how each can be accessed from the other. This paper presents a systematic framework of exploring Mutual Augmentation and applying this concept to support collaboration, communication, and coordination of architectural design beyond single real/virtual space.

Figure 2. Examples: (a) Augmented reality system (Wang et al. 2005); (b) Augmented virtuality system (Regenbrecht et al. 2004)

The concept of structured MA mega-space also opens up a key direction for future research into collaborative virtual environments (CVEs), AR and AV. This paper seeks to investigate how the concept of Mutual Augmentation could be integrated into the traditional CVEs concepts and development to improve the practice of designing in virtual environments.

Next section presents the MA Topology and explains the MA concept through case illustrations in architectural design. The third section presents the fundamental properties of RV interfaces in MA.

2. Recursive Hierarchical Mutual Augmentation Construction

This part investigates the alternatives of spatial topology which spans real and virtual spaces in a structured MA mega-space. Cases in architectural design/collaboration are exemplified and discussed for certain selected topologies.

2.1. HIERARCHICAL TREE

This section introduces the notion of the Mutual Augmentation construction, providing motivation for the subsequent more theoretical treatment. Figure 3 provides a simplified example of what a hierarchical representation of Mutual Augmentation construction might look like. There are two ways of adding spaces: Real (R) and Virtual (V), which could also be added together. MA hierarchical tree construction mainly consists of three legends: real subspace (solid line), virtual subspace (dashed line), and formed space/node (black dot). Each node represents a specific formed mega-space.

The tree hierarchy that is generated by the recursive application of a simple set of Mutual Augmentation rules could yield combinations with properties that strongly reflect their recursive hierarchical construction. Noting that the first mega-space may be conveniently represented by the node of a rooted tree (starting from a void space) as illustrated as "0" in Figure 3. The second level of mega-space is formed by adding subspaces (either real or virtual) onto the above mega-space. Therefore, the rule is set as: the subsequent mega-space at the immediately lower level is formed by superimposing the relevant real and/or virtual subspace onto the mega-space at the immediately higher level. The rule can be applied repeatedly for i = 1, 2, 3…, n times starting from a void space "0", and using the mega-space from a previous node as the starting point for the next node. For example, the mega-space on the bottom of the hierarchy in Figure 3 could be as complicated as VRVRRVRVVR, which has five real spaces and five virtual spaces interweaved and inter-overlaid and inter-augmented with each other. Not each node inside the tree could be matched to a counterpart of a realistic application scenario in architectural design, but might matter in future as technology advances.

It is possible that the very real space which is augmented in an AR space could meanwhile augment another virtual space to create a resulting AV space. Likewise, the very virtual space that is augmented in an AV space could augment a real space and thus create an AR space. Therefore each intermediate node in the hierarchical tree actually augments its immediately higher-level node and meanwhile is augmented by its immediately lower level node(s). For example, in the case of node "a" (RV) in Figure 3, it augments the node "c" (R) with a virtual subspace represented by a dashed line and are augmented by "g" (RVR) with a real subspace and by "h" (RVV) with a virtual subspace.

The real extreme in the RV continuum in Figure 1 actually could be represented by node "c" (R) in the Figure 3. Likewise, the other extreme which is virtual environment, corresponds to the node "d" (V) in the Figure 3. The AR example (Wang et al. 2005) shown in Figure 2 actually corresponds to the node "a" (RV) in the Figure 3 because a virtual mechanical design is inserted into the designers' common real working/viewing environment. The AV example (Regenbrecht et al. 2004) in Figure 2, actually fits to the case of node "b" + "e" (VR+VV) on the same level, but under the same previous mega-space because there are two types of subspaces inserted into the base environment "d": real video image of remote collaborators for note "b" (VR) and virtual car product design for note "e" (VV).

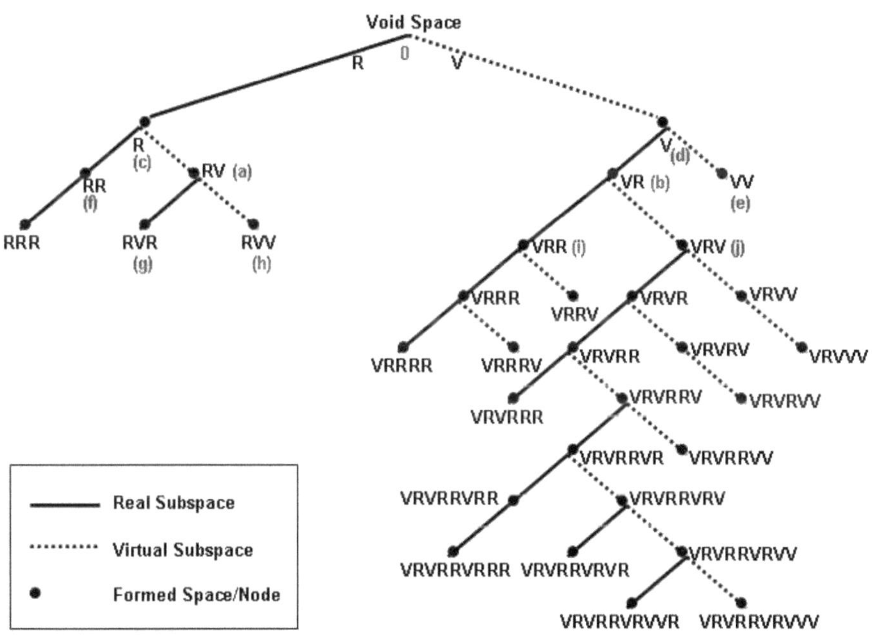

Figure 3. A simplified example of recursive hierarchical mutual augmentation construction

Two segmented spaces in two independent/individual mega-spaces could also metaphorically augment with each other although they are not structurally located along one path in the recursive hierarchical MA construction. A spatially segmented interface links the two spaces through multiple non-adjacent segments (these can themselves be property segmented). For example, the real design documents and experts of a specialty service (real entities in one mega-space) in one project could be borrowed into another project (virtual environment in another mega-space) by texture-mapping them into the appropriate positions in the virtual design environment with appropriate format (e.g. experts as videoconferencing; real design documents as real images). Theoretically reflected in the recursive hierarchical MA construction in Figure 3, for instance, the virtual space in the node "h" (RVV) could augment the real space in the node "i" (VRR), forming another resulting Augmented Reality mega-space. As explained above, the hierarchical tree representing a recursive MA construction could be much topologically complicated and involve much inter-augmentation among any nodes inside the tree.

In the following subsection, one case is illustrated to demonstrate why this hierarchy is potentially interesting and thus motivates more theoretical investigation. By introducing MA into collaborative virtual environments across real and virtual spaces, the resulting mega-space could support architectural designers' social interaction and convert digital communication media from being socially conservative to a more generative and familiar form as in real space.

2.2. CASE ILLUSTRATION IN ARCHITECTURAL DESIGN

Based upon Milgram's exploration of the Reality-Virtuality continuum (Milgram et al. 1999), an MA continuum is formulated from certain nodes identified from Figure 3. The MA continuum spans from a completely real space (mode "c") and a completely virtual one (mode "d").

2.2.1. Mutual Augmentation Continuum

A simplified case of MA continuum is illustrated in Figure 4 by allowing only one real and/or one virtual space registered into a predominantly real or virtual substratum space (e.g. mode "a"), to schematically demonstrate a selection of scene composites that could be encountered when one play with combining real and virtual spaces. At a global level, Figure 4 corresponds to the RV continuum along which any number of virtual and real spaces could exist. Furthermore, each mode in this simplified case could find a corresponding counterpart in the hierarchical tree in Figure 5 with the same representation letter. In terms of earlier examples, for instance, the AR example in Figure 2 could be considered to correspond to the mode "a" in Figure 4, in the sense that it has a predominantly real environment as substratum with a few virtual objects superimposed. The AV example in Figure 2, furthermore, would correspond to the mode "b+e", for analogous reasons.

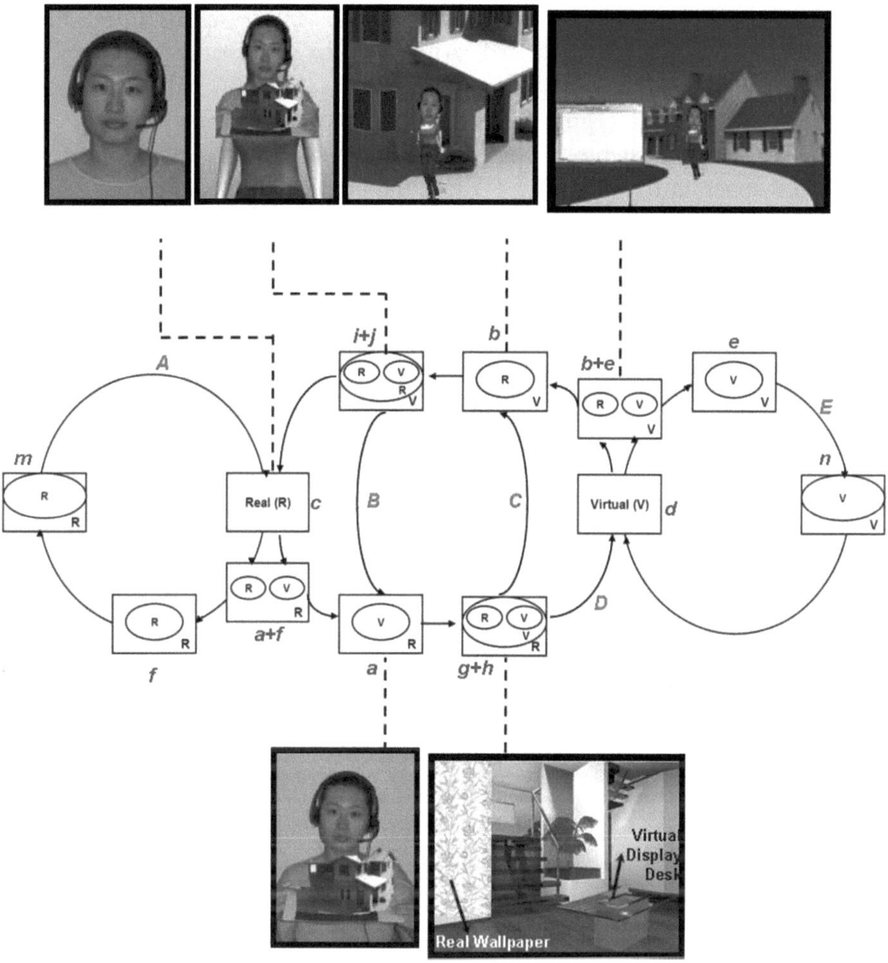

Figure 4. An example of Mutual Augmentation continuum: illustration of MA combination spaces as experienced through a journey

From Figure 4, it is also shown that real and virtual spaces can "flow" into each other recursively (Milgram et al. 1999). Another important aspect of the schematic representation of Figure 4 is the essentially trajectory nature of the MA continuum. Figure 4 illustrates that there are mainly five interesting trajectories along the transverse between the modes "c" and "d": two self- trajectories "A" (real-to-real: "c" –> "a+f" –> "f" –> "m" –> "c") and "E" (virtual-to-virtual: "d" –> "b+e" –> "e" –> "n" –> "d"), and three in-between trajectories "B" ("c" –> "a+f" –> "a" –> "g+h" –> "b" –> "i+j" –> "c"), "C" ("d" –> "b+e" –> "b" –> "i+j" –> "a" –> "g+h" –> "d"), and "D" ("c" –> "a+f" –> "a" –> "g+h" –> "d" –> "b+e" –> "b" –> "i+j" –> "c"). As illustrated in the self-trajectory "A" and "E", we turn the next doorway into a virtual portal from the mode "b+e", depicting an adjoining virtual presentation bulletin board. Alternatively, we could turn to a real portal by following the in-between trajectory "B" or "D". Likewise applies in three trajectories diverging from mode "c" (for trajectory "A", "C", and "D"). Clearly, it is possible to continue in this manner, enter completely into the virtual space in the mode "a+f", and thus traverses the trajectory "C" or "D" to get back to real space "c". Eventually along the two self- trajectories, if the entire visible image, or view port, consisted of virtual/real objects, one could argue that we had arrived (returned) at the completely virtual/real case of mode "c" and "d" again.

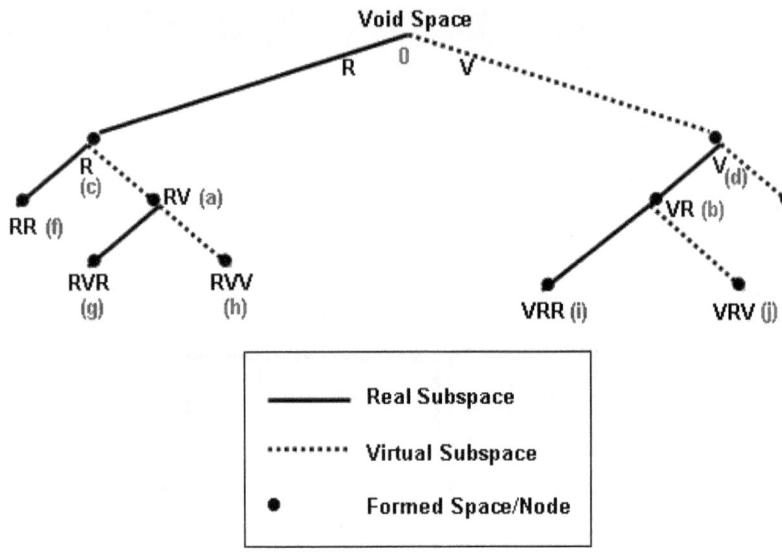

Figure 5. The recursive hierarchy of the case illustration

2.2.2. Case Illustration in the Context of Design

Now, we begin to use a case illustration to verify how the MA concept is applied in the context of architectural design collaboration. In the following we present an analogous case to concretely demonstrate the power of transitions in Figure 4. What we shall do is to illustrate what a journey along the MA continuum might look like, as we travel along some trajectories in Figure 4. The point of departure is mode "d", which shows a completely virtual residential area to give me an overall sense of the layout of houses that are proposed to be built. It is assumed that I, the actor of the journey, am the chief architect of this area. To continue the journey, we purposely insert a real space (video of a remote house designer attached to a virtual avatar standing in front of a house) and a virtual one (a design information and documents presentation bulletin) into the virtual residential area, thus forming the mode “b+e”. The virtual space could expand and eventually end up with another completely virtual space back to the mode “e”. If I choose the self-trajectory “E” by stepping into another virtual space, then I will be involved into a virtual presentation board for discussion of issues such as urban planning and environmental regulations or other rules. If I select the in-between trajectory “B or “D”, then I could communicate with the remote house designer whose appearance is displayed as a real-time video appearance texture mapped to the virtual avatar standing in front of a specific house of interests for further inspection as shown in the mode “b”. Thus an AV scene has been created with the virtual space as the registration base for the real entities upon it. As I approach the real portal framed by the video window by zooming in, the composite image becomes proportionately more real and less virtual. Finally, as I advance all the way through the real portal, in the mode “b”, I enter into real environment/real video (mode “i”). It is not the end and as illustrated in Figure 4, if I look in further, it is found that a virtual house is superimposed onto the hand of the designer in the video (mode “j”), thus an AR scene has been created with the real video screen as the registration base for the virtual entities upon it. Next, I could choose from the mode “i+j” to continue talking with the designer only by following the trajectory “D” and then reaching the mode “c”. Alternatively, as I approach the virtual house by zooming in, the composite image becomes proportionately more real and less virtual. Finally, I could advance all the way and “step” into the video and click the door of the virtual house and virtually entering the completely virtual house. For that, I am actually following the trajectory “B” and reach the mode “a” as the next step. Inside the virtual house as illustrated in the mode “g+h”, I encounter two choices again: one is to look at the digital design specification on the virtual display desk (follows trajectory “D” and ends at the mode “d”; be occupied into another virtual space) and the other one is to choose the real wallpaper samples represented by the real photos stored in remote supplier’s repository (follows trajectory “C” and reach the mode “b” again). Real images of wallpapers can be captured in real-time and texture-mapped onto the virtual walls to decorate it with much of the richness of the real world. Theoretically, the story could continue indefinitely along the MA continuum and reach the necessary stop mode.

3. Fundamental Properties in RV Interfaces

The concept of Mutually Augmentation connects distinct real and virtual spaces by creating bi-directional RV interfaces between them. A set of properties associated with RV interfaces in the context of architectural design are identified in this section, based on Mixed Reality boundaries theory by Benford et al. (Benford et al. 1996; Benford et al. 1998; Koleva et al. 1999). In their approach, the real and virtual spaces are not overlaid, but instead are distinct but adjacent. In contrast, the MA approach involves distinct but overlaid real and virtual spaces. These two approaches do share certain common properties with each other. The purpose of identifying these properties is to provide an analytic framework for supporting the design and analysis of RV interfaces and MA mega-spaces for a broad range of cooperative activities in architectural design. Examples of theses activities are product/design presentation, distributed design review, design document spaces, design document collaborative editing, etc. Different cooperative activities apparently involve varying requirements for communication, awareness, and even privacy (Benford et al. 1998). These properties are discussed in the context of architectural design below.

3.1. INFORMATION ACROSS RV INTERFACE

There are two major types of sensory information that can pass between the overlaid spaces in MA, which are visual and audio information. Visual quality determines the amount of visual information that is allowed through the interface and depends on the presentation format and level of graphical detail (Benford et al. 1996). For instance, a real remote building site could be transmitted back via computer network and dynamically textured mapped onto the corresponding virtual site in a virtual design environment with high fidelity format as a monitoring video captured by camera, or with low fidelity format as a still image. What audio information is permitted through the interface is determined by the way of rendering the audio information (Benford et al. 1996). For example, audio like project coordinator's announcement/discussions could be projected to a public system in the virtual design environment so that its effects are amplified to reach all the virtual design team members. Another example is to locate and render the real unprocessed building sound design in a spatially consistent manner to test its functionality in the virtual building. The issue of spatial consistency is a very important one as it affects the level of details to which participants on opposite sides can establish mutual orientation.

3.2. SPATIAL FACTORS OF RV INTERFACES

The spatial factors of RV interfaces include position, orientation, geometry, translation, and rotation. These spatial factors are elaborated in the following subsections.

3.2.1. Position and Orientation

Position and orientation describes the placement of the RV interface within the connected spaces. For example, one RV interface could be vertically located onto a virtual wall so that designers could assess the atheistic effects of proposed wallpapers by texture-mapping the real image of wallpaper samples from suppliers. A horizontal location involving projection onto a virtual desk or board could establish the boundary as a shared drawing surface or a platform to review real design documents which are most relevant to the facility the designers are standing in.

3.2.2. Geometry

Geometry determines the contour/shape of RV interfaces. If the display for the RV interface is large enough, the image of real space (real existing surroundings and landscape) might even be presented as a direct and smooth extension of a virtual proposed building. The geometry could also be a door-shaped/looking if this interface intends to lead designers to another virtual room where interior design would be implemented by another design team.

Another important factor of geometry is dimension of the RV interface: 2D, 3D, and even 4D (3D + time). For example, a 3D interface as a bulletin board could be constructed with different facets displaying technical information for different specialty services such as HVAC, safety, mechanical, etc. Time element in 4D refers to when and for how long the interface is in existence. Interfaces may be scheduled to appear at specific times to support the pre-planned nature of many activities (e.g. face-to-face meetings through embedded videoconferencing), and then hide in other times (Koleva et al. 1999). The time element of an interface could therefore be determined by the service nature of the interface. For example, if the interface is devised for remote site surveillance, its time element should be set as long-term duration. If the interface is only designed to serve a specific public meeting, its duration should be aligned with the schedule of the meeting.

3.2.3. Translation and Rotation

Translation and rotation of RV interfaces could also be realized for special purposes. RV interfaces could be static, connecting two fixed spaces. RV interfaces could also be dynamic with users steering through the connected spaces (Benford et al. 1996). For example, the participants could follow a pre-defined trajectory for a tour-like inspection for a building facility.

3.3. INTERFACE TRAVERSABLILITY

Traversable interfaces enable users to virtually cross from one space to the other. Traversable interfaces provide a mechanism for people to dynamically relocate themselves along the RV continuum (Koleva et al. 2000) and people located in one space can transverse into connected spaces. Traversable interfaces can allow people to virtually move back and forward through various modes in the MA construction tree, re-positioning them along the

MA continuum, driven by their design task, interest, and focus. For example, at one moment they may be primarily located in the mode “g” in Figure 3, with a view back into the augmented virtual environment in the mode “a”. They may then traverse the interface and find themselves located within the mode “i” in Figure 3, with a view back into the real environment in the mode “b”. MA spaces could be public where every participant can have access to the same pool of resources. MA spaces could also be private where only authorized participants can have access. Certainly participants can actually transverse from a public space through an interface into a private space, and vice versa.

There are various techniques and methods such as immersive displays (e.g. head-mounted display) combined with trackers that allow a designer in one space to enter into another space. The designer might need to change the techniques to interact when he/she is trying to cross the interface. In addition, related collaborators in different spaces might transform their visual representations as one designer is crossing an interface from one space to the other. We now go back to the case depicted in Figure 4 to show how people can virtually transverse between interfaces. I am the designer in the real environment. I am traversing from the space “a” to the space “g+h”. In the space “a”, I see my remote collaborator as a real human through the interface enabled by the telepresence video view. I then “step” into the virtual space “g+h” through the interface technically enabled by the head-mounted display, large projection devices, or even CAVEs (cave automated virtual environments). At the same time, I see my collaborator as virtual avatar that emerges when I enter the virtual space “g+h”.

4. Conclusions

This paper developed a novel concept – Mutual Augmentation (MA) where AR and AV co-exist to form a seamlessly integrated mega-space by sharing certain real/virtual entity. This paper also presented a systematic framework of exploring MA for supporting architectural design beyond traditional single real/virtual space. A case illustration was discussed to explain how the MA concept approach is applied in the context of architectural design collaboration. The case illustration provided an enhanced understanding of how MA-based design environment might be exploited to facilitate the work of architectural practitioners. The MA concept also opens up a key direction for future research into Collaborative Virtual Environments, AR and AV.

References

Benford, S, Bowers, J, Fahlen, LE, Mariani, J, and Rodden, T: 1994, Supporting co-operative work in virtual environments, *Computer Journal* **37**(8): 653-669.

Benford, SD, Brown, C, Reynard, G, and Greenhalgh, C: 1996, Shared spaces: transportation, artificiality and spatiality, *Proceedings of Computer-Supported Cooperative Work (CSCW '96)*, ACM Press, pp. 77-85.

Benford, SD, Greenhalgh, C, Reynard, G, Brown, C, and Koleva, B: 1998, Understanding and constructing shared spaces with Mixed-Reality boundaries, *ACM Transactions on Computer-Human Interaction* **5**(3): 185–223.

Koleva, B, Benford, SD, and Greenhalgh, C: 1999, The properties of Mixed Reality boundaries, *Proceedings of the Sixth European Conference on Computer-Supported Cooperative Work*, pp. 119.

Koleva, B, Schnidelbach, H, Benford, S, and Greenhalgh, C: 2000, Traversable interfaces between real and virtual worlds, *Proceedings of CHI '2000*, ACM Press, New York, pp. 233-240.

Milgram, P and Kishino, F: 1994, A taxonomy of Mixed Reality visual displays, *IEICE Transactions on Information Systems* E77-D, 12.

Milgram, P and Colquhoun, H: 1999, A taxonomy of real and virtual world display integration, *in* Y Ohta and H Tamura (eds), *Mixed Reality: Merging Real and Virtual Worlds*, Ohmsha Ltd and Springer-Verlag, pp. 5-30.

Nakanishi, H, Yoshida, C, Nishimura, T, and Ishida, T: 1996, Freewalk: supporting casual meeting in a network, *Proceedings of the ACM Conference on Computer-Supported Cooperative Work (CSCW '96),* ACM Press, New York, pp. 308-314.

Regenbrecht, H, Lum, T, Kohler, P, Ott, C, Wagner, M, Wilke, W, and Mueller, E: 2004, Using Augmented Virtuality for remote collaboration, *Presence* **13**(3): 338-354.

Reynard, G, Benford, S, and Greenhalgh, C: 1998, Awareness driven video quality of service in collaborative virtual environments, *Proceedings of the ACM Conference on Human Factors in Computing Systems (CHI '98),* ACM Press/Addison-Wesley Publishing Co., Los Angeles, CA, pp. 464-471.

Wang, X and Dunston, PS: 2005, System evaluation of a Mixed Reality-based collaborative prototype for mechanical design review collaboration, *in* L Soibelman and F Pena-Mora (eds), *CD Proceedings of 2005 ASCE International Conference on Computing in Civil Engineering*, American Society of Civil Engineers, New York, 9 pages.

CONCEPTUAL MODELING ENVIRONMENT (COMOEN)

A 3D user interface for integrating the use of tangible tools into conceptual modeling

CHIH-CHIEH SCOTTIE HUANG
National Taiwan University of Science & Technology, Taiwan

Abstract. Conceptual modeling is an actively creative stage in a design process. Through hand modeling and manipulation of different kinds of modeling tool kits for specific materials, designers are able to generate forms. This article presents a tangible human-computer interface of a C-StressBall for form manipulation and a C-BenchWhirler for visual control. They create a new way of interaction between the virtual world and the physical space. They are aimed to ease the operation in design process by using CAD.

1. Introduction

1.1. CONCEPTUAL MODELING IN ARCHITECTURE DESIGN

The concept in the early phase of architecture design is considered as the key direction force of design creativity (Huang and Liu 2001). Designers can think over detail design of forms by manipulating models in the real world and switch the perspectives of designed forms freely (Lee 2002). While developing concepts, designers usually generate different aspects of visualized thinking by creating conceptual models (Goldschimidt 1994; Liu 1996; Schön and Wiggins 1992; Suwa et al. 2001). Tangible operations of hand gestures help in design thinking of solid models. In traditional design process, clay, foam and paperboard are generally used in creating conceptual models.

Tangible sense is a communication tool. It is helpful to enhance hand gesture and express more creative ideas by the senses of solidness by touching the material and transforming the spatial ideas into design models (Bolt and Herranz, 1992; Sturman and Zeltzer 1993; Hinckley et al. 1999).

A Dong, A Vande Moere & JS Gero (eds), CAADFutures'07, 31–43.

Nowadays, although a CAD (Computer-Aided Design) system is deeply involved in the design process, a designer still needs to adapt to the CAD system. One of the major obstacles is the lack of tangible operations.

1.2. USING CAD IN CONCEPTUAL MODELING

Using physical materials, a designer can handle direct carving, piling and modeling, and forms can be developed easily. However, manipulating objects in real world is limited by physical dynamics. Therefore, it is hard to generate free form with a high degree of freedom. While fabricating free forms, a designer has to overcome material constraints, fabrication difficulty, and time-consuming labor efforts of cutting and gluing. Fortunately, existing CAD systems (such as Maya and Max) contain diverse functions and high capacity of computing power. It becomes easier to overcome the traditional limitation of free form development (Lin 2000). Furthermore, it becomes possible to have a way to create form more freely in the virtual environment.

Although a CAD system provides advantages in versatile functionalities, it causes alienation in the design behaviors of designers during the design process (Won 1999; Wong 2000; Brady 2003). The operation of the GUI (Graphical User Interface) goes through mouse and keyboard. The situation causes difficulty in adapting to the new system while lacking the sense of real space (Lee et al. 2003). Rather trivial efforts with real materials need to be extracted into long steps in CAD system. Extra cognitive load leads to the gap of design thinking and command manipulation. It indeed takes extra effort in planning rather than form generation (Figure 1).

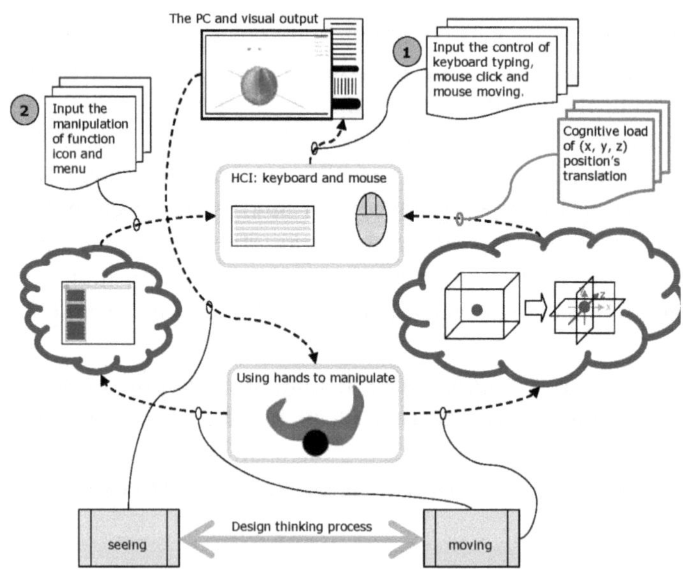

Figure 1. Cognitive loads in design process

The coordination of input/output devices as the medium constructs the framework of human and information (Hsu 1993; Trewin et al. 1999). However, the existing pattern of human-computer interaction does not satisfy our direct form manipulation (Foley 1987). As a result, a designer cannot really lay focus on the design issues.

1.3. GOAL OF THE DESIGN

Some researchers have pointed out that the traditional GUI interaction cannot satisfy the needs of a designer anymore, especially in the early phase of the design process (Gross and Kemp 2001; Tamotsu and Naomasa 1994). CAD needs to have a new solution for resolving the limitation of graphical user interface. In 1991, Mark Weiser (1991) published an article on his vision of Ubiquitous Computing, illustrating a different paradigm of computing and HCI (Human Computer Interaction) which pushes computers into the background and leaves only the valuable information directed to the users. In 1997, Ishii (1997) proposes tangible bits which bridge the gap between cyberspace and the physical environments. Tangible media provide meanings to practical usage through input/output interface. They create a new way of interaction between the virtual world and the physical space.

This research points out some deficiencies with the current CAD systems and proposes a resolution of interaction model which fits with the original behaviors of design practices. The aim of the research is to target the following points: 1) Redesign a CAD system that fits in with the early phase of design process; 2) Use TUI (Tangible User Interface) to replace current GUI which is hard to operate in terms of HCI; 3) Construct a working prototype which is suitable for a design environment. C-StressBall and C-BenchWhirler are introduced here as two new tangible interface. They are aimed to ease the operation in design process.

2. Approach

Compared to the traditional physical modeling tools, mouse and keyboard of the current CAD system are difficult for design use, even though the digital tools have brought up many potentialities. The traditional modeling tools are actually very complete such as pottery tool kits, ribbon tools, box wood modeling tools, and so on (Figure 2). Moreover they assist in visual thinking by coordinating with the position of the benchwhirler. These traditional modeling tools have existed through human civilization and evolved for a long time to develop the detailed functions in the model-shaping process. And, these tools have a unique characteristic: the users could understand their characteristic easily through the sense of touch. By different strength and angles, a user can learn how to use them correctly. After studying for a short time, people may get used to them and directly create their work.

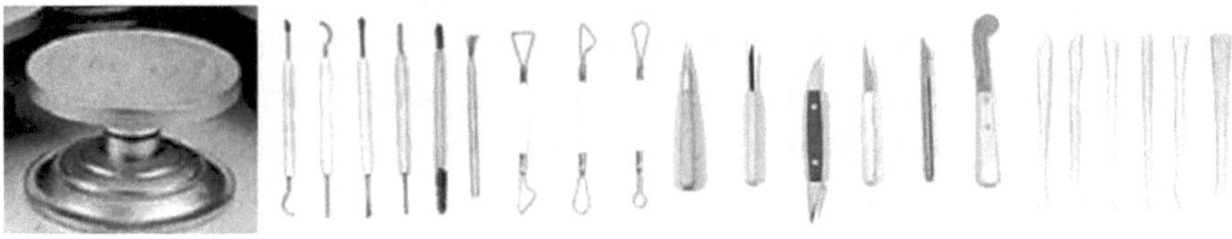

Figure 2. Traditional physical modeling tools

These kinds of ease in usage and exquisite manipulation are not provided in GUI. On the contrary, they are the features of tangible objects. Therefore, how to design the operation of the tangible objects, and how to establish contact with the tangible's features and the modeling behaviors in virtual environment are our research focuses. In this article, we present two physical tangible tools: C-StressBall and C-BenchWhirler combined with the COMOEN (COnceptual MOdeling ENvironment). Together, they offer a set of new methods of modeling.

2.1. REALISTIC INTERACTION

The concepts of C-StressBall and C-BenchWhirler come from the traditional modeling tool kits and C-BenchWhirler. We are providing the exquisite sense of touches by hand during the process of modeling. C-BenchWhirler is a circular turntable to make fast and easy adjustments. C-BenchWhirler provides a way of revolving the turntable with the hand, which will rotate the objects in the virtual environment (Figure 3A). As the turntable is rotated, it places objects on the C-BenchWhirler along with rotation.

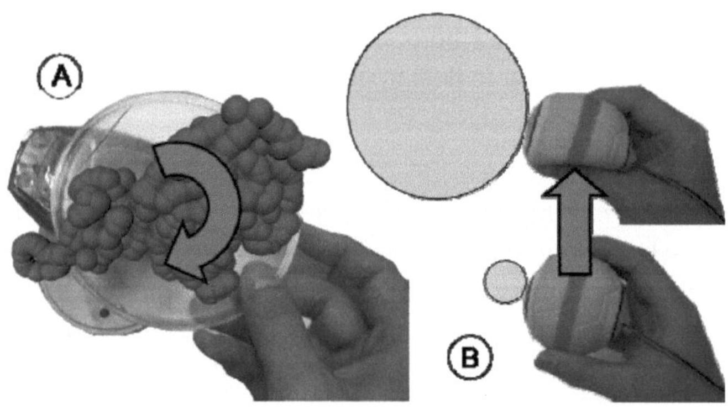

Figure 3. Interaction of tangible tools. (A) C-BenchWhirler provides the function of rotating a virtual object; (B) Through the extrusion of hands, C-StressBall provides the function of creating solid ink

C-StressBall supplies a surface of sphere for designers to hold with the fingers and extrude the substances for design. C-StressBall is like a container which is full of jelly ink. Squeezing the C-StressBall would make the virtual objects come out. C-StressBall responds to the squeeze pressure by creating different sizes of ink dots (Figure 3B). Following gesture activities, C-StressBall makes models in any location of COMOEN.

2.2. SCENARIO

Here, we have the following scenario planned:

The designer takes C-StressBall and moves in the space. At the same time, C-StressBall follows the movement on the screen in front of the desk. Just like a mirror, it reflects movements directly. On the screen, the spheroid changes according to the hand pressure, like the actual feeling from which the objects crowd out from hands. So, the designer can create three-dimensional forms in the space according to feeling, and organize his design inspiration. On the tabletop, there placed C-BenchWhirler. The designer occasionally rotates the turntable, and the virtual objects moved along with the rotation of turntable. The designer investigates the forms with different angles while rotating the C-BenchWhirler. And C-StressBall is still used in consolidating the ideas at the same time.

In the process, the designer does not realize he is using CAD, but he knows it is an intuitive modeling environment. We put forward the concept of a tangible tool via a CAD system, and offer users to operate CAD information from the tangible tools. The designer can obtain a higher level of satisfaction out of the design process of COMOEN.

3. Implementation

3.1. SYSTEM OUTLINE

In software, we utilize MEL (Maya Embedded Language) to program new functions as plug-ins for the Maya 3D environment. In terms of hardware, Matrox CronosPlus image capture board is used for retrieving computer vision data from two CCD cameras, in order to obtain the actual spatial position. The functions of optics inductor from mouse and the infrared ray receiver from IRX board offer the sense of touch operation. Through the serial port, the sensed data are sent to the computer. In terms of CAD system, we use the 3D virtual environment in Maya. In COMOEN, tangible tools include C-StressBall and C-BenchWhirler on the table. And the 3D image is projected in front the table (Figure 4).

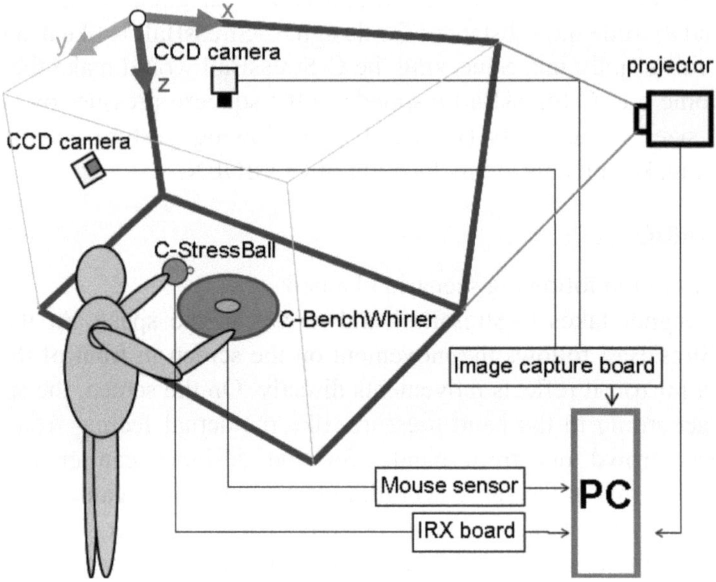

Figure 4. Framework of COMOEN

3.2. INPUT AND OUTPUT SETUP

3.2.1. Input of Tangible Tools

C-StressBall is made from a hollow plastic ball. The C-StressBall can be easily caught and pinched by hands. After pinching the ball, C-StressBall can resume its original figure in real-time. The ball is equipped with an Infrared (IR) Distance Sensor inside. When pressing the ball, the IR Distance Sensor can capture the pressure level from the distance of the interior surfaces. Greater pressure creates a larger spheroid. The other way round, minor pressure creates a smaller spheroid. With this principle, C-StressBall can create the spheroid of different size.

In order to get the information of spatial position one CCD camera is placed on the (x, y) plane and the other on (y, z) plane separately. Through t connecting CronsPlus board and using MIL (Matrox Image Library), the system detects the images derived from both cameras under Visual Studio operational environment. The LED light is recognized and points out coordinates (Figure 5) based on an illumination value. Hence, we can obtain the position of C-StressBall in the space.

Figure 5. Spatial input interface

C-BenchWhirler offers a round rotary table on the desk, and an IR sensor under the table to detect turning actions. IR sensors detect the directions and the distance when C-BenchWhirler rotates. The edge that catches the rotary table through hand can rotate all objects in virtual environment.

3.2.2. Output of the Virtual Environment

In Maya environment, the mouse has been repackaged into C-BenchWhirler and uses the rotation function in the existing Maya software. In order to obtain the spatial coordinate information, we use the image based spatial input interface to obtain the position information. A txt file format is used save the information of (x, y, z) position and pressure strength from the IRX board (Figure 6). The C language is used to program new functions in Maya so that Maya can use the information in virtual 3D environment from the txt file (Figure 6).

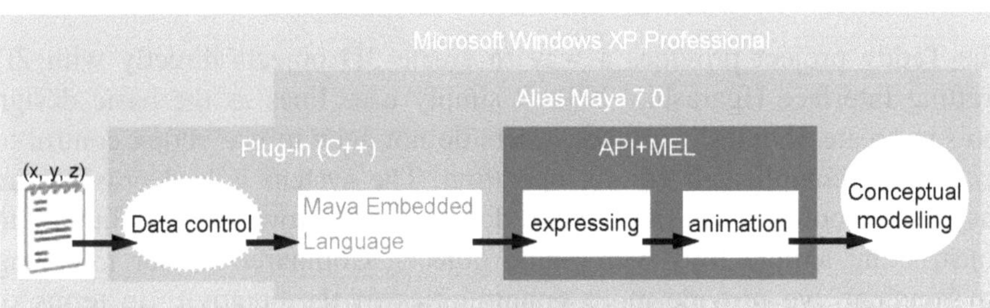

Figure 6. Software architecture

In Maya, we use MEL to create a new function, which is to get the information of position and pressure level from C-StressBall. That new function makes modeling activities work. In the program, it reads the value of (x, y, z) position and radius from txt file. Then, use the received values in sphere command and execute command in Maya. We named these process "post1". For real time animation, "post1"command set to immediate execution. Finally, COMOEN can translate the operation of tangible tools into modeling commands.

4. Discussion

4.1. CURRENT OPERATION PROBLEMS IN EXISTING CAD SYSTEM

The personal computer provides the possibility for users in creating, editing and saving complicated data structure. These functionalities extend the field of human's imagination which might overcome the constraints of gravity and enhance design thinking in various from development.

3D modeling system based on parameter controls is difficult to integrate digital data and design thinking. The traditional method starts with drafting in pen and paper. And then the drafts would be developed and converted into 3D models. However, the detailed information such as design instincts and art expression could be lost during conversion.

In our example project, we address the contextual environments. The user activities in the physical world could be captured into spatial coordinates and represented with vertex and line extrusion in digital world.

Precision of size is the not key point of 3D modeling. The point is to provide an easy and efficient way to define the clear relationship in the locations of objects. The relationship is in fact the focus of communication between physical and virtual space. TUI has more direct manipulation of objects rather than GUI. Our goal is to identify a better way to establish the link between the tangible and the virtual.

4.2. NEEDS OF DESIGNERS IN THE EARLY PHASE OF DESIGN PROCESS

The Teddy project provides a way to create 3D objects directly with 2D drafting interface (Igarashi 1999). It simply uses lines as the basic design tools to create 3D mesh surfaces. Users do not need to use vertex control to accomplish complicated editing operation. The system indeed provides an easy and smooth way in the specific design phase. However, it is limited to constructing simple toys with round objects. Compared to our modeling environment, we provide more opportunities of the creativity in terms of spatial perspectives. Our system will be more helpful for architects to obtain a better sense of space.

In a traditional CAD system, it is insufficient for designers to fully bring creativity. Surface drawing project is a tool which fits more on artists' requirements (Schkolne 2001). It provides the functions of line-drawing and doodling to create 3D models. By repeated uses of various physical hand tools, users can get instant feedback of moving, extending and deleting objects. The specific modeling method is getting closer to the behaviors of artwork creation. Compared to our tool, it is more complicated and has more constraints. In our modeling environment, we have reduced the complexity by providing two simple tools. For instance, C-StressBall can create objects with different sizes and positions and identify the spatial relationship of objects through pressing a ball by hand. Users can create handcraft-like objects with sense of space in a few minutes.

4.3. USING TANGIBILITY TO ACHIEVE PROPER MODELING OPERATION

Triangles system is a set of tool kit that will integrate digital and physical environment (Gorbet 1998). It allows users to manipulate complicated digital information by hands. By placing the triangle tool kit, the composition of the triangles will be immediately translated into digital data that represent the physical structure and organization of the units. Compared to our C-StressBall and C-BenchWhirler, we are reaching an intuitive operation by sorely pressing, moving and rotating objects. In our daily life, the action of pressing is usually indicating volume control. Just like calligraphy, more pressure the brush is placed, larger the spot is. Calligraphy writing expresses the aesthetics by the tracks of pressure and directions. The design of C-BenchWhirler is trying to emulate to the experiences of turning table in daily life. By a natural and intuitive way, users could realize how to control the rotation of a virtual object with proper strength of hands.

Our research is not to addressing the precision of the data, but to realize how to improve the design development by tangible media in the early phase of design process. In the project of Surface Drawing, it provides too many options of tools that might cause heavier metal loading for users while switching the tools (Schkolne 2001). It is relatively complicated to use. Nevertheless, we are trying to provide an intuitive and easy way for users by addressing the most efficient modeling operation modes.

4.4. THE MEANING OF DIGITAL INFORMATION OF TANGIBLE TOOLS

Physical units are very recognizable and meaningful in the physical world. Playing with the units would provide instant interactions with tangible senses and actions. Adjusting the weight center, balance and the external force on the objects would allow subtle and tender control. The application of C-StressBall and C-BenchWhirler in fact does not only help to understand the geometrical relationship but also extends your emotional senses onto the objects you create. It will train the users a new skill and provide a brand new experience in creation activity. The rich interaction with the digital media does help in covey the original ideas of the designer.

This research is trying to transfer physical objects from passive units to proactive tools. They can be recognized and interpreted as composition and organization structure by computer system. Furthermore, they can be manipulated subtly. In the case of Triangle, simple triangle units are applied (Gorbet 1998). All the physical units relate to certain digital information behind the scene.

We are providing a solution to handle digital information by human hands which matches to the creative work in the physical world. Eventually, two students from the design school are recruited for an informal testing, Figure 7. One of them is quite familiar with 3D software. The other is a novice for 3D application. Only in two minutes, both designers develop interesting concept models, Figure 8. In the process, the designer uses the ink spheroid which C-StressBall. At the beginning of the experiment, ink spheroids are displayed with the structure of the form. Based on the form structure, the target is changed to focus on the details. Designer starts using more small spheroids in order to refine the form. The design outcome matched their imagination and was not limited in their initial forms. After using C-StressBall to create concept models, the designer can achieve a proper model through the consideration of volume and size. Surplus spheroids produced in the design process are also valuable for a designer. They offer development-oriented possibilities for the design. C-StressBall and C-BenchWhirler successfully helped in getting easier and more direct interaction with 3D virtual objects and handling them better in virtual space.

Figure 7. The participants in an experiment

5. Conclusion

This system is only utilizing the existing “sphere” modeling function in Maya. Through tangible operation, COMOEN provides high level design capability and reaches high efficiency in modeling. A round shape provides a good sense of sight and simply represents the relationship of the mass in the design process. Traditional modeling methods using clay and cardboard take a lot of effort. In COMOEN, it is easy to operate and help a designer to present the concept more easily.

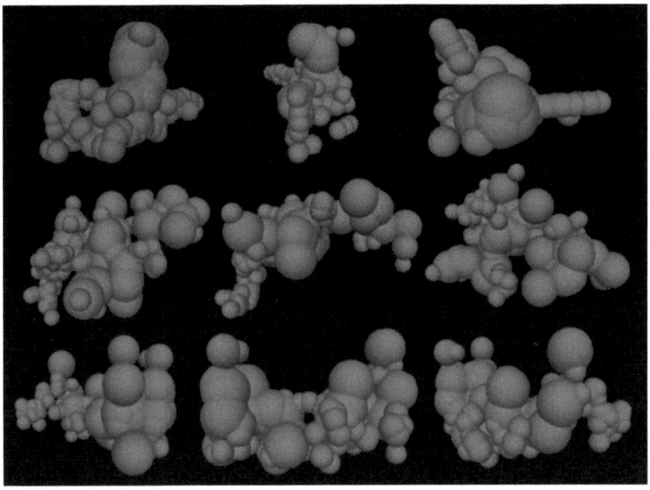

Figure 8. Subjects shaped in COMOEN

COMOEN integrates tangible tools for the spatial modeling behaviors. With C-StressBall and the viewing options provided by C-BenchWhirler, they provide a new conceptual modeling method with touch senses enhanced. We also emphasize that both of the modeling actions are needed in our physical environment. This system provides a new channel for the communication between designer and CAD system. It is a rather intuitive interaction implemented from tangible interface that would make designers manipulate as operating simple physical tools. We find the strength of using the senses of touch. The touch senses succeed in impelling the designer to have their design details more thoroughly.

In our implementation, a working prototype is used to present the possibility. In technology side, all we use is common and ready-made components. Through the meaningful tangible manipulation provided here, we could leave out GUI manipulation. Instead, it would promote itself with high level creation along with CAD system. In the near future, the technology of image recognition and hand sensing will be integrated.

References

Bolt, RA and Herranz, E: 1992, Two-handed gesture in multi-modal natural dialog, *Proceedings of ACM symposium on User interface software and technology*, Monterey, California, USA, pp. 7-14.

Brady, DA: 2003, Ideation: Metaphorical Explorations and Digital Media, *Proceedings of eCAADe conference*, Australia, pp. 187-190.

Chang, CT: 2005, *Some Phenomena of Tactile Sensation in Study Models,* MS Thesis, National Chiao Tung University, Hsin- Chu, Taiwan.

Foley, JD: 1987, Interfaces for Advanced Computing, *Scientific American*, pp. 126-135.

Gorbet, MG, Orth, M, and Ishii, H: 1998, Triangles: Tangible Interface for Manipulation and Exploration of Digital Information Topography, *Proceedings of the SIGCHI conference on Human factors in computing system*, Los Angeles, California, USA, pp. 49-56.

Gross, MD and Kemp, A: 2001, Gesture Modeling-Using Video to Capture Freehand Modeling Commands, *Proceedings of CAAD Futures conference,* Eindhoven, pp. 271-284.

Goldschmidt, G: 1994, On visual design thinking: the vis kids of architecture, *Design Studies* **1**(15): 158-174.

Hsiang, SH: 2005, *Using hand movement system to operate 3D design objects in virtual environment,* MS Thesis, National Chiao Tung University, Hsin- Chu, Taiwan.

Hinckley, K and Sinclair, M: 1999, *Touch-Sensing Input Devices*, Microsoft Research, Redmond.

Huang, SY and Liu, YT: 2001, Some phenomena of creativity in design with computer media: Interview with Eisenman and cognitive experiments, *Computational and Cognitive Models of Creative Design V*, University of Sydney, Sydney, pp. 241-262.

Hsu, J: 1993, The Encyclopedia of Virtual Environments, Produced by the students of Dr. Ben Shneiderman's CMSC 828S Virtual Reality and Telepresence Course.

Ishii, H and Ullmer, B: 1997, Tangible Bits: Towards Seamless Interfaces between People Bits and Atoms, *Proceedings of the SIGCHI conference on Human factors in computing system*, pp. 234-241.

Igarashi, T, Matsuoka, S, and Tanaka H: 1999, Teddy: a sketching interface for 3D freeform design, *Proceedings of ACM conference on Computer graphics and interactive techniques*, pp.409-416.

Lee, HL: 2002, *A comparative study on concept development process using computer and conventional media*, MS Thesis, National Chiao Tung University, Hsin- Chu, Taiwan.

Lee, CH, Ma. YP, Jeng. TS: 2003, A Spatially-Aware Tangible Interface for Computer-Aided Design, *NCKU Press*, Tainan, Taiwan.

Lin, CY: 2000, *A study of computer models in terms of space and media*, PhD Thesis, National Chiao Tung University, Hsin- Chu, Taiwan.

Liu, YT: 1996, Restructuring shapes in terms of emergent subshapes: a computational and cognitive model. *Environment and Planning B: Planning and Design*, pp. 313-328.

Schkolne, S, Pruett, M, and Schröder, P: 2001, Surface Drawing: Creating Organic 3D Shapes with the Hand and Tangible Tools, *Proceedings of the SIGCHI conference on Human factors in computing systems*, Seattle, Washington, USA. pp. 261-268.

Schon, DA and Wiggins, G: 1992, Kinds of seeing and their functions in designing, *Design Studies* **13**(2): 135-156.

Sturman, DJ and Zeltzer, D: 1993, A Design Method for "Whole-Hand" Human-Computer Interaction, *ACM Transactions on Information Systems* **11**(3): 219-238.

Suwa, M, Gero, JS, Tvesky, B and Purcell, T: 2001, Seeing in to sketch: Regrouping parts encourages new interpretations, *Visual and Spatial reasoning in Design* **2**: 207-219.

Tamotsu, M. and Naomasa, N: 1994, Direct and intuitive input device for 3-D shape deformation. *Proceedings of the SIGCHI conference on Human factors in computing system*, Boston, pp. 465-470.

Trewin, SP and Pain, H: 1999, Keyboard and mouse errors due to motor disabilities, *International Journal of Human-Computer Studies* **50**(2): 109-144.

Won, CJ: 1999, The comparison between visual thinking using computer and conventional media in the concept generation stages of design, *Automation in Construction* **10**: 319-325.

Wong, CH: 2000, Some phenomena of design thinking in the concept generation stage using computer media, *Proceedings of CAADRIA conference*, Singapore, pp. 255-264.

SIMULATION OF AN HISTORICAL BUILDING USING A TABLET MR SYSTEM

ATSUKO KAGA, MASAHIRO KAWAGUCHI,
TOMOHIRO FUKUDA
Osaka University, Japan

and

WOOKHYUN YEO
Yonsei University, South Korea

Abstract. To depict characteristics of historical buildings, digital archives must display visual information about structures and their construction. This study defines the components used for three-dimensional (3D) models of framework construction. Framework construction has heretofore portrayed structures through animation using VHS or Hi-Vision video. This paper describes a method to facilitate exhibition through interactive simulation using animation and real-time images. Furthermore, a Tablet MR can be used as an effective simulation tool for studying historical buildings in on-site models. For education about historical wooden-framework architecture, increased interactive potential according to users' needs will be increasingly necessary.

1. Introduction

Many historical buildings exist throughout Japan. Wooden framework construction is a common feature of older historical buildings. To enable anyone to understand the characteristics of such historical Japanese buildings, digital contents using visual information about construction and structure are needed. Such substantial digital content is useful in construction training, and can aid in the understanding of historical buildings through exhibition. In Japan, to introduce construction methods used in ancient Buddhist architecture, physical models play an important role. A ready grasp of old construction methods is achieved through the display of three-dimensional models.

A Dong, A Vande Moere & JS Gero (eds), CAADFutures'07, 45–58.

2. Building a Historical Archive Using Digital Information

Several digital archives have been made of historical buildings with wooden framework architecture (Tang 2001; Tang 2002; Shih 2004). Particularly in regard to digital archives of wooden framework architecture, for improved understanding of structures, there is much that must be explained related to the framework construction and joints of components, in addition to the external and internal views. The contents and expression methods are surveyed based on the example of a digital archive of a historical building with wooden framework architecture (Yeo 2003).

First, we introduce the digital archive, created in 1987, of Suzakumon. As the main gate of Nara, a historical capital of Japan, Suzakumon existed in the 8th century. There, foreign envoys were greeted and sent off; celebratory events were held by the Emperor. Although this gate disappeared, it was restored in 1997. No data related to the structure of Suzakumon gate survived. A 3D model was created based on a proposal which estimated the appearance of the framework and the detailed components of Suzakumon gate from ruins and archaeological information by the Nara Cultural Property Research Institute. Rules about the combination and processing methods of components were extracted. These rules were added to the definition of the model on a computer, thereby producing a digital archive. In the digital archive of Toshodai-ji (1997), to create a 3D model and to explain the detailed structure of an auditorium, an animation was created using Hi-Vision. A joint and framework construction was created using CG animation in a 3D model in the digital archive of Ueno Kanei-ji (1998). Both were used as teaching material for architecture students. An example of the traditional architecture of Japan expressed using still images and Hi-Vision is shown in Figure 1.

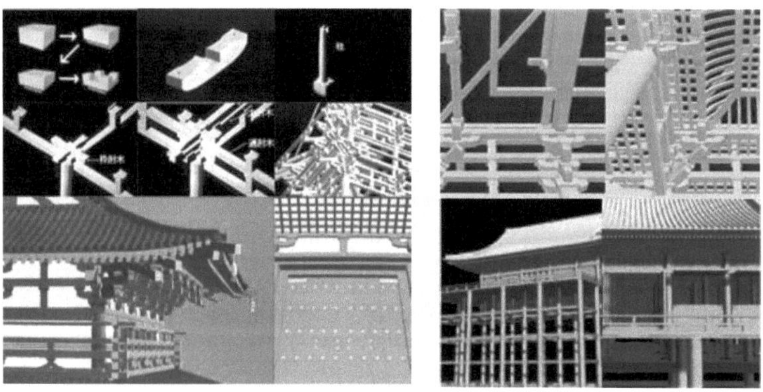

Figure 1. Traditional architecture of Japan expressed using a still image and Hi-Vision

To date, most digital material that is related to historical buildings has been produced for a specific purpose. Their video media formats have been VHS, Hi-Vision video, and digital video. Important historical buildings are used in various fields, such as architecture, history, and sociology; they are also of cultural and technical interest. However, the available data are inadequate for addressing such varied demands. A better form of a digital archive that is applicable to various uses was considered. A digital archive which can respond to various media was created for the five-storied pagoda in Kyoto To-ji.

3. Preparation of the Digital Archive

As a sample of a digital archive for carrying out an interactive simulation, data related to the five-storied pagoda in To-ji, Kyoto city were prepared. The pagoda was surveyed using past research about interactive digital archives (Yeo 2003). This building is a national treasure and was registered with the World Heritage Foundation in 1994. It is a five-storied pagoda and is used as the symbol of Kyoto. Its height of 54.8 m makes it the tallest wooden five-storied pagoda in Japan. The present five-storied pagoda, built in 1644, is the 5th generation. The foundations date from the end of the 9th century; it was built making full use of the best construction technology of the Heian era. This five-storied pagoda has withstood earthquakes and typhoons, which are common in Japan. It is difficult to acquire detailed information on the structure of this five-storied pagoda from reference books.

As the first step, information about the pagoda was collected in co-operation with the cultural property public assistance section in the Kyoto Prefecture board of education. Then, based on that information, we prepared a 3D model with detailed internal and external perspectives. The photographic data obtained in the information gathering stage were used for 3D-model data texture mapping. Using this technology, the created data became highly realistic. The detailed 3D form at the time of erection was recreated and expressed using texture mapping based on old references. This precise digital archive is useful for educational purposes.

4. Development of an Interactive Digital Archive

By digitizing data, a digital archive alleviates the problem of informational degradation and informational loss; moreover, it can promote the reuse of data. A digital archive records quality digital images and maintains them in the form of multimedia, databases, etc., which can become important historical, cultural, and scientific resources. The media of the digital archive taken up in the preceding chapter have so far been restricted to animation and still images. Virtual reality (VR) technology and its systems have been developed as effective means of design simulation or presentation in the environmental design field (Lou 2003; Kaga 2005). Therefore, we specifically examined real-time simulation, which enables free movement inside a 3D virtual space, as the medium of the new digital archive. Real-time simulation enables construction of an interactive knowledge database using 3D space (Figure 2 and 3). The resultant digital archive was used for sharing of interactive knowledge and for television broadcasts. VirtoolsDev of Virtools was used as the base software to recreate a local environment in 3D space through real-time simulation.

DirectX API, which realizes real-time rendering, was used for this on a PC. It was equipped with a Virtools player as a plug-in to a commonly used web browser. Visual programming with VirtoolsDev is achieved by connecting the program put together for every function of the series

Figure 2. Five-storied pagoda: outside (Left), and inside (Right)

Figure 3. Present figure of five-storied pagoda (Left). A rendition of the five-storied pagoda when it was first constructed (Right)

"Behavior Building Block" as an event flow. Furthermore, if a "Building Behavior Block" has not been prepared beforehand, a user can newly develop it using C++.

The following items describe the interface functions of the scene (Table 1).

TABLE 1. Interface functions of the scene

Interface Function	Details
Walkthrough	Enables free movement in space while observing the surroundings. It supports the ability to view objects in many directions. Both the interior and exterior of the building can be viewed separately. If the interior view is too narrow, the viewing angle can be adjusted (Figure 4).
Section & Plane Display	Cuts the building and to show a section at any point elevation or plane. The section is displayed in a perspective mode to determine the depth easily (Figure 5).
Show or Hide Main Materials	Shows or hides materials classified into groups. Concealed objects or materials, such as those by an external wall, become visible (Figure 6 Left).
Parts Information Display	Shows basic information related to various literature, i.e., what were used and for what purpose (Figure 6 Right).

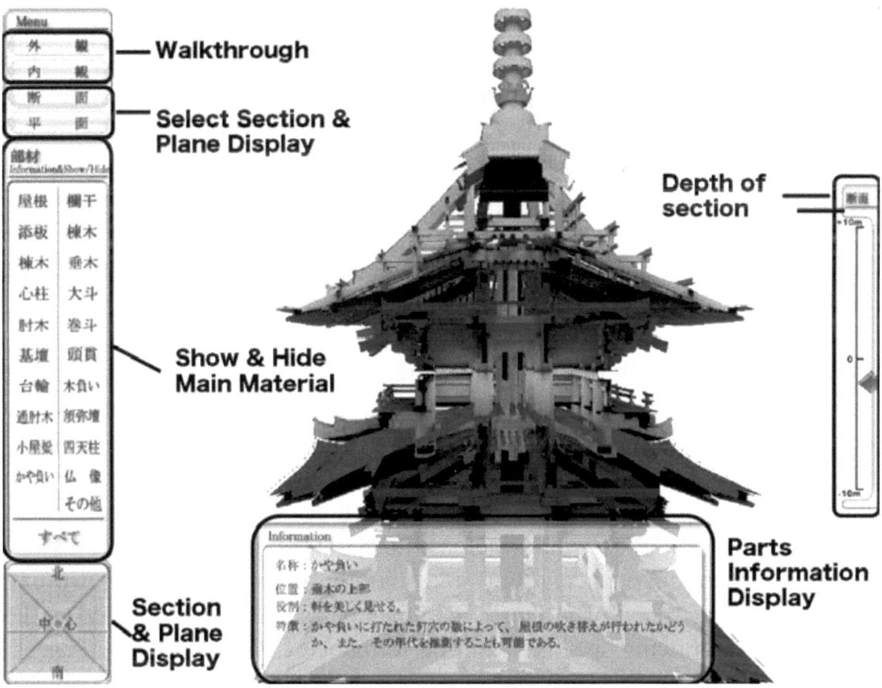

Figure 4. Interface of the VR system

Figure 5. Walkthrough outside (Left), Inside (Middle), Section display, Elevation (Right)

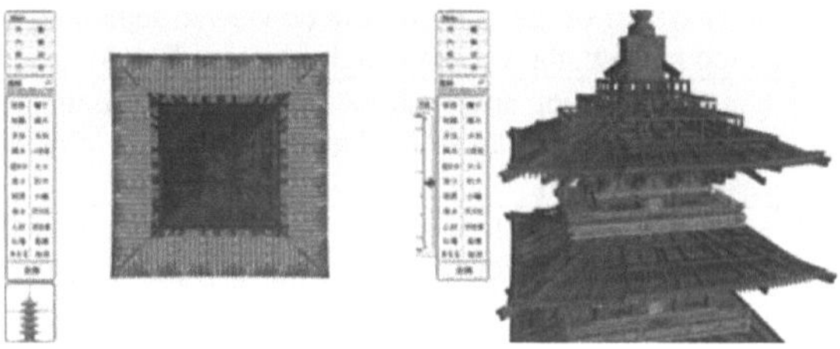

Figure 6. Section display, Plan (Left), Show or Hide main materials (Middle) and Part information display (Right)

Generally, existing 3D games or real time simulations use Level of Detail (LOD) technology, which simplifies data according to the distance between a viewpoint and an object. However, in this digital archive, because accuracy was necessary to portray the data of the whole five-storied pagoda, technology which visualizes only the visible area was emphasized. Regarding the arbitrary cross-sectional form of a five-storied pagoda, and the names and roles of components, this information can be displayed interactively when a user requires it.

For example, the pillar that supports the center of a tower (Shinbashira) was not combined with the structural objects of the five-storied pagoda. For that reason, the five-storied pagoda can be called a flexible structure, which has excellent durability during an earthquake. Those aspects of this structure can be understood easily by anyone through a simulation using a clipping function. Moreover, if this archive were to include data of a Buddhist image, the number of polygons would increase to 830,000. For users to enjoy the interactive operation of this archive and smooth movement of the viewpoint, a frame drawing speed of at least 12 frames per second (fps) is needed. To realize such a drawing speed, a high-performance CPU, a Graphics Processing Unit (GPU), and memory are important.

5. Simulation of Historical Buildings On-site

Real-time simulation of the historical building described in Section 4 is assumed for use at alternative sites, such as exhibition spaces. Such a display range of VR is a part of the visible range of humans. One problem with VR is that adjustment of a flexible human viewpoint cannot be performed and that the grasp of the scale or slopes is difficult. However, when only ruins exist and are used to build a 3D model, the historical building can be recreated in the real world intuitively by having someone go there and unite the VR image and on-the-spot photographic images.

On the other hand, when a historical building exists, because someone has visited the site and the VR image and on-the-spot photograph images are used together, it is expected to be possible to understand the internal structure visually and to get a feeling of its scale. Furthermore, if someone were to visit the site and on-the-spot photographic images and the VR image are united with mixed reality (MR) technology, it would be possible to add visual information to the framework construction or components. Because information can be understood on a scale of real space, information can be offered effectively.

5.1. SYSTEM DESIGN AND CONFIGURATION

5.1.1. MR Technology

Mixed Reality (MR) is also called compound reality. P. Milgram and F. Kishino present an explanatory figure similar to the one shown in Figure 7.

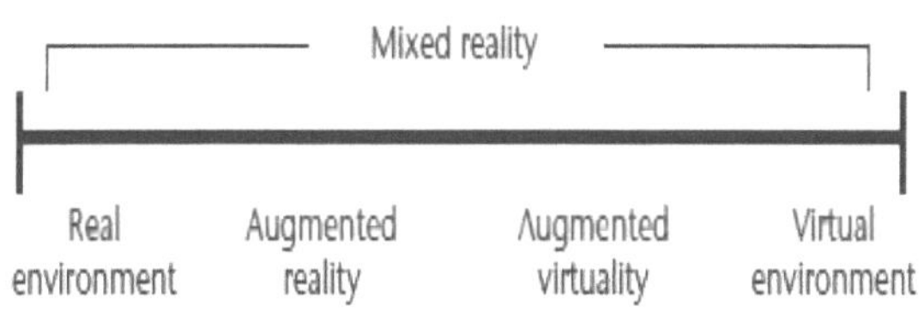

Figure 7. Relation of being as virtual as real by Milgram

Kato (1999), You (1999), and Behringer (1999) conducted research into locating objects in mixed reality space accurately. However, few examples exist of effective use of this simulation technology for a historical building. This research is directed primarily toward construction simulation using a mixed reality system rather than tracker locating. Ito (2005) described the availability of MR in the examination of a city space, and has classified MR according to characteristics like those shown in Table 2.

TABLE 2. Input/output classification (D: Dynamic/S : Static)

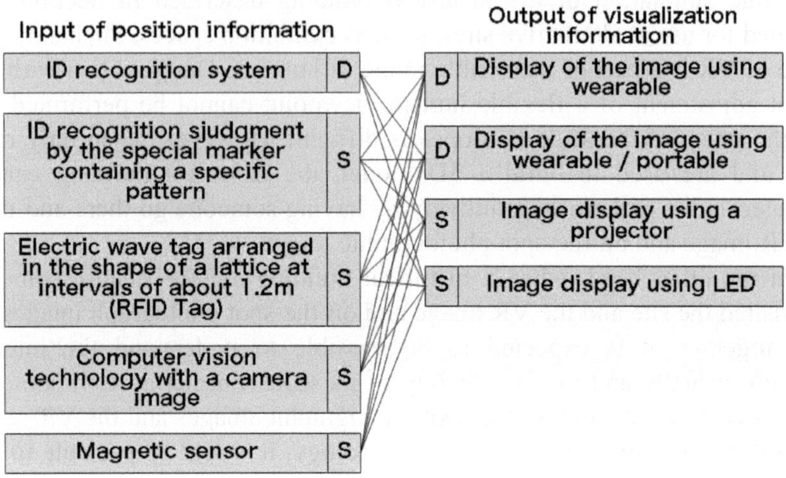

The DD type follows in the footsteps of operations in space, and mobile ones, wearable, etc. using an apparatus carried in the body for informational dynamic acquisition or presentation. Neither pattern matching nor an environmental embedding type sensor is used for this. Therefore, it is considered to be applicable also to object grounds, such as historical buildings.

Therefore, to realize an on-site simulation, an experiment in system configuration was conducted and a prototype system was tested with particular emphasis on MR technology of grouping together on-the-spot photograph images and VR images in real time.

5.1.2. System Outline

Fukuda summarizes the "Tablet MR" system configuration as follows (Fukuda 2006). To realize MR technology, the system configuration must synchronize the aspect of view and the positions of the live camera and the VR camera; therefore, an external device is used. Consideration was given to the composition of the apparatus to apply technology of MR in the field of environmental design in which the simulation of historical buildings is also included. The 3D sensor is used for detection of the direction. High-precision GPS is used for detection of position information. Moreover, instead of the Head-Mount Display (HMD), which is currently generally used, a tablet PC was used as the display device for the MR image so that perusal and operation by more than one person is possible. To interlock each device, software development was carried out to allow adjustment and use of each external device. An antenna and a receiver are required for GPS. Also needed are a PDA and a receiver for control of communication using a

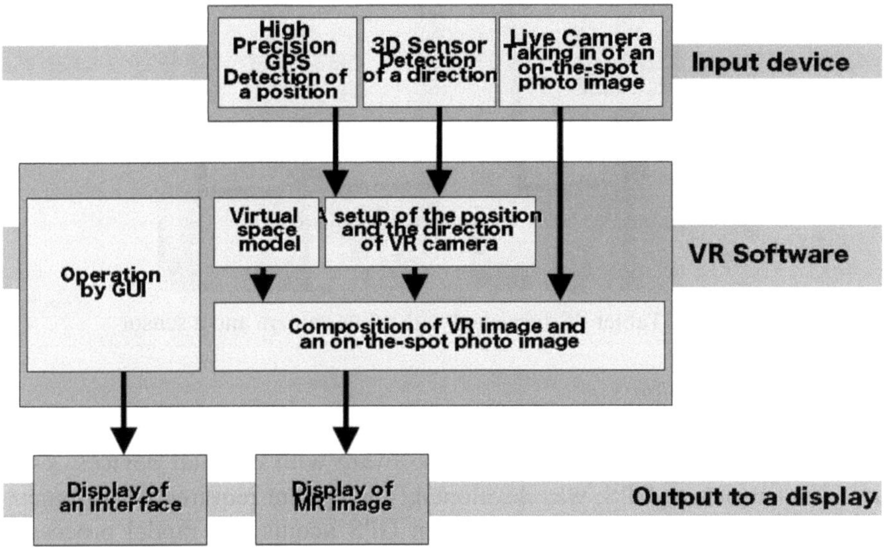

Figure 8. System outline (Fukuda 2006 – Appendix)

Bluetooth device. The interface for operating the MR space according to the purpose was implemented (Figure 8).

5.1.3. Hardware Design

Moreover, a frame incorporating a live camera, a 3D sensor, and a Tablet PC was designed and created, producing a "Tablet MR" system prototype (Figure 9). This was designed to be used with a tripod; therefore, it is useful even if a user must leave it to walk somewhere. The apparatus composition of the completed Tablet PC is shown in Figure 10.

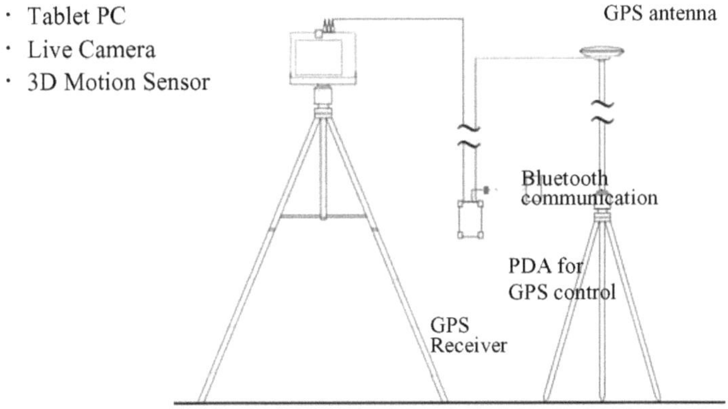

Figure 9. System Configuration (Fukuda 2006)

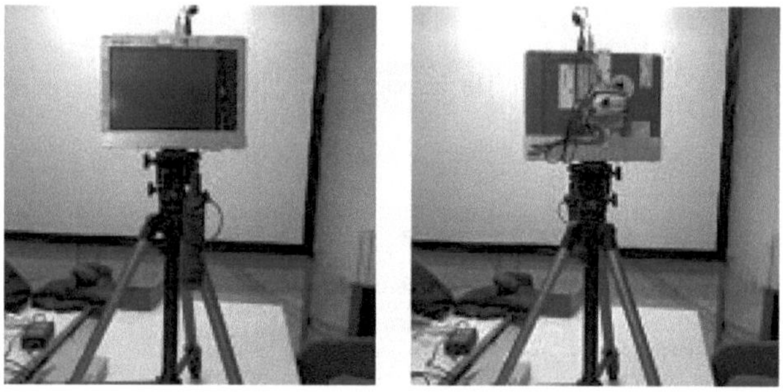

Figure 10. Tablet PC furnished with a live camera and a sensor

5.1.4. Software Design

The software design was developed based on the VR system described in Section 4. Otherwise, communication software with external devices, such as a 3D sensor and GPS, was developed. The system required development of a module to acquire GPS data. Then GPS acquisition model processes GPS data into a format that are is treated as digital data transmitted from the 3D sensor. These were developed using the Software Development Kit (SDK) which used Visual C++ language of Visual Studio (Microsoft Corp.)

5.1.5. Development of the Operating Function

The following MR console was added to the system created in Section 4 at the interface so that it might correspond to the Tablet MR system (Figure 11). The use flow of the system is as depicted in Figure 12. The scenery used in the system is shown in Figure 13. To maintain portability, the antenna and the receiver were made sufficiently small to be put into a rucksack and carried. When the system is fixed, it rotates by attaching it to a tripod.

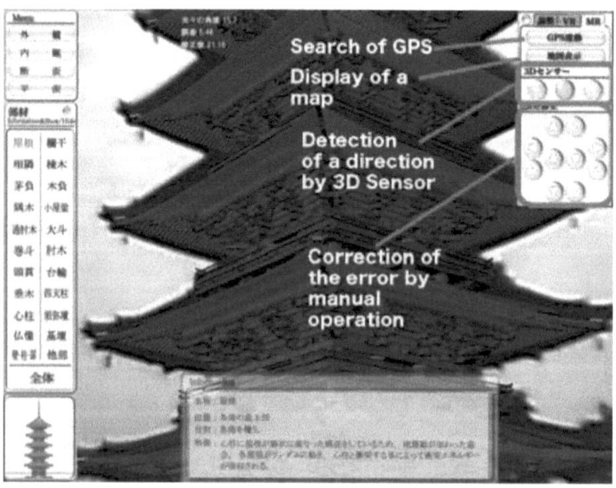

Figure 11. Interface of "Tablet MR" system

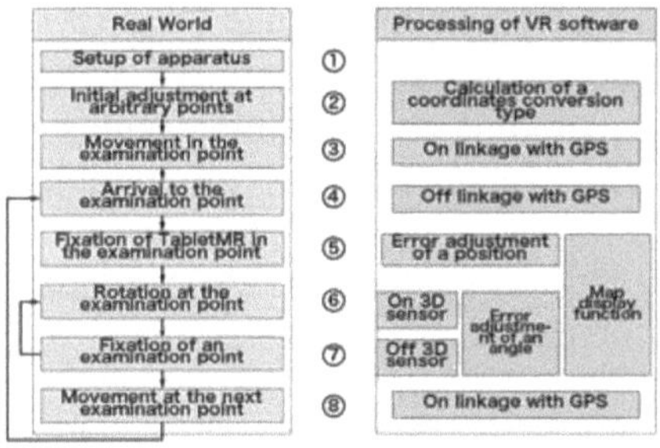

Figure 12. Use flow in "Tablet MR"system

Figure 13. Use scenery of the system

5.2. SYSTEM EXPERIMENT

Using the To-ji contents described in Section 4, the author visited the original site and used this system. The number of polygons of the real-time simulation first required reduction because of a problem with the display performance of the tablet PC display device at the time of content creation. Although smooth drawing was impossible, it was calculated that a satisfactory drawing speed was about 4 fps. This was done in an actual proof experiment using other digital contents at the time of operation. Therefore, although it was 830,000 polygons in full size, the data needed to be reduced by half, to about 400,000 polygons, to assure 4 fps operation. Then, the outer wall and fittings, which were shown in the original condition, were made invisible. Moreover, for some components of the historical wooden structure, most notably Taruki and Masu, which are components with many polygons because they have curved surface forms, transposition was made to a model which reduced the number of polygons. In the experiment, the display of the components inside the building and the description display of components were carried out, placing a tripod at a point which provided a general view of the five-storied pagoda, and moving the Tablet MR system to it (Figure 14). The tablet MR system is operated by the tap of the stylus of a tablet PC attachment. Therefore, the button interface realized the trigger of a fundamental function such as GPS, a 3D sensor, or an error-correction program. When, in an experiment, the view angle of the VR camera was changed to 36 degrees, it was found that there was almost no difference in vision in comparison to a live camera image (Figure 15). As a result of the experiment, data related to the framework construction and components were perused in a state matching the appearance and scale of the five-storied pagoda (Figure 16). The contents of the structure can be understood by building up the structure from the foundations on an on-the-spot photo image.

Figure 14. Study by "Tablet MR" system

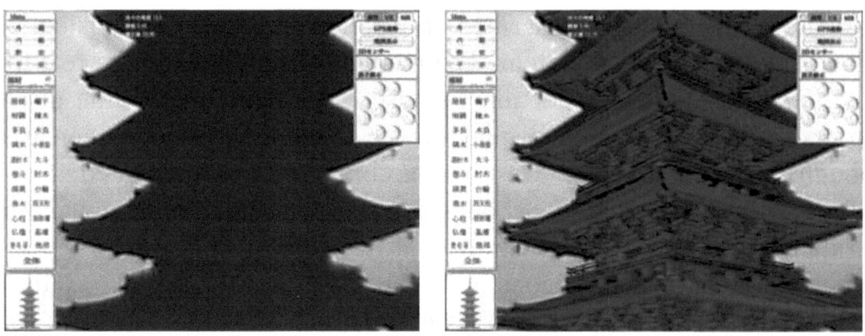

Figure 15. Gap with VR and an image of five-storied pagoda. Left: Before composition with VR and an image, Right: Composition with VR and an image

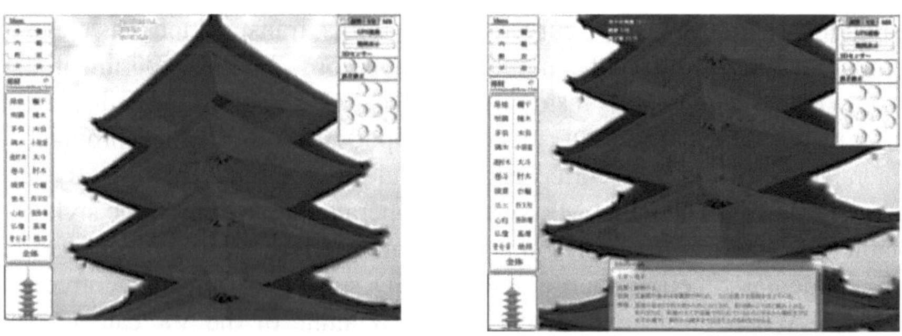

Figure 16. MR capture image of five-storied pagoda

6. Conclusion

First, the wooden framework architecture was reviewed in regard to the content and expression method of digital archives of Japanese historical buildings. The definition of the components using a 3D model or framework construction was given. A description was given of the animated joints, etc., with Hi-Vision TV, and of the structure, which can explain the framework construction interactively in a real-time simulation. Furthermore, the possibility was raised that the Tablet MR system can be used effectively as a simulation tool for historical buildings in on-site models. It is thought that, in the interests of education about Japanese historical buildings, the increased interactive potential according to users' needs will be increasingly necessary.

In future studies, many more simulations will be made and the system will be improved further until it is ready for use with interactive contents as an on-site model simulation tool. Improvement of the interactive contents and the on-site model simulation tool will contribute to the smooth advancement of e-learning related to historical buildings.

Future research subjects might include the device-related subject of improvement in the 3D-sensor accuracy. Then, for GPS, to improve protability, the antenna must be miniaturized and made lighter. Moreover, in MR, there is a fault in which the object which is in front of the VR image actually disappears because the VR image is overlapped and displayed on top of the object. Development of a technique to remedy that problem is also desired. In addition, it is necessary to prepare an environment so that examination of the system functions can be performed.

Acknowledgements

The data of the five-storied pagoda used by this research was created in collaboration with Dr. Byun, C. and Prof. Ikegami, T, Faculty of Fine Arts, Kyoto City University of Arts.

References

Yeo, W, Lou, C, Kaga, A, Sasada, T, Byun, C and Ikegami, T: 2003, An Interactive Digital Archive for Japanese Historical Architecture, *CAADRIA 2003*, Thailand, pp. 513-522.

Tang, SK, Liu, YT, Lin, CY, Shih, SC, Chang, CH and Chiu, Y-C: 2001, The visual harmony between new and old materials in the restoration of historical architecture: A study of computer simulation, *CAADRIA 2001*, Sydney, pp. 205-210.

Tang, SK, Liu, YT, Fan, YC, Wu, YL, Lu, HY, Lim, CK, Hung, LY and Chen, Y: 2002, How to Simulate and Realise a Disappeared City and City Life? - A VR Cave Simulation, *CAADRIA 2002*, Malaysia, pp. 301-308.

Shih, NJ, Lin, CY, and Liau, C Y: 2004, A 3D Information System for the Digital Preservation of Historical Architecture, Architecture in the Network Society, *eCAADe2004*, Copenhagen, pp. 630-637.

Lou, C, Kaga, A, Sasada, T: 2003, Environmental design with huge landscape in real-time simulation system - Real-time simulation system applied to real project, *Automation in Construction*, **12**(5): 481-485.

Kaga, A and Sasada, T: 2005, Interactive Environmental Design using 3D Digital City Archives, *CAAD TALKS 4, Insights of Digital Cities*, ARCHIDATA, Taipei, pp. 211-228.

Byun, CS: 2003, New possibility of the digital archives in a wooden old building: computer graphics of the new possibility five-storied pagoda in the Kyouou-gokoku-ji Temple of the digital archives in a wooden old building, Kyoto City University of Arts.

Milgram, P. and Kishino, F: 1994, A Taxonomy of Mixed Reality Visual Displays, *IEICE Transactions on Information Systems* **E77-D**(12): 1321-1329.

Kato, H, Billinghurst, M, Asano, K, Tachibana, K: 1999, An Augmented Reality System and its Calibration based on Marker Tracking, *Transactions of the Virtual Reality Society of Japan*, **4**(4): 607-616.

You, S, Neumann, U and Azuma, R: 1999, Hybrid Inertial and Vision Tracking for Augmented Reality Registration, *Proceedings of VR '99*, pp. 260-267.

Behringer, R: 1999, Registration for Outdoor Augmented Reality Applications Using Computer Vision Techniques and Hybrid Sensors, *Proceedings of VR '99*, pp. 244-251.

Ito, S: 2005, A study on informational space of wide range area –Based on mixed reality–, *Journal of Architecture and Planning* **590**: 87-94.

Fukuda, T, Kawaguchi, M, Yeo, W and Kaga, A: 2006, Development of the Environmental Design Tool "Tablet MR" on-site by Mobile Mixed Reality Technology, *eCAADe2006*, Greece, pp. 84-87.

BECOMING EDUCATED

DIDACTICAL INTEGRATION OF ANALOG AND DIGITAL TOOLS INTO ARCHITECTURAL EDUCATION

From the geometric sketch to the rapid prototyping manufactured artifact

MILENA STAVRIĆ, HEIMO SCHIMEK
AND ALBERT WILTSCHE
Graz University of Technology, Austria

Abstract. This paper describes the new syllabus of the course "Methods of representation" that has evolved in the first year of architectural study at our university. Due to the rapidly growing digital possibilities students need to know/learn the new topics and tools which are relevant in modern architectural design practice. Our students should be empowered rather than overwhelmed by the arsenal of digital tools available today. In this course we try to define the essential skills in representation which we achieve through the synthesis of digital and analog methods and tools. Digital and analog methods and tools we use are: study and construction of complex geometry, observation and analysis of organic forms and their representation through hand drawing, collaborative work through peer-to-peer learning on our web interface, NURBS-modelling, rapid prototyping and desktop publishing.

1. Introduction

Architects are constantly searching for new tools – digital inspiration – in other disciplines and manufacturing processes and they are seeking for a combination of analog and digital tools in order to define an aesthetic which can reflect the new phenomena in architectural computing. Due to these rapidly growing digital possibilities, students of architecture need to know/learn the new topics and tools which are relevant in modern architectural design practice. They should be empowered rather than overwhelmed by the arsenal of digital tools available today.

A Dong, A Vande Moere & JS Gero (eds), CAADFutures'07, 61–70.

2. Design Education

Modern architectural design education has to teach students how to apply the knowledge and skills of digital techniques and methods using digital and analogue tools by emphasizing the understanding and research of specific characteristics of different media. Digital tools modified the approach to the design process and today they are an undeniable part of design. The new technology provides the designer a way to control and integrate all steps of the design process starting from the sketch on a digital table to the virtual 3D product and finally to the physical model. This is called integrated 3D design process chain and the direct link between CAD and CAM is known as integrated technology. The new possibilities create pros and cons. On the one hand the designer manages the whole process by himself. On the other hand it is necessary to know how to handle with all the used techniques.

For the first steps of designing one still uses two dimensional representation tools (paper or digital tables for sketches and screens for the 3D models) to externalize and represent the "three dimensional ideas in mind". From our experience there is a great lack of knowledge in the area of spatial thinking and visualising and transferring this knowledge onto a "technical medium" Piegl (2005). Therefore we put a main focus on the improvement and training on this by using a funded geometric education to develop the spatial and visual reasoning.

Because of the importance of the above mentioned in the "new architecture practice" we implemented the following in the curriculum "Methods of representation" already in the first year of architectural study.

In a first stage students are instructed in funded geometric knowledge and trained in developing spatial and visual thinking. In a second (progressive) stage integrated design process and integrated technology is taught. Our course covers a wide range from handmade sketches to rapid prototyping produced products.

From our point of view this is a new approach to the understanding of CAAD teaching because in combination with funded geometric instructions we teach integrate both analogue and digital techniques .

3. Representation

In the past three decades a great number of publications have described, explored and summarized a relationship between representation and design process. Representation and design can be examined by categorizing them from a number of perspectives. For our research, two approaches are relevant: external representation in visual reasoning and representation as a tool for design visualization. We choose these approaches because architects are constantly confronted with spatial shapes and structures, with internal and external representation and with the communication of this matter. The link between visualizing an idea in mind and its externalized transfer in order to be aware of oneself and to communicate with others is a very complicate subject-matter. This must be trained from the very beginning of architectural education. The visual representation on a two dimensional medium and the converse way of understanding a sketch or drawing and their transformation into a spatial form in mind are the crucial points thereby.

3.1. EXTERNAL REPRESENTATION OF VISUAL REASONING

From a psychological point of view, our design thinking operates through externalized representation in visual reasoning (Oxman 2002). Visual reasoning and visual cognition may be considered as a keystone of design emergence. Visual cognitive richness is related to perceptual components. Perceptual components, according to Marr (1982) are shapes, which in design have a function of representation of the physical object. The characterization of these shapes is mainly based on their geometrical properties and relation between a geometrically derived secondary-form to its primary shape (Liu 1995). The ability to represent these shapes, their interpretation and reinterpretation is a central point of creativity. Thus, in a design process also shape ambiguity makes a creative process possible. Ambiguity may enable new interpretation of existing shapes and gives new meaning to the design process (Figure 1).

For our methodological approach in our second stage of teaching, tthe heoretical foundation can be found in Eizenberf's, analysis→ transformation→synthesis method (Knight 1999). With the appropriate

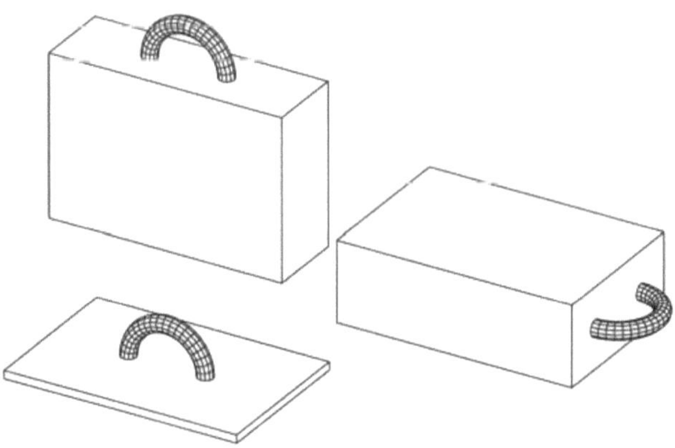

Figure 1. New configurations of the same shapes enable various interpretations

geometric grammar, free computational forms based on NURBS technology we established a process for generating organic forms. Through shape generation by basic geometry we refer to the design process as a non-accidental phenomenon. We agree with Oxman (2002) who proposes that basic knowledge guides design. Therefore we say that knowledge of geometry and its grammar guides the students to transformational emergence.

Students start with an analysis of organic forms, as a representation of an abstract architecture and form. A second part is the extraction of rules by emphasizing the understanding of geometry, and then playing with these rules and eventually formulate own rules for design that satisfy a given program.

3.2. REPRESENTATION AS A TOOL FOR DESIGN VISUALISATION

The choice of a representational medium as a tool for design visualisation has a huge impact on the character of the design results. The long tradition of Euclidean geometry and a traditional medium for representation (paper) led to the consequence that architects "drew what they could build, and built what they could draw" (Mitchell 2001). New digital tools have opened new tracts and possibilities of representation of non-Euclidean geometries. Today the question is no longer whether a particular form is buildable or not, but rather the deduction of new instruments of practice (Kolarevic 2003). The development of tools is dependent on design theories and vice versa. The protagonist of the radical conceptual and formal architectural research from the early 1980 is Zaha Hadid, who found in new media a helpful tool which was already established as an architectural language. For many designers in the second half of 1990ies new digital tools inspired the conceptualization of new digital esthetic and a new terminology was adopted like hyper surface design, blob architecture, parametric architecture, hyper body etc. (Oxman 2006). Therefore the medium of representation defines and limits the design process and enables or disables the continuum from design process to production.

Today's digital representation media enable us to represent a wide range of complex geometric forms with constructing complexity (Mitchell 2005) like organic forms.

4. Didactical Methods

"A creative person is one who can process in new ways the information directly at hand – ordinarily sensory data available to all of us. A writer needs words, a musician needs notes, an artist needs visual perception, and all need some knowledge of the techniques of their crafts. But a creative individual intuitively sees possibilities for transforming ordinary data into a new creation, transcendent over the mere raw materials." (Edwards 1989)

We propose to redefine didactic methods to teach the use of new digital tools at an early stage of design education. Geometry is the core of most digital designing tools, a basis for understanding and performing handmade (analog) representations of design ideas, processes and structures. A number of enquiries worldwide (Saito 1998, Leopold 2001) proved direct connection between the study of the subject matter of space geometry and the improvement of visual spatial intelligence (Gittler 1998) as one of the most important abilities for an engineer. Hence it was obvious to us to build up the training of analog and digital tools as well as the introduction of design processes on a geometric framework.

Austria has a long tradition and great experience in teaching geometry in high school and university. Students are both instructed in hand made geometry which means space geometry constructed by pencil, ruler and compasses and in using CAGeometricD tools. CAGD-tools have been used for over than fifteen years. Not all the students choose the "geometric way" in high school. Consequently universities get experienced and unexperienced students in geometry. At a first stage we try to equate the gap of geometric knowledge with additional courses obligatory for the non experienced ones.

We take this great "educational advantage" as a base for further instructions of geometry at university. We build up a solid base in geometry with the help of the following tools: geometric freehand sketches; constructive space geometry; and, 3D-CAD-Packages.

In this phase students learn to carry out many topics from simple freehand sketches up to the modelling of complex 3D-structures derived from platonic shapes (see section Geometry). We engage the students to constantly evaluate the tools used in the course. They should identify the pros and cons as well as the grammar of these tools and how they can be used properly (Mark 2002). During this phase we conduct ex-cathedra teaching and no creative input from the students is expected. Students have to learn fundamentals first in order to develop their own ideas later on. The students reported that just the combination of analog and digital tools enables them to get a deeper insight. The result of a survey among 150 students shows that 75% think that 3D-modelling on the computer leads to better understanding of 2D-representations of 3-dimensional objects but at the same time 80% consider that hand made construction of geometry plays an equal important role.

The second phase is dedicated to the design process. On the basis of the geometric principles of the first phase the students should now be prepared to develop and present their own ideas and first digital products and finally build them using traditional output and rapid prototyping machines.

Now geometry plays again a significant role. The design process is now supported by geometric thinking, analyzing and problem solving which was trained before. Whatever strategy the students choose, it is independent of the tools involved if the process is set up on geometric principles.

Because of the complexity of architecture design we select issues which have the same characteristic as architecture design but in a more appropriate scale. We take organic forms like flowers, fruits, bones etc. and their structure to represent architecture. 3D modelling of organic forms enhances the students' capability of developing free form design almost without limitation of functional characteristics. The didactical set up is funded by Eizenberf's method (see Section 3.1). Students start with observation, analysis and sketches of organic forms followed by the modelling of individual chosen forms in a 3D-CAD-Program. After that they create their own hybrid forms by taking (downloading) design parts from colleagues' work (Figure 2).

Figure 2. Analysis, generation and transformation of freeform surfaces

5. Geometry

In the first phase the students receive instructions in sketching and constructing axonometric and perspective views of 3D geometries. Additionally shadow constructions and reconstruction of perspective views are used to demonstrate the connection between a space configuration and its two dimensional representation (Figure 3).

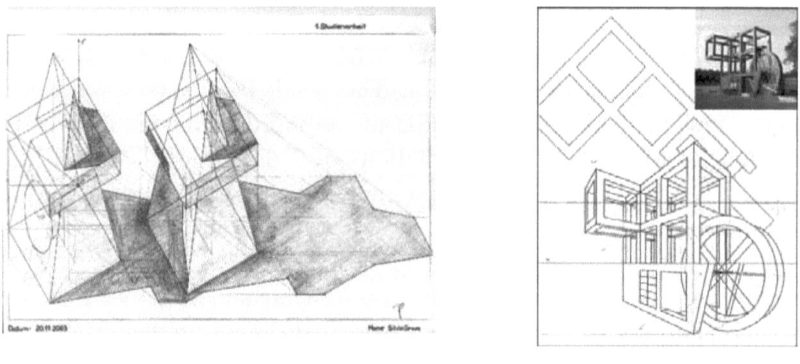

Figure 3. Hand constructions

Besides this we apply 3D-CAD-software to train solid modelling with standard primitives like boxes, spheres, cylinders and objects created by extrusion (Figure 4).

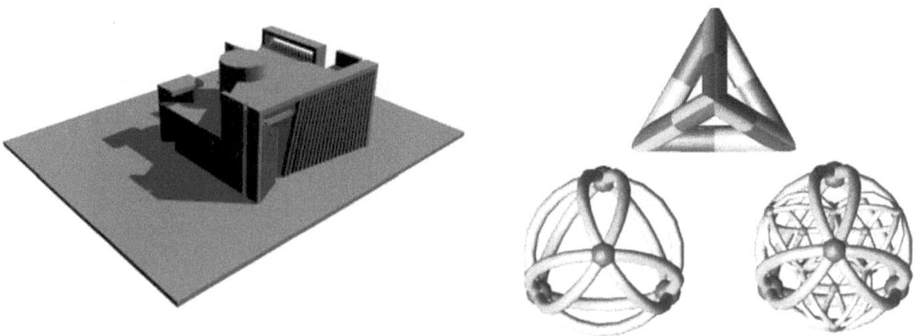

Figure 4. Solid Modelling with standard primitives and "platonic" shapes

In the second phase (the design part) we use again sketching as a natural human tool to communicate first design ideas and as a companion for the whole process.

For the generation of organic forms we consider freeform surfaces – Bezier- and NURBS technology – as an appropriate geometric and digital tool. Students get instructions in the theory of freeform surfaces, which means generation, algorithms (e.g. Casteljau-algorithm), data structures, C1- and C2- continuity, blending, etc.

6. Output – Rapid Prototyping

Since students today are "Naturally born computer users" (Pongratz and Perbellini 2000) we fully agree with Kvan (2004) and teach students a deeper understanding of the use of digital media right from the beginning of their career and not just before they graduate in advanced classes.

We do not consider digital tools as extensions to manual skills or digital design teaching as service role but rather as a holistic integration of computational design methods into architectural design culture.

It has become unquestionable to integrate Rapid Prototyping technology besides the more traditional output machines into the curriculum which we started three years ago with two CO2 Laser Cutters followed by an ABS plastic 3d printer and a CNC milling machine. After three years of employment of these machines within the digital design education we identified very clearly: Rapid Prototyping Technology, more precisely 3D-printers can be used to enhance the involvement into the architectural design process and motivate students tremendously through fully integrated

3d-process chains (Schodek 2005) where students are enabled to review their work constantly with a physical model (cause-impact). Additionally students are engaged to use the machines independently in an experimental way (Figure 5).

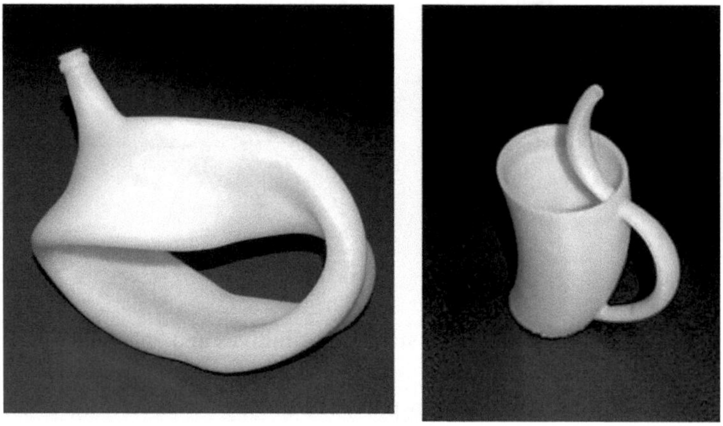

Figure 5. Printed ABS-models

Unfortunately production time and cost does not allow using RP to educate a large number of students (the course "Methods of representation" is taken by more than 180 first year students every year).

But we assume that like other technologies (for an A3 laser printer you had to pay the price of luxury car) rapid prototyping will become more affordable and faster very soon. Then a larger number of students will be able to make expedient use of RP-machines in their architectural education.

7. Collaboration – Single Work

In our courses we established a database founded website at http://iam.tugraz.at/dm0/s06 which is both a presentation and communication tool. Every step of student's work is saved and documented by upload. Evaluation of students work can be executed by the teachers and the students themselves can compare and exchange their work with each other. But above all this web based system is a tool for creative and collaborative work where users have the possibility to learn from each other and it serves as a forum for exchanging experience, to keep track and discuss architectural design teaching.

8. Evaluation

The course "Methods of representation" is evaluated every year by TUGonline" – a information management system at the University of Technology in Graz (Austria). The outcome of the last two years shows that students are very satisfied with the course especially with the diversified content, various interesting examples, the tutorials, the organization of the course and the regular updated web site.

9. Conclusion and Outlook

New media has changed the way how we design today. This radical change has to be reflected in design education as well. However we consider analog tools as an essential complement to digital media. This paper shows how we merge both the digital and the analog within the curriculum of our teachings and research. Equipped with this knowledge we can face the challenge of identifying the core in an overwhelming pool of information. Solely if we understand the principles of geometry, the language of shapes, we can capitalize on the full potency of digital media.

Acknowledgements

Urs Hirschberg initiated this course 3 years ago at the Faculty of Architecture, Graz (Austria). During these years the course has developed and adapted constantly. Deeply involved in the teaching of this course along with the authors are Otto Röschel, Christian Pagitsch and Richard Dank. Thanks to our tutors and all students who took part in the studies. Additionally the authors would like to thank the referees for their comments which have helped to improve the paper.

References

Edwards B: 1989, *Drawing on the right side of the brain*, Putnam Publishing, New York.

Gittler G, Gluck J: 1998, Differential Transfer of Learning: Effects of Instruction in Descriptive Geometry on Spatial Test Performance, *JGG* **2**(1): 71-84.

Knight T: 1999, *Applications in architectural design, and education and practice*, Report for the NSF/MIT Workshop on Shape Computation, MIT Cambridge.

Kolarevic, B (ed): 2003, *Architecture in the Digital Age: Design and Manufacturing,* Spon Press, London.

Kvan T et al.: 2004, Ditching the Dinosaur: Redefining the Role of Digital Media in Education, *International Journal of Design Computing* **7**.

Leopold C et al.: 2001, International Experiences in Developing the Spatial Visualisation Abilities of Engineering Students, *JGG* **5**(1): 81-91.

Liu, YT: 1995, Some phenomena of seeing shapes in design, *Design Studies* **16**(3): 367–385.

Marr, D: 1982, *Vision*, W.H. Freeman, San Francisco.

Mark, E et al.: 2002, Theoretical and Experimental Issues in the Preliminary Stages of Learning/Teaching CAAD, *in* K Koszewski and S Wrona (eds), *eCAADe 2002*, Warsaw, pp. 205-211.

Mitchell W, 2001: Roll Over Euclid: How Frank Gehry Designs and Builds, *in* J Fiona Ragheb (ed), *Frank Gehry, Architect,* Guggenheim Museum Publications, New York, pp. 352-363.

Mitchell ,W: 2005, Constructing Complexity, *in* B Martens and A Brown (eds), *CAADFutures2005*, Springer, Vienna, pp. 41-50.

Oxman, RE: 2002, The Thinking Eye: Visual Re-Cognition in Design Emergence, *Design Studies* **23**(2): 135-164.

Oxman, R: 2006, Theory and Design in the First Digital Age, *Design Studies* **27**(3): 229-265.

Piegl, LA: 2005, Ten challenges in computer-aided design, *CAD* **37**(4): 461-470.

Pongratz C, Perbellini M: 2000, *Natural born CAADesigners*, Birkhäuser, Basel.

Saito T et al.: 1998, Relations between Spatial Ability Evaluated by a Mental Cutting Test and Engineering Graphics Education, *Proc. 8thICECGDG*, Austin, pp. 231-235.

Schodek, D et al.: 2005, *Digital Design and Manufacturing*, John Wiley and Sons, Hoboken, New Jersey.

AESTHETIC DATA VISUALIZATION AS A RESOURCE FOR EDUCATING CREATIVE DESIGN

From information visualization over ambient display to data art

ANDREW VANDE MOERE
University of Sydney, Australia

Abstract. Data visualization is usually considered an expert field reserved for the computer science or data analysis specialist. In contrast, in this paper we argue that the approaches and theories from data visualization can form a rich contextual resource for teaching creative design principles to students. A conceptual data mapping model is proposed that describes a continuum between 'traditional' data visualization applications and more artistically inclined works of 'visualization art'. This model is useful to clarify conceptual relationships between different visualization design approaches, ranging from traditional data representation applications over to ambient displays to visualization art experiences. This exchange of insights from related scientific and artistic fields forms the foundation for potential collaboration initiatives in research or educational contexts. Subsequently, this aesthetic data visualization model is explained and illustrated by various student works accomplished in several creative design visualization course units.

1. Introduction

Visualization aims to represent data graphically in order to exploit high-bandwidth human perceptual and cognitive capabilities. Accordingly, a visual representation generally aims to empower humans to detect patterns and derive interferences out of visual form. Two important visualization categories exist. Scientific visualization is concerned about the accurate or more effective simulation of data that has a natural geometric structure. Typical examples include the visual depiction of human anatomy, weather patterns or the dynamic behavior of materials. Conversely, data visualization

A Dong, A Vande Moere & JS Gero (eds), CAADFutures'07, 71–84.

deals with so-called abstract data, which has no physical presence in reality, such as measurements in economic, networking or social sciences.

Information aesthetics is an emerging field that analyzes the aesthetics of information access as well as the creation of new media works that beautify information processing (Manovich 2001). Its practice consists of data representation and interfacing applications that are situated between the realm of functional data visualization, and the more subjectively loaded nature of fine arts.

One should note that many 'traditional' data visualization algorithms, solutions and visual styles demonstrate levels of genius and creativity. However, until today, the field has shown little understanding of typical creative design considerations such as the subjective value or purpose of visual aesthetics, intrigue or pleasure. Tensions seem to exist between the 'traditional' data visualization field, typically focused on developing high-end applications for research and commercial enterprises, and more 'artistic' approaches, which aim for a non-expert audience attending art exhibitions or browsing theme-specific websites. Although both fields investigate new ways of representing data, misunderstandings tend to arise when respective works are reviewed with identical assessment criteria. Therefore, a basic understanding about the commonalities and inequalities between both fields is required to better appreciate their motivation, purpose and significance, to facilitate accurate reviewing processes, and to allow for a more useful exchange of relevant knowledge that would benefit both.

Currently, several design schools have integrated sophisticated data visualization themes in their educational and research curricula, of which the most prominent examples probably include MIT's Sociable Media Group, NYU's Interactive Telecommunications Program or IVREA's Interaction Design Institute. Even in the field of architecture, one can observe conceptual data visualization influences, ranging from infographical representations arising from site analysis studies to large-scale data-driven building facades that reflect information ambiently in public space, as shown in Figure 1. The focus on data visualization within a creative design education context is meaningful in at least three ways. Firstly, the intrinsic use of real world data provides students with a genuine purpose and relevant design context. As the designed object conveys 'real' (versus arbitrary, mock-up or random) data that contains some sort of relevant measurements, an intrinsic creditability to the designed artifact is provided. Secondly, the development of visually attractive and directly tangible objects arising from highly abstract themes and concepts seems to challenge and motivate typical design students. Accordingly, 'inventing' a new visualization method can be contextualized as a typical design process that should comply to Vitruvius'

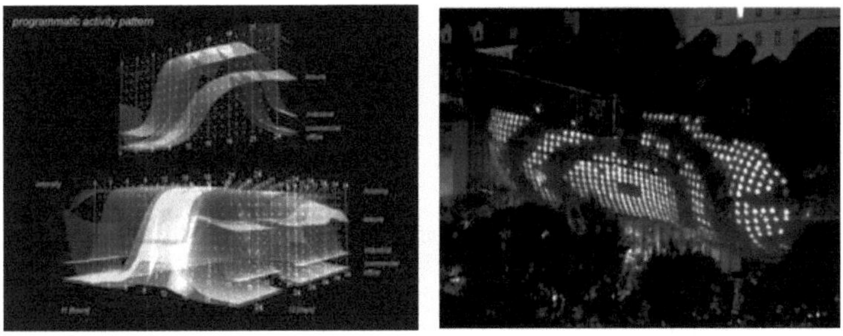

Figure 1. Data visualization influences in architecture. Left: a data visualization used for an architectural site analysis (van Berkel and Bos 1999), Right: modal.patterns, a large-scale interactive façade that translates text data into abstract visual and audio animation sequences (Gaviria 2006)

basic principles: a 'good' visualization needs to be functional (*utilitas*), effective (*firmitas*) as well as beautiful (*venustas*).

For instance, a seemingly meaningless object tends to be understood differently by onlookers once it is clear its design is based on data: as its 'purpose' is revealed, people typically wish to decrypt any 'hidden' data patterns, and to reveal its visual presence in the context of the data attributes. Accordingly, by merging artistic and functional design considerations, students are challenged to consider the purpose of aesthetics, and the emotional connotations provoked by purely functional objects.

Based on the natural tension between data visualization and visualization art, this paper aims to describe the virtue of data visualization as a resource for educating creative design principles. It relates the qualitative differences to a simplified model of data mapping, and illustrates the spectrum between both fields in the context of several creative design student works.

2. Data Visualization versus Visualization Art

This section defines some of the qualitative differences between data visualization, an established academic field inspired by the fields of computer science, psychology, semiotics, graphic design, cartography and art, and what we coin as 'visualization art', an emerging field that is more inspired by interactive art, new media, graphic design and social sciences. As shown in Figure 2, even for the same dataset (i.e. genetic code), different visualization techniques exist, each with their own unique purpose, and each using creative design principles differently. While traditional data visualization allows for the interactive exploration of genes and their functional relationships, more aesthetic approaches aim for overwhelming the audience with the huge size or almost randomness character of the collection of genetic code.

Figure 2. From data visualization over visualization design to visualization art. Left: Circos, a visualization of functional relationships within a genome (Krzywinski 2006), Middle: 13 million letters of genetic code of Chromosome 21 on a single poster (Fry 2002), Right: DNA space, a generative artwork animation using a DNA sequence as a dynamic data structure (stanza 2003)

2.1. DATA VISUALIZATION

Data visualization most often is described as "…the use of computer-supported, interactive, visual representations to amplify cognition" (Card, Mackinlay and Shneiderman 1999). *Computing* facilitates the automatic creation of visualizations, away from time-intensive hand-drawn methods. *Interactivity* allows users to form individual hypotheses on-the-fly, which can then be tested and reformulated in an iterative, and therefore necessarily interactive, way. Importantly, according to this definition, data visualization has a single purpose: to increase the *human understanding* of data. Data visualization therefore focuses on methods that reveal *patterns* hidden inside the dataset, such as the similarities between different multiple data items, those that are significantly different, and the detection of specific tendencies or trends. Data visualization thus specifically looks *in* the data to derive useful information, meaning or knowledge, and potentially allows for the detection of their underlying principles. Data visualization research is generally treated as a typical engineering issue, without any consideration whether such techniques can also be used for creative design purposes. Instead, its research aims to optimize functional requirements, for instance whether users can understand the representations *effectively*, that is the accuracy and completeness with which users achieve specific tasks, and *efficiently*, that is the resources expended in relation to the effectiveness criterion, such as the required time or computational power (van Wijk 2006).

2.2. INFORMATION AESTHETICS

In recent years, a stream of mainly young and self-motivated people is experimenting to visualize fashionable real-world datasets in 'artistic' ways (Judelman 2004; Vande Moere 2005). Independent from institutional or commercial pressure, their visualizations demonstrate the initiative, enthusiasm, interest and skill to tackle complex issues that were previously reserved for the visualization researcher or developer. Captured in the relative limited fame of online weblogs or art exhibitions, their contributions seem to be somewhat ignored by the academic world. Why have these more creative data visualizations apparently become fashionable recently?

In the *information society* of today, people are literally surrounded by data. Each single email message, phone conversation or purchase is tracted, recorded and stored. Data is continuously accumulated, almost never deleted. It has become clear that our modern society generates data faster than technology can analyze it. While many sophisticated technologies exist for generating, communicating, filtering, storing and querying data, it is still an open question how this information can be best represented for humans to to understand. In spite of ultra-fast networks and increasingly huge displays, only few visualization techniques have been shown to successfully communicate insight. This problem has become a natural challenge that initiated several research projects and commercial ventures, and equally forms an ultimate challenge and motivation for a creative designer.

Recently, several *software tools* have been marketed that are specialized in the creation of high-end visual applications. Ranging from free, community-supported open-source initiatives (e.g. *Processing*, *vvvv*) to commercial enterprises (e.g. *MAX/MSP Jitter*, *Virtools, Macromedia Flash*), these authoring tools are becoming increasingly affordable, more powerful, better supported and easier to use. The concept of "visual programming", the process of connecting so-called "programming blocks", allows the on-the-fly creation of complex computer programs. In fact, visual programming has finally allowed software development to resemble to *sketching*, a typical design activity which is inherently elaborate and cyclic (Lawson 1997). By hiding low-level technical and programmatic complexities, these new software tools facilitate the creation of sophisticated data-driven visualizations by people not necessarily schooled in computer science or software development principles.

Typical creative professions, either by self-learning or by education, have become ever more *proficient* in typical computer science skills, including programming techniques, database management and computer graphics principles. Accordingly, creative design is increasingly borrowing from the newest developments in computer science research.

Relatively large and complex, but also *interesting datasets* have become increasingly accessible. Naturally, most used datasets originate from fields that trickle human curiosity, ranging from social networking (e.g. del.icio.us, Technorati), socially and environmentally relevant statistics offered by governmental (census data, Bureau of Statistics) and non-governmental organizations (e.g. Gapminder, Greenpeace), or even Right to Information

Acts (e.g. Enron email traffic log) and involuntary corporate leaks (e.g. AOL search, credit card financial information).

Online content creation and *sharing* has matured in so far that the efforts of independent visualization developers are relatively easily distributed and recognized in online newsgroups, forums, weblogs, wikis, portals or other content curation aggregators. At the same time, several reputable companies such as online news (e.g. CNET, digg.com), search engines (e.g. Google Trends), and shopping portals (e.g. Browse Goods) have started to integrate novel visualization approaches in their web interfaces. These developments are noteworthy, as they illustrate the recent shift of visualization outside of specialist business applications, reaching into the popular (online) culture.

3. Data Mapping

3.1. THE DATA MAPPING PROCESS

As mentioned before, data visualization focuses specifically on the representation of so-called *abstract* data, which is characterized by its lack of physical presence. Such datasets are mostly of technological nature and invented by humankind, ranging from stock market quotes over functional DNA sequences to sensor reading logs. Exactly because such datasets have no intrinsic visual form, a *metaphor* is required to translate its values into a representation that can be more easily comprehended by humans. It is exactly the invention of such elegant metaphor that forms an interesting problem from a creative design perspective. Following steps can be recognized in the use of data mapping metaphors (North 2005):

- **Data Mapping.** Data mapping applies a set of predefined rules to the numerical and textual values contained in the dataset. These rules define exactly how specific data attributes are represented. Typically, each data item (e.g. database row) within a dataset corresponds to a unique visual entity, such as a point, line, polygon or 3D object. Each visual entity is then manipulated (e.g. position, direction, color, size, shape) according to the specific data values it represents. Users can then observe the resulting constellation of transformed visual entities, and detect apparent visual patterns (e.g. outliers, clusters, tendencies) that reflect meaningful phenomena in the data. Typically, each data visualization technique is uniquely characterized by an original set of data mapping rules.
- **Visual Transfer.** This phase considers the transmission of the resulting visualization from the presentation medium, via the eye, to the human brain. It focuses on how humans visually perceive the world, and thus considers aspects from cognitive studies, such as human perception, color theory, visual bandwidth or Gestalt Laws. The optimization of visual

transfer aspects directly influences the data visualization performance, i.e. whether it can be easily perceived and understood.

- **Inverse Data Mapping.** Before a user can interpret the resulting representation, one needs to 'understand' the used data mapping rules. This means a user 'inverses' the data mapping rules that were applied: visual attributes, such as position, color, size and shape, are 'reverted' into meaningful mental constructs: objects close by each other are seen as 'related', those with an equal color are considered from the same category, and so on. What are essentially a collection of visual entities and attributes is 'interpreted' as meaningful information, producing insight where there was none before.

3.2. FROM DATA VISUALIZATION TO VISUALIZATION ART

The abstraction of a data mapping metaphor can vary between intuitive and immediately understandable versus obtuse and ambiguous. In this paper, we argue that the main difference between a functionalistic and an artistic data visualization is its data mapping approach. Accordingly, 'traditional' data visualization is concerned with the accurate depiction of small patterns, seeking insights 'within' the dataset. Visualization art, in contrast, exploits the representational power of data to communicate insights 'about' the dataset, often transcending any meaningful patterns that might occur in it. Accordingly, data visualization tends to use data mapping metaphors that depict the dataset objectively, using a metaphor that is immediately inversable to meaning hidden inside the dataset. Visualization art tends to use concepts that deal with the dataset as a whole, using metaphors that can be imaginative and so ambiguous that inversing becomes unpredictable, potentially to the extent of being arbitrary. However, the ambiguity of visualization art deliberately puts the responsibility of interpretation (and misinterpretation) by the viewer instead of the designer (Gaver, Beaver and Benford 2003), forcing onlookers to focus on the meaning of the dataset (or the data mapping itself), instead of revealing detailed, expert information that might be hidden inside the data itself. One should note that this conceptual model is based on the phenomenal observation of a visualization artifact, which can differ with what the developer had actually intended.

4. Data Mapping in Creative Design Education

The data visualization context in educating creative design is demonstrated by the illustrations of this section, which are primarily based on coursework student works produced between 2004-2006 at the Key Centre of Design Computing and Cognition at the University of Sydney. These figures show how data visualization can be used to introduce students with a wide range of design challenges, ranging from expert tools to interactive art works.

4.1. DATA VISUALIZATION

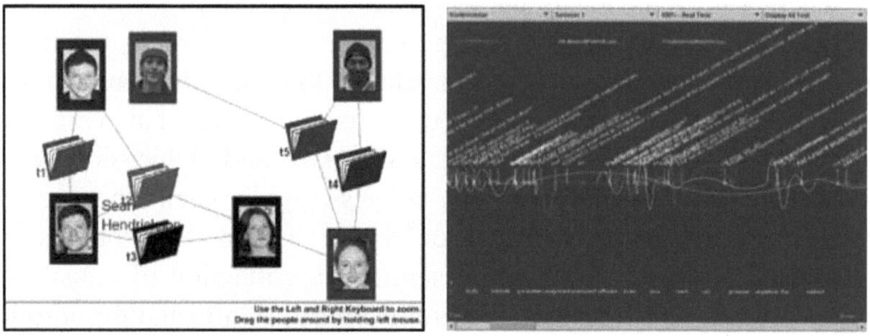

Figure 3. Infodesign course results. Left: activity health display displaying active collaboration between people and the according stress levels (Author: Jason Green). Right: online chat text visualization based on keywords (Author: Andrea Lau)

Data visualization is specifically used for 'complex' datasets, typically containing a very large amount of data objects, which have multiple data dimensions that might change over time. Its purpose is to increase the understanding the phenomena present in the dataset, so users can derive useful information, make informed decisions or communicate knowledge about it. The design of an appropriate data mapping metaphor is mostly motivated from task performance considerations, with a strong focus on the accurate and objective depiction of data values. Few research approaches have even proposed automated techniques that recommend the most effective data visualization method according to specific dataset characteristics (Bergman, Rogowitz and Treinish 1995; Healey, Amant and Elhaddad 2000). The integration of creative design aspects is mostly neglected, except of some attention to "usability" or "user experience" effects. While some evaluations might question users whether they find the visualizations 'enjoyable' to use, any aspect of deliberate creative or aesthetic design seems to be considered as an superficial add-on, mostly to convey the aspect of coolness or novelty. Accordingly, only few visualization approaches have reported a collaboration with designers or artists (Healey and Enns 2002; Keefe, Karelitz, Vote et al. 2005). Their outcomes show a strong appreciation of the typical creative design process and the focus on re-questioning of what is considered as common knowledge. However, as shown in Figure 3, design-influenced data visualization can be easily used within the context of professional applications, and might seem most beneficial in terms of user experience.

In short, data visualization is concerned about specific patterns hidden in abstract datasets ('what', object), for the purpose of increasing insight in the data ('why', purpose), using the method of data mapping rules that can be interactively manipulated by users ('how, methodology).

4.2. VISUALIZATION DESIGN

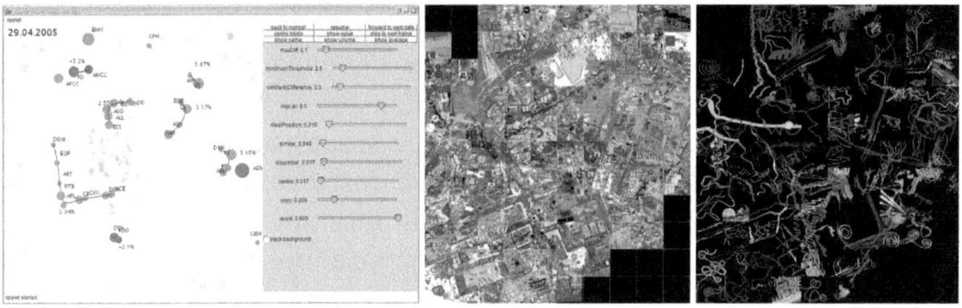

Figure 4. Left: Infoboids, a self-organizing visualization design using the concept of swarming to convey the dynamic nature of the New York Stock Exchange over time (Authors: Andrea Lau and Andrew Vande Moere), Right: infoscape course results, a collaborative geographical map of the University campus created by 100 students

Visualization design tends to represent data in a more iconographic way, devoting as much emphasis on the beautification as on the clarification of the dataset. By doing so, specific data simplifications often occur. Details might get lost, so that the resulting visual representation might only highlight a few dataset aspects instead of conveying the complete dataset. For instance, a typical visualization design might specifically depict the sheer size of a dataset, rather than inventing an effective way to overcome this specific complexity. Accordingly, the data mapping integrates design considerations as an inherent quality that emphasizes specific, predefined data characteristics and engages users by its visual aesthetics. In Figure 4, two such visualization designs are shown. On the left, infoboids combines the self-organizing nature of swarming to illustrate the dynamic characteristics of a Stock Market dataset. Companies that experience similar stock market quote changes over time flock closely together, while dissimilar companies are repulsed. On the right, the infoscape landscape depicts the collaborative efforts of more than 100 undergraduate students that 'captured' abstract features discovered on our university campus on a shared map. These particular visualizations differ from traditional data visualization in their intended purpose: non-expert users can feel compelled by the relatively simple but intriguing visual metaphors and consider investigating them over a longer period of time than professional data visualization tools. These applications still represent complex datasets, but invite onlookers for exploration and interpretation.

Visualization design is concerned about extrapolating specific data dimensions, for the purpose of highlighting specific data patterns (while diminishing others), using data mapping techniques that integrate aesthetics, have limited interaction, but still are relatively easily understandable.

4.3. AMBIENT DISPLAY/INFORMATIVE ART

Ambient display is an emerging visualization direction that aims to communicate information in the periphery of human attention. Ambient displays are generally meant as architectural, physical interfaces between people and information, positioned in public spaces such as an office or a hallway, translating data in a calm, non-intrusive experience (Wisneski, Ishii, Dahley et al. 1998). Because ambient displays are used in a public context, creative design is exploited for functional purposes, for instance to adapt the physical design to the physical environment or usage context (Mankoff, Dey, Hsieh et al. 2003). Creative design is required in order to merge the display in the physical surroundings, in order to augment the acceptability of the general public, and to be able to entice the audience repeatedly over long periods of time. An ambient display data mapping is unique in that it deliberately 'hides' data behind a metaphor that requires time and effort to understand. Because of its size and context, an ambient display often hasarchitectural qualities (see Figure 5). For instance, an ambient display can consist of a complex wallpaper pattern that adapts to dynamic data streams in real time, such as network traffic or shopping habits. Here, students experience the relevance of real data, and learn how it can be represented in a non-intrusive way within a spatially relevant context. Creative design considerations become an integral part of the display, and ultimately determines whether the information representation is boring and undecipherable, or in contrast, pleasant and intriguing to learn and discover over a long period of time.

In short, ambient display is concerned about relatively simple datasets with few data dimensions, for the purpose of informing people in a non-intrusive way within a physical context, using non-interactive data mapping techniques that are potentially not immediately understandable, but highly enjoyable. This ambiguous approach aims to appeal human curiosity and

Figure 5. Infostudio course results. Left: a large-scale ambient installation showing real-time network traffic flowing through the architecture building (Authors: H. Cauchi, C. Lau, M. Page, and M. Tracey), Right: a spatial plant-like projection conveying real-time shopping behavior (Authors: H. Nguyen, J. Song and D. Xu)

allows for multiple, potentially conflicting interpretations (Gaver, Beaver and Benford 2003). It is different from common data visualization in that data shifts to the background, and patterns are more subtly depicted. The quality of such display depends on how it is adapted to its surroundings and is able to intriguingly 'reveal' information over a long period of time.

4.4. VISUALIZATION EXPERIENCE

Some data depictions focus beyond the visual sense, and instead attempt to stimulate alternative human senses, such as touch, smell, taste or sound. Such *visualization experiences* or *non-visual visualizations* can even be used in addition to the visual sense, and explore novel ways of conveying and interacting with information. As shown in Figure 6, such approaches can encompass new human-computer interaction interfaces such as a DJ turntable as a way to 'scratch' through time-varying data, or physical objects that move, wiggle or change temperature depending on human emotions communicated during online chat conversations. These visualizations are not concerned with depicting exact dataset values or meaningful patterns such as in the previous visualization categories, but rather exploit the use, presence and context of data to convey a specific dataset-related message: here, to 'playfully browse' time-varying data in a similar way to mixing music, or using complex motion typologies of physically moving objects or the cold/hot temperature alterations of a computer mouse as ways to 'more naturally' communicate human emotions than just static visual diagrams. This approach shows how educating creative design can act as a real research medium, as students explore new interaction or presentation media using the latest technological advances through the process of designing. Consequently, the presence of data is exploited as a relevant design context to communicate a strong, artistic message that is related to the dataset's meaning. Instead of revealing patterns 'in' data, a visualization experience is

Figure 6. Infodevice course results. Left: Data Scratching, exploring time-varying data by video jockeying (Author: Sheryl Soo), Middle: Dino, an egg-shaped device that moves in reaction to emotions during online chat conversations (Author: James Kim), Right: FeelMouse, a computer mouse that alters temperature depending on textual emotions (Author: Irene Chen)

thus more concerned about conveying the underlying meaning of the data in a thought-provoking way.

In short, a visualization experience is concerned about providing a (often multi-sensory) experience based on a creative design exploration, for the purpose of communicating a relevant conceptual theme that is related to what the data, seen as a holistic, socially relevant entity represents. It uses novel and often partly interactive data mapping techniques that are engaging and enjoyable. The quality of a visualization experience is generally dependent on its artistic expression, its originality and the relevance of the design rationale in the context of the chosen dataset.

4.5. VISUALIZATION ART/DATA ART

As the most 'extreme' form of data visualization, *data art* or *visualization art* foregoes any consideration of useful interpretation or understanding. Instead, data is used as an abstract textual or numerical source, similar to binary code or a matrix of parameters that control an algorithm. Data mapping is interpreted as a pure, literal form of translation, without consideration whether the outcome is understandable or even accurately perceivable. As shown in Figure 7, data art can be used to introduce students with complex generative programming algorithms of 3D animation effects, at which typically arbitrary numerical values are replaced with 'real' values from well-chosen data streams. For real-time, time-varying data, each program execution becomes unpredictable and emergent, and might even be different from what the designer originally had intended. Potential applications might include software screensavers, aesthetic public displays or music video animations.

The inherent connotations to the expectations and qualities of traditional visualization make these works stand out from other generative art works: although such visualizations are not concerned about patterns or meanings of

Figure 7. Infodemo course results. Left: a 3D animation based on data retrieved from a music group fan website called "Thursday" (Author: Sean Pieres), Right: recursive visual patterns based on real-time weather information (Author: Andrew Wallace)

the dataset, onlookers nevertheless expect such sort of purpose. Such approaches ultimately aim to reveal the 'essence' deeply hidden inside data: by revealing that seemingly random visual effects are actually induced by real data, onlookers start to interpret it differently, and become motivated to search (unsuccessfully) for the occurrence of any visual patterns.

Visualization art is thus concerned about providing a (often multi-sensory) user-engaging experience based on explorative creative design considerations, for the purpose of inducing a generative process that resembles a data mapping algorithm, by literally (and potentially non-effectively) translating data values into visual form. The quality of such works is based on how visual patterns are correlated with data phenomena, the occurrence of emergent effects, originality and dataset relevance.

5. Conclusion

In this paper, we described different forms of data representation according to their data mapping focus, hereby identifying the qualitative differences between functional, traditional data visualization to the more purely aesthetic forms of visualization art. It identified the rich potential of data visualization as a broad and freely interpretative resource for teaching creative design. This data mapping model enables teachers and students to exploit the various interpretations of data visualization to introduce different forms of creative design, ranging from functional, objective considerations in professional tool development to critical, artistic statements in generative new media art. In addition, it has been shown that data visualization can provide for a real-world and relevant design context, enables the creation of immediate and tangible artifacts, and can provide a rich platform of interpretation, similar to art but mostly with some sort of identifiable intended real-world purpose. A better understanding of the qualities related to the different data mapping categories allows for artistically motivated works to be more correctly interpreted and appreciated, so they can be more accurately reviewed and assessed according to their intended purpose and creative design rationale.

By integrating creative design considerations in data visualization applications, valuable tools can be developed that address the emotional experience and mental engagement of users, instead of solely focusing on traditional task effectiveness metrics. As an increasing number of independent and self-motivated data visualization works are emerging, especially in the fields of ambient display, sociable media, Internet applications and info-aesthetic visualizations, creative design education should seize this opportunity to school a new generation of data-aware visualization specialists that can make our information society a more sustainable and enjoyable place to live in.

Acknowledgements

We would like to thank all the students who participated in the different creative design data visualization courses at the Key Centre of Design Computing of the University of Sydney, and especially those that authored the projects that were used as illustrations in this paper.

References

Bergman, LD, Rogowitz, BE and Treinish, L: 1995, A rule-based tool for assisting colormap selection, in *Proceedings Visualization '95*, pp. 118-125.

Card, SK, Mackinlay, JD and Shneiderman, B: 1999, *Readings in Information Visualization: Using Vision to Think*, Morgan Kaufmann, San Francisco, CA.

Fry, B: 2002. Genomic Cartography: Chromosone 21. International Center of Photography, New York.

Gaver, WW, Beaver, J and Benford, S: 2003, Ambiguity as a Resource for Design, in *Conference on Human Factors in Computing Systems (SIGCHI)*, ACM, pp. 233-240.

Gaviria, AR, 2006, modal.patterns at Kunsthaus Graz. Graz, Austria.

Healey, CG, Amant, RS and Elhaddad, MS: 2000, ViA: a Perceptual Visualization Assistant, *AIPR Workshop: 3D Visualization for Data Exploration,* SPIE, pp. 2-11.

Healey, CG and Enns, JT: 2002, Perception and Painting: A Search for Effective, Engaging Visualizations, *IEEE Computer Graphics & Applications* **22**(2): 10-15.

Judelman, G: 2004, Aesthetics and Inspiration for Visualization Design: Bridging the Gap between Art and Science, *International Conference on Information Visualisation (IV'04).* IEEE, London, UK, pp. 245 -250.

Keefe, DF, Karelitz, DB, Vote, EL and Laidlaw, DH: 2005, Artistic Collaboration in Designing VR Visualizations, *IEEE Computer Graphics & Applications* **25**(2): 18-23.

Krzywinski, M: 2006, Circos - Circularly composited genome data and annotation generator http://mkweb.bcgsc.ca/circos/ January.

Lawson, B: 1997, *How Designers Think*, Architectural Press, London.

Mankoff, J, Dey, A, Hsieh, G, Kientz, J, Lederer, S and Ames, M: 2003, Heuristic Evaluation of Ambient Displays, *ACM Human Factors & Computing Systems*, pp. 169-176.

Manovich, L: 2001, Information and Form http://www.manovich.net/ia/, January 2007.

North, C: 2005, Information Visualization, *in Handbook of Human Factors and Ergonomics*, John Wiley & Son, New York, pp. 1222-1246.

Stanza: 2003, Generative DNA Space http://www.genomixer.com/dnaspace/, January 2007.

van Berkel, B and Bos, C: 1999, *Move - UN Studio*, Architectura & Natura, Amsterdam.

van Wijk, JJ: 2006, Views on Visualization, *IEEE Transactions on Visualization and Computer Graphics* **12**(4): 421-432.

Vande Moere, A: 2005, Form follows Data: the Symbiosis between Design and Information Visualization, *CAADfutures*, OKK Verlag, Vienna, Austria, pp. 31-40.

Wisneski, C, Ishii, H, Dahley, A, Gorbet, M, Brave, S, Ullmer, B and Yarin, P: 1998, Ambient Displays: Turning Architectural Space into an Interface between People and Digital Information, *Workshop on Cooperative Buildings (CoBuild '98)*, pp. 22-32.

IS A DIGITAL MODEL WORTH A THOUSAND PICTURES?

IVANKA IORDANOVA, TEMY TIDAFI
AND GIOVANNI DE PAOLI
University of Montreal, Canada

Abstract. This communication addresses the use of a new type of referents database in the context of an architectural design studio. It discusses the results of design experiences held with the objective to study the cognitive effects of a teaching approach based on precedents and metaphors available as interactive and reusable digital models to students. The introduction of this referent-based approach is inspired by three major principles: the largely accepted fact that the creative work of architects is highly supported by referring to precedents and metaphors; the use of algorithmic digital methods to encapsulate architectural knowledge; and the constructivist approach to architectural design education. The study finds that the role of the modeled referents is helpful for the design studio learning, and that they are most creatively used when internalized by the student.

1. Introduction

This communication addresses the use of a new type of referents database in the context of an architectural design studio. It discusses design experiences held with the objective to study the cognitive effects of a teaching approach based on referents available as interactive and reusable digital models to students. In other words, if a picture is worth a thousand words, is a digital model worth a thousand pictures in the context of architectural design education?

Based on previous work, this article reports a qualitative study performed with students in architecture given the possibility to use a library of referents during their work on a design task. Together with visual material, the library included algorithmic and parametric models of architectural know-how. The communication consists of five main parts: a first one giving the background for the study; a second one, discussing the methodology used; a third one presenting the observations held; a fourth one showing some results, and finally a discussion together with the future avenues of this research.

A Dong, A Vande Moere & JS Gero (eds), CAADFutures'07, 85–98.

2. Background

The introduction of this referent-based approach is inspired by three major principles: the largely accepted fact that the creative work of architects is highly supported by referring to precedents and metaphors; the use of algorithmic digital methods to encapsulate architectural knowledge; and the constructionist approach to architectural design education.

2.1. ON THE ROLE OF ARCHITECTURAL REFERENTS

We use the term referent to indicate all kinds of objects or phenomena to which an architect would eventually refer, either for inspiration (in metaphors) or for finding 'how-to' information (in precedents) during a design process. The distinction between metaphors and precedents is important but we will not specifically discuss it in this paper. We prefer the term 'referent' to 'reference' because of its more specific meaning in design.

The role of referents in architectural design and in design learning is largely described in the literature. Without going into any details, we will mention some main aspects revealed in the numerous studies on the theme. The role of analogical transfer (which is the cognitive mechanism of metaphors and precedents) is crucial for the processes of recognition, classification and naming (Minski 1985). In an architectural context, Léglise (2000) states that a person best perceives and understands new things based on analogies with past experiences. With the words of Schön (1988), the 'Design World' of architects consists of referents and "things to think with", that embody implicitly architectural know-how. Oxman (1994) speaks of knowledge chunks, indicating by this term the design knowledge on precedents. According to Kalay (2004) referents and cases offer holistic knowledge and provide a shortcut to a solution of a complex problem. These last three examples are particularly important in the context of our study because they provide a direct link between a referent and architectural know-how.

Reconsidering referents form a digital point of view, brought up the idea of augmenting their cognitive role by providing digital models rather than only text and pictures.

2.2. ON ALGORITHMS, OR THE NEED FOR ARCHITECTURAL KNOW-HOW

Whilst in the time of Vitruvius or during the Middle Ages architectural and building knowledge was directly transferred from master to apprentice architect, with the separation of architects as a profession, and with their alienation from the construction site, visual referents began playing a much more important role. This trend was enormously boosted in recent years by the Internet. Nowadays architectural culture is extremely visual, this way taking advantage of the powers of a 'visual thinking' and, in the same time, often suffering from lack of information on the 'why' and 'how' of a drawing or picture. At the same time some authors find an increased insufficiency of architectural knowledge in young architects, blaming partially the computer for this (Akin 2002, Fernandez 2002).

These considerations lead us to the second principle applied to the referents: the introduction of algorithms in the digital architectural models. Made accessible by the introduction of computer technology into architectural practice, algorithms now have their place in the avant-garde of the profession (Abel 2004, Terzidis 2006). Some promising introduction of algorithmic generation of forms is made in architectural studios as well (Yakeley 2001, Weinand 2004, Tidafi and Iordanova 2006). The differences between algorithmic approaches and methods accommodating the 'paper-and-pen' way of thinking in architecture are underlined by Oxman (2006). Giving clear preference to 'digital thinking' when designing on a computer, the author enumerates three paradigmatic classes of digital models that could enrich the design methods of an architect with methods made possible by computers: formation, generation, and performance. All these have parametric modeling and algorithms as a creation base.

Using algorithms when designing brings at least two advantages: being able to define a generating rule or a process instead of representing one of its final instances; and having the possibility to produce multiple instances by intervening in the process description, this way stimulating a process of creative exploration of the design proposition. From an educational point of view, algorithms give the possibility to encode architectural knowledge linked to rules and laws (structural, climatic, compositional, etc.). It makes possible as well to encapsulate processes and to be able to visualize and test them as simulations in the time (energy optimization, manner of production, etc.).

In order to be able to explore different solutions based on variations of generating algorithms, students should be able first to encode them. According to some authors (Yakeley 2000), programming has a stimulating impact on design thinking. From our experience though, it is difficult, to introduce it directly in a digital studio, and not less unattainable to convince students used to visual and tactile manipulations when designing, of the interest of some programming. So, a more accommodating solution, having as well its own advantages, was working with pre-modeled examples. This way, students can see some visual aspects of the algorithmic model, together with its description. Often, the model would be linked to a real architectural precedent or a metaphor, thus providing a rather complete referencing basis: textual description of the 'what and why', model of the 'how', and visual representations. The fact that the 'how' is presented by an algorithmic digital model gives the possibility for its reuse by students in a new design situations. The validation of this approach is one of the objectives of this study.

The introduction of referents modeled in an algorithmic way to the digital studio pursues a double objective: educating students in a new way of design design thinking (based on process rather than on result) that could be complementary to traditional methods of design; as well as providing architectural know-how linked to design process and 'performative' architecture.

2.3. ON THE CONSTRUCTIONIST APPROACH TO EDUCATION

A third main inspiration for this research was the constructivist methodology giving the grounds for the constructionist educational approach, as well as for the digital modeling techniques taught to students. According to Piaget (1970) and Schön (1988), learning is especially effective when using know-how in a constructionist way (to create something new with it). With the words of Schön, architectural design is a process of 'reflective conversation with the materials of the situation' that uses different types of referents, including the past experience of the creator. These two studies lead us to the idea that it could be advantageous for the students to be given the possibility to design using referents containing architectural know-how, and being able to immediately reuse this know-how in their educational design projects. Based on previous work, the modeled referents encapsulate only 'chunks' of knowledge, in order to permit greater flexibility and to comply with constructivist memory structure theories (Minski 1985). This way, interactive "chunks of knowledge" serve as referents during the process of design. The The constructivist approach is omnipresent in the methodology chosen for this research.

3. Methodology

The methodology identified for this study is purely qualitative and participative. This is motivated by the complexity of the research domain (design and education), as well as by the will to be able to study in depth a small number of participants (10 students) (Creswell 1998). The methodology part of the study will discuss three aspects: the methodology used for the creation of the referents library, the pedagogical approach introducing it into the digital studio, as well as the validation methodology.

3.1. THE REFERENTS LIBRARY

In the development of the proposed library, we have taken into account some recent studies on new computer methods for architectural education that look for a way to integrate precedents into the architectural studio in an intelligent and intuitive way. But rather than proposing computer assistance based mainly on visual information on precedents, combined with keywords and "concepts" manipulation and association (Oxman 2004; Kocaturk and Veltkamp 2005), the digital-models referents library offered in our approach is directly linked to a modeling program and allows for knowledge transfer from a precedent to the new design.

3.1.1. The Models

What is, in our comprehension, architectural know-how? It is the knowledge and the methods of work of an architect, that are perceivable in the actions posed during the design process (Tidafi 1996). It includes the following dimensions: (1) scientific knowledge: building rules (structural, climatic, physic), urban regulations, functional organization, etc.; (2) artistic knowledge: styles, formal composition, etc.; and (3) methods-of-design knowledge. Examples of all these dimensions can be found as encoded knowledge in the modeled referents.

3.1.2. The Library Integration

In previous work, we have already defined a modeling methodology for a similar kind of digital 'object types' (in the sense of Schön (1988)). But then, the proposed 'teaching assistant' was not integrated in free-modeling software. Now, the referents library is a free standing unit (a structure of folders), but can be accessed through a browsing interface of the main modeling software, Cinema4D in this case (Figure1).

This gives the possibility to have visual representations (large thumbnails) of the models, as well as to be able to directly open or "merge" the referent model into the current scene. It also allows combining the use of

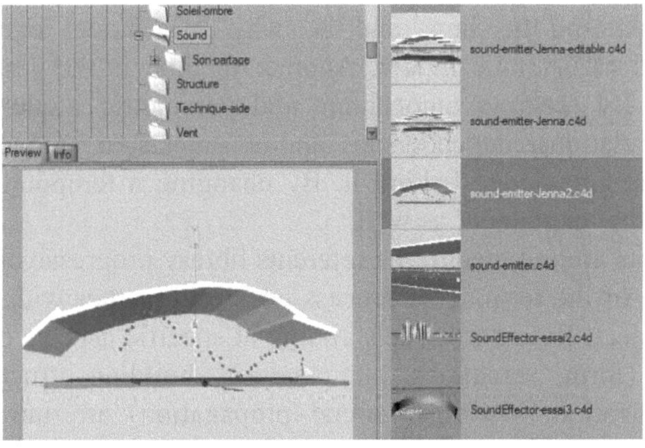

Figure 1. Integration of the referents library in a modeling software program

referent models and the know-how encoded in them, with other more traditional methods of design like free modeling and CAD.

One of the major concerns in researches on precedents databases is the possibility to personalize used referents and to keep track of visited items together with the connections (the analogies) that have lead to them in order to be able to create 'conceptual maps' for future use. This functionality is present in the proposed referents library through the creation of a named and dated entity keeping links to the concepts 'searched for' (Figure 2).

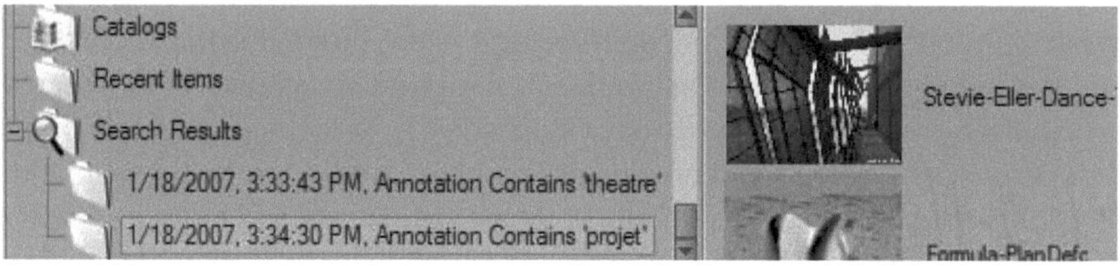

Figure 2. Personal annotation of referents and saving search results

Models, visual information (picture and drawings), textual descriptions, video recordings and sound files are organized in the same library structure provided by the tutor, but customizable by the student.

3.2. THE PEDAGOGICAL APPROACH

As we already mentioned, the pedagogical approach used in the studio is mainly based on the constructionist theory of education. Simultaneously, it integrates the opinion that even though architects are used to work with implicit knowledge (Lawson 1979), this is not as appropriate for design education (Akin 2002; Oxman 2004). Therefore, we provide the students with referent models whose design know-how can be made explicit. Two methods are used for this. One is including in the library a video and voice recording explaining the 'how' and the 'why' of a model together with its creation as an algorithmic model. Another method is the structure of the model itself. By creating algorithmic and parametric models with clear structure of relations, dependencies and/or objects, a student is able to understand the knowledge behind it. By changing a temporal component, processes can be 'explained' as well.

The students are initiated to the referents library progressively, starting at the beginning of the term. This process goes on together with the work on the studio project. Referent models aiming at specific aspects of the project development (form, semantics, site analysis, building structure, passive energy optimization, visibility, sound propagation) are introduced each week, thus bringing the students' attention to them (Figure 3: showing an example of a modeled 'chunk of knowledge' from a precedent interesting from structural point of view). This way, both learning algorithmic design, and getting used to working with model-precedents is simultaneously achieved.

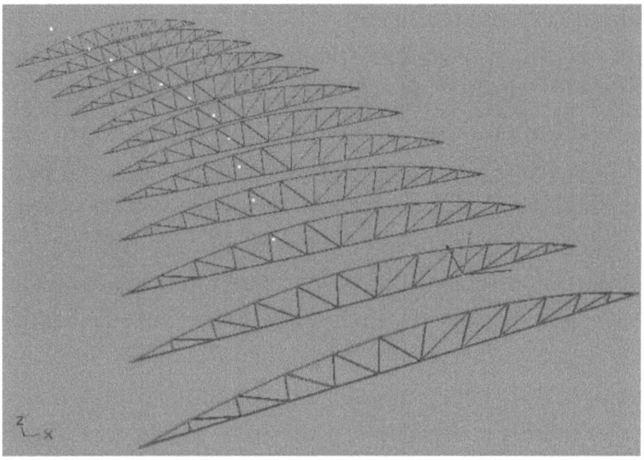

Figure 3. Parametrically created and distributed metal trusses (similar to the structure of the waterloo station by nicholas grimshaw & partners)

3.3. VALIDATION METHODOLOGY

The validation experiences in the design studio adopted qualitative methodology combining case study with grounded theory (Creswell 1998). An observation protocol of team work was chosen for the natural and instant verbalization it provides, compared to concurrent and retrospective protocols. The teams consisted of two students working on one computer but with two mice for better digital interaction with it. Exhaustive data collection included a screen session recording and a video-camera recording of the students' activities. The term project is taken into consideration as background information. This was made possible thanks to regular presentations of the project advance, and to a 'web-diary' kept by the students.

A data analysis coding scheme aiming at finding out some cognitive effects of the design teaching approach is developed aiming at a better understanding of the observed design processes. Specifically observed phenomena are: (1) emergence of design ideas, (2) 'use' of referents, (3) contents of the analogical transfer from a referent, (4) moments of 'reflective conversation'.

When a referent is 'used' (referred to), its type is identified:

- from the referents library: visual (picture or drawing), textual, algorithmic model;
- previous experience;

- architectural precedent (just mentioned);
- metaphor (just mentioned).

The role of the 'used' referent for the design idea is determined as well: emergence, support or concretization.

The content of the analogical transfer is especially important for the validation of the possibility for know-how transfer when using modeled referents. The types of content 'looked for' are linked to the three aspects of architectural know-how we have defined earlier in this paper: scientific knowledge, artistic knowledge and methods-of-design knowledge.

The analogical transfer can be successful or not: this was determined by the level of accomplishment of the task it was intended for. Another point of interest is the degree of novelty in the designs where referent-models have been reused. In order to determine this delicate aspect, 'new-design' criteria have to be defined. For the purposes of this study, only one criterion was considered: a reasonable difference in the form between the referent and the design object (which was evaluated by the participants in the study).

At the end of the recorded experiences, questionnaires were given to the students in order to ask for their level of satisfaction with the result of their work, as well as on the interest they find in the library of modeled referents.

4. Observations and Data

Ten students (5 male and 5 female) from the third year of architectural education participated in the digital studio. The modeling software used for the project was new to them. During the 10th week of the term, the same students were given 2,5 hours to complete a design task (only in the conceptual stage) working in teams of two. They were encouraged to briefly review the referents library before starting work on the project. In addition to the already introduced models of referents, new ones covering the design task domain (*Summer Theater with an Exhibition Space*) were included.

The recorded material was synthetically transcribed (design actions, conversation, gestures) and then coded according to the identified scheme. Qualitative methodology implies not a statistical analysis, but rather an interpretation of the data, the objectivity being assured by other researchers interpreting the same data.

A general observation on the digital design methods used was that parametric generation of design was successfully used by three (of the five) teams. Two of these teams were working exclusively parametrically (Figure 4 and Figure 5). The remaining two teams were trying to use parametric forms and distributions in the context of their architectural task, but with little success.

Figure 4. The project of Maude Halle Saint-Cyr and Nicolas Bocobza realized during the observations

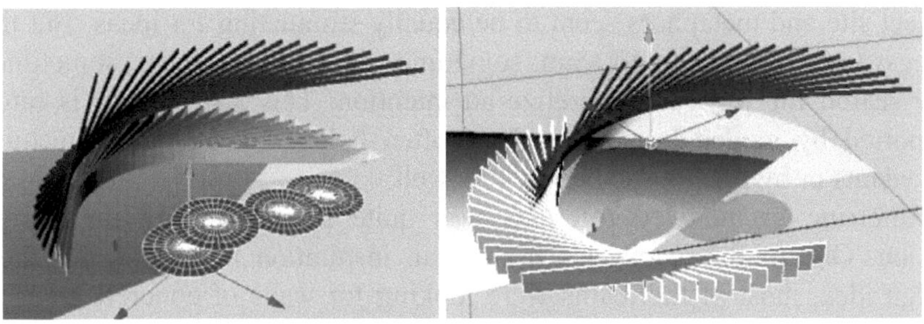

Figure 5. The project offering dynamic configurations (observation project of Jerome Taillandier and Rachid Saghir)

The situation was different regarding the term projects of the same students. There almost all of them (nine) have extensively used parametric and algorithmic methods during the design process. This difference could be partially attributed to the time constraint during the observation experience.

5. Results

After having described the general picture of the students design work, we will represent and discuss each of the observed phenomena.

5.1. EMERGENCE OF DESIGN IDEAS

Only major design ideas were observed. Two main 'patterns' were identified: (1) general definition of the project from the very beginning of the design period, after which only minor ideas emerge while the objective is the representation of the 'project idea'; and (2) identification of the leading principles (or forces) for the project, after which the design is guided by an exploration process. The first 'pattern' was noticed in the teams not working parametrically, and generated ideas less in number (six for each of the teams) and mainly at the beginning of the design work. The second one was present in the teams using parametric digital methods, and generated respectively 12 and 16 ideas for the two teams.

5.2. USE OF REFERENTS

Out of the 50 major design ideas identified during the work of the 5 teams, 38 were linked to use of referents. As reported by Leclercq and Heylighen (2002), a large part of the objects and phenomena students referred to, were not coming from the provided referents library, but from prior knowledge or experience. Thus, 28 of the referents that have provoked a design idea were from the referents library (11 images and 16 models). Nine metaphors were used, 3 of them being evoked by a model of the referents library.

Students' design methods varied a lot in terms of referent use. Images, project site and metaphors seem to be equally stimulating for ideas. But the process varies from team to team: sometimes they look for ideas, sometimes they search for ways to concretize an intention. This last process is often supported by modeled referents. It is often helped by other architectural precedents or by previous experience as well.

Referring to modeled referents was quite present during the design session. One of the teams got from it an inspiration in support for their design idea; most of the teams were looking for ways of concretization of their intentions. More extensive use of the modeled referents could be seen during the work on the studio project. After the introduction of each part of the referents library, the students were taking the time to explore the models and to eventually integrate an emerged idea into their term project. In the answers to the questionnaire, the models were qualified as very useful and enriching.

5.3. CONTENT OF THE ANALOGICAL TRANSFER

The content of the intended analogical transfer (when using referents) was covering mainly scientific knowledge and methods-of-design knowledge when modeled referents are used. The tendency was to witness more artistic knowledge and 'experiential' transfer, when images were discussed or architectural precedents mentioned. These results are supported by the data coming from the term project. In fact, both scientific knowledge and methods-of-design knowledge were used by the students for project exploration.

The level of success of the transfer of know-how embodied by the referent was quite high. The reuse of modeled referents was sometimes hampered by technical difficulties (not knowing the functions of the software used). The situation was much better during the studio project when the time constraint was not present, and where students could ask the tutor for help. In fact, three times during the observations, one of the team members was asking to watch the explicative video in order to find out how to use a modeled referent, but the other member of the team declined the request because of the time limits.

A known danger of reuse of models is imitation, or directly copying from the referent. The study of the students' projects according to the established 'new design' criteria, gave a satisfying result. This is especially well observable when methods-of-design knowledge are transferred (Figure 6).

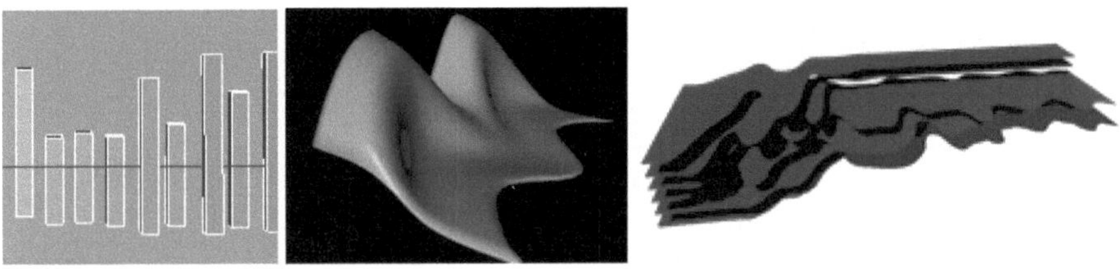

Figure 6. Comparison between a referent model in the library (left) and two students' variations (middle and right)

Figure 7. Form generation influenced by music: (top left) exploration based on a modeled referent; (top right) idea for the project; (bottom) the final project (work of Jerome Taillandier)

In the example on Figure 7, the exploration made with one of the referent models gave place to a main design idea of the studio project of the student.

The degree of novelty should be considered in a slightly different way when scientific knowledge is transferred. Some formal aspects of the newly designed object may remain similar. In the project shown on Figure 8, visibility and acoustic parameters determine the relatively similar slopes of the audience's seats in the concert hall. The advantage taken from the modeled referent here is the possibility to realize the project according to the encoded knowledge, and at the same time, to be able to vary the available parameters within permitted limits in order to find an optimal solution.

Figure 8. Concert hall: (top left) modeled referent, (top right, bottom) new project in plan and in perspective (work of Jerome Taillandier)

5.4. MOMENTS OF 'REFLECTIVE CONVERSATION'

The moments of reflective conversation were the most surprising part of this study. They were almost exclusively the result of parametric and algorithmic explorations of the design object or parts of it. Sometimes, the exploration was initiated by a reference to a model; other times simply by the application of an already learned digital method. The common point is the dynamic, interactive and continuous modification of the design object, assisted by computer algorithms. The teams working with parametric methods had most of their ideas emerged in this way.

6. Discussion

The referents library was a precious help for the students as well as for the tutor during the studio work. It was noticed that some of the models played a role similar to this attributed to metaphors – design inspiration; while others were transferring design know-how as architectural precedents are supposed to do. The new moment is the possibility to reuse this encoded know-how and to be able to exploit it as a basis for design exploration. This way, functional, structural and performative aspects of the future building, can be considered from the very beginning of a design process; and even more, can participate in the form generation of the architectural space.

Whilst all students stated that modeled referents were extremely helpful to their studio learning, their ways of using them during the design observation session differed a lot. The processes varied from (1) merging the model into the current project and changing its structure or parameters; to (2) internalizing the modeled referent thus making the encoded know-how completely 'operational'. One explanation to this difference (other than time passed for learning) could be the background of the students. Some of them come to architecture after a scientific profile of education, others – from art or even from humanities. Another link could be possible with the cognitive learning type of the students. Thus, learning in an analytical way could require different support than learning in a holistic way; and similarly to visual or verbalizing cognitive styles.

There are some aspects of the methodology of this study that have to be further developed. For example, a more precise validating method should be defined to study the observation that know-how transfer is not on the same level from a picture or from a modeled referent. In the future, the study can go into more depth into the cognitive learning processes and their implication to the referents library development and use.

Generally, we can conclude that algorithmically modeled referents are very useful for digital design learning. They are most creatively used when internalized to a certain extent by the student. From this moment on, they can offer the advantages of design exploration based on the knowledge coded in them, and thus, stimulate a process of 'reflective conversation' with the situation. This way, they are worth a thousand pictures.

Acknowledgements

We thank the students from the ARC-3011 digital studio of the 2006 fall term for their participation in the observations. Special thanks as well to the professors from the School of Architecture at the Université de Montréal, participating in the Digital Pedagogy research project sponsored by SSHRC and lead by Prof. De Paoli.

References

Abel, C: 2004, *Architecture, Technology and Process*, Boston, Elsevier.

Akin, O: 2002, Case Based Instruction Strategies in Architecture, *Design Studies* **23**(4): 407-431.

Creswell, J: 1998, *Qualitative inquiry and research design: Choosing among five traditions,* Sage Publications, Thousand Oaks, CA.

Fernandez, P: 2002, Approches méthodologiques et modes opératoires dans le processus de conception architecturale, *in* M Borillo & J-P Goulette (eds), *Cognition et création: Explorations cognitives des processus de conception*, Mardaga, pp. 97-118.

Iordanova, I and Tidafi, T: 2005, Using historical know-how to model design references: digital method for enhancing digital design teaching, *in* B Martens and A Brown (eds), *CAAD Futures 2005,* Springer, Vienna, pp. 197-206.

Kalay, Y: 2004, *Architecture's New Media,* The MIT Press, Cambridge.

Kocaturk, T and Veltkamp, M: 2005, *Interdisciplinary Knowledge Modelling for Free*-Form *Design.* Paper presented at the CAAD Futures 2005, Vienna, pp. 465-473.

Lawson, B: 1979, Cognitive Strategies in Architectural Design, *Ergonomics* **22**(1):59-68.

Leclercq, P and Heylighen, A: 2002, 5.8 Analogies per Hour, *in* J Gero (ed), *Artificial Intelligence in Design '02*, Kluwer Academic Publishers, Dordrecht, pp. 285-303.

Léglise, M : 2000, Conception assistée: modélisation et interprétation, *in* G De Paoli and T Tidafi (eds), *Modélisation architecturale et outils informatiques entre cultures*, Acfas, Les cahiers scientifiques, pp. 51-66.

Minski, M: 1985, *The Society of Mind*, Simon and Schuster, New York

Oxman, R: 1994, Precedents in design: a computational model for the organisation of precedent knowledge, *Design studies* **15**(2): 141-157.

Oxman, R: 2004, Think-maps: teaching design thinking in design education, *Design studies* **25**(1): 63-91.

Oxman, R: 2006, Educating the Digital Design Thinker, *Communicating Spaces 24th eCAADe Conference Proceedings*, Volos, Greece, pp. 198-205.

Piaget, J: 1970, *Le structuralisme*, Presses Universitaires de France - PUF, Paris.

Schön, D: 1988, Designing: Rules, types and worlds, *Design studies* **9**(3): 181-190.

Terzidis, K: 2006, *Algorithmic Architecture* Architectural, Oxford.

Tidafi, T: 1996, *Moyens pour la communication en architecture - Proposition de la modélisation d'actions pour la figuration architecturale.* Ph.D. Thesis, Université de Montréal, Montréal.

Tidafi, T and Iordanova, I: 2006, Experimental Approach in an Architectural Design Studio, *Communicating Spaces 24th eCAADe Conference Proceedings*, Volos, Greece, pp. 852-858.

Weinand, Y: 2004, *New Modeling*: Presses polytechniques et universitaires romandes.

Yakeley, M: 2000, *Digitally Mediated Design: Using Computer Programming to Develop a Personal Design Process*, Unpublished Doctoral Thesis, MIT, Boston.

LEARNING BY DOING IN THE AGE OF DESIGN COMPUTATION

MİNE ÖZKAR
Middle East Technical University, Turkey

Abstract. A design teaching approach of integrating the notions of design thinking and computing in the first year of architectural design education is introduced and discussed. The approach aims to enhance and bring up-to-date the educational practice of "learning by doing" in the first year foundations curriculum. In the studied example, the analytical phases of thinking in a simple design task are systematically and visually recorded. This documentation is incorporated to the design process as a means for the students to consciously reflect on their design thinking.

1. Introduction: Learning by Doing before Computing

Learning by doing, or experiential learning, is a phrase that is representative of the pedagogy articulated and advocated a century ago by the American philosopher and educator John Dewey (1916) as part of an agenda of implanting democracy in education. This pedagogy is based on the general idea that hands-on experiences leave deeper marks towards the development of the creative individual than those induced by uniform second-hand knowledge. Recognizing artistic activity as a mode of intelligence, John Dewey devotedly promoted the hands-on nature of artistic production as the primary means for elementary education (Eisner 1972).

The above point of view finds its parallel in the way William James (1908) couples learning with the ability, endorsed by the senses, to discover new part-relations as two indispensable parts of reasoning. Along this line, learning by doing within the extent of this paper specifically implies the using of the hands in coordination with the eye, and the other senses where necessary, to govern tools within a context of artistic production.

Learning by doing in the Modern framework is manifested most articulately in Dewey's writings and his efforts at the Teachers College at Columbia University between the years 1905-1930 to establish active learning in education. Historically it is traced back to the pedagogics of early 19th century child educators Johann H. Pestalozzi and Friedrich Froebel who

A Dong, A Vande Moere & JS Gero (eds), CAADFutures'07, 99–112.

separately started the kindergarten tradition in which children draw, make, build, play, and at the same time learn through sensory experiences of all kinds (Naylor 1985). Hands are at work in supplement to the eyes in acquiring not just abstract knowledge but also experienced (tested and personalized) knowledge. To make it all possible, "doing devices," the tools, procedures, media or game objects incorporated by the educator as the means to *do,* are essential to this method (Schank 1995).

2. Learning Design by Making

Dewey's legacy and learning by doing is today at the core of a widely practiced model of design education with the design studio at its center. It is yet open to improvement and thus has been a critical reference to multiple studies in artificial intelligence and education sciences, as well as those in the fields of design computing and design inquiry, notably by Gero (1999).

A design studio is ideally an atelier, open 24 hours, inhabited and kept by the students. It is an environment where students test out theories, ideas, materials, constructions, and similar productions as part of their design processes. Because it is a shared space, students are able to work together, and follow each other's processes.

In pedagogical approaches from the lineage of the Bauhaus, experiential learning in the studio is rigorous especially in the first year of instruction when the subject matter is the first encounters with *the means of doing*. The foundations curriculum, which starts off the design education, encourages learning by *making*, where *making* implies literally the hands-on production. Directly involving the tools and materials, this approach aims to develop "that craft" which a designer must possess: creating while constantly testing out visual or spatial outcomes of ideas. The subject matter learnt is *making* itself in the very broad sense: how one *makes,* as part of designing rather than making a particular object in a particular way. This generalized experience implanted in the very first year of architecture education is adaptable to other contexts to come in the advanced years of education.

Today, tending towards the integration of digital tools, architectural design education is going through a transformation. Design students are now immersed in working with digital tools as much as and even more than in working with traditional design tools. The common ways in which they make their design models, the materials and the ways of production that the aspired architecture profession deals with are changing. Digital fabrication is becoming more and more the key to integrated design solutions.

From the point of the educator, the means to teaching design are altering in parallel with the tools. How the notion of making in the studio prevails in the age of technology remains to be investigated, along with how learning by digital fabrication is a continuation of the making learnt in the first year.

Rather than yielding to CAAD as advanced ways of designing and as an add-on to architectural design curricula, educators can transform the common tools of the profession. Garvey (1997) suggests interdisciplinary links, in order to sustain the richness of hand-mind relations across media in art and design education. Along similar lines, Ivanka and Temy (2005) propose to reconsider the traditional design teaching ways within a modern view, in order to make the most of what has been long tested.

Traditional design tools such as technical drawing, cardboard modeling, and freehand sketching are usually introduced to students in the first year as means to work on design tasks. Then again, if *making* is to find a way into digital culture as implied above, digital tools should make their way into design education at this very fundamental level. Not to overload the already intense curriculum of the first year by introducing computers as a primary medium for design, this introduction may consist of the theoretical framework that enables one to make the most of tools in general. The traditional tools can be enhanced via design computability as a technique for governing the design process.

Building on discussions of 'learning design by …', this paper inquires which aspects of design computability can be introduced at the level of the first year. It is a proposal for first year curricula in schools that tend towards digital fabrication in senior level design studios. The motivations and results of strategies tried in a first year design curriculum are discussed through a sequence of basic design assignments and the contents of a supplementary course that puts emphasis on analytical thinking in design.

3. Learning Design by Digital Fabrication

Students in the first year of their architecture education, learn to experiment with materials and tools effectively for the first time. In the basic design curriculum, forms, materials and tools are all abstract, due to the reason that, independently from all these ingredients, the subject matter of teaching and learning is mainly what Cross (1988) has named the "designerly way of thinking."

Nevertheless, what is considered to be design tools is fast developing. Architects and architecture students are getting acquainted with technologies used in other disciplines such as engineering, which are keen on the integration of design with the production process. In the last few decades, architecture students have come to experiment with new technologies in their design studios. They are able to construct models out of planes of cardboard pre-designed and pre-cut in the laser cutter according to a production plan. This saves time and provides the desired precision. Alternatively, models can be printed in one-piece solids or in separate solid pieces later put together by the student. More and more, students are also designing the formwork to produce their unique design elements. They are able to scan and transport information from the hand-made models into the digital medium and mold them into new forms, adapt them to new constraints that emerge during the design process. Additionally, students are knowledgeable in programming, able to quantitatively construct complex parametric designs, represent these in precise virtual models, and to directly instruct prototyping production.

The objectives of production converge on feasibility, efficiency, optimization, and rely on repeated elements. Designers' effort to grasp, accept, and embrace this methodology is understandable from a practical standpoint in the architectural profession. However, inescapably, the availability of advanced tools in architecture schools transforms the taught conception of the design process to one that is overwhelmed by the goal of production.

If "learning by doing" in the first year design studio is simply getting acquainted with how to do design in general, then "learning design by making" is getting acquainted with how to work with materials towards a product. If one continues this word play, "learning design by digital fabrication," a more specialized version where digital tools are employed for the act of *making*, is getting acquainted with working in a particular medium towards a particular product. In this third *learning*, the making process is invaluably transparent due to the precision required. The hanging question seems to be how the "designerly way of thinking" and design methods are then effected. Is there a divide from "learning design by making" in the first year studio to "learning design by digital fabrication" in the later years?

From the point of view of a first year design educator, if the student is acquainted with the analytical aspect of the digital medium as a part of how to design rather than simply how to produce a design, then there is no divide. This study thus proposes to raise awareness in the first year students regarding the analytical thought processes in design, and shift the focus of value in digital fabrication and digital design from the goal of production to analytical thinking.

4. Learning Design by Analysis and by Computing

The foremost inquiry of the paper is regarding which aspects of design computability can be introduced at the level of the first year. Discussions on this matter have already been ongoing, ranging from how to handle the varying backgrounds of first year students to how to adapt architectural computing to early stages of education (Mark, Martens and Oxman 2003). Here, the framework and the results for strategies tried in a first year design curriculum are described through the examples of two basic design assignments and the contents of a supplementary course from the first year architecture curriculum at Middle East Technical University.

The approach presented here methodologically emphasizes the analytical modes of design thinking. Rather than the designed products, the student process and experience, as manifested through the documentation they were required to produce in the process, is the subject of investigation to reflect on the learning outcomes.

4.1. BUILDING UP A NEW VOCABULARY

The scope of the course titled Introduction to Information Technologies and Applications expands over various topics from basic knowledge of computer hardware to constructing algorithms. It is currently run in parallel with the design studio and is utilized as a venue to introduce the very basic notions of computation to the first year architecture students. Here only those topics that are directly pertinent to the described studio exercises will be mentioned.

Following a general acquaintance with the basic notions of hardware and software, programming languages, defining variables, procedures and commands, conditional statements, students are introduced to the notion of constructing algorithms. Students first practice constructing algorithms for tasks not related to the design world as they know it. Examples are as general as cake recipes and M Resnick's LOGO turtle mowing a lawn. These exercises convey the unforgiving aspect of computing that every ingredient must be defined and called upon that definition.

The notion of algorithm is then inquired in relation to the two dimensional compositions assigned in the studio. The question whether it is possible to write an algorithm for a basic design or not is posed. Students are introduced to the concept of visual computing as defined both technically and philosophically by Stiny (2006) in the theory of shape grammars. Three key technical aspects of the theory are discussed: visual rules, part relations and Euclidean transformations. Repetitive exercises of simple visual computations and of determining symmetry groups of various shapes are done in order to grasp ubiquitous part relations and Euclidean transformations. Most importantly, the philosophy behind the theory, in reference to James' description of reasoning based on the utility of the senses as well as learning, is put to practice by referring students to thinking about visual rules, and part-whole relations in their basic design work.

4.2. BUILDING A LIBRARY OF DESIGN ELEMENTS

Basic design exercises are not as meticulously carried out as, but are very much like, concept design games where certain aspects of the design process are isolated (Habraken and Gross 1988). The isolation draws attention to the notion that is to be taught. In the series of exercises described below, the abstract, analytical, systematic thinking is recorded and thus isolated as an aspect in grasping design computing.

In the second half of the fall semester of 2005, as part of the basic design curriculum, first year architecture students at Middle East Technical University are assigned the task of a three dimensional composition to be built of planar elements in a duration of two weeks. The student-teacher ratio is 67:5. Initial constraints defined to the students are regarding the use of only two different types of planar shapes, the minimum and maximum numbers of discrete planar elements to be used in the overall design, the minimum and maximum sizes allowed for the finished design, and the use of single material which was cardboard. Students are to come up with two different planar shapes of their choice. The task of producing the pair entails experimentation with possible spatial relations between the two. As students are producing these pairs in numbers out of cardboard, they are asked to develop a library of relations that were tried out and found viable.

Developing a library of relations stands for a categorical documentation of spatial relations physically tried between the elements. Following in principle the practices of shape grammar studios, especially run and discussed by Knight (1999) where spatial relations of a limited number of basic shapes are enumerated to show all possibilities, this exercise differently serves to identify the possible meaning of each selected relation in the context of creating a composition. Stiny (1980) has already pointed out the interaction between the hand and the eye in putting together the blocks in the series of hypothetical Kindergarten exercises to make sense out of the object. Exemplified in the student work similarly but in relation to the composition problem, a possible way to group relations is according to whether they form a defined volume in between the two elements or not. Another one is according to whether a relation is introverted, or extraverted, opening up the edges for new connections with other elements.

For this documentation, orthographic projection drawings are encouraged, whether in pencil or on computer, as a means of abstracting relations and highlighting particular formal properties of the shapes in relation. Each relation is represented in an orthographic set of plan and front side, with alternative second side view. That the elements were planar helps in isolating the faces and the perpendicular edges in relation and how they vary in relation to one another throughout a specified category. For example, in the libraries shown in Figure 1, it is possible to follow how the position of the second element varies in relation to the other, by looking at the *lines* moving across the *planes*.

The libraries in Figure 1 represent the typical response of the students to the assignment. Although asked to try out "as many spatial relations as possible", students draw mostly an average of eight. Drawing, a task they are not yet very proficient in yet, has proven to be difficult and thus tedious. However, the response received is quite sufficient for discussions in the studio regarding the posed issues.

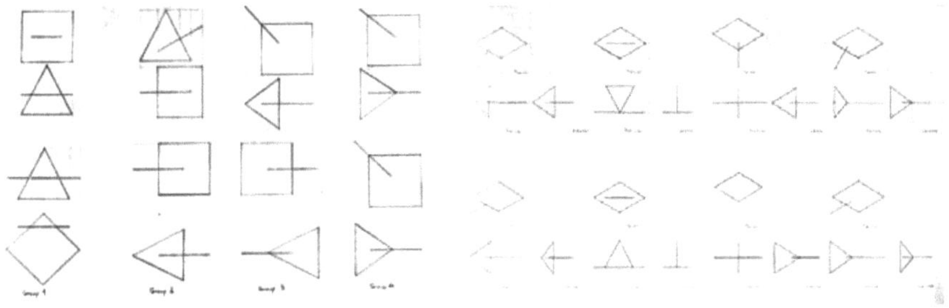

Figure 1. Libraries of relations between a rectangle and a triangle as developed separately by Ozan Sürmelihindi and Tunahan Çörüt

In the libraries, categories are left entirely to the student to decide. Rather than a goal, the task of categorizing is the means to get the students to think twice about the spatial and formal qualities of the elements and the relations between them.

While students are forming this library of pairs, they are simultaneously expected to work towards organizing a large number of these into a whole. Students are already experienced from the earlier half of the semester regarding strategies in composing, for example, the notions of unity, rhythm, grouping, linear versus central development, etc. The drawn analyses are posed ideally to help students in deciding on organization strategies. For example, a symmetric relation could induce a symmetric composition if it is located centrally, or another volumetric one grouped with two of the same kind could induce a rhythmic element. Works shown in Figure 2 are examples to what the end products of the design task looked like. Nevertheless, this paper puts emphasis on the process illustrated in Figure 1.

Figure 2. Designs produced by Ferayi Öztürk, Ayça Turgay and Gülistan Durmaz

The task of forming a library on the side is used in this exercise to emphasize the analytical aspects in design thinking and how analysis feeds synthesis. Considered together with the exercises and discussions in the non-credit course, the representations of spatial relations between the elements of design in the libraries are proposed to manifest the rules of visual and spatial thinking students employ in their designs. As an example, in the photograph that is first from left in Figure 2, the relation of the quarter circle and the square is repeated to achieve a rhythm of twos and threes elements as well as symmetry along the diagonal of the square. Overall this repetition helps the student achieve the unity in the overall composition.

It should be noted that the library in this case does not work as a fixed set of variables as the students learn to define in programming. This difference is emphasized in the discussions in the studio. In the assignment, the design elements are discrete and come together in an additive process of design. Nonetheless they are not fixed in the beginning of the task. The students are instructed that they can add or subtract relations (groups of design elements) from the library.

In the fall of 2006, the same task of working with a library of relations is tried out within the context of a more complex design assignment in the basic design studio with another group of architecture students. On the negative side, the student-teacher ratio is now 80:2. On the positive side, in addition to taking the supplementary course in parallel to the studio, this second group of students has already once before experienced building up a library of design elements within an assignment of creating a three-dimensional composition out of three-dimensional solid elements of five kinds. Before continuing with the case to be discussed, it may be worth mentioning the first experience this group of students has had with forming a library.

In the second half of the semester, students are once again instructed to create libraries while they are working on a three-dimensional composition. This time, the given design elements are three-dimensional solids. Orthographic projection drawings are again encouraged. When the products in the two consecutive years are compared, it is seen that students have been more successful in representing the relations between planar elements than those between three-dimensional ones. Drawing solids in orthographic projection and categorizing them according to formal properties prove to be even more difficult than drawing and analyzing planes. In the light of the results of both years, the success of the students in documenting is connected to a few factors. One of these factors is the complexity of the design elements. Another and possibly the strongest factor is the confidence the students have in doing the task. The task is openly explained to them when the exercise is given out, articulating and emphasizing the role of documentation, the format of documentation and how it is expected to reflect to their design thinking. Nevertheless, students may not follow these instructions properly that seem tedious and useless at first.

For the group of 2006, the first attempt to work analytically through a library of relations has not been as successful as in 2005 in terms of the amount of work produced and the effort students seemed to put in. Apart from having the students deal with two dimensional forms as explained as an advantage in the previous paragraph, in 2005, the particular assignment was better synchronized with the topic of visual computation studied in the supplementary course. Nevertheless in 2006 as well, the exercise serves to build up an experience of what was expected from the students for the next time. They are given a second chance at trying the task out, in the final assignment of the semester.

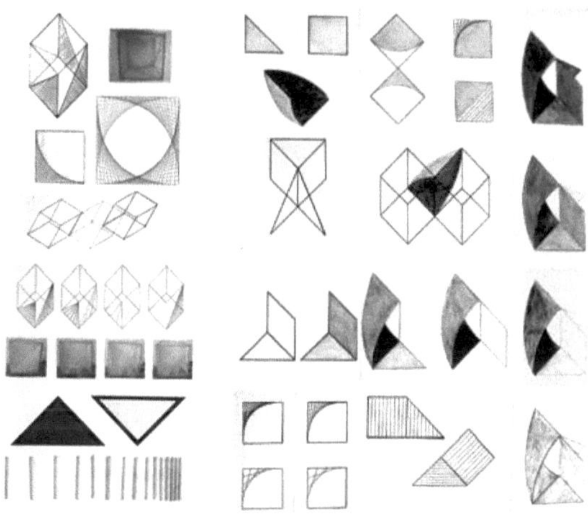

Figure 3. İlkay Güryay illustrates how she derives her design elements on the left, and the final presentation of her library of relations of elements on the right side

The final assignment is complex in gathering as much of the knowledge and experience they have accumulated throughout the semester. The analytical part described here covers only a small section of the whole assignment that lasted for five weeks. The assessment criteria for the three dimensional compositions to be achieved at the end are formed by each student for his or her project in the first week. The initial task is studying a short story of choice and deriving its five main spaces. The student was expected to interpret the relations of these spaces within the story and represent them spatially in a series of abstract models. In addition to each student's unique set of criteria thus formed, some of the external criteria for assessment are how much the student is able to carry out a concept between different modes of abstraction and how he or she is utilizing the elements of design in creating variation in a continuous spatial organization. The three week process discussed here starts after this stage of establishing the criteria for assessment.

In this assignment, the task is a three-dimensional volumetric composition to be constructed out of design elements of two geometric groups: rigid linear elements and surfaces. As stated in the previous paragraph, each student derives these elements from a study in the preceding stage within the same assignment. Once this first attempt at defining the elements was achieved, the students are once again expected to utilize the method of constructing a library of relations of elements to help them proceed with their design. Figures 3 and 4 separately show the processes of deriving the elements and the final stage of the library by two different students.

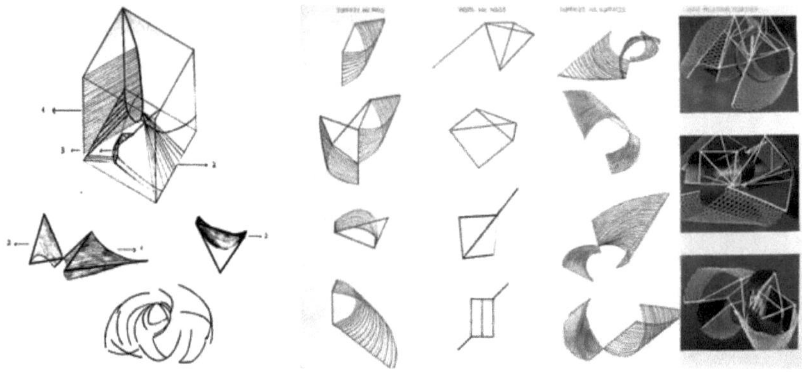

Figure 4. Seçil Binboğa illustrates how she derives her design elements on the left, and the final presentation of her library of relations on the right side

These libraries consist of singular elements, pair relations and relations of larger groups of elements. The means of representation here are not prescribed to the students, but according to their developed graphic communication skills, they are able to represent the design elements in axonometric, or perspective constructions rather than in orthographic drawings, which have proven to be insufficient for solids. In the case of establishing categories in the library of relations, the student whose work is shown in Figure 3 has chosen to keep the point of view in the perspective drawings consistent throughout the presentation as to be able to compare the variations between the relations shown.

The many shapes in Figures 3 and 4 only show the elements in the library. The students were not asked to show the shape computations as they are not equipped with a formalism such as shape grammars. However with the assigned task of developing a library of relations, they were guided to systematically approach design and introduced to computing that is intrinsic to design. The performed computations would have been clear if the students were given more time to dwell on and document the relation between their library of elements and the final outcome. Figure 5 gives two other examples to illustrate the varying interpretations of the assignment by the students.

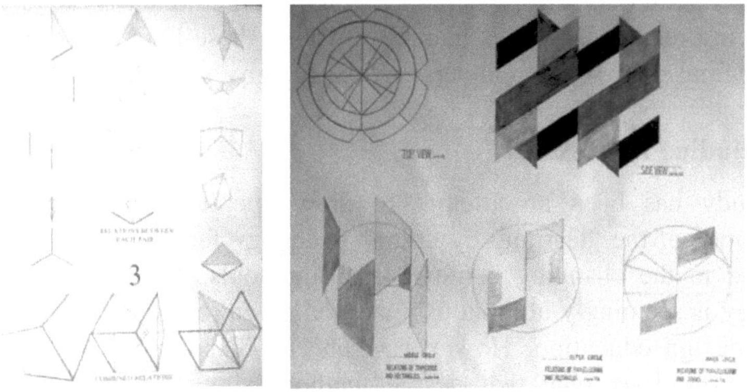

Figure 5. Process drawings by Başak Yüncü and Yasinalp Örsel

There are also other properties of design elements, which the students feel obliged to represent as they play into the variation of parts. Materials specified in each case are rendered and the types of linear and planar elements are shown separately and in relation to one another.

As mentioned in the previous section, in the supplementary course, the students are introduced to the notion of defining the variables. In the design exercise, they define the variables, but since these are visual, they change from time to time according to changing perception in the changing whole.

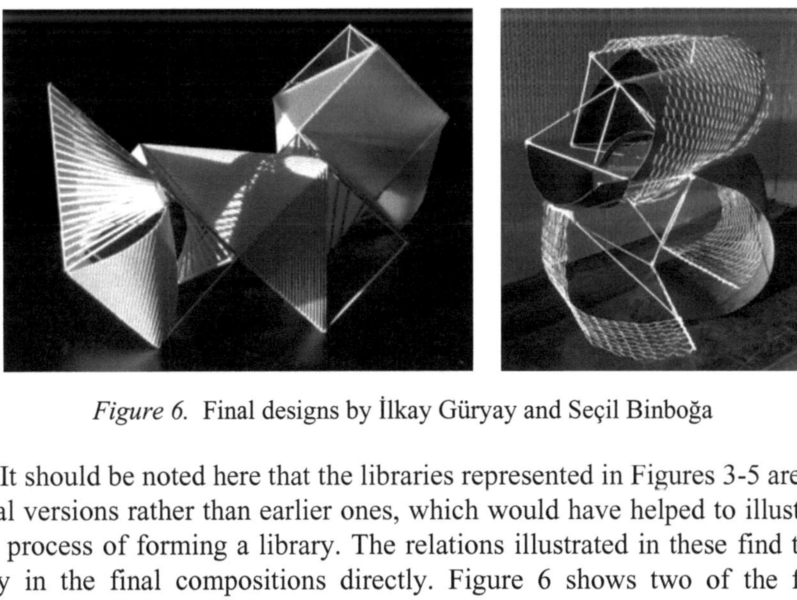

Figure 6. Final designs by İlkay Güryay and Seçil Binboğa

It should be noted here that the libraries represented in Figures 3-5 are the final versions rather than earlier ones, which would have helped to illustrate the process of forming a library. The relations illustrated in these find their way in the final compositions directly. Figure 6 shows two of the final designs produced in the studio corresponding to the two libraries illustrated in Figures 3 and 4. In both, the relations between the parts of the composition are those described in the libraries. Even if the process is not shown in its full dynamics, where ideally a dynamic library is the tool to test out varying relations towards making a whole, these libraries, snapshots of the very final stage serve to understand the design analytically.

5. Concluding Discussions

This study has been an attempt to draw attention once again to the significance of the "learning by doing" pedagogy for design education, but this time in the changing context of design tools. At a first glance, the pedagogy is seemingly ubiquitously applied given the common studio practice in design education. However when considered in terms of what is being learnt, it is seen that design methods show variance in between different years of education, i.e. between the first year instruction and advanced levels of instruction where digital tools are used. Hence, a way to instruct design as a computation process throughout the years is proposed in order to update the first year curricula of learning by doing.

Recognizing the line of thought that links Dewey's motto for hands-on education to Stiny's take on spatial thinking, this paper advocates an understanding of design computing that is thriving on the uncertainties of perception and dynamics of design thinking. Its original contribution is claimed to be in the formulated and experienced process of the students. Following the framework proposed and propagated by Stiny to include the sensorial experience of the subject in computing and referring to Özkar's previous study (2005), the experimental approach described in this paper aims to develop ways for beginner design students to talk about their design process and thus learn designing as a conscious activity of organizing relations. The students are asked to put emphasis on the analytical activity during very basic design tasks, and are guided in terms of how to document this analytical activity. Using analytical tools such as orthographic drawing are encouraged to capture design rules in visual and spatial ways. Maintaining a balance between analysis and creative hands-on design thinking is deemed imperative.

Learning by doing can be articulated and rephrased in the framework of this paper as both learning design by computing and learning computing by design. Computing is also proposed as the foundation of working with other analytical tools as digital fabrication in later years of education.

In this study three main limitations were observed and left to further explorations in subsequent work. Firstly, the study only focuses on design as composition in the context of the first year curriculum, in an attempt to isolate certain aspects of designing. Secondly, although it dwells on issues of computation, it does not yet introduce the full use of computers in the first year design studio as it entails social implications as well as being a technical issue as demonstrated by Taşlı-Pektaş and Erkip (2006). Thirdly, it does not yet fully utilize the formalism proposed by the theory of shape grammars. The representations tried out by students are not formal but nonetheless accepted in this study as visual rules. They are supplemented with numerous verbal representations, which may be incorporated into the grammar mathematics through Weight algebras in future work. Allowing for personal narrations as much visually as possible is believed to be a significant step taken at this point.

Another topic to be considered in detail in further research is the student factor. The complex, unpredicted and varying responses of the student body to education presents difficulties in doing research through teaching. For instance, students may refuse to follow instructions if they see it to be useless or too much work for them. Nevertheless, for the comparative thinking that is aimed to be conveyed to them, they need to produce many examples. Here rises the possibility of introducing a tool, for example the computer, to help them enjoy the task and at the same time faster produce what is asked for.

Trying an updated version of 'learning by doing' suggestive of systematic thinking in design education in established institutions prove to be difficult. Traditionally the basic design studio is guided by the understanding that the individual is to develop one's own methods of design through experimenting within the act of creating. Students are mostly expected to create without a given method as they are to develop their own. The general fallback is that a high ratio of students lacks confidence upon feeling unable or not gifted. Moreover, the curriculum lacks other supplementary courses that would serve the studio in terms of teaching the contemporary context of architectural design in relation with the tools the technologies have to offer. The methodology in education that is tried here is the introduction of guidance to learning by doing in the age of design computing. The assignments described are attempts to negotiate between the traditionally tested methods of design teaching and the futuristic models, and to indicate the possibility of change without much compromise. In spite of this optimistic standpoint, it is the personal position of the author that required courses supplementary to the first year design studio should be fast updated to introduce the contemporary context of architectural design and the contemporary status of design tools available. Clinging to hopes of timeless values may just be currently debilitating design education. Educators should learn from the past as well as from the future to update their outlook on design.

Acknowledgements

The author would like to acknowledge Selahattin Önür, Tuğyan Aytaç Dural, Nihal Bursa, Nicolai Steinø, Derin İnan, Başak Uçar, Pelin Yoncacı in reference to the preparation and execution of the design exercises, and Arzu Gönenç Sorguç in reference to the preparation and coordination of the non-credit course.

References

Cross, N: 2001, Designerly Ways of Knowing: Design discipline versus design science, *Design Studies* **17**(3):49-55.

Dewey, J: 1944 [1916], *Democracy and Education*, Free Press, New York.

Eisner, EW: 1972, *Educating Artistic Vision*, The Macmillan Company, New York.

Garvey, GP: 1997, Retrofitting fine art and design education in the age of computer technology, *ACM SIGGRAPH Computer Graphics,* **31**(3): 29-32.

Gero, JS: 1999, Constructive Memory in Design Thinking, *in* G Goldschmidt and W Porter (eds), *Design Thinking Research Symposium: Design Representation*, Cambridge, MIT, pp I.29-35.

Habraken, NJ and Gross, MD: 1988, Concept design games, *Design Studies*, **9**(3):150-158.

Ivanka, I and Temy, T: 2005, Using Historical Know-how to Model Design References: A Digital Method for Enhancing Architectural Design Teaching, *in* B Martens and A Brown (eds), *Computer Aided Architectural Design Futures 2005*, Springer, Netherlands, pp. 179-206.

James, W: 1983, *Principles of Psychology*, Harvard University Press, Cambridge, MA.

Knight, T: 1999, Shape grammars in education and practice: history and prospects, *International Journal of Design Computing* 2.

Mark, E, Martens, B and Oxman, R: 2001, The Ideal Computer Curriculum, *in* H Pentilla (ed) *Architectural Information Management, 19th ECAADE Conference Proceedings,* Helsinki, Finland, pp. 168–175.

Mark, E, Martens B and Oxman, R: 2003, Preliminary stages of CAAD education, *Automation in Construction, Design e-ducation: Connecting the Real and the Virtual*, **12**(6):661-670.

Naylor, G: 1985, *The Bauhaus Reassessed: Sources and Design Theory*, The Herbert Press, London.

Özkar, M: 2005, Lesson 1 in Design Computing Does not Have to be with Computers: Basic Design Exercises, exercises in visual computing, *in* J Duarte, G Ducla-Soares and AZ Sampaio (eds), *eCAADe 23 Digital Design: The Quest for New Paradigms*, Technical University of Lisbon, Lisbon, Portugal, pp. 679-686.

Schank, RC: 1995, *What We Learn When We Learn by Doing. Technical Report ILS Technical Report No. 60*, Institute for Learning Sciences, Northwestern University.

Stiny, G: 1980, Kindergarten grammars: designing with Froebel's gifts, *Environment and Planning B*, **7**:409-462.

Stiny, G: 2006, *Shape: Talking About Seeing and Doing,* MIT Press, Cambridge, MA.

Taşlı Pektaş, Ş and Erkip, F: 2006, Attitudes of Design Students Toward Computer Usage in Design, *International Journal of Technology and Design Education* **16**:79-95.

BECOMING DESIGNED

TOPOLOGY OF URBAN ENVIRONMENTS

Graph construction from multi-building floor plan data

EMILY WHITING, JONATHAN BATTAT AND SETH TELLER
Massachusetts Institute of Technology, USA

Abstract. This paper introduces a practical approach to constructing a hybrid 3D metrical–topological model of a university campus or other extended urban region from labeled 2D floor plan geometry. An exhaustive classification of adjacency types is provided for a typical infrastructure, including roads, walkways, green-space, and detailed indoor spaces. We extend traditional lineal techniques to 2D open spaces, incorporating changes in elevation. We demonstrate our technique on a dataset of approximately 160 buildings, 800 floors, and 44,000 spaces spanning indoor and outdoor areas. Finally, we describe MITquest, a web application that generates efficient walking routes.

1. Introduction

We describe a representation and navigation system to support the walking traveler. While many online mapping tools offer powerful route searching functions, they are targeted at automobile travel and model only locally one-dimensional street networks. Current applications are unable to represent continuous indoor and outdoor spaces fundamental to a complex of buildings. Building interiors present the additional challenges of complex connectivity, changes in elevation, and movement through large open spaces.

Metrical-topological models describe the shape and connectivity of space, and are useful underlying tools for wayfinding. We introduce a new approach for constructing metrical-topological models of outdoor and indoor environments from labeled floor plan geometry. We provide an exhaustive classification of adjacency among rooms, corridors, and outdoor spaces, and describe an out-of-core algorithm for construction of a corresponding graph. We demonstrate our method on data from a university campus comprising over 160 buildings, 800 floors, 37,000 indoor and 7,000 outdoor spaces.

A Dong, A Vande Moere & JS Gero (eds), CAADFutures'07, 115–128.

"walking route from building W1 (Ashdown House) to room 1-190"

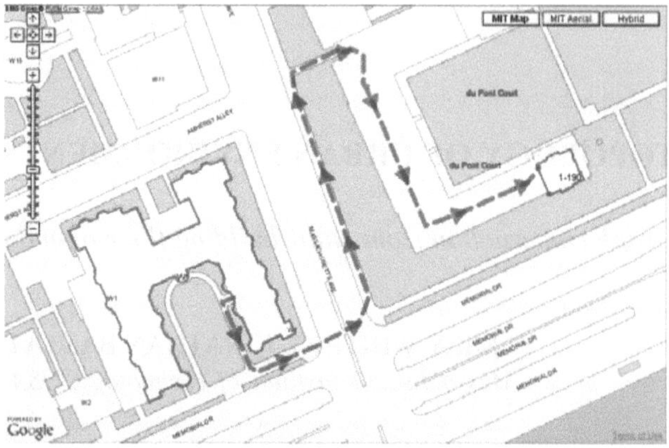

Figure 1. The user made the query shown at left; our method produced the result on the right. Our contribution is to compute efficient routes that seamlessly combine indoor and outdoor paths, allow different levels of granularity for source and destination, and cross 2D spaces not limited to the linear travel of automobiles

1.1. RELATED WORK

Substantial work has been done on extracting graph representations of street networks using digitized road maps (e.g. Haunert and Sester 2004; Gold 1997). However, these techniques are limited to 1D paths with a single direction of motion, constant width between opposing boundaries, and point intersections. The MIT Stata Walking Guide (Look et al. 2005) used a manually constructed graph to support route-finding and written walking directions between different locations in MIT's Stata Center. Lee (2004) addressed the problem of automatic graph construction from floor plans using a model derived chiefly from hallway elements which share similar properties to 1D street networks.

We build on work by Funkhouser et al. (1996), Nichols (2004) and Kulikov (2004) on automatic interpretation of floor plan data in a campus environment. Their system analyzes floor plans to derive a hybrid metrical-topological environment representation. Our paper addresses the additional issue of vertical connections (stairs, ramps and elevators), and generates a more complete topological representation of an entire campus. Our contribution is to extend existing methods to 2D spaces such as lobbies and open lounges, and to vertical movement via stairs, elevators and ramps. Our methods involve automated construction of an underlying graph data structure, the topology of which is generated robustly from arbitrarily shaped spaces and varied connectivity types present in raw floor plan data. Further, in contrast to prior work that applied to networks within enclosed buildings, our system extends the graph structure to multiple buildings and adjacent outdoor terrain.

Summarizing, this paper makes the following contributions:

- Methods for inferring and storing a metrical-topological data model representing an extended, indoor/outdoor multi-building environment.
- A framework for constructing graphs of environments too large for processing in one pass.
- A prototype application for generating efficient fine-grained routes for a walking traveler.

1.2. DATA CORPUS

The input to our system is a set of floor plans in DXF format. We base our computations on floor plans because they are a generally available source of geometry data and follow strict conventions, such as unique space names, consistent room use codes, and implied adjacency information. Each construction floor plan is segmented into functional layers such as room contours, floor extents and exterior walls, enabling streamlined parsing.

To derive the physical layout of the terrain, we extract additional input from a *basemap* DXF. The basemap specifies position and orientation for building footprints, along with other physical infrastructure such as locations of sidewalks, streets and grass. For the purpose of route generation (Section 4), we segment basemap regions into units of similar area (Kulikov 2004).

We pre-process the basemap and floor plan geometry to remove degeneracies such as self-intersecting polygons and repeated edges.

1.3. SYSTEM OVERVIEW

Our system comprises a central database for storing geospatial elements, and a set of modules designed for specific read/write operations (Figure 2).

Input modules. Input modules populate the data model by extracting information from common data sources. A DXF parser reads geometry data from raw DXF files, and populates the data model with pertinent information such as building footprints, Space contours, and Portal locations. Section 2 reviews the design of the data model for representing geometric and topological features, and Section 3 describes floor plan conventions used by the DXF Parser to recognize Portal locations.

Derivative modules. Derivative modules operate on the data corpus to derive richer geometric and topological information. For example, graph construction is performed by the Portal Linker (Section 3), the Location Server operates on the graph for path finding functions (Section 4), and an additional module generates Space triangulations.

Output modules. Output modules act as intermediaries between the geospatial database and external applications. For example, the visualization

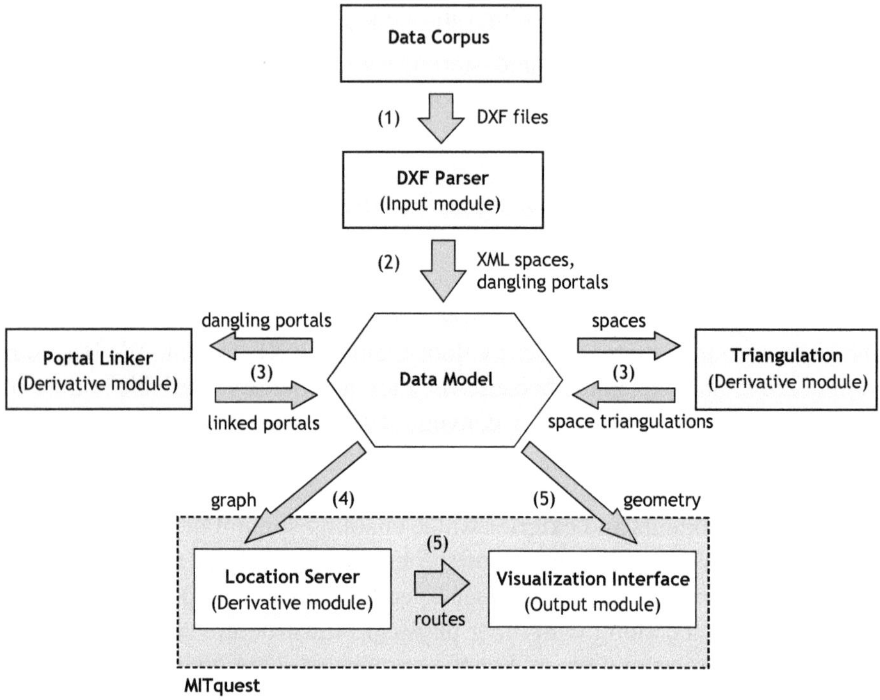

Figure 2. Project overview with ordering of operations. (1) input DXF files to the DXF Parser, which (2) converts data to our Space and Portal representation. (3) construct Space triangulations and Space-Portal linkages. (4) generate routes from the Space-Portal graph and (5) visualize the route on a map

interface is combined with the Location Server to produce MITquest, a web-based service providing walking routes (Section 4).

2. Data Model

Our data model represents containment relationships with a tree data structure, and connectivity relationships with a graph structure. The basic elements of the data model are *Spaces* and *Portals.* Each Space represents a contiguous physical region such as a room, corridor, sidewalk, or patch of outdoor area. Each Portal represents an adjacency, such as a door, elevator, or stairwell connecting two Spaces.

2.1. SPATIAL HIERARCHY

We organize Spaces into a tree hierarchy to represent containment relationships. The root element is the terrain which has individual buildings as children nodes; buildings have floors as children nodes; and so on. Each node has properties such as its name and polygonal contour. We use the

XML file format to represent this hierarchy because of its ability to store information in a tree-based structure, and for ease of transfer over the web.

2.2. SPACE-PORTAL GRAPH

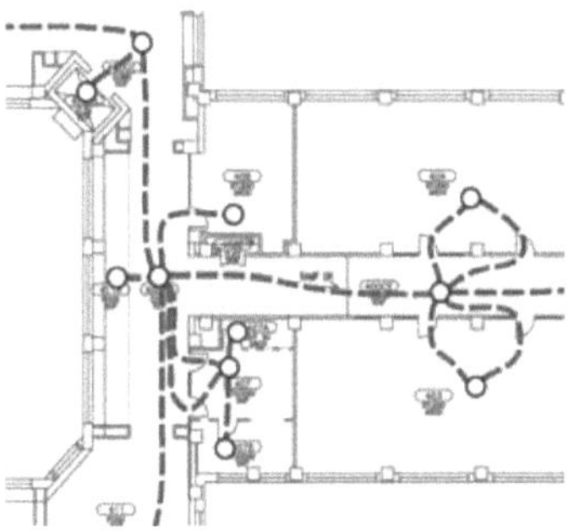

Figure 3. Graph superimposed on floor plan. Spaces are nodes and Portals are edges

Locations and adjacencies are represented with a graph data structure containing a node for each Space and an edge for each Portal (Figure 3). The graph is directed: each edge $e(v_1, v_2)$ has a source and destination Space v_1 and v_2 respectively. This captures the fact that certain Portals such as security doors allow exit but not unconditional reentry. Each Portal has a weight: the distance between the centroids of the Spaces it connects. From the floor plan input, our goal is to produce a connected graph of all rooms, hallways, sidewalks, streets, and other Spaces within the modeled region.

2.3. DATA ELEMENTS

We now describe the representation of each element in our data model.

Floor. In the tree hierarchy, Floors embody the containing region for a set of Spaces, and are the parent element of all Spaces on that Floor. Each Floor has a set of contour points defining its polygonal boundary.

Space. Each Space has a unique room identifier, a type (e.g. classroom or lobby) and a polygonal boundary derived from the floor plans. From the contour we compute a constrained Delaunay triangulation (Lischinski 1994) and an axis-aligned bounding box (Figure 4 on the right). We analyze each Space to determine which Portals originate from or terminate within that Space, and to compute a height differential for each entry-exit Portal pair in the Space.

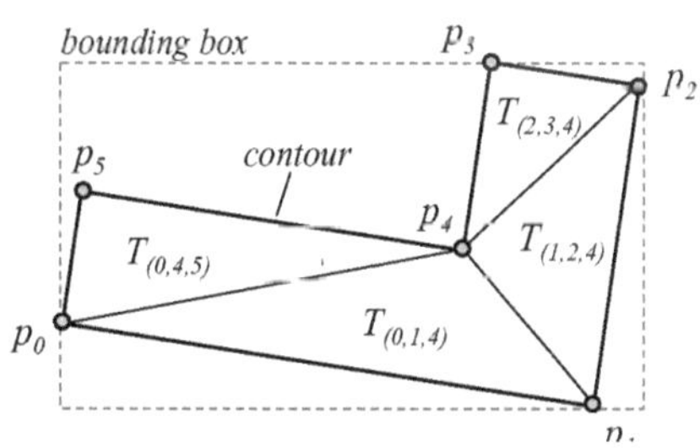

Figure 4. Geometric properties of spaces are a set of contour points, a triangulation and a bounding box

Portal. Each Portal has a source Space, a destination Space, and a classification as either Horizontal or Vertical (Figure 5). Vertical Portals

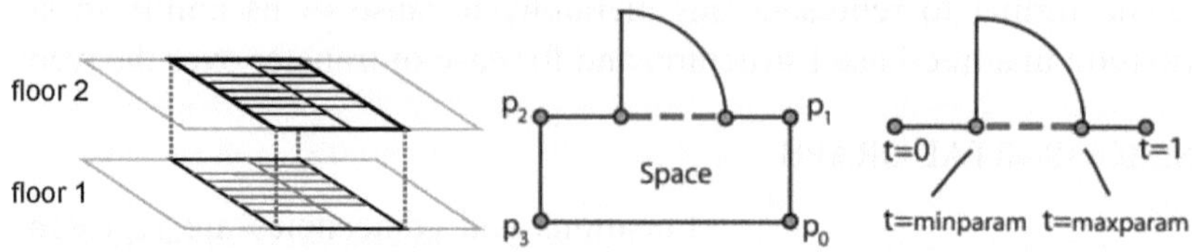

Figure 5. (left) Vertical Portal: two overlapping staircases; (right) Horizontal Portal with extent defined by a space edge (p_1, p_2) and an interval (t_1, t_2) on this edge

connect adjacent floors and have type Elevator, Stair or Ramp. They inherit a contour from their source Space (e.g. an elevator Portal has the same shape as the elevator itself).

Horizontal Portals include connections between Spaces on the same floor, connections between buildings, and connections between adjacent basemap Spaces. Each Horizontal Portal is represented as a line segment incident on its parent's contour. (We say that two polygonal contours are "incident" if they share part of at least one boundary segment).

3. Topology Construction

This section describes the procedure for populating the data model with adjacency information. This involves constructing Portals whenever a pair of Spaces is found to be adjacent and no physical barrier prevents direct traversal from one Space to the other. The main challenge faced is the massive size of the dataset, in our case comprising millions of geometric primitives. Rather than process the entire dataset at once we process one floor at a time. Computations that require data outside the active floor are deferred to a later stage using *dangling portals* – Portals that have a source Space but a temporarily unspecified destination Space.

In a first pass, our algorithm processes one floor plan at a time. Portals whose source and destination are contained within that floor are fully linked, while any Portal that requires data outside the floor is created as dangling. In a second pass, a Portal Linker matches pairs of dangling Portals. Section 3.1 reviews the various Portal types. Section 3.2 describes the procedure for linking dangling Portals.

3.1. PORTAL TYPES

Portals may be *explicit* or *implicit*, and may be *horizontal* or *vertical.*

Explicit Portals. Explicit Portals, a type of horizontal Portal, represent connections between Spaces that are physically separated by a barrier (e.g. a doorway through a wall). In our source floor plans, each explicit Portal is indicated by a circular arc (Figure 6). We use geometric proximity to determine each Portal's source and destination Space. If the door segment is

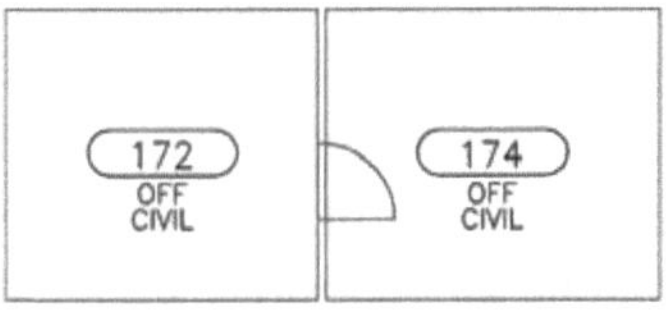

Figure 6. Explicit Portal. Source and destination Spaces are determined by proximity

incident on the floor contour, this indicates a destination Space outside the building, and the Portal is created as dangling.

Implicit Portals. Implicit Portals, another type of horizontal Portal, represent connections between Spaces with no physical barrier. For example, the photo in Figure 7 shows a large open area outside a cafe. Although there is no wall between the corridor and the café tables, the two regions are defined separately in the floor plans to differentiate between circulation zones and food services. We identify implicit Portals by an incident edge between two Space contours. Similar to explicit Portals, if a Space is coincident with the floor contour, the Portal is left dangling for connection to an abutting building.

Basemap Portals are implicit Portals. Any two basemap Spaces whose boundaries share any portion of a boundary segment are considered adjacent.

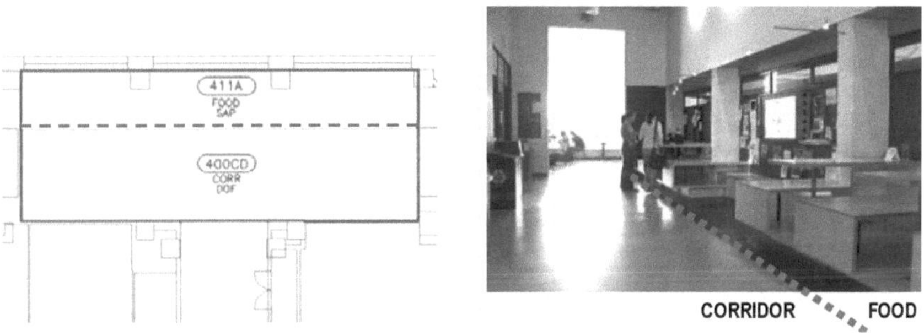

Figure 7. Implicit Portal identified by an incident edge between Space contours (dotted line). Although no physical barrier exists, the Portal places an implicit divide between the corridor and café tables (photo)

Vertical Portals. Vertical Portals connect adjacent floors in multi-story buildings. We identify vertical Portals by searching for stair, elevator and ramp Spaces. Since source and destination Spaces typically lie on separate floor plans, vertical Portals are initially dangling.

3.2. LINKING DANGLING PORTALS

The three types of dangling Portals are building-to-building, building-to-basemap, and vertical. This section discusses the linking procedure for each.

Building Connections. Building Portals model connections between abutting buildings, such as continuous corridors or breezeways. Dangling building Portals are resolved later by finding proximal Space pairs.

Basemap Connections. Connections from buildings to the basemap are handled analogously, with the additional constraint that only explicit Portals are assumed to link an interior Space to the campus terrain. For each dangling Portal leading out of a building, we search for the closest basemap edge. When a match is found, the Portal is linked, and an oppositely-directed Portal is constructed from the basemap Space to the building interior.

Vertical Connections. Two stages are involved in linking vertical Portals. First we construct an ordered list of floors for each building, assuming consecutive floors are vertically adjacent. Second, for each ordered pair of floors, we find stair and elevator Spaces whose axis-aligned bounding boxes overlap in plan view (Figure 8a). Two oppositely-directed Portals are constructed representing upward and downward movement respectively.

Mezzanines present a special case when determining floor adjacencies. A staircase may connect either to a mezzanine or to the full floor above (Figure 8b). To determine the proper connection we cast a ray upward from the bottom-most staircase. If the ray lies outside the mezzanine extents then the mezzanine can be ignored.

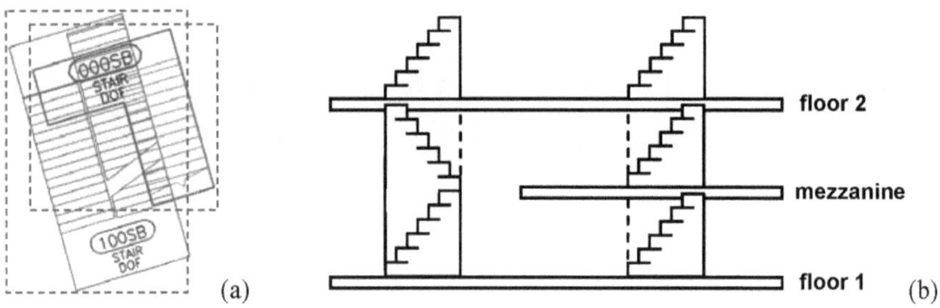

Figure 8. Vertical Portals. (a) plan view of stairs on adjacent floors. Axis-aligned bounding boxes (red) overlap; (b) mezzanines in the floor stacking sequence

TABLE 1. Summary of Portal types and detection/linking methods

Type	Connection	Test
Implicit	Intra-Floor	Incident edge between two Space contours
	Inter-Building	Incident edge between Space and Floor contour
	Intra-Basemap	Incident edge between two basemap Space contours
Explicit	Intra-Floor	Door arc proximal to two Space contours
	Inter-Building	Door arc proximal to Space and Floor contour
Vertical	Inter-Floor	Axis-aligned bounding box overlap

4. MIT Route Finder

To demonstrate the practical value of our fine-grained metrical-topological model, we developed MITquest, a prototype application that generates efficient walking routes between any two locations on the MIT campus. The route generation problem is divided into three sub-problems: finding a sequence of Spaces that efficiently connects the source and destination (Section 4.1); finding the actual path through each Space (Section 4.2); and combining these results into a route to be displayed to the user (Section 4.3).

4.1. SPACE PATH

The first step determines an efficient sequence of Spaces connecting the source and destination in the Space-Portal graph (Figure 9). With each Portal's edge weight set to the distance between adjacent Space centroids, the Space sequence is determined by applying Dijkstra's shortest-path graph search algorithm (Cormen et al. 2001).

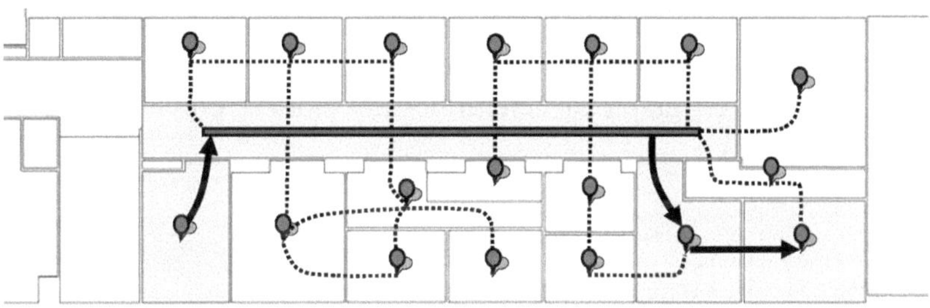

Figure 9. Example Space-Portal graph. Edges (dotted lines) are placed between Spaces (red nodes) connected by Portals. Edges are weighted by centroid-to-centroid distance. Solid arrows represent traversed edges between the start and end Spaces

4.2. POLYLINE PATH

The second step determines a metrical path *through* each Space in the route. The challenge is to handle non-convex Spaces where a simple straight line between Portals may intersect the boundary.

To extract the lines linking Portals, we use a method by Joan-Arinyo et al. (1996) that approximates the medial axis (Lee 1982; Latombe 1991). In practice, this implementation has lower computational cost and yields nearly equivalent results. We construct a graph inside each non-convex Space by placing straight line segments between midpoints of shared triangle edges (Figure 10). To find the shortest path between any pair of Portals, we then run Dijkstra's algorithm on the resulting graph. The effect is a natural-looking path that follows the shape of the Space. This method is fast because we pre-compute triangulation data when we parse the DXF file.

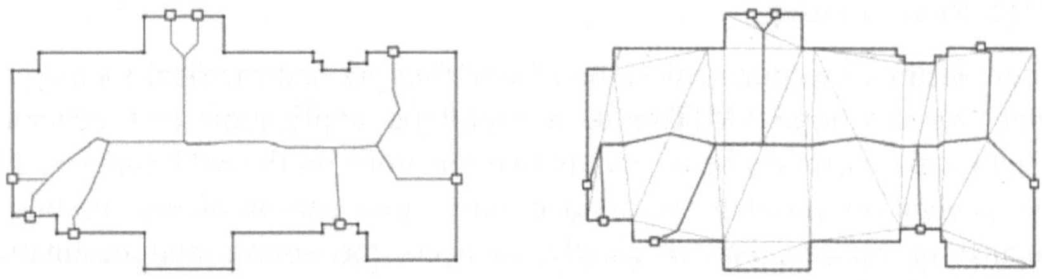

Figure 10. Internal graph connecting Portals for a typical room contour. We approximate the medial axis by connecting midpoints of shared triangles edges

4.3. ROUTE GENERATION

Finally, we combine the Space sequence and polyline paths to generate efficient routes. To do so we must determined the polyline path through the entire sequence of Spaces. We first determine the union of intra-Space graphs (Figure 11). The graphs are combined by merging corresponding Portal nodes between each pair of adjacent Spaces. When multiple matches are available, nodes are paired by geometric proximity. Dijkstra's algorithm is run on the merged graph to determine the shortest polyline path from source to destination.

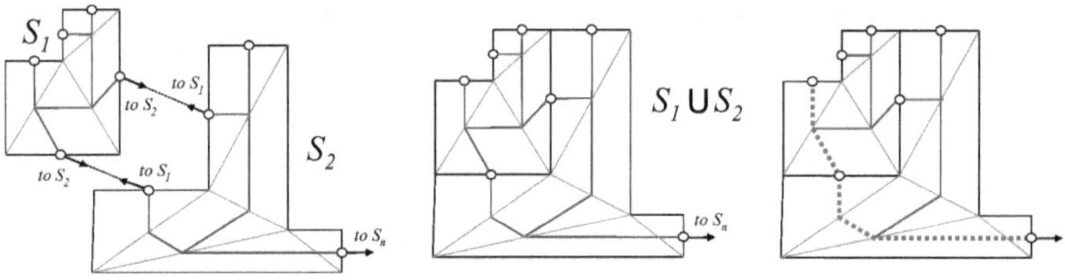

Figure 11. Combination of internal graphs for Spaces S_1 and S_2. The two graphs are connected at corresponding Portal nodes. Dijkstra's algorithm searches the combined graph to find a path through the Space sequence

4.4. PATH RELAXATION

Once the polyline path has been determined, a final shape simplification process is applied. This stage reduces the number of segments in the path to yield a cleaner looking map, while leaving the overall shape of the route intact. For each Space, we step through the path removing interior points. When a removal causes the path to intersect the Space boundary, we re-insert the point, and repeat the process with an updated starting position. The process is demonstrated in Figure 12. Our approach is similar to that of Agrawala (2001) in shape simplification of road maps, with the difference that we maintain overall shape by constraining the route within the Space boundaries.

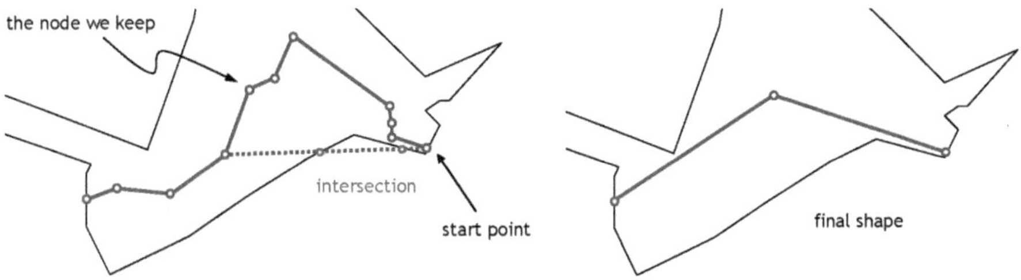

Figure 12. The path relaxation process removes interior points, while ensuring that removals do not cause the path to intersection the Space boundary

4.5. ROUTE CONSTRAINTS

Route constraints are implemented by selectively restricting undesirable Space and Portal types in the campus graph. For example, "paved" routes prohibit Portals leading to grass or construction on the basemap, but allow streets, sidewalks, and any indoor Space type. "Rolling" routes are additionally constrained to traverse only elevators and ramps when moving vertically within buildings.

5. Results

We have implemented our route visualization tools as an interactive web-based application modeled after the Google Maps API. The interface allows users to specify source and destination points at varying levels of granularity, either by building, room or a combination. We illustrate a few representative scenarios in the following Figures.

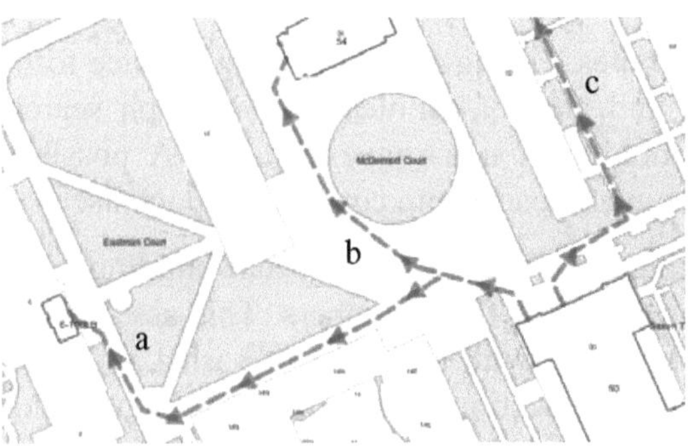

(a) "building 50 to room 6–100"

(b) "building 50 to building 54"

(c) "building 50 to building 66"

Figure 13. Outdoor routes crossing a large courtyard, resulting from queries (a)–(c). The multi-directional walking routes exploit the 2D nature of the terrain

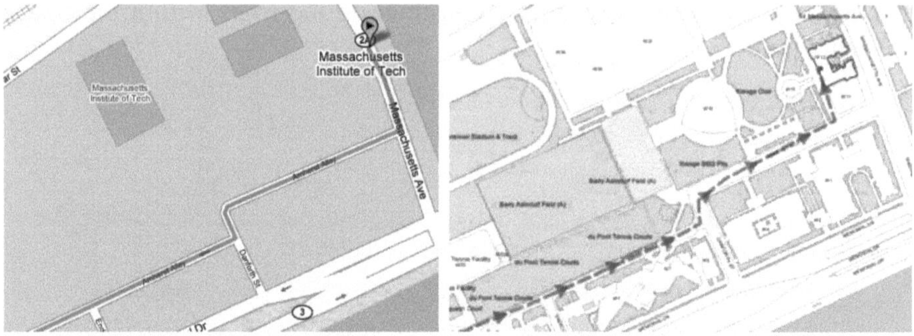

Google Maps route to address: "50 Massachusetts Ave. Cambridge MA"

Our result from query: "building W84 to building W13"

Figure 14. Increased level of detail of MITquest in comparison to google maps. Our outdoor route employs the nearest building entrance rather than a street address

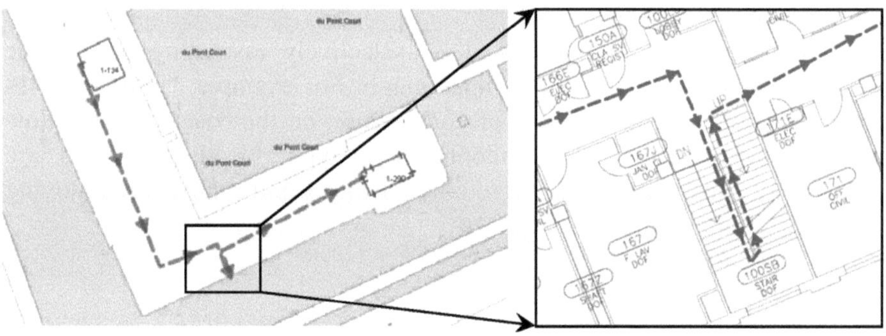

Figure 15. Indoor route with vertical segment: "room 1-134 to room 1-290". The route goes through 1st and 2nd floor corridors, ascending a staircase along the way (detail). Visualization of height differences is an area for future work

5.1. POSSIBLE EXTENSIONS

Non-Convex Spaces. Shortest routes leaving and re-entering a Space form a cycle in the Space sequence, and are not handled by our graph search algorithm. This scenario arises only with non-convex Spaces. A possible extension is to break up all non-convex Spaces into convex components.

Misaligned Floors. When linking Portals between adjacent buildings, we assume that connections occur at identical floor numbers. This assumption does not always hold in an environment with buildings of varied ages and styles. An alternative is to determine elevations from grade and impose the constraint that connections occur at identical elevations.

Graphical Identifiers. The DXF Parser relies on a labeling scheme specific to MIT. A remaining challenge is to incorporate more universally applicable graphical identifiers. For example, a staircase is more commonly represented by a sequence of closely spaced line segments than by a "STAIR" label.

IFS and OpenGIS. Our data model and gr aph construction routines were developed for efficient performance on the MIT campus data corpus. Future developments could improve interoperability with existing IFC (Liebich and Wix 2000) and OpenGIS (OGC 2007) tools.

6. Conclusion

This paper makes three contributions. First, we describe a data model for storing geometric and topological properties of the built environment. Second, we provide an exhaustive classification of adjacency types for an urban infrastructure, and methods for inferring topological relationships from floor plan geometry. Third, we present MITquest, a prototype application that demonstrates how our data model can be used to generate walking routes spanning interior and exterior environments. The MIT campus is used as a test-bed which is representative of many urban datasets and demonstrates that our algorithms are readily usable.

The work presented in this paper could help answer numerous practical questions in architectural design. What are the common navigation paths within an environment? Do they provide adequate circulation capacity? Are landmarks effectively placed in the environment to aid navigation? Does a building provide appropriate facilities for access and navigation by people with disabilities? Directions for future research include automated landmark identification, improved route visualization, incorporation of object-oriented building models using IFC, and integration of our local environment models with global urban features.

References

Agrawala, M and Stolte, C: 2001, Rendering Effective Route Maps: Improving Usability Through Generalization, *Proc. ACM SIGGRAPH 2001*, pp. 241-249.

Bell, J: 2003, *An API for Location Aware Computing*, Master's Thesis, Massachusetts Institute of Technology.

Bern, M and Eppstein, D: 1992, Mesh generation and optimal triangulation, *in* F Hwang and D Du (eds), *Computing in Euclidean Geometry*, World Scientific, Singapore, pp. 23-90.

Cormen, T, Leiserson, C, Rivest, R and Stein, C: 2001, *Introduction to Algorithms – 2nd ed.*, The MIT Press and McGraw-Hill, Cambridge.

de Berg, M, van Kreveld, M, Overmars, M and Schwarzkopf, O: 1998, *Computational Geometry: Algorithms and Applications 2nd ed.*, Springer-Verlag, Berlin.

Funkhouser, T, Séquin, C and Teller, S: 1992, Management of Large Amounts of Data in Interactive Building Walkthroughs, *Proc. 1992 Symposium on Interactive 3D Graphics*, pp. 11-20.

Funkhouser, T, Teller, S, Sequin, C and Khorramabadi, D: 1996, The UC Berkeley System for Interactive Visualization of Large Architectural Models, *Presence: Teleoperators and Virtual Environments* **5**(1): 13-44.

Gold, C: 1997, Simple Topology Generation from Scanned Maps, *Proc. Auto-Carto 13, ACM/ASPRS*, pp. 337-346.

Google: 2007, *Google Maps API.* Retrieved from http://www.google.com/apis/maps/.

Guibas, L and Stolfi, J: 1985, Primitives for the Manipulation of General Subdivisions and the Computation of Voronoi Diagrams, *ACM Transactions on Graphics* **4**(2): 75–123.

Haunert, J-H and Sester, M: 2004, Using the Straight Skeleton for Generalisation in a Multiple Representation Environment, *Proc. ICA Workshop on Generalisation and Multiple Representation.*

Joan-Arinyo, R, Perez-Vidal, L and Gargallo-Monllau, E: 1996, An Adaptive Algorithm to Compute the Medial Axis Transform of 2-D Polygonal Domains, *in* P Brunet and D Roller (eds), *CAD Tools for Products*, Springer-Verlag, Berlin.

Kulikov, V: 2004, *Generating a Model of the MIT Campus Terrain*, Master's Thesis, Massachusetts Institute of Technology.

Latombe, J: 1991, *Robot Motion Planning*, Kluwer Academic Publishers, Boston.

Lee, DT: 1982, Medial Axis Transformation of a Planar Shape, *IEEE Trans. Pattern Analysis and Machine Intelligence* **PAMI-4** 363–369.

Lee, J: 2004, A Spatial Access Oriented Implementation of a Topological Data Model for 3D Urban Entities, *GeoInformatica* **8**(3): 235-262.

Liebich, T and Wix, J (eds): 2000, *IFC Technical Guide – Release 2x*, International Alliance for Interoperability.

Lischinski, D: 1994, Incremental Delaunay Triangulation, *in* P Heckbert (ed), *Graphics Gems IV*, Academic Press, Boston, pp. 47-59.

Look, G, Kottahachchi, B, Laddaga, R and Shrobe, H: 2005, A Location Representation for Generating Descriptive Walking Directions, *Proc. 10th International Conference on Intelligent User Interfaces*, pp. 122–129.

Lynch, K: 1960, *The Image of the City,* The MIT Press, Cambridge.

MassGIS, Office of Geographic and Environmental Information: 2006, *Datalayers/GIS Database Overview.* Retrieved from http://www.mass.gov/mgis/spc-pts.htm.

Nichols, P: 2004, *Location-Aware Active Signage,* Master's Thesis, Massachusetts Institute of Technology.

Open Geospatial Consortium, Inc.: 2007, *OpenGIS Specifications (Standards)*, http://www.opengeospatial.org/standards/.

Roush, W: 2005, *Killer Maps*, Technology Review **108**(10): 54–60.

Timpf, S and Frank, A: 1997, Using Hierarchical Spatial Data Structures for Hierarchical Spatial Reasoning, *in* S Hirtle and A Frank (eds), *Spatial Information Theory,* Springer, Berlin, pp. 69–83.

Varadhan, G and Manocha, D: 2002, Out-of-Core Rendering of Massive Geometric Environments, *Proc. IEEE Visualization*, pp. 69–76.

DISCOVERING COMPUTATIONAL STRUCTURES IN ARCHITECTURE

An exploration

GANAPATHY MAHALINGAM
North Dakota State University, USA

Abstract. The linkage between the worlds of Architecture, which involves the design and construction of the built environment, and Computer Technology, which involves practical applications of computation, still has a vast, as yet untapped potential. What if the implications of the linked term, 'computer-architecture,' are explored to reveal its full scope? This paper describes a unique method to analyze and code works of Architecture in a way that enables one to discover hidden computational structures in the works of Architecture. The case being made here is that the inherent structures of architecture may be computational structures as well.

1. Introduction

The term 'computer architecture' is often used in the computer industry and refers specifically to the design of computer systems, both hardware and software. Even Bill Gates, the head of Microsoft, prefers the title Chief Software Architect. This linkage between the worlds of Architecture, which involves the design and construction of the built environment, and Computer Technology, which involves practical applications of computation, still has a vast, as yet untapped potential. What if the implications of the linked term, 'computer-architecture,' are explored critically to reveal its full potential?

A work of architecture is created after an intense design process. The resultant architecture has embodied in it various formal structures (i.e., structures that articulate a particular form). The really interesting question is, are these formal structures, feasible computational structures as well? If the answer is yes, this will truly bring the world of Architecture into the world of computation! This project sets out as its main goal to discover and verify

A Dong, A Vande Moere & JS Gero (eds), CAADFutures'07, 129–137.

if the formal structures embodied in works of Architecture could serve as computational structures as well.

This project is the next in line of a long list of investigations completed by Mahalingam in the last decade linking the worlds of computation and architectural design. For his doctoral work Mahalingam successfully created an algorithm for the design of proscenium-type auditoriums. The algorithm was incorporated in object-oriented software for the design of proscenium-type auditoriums using the Smalltalk programming language and the VisualWorks software development environment. (Mahalingam 1998, 2000). As a part of his doctoral investigation, Mahalingam also proposed a paradigm for the representation of architectural design entities as virtual computers (Mahalingam 1997). This was a significant attempt to look at architectural entities as computational devices. In a subsequent investigation, a model was proposed for the parallel computational processing of load transfer in rectangular structural systems for architectural design (Mahalingam 1999). A project was also completed where a programming language was proposed for architectural design with the complete Backus-Naur notation for the language (Mahalingam 2000). In a more recent project, a new model was proposed for the sensor-based control of the propagation of sound in spatial enclosures based on an algorithmic model for sound propagation simulation developed earlier (Mahalingam 1999). This project involved the modeling of the components involved as an elliptical graph called an *optimation* (Mahalingam 2005).

In a recent seminal paper, which has generated the main idea for this research project, a paradigm was presented for the representation of different aspects of architectural design using connections-based models (Mahalingam 2003). The paradigm suggested a uniform representation of spatial layouts, circulatory systems, egress systems, structural systems and environmental control systems in architecture using three-dimensional networks or graphs. The argument was made that these three-dimensional networks or graphs reveal the architectonics underlying their composition, and by extension, could be the basis of computational frameworks. In this project, the author has simulated the behavior of a computational structure in the form of a virtual finite state machine (VFSM) that is based on works of physical architecture to see if the VFSM could be the basis of new computational tasks in architectural design such as the simulation of fire spread in a building, load transfer in structural systems, sound propagation in spatial enclosures, and heat transfer in buildings, to name a few.

2. Methodology

The way this was accomplished is as follows:

2.1. ANALYSIS

The first step was to analyze a work of Architecture (i.e., part of the built environment) so as to reveal its underlying systems, such as structural systems, circulation systems and arrangements of spaces. Three projects, Figure 1, by the architect Frank Lloyd Wright from around the U.S.A. that were analyzed earlier by March and Steadman (1971) were selected by the author. Each of these works of Architecture had been analyzed to reveal the 'invariant' relationships in their arrangement of spaces. Other examples of some of systems that could have been included in the analysis are structural systems, circulation systems, egress systems, HVAC systems, plumbing systems, etc. These were not attempted in this initial implementation.

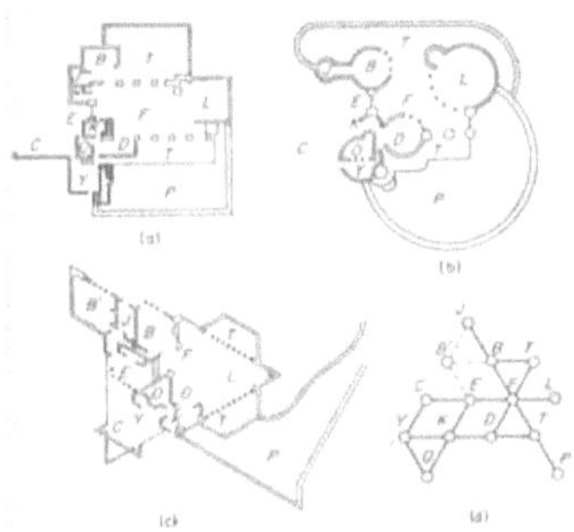

Figure 1. Three different floor plans of architectural works designed by the architect Frank Lloyd Wright showing the identical graph of space adjacencies derived from each one of them (from March and Steadman 1971)

2.2. CODING

The next step was to code the spatial arrangement system as a diagram comprising nodes and links, i.e., as a graph. The spatial arrangement system uncovered in the analysis phase was coded as an adjacency graph comprising 'nodes' and 'links', Figure 2.

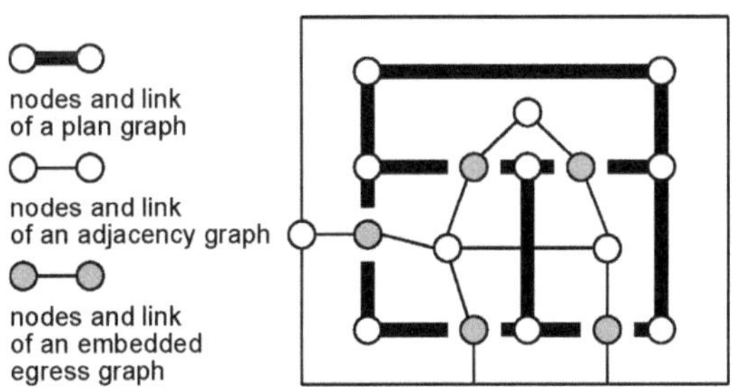

Figure 2. Encoding of an architectural plan as a graph showing how different features are embedded hierarchically

2.3. VFSM GENERATION

The next step was to use the graph that was uncovered in the previous step to model a virtual finite state machine (VFSM), Figure 3. The graph was used as a template for the generation of a VFSM using commercial software (StateWORKS for VFSM simulations).

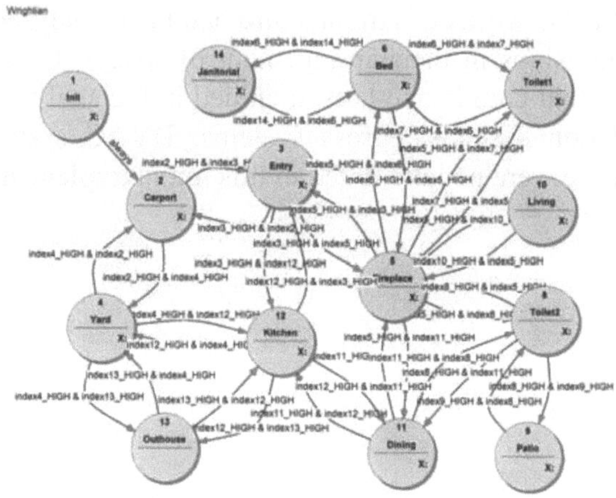

Figure 3. The state diagram of a virtual finite state machine (VFSM) based on the 3 architectural works by Frank Lloyd Wright that share the same adjacency graph for the spaces that they contain. The finite state machine is used to determine computationally if fire has spread from one space to another, given the occurrence of fire at the various locations

2.4. SIMULATION

The next step was to simulate computations using the VFSM and see what computational structures could be derived from the works of Architecture. The VFSM was used to simulate the spread of fire in the buildings, a computational task in architectural design that could be mapped easily onto the VFSM.

2.5. TESTING

The last step was to test to see if the computational structures could be used to form the basis of new computer software for architectural design (i.e., the spread of fire in a building). The efficiency of the VFSM in performing the computational task attempted was demonstrated. The suitability of the VFSM for new computational tasks in traditional computation as well as other computational tasks in architectural design will be explored in the future.

3. Implementation

The spatial arrangement of three works of architecture by the architect Frank Lloyd Wright which were analyzed earlier and coded as adjacency graphs were used in the implementation. Incidentally all three works had the same underlying adjacency graph. The software StateWORKs (Wagner et al. 2006) was then used to generate a virtual finite state machine (VFSM) that was based on the adjacency graph of the spatial arrangement.

A particular computational implementation was then mapped onto the VFSM. This was a computation that would determine if fire spread to a particular space given the occurrence of a fire in another space. The nodes of the graph (the spaces) were each assigned a range for a flammability value. This flammability value was modeled as a 'switchpoint' that would switch on and off based on whether the fire in that space crossed the high or low threshold value. If the intensity of a fire in that space exceeded the flammability value's high threshold then the space caught fire. Conditions were set for the fire to transmit from one space to another. This was modeled as state transition conditions in the VFSM. A system was then set up to input the intensity of a fire in each of the spaces. A simulation was then run, whereby one could input the intensity of a fire in each of the spaces using a numerical input dialog box and see if it spread to the other spaces, which was indicated in an output monitor that indicated that a fire had occurred in that space. The whole process of the spread of the fire was a computation of state transitions in the VFSM.

In a real world scenario, the system for the input of the intensity of the fires could be linked to a real digital input using a communication port in the computer, and the output signal that a fire had occurred could be used to activate an alarm using another communication port in the computer. This capability to link digital inputs and outputs to communication ports on the computer is inherent in the StateWORKS software system. This VFSM could effectively form the engine of a real fire alarm system in each of the buildings analyzed.

If one had to develop software for the prediction of fire spread in the architectural design by inputting flammability values for each of the spaces, starting fires of various intensities in the various spaces, and predicting where the fire would spread, then this VFSM could be used as an engine for the development of the software. The StateWORKS software system allows you to generate such software engines for runtime control systems with full control of I/O (input/output) such as WinStExec, StExec, LinuxExec and a diskless RTOS (real-time operating system) environment, which can be used for software development using other IDEs (integrated development environments). The conditional transitions from state to state in the VFSM could also be used to model systems such as Bayesian networks that are based on the VFSM. The state transition conditions could then incorporate probabilistic triggers.

Also other computational systems, such as heat transfer from space to space, could also be mapped onto the same VFSM. Instead of the ‘flow’ of fire, the ‘flow’ of heat from space to space could be computed using the same VFSM. The conditional transitions in the computational ‘flow’ from space to space could be modeled based on the heat transfer properties between the spaces.

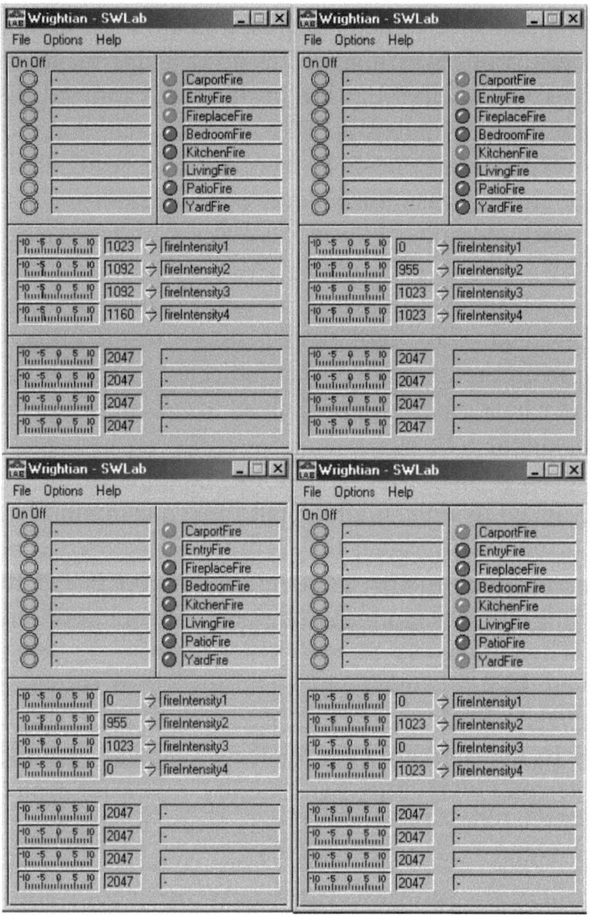

Figure 4. Screen shots of the VFSM runtime computation monitor in StateWORKS that monitors the Wrightian VFSM. The indicators in green show where the fires have occurred and the numerical values are the intensity of fires that have been mapped to the various spatial locations in the Wrightian houses

4. Intellectual Merit of the Project

The intellectual merit of this project is that it makes a unique proposal to analyze and code works of Architecture in a way that enables one to discover hidden computational structures in the works of Architecture. It is hoped that the project will provide valuable insight into the architectural basis of computational structures.

During the process of architectural design, various formal structures (i.e., structures that articulate a particular form) are generated and integrated to define the design of a building. These formal structures determine the spatial layout of structural systems, circulation systems, egress systems, arrangement of spaces, HVAC systems, plumbing systems, etc. in a building. All these formal structures are integrated in the design process to create the design of a functional building. These formal structures satisfy many constraints and meet many performance criteria in different domains. As such, they are very complex design constructs. If these formal structures could be shown to be feasible computational structures as well, then the rigor and complexity of the architectural design process could be brought to bear on the design of software systems. If a particular formal structure derived from a work of Architecture is shown to be a computational structure as well, then the methodology of the architectural design process that resulted in that formal structure could be studied as a viable software design process. This will bring the whole body of design methods used in the architectural design process into the world of software design. Conversely the research process will also yield computational structures for the design of architectural entities, thereby enabling the creation of new kinds of computer-aided design systems in Architecture.

The broader impact of this research project will be to amplify the interdisciplinary relationship between Architecture and Computer Science and provide practical benefits such as the creation of new kinds of software for both traditional computational tasks and for architectural design. Though the methodology described in this project aims at discovering hidden computational structures in Architecture, it can be adapted to discover hidden computational structures in other fields such as Engineering and Biology, thereby enriching the field of computation.

5. Conclusion

The project described in this paper has successfully shown how you can take a formal structure from Architecture and convert it into a computational structure. It has also shown how this computational structure can be used as an engine to develop hardware and software systems for applications such as the monitoring of fire spread in a building. This is the proof of concept for discovering computational structures in architecture. The project still has to demonstrate that these computational structures, which are derived from works of Architecture, can be feasible computational structures for tasks in traditional computation They hold the promise of serving as meta-computational structures for computational applications in architectural design, but have yet to be shown to enable other computational tasks such as sorting and searching, which are often considered benchmark tasks in Computer Science.

In his landmark book, Hillier presented the case that "space is the machine." (Hillier 1996) This book has a strong connection to this project. However, Hillier was specific in referring to his theory as a "configurational theory of architecture," and not a "computational theory of architecture." In a chapter devoted to the topic, he made the case for "non-discursive techniques," that were neutral in the analysis of space and form, thereby aiming for a "universal" understanding and the development of an "internal" theory of architecture. Is Hillier's machine a computer? If this is the case, the 'configurations' of architecture become viable 'computational structures' as well. This project reveals the intriguing possibility that this may be the case. As this project unfolds, more involved issues related to discovering computational structures in architecture are bound to emerge, which need to be thoroughly investigated.

The results of this research project are intended to be used as the foundation for an interdisciplinary Honors seminar course at our university titled, "The Architecture of Software Systems." This course will extend this inquiry and develop it further. The Honors program at our university is based on selective admission and attracts the best and brightest students in the university who have a natural inclination for interdisciplinary studies. Courses are typically taught by a team of two or more faculty members from different disciplines. Mahalingam and a faculty member from Computer Science intend to teach the Honors course together. Their cross-disciplinary collaboration on the subject will make them effective teaching colleagues. The course will stimulate motivated students to pursue and extend research ideas in this area of inquiry further by exposing them to the state-of-the-art in this field.

Acknowledgements

The developers of the StateWORKS development tool have opened up this new avenue for research in the field of computer-aided architectural design. StateWORKS allows researchers to study computational modeling problems in architecture by building and testing tractable solutions in the form of virtual finite state machines that can be implemented in both software and hardware.

References

Hillier, B: 1996, *Space is the machine*, Cambridge University Press, Cambridge, England.

Mahalingam, G: 2005, A Computational Model of a Sensor Network for the Optimization and Control of Acoustical Performance Criteria in Spatial Enclosures, *Proceedings of CAADRIA 2005*, New Delhi, pp. 475-483.

Mahalingam, G: 2003, Representing Architectural Design Using a Connections-based Paradigm, *Proceedings of the ACADIA' 2003 Conference*, Indianapolis, Indiana, pp. 269-277

Mahalingam, G: 2001, POCHE: Polyhedral Objects Controlled by Heteromorphic Effectors, *in* B deVries, J van Leeuwen and H Achten (eds), *Proceedings of the CAAD Futures 2001 Conference*, Kluwer Academic Publishers, Dordrecht, pp. 603-614 .

Mahalingam, G: 2000, The Algorithmic Auditorium: Automating Auditorium Design, *Proceedings of the ACSA Technology Conference 2000*, MIT, Boston, Massachusetts.

Mahalingam, G: 2000, Computing Architectural Designs Using An Architectural Programming Language, *Proceedings of the eCAADe 2000 Conference*, Weimar, Germany, pp. 125-130

Mahalingam, G: 1999, A Parallel Processing Model for the Analysis and Design of Rectangular Frame Structures, *Proceedings of the ACADIA 99 Conference*, Snowbird, Utah, October, pp. 346-347

Mahalingam, G: 1999, A New Algorithm for the Simulation of Sound Propagation in Spatial Enclosures, *Proceedings of the Building Simulation '99 Conference*, Kyoto, Japan, paper D-19.

Mahalingam, G: 1998, The Algorithmic Auditorium, *Proceedings of the CAADRIA '98 Conference*, Osaka, Japan, pp. 143-152.

Mahalingam, G: 1997, Representing Architectural Design Using Virtual Computers, *Proceedings of the ACADIA '97 Conference*, Cincinnati, Ohio, pp. 51-61.

March, L and Steadman, P: 1971, *The geometry of environment: An introduction to spatial organization in design*, RIBA Publications Ltd.

Wagner F, Schmuki, R, Wagner, T and Wolstenhilme, P: 2006, *Modeling Software with Finite State Machines: A Practical Approach*, Auerbach Publications, Taylor & Francis Group, New York, New York.

PLASTIC SURGERY IN THE EVOLUTIONARY DESIGN OF SPATIAL FORM

MICHAEL A ROSENMAN AND NICHOLAS PREEMA
University of Sydney, Australia

Abstract. This paper presents a methodology for producing good solutions for spatial form for non-routine design more efficiently. The methodology is based on augmenting a conventional evolutionary design approach with a method for improving suboptimal design solutions using domain-specific knowledge. This approach is based conceptually on the practice of plastic surgery, i.e. making minor adjustments to an entity, based on some desired qualities. While a conventional evolutionary design approach can produce reasonably good design solutions in an environment of knowledge uncertainty, plastic surgery, using domain-specific knowledge to manipulate the phenotype, can further improve such solutions in an efficient manner. This paper demonstrates how such a technique can be applied to the generation of spatial form.

1. Introduction

Design is characterized by the generation of form in response to some functional needs In architecture this form can be either spatial or physical (material). In either case, the generation of form can be implemented by placing a number of primitive elements in various combinations. In the case of spatial form, this constitutes the placement of a number of units of space together to produce required spaces. In non-routine design, the form required for a particular problem is not exactly known and a method, which can allow for the generation of many possible forms is advantageous as it can lead to unanticipated solutions.

Non-routine design tasks are characterized by the lack of knowledge available for their immediate solution (Coyne et al. 1990). Thus knowledge-lean approaches, such as evolutionary computation methods, are well suited to the task of non-routine design (Rosenman1996a; Bentley 1999, 2003; Koza et al. 2004). Evolutionary computation methods are characterized by

A Dong, A Vande Moere & JS Gero (eds), CAADFutures'07, 139–152.

their ability to arrive at reasonable solutions fairly quickly to begin with but then needing many generations to make subsequent small improvements, (Goldberg 1989; Parmee and Denham, 1994). A great deal of effort can be expended to make a small (but maybe critical) improvement and, in general, there is no guarantee that such an improvement will be found. In addition, in non-routine design, it is not always possible to perfectly specify the fitness function such that optimal or very good solutions will be found since the design task is not well-known. This paper argues that, even in such conditions, it is possible to obtain reasonable solutions within the bounds given and then, using these resulting solutions as a guide, make improvements to obtain better solutions.

Plastic surgery is a practice whereby features of an entity (generally a human) are altered to improve the appearance of that entity. In all cases, the effect is on the phenotype, i.e. the entity itself, and there is no change to the genotype (DNA). Since evaluation is done on the phenotype, any improvement to the phenotype gives the entity a better chance of survival or attaining its goal, e.g. attaining self esteem, attracting other entities, etc. Plastic surgery is generally done to correct minor features, e.g. making a nose smaller, etc. An entity exists, that is, it has been generated in some way, but is defective in some features and minor corrections are made (to the phenotype) to improve it. Specialized knowledge is required to recognize the defects and to modify the phenotype. Different domains require different specialized knowledge.

A conventional evolutionary method may be used, in situations where the form required is not known a priori, to produce possible solutions which are reasonably good but need some improvement. Once the solutions are produced, they can be examined and, where suitable, improved by making small modifications to the phenotype. This paper presents an approach that has the potential to significantly improve the ability of evolutionary design processes to produce good design solutions. While, an improvement in computational efficiency is important, it is more a case of the ability to actually produce solutions of high quality.

2. Evolutionary Design

While knowledge-rich approaches can solve problems where the problem is well defined and the knowledge and methods required are also known, they operate in specific problem areas with little capacity for producing innovative solutions. On the other hand, while knowledge-lean methods, such as evolutionary design, are good for discovering possible reasonable solutions where little knowledge is known a priori regarding the form of the solution, they are generally computationally expensive and may not be able to make the necessary improvements in a reasonable time with reasonable resources. Additionally, in an environment where there exists little a priori knowledge, it is not always possible to perfectly specify the requirements, i.e. formulate a 'perfect' fitness function.

The proposed approach combines knowledge-lean and knowledge-rich approaches to increase the efficiency of producing good design solutions in a non-routine design problem environment. The conventional evolutionary computation approach generates reasonably good solutions within given initial specifications and the proposed plastic surgery makes small modifications to those solutions based on local knowledge of the problem.

3. A Design Representation for Spatial Form

In its simplest mode, the construction of form can be thought of as the set of decisions for locating a set of cells of substances, where a substance may be physical (composed of a physical material) or virtual (e.g. composed of graphic entities or pixels). The construction of a spatial entity may be considered as the allocation of a number of cells of a physical substance composed of a 'space' material. In an evolutionary design approach, a gene selects a module of substance and allocates it to some location. In the approach of Rosenman (1996a, 1996b, a gene locates a module of substance relative to another module. A gene, GN, is thus (M_1, M_2, L_{12}) where M_1 and M_2 are two modules of some substance and L_{12} is the operator for locating module M_2 relative to module M_1. A module, M_i, may be a single unit cell or a set of unit cells already grouped and, in general, M_1 and M_2 need not be composed of the same substance. In the design of spatial form, S will be a single substance composed of space.

Since spatial form can be represented as the shape of spatial composition, the aim being to produce shapes suitable for various functions. A cellular composition of space units can be represented as a composition of elementary polyhedral or polygonal units (Rosenman 1995, 1999).

4. The Design Solutions

When a number of squares are joined randomly the resulting shapes (polyminos) are not likely to show much regularity, especially if the number of squares is large. Figure 1 shows 40 random generations of 16-unit polyminos.

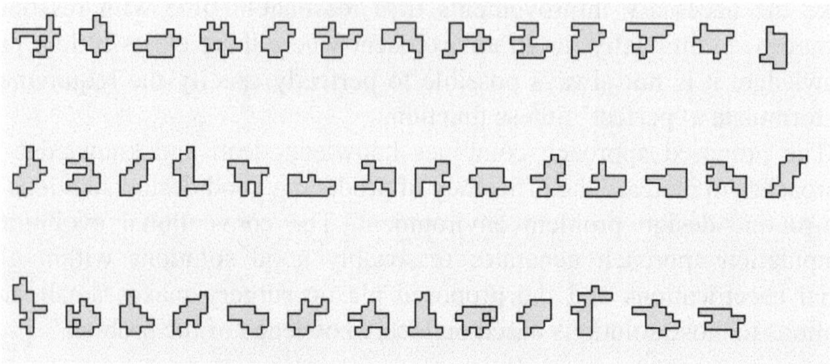

Figure 1. 40 random generations of 16-unit polyminos

The objective for architectural spaces will be to produce a shape with a contour having reasonably smooth edges. Figure 2 (a) shows a configuration of 12 cells that may arise after a number of generations. To produce an improvement such that the protrusion is removed and the indentation is filled (leading to a square in this case), Figure 2 (b), may take a great deal effort from the evolutionary computation process especially where the number of cells is large, e.g. >=100. While we can see that removing the protrusion and filling in the indentation would lead to a good solution, the evolutionary system based on random genetic operations (crossover and mutation) on the genotype may not be able to produce the required solution within a feasible timescale.

(a) an almost 'perfect' solution (b) an improved solution

Figure 2. Improvement of a design solution

As stated previously, in an environment of non-routine design, it will generally not be possible to accurately state the precise requirements nor translate them into a fitness function capable of precisely driving the evolutionary system to perfect solutions. The example in Figure 1 has only 16 cells. However, if the scale of the cells in Figure 1 were reduced by a factor of 10, allowing for increments in length of say 10cms rather than 1m, the total number of cells would be 1600. For a large number of cells, the evolutionary process, will, after a number of generations, give some indication of possible satisfactory shapes but will, usually, not be able to perfectly smooth out all the protrusions and indentations. For example, the fitness function may be based on minimizing the perimeter to area ratio since this will tend to produce compact shapes and tend to minimize long perimeters. However, one will find that, with a large number of cells, the number of cells at the perimeter is small compared to the number of interior cells which are fairly well compacted. Thus most of the solutions will show a fairly high score for that fitness function. The process will not be able to make any significant improvement in any reasonable time.

Although it may be argued that one should find a more precise fitness function, this is not always possible. The approach taken here shows that it is possible to postulate some reasonable fitness function which drives the evolutionary system towards reasonably satisfactory solutions. Then, the strategy is to improve these solutions as required.

5. Plastic Surgery in Evolutionary Design

In an evolutionary system, selection acts with respect to the phenotype. Those members whose phenotypes are judged to be well-suited to their environment will have a better chance of survival and of propagating their genes (Janssen et al. 2002). Thus any improvement in the phenotype, regardless of any change in the genotype, will improve that member's chance of survival and propagation. Of course, this improvement will not be transmitted to the member's descendants. In a design domain the fitness of the design is what counts, how it got to be that way is secondary.

The Merriam-Webster (2006) dictionary states that plastic surgery is:

"surgery concerned with the repair, restoration, or improvement of lost, injured, defective, or misshapen body parts"

Plastic surgery is aimed at improving the organism's survival in its environment, where survival may mean the organism's perceived state of happiness or its improved ability to attract partners as well as its improved ability to function better.

In this work, plastic surgery is proposed as a solution to improving a phenotype (design solution) generated through an evolutionary computation method. The modifications should be limited to relatively small remedial improvements. While it may be possible to make large alterations, this seems to be too large a departure from the solutions found leading to different forms and is not the aim of this work.

While an example in the domain of the generation of smooth polygons will be used to demonstrate the concepts, this paper suggests that the general principles of plastic surgery could be applied to other domains since design is seen generally as a process of locating suitable elements in a certain configuration.

6. Methodology

The implementation of plastic surgery consists of several transformation functions. There exist various smoothing algorithms mainly in image processing, where they are used to produce smoothed surfaces from polygonal or noisy surfaces (Hoppe 1996; Volino and Thalman 1998; Hobby 1998). Algorithms such as Potrace (2006) transform bitmap images into vector graphics. Another process uses sampling for anti-aliassing in ray tracing (Rossignac and Borrel 1992). Sampling works by overlaying a grid of larger cells on the form. Each cell is analyzed to determine what percentage of the cell is occupied. Cells with 50% or more occupation would be filled in completely, while those with less than 50% occupation would be left empty. The small-increment method is closer to the philosophy of making minor repairs rather than large-scale modifications and results in shapes closer to the original shapes than the sampling method which results in ‘major reconstructions’.

Modifications can be carried out to various levels of refinement, i.e. with respect to the number of units to be treated. Figure 3 shows the various examples (defects) which may require modification.

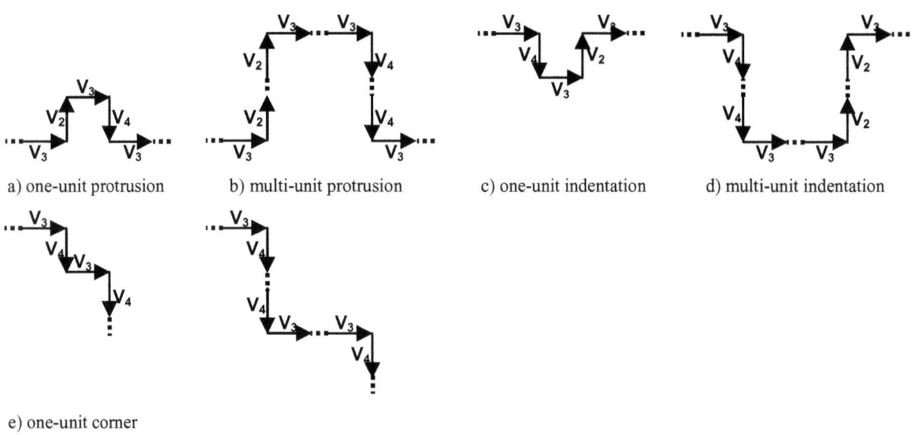

Figure 3. Cases for modification

These include protrusions, indentations and corners, ranging from one unit to several units. The number of units in each direction may depend on the scale, i.e. the total number of units in a shape. While Figure 3 shows defects on one edge or corner only, the defects may occur on any of the four edge or corner directions (for polymino shapes).

Figure 4 shows the rules for plastic surgery, i.e. modifying the phenotype (shape) according to the type of defect (protrusion, indentation or corner) and the number of units to be rectified in the two directions. Again, it should

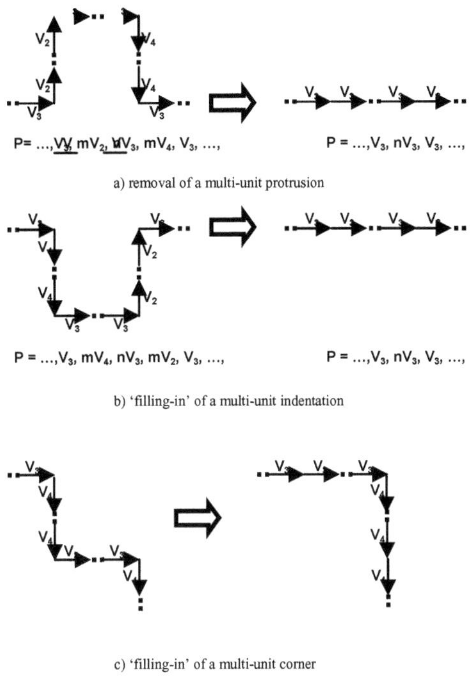

Figure 4. Rules for plastic surgery of defects

be noted that the defect may occur in any direction so that the depth and width of a defect are local to the particular direction.

The level of refinement is set by setting the depth and width, in terms of number of units, for the plastic surgery to take effect. The degree of refinement and the order of implementation of the operations will determine the final result. Different parameters and sequences will produce different results. In the physical world it is not possible to try several alternatives, whereas in a computational process it is possible to try alternatives and select among them depending on the result. Figure 5 shows two different sequences of operations on a shape of 50 units based on the following operations or rules:

Rule 1:	Defect = protrusion	max depth = n	max width = 1
Rule 2:	Defect = indentation	max depth = 1	max width = 3
Rule 3:	Defect = corner	max depth = 1	max width = 1

Rule 1 states that all protrusions of width 1 unit, no matter their depth, are to be deleted.

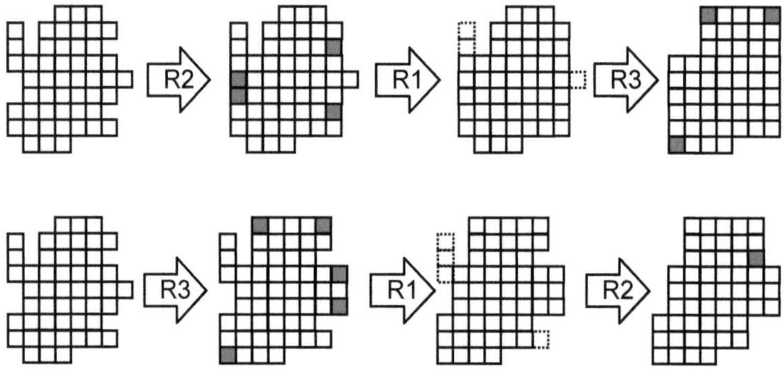

Figure 5. Two different sequences for plastic surgery

The shaded and dotted units show the units added or trimmed. The first solution has grown from 50 units to 54 units whereas the second solution has increased to 52 units. The size of the resulting solution depends on the number of units trimmed or filled. Since the number (size of the element) may be critical, some constraints may need be applied regarding the number of units trimmed or added or the number of elements trimmed may need to be balanced by the number of elements added (and vice versa). In a very large number of units, the number of units adjusted may not makes a significant change to the size of the shape since the number of units on the perimeter is small compared to the total number of units.

A method for recognizing which shapes are suitable for plastic surgery is based on the measure of fitness of the shape as well as on a measure of the number of defective units with respect to the shape's perimeter.

7. Implementation Example

An example in the domain of room designs was implemented. Rooms need not necessarily have rectangular shapes nor do they necessarily have to have 'smooth' walls. They may have recesses but generally these need to be large enough to accommodate furniture such as bookshelves etc. So, in general, small protrusions and recesses in the perimeter are not acceptable. The aim is to generate shapes for a room of 18 m^2. With a square unit of 1 m $\times$ 1 m there would be only 18 units and the variations in acceptable dimensions of length and width would be quite limited. Therefore, a variation of 300 mm in each dimension was set to allow for a wide range of possible dimensions. This results in the arrangement of 200 square units of 300 mm $\times$ 300 mm.

7.1. FITNESS FUNCTION

The fitness functions used were those used in Rosenman (1996a, b). A function that tends to smooth the perimeter is that of minimizing the perimeter. The minimum perimeter of a polymino shape is ideally a square. While not all given areas (e.g. 200 units) can form squares, using this fitness function will tend to make shapes more compact, thus reducing the length of the perimeter. The aim of room design is not to necessarily produce square or rectangular shapes but to use the fitness function to drive the evolutionary process towards such shapes, generating other suitable shapes in the process. Another measure of the smoothness of the perimeter is that of minimizing the number of corners. The minimum number of corners of a polymino shape is 4. Obviously a square has both the minimum area and the minimum number of corners. This function has a tendency to prefer L-shapes over T-shape. Both these shapes will have the same perimeter to area ratio but the L-shape has six corners compared to eight for the T-shape. While the first function tends to prefer more compact shapes, the second function will assign a maximum value to a rectangular shape no matter what its proportion.

For the first function, minimizing the perimeter to area function, the fitness is given by:

$$f1 = (MaxP - P / MaxP - MinP) \times 100 \quad (1)$$

where

$f1$ = fitness function wrt minimum perimeter to area
$MaxP$ = maximum possible perimeter for a shape of n units
P = perimeter of generated shape
$MinP$ = (ideal) minimum perimeter of a shape of n units

and

$Min\ P = 4\sqrt{n}$ (ideal square)
$MaxP = 2n + 2$ (e.g. shape of 1 unit width and n units length)

where

n = number of units

For the second function, that of minimizing the number of corners, the fitness is given by:

$$f2 = (Max\ C - C / MaxC - 4) \times 100 \quad (2)$$

where

$MaxC$ = maximum possible number of corners for a shape of n units
C = number of corners of generated shape

and

$MaxC = 2n$ (e.g. fully stepped shape)

Both functions use a ratio of the range of possible values to determine the normalized percentage fitness of the shape. The total fitness is given as:

$$TF = (f1 + f2) / 2 \quad (3)$$

Different weightings could be used for each fitness function to influence the shape towards one or the other but for this example a simple weighting of 1 for each has been used for simplicity.

7.2. METHOD

A C++ program for Windows was written to generate and evolve a population of polymino shapes using a genetic algorithm based on cell addition using the edge vector representation discussed previously and then to perform plastic surgery. The inputs to the generation and evolution are: the number of units, the number of members of the population and the maximum number of generations to be run. The genetic algorithm may terminate before the maximum number of generations is reached if it converges or remains stable. A run converges if the average fitness is within 5% of the best fitness and remains stable if there is no significant change in the best solution or average fitness over a specified number of generations. Simple one-point crossover was used with the best of the two populations (parent and child) kept to preserve the best solution. The remaining members of the new generation are selected using the roulette wheel method. The inputs to the plastic surgery are the width and length of the three repair cases (protrusion, indentation and corner) specifying the scale of the repair.

The program was run several times with the following parameters:

No. of units 200
Population 40
Max. no. of generations 60
Max. depth 1
Max width 3

7.3. RESULTS

Results were similar over a number of runs. Figure 6 shows the results of one of these runs. Figure 6 shows a typical growth in fitness over the 60 generations using the conventional evolutionary process. The average fitness of the population is 72.6%. As can be seen from the graph, the population has arrived at a fairly stable state and it could take a very large number of

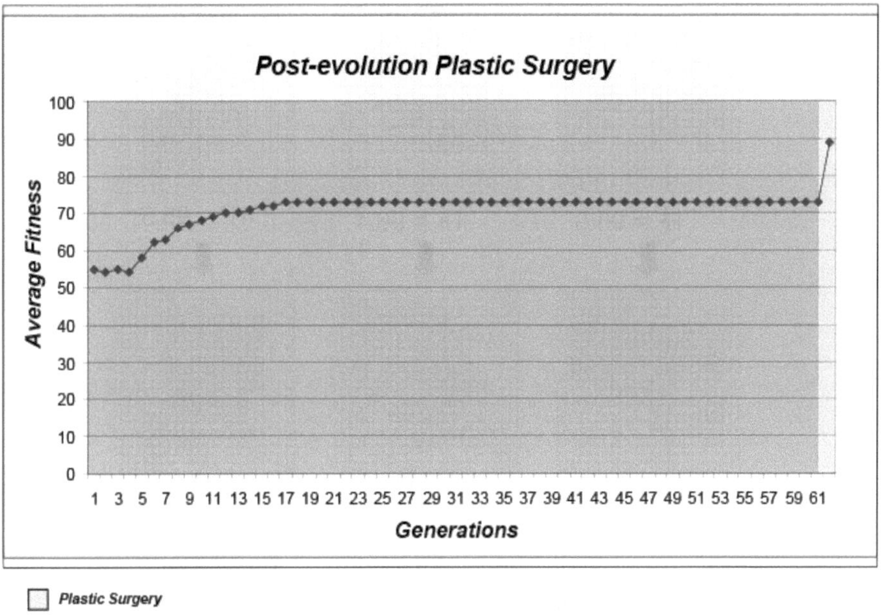

Figure 6. Effect of plastic surgery after the evolutionary process

additional generations to produce any improvement (if any is possible). After the application of plastic surgery, the average fitness jumps to 89.3%. This is a 23% improvement.

Figure 7 shows three of the shapes subjected to plastic surgery. It can be seen that these three members, previous to the plastic surgery, had a high fitness (95.6 to 96.6) even though their shapes are not all that good. The first shape is better than the other two but still has some small changes in direction in the upper left-hand part. The relatively high fitness values are due to the fitness function used which, in part measures the compactness of the shape. Since a large proportion of the shapes is indeed compact, the fitness values are high and there is little pressure to improve them. In the previous work (Rosenman 1996a, b) where only relatively small number of units were used (maximum 25) this problem did not exist. It can be seen that while the application of the plastic surgery has improved the fitness values, its main contribution is in producing better shapes, i.e. shapes with fewer small protrusions, etc. No method was used to ensure that the size of the shape (room) remained the same and the first shape has increased to 208 units, the second to 206 and the third to 207, an increase of less than 5% in all cases. Note that while none of the shapes shown are rectangles, nevertheless they could be suitable as rooms in certain instances.

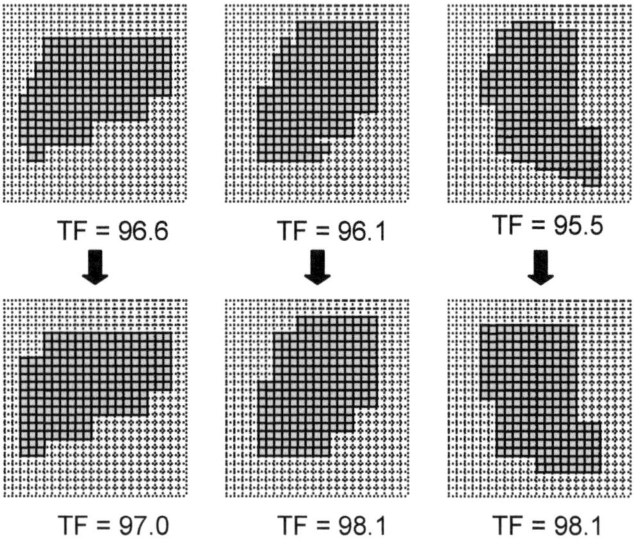

Figure 7. Members from the run before and after plastic surgery

8. Summary

This paper has presented a method of generating spatial forms using an evolutionary approach. It has argued that evolutionary design methods are suitable approaches for non-routine design generation since they are knowledge-lean and hence suitable for situations where there is little a priori knowledge available regarding any associations between the requirements and the form to be generated. An example using square cells was used for simplicity although the approach could be generalized to 3-D polyhedral shapes. However, it was argued that for complex objects with large number of cells, and with possibly imprecise fitness functions, the solutions arrived after a reasonable effort may still need improvement. It was shown that, although, the solutions obtained are reasonable, i.e. they will show the general direction of the form to be achieved, they need minor modifications to achieve more satisfactory results.

The results of the implementation of the example show that plastic surgery is a useful method for efficiently improving design solutions where the evolutionary process has achieved stability. Plastic surgery is seen as a knowledge-based mutation of the form (phenotype). Though illustrated in the context of the 2D cellular formation of shapes and the smoothing of irregular perimeters, it is a general concept applicable to 3D forms and other applications. Other applications will need to use domain specific knowledge for their repair rules.

9. Future Work

It was argued that design, in general, is the allocation of units of substances to create form and that non-routine design suffers from incomplete knowledge. Thus, while this work is specific to space layout, the concept of generate-and-fix is more general. Each domain, however, needs its domain-specific knowledge to specify fitnesses, recognize defects and provide methods for repair. Future work will generalize the approach to other design domains. This will require that one takes into consideration the allocation of units of different substances and the repair of the whole. This will mean deciding not only what form needs to be repaired but what substance should be used.

As in the human example, any modification to the phenotype (design solution) is not transmitted to the genotype. Any 'children' may carry the defective genes and reproduce the same defects. However, in design, if the modified design solution is the final solution required, and no more processing is to take place, then this does not matter as the genotype was just the means to the end and is no longer of any interest. However, if the modified design solution is only a part solution and is required to take part in further evaluation, e.g. as a component in a hierarchical system, a problem exists since all evolutionary operations are carried out on the genotype. In that case, genetic re-engineering of the genotype will be required. Future work will look at the implementation of the re-engineering method for various stages of an evolutionary process.

References

Bentley, PJ (ed): 1999, *Evolutionary Design by Computers*, Morgan Kaufman, San Francisco, CA.

Bentley, PJ: 2003, Natural design by computers, *Proc of the AAAI Symposium on Computational Synthesis*, Stanford University, Palo Alto, CA.

Coyne, RD, Rosenman, MA, Radford, AD, Balachandran, MB and Gero, JS: 1990, *Knowledge Based Design*, Addison-Wesley, Reading, Mass.

Goldberg, DE: 1989, *Genetic Algorithms in Search, Optimization and Machine Learning*, Addison-Wesley, Reading, Mass.

Hobby, JD: 1998, Smoothing digitized contours, *Theoretical Foundations of Computer Graphics and CAD*, pp. 777-793.

Hoppe, H: 1996, Progressive meshes in computer graphics, *SIGGRAPH '96*, pp. 99-108.

Janssen, P, Frazer, J and Ming-Xi, T: 2002, Evolutionary design systems and generative processes, *Applied Intelligence* **16**: 119-128.

Koza, JR, Jones, LW, Keane, MA, Streeter, MW and Al-Sakran, SH: 2004, Towards automated design of industrial-strength analog circuits by means of genetic programming, *in* U-M Oreilly, RL Riolo, G Yu and W Worzel (eds), *Genetic Programming Theory and Practice II*, Klewer Academic, Boston, Chapter 8, pp. 121-142.

Merriam-Webster: 2006. Retrieved December 4, 2006 from http://www.m-w.com/.

Old, RW and Primrose, SB: 1994, *Principles of Gene Manipulation: An Introduction to Genetic Engineering (studies in Microbiology)*, Blackwell Science 5th ed, Oxford, UK.

Parmee, IC and Denham, J: 1994, The integration of adaptive search techniques with current engineering design practice, *Proc.of Adaptive Computing in Engineering Design and Control '94*, University of Plymouth, Plymouth, pp. 1-13.

Potrace: 2006, Transforming bitmaps into vector graphic. Retrieved December 4, 2006 from http://potrace.sourceforge.net.

Rosenman, MA: 1995, An edge vector representation for the construction of 2-dimensional shapes, *Environment and Planning B:Planning and Design* **22**: 191-212.

Rosenman, MA: 1996a, The generation of form using an evolutionary approach, *in* JS Gero and F Sudweeks (eds), *Artificial Intelligence '96*, Kluwer Academic, Dordrecht, The Netherlands, pp. 643-662.

Rosenman, MA: 1996b, A growth model for form generation using a hierarchical evolutionary approach, *Microcomputers in Civil Engineering*, special issue on Evolutionary Systems in Design, **11**(3): 161-172.

Rosenman, MA: 1999, A face vector representation for the construction of polyhedra, *Environment and Planning B: Planning and Design* **26**: 265-280.

Rossignac, JR and Borrel, P: 1992, Multi-resolution 3D approximations for rendering complex scenes, *in* B Falcidieno and TL Kunii (eds), *Geometric Modelling in Computer Graphics*, Springer-Verlag, Genoa, Italy, pp. 455-465.

Volino, P and Magenat Thalman, T: 1998, The SPHERIGON: A simple polygonal patch for smoothing quickly your polygonal meshes, MIRAlab Copyright Information. Retrieved December 4, 2006 from http://www.miralab.unige.ch/papers/50.pdf.

A SYSTEM FOR PROVIDING CUSTOMIZED HOUSING

Integrating design and construction using a computer tool

DEBORAH BENRÓS, JOSÉ P DUARTE
AND FERNANDO BRANCO
Technical University of Lisbon, Portugal

Abstract. This paper describes a system for generating customized mass housing. The aim is to provide dwellings at an affordable cost with recourse to mass production and yet guarantee that they are tailored to their users. It combines two systems, a rule-based design system and a prefabricated building system. The integration of both systems is achieved through the development of a computer tool to assist designers in the various stages of the housing design process. This tool produces three kinds of outputs: three dimensional models, construction drawings, and a list of construction elements, including their cost and information for manufacturing.

1. Introduction

A considerable amount of studies was developed over the last decades to improve housing conditions, diminish final costs, and customize dwellings. Professionals from different fields presented different approaches. While architects are interested in functionality, aesthetics and ergonomics, engineers are more concerned with structural systems, ease of construction, and overall costs. The role of the client in the housing provision process is increasingly smaller. The great majority buy ready-to-use dwellings, hoping for a greater level of versatility that could allow them to personalize their homes.

In the recent past, efforts have been made to integrate all these different, and sometimes conflicting, interests and still provide for a doable, affordable and customized dwelling. During the second quarter of the twentieth century architects like Le Corbusier, Walter Gropius, and other modernist architects proposed housing designs that employed prefabricated elements in an effort to accelerate construction and diminish costs in large scale mass housing.

A Dong, A Vande Moere & JS Gero (eds), CAADFutures'07, 153–166.

These approaches were put in practice in the devastated post second world war Europe.

In the 1960's, Habraken developed the theory of supports (2000). This theory proposed a matrix system that included a tartan grid based on which modular elements were created and combined to generate dwellings. Functional spaces were considered as design elements and manipulated like building elements. Designers were supposed to developed specific rule systems that they could manipulate to design different housing solutions, thereby promoting diversity and customization. The theory also foresaw the recourse to prefabrication, using standard elements, to permit greater efficiency in the construction process and controlled final costs. However, the system implementation depended on the rigorous establishment of design rules and on the correct and efficient manipulation of such rules.

In the 1990's, Duarte proposed a framework to overcome limitations in the implementation of design and building systems (1995), which foresaw the use of computers systems to assist in the design and construction processes. He illustrated this framework with the development of a computer program for exploring housing solutions within Siza's Malagueira style, whose compositional rules were inferred after careful analysis (2001; 2005). This program first helped the user to establish a housing program based on user and site data, and then generated a solution that matched the program, which took the form of a three-dimensional model.

The subsequent logical step was to facilitate the construction process. A great amount of the designer's effort and time is invested in drawing, detailing, and organizing construction data. Another share of time is spent in expensive and long on-site construction tasks. The goal of the present work is to contribute for diminishing the time and labour spent in such tasks. This is achieved by automatically generating construction drawings, once the design is settled, and by producing files that compile the data required for automated production, including bills of construction elements.

The motivation for developing the current work was the difficulty faced by designers in the use of a sophisticated light-weight prefabricated system produced by the British firm Kingspan. The richness of this system permits to construct a great variety of buildings, but its complexity jeopardizes its use in practice, thereby diminishing its commercial potential. The strategy to overcome this limitation was twofold. First, it was to develop a housing design system that permitted to design mass customized housing based on the Kingspan building system. And second, it consisted in creating a computer system that allowed the easy exploration of the universe of solutions and the automatic generation of information for fabrication. From the commercial viewpoint, the idea was to provide the firm with a new business model that enabled it to sell its product and gain market share.

Due to time constraints, however, it was not feasible to develop a new design system. Therefore, the solution was to look for an existing system that fulfilled the intended goals—the generation various dwellings—and was compatible with the Kingspan building system, thereby enabling to demonstrate the proposed model to the client. This system was the ABC system conceived by the Spanish architect Manuel Gausa.

2. Methodology

The development of this project can be divided into three stages: first, the establishment of the rule system; second, the coding of such a system into a computer program; and, third the assessment of the program.

The first work stage combined the selection, study, and adjustment of the design system to the construction system. The design system was adapted from the conceptual idea of the ABC design system conceived by the Manuel Gausa, the leader of Actar. This design was never materialized since it was created for the Ceuta competition in 1994, but it was object of analysis by leading architectural publications. It stands out due to its innovative approach that applies prefabricated systems to mass housing while giving the final user the opportunity to customize the dwelling with serial elements without the risk of overpricing the final result. The system borrows its name from the acronym of the functional units used in the design of dwellings: *Armario*, *Baña*and *Coziña* (storage, bathroom, and kitchen.)

The design of dwellings is not imposed by the architect, but suggested according to a set of conceptual rules. These rules predefine possible relations between functional spaces and control geometrical proportions. In addition, they define the external building envelope by reflecting the design of the interior layout. The original system yielded apartments with one or two bedrooms, whose spectrum of possible configurations was demonstrated in the form of a combination grid (Figure 1).

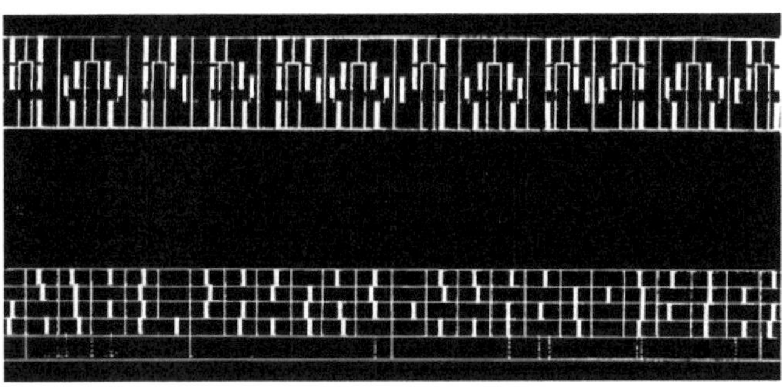

Figure 1. Compositional grid designed by Manuel Gausa to illustrate how layouts can result from the different placement of functional units; the top row shows layouts in plan and the one bellow shows the corresponding section (Gausa 1998)

The construction system is based on the Kingspan building system developed by the British firm Kingspan. It is a prefabricated building solution that presents two features, a steel cold formed structure and an envelope constructed with standard finishing elements. It is a complete system that can become too complex, hence the difficulties of penetration in the architectural market. Nevertheless, it is a versatile building scheme with high dimensional tolerances. It can be adapted to different geometries and its modular characteristics also permit the use of other standard finishing materials and envelope solutions. It presents some conditionings in terms of number of floors, maximum length, height, and thickness. For instance, the maximum number of floors is 6, and the pillar and beam grid cannot overtake 12 × 4.5 × 3.5 m.

The rules of both the design and the construction systems were identified and systematized, and then encoded into the computer program. This was developed in AutoLISP, a dialect of common LISP, using VisualLISP, an editor that runs within Autodesk's AutoCAD since the 2000 version. The computer program is composed of a number of functions, each being responsible for a specific task (for instance, the layout of a certain functional unit) or for the representation and geometrical construction of a particular building element (like a window frame, for example.) The program operates in three stages. The first is targeted at the development the three dimensional model of the housing units and the building; the second stage aims at creating bi-dimensional representations; and the third stage consists in the quantification and listing of all the construction elements required to erect the building.

3. Design and Constructive System

The final design system is an upgrade from the one proposed by Gausa (1998, 1999), since it was necessary to increase the flexibility of the system concerning the number of rooms, the total area of each housing unit, and the number of floors. After these alterations, the universe of solutions was enlarged to encompass the design of studio flats up to four-bedroom apartments, with areas ranging from 50 to 150 m^2, and the design of buildings with one up to six floors (the maximum number allowed by the structural system.) Despite the alterations, the basic compositional and spatial relationships remained untouched, thereby preserving the underlying architectural concept. Namely, the altered system retained major conceptual ideas from the original one, such as the spatial distribution principles, the functional units placement scheme, and the façade design rules.

The adaptation of the construction system did not require the need to perform any major changes and it was directly applied and coded into the computer program. This could be explained by the already mentioned versatile features of the system, which possesses a modular and orthogonal geometry with high dimensional tolerances that makes a wide variety designs feasible. The structural layout follows simple rules that rely on major spatial vertexes to free the interior from structural constrains and keep it fluid as required by the design system. The secondary framing occupies the inner spaces of external walls and partitions, thereby diminishing their visual impact on the internal space.

The functioning of the design system can be illustrated by a set of rules that determine the internal layout of the dwelling, depicted in Figure 2, and a set of spatial confinement and wall placement rules, shown in Figure 3.

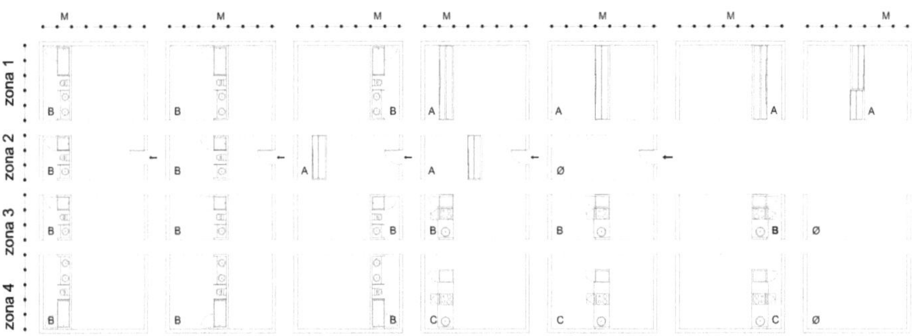

Figure 2. Spatial system: matrix after Gausa's original drawings illustrating several possibilities for placing functional units and used to infer their placement rules. Legend: A-storage, B-bathroom, C-kitchen, Ø-open-space

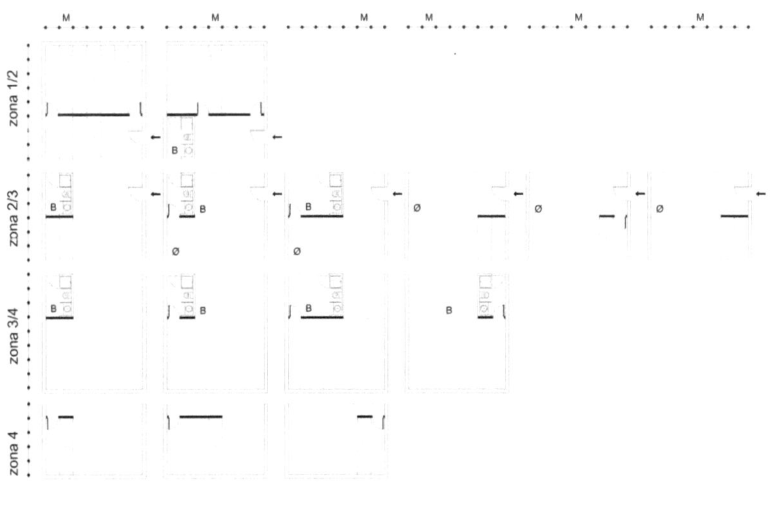

Figure 3. Spatial system: matrix after Gausa's original drawings illustrating several possibilities for creating spaces by placing partitions and doors and used to infer the delimitation rules

The spatial distribution is defined by the designer according to the following premises: every dwelling has to include at least one functional unit of each kind (storage, bathroom, or kitchen); living or sleeping spaces are adjacent to the façade to ensure natural lighting and ventilation, while circulation and services are located in the inner core of the dwelling. With this in mind, the designer can create different dwellings by placing the three functional units on different locations. Spaces are defined by the position of such units. The spectrum of possible placements are described in the scheme and coded into the program, which does not allow any other combination.

The internal layout is established based on two aspects: first, the predefined housing program or design brief and second, the preferences of the designer in terms of spatial distribution. The design brief is input during the initial steps of operating the computer program. The program assists the designer and enquiries about the number of bedrooms and overall area of the dwelling. Based on this information, the internal distribution is defined step by step from the so called zone 1 or sleeping area, to zones 2 and 3, corresponding to access, circulation and services, and finally, to zone 4 or the living area. The same sequence is followed during the generation of the dwelling when the computer program asks the user to place different units on different locations and assists him in this task to guarantee an acceptable final result.

Success is guaranteed by a well established set of rules that define all the acceptable relationships among adjacent spaces. For instance, in zone 1 or the sleeping area, three types of spaces may be placed: a bathroom, a storage unit, or a simple sleeping space. In addition, there are three different locations for the chosen unit, each resulting on a different spatial arrangement. In a similar fashion, zone 2 can host a bathroom, a storage unit, or an open space. However, the placement options are constrained by the presence of the entrance, which does not allow the creation of a small space close to the entrance door. Other rules can be extracted from the table in Figure 2; some address aesthetical aspects and others functional matters, such as circulation, environmental aspects, or hygiene.

Once the basic spatial layout is defined by the user, the computer program completes the interior design with the placement of walls and doors as shown in Figure 3. In this task, the program takes into account the use of a particular space, but also those of adjacent spaces. Sleeping spaces are always confined by walls, except in studio apartments where space is completely fluid. Similarly, services like washing spaces are limited and enclosed by walls to guarantee water proofing and privacy. Kitchens are delimited by walls and doors according to the house typology and the corresponding required area. Other rules can be inferred from the table in Figure 3, like those for placing a door to a given space when the most immediate location is occluded by an adjacent space. All these rules are encoded into the program and illustrated in the table.

The design of the façade is a reflection of the layout of inner spaces. This means that the placement of the functional units predetermine the placement of opaque façade panels and a colour code associated with the unit type is used to colour the panel. The remaining façade panels consist of transparent glass windows to provide for natural lighting and ventilation.

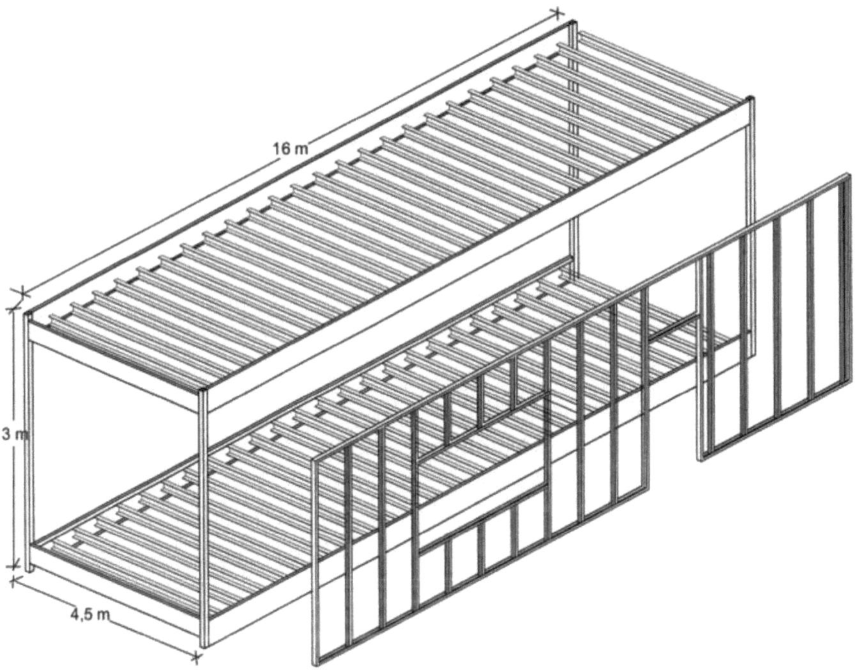

Figure 4. Structural and framing system from the Kingspan building system. Typical prefabricated grid with maximum dimensions

The Kingspan building system is a complete construction system composed by three subsystems: a structural system, a framing system, and a lining system.

The structural system is composed of galvanized steel elements that form a pillar and beam orthogonal supporting frame. These elements are manufactured by cold forming or simply by hot rollers and transformed into linear elements with diverse standard sections. These vertical and horizontal elements form a three-dimensional grid that frames each portion of interior space called a zone in the design system. The maximum grid dimensions are 4,5 m × 16 m × 3,5 m for the width, length, and height, respectively, as shown in Figure 4. The structural system can support up to six storeys, but structural reinforcement is recommended for more than three levels.

The framing system acts as a secondary reinforcement to the structural system and occupies the gaps between main structural elements, both in external walls and slabs. Cold-rolled galvanized C and I sections are used repeatedly to conceive the framing. I sections are used as main support, in beams and pillars, while C sections are used as wall and façade studs and slab supporting elements.

The lining system depends on the choices of the designer and the materiality of a specific housing design. The internal lining and ceiling systems are prepared to adapt to various layouts and introduce most of the standard manufactured finishing products available on the market. However, for this particular project it was chosen coloured glass-fibre reinforced concrete panels and aluminium window frames for the façade, and concrete prefabricated panels for the side walls. The interior walls and ceilings are finished with plaster boards, and the floor is levelled with a light concrete layer finished with wooden boards in living and circulation spaces and with tiles in wet spaces.

4. Computer Program

The integration of the design and the construction systems into a single platform is possible thanks to a computer program that assists the designer in the conception of dwellings. As mentioned in Section 1, some of the major shortcomings and drawbacks of past design systems stemmed from difficulties in applying their rule sets, often extensive and complex, in an accurate and efficient manner. In the current case, many of the design aspects valued by designers, such as harmony of spatial proportions, functionality, salubriousness, structural stability, or even building codes[1] are encoded into the computer program, which assists in and evaluates each design move.

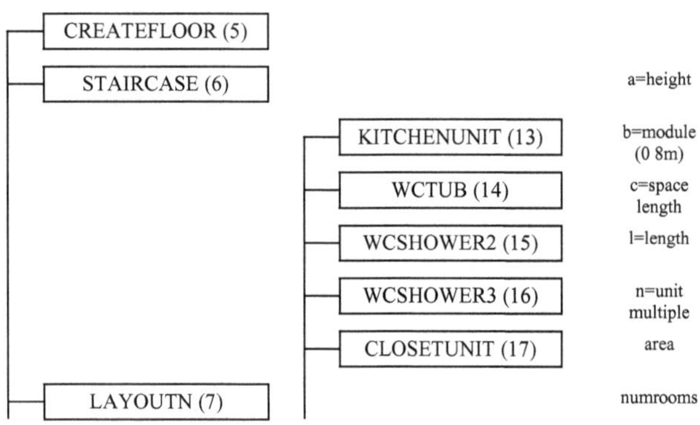

1 The current design system encodes the principles defined in the Portuguese building regulations, called REGEU – "Regulamento de Edificações Urbanas".

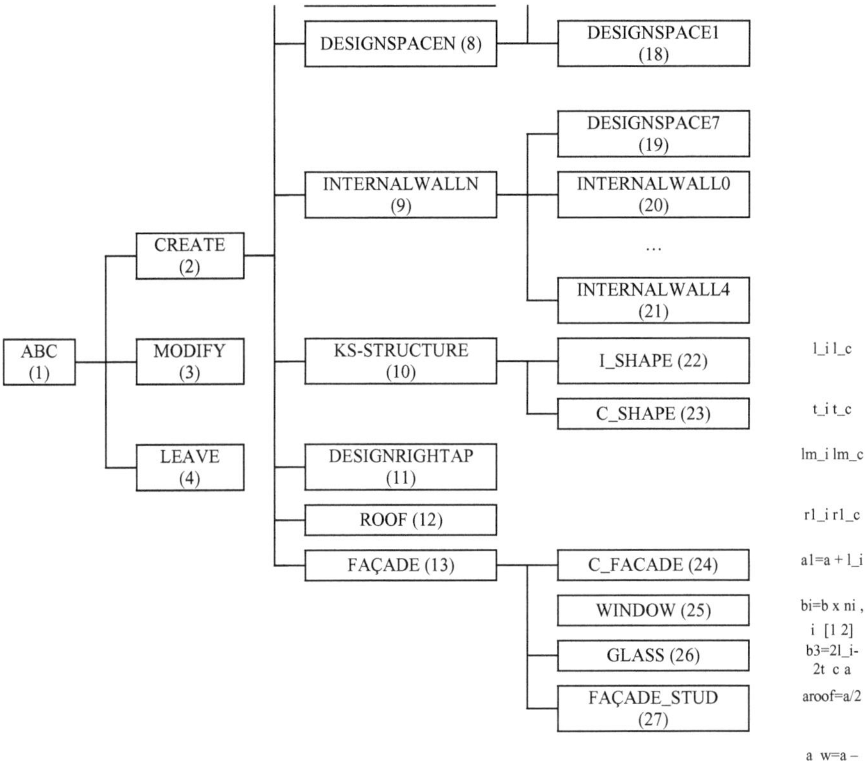

Figure 5. Computer program structure – functional diagram

The structure of the computer program is diagrammed in Figure 5. The main function, called ABC, is responsible for activating the program and initiating the Create, Modify and Leave cycle. The Create function generates the housing building design. This function starts by enquiring about basic building features such as the number of floors and floor height. This is followed by the activation of the function Createfloor, which will repeatedly run until the specified number of floors is designed. This function is responsible for the design of common spaces, including stairs, lifts, and circulations, as well as for the design of each housing unit, starting with left side one. For each dwelling, the interior design will evolve from zone 1, the sleeping area, to zone 2, the access area, to zone 3, the service area, and finally, to zone 4, the living area.

Design at this stage is assisted by the functions LayoutN and DesignspaceN (with N < 7). The former is responsible for the placement of the perimeter wall, and the latter for the assignment of functions to spaces. DesignspaceN depends directly on the functions Kitchenunit, WCunit, and Closetunit, which generate different types of functional units to equip each dwelling with the basic services, namely, kitchen, bathroom, and closet. It also prompts the user to select functional units and to specify their correct location within zones.

Once the available dwelling area is packed with the selected spaces, the computer completes the design by assessing the resulting spatial distribution and then by placing appropriate boundaries among spaces – doors, walls, or partitions – according to the rule system illustrated in Figure 3. The function Designrightap performs a cycle where the functions just described are recalled and mirrored in order to design the right side dwelling.

Once the floor is completed, the KStructure is responsible for the erection of the Kingspan building system dimensionally adapted to the generated design. This function will call sub-functions like I-beam, C-stud, and other sub-functions that are responsible for modelling particular elements. I and C sections are placed both horizontally and vertically to form frames that are parametrically defined in the function and then adjusted to specific spans.

The façade is designed according to the inner placement of functional units. Opaque panels are aligned with the units and placed by the function Façade. Façade is also responsible for designing and modelling window frames, glass panels, and structural studs calling upon the sub-functions C-stud, Window and Glass. The process is repeated for each floor until it ends with the placement of the roof above the top floor by the function Roof.

The design process can be monitored by the designer and client in real time with great precision since a three-dimensional model of the design is created in parallel to the decision making process (Figure 6). This allows the modification of undesired solutions or the comparison among different ones, which are enabled by activating the Modify function or the Create function, respectively. Once the user and the client are satisfied with the design, they can exit the program by activating the Leave function. Previously saved solutions can be later retrieved and modified as well.

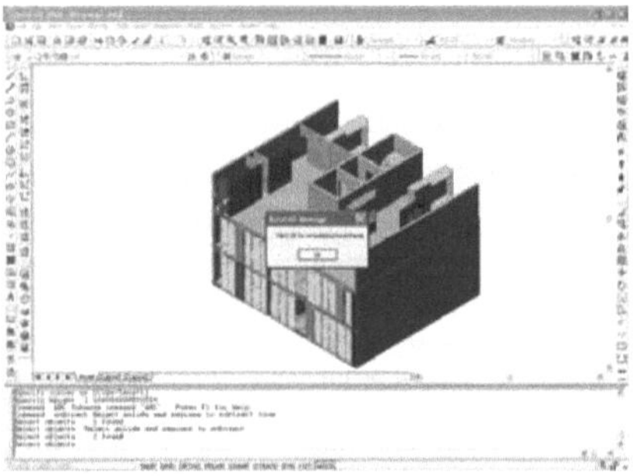

Figure 6. A 3-dimensional model of the evolving design is displayed to facilitate assessment and decision-making

There are three different outputs of the computer program: the three-dimensional model just mentioned, but also bi-dimensional drawings and bills of quantities (Figure 7, top). The main purpose of the three-dimensional model is to facilitate visualization and assessment of the design by the designer and the client, which can take several forms with increasing levels of sophistication. It can be used for immediate visualization within AutoCAD, it can be exported into rendering software to obtain photo-realistic views (Figure 7, bottom), or into a virtual reality system for virtual walks-through. It also can be utilized to generate a physical model using a rapid prototyping machine. The bi-dimensional drawings can be used as licensing drawings for approval of the design by the town hall, or as construction drawings to guide the construction of the building, following standard procedures.

The bill of construction elements is used to facilitate budgeting and manufacturing. For each element modelled by the computer, a record is

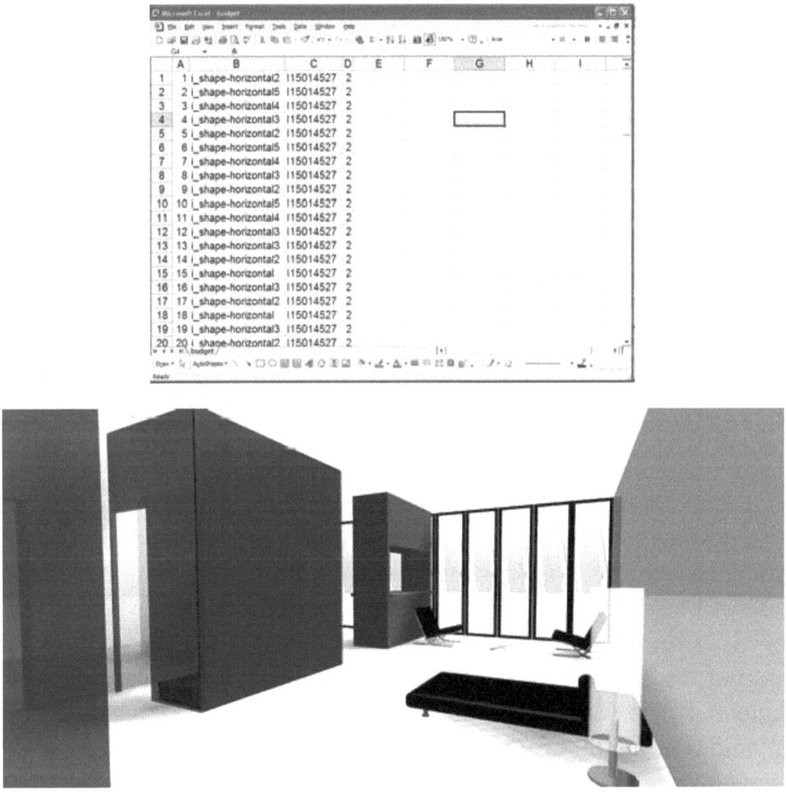

Figure 7. The output of the program includes a bill of construction elements (top), and a 3D model that can be exported to rendering software to create photorealistic views (bottom)

inserted in a list that compiles every element, its numerical reference, and its dimensional features. This list is converted by the function Record and saved as an .xls extension file, the standard EXCEL file format, which can be opened with MS Office to assess and control the overall budget. The same list can be used for automated production of prefabricated elements with the specified dimensions in the right quantity.

5. Conclusion

The aim of this study was the creation of a system to explore tailored housing solutions and to produce documentation for mass-producing them using prefabrication as a way of rationalizing construction and controlling costs. The way chosen to guarantee the efficient application of the underlying design and construction systems was the development of a computer program that encodes both systems. This program can assist the designer and help to minimize the time and effort spent in conceiving, drawing, detailing, and budgeting solutions. The program also facilitates the participation of the client in the design of his or her own dwelling as a decision maker. Customization and diversity in mass-housing become goals that can be achieved without overpricing the final result since design and fabrication are partially automated.

The proposed system is in line with previous approaches, but it goes one step further. In a paper called Design Machines, George Stiny and Lionel March (1981) proposed a theoretical model for the automated production of artefacts. The model foresaw the automation of both design and fabrication. This model was implemented by Wang and Duarte (2002) who developed a program that permitted the generation of 3-dimensional abstract objects using shape grammars (Stiny 1980) and the fabrication of the corresponding physical models using rapid prototyping. Later on, Duarte (2001; 2005) proposed a theoretical model for the automated production of dwellings called discursive grammar. This model foresaw the automated generation of housing designs that matched given criteria within a given design language. The model's validity was illustrated with an implementation developed for the case of houses designed by the architect Alvaro Siza at Malagueira. The model also foresaw the use of computer aided-manufacturing to produce houses, but the link between design generation and fabrication was yet to be implemented. The current system establishes such a connection.

In addition, there are three important differences between the two implementations. First, in the previous implementation, the rules of the design system were codified using a shape grammar, whereas the current one relies on parametric design. Shape grammars constitute a well-defined formalism that facilitates the process of devising, structuring, and applying rules systems that define languages of designs. A grammar permits to explain the features of designs in a language, to say whether an unknown design in that language, and how to generate new designs in the same language. However, shape grammars are difficult to implement in the computer because they require one to solve difficult technical problems, linked to shape recognition and rule application. On the other hand, there is no clear formalism to develop parametric systems of designs and one has to rely on his or her intuition to do it. Moreover, parametric design does not offer a rational explanation of how designs are categorized and generated. Nevertheless, once a parametric model is devised, it is much easier to implement and apply in the computer. Because the design system was purposefully devised by the architect and thus its rules were very clear, and because the current research had very practical goals, it was decided to develop a parametric model, instead of a shape grammar.

The second difference is that in the previous implementation there was a clear separation between the generation of the housing program and the generation of the corresponding solution, whereas is the current one there is not. Such a separation permitted greater flexibility and interaction in the definition of housing specifications, but implied that the user only visualized the impact of his choices at the end of the specification process, after making all the decisions and the program generating the solution. By evolving the 3D model while the user made choices, it was possible to visualize the result and correct it immediately, thereby making it easier and faster to tailor the design to the family needs

The third difference is that in the previous implementation the generation of designs was fully automated and the user could be the architect or the client, whereas the current one was targeted at the architect right from the beginning. As a result, it was developed as a design support tool and the degree of automation is considerably lower. This avoided complex technicalproblems such as shape recognition and optimization and made programming easier. Because the role of the architect is more apparent, the use of the tool is likely to be more accepted by the architectural community.

Acknowledgements

The authors would like to thank the support and interest of the Foresight and Innovation Department of the Ove Arup office in London and, particularly, Chris Luebkeman, Alvise Simondetti and Kristina Shea. This project was developed partially at Ove Arup in London and at Instituto Superior Técnico in Lisbon.

References

Duarte, JP: 1995, *Tipo e módulo. Abordagem ao processo de produção de habitação*, LNEC, Lisboa.

Duarte JP: 2001, *Customizing Mass Housing: A Discursive Grammar for Siza's Malagueira Houses*, Ph.D. Thesis, Massachusetts Institute of Technology, Cambridge, MA.

Duarte, JP: 2005, A discursive grammar for customizing mass housing; the case of Siza's houses at Malagueira, *Automation in Construction* **14**: 265-275.

Gausa, M. 1998, *Housing new alternatives, new systems*, ACTAR and Birkhäuser, Barcelona.

Gausa, M. and Salazar, J: 1999, *Singular housing, the private domain*, ACTAR and Birkhäuser, Barcelona.

Habraken, N.J: 2000, *El Diseño de soportes*, Editorial Gustavo Gili, Barcelona.

Stiny, G: 1980, Introduction to shape and shape grammars, *Environment and Planning B: Planning and Design* **7**: 343-351.

Stiny, G. March, L: 1981, Design machines, *Environment and Planning B: Planning and Design* **8**: 245-255.

Wang, Y, Duarte, JP: 2002, Automatic Generation and Fabrication of Designs, *Automation in Construction* **11**(3): 291-302.

ALGOGRAM: AUTOMATED DIAGRAMS FOR AN ARCHITECTURAL DESIGN STUDIO

CHRISTIANE M HERR AND JUSTYNA KARAKIEWICZ
University of Hong Kong, Hong Kong

Abstract. Building on a previously presented theoretical model for the integration of cellular automata into the design process, this paper introduces cellular automata as architectural design process support in the form of automated conceptual diagrams. This approach is the outcome of a series of successive software implementations, which are briefly outlined in terms of key features and observations made during their applications. The main part of the paper focuses on *Algogram*, the latest implementation, and its application in a second year design studio. The integrated concept of abstract representations, automated design exploration and individual interpretation is introduced as *automated diagram*.

1. Introduction

Among generative design strategies available to architectural computing, cellular automata (CA) have been described as an approach to support design by facilitating the generation of complex patterns (Chase 2005). CA were originally invented as mathematical games by Ulam (Schrandt and Ulam 1970) during the 1940s, and subsequently applied in a variety of fields to simulate complex processes based on the parallel and local interaction of elements. Previous applications of CA in architectural design have emphasized representations of form with cells depicting building volumes in a variety of ways. In the work of Coates et al. (1996), Krawczyk (2002) and Watanabe (2002), CA are used as generative tools to produce variations of building form (see Figure 1). The CA systems employed in these examples are based on uniform Cartesian grids with cubic cells, usually with very few cell states. Binary cell states such as "zero" and "one" or "dead" and "alive" are often translated into volumetric representations of matter or voids, resulting in three-dimensional forms that are then interpreted as building mass.

A Dong, A Vande Moere & JS Gero (eds), CAADFutures'07, 167–180.

Figure 1. CA as form generators in the work of Coates (left), Krawczyk (middle) and Watanabe (right)

In the early, conceptual design stages, architects typically use visual representations such as sketches and diagrams, which relate more to concepts rather than objects (as discussed in Section 3 below). The direct association of CA-generated shapes with building form as in the examples cited above may thus be premature and limiting. The approach taken here builds upon a previously proposed extended CA model that has been adapted for architectural design purposes (Herr and Kvan 2007). It builds on the design process model proposed by Schön (1983), which is extended to include CA-based design support as part of the design move and offers CA support in form of optional, small-scale steps to an otherwise conventional design process. To explore the implications of this approach and further develop the underlying theoretical assumptions, a series of four software implementations were developed and tested with architecture students in design studio and workshop settings. It was not the purpose of this study to optimize a specific tool. Software implementations instead served as platforms to explore an approach to CA-based design processes and provided mainly qualitative data for this study. As a result of outcomes from the software implementations, this study progressed from an initial focus on CA as generators of building form to an emphasis on rule-based support of diagrammatic representations. This paper first briefly presents the explorative research process that led to the application of CA-based design support in form of automated diagrams. The final implementation, *Algogram,* and its application in a second year design studio are described in more detail in the second half of the paper.

2. Exploring CA-based Modeling of Form and Relationships

The first three implementations of the initially proposed extended CA model (Herr and Kvan 2007) indicated several shortcomings of the approach. They are briefly summarized below to provide the background of the subsequent development of *Algogram*, which discussed in more detail in Section 4 and 5. Following a previously published initial pilot study (see Herr and Kvan 2005), the first implementation was used by 23 graduate architecture students in the initial phase of a design studio at The University of Hong Kong in late 2005. Implemented in *3DStudio MAX Script*, the tool offers its users a graphical interface to CA-based modeling functions to complement conventional three-dimensional modeling in *3DStudio MAX*. A wide variety of geometrical objects can be defined as cells, and then be assigned user-defined rules. The main purpose of this studio test was to explore how students would use and adapt CA-based software in their individual design processes, and how this would affect their design outcomes. While students readily experimented with the use of rules and incorporated the forms generated by the software into their projects, some have questioned the disruption rule definitions caused in their thinking process as well as the lack of predictability in the generated outcomes. What was on the one hand perceived as an interesting new method also discouraged students who previously had used computers only in deterministic ways to illustrate previously developed ideas. Most students however eventually engaged in an exploratory mode of design experimentation instead of a goal-driven one (see Figure 2). As a consequence, students expressed their wish for generative functions that would require less detailed rule definitions but would generate more complex and less predictable form.

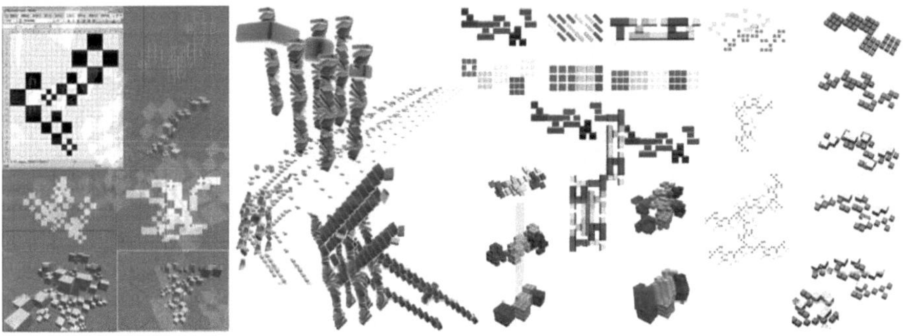

Figure 2. Exploratory design results generated with CA-based design support

In the following software implementation, named *Tofu Automata Generator*, rules were encapsulated into a set of predefined functions, which were geared towards quickly and more easily generating a variety of intricate geometric configurations. For this purpose, the available basic geometries were limited to box shapes only, which could be defined as "matter", "void", "neutral" or "context". Instead of complex neighborhood definitions, the software gives users the option of manipulating geometries by relating geometric transformations to the different object types mentioned above. The *Tofu Automata Generator* was tested in a design workshop with 17 graduate architecture students at National Cheng Kung University in Taiwan. Results from the workshop indicated shortcomings resulting from a focus on immediate form representation (see Fischer and Herr 2007). To achieve their design intentions, students often used the software in ways unintended by the developer, or re-interpreted forms or functions in the *Tofu Automata Generator* into new concepts and meanings. This kind of misappropriation, however, tended to fit individual design concepts better than the intended modes of software use, and produced a greater variety of design outcomes than expected. It thus indicated the necessity of encouraging individual interpretations in CA-based design support software. As a result of this implementation, flexibility in design support tools emerged as a main concern, as designers are likely to diverge significantly from the mode of use anticipated by software developers.

The third software implementation was used to support an individual graduate student of architecture at The University of Hong Kong. Her design project included a rule-based way to generate city models, which had much in common with CA systems. The software developed to support her design enabled the student to generate varieties of options by first setting up a set of neighborhood rules. These rules could then be modified by manipulating several parameters relating to the composition of land use functions in the given city model (see Figure 3).

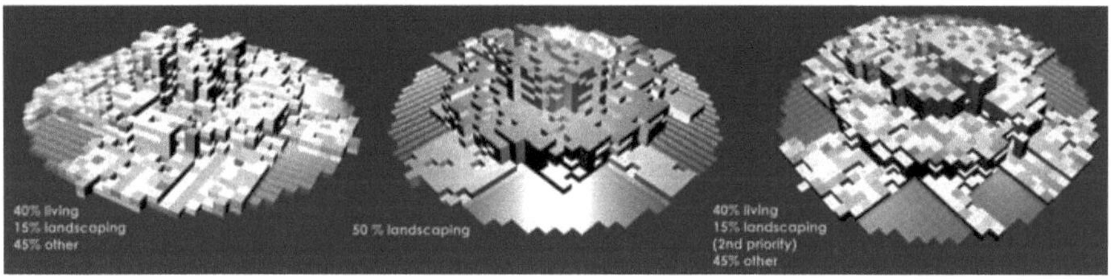

Figure 3. Peggy Louie: *KCRC station new town* proposals

As in the previous implementations, the use of CA-based design support was combined with manual modeling to allow for exceptions from rule-generated form if desired. Outcomes generated by the software could be read in different ways. While the student's intention was to generate diagrams of urban context to be further interpreted when translating them into form, the cube-based volumes of the graphical representation invited the misconception of the three-dimensional models as directly representing physical form. This however led to new insights: it demonstrated how form generated through CA could play a more abstract and conceptual role in the early design process. Aspects central to this implementation were diagrammatic representations that were intended to provoke further interpretation as well as a focus on element relationships rather than form. These features provided the core of *Algogram*, the following software implementation, and a new focus of the study.

3. Sketches, Diagrams and Automated Diagrams

In architectural design, the established design aid of choice for generating novelty is sketching (Fish 1996), which is used at all stages of the design process, from initial ideas to refinements of the final shape. Sketches work by enabling designers to externalize their thinking into graphic representations that provide visual cues for revision and refinement of design (Suwa and Tversky 1997). Schön (1983) describes the design process as "reflection in action", with the designer engaged in a conversation with the design problem. This conversation consists of recurring cycles of framing, moving and reflection, in which the designer "sees" and then "moves" design objects in a representation of the design problem in question.

To support this creative reasoning process, architects employ visual representations such as sketches and diagrams that generate multiple interpretations by enabling different modes of seeing (Wiggins and Schön 1992). Though sketches are frequently described as "talking back" to the designer (Schön 1983, Goldschmidt 2006), in traditional sketching it is indeed the designer himself who interprets what he sees, perceiving this perspective change as "backtalk" of an active conversation partner. In the proposed CA-supported design process, the role of the computer during the early design stages is to enrich this dialogue between designer and visual representations (see Glanville 1999, p. 88) by actively producing feedback that invites reinterpretation by the designer. In this study, CA are used to activate computer-based representations employed in conceptual design.

Drawings produced in the early design stages have been described as typically pertaining to two different types: sketches that aim to capture as well as generate design concepts and guiding principles, and sketches depicting physical form (Do and Gross 2001). Sketches that are used in the development of early design concepts frequently employ symbolic representations and focus more on relationships of basic design components than on building shape. This type of sketch is commonly termed conceptual diagram, recognized for its explanatory power as well as for its versatility in developing design ideas at a conceptual level (Phillips 2006). As drawings frequently exhibit characteristics of both types of design representation however, the distinction between diagrams and sketches remains blurry.

The emphasis on relationships of elements typically found in diagrams relates to a similar emphasis in CA systems. When introducing CA as design process support, this emphasis on relationships may be used to apply CA to provide rule-based diagrammatic representations to aid in the early, conceptual design stages. Such CA-based diagrams – or *automated diagrams* – are not limited to representing physical shape but potentially allow for multiple interpretations and mappings. Automated diagrams may be best suited for idea development during the early design process, when concept framing and re-framing are more important than thinking about detailed building form (see Goel 1995, p. 193 ff). Two aspects are central to the concept of automated diagrams: Abstract and somewhat ambiguous diagrammatic representations can suggest issues and perspectives for consideration without imposing solutions (Gaver et al. 2003, p. 240). The automated component of such diagrams may be used to give such diagrammatic representations the capability to actively respond to configurational changes initiated by the designer. In this approach, the computer is not utilized merely as a tool to execute predetermined and deterministic commands but as medium in the sense of Glanville (1992).

4. Algogram

Algogram provides design support for the conceptual design of architectural programmes. It has been developed as a design aid that explores the potential of linking generative design, diagrams and cognitive research, resulting in the concept of automated diagrams. Ambiguity of representations and open-ended interpretation by the designer are recognized as central to early, conceptual design (Dogan and Nersessian 2002). In this context, the role of the computer is primarily to provide automated representations that support thinking and reflection in terms of relationships. *Algogram* aims to give designers an opportunity to work with generative CA-based processes while avoiding determining outcomes in terms of form too early in the design process. *Algogram* provides a generic way of representing architectural functions and their relationships, which is related to both bubble diagrams – not so much in their functional, but in their generative capacity as described by Emmons (2006), and Venn diagrams. Architectural functions are represented as spheres instead of cubes or squares to avoid premature visualizing of diagrams as possible building forms. Spheres relate more to diagrammatic representations of functions already known to students, such as bubble or Venn diagrams, while box shapes could easily be interpreted as physical building form. Representations in *Algogram* were intended to be somewhat ambiguous, such that students would be encouraged to reinterpret the diagram while developing their design concepts. The diagrammatic representations can be manipulated either manually or by establishing automated relationships between elements by defining rules. Rules in *Algogram* are used to numerically control relative positions of spheres and their intersections in three dimensions. Within the framework of the diagram, meaning is established by adding user-defined text labels and colours to generic spheres. To translate representations into architectural form, users need to interpret the resulting diagrams, which remain at a relatively abstract level to encourage individual design solutions.

Algogram was developed for a studio project at The University of Hong Kong. The architectural approach taken in this studio project - and implemented in *Algogram* - seeks to evade the limits of prescriptive typologies developed from the modernist motto of "form follows function", exemplified by the examples given in AJ Metric or Neufert books. Following these examples likely results in buildings based on preconceptions, which hampers innovation and prevents re-interpretation of architectural programmes. Instead of solving design problems as quickly as possible, students were encouraged to re-think the initial problem statement, with the intention to lead students to re-frame the given problem.

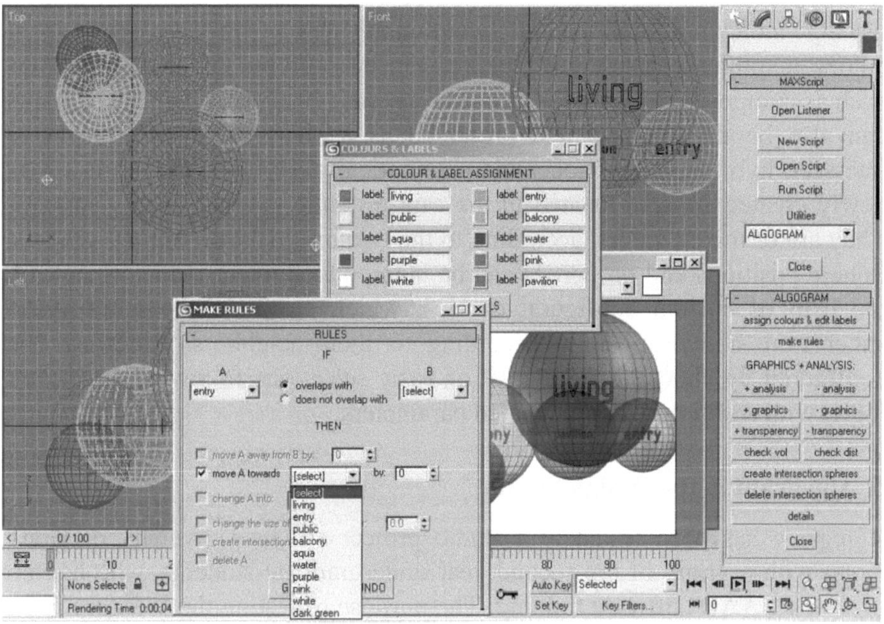

Figure 4. Algogram user interface

Algogram builds on the concept that architectural programmes are rarely stable and often need to be changed or reconfigured throughout the design process. The software supports experimentation with combinations of functions that may co-exist and develop in unusual ways to create different and often unpredictable results. To heighten students' awareness of the potential of interactions between functions, we introduced the term "hybrid". Hybrids in this context are opportunities for creating spaces that can be adapted for different uses and allow space to be reinterpreted for different functions. Such spaces are not typically found in traditional architectural programmes and can be generated by adjoining architectural functions that create unconventional synergy. In this way, a typical hybrid may for example be created by two overlapping spheres labeled "performance" and "water". In diagrams produced with *Algogram*, hybrids are a source of ambiguity intended to stimulate individual interpretation by the students, both during the conceptual design stages and also when translating into architectural form at a later stage in the design process.

Algogram is implemented as a utility in 3DStudio MAX (Figure 4), where it is accessible as an alternative to manual three-dimensional modeling. The three main components of the user interface are graphical representation functions, analysis functions and rules. To compose an "algogram", users start by drawing spheres, which are then assigned colors from a predefined selection. Colors can be labeled with customizable names, usually indicating architectural programme items. Once assigned with colors, diagrams consisting of spheres can be analyzed for their properties such as composition, sphere volumes or distance between spheres. Diagrams can also be decomposed and presented as a chart overview. If spheres intersect, hybrids can be generated automatically. Hybrids are expressed as newly created spheres located in the centre of the overlap of two spheres. They are of mixed colors, according to the two original overlapping spheres. Sphere positions and properties can be manipulated either manually or with the help of custom configurable rules, which enable users to transform spheres in size or position according to their neighbors. Rules can be configured by choosing from a set of basic selections following an if/then logic, with additional, more detailed parameters.

5. Algogram in the Design Studio

Algogram has been tested in a studio project at The University of Hong Kong with a group of ten second year undergraduate students, who had no previous CAAD software training. The purpose of testing the software in an applied design studio setting was to investigate two aspects of using *Algogram* in the early design stages: first, how students integrated the software into their individual design processes, and second, how this affected the outcomes. The project brief for the studio, which included several other student groups as well, called for the design of a school for a given site in Hong Kong, with particular consideration of urban and landscape context. The students were introduced to *Algogram* and *3DStudio MAX* during the early, conceptual design phase, which lasted for about two weeks. At this point, most students switched to traditional sketching and drawing tools for developing both programme and physical form of their buildings in greater detail. After the concept development phase, students were interviewed for their experiences during the design process as well as for their opinions on the usefulness of the software and suggestions for improvements. Students responded well to the software and readily developed their concepts using the abstract representation in *Algogram*, even without prior CAAD knowledge. As *Algogram* provides only abstract sphere geometries, students had to conceptualize their school in terms of programme, without considering form (see Figure 5).

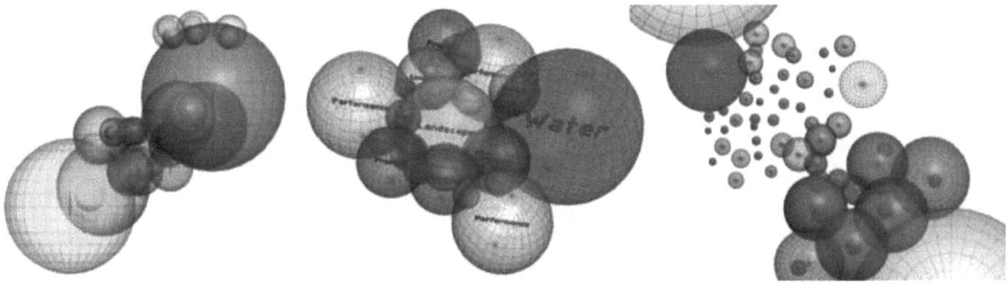

Figure 5. "Algograms" by Finnie Yu (left), Ho Wing Ho (middle), and Claire Fu (right)

The intention behind this strategy was to extend the conceptual design stage in order to allow a more thorough exploration of ideas and to prevent premature decisions. In terms of design process, this extended period of conceptual diagramming was aimed at encouraging the initial framing and re-framing of design problems instead of solving a problem as quickly as possible. In terms of architectural design approach, this strategy aimed to increase students' awareness of interactions between functions and their role in conceptualizing new and context-specific architectural typologies. The expected outcome in the studio test was for students to engage in an explorative design process, negotiating between definitions of element relationships through rules on the one hand and individual interpretation of ambiguous graphical representations on the other hand. Data on the studio test was collected in form of student results, field notes, samples from other second year students who did not use *Algogram*, interview feedback as well as student sketches produced during the studio.

6. Studio Observations and Discussion

The studio test of *Algogram* aimed at open-ended qualitative feedback on how the software integrated with the students' design processes and aims. Design outcomes of student projects in the group using *Algogram* were slightly different in nature than results from other student groups in the same studio project. This is likely an effect of the particular design approach encouraged, with an extended conceptual design phase and further enforced by the use of *Algogram*. Since student results tend to be shaped by the varying teaching styles and preferences of design tutors, however, this assessment of student work from groups working with or without *Algogram* is merely indicative. It is based on samples of student outcomes from three other groups as well as field notes from these groups' design critiques. Design proposals from other groups tended to separate functions rather than considering their potential interactions within a building. Students instead focused on developing unconventional exterior building form. Reviewers of other groups' work often criticized the lack of reflection of urban context, which students tended to consider only in terms of composition, with functional aspects frequently ignored. The focus on functions in the student group that used *Algogram* seems to have encouraged students to integrate their design concepts more closely with surrounding urban and landscape context, with many diagrams emphasizing sphere labels such as water, hill, planting, public or private. Most students in the group using *Algogram* had strong individual design concepts that came out of a reconsideration of conventional building programmes. Students subsequently used these programme-oriented concepts to generate unique and site specific building typologies.

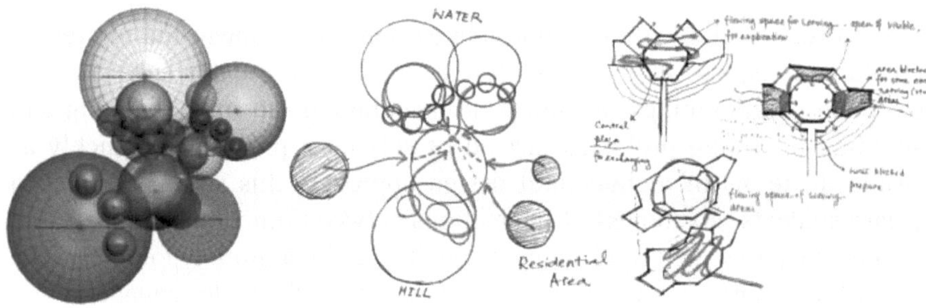

Figure 6. Translation of "Algograms" into building form by Finnie Yu

When switching to other design tools and media to develop building form, most students used the latest stages of their "algograms" to guide their form development processes (Figure 6). In many cases, buildings closely resemble the three-dimensional concept diagrams in terms of composition, not however in terms of building form. It appears that after the conceptual diagramming phase, concepts were regarded as sufficiently fixed, and students focused mainly on the translation of diagrams into form. In the interviews, all students described using the software as generally helpful for their design processes, while the reasons given varied. "Algograms" were seen as useful in finding and organizing relationships between functions within a building programme. They were also described as reminders of design potential, especially when considering and interpreting hybrids. The simplicity of the graphical representation was also perceived as helpful, since it allowed for conceptual clarity in the beginning of the design process. Most students appreciated the hybrids as source of inspiration, often describing it as the most important feature of *Algogram.*

It seems that students were happy with the ambiguity of hybrids when interpreting entire diagrams, but when hybrids were separated from their context, such as in the analysis chart overview, students perceived them as confusing. Sphere sizes in *Algogram* can be interpreted in several ways. Initially, students were introduced to sphere sizes as indicators of physical volumes allocated to a particular function. As their design progressed, however, students increasingly developed their own understandings. Many students switched to an interpretation that saw sphere sizes as a sign of importance and relative sphere distances as indicator of mutual relevance in a building programme. Students also reported frequent use of mixed representations, interpreting sphere sizes in some cases as representing physical size, in some cases as representing importance and in yet other cases in yet other ways - all within the same "algogram". In this sense, ambiguity in "algograms" encourages and supports individual construction of meaning and design thinking. Of the analysis functions, the chart overview was described as especially useful, as it allows a visual overview of the number and type of spheres contained within a diagram.

The rules function received mixed comments: While some students regarded rules as very important, especially in the early diagramming stages, most students considered the interface for rule configuration in *Algogram* too restrictive and exact. They suggested providing rules that could be used in more intuitive ways in the early design stages. This echoes a description by Schön (1988), who characterized rules in design as largely implicit, diverse, contextually dependent and subject to exceptions and modifications. The most frequently mentioned drawback to the use of rules, however, was that similar to rules in classic CA systems, rules in *Algogram* affected all spheres of the same type in the same way. After an initial diagramming stage, in which only one or very few spheres of a given type exist at the same time, "algograms" quickly become more differentiated as relationships between architectural functions are further developed. In a more differentiated diagram, however, uniform rules do not apply any more.

In the final design critique, the majority of students explained their design process as well as their concepts using "algograms" in their presentations, with additional conceptual diagrams used in translating diagrams into building form. Students often used vocabulary introduced through *Algogram* to explain their design concepts. Similarly, student sketch books often showed hand-drawn diagrams using circles and labels similar to those in the software. In some cases, students reverted back to this notation even later in the design process when revising their design schemes at a fundamental level. These results seem to indicate that working with *Algogram* provided students with a notation and vocabulary that they felt comfortable to use in conceptual design development. Students typically described "algograms" as helpful in the three-dimensional development of their schemes, and as more appropriate to concept development than bubble diagrams. The latter were thought of as appropriate for functional planning issues where architectural programme elements are considered in terms of numbers rather than spatial qualities.

According to the interviews, none of the students felt limited by the software in pursuing individual design ideas. Most positive comments on *Algogram* relate to its potential to provide students with representations of their design concepts while at the same time giving enough room for individual interpretations. In comparison to the utility of immediate visual representations, though, CA-based rules as implemented in *Algogram* seem to be marginalized, in particular past the initial diagramming stages. During the final design critique, it became apparent that the same properties of "algograms" that are perceived useful by students during their design processes can result in ambiguous and vague elements in presentations that other students, tutors or critics not familiar with the particular design project find difficult to follow. *Algogram* teaches students to recognize the value of ambiguity in design representations during the design process, but also requires students to consciously reduce ambiguity in presentation materials intended to communicate the design to others. In summary, the processes and outcomes of the design studio differed from initial expectations in several ways. The students' explorative design processes depended heavily on representations inviting individual interpretations and much less on the use of formalized rules. They instead preferred intuitive manipulation of geometry and avoided numeric parameter settings. Students embraced the open-ended aspects of the software, namely the ambiguity of hybrids as well as individual interpretation of sphere sizes and positions in abstract graphic representations. In comparison to the previous software implementations, students working with *Algogram* focused more on concept development than building form. The step of translating conceptual diagrams into form, however, appeared to be of considerable difficulty to the students.

7. Conclusion

From an initial focus on supporting design with CA-based form generators, software implementations in this study have developed to embrace diagrammatic representations. This emphasis on CA-based design support as providing automated diagrams for conceptual design resulted in the latest implementation, *Algogram*. Abstract diagrammatic representations were found to be helpful in the early design stages, as they encourage students to develop multiple individual interpretations and allow for an extended process of framing and re-framing design problems. This leads to a prolonged conceptual development stage and prevents a premature transition to the level of physical building shape. Comments in student interviews indicate that students embraced the ambiguity inherent in the abstract spheres in *Algogram* diagrams to develop a variety of individual interpretations. While aiding students' design processes in this way, the ambiguity in even relatively simple configurations of spheres rendered outcome presentations to outsiders surprisingly challenging.

The generative potential of the proposed automated diagram model was found to be more a consequence of the abstract and partly ambiguous representations employed than it was a consequence of using CA-based rules. Uniform rule sets were perceived as helpful in the early setup of conceptual diagrams, but students criticized uniform rules as inadequate for more differentiated diagrams produced later in the design process. Students commented that rules should be implemented to be used in a more intuitive way, in particular without manual setting of parameters in numeric form, as this interrupts the design process. This leads to a question for further research: How can rules be integrated in a somewhat less precise and more intuitively controllable way, such that relationships between elements can be manipulated without requiring detailed definitions or numerical input? An open question also remains on how initially uniform rule sets can become more local and specific to allow for processes of differentiation in automated diagrams. Overall, *Algogram* supported students not only in developing individual design solutions, but also in exploring architectural typologies beyond their initial preconceptions.

Acknowledgements

We would like to acknowledge the support and feedback by our colleagues and students at The University at Hong Kong, in particular Peggy Louie, Yunyan Jia and Janice Affleck, and at the Department of Architecture at the National Cheng Kung University. We are particularly grateful to the following students who have used Algogram in their studio work during the fall 2006 semester: Wu Tsz Ching, Zhang Jia Heng, Kwong Yan Kit, Ho Wing Ho, Yu Yuk Fan, Fu Hui Yan, Lee Man Yeng, Luk Lai Fun, Lo Yee Cheung and Kwan Chun Sing. We also thank Prof. Thomas Kvan for his feedback and guidance over the course of this study. This research is supported by a PhD scholarship granted by The University of Hong Kong.

References

Chase, S: 2005, Generative design tools for novice designers: Issues for selection, *Automation in Construction* **14** (6): 689-698.

Coates, P, Healy, N, Lamb, C and Voon, WL: 1996, The Use of Cellular Automata to Explore Bottom-Up Architectonic Rules, paper presented at *Eurographics UK Chapter 14th Annual Conference held at Imperial College London/UK.*

Do, EY-L and Gross, MD: 2001, Thinking with Diagrams in Architectural Design, *Artificial Intelligence Review* **15**(1-2): 135-149.

Dogan, F and Nersessian, N: 2002, Conceptual diagrams: representing ideas in design, *in* M. Hegarty, B. Meyer and N.H. Narayanan (eds), *Diagrammatic representation and inference*, Springer, Berlin, pp. 353-355.

Emmons, P: 2006, Embodying networks: bubble diagrams and the image of modern organicism, *The Journal of Architecture* **11**(4): 441-461.

Fischer, T and Herr, CM: 2007, The architect as toolbreaker? Probing tool use in the practice of generative design, *CAADRIA 2007*, forthcoming.

Fish, JC: 1996, *How Sketches Work - A Cognitive Theory for Improved System Design*, PhD thesis, Loughborough University of Technology.

Gaver, WW., Beaver, J and Benford, S: 2003, Ambiguity as a resource for design, *Proceedings of the Conference on Human Factors in Computing Systems*, 5-10 April 2003, Fort Lauderdale, FL. ACM Press, New York, pp. 233-240.

Glanville, R: 1992, CAD Abusing Computing, in Proceedings eCAADe 1992, Polytechnic University of Catalonia, Barcelona, pp. 213-224.

Glanville, R: 1999, Researching Design and Designing Research, *Design Issues* **15**(2): 80-91.

Goel, V: 1995, *Sketches of Thought*, MIT Press, Cambridge, MA.

Goldschmidt, G: 2006, The Backtalk of Self-Generated Sketches, *Design Issues* **19**(1): 72-88.

Herr, CM: 2003, Using Cellular Automata to Challenge Cookie-Cutter Architecture, *in* C Soddu (ed), *The 6th International Conference on Generative Art 2003*, Generative Design Lab, DiAP, Politectnico di Milano University, Milano, Italy, pp. 72-81.

Herr, CM and Kvan, T: 2005, Using Cellular Automata to Generate High-Density Building Form, *Proceedings of the 11th International Conference on Computer Aided Architectural Design Futures, Vienna*, pp. 249-258.

Herr, CM and Kvan, T: 2007, Adapting cellular automata to support the architectural design process, *Automation in Construction* **16**(1): 61-69.

Krawcyk, R: 2002, Architectural Interpretation of Cellular Automata, in C Soddu (ed), *The 5th International Conference on Generative Art 2002*, Generative Design Lab, DiAP, Politectnico di Milano University, Milano, Italy, pp. 7.1-7.8.

Phillips, A: 2006, Lines of Inquiry: diagrams as catalysts in creating memorable architecture, *Architectural Review* **219**(1307): 68-73.

Schön, DA: 1983, *The reflective practitioner: how professionals think in action*, Basic Books, New York.

Schön, DA: 1988, Designing: Rules, types and worlds, *Design Studies* **9**(3): 133-43.

Schrandt, R and Ulam, S: 1970, On Recursively Defined Geometrical Objects and Patterns of Growth, *in* A Burks (ed), *Essays on Cellular Automata*, University of Illinois Press, Urbana, pp. 232-243.

Suwa, M and Tversky, B: 1997, What do architects and students perceive in their sketches? A protocol analysis. *Design Studies* **18** (4): 385-403.

Watanabe, MS: 2002, *Induction design: a method for evolutionary design*, Birkhäuser, Basel.

Wiggins, G and Schön, DA: 1992, Kinds of seeing and their function in designing, *Design Studies* **13**(2): 135-156.

BECOMING KINÆSTHETIC

USE OF A MOBILE ARCHITECTURAL GUIDE

ALEXANDER KOUTAMANIS
Delft University of Technology, The Netherlands

Abstract. A mobile architectural guide assists architectural tourists in selecting, navigating to and recognizing architectural sights. The guide supports such tasks by means of domain knowledge, design documentation and contextual information organized into navigation modules, architectural information systems and learning modules.

1. Visiting Architecture

Modern information and communication technologies support access to all kinds of information from virtually any place in several continents. Access to online information is no longer restricted to conventional computing devices: mobile telephones and other lightweight wireless devices are becoming increasingly popular for information processing on the road or in the field. Despite the obvious limitations of screen size, processing and storage capacity, such devices are generally capable of supporting interaction with the majority of documents used in professional settings. The current focus in mobile information processing seems firmly fixed on 'social' applications but there is a discernible increase in more conventional professional applications (Kaga et al. 2006; Matsumoto et al. 2001; Tedrumpun and Nakapan 2004; Wang and Shih 2002) –even if it may have come rather late, as we can judge from the recent stagnation in the development of palmtop hardware and software. Somewhere in between social and professional applications we encounter informative and educational applications which make use of professional information for non-professional purposes and use technologies marketed for personal entertainment and communication.

Digital architectural guides are an example of such applications. Even though copyright issues form obstacles of increasing magnitude and complexity, there has been substantial even though unsystematic digitization of information on architecturally important buildings. Online resources concentrate mostly on visual documentation (scanned drawings,

A Dong, A Vande Moere & JS Gero (eds), CAADFutures'07, 183–195.

photographs, three-dimensional models), while only a few have been designed as architectural guides, with a complete presentation of a building and its context in mind (including maps and instructions on how to get there, e.g. www.galinsky.com). Nevertheless, with the plethora of navigation services and maps on the Internet the addition of visiting information to databases of buildings has become quite straightforward (e.g. www.greatbuildings.com).

An architectural guide must fulfill a number of requirements. It should provide concise but unambiguous information that facilitates identification and a fundamental understanding of a building. It should be legible, lightweight and comprehensive. It should support searches and browsing from various points of view and entry points, e.g. location, style, architect, type etc. All these functions and constraints relate to the activities of visiting one or more buildings either casually (as part of various tourist attractions) or specifically (as architectural tourist). Paper guides remain a favorite among architectural tourists but are often criticized for the quality of their visual documentation (small size, vagueness, incompleteness or lack of photographs and drawings), for their coverage (i.e. being overly selective, arbitrary or not up-to-date) and the precision and accuracy of contextual information (especially the part that supports finding a building). Most complaints derive from the analogue nature of publications on paper and the low periodicity of architectural guides (Koutamanis 1998). It is therefore surprising that there has been so little attention for digital guides, especially on mobile devices which can be carried around just like their paper counterparts.

In recent years there has been some interest in architectural guides on mobile devices but mostly from mobile telephony providers or related service providers (cultural or tourist). It is already possible to make architectural walks with one's own mobile phone providing textual or aural instructions and commentary in several cities (www.talktomenl.nl, www.walkthetalk.hk). In CAAD research there is only one known relevant research project, thankfully with extensive ambitions and many facets (Berridge and Brown 2002; Berridge et al. 2002; Brown et al. 2006). The wide general interest in technologically related subjects like ubiquitous computing and smart buildings has returned interesting ideas on e.g. interaction with information and navigation, especially in confined environments like museums and historical areas (Bruns et al. 2005; Jeng 2005; Nomura and Kishimoto 2005, Shen and Teng 2005), but no architectural guides as primary products. Interest in guided navigation with information feedback has been higher in other fields, with emphasis mostly on general computational and cognitive issues (Abowd et al. 1997; Cheverst et al. 2000; Persson et al. 2002).

In addition to their educational value, digital architectural guides present new research opportunities: by making already available digital information accessible for mobile use we not only extend the utility of digital documentation and explore the potential of mobile information processing (Berridge et al. 2003) but also investigate the wider usability and applicability of existing representations and information systems towards more effective and efficient fundamental solutions to information and modeling problems (Knight et al. 2006). The two questions of how to make existing information available for mobile processing and what information is necessary for mobile architectural applications are central to our research into the development of a mobile architectural guide.

2. A Mobile Architectural Guide (MAG)

MAG is a modular system that has been implemented on a number of mobile platforms (palmtop computers and smartphones with various operating systems). In general lines MAG consists of:

1. Architectural information systems containing multimedia descriptions of the sights: texts, drawings, photographs, video etc. that present a building, its context and background to an architectuaral public.
2. Navigation modules that permit location identification, support orientation and assist organizing a trip to a number of sights.
3. Learning modules that register, remember and re-use user preferences and search patterns.

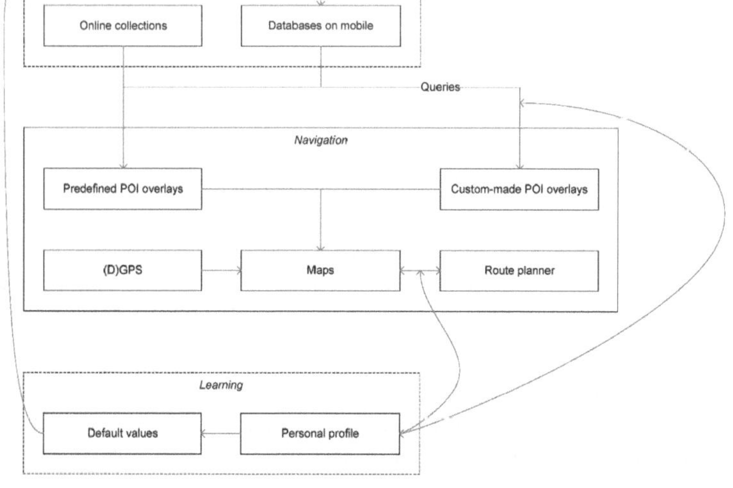

Figure 1. MAG outline

The main intention concerning MAG use is to assist architectural tourists in identifying and navigating to architectural sights. Such information could be also made available to other tourists with a casual cultural interest in architecture but the demands of the architectural visitor are significantly higher and result into more challenging specifications and problems.

The architectural information systems of MAG can be purpose-made databases on a mobile device as well as external online collections, which are connected to the MAG either directly (e.g. as a hyperlink to a web page) or through a linking database on the mobile device. The connection mode depends on the structure of the external collection, i.e. support for direct retrieval of relevant items (e.g. by having a standardized content subdivision into separate web pages). Problems relating to the size of items to be retrieved have been left outside the scope of the first implementations of MAG.

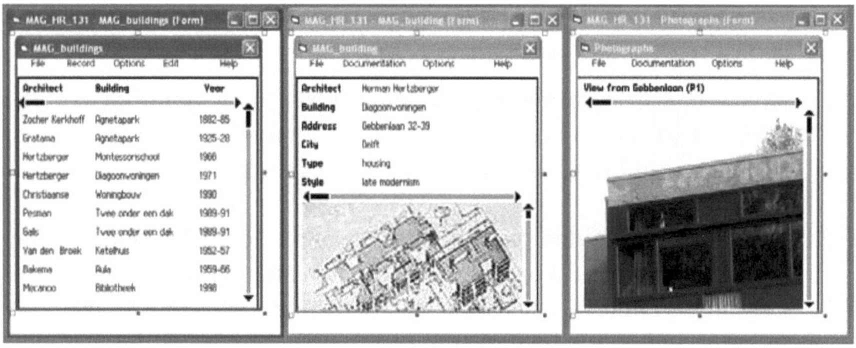

Figure 2. Mobile architectural database in MAG

The navigation modules are built on top of existing navigation systems that provide the general functionality a tourist requires. With respect to navigation there are three main options: (*i*) smart tagging of architectural sights, (*ii*) use of mobile phone network cells, or (*iii*) use of mobile navigation systems based on satellite global positioning (GPS) or combined satellite-terrestrial differential global positioning (DGPS). We have chosen for the third option because it needs no dedicated infrastructure, offers greater accuracy, precision and sensitivity, and links seamlessly architectural interests with general tourist support (Koutamanis. 2006). This also means that users can add a MAG to their own navigation system and reduce learning time and cost. The main disadvantage of dependence on external commercial R&D is alleviated by linking navigation systems with MAG by means of universal overlays of points of interest (POI). Such overlays can be used with practically any navigation system and form a logical extension of the architectural databases in MAG (i.e. a summary of pragmatic information: textual and geographic data for identifying a building and its location).

The learning modules facilitate interaction with the MAG by recording and re-using user input and interaction with different modules. Consequently, the learning part of MAG forms an interconnected network of modules distributed in overlay facilities (e.g. where users enter their own POI), the navigation system (e.g. registration of transport mode preferences and success rate in actually visiting the scheduled sights), and especially in architectural information systems, where users can not only add new sights but also define selection criteria that reflect their individual interests in particular architectural styles, periods, architects, building types etc. Our interest in learning lies mainly in its important for the efficiency and effectiveness of user interaction with MAG – two primary concerns in mobile information processing. Being able to anticipate user actions reduces response time and redundancy in the options offered at any given moment without diminishing the flexibility and comprehensiveness of the overall system.

Figure 3. MAG architectural sights overlay in a navigation system map (detail)

3. Navigation: Routing

The focus of the present paper is primarily on the navigation modules and secondarily on the architectural information systems in their capacity of information sources that support orientation and recognition. This combination supports both local and global navigation capabilities, i.e. respectively enables effective and reliable interaction with the built environment (including understanding of one's own motion, recognition and avoidance of obstacles, and achieving a stable mental image of the environment) and facilitates the development of mnemonic structures with reference to the environment (Fermüller and Aloimonos 1995). In the case of the MAG we are interested in the first (local navigation capabilities) as a practical necessity and in the second (global capabilities) as the ultimate goal of an architectural navigation and information aid.

In a typical MAG implementation navigation relies on a commercial satellite navigation system in a palmtop computer or smartphone. Buildings in the architectural information system are imported to the navigation system as POI overlays. Each POI serves not only as identification of the building and its location but also as a dynamic link to the architectural information system, so that users can move seamlessly between the navigation and the information systems. The number of architectural overlays depends on a small number of criteria, primarily the number of architectural sights in a guide and the diversity of building styles and types in the information system. Users of databases on the mobile device can define their own POI overlay distribution on the basis of queries and reports in the database which can generate new overlay files. Such actions have an impact on the system's learning, as the queries and overlays are included in the particular user's profile.

Navigation operates in two different modes. The first is based on the identification of intervening opportunities and forms a straightforward application of capabilities existing in many commercial systems: the navigation system alerts the user to the existence of an architectural sight in the area on the basis of dynamic proximity (i.e. taking into account the direction and speed of movement). Users have then the option of adapting their current route so as to visit the building. The second mode is planned visits and tours. In this mode users start either in the navigation or the architectural information system with a selection of buildings and organize a route that allows them to visit every building in the selection. The route can be the shortest one, thematic, chronological or any other order supported by the architectural information system and can utilize any transportation means supported by the navigation system.

Combining such criteria for ordering architectural sights in a reasonable route is a complex process which may be poorly supported by route planners in commercial navigation systems. To compensate for eventual limitations and integrate the required domain knowledge we have added a sorting module that organizes the results of a query on the basis of multi-criteria techniques. The purpose of this module is to allow the user to consider his priorities and minimize unnecessary complexity in the route. The latter is performed by means of a preliminary evaluation of the routes proposed by the navigation system on the basis of a topological analysis we have previously applied to pedestrian circulation in buildings (Koutamanis et al. 2001). This evaluation reduces self-intersections in route and draws the user's attention to lengthy links between nodes in the route.

One of the reasons why such preprocessing and evaluation is necessary is the difference between proximity and accessibility: architectural sights may be next to each other and yet separated by major obstacles such as a railway line or a waterway that do not afford crossing in the immediate vicinity. The MAG is particularly sensitive to such problems that might spoil architectural touring with irrelevant time-consuming and cumbersome activities. Preprocessing of routes to architectural sights is more extensive when the complexity of their physical context makes navigation and identification of the route too cumbersome. In such cases the building has an own local navigation overlay that presents a number of options and connections, e.g. pedestrian footpaths leading to the building from the nearest public transportation stops or a parking lot (Figure 5).

Figure 4. MAG routes: corrected route linking three sights by car

Figure 5. MAG routes: local navigation options focused on a single sight

Connecting local navigation options to the mental maps made by tourists and (in the terminology of Lynch) place legibility is questionable. It could be argued that these options and interaction with routes proposed by a navigation system in general antagonizes the paths tourists perceive. It is not uncommon that users of navigation systems have difficulty mapping the visual representations of a route on a map to the scenes they perceive. The pseudo-three-dimensional projections currently in vogue do little to reduce this difficulty. It could be further argued that navigation aids should focus more on landmarks, edges, nodes and other places where visual and other cues combine to assist place legibility and the formation of reference frameworks. Such important questions are left out of the scope of the first implementations of MAG, which is restricted to more practical navigation issues. Local navigation support is therefore adapted to the strengths and possibilities of the host navigation systems. One notable exception that may provide a glimpse of a more coherent and effective investigation of place legibility is orientation support. The reasons for providing such support remain nevertheless practical.

4. Navigation: Orientation

Even when routing problems are satisfactorily solved, the architectural tourist may still experience difficulty reaching a building as a result of orientation problems. In an unknown environment one often has difficulty identifying the right direction, especially under inconvenient conditions (e.g. cloudy skies, insufficient or confusing road signboards, obscure paths). Orientation problems are compounded by the inability of (D)GPS-based navigation systems to identify directions or even the current location when the user is stationary or moving slowly. The resulting uncertainty may lead to frustration and distrust of the navigation system and the MAG.

Our approach is to provide information that supports effective, efficient and reliable orientation. Such information consists of local overlays that focus on the accessibility of a building (Figure 5) and visual descriptions of the context at critical points (nodes) in a route (crossroads, public transportation stops, parking lots), such as photographs of easily recognizable landmarks taken from these points and panoramic views. These photographs are annotated with indications of the cardinal directions and the road leading to the target of the route or other significant points (Figure 6).

Figure 6. Orientation panorama with navigation instructions

An alternative to static panoramas are short panoramic videos (pan shots), which can also indicate movement towards the next target (traveling or zoom shots of a building, landmark, crossing etc.). Such videos can be surprisingly small in storage size, efficient in use and quite legible on the small screens of mobile devices, frequently performing better than static panoramas in terms of recognition.

5. The MAG in Use

Experimental use of the first versions of the MAG focused on a few small geographic areas containing 12-36 architectural sights. The developers of the system were familiar with some of these areas and first-time visitors to others. This combination allowed for evaluation on the basis of established experiential expectations as well as general functional specifications. The navigation and information support provided by the MAG was appreciated by users in all cases, as it supported a higher precision in recognizing a building and its environment than analogue guide books. Such support was particularly useful in cases where precise identification of an architectural sight was made rather tentative by later buildings in the immediate area that imitated the morphology of the eponymous ones. The MAG assisted in the resolution of such problems by providing not only precise navigation aids but also more extensive information than guide books.

The routing aids included in the MAG were useful in two respects. The first was the ability to make selections of buildings either in the navigation or the architectural information system. The existence of multiple entry points allowed users to interact flexibly with the MAG, even extensively adapting routes on the way. The domain knowledge in the architectural information systems was intensively used, as it supported transparent selection on the basis of different criteria. The second was avoidance of topographical features that spatially separated a selection of buildings into two or more subgroups. Elevated railway lines and rivers were probably the hardest obstacles because the existence of respectively passageways on ground level and bridges meant that unsupported route planners could suggest routes that seemed logical because they did not contain long links. On the other hand, users have commented that by attempting to make routes more efficient one may sacrifice the coherence or consistency of a thematic architectural tour. Such choices are quite transparent in the queries but user interaction with a mobile device appears to afford too little time for reflection and elaboration. Most users tended to avoid cyclical routing processes.

One of the critical observations made during early use of the MAG is that architectural images may be removed from normal everyday perception of the built environment: they often relate strongly to canonical representations and views which explain aspects of design rather than present the appearance of a building from trivial viewpoints that may nevertheless assist recognition. The inclusion of photographs and video in the documentation may resolve most related problems of the architectural tourist but at a cost: increase in the redundancy of information in the MAG requires more storage space and relatively high processing capacity (especially for efficient transitions between modules and programs). Arguably more significant is that, as architectural tourists also want to understand and analyze the buildings they visit, users are directly confronted with this redundancy. Multimedia techniques can make relationships between information items transparent but cannot resolve problems of inconsistency, incompleteness and overload.

The ability to add as much information as possible (available) to a digital information system does not mean that the system becomes more informative. While we firmly believe than practically all users can use their cognitive faculties to discriminate between relevant and irrelevant, crucial and trivial information on the basis of variable personal criteria, we do not want to succumb to the temptation of developing an all-encompassing documentation system for architectural monuments. We do not have the illusion that a user can learn a building from a guide book (even if digital) and a visit. Consequently we restrict the applicability of the MAG to support for finding and recognizing the building, and to explaining salient aspects and interesting features like construction details and development stages that might become apparent during a visit. This also means that we had to resist suggestions to include more information on the context of buildings (e.g. extensive historical reviews of city parts).

A second critical user observation is that current navigation systems contain incomplete cartographic data for cyclists and pedestrians. As a result of the mapping systems used for the collection of such data, cycle and pedestrian routes may be adequately documented only if they are close to motorways. This has consequences for the clarity and efficiency of the last parts of a route (near a building). The MAG compensates for such limitations by means of additional local information (Figure 5). These improve the effectiveness and reliability of the system without significant loss of efficiency, even on less powerful mobile devices (especially if added to the navigation systems as overlays).

6. Discussion

From a technical viewpoint the MAG is essentially similar to multimedia systems we have been developing for different purposes and platforms since the mid-1990s. Current mobile devices present few technical problems to the development of such systems, even with demanding types of information like three-dimensional models and video. The usual complaint of small screen sizes presented few obstacles to the design and development of the various MAG versions because the spatial resolution of current devices is generally sufficient for the visual information we need in a digital guide for architectural tourists.

The extensive use of existing digital building documentation in the MAG caused few technical problems but also made evident essential differences between design information and the perception of real buildings. These differences range from the variable abstraction used in architectural projections (which makes many drawing scales inappropriate as conveyors of spatial information) to that most viewpoints used in architectural projections are far removed from those where a visitor can actually stand. Such differences point to the fundamental dichotomy of technical and presentation aspects in architectural representation.

In subsequent versions of the MAG we intend to address such issues by focusing more on three-dimensional models that integrate different projections and perspective transformations of two-dimensional images so as to match visitors' viewpoints. Such representations also have a more direct relationship with advanced Euclidean and projective representations proposed in visual navigation studies (Riseman et al. 1997; Robert et al. 1997), as well as with mental spatiotemporal representations of visual memories (Aloimonos et al. 1995; Nelson 1997). Another area of improvement concerns the application of automated visual recognition to the recognition of objects. Recent advances suggest that mobile devices could accommodate feature-based systems that can distinguish between members of one or more classes (Föckler et al. 2005). Resolution issues may impede recognition of a building as a whole but identification of particular or typical elements and salient features such as classical columns of a specific order seems to be feasible also for MAG. Recognition of such features presents new opportunities for learning (machine and human) as well as new possibilities for search entries.

Another extension that was actually suggested by an anonymous reviewer of this conference is the use of MAG to study mental maps and place legibility. The purpose of this is twofold: on the one hand the improvement of local navigation and orientation without resorting to predetermined paths and on the other the refinement of our understanding of architecture in context. The first seems feasible despite the limitations of mobile devices and host navigation systems but the latter may require significant technological additions for registering and analyzing human behavior. In the resulting system MAG will probably play a secondary role.

The main operational problem of MAG remains maintenance, in particular of the contextual information that contributes to identification, orientation and recognition. Given the growing popular interest in navigation systems, we expect that we can rely on their developers for up-to-date cartographic data and improvements in route planning. However, we also expect that our own additions will remain at least partially useful and that they will require similar periodic verification and improvement.

References

Abowd, GD, Atkeson, CG, Hong, J, Long, S, Kooper, R and Pinkerton, M: 1997, Cyberguide: A mobile context-aware tour guide, *Wireless Networks* **3**(5): 421-433.

Aloimonos, Y, Fermüller, C and Rosenfeld, A: 1995, Seeing and understanding: representing the visual world, *ACM Computing Surveys* **27**(3): 307-309.

Berridge, P and Brown, A: 2002, A touring machine, *Connecting the Real and the Virtual - design e-ducation. 20th eCAADe Conference Proceedings,* eCAADe, Warsaw, pp. 488-493.

Berridge, P, Brown, A and Knight, M: 2002, One city to go, in AME Rafi, CW Khong, M Neo, KT Neo and SNAS Ahmad (eds) *CAADRIA 2002. Proceedings of the 7th Conference on CAAD Research in Asia,* CAADRIA, Cyberjaya, pp. 57-64.

Berridge, P, Koch, V and Brown, AGP: 2003, Information spaces for mobile city access, *International Journal of Architectural Computing* **1**(1): 34-45.

Brown, A, Knight, M, Chen, Y-H and Saeed, G: 2006, City information delivered to mobile digital devices - reflection on contemporary potentail and problems, *in* V Bourdakis and D Charitos (eds) *Communicating space(s),* eCAADe, Volos, pp. 146-150.

Bruns, E, Brombach, B, Zeidler, T and Bimber, O: 2005, *Enabling mobile phones to support large-scale museum guidance*, Bauhaus University Weimar.

Cheverst, K, Davies, N, Mitchell, K, Friday, A and Efstratiu, C: 2000, Developing a context-aware electronic tourist guide: some issues and experiences, *Proceedings of the CHI'00. ACM international conference on human factors in computing systems,* ACM Press, New York, pp. 17-24.

Fermüller, C and Aloimonos, Y: 1995, Vision and action, *Image and Vision Computing,* **13**(10): 725-744.

Föckler, P, Zeidler, T, Brombach, B, Bruns, E and Bimber, O: 2005, PhoneGuide: museum guidance supported by on-device object recognition on mobile phones, *International Conference on Mobile and Ubiquitous computing (MUM'05).* ACM Press, New York, pp. 3-10.

Jeng, T: 2005, Advanced ubiquitous media for interactive space, in B Martens and A Brown (eds) *CAAD Futures 2005,* Kluwer, Dordrecht, pp. 341-350.

Kaga, A, Miyagawa, A, Kawaguchi, M, Yeo, W and Fukuda, T: 2006, Landscape evaluation system using a 3D space model and a cellular phone with GPS camera, *in* A Kaga and R Naka (eds) *CAADRIA 06. Proceedings of the 11th Conference on CAAD Research in Asia,*CAADRIA, Kumamoto, pp. 503-512.

Knight, MW, Brown, AGP and Smith, JS: 2006, Digital terrain meshes from GPS in urban areas: A practical aid to city modelling, *in* A Kaga and R Naka (eds) *CAADRIA 06,* Kumamoto, pp. 443-451.

Koutamanis, A: 1998, Information systems and the Internet: towards a news counter-revolution?, *4th Design and Decision Support Systems in Architecture and Urban Planning Conference,* Eindhoven.

Koutamanis, A: 2006, Contextual awareness in mobile information processing, *in* V Bourdakis and D Charitos (eds) *Communicating space(s),* eCAADe, Volos, pp. 152-159.

Koutamanis, A, van Leusen, M and Mitossi, V: 2001, Route analysis in complex buildings, *in* B de Vries, J van Leeuwen and H Achten (eds) *CAADFutures 2001,* Kluwer, Dordrecht, pp. 423-430.

Matsumoto, Y, Onishi, Y, Yamaguchi, S and Morozumi, M: 2001, Using mobile phones for accelerating interaction, *in* H Penttilä (ed) *Architectural information management,* eCAADe & Helsinki University of Technology, Espoo, pp. 311-316.

Nelson, RC: 1997, From visual homing to object recognition, *in* Y Aloimonos (ed) *Visual navigation,* Lawrence Erlbaum Associates, Mahwah, New Jersey, pp. 218-250.

Nomura, Y and Kishimoto, T: 2005, Visualization of tourists' behavior and activity using GPS and GIS in Kamakura City, *in* A Bhatt (ed) *CAADRIA 2005*, Seoul, pp. 320-327.

Persson, P, Espinoza, F, Fagerberg, P, Sandin, A and Cöster, R: 2002, GeoNotes: A location-based information system for public spaces, *in* K Höök, D Benyon and A Munro (eds) *Designing information spaces: The social navigation approach,* Springer, London.

Riseman, EM, Hanson, AR, Beveridge, JR, Kumar, R and Sawhney, H: 1997, Landmark-based navigation and the acquisition of environmental models, *in* Y Aloimonos (ed) *Visual navigation,* Lawrence Erlbaum Associates, Mahwah, New Jersey, pp. 317-374.

Robert, L, Zeller, C, Faugeras, O and Hébert, M: 1997, Applications of nonmetric vision to some visually guided robotic tasks, *in* Y Aloimonos (ed) *Visual navigation,* Lawrence Erlbaum Associates, Mahwah, New Jersey, pp. 89-134.

Shen, Y-T and Teng, T-S: 2005, Personal mobile device for situated interaction, *in* A Bhatt (ed) *CAADRIA 2005*, Seoul, pp. 382-387.

Tedrumpun, T and Nakapan, W: 2004, Site measurement with combination of pocket PC and global positioning system for preliminary architectural design process, *in* J-W Choi and HS Lee (eds) *CAADRIA 2004*, Seoul, pp. 717-726.

Wang, P-H and Shih, N-J: 2002, A preliminary application of a PDA-based OODB system for construction information management, *in* K Kosszewski and S Wrona (eds) *Connecting the real and the virtual - design e-ducation,* eCAADe, Warsaw, pp. 306-309.

UNREAL STUDIO

Game engine software in the architectural design studio

SEAN PICKERSGILL
University of South Australia, Australia

Abstract. This paper investigates the relationships between conventional modes of architectural design, those represented through and mediated by Cartesian schema, and the radical organization of spatial experience available through the use of NURBS modelling. This is examined particularly through a study of how game engine software and the appropriate editors are able to accommodate the properties of both. Within this software the first-person view attempts to provide a normalised experience of the VR environment (usually a game), yet there is significant scope for experiencing radically 'other' spatial and topological presences. Whilst considerable work has been done in the use of participatory digital spaces, there is the opportunity for examining the manner in which a highly stylised medium such as Unreal Tournament can productively assist the architectural design process.

1. Introduction

By using a number of experimental maps created in the Unreal Tournament 2004 Editor, modified to remove the aggressive elements in the HUD (Heads Up Display), this paper will present an analysis of the emergent ontological qualities of working and thinking in a game-space, Figure 1, as distinct from those spaces currently typified as the technical domain of avant-garde architectural practice – complex geometry and NURBS modelling. The ability to create and script an environment that is present and interactive fundamentally transforms the manner in which architectural design may be approached. Beyond the fascination with complex geometries for their own sake, the manner in which the use of game-engine software is a performative medium gives it a temporality and indeterminacy absent from more controlled representations. Further, functional gaps in the available

A Dong, A Vande Moere & JS Gero (eds), CAADFutures'07, 197–210.

technology – BSB holes (problems with reading form caused by ambiguous rendering priorities), video card properties – may be exploited to get a glimpse of aesthetic qualia that digital theory is still attempting to articulate, the experimental nature of this work permits an immersive optical activity and, through scripting, encourages new kinds of haptic practices (Wardrip-Fruin and Mountfort 2003). This paper will summarise the analysis of studio work by referring to interests in flow, surface and indeterminacy – interests that are typical of architectural work influenced by readings of philosophers of presence (Massumi, de Landa) who have attempted to clarify how the experience of the digital is a unique event.

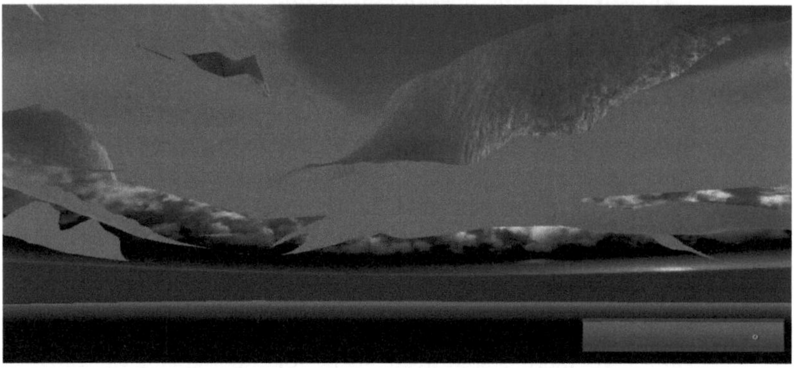

Figure 1. Unterwasser, unreal game space

Until recently there have been clear extant, though under-discussed, conventions in the understanding of the role of representation in architecture. Up to the onset of digital practices, these conventions preserved a dilemma regarding the manner in which architecture represented itself. Given that, essentially, the media of representation had not changed since the Renaissance, the issue turned often on the similarities of the explorations of graphic architectural practice to similar ideas in the visual and graphic arts. The strength of this debate was the recognition and celebration of the fact that the graphic practice of architectural representation had developed autonomous critical discourses that looked past the media of its presentation in order to concentrate on the referent of the work. This is not always the case. Daniel Libeskind's Gnostic/Kabbalistic constructions: *Three Lessons in Architecture*, or alternatively the datascapes of MvRdV present clear critiques of conventional architectural representation. In many respects the strength of this critical practice on the nature of architectural language – the vicissitudes of the referent – reaches a self-reflexive apogee in the work of Peter Eisenman in the seventies. Alberto Pérez-Gómez's *Architectural Representation and the Perspective Hinge* is a liminal study in this respect – giving a damning assessment of the properties of the digital before the medium had established a body of critical practice worthy of discussion (Pérez-Gómez and Pelletier 1997). Key to Pérez-Gómez's book was the ineluctable relationship between the medium of representation (drawing in its many forms) and the architectural work's role as a general indicator of trends towards, for example, precision, instrumentality and categorisation. Indeed in a previous book, *Architecture and the Crisis of Modern Science*, Pérez-Gómez explicitly identifies the relationship between drawing practices in the work of Soufflot, Guarini, Durand and others and the development of categorisation and functionalism in architecture.

2. Applying the Applications – NURBS Modelling and Beyond

The advent of digital mediums, from the precision of 2D applications such as AutoCad and the collagistic opportunities of Photoshop to the use of NURBS modelling has significantly changed the manner in which these questions have been addressed in studio work within schools of architecture. The use of CATIA, 3DSMax, Rhino, Solidworks and Maya has unleashed an array of complex geometries within speculative architectural design work without a proportionate examination of why these geometries might be appropriate or otherwise. The questions for theorists of architecture are whether the same semantic relationship between form and meaning holds in this new, more complex environment. The formal complexity of this work, from the para-organic forms of Greg Lynn, Hani Rashid and Lars Spuybroek to the myriad fluid-form children of this practice now emerging in architecture schools around the world, is only partially understood.

What is clear is that the process of theorizing the work follows the same paradigm as that of the Modern distinction between objects, method and meaning. As with the example from Pérez-Gómez, the work is often explained as a consequence of its method of production, with a number of metaphorical similarities exploited to present its theoretical depth. The flow of a surface is compared with the phenomenological flow of the eye over it; the liquidity of a plan is compared with the patterns of programmatic use by persons over a period of time; the indeterminacy of where vertical and horizontal planes might meet is compared with ideas on how multi-centred the post-renaissance individual is; the complexity of the structural geometry required is connected to the fusion of form and meaning extant in the Gothic – ensuring an impression of historical continuity as well. In addition, the ability of NURBS surfaces to precisely accommodate the complex algorithms necessary for the determination of double curvatures, folds, and other motile surfaces which can then be incorporated into CAM procedures allows the architectural work to sit credibly in a materialist economy. In this sense the perennial question, 'But, can it be built?' is also answered.

This being the case, work such as Gehry's is explained as being 'sculptural' in a populist sense, or 'spatially and phenomenally provocative' in the language of architectural criticism touched on above. The relationship between means of production and meaning is clear – the use of 3d applications is focussed on allowing the architect to unleash some sort of mystical *Kunstwollen,* literally a 'will-to-form' that attempts to describe the (somewhat Nietzschean) movement by which appropriate form is chosen by the artist/designer. The most important early digital example of this was Bernard Cache's *Earthmoves: The Furnishing of Territories*, in which the subtle argument for folding and replication eventuated in a number of projects whose final form was determined, ultimately, by a form of post-critical 'choice'. Choosing a single iteration of his designs for CNC milling from an infinite number of variants was a trivial precipitate in comparison with the realisation that the process of coming-to-form was inherently chaotic and performed no representational or semantic function (Cache 1995). To be cynical about this however risks forgetting the very legitimate arguments that the process of identifying patterns of use that in themselves are enlightening. Just as the minimalism of Mies differs subtly from that of Ludwig Hilberseimer or Ernst May, so too the florid emendations of Preston Scott Cohen or Lise-Ann Couture may contain subtle, but revealing differences as yet unarticulated.

When this relationship is resisted and the expressive fallacy of concentrating on the designer and their supposed intentions is put aside, there are two options. Either one reads the work *sui generis*, assuming that it appears as some effect of 'the digital' as a natural event, or one looks to processes that might provide form without selections of choice, *Kunstwollen* again, being made. The use of viral algorithms in architectural design to theoretically remove the selectivity and stylisations of the design process remains a method that tends towards the same theoretical ground as Serialism in art and music. Highly structural, it resists the transactional relations of meaning that Structuralism generally sought to uncover, but without the same type of reflexivity central to a discipline such as anthropology. The hypersurfaces of Stephen Perella and Marcus Novak attempt to circumvent a simple transaction between form, process and meaning as an issue of sequential apperception. Mark Jackson writes perceptively on this process, identifying the undeveloped reliance on mind/body split that remains resolutely Cartesian – and hence a form of fetishization of the reader rather than the author with all the transferred anthropomorphism that that may entail. Better, for Jackson, are the analyses of Greg Lynn who identifies the exact, anexact and inexact as iterations of the possibilities of complex digital modelling undertaken over time – introducing the opportunity for recognising architectural form as a dynamic system (Jackson 2002). Whilst Jackson's essay concentrates on the issue of the 'diagram' that emerges from this study and the commentary on this provide by Zizek and Massumi, there is also, I argue, opportunity to read the environment of digital production cr eated within Game environments.

3. Gaming

The parallel development that has occurred within digital media, specifically the enormous rise of game environments in which players participate as first or third person avatars performing actions is as varied as the entertainment media industry can devise. Significantly too the code for these environments, the manner in which they organise uv mapping, field of vision rendering, frame rates is allied to the representational 3D modelling media identified above, Figure 2.

Figure 2. Suspiria

Gaming of course continues to be regarded as a threat to social cohesion and democratic experience because of the violent and anti-social thema of most its products, the particularly disembodied nature of community it embraces, and a residual 'parental' chauvinism towards the idea of games. Of course the critical community of gaming has not addressed these issues to a broader audience for a number of reasons. Principal of which is the sheer economic force of the current product, it needs no explanation or attempt to reinterpret it as part of positive, reflective artistic culture because it is part of a significant 21st century economy for which these questions are no longer crucial. Secondly there is an internal ongoing debate within the gaming community regarding the narratival and/or ludic aspect of games. Are games representative of fictional production generally and open to the body of critical commentary developed within literary studies, or are they simply a form of dissociative experience that temporarily and innocently disengages the player from everyday experience and places them in a contained, speculative space of pre-determined operations (Frasca, 2003)? Significantly the understanding of how this discussion should evolve is not considered to lie outside of the gaming itself – it is a function of the qualities of contemporary gaming practice and not literary studies or neuroscience. Gonzalo Frasca looks towards an emergent critical practice that is unique to the structural properties of the game experience.

Yet this is difficult to achieve in the short term because of the rapidity with which generational change is occurring within the commercial games marketplace. For example the narratival simplicity of *Doom 3* is presented as evidence, along with its technical sophistication and economic power, that ludic aspects are paramount. The rejoinder to this does not come from a meta-discourse on the nature of fictional engagement, but from the fact that the successor blockbuster, *Half Life 2*, contained considerably more storyline (*and* a better physics engine and particle shader).

It is a matter of historical record now that along with the gaming industry, digital architectural culture has developed enormously. And while Pérez-Gómez had had considered suspicions regarding a practice that so clearly presented the textural qualities of the medium as limited in their aesthetic-critical effect, the very thin-ness of this effect coincided with the emergence of discussions of surface (Perella 1998).

So it is worthwhile investigating aspects of the representational practice of computer games to see the manner in which theoretical crossovers between it and architecture take place. For not only do most 3D games take place in environments that attempt to imitate aspects of the 'real' world, they also invoke ideas relative to the temporal moment of architecture either as historical fragments, future utopian/dystopic places, or the current world. They involve the presence of the gaming subject as either a first-person, third person or omnipresent figure; they create simulations of physics recognisable as being terrestrial, ambient sound and weather effects; and they also include complex animation sequences that either figure as part of the dynamic qualities of the environment, or are used as filmic cut-scenes within game-play.

I take the position that architecture, as a discipline, enjoys a culture of enquiry directed not only at the built environment and those projects that specifically are directed at construction in a traditional sense, but more generally in the practice of using architectural design as a mode for representing and exploring an embodied form of thinking. For this reason, the infinite expanse of the digital game environment represents a land beyond the looking glass whose architectural culture is yet to be recognised.

4. Applying the Applications – Game Modelling

Central to these environments is the creative process of 3D modelling packages such as 3D Studio Max, Maya, Lightwave, Solidworks, etc, the game engines used to paint 3D space within gameplay, pc videocards that assist the CPU's in this process, and the editing suites (often associated with the game engine) within which these environments are created. A typical example is the game *Unreal Tournament 2004* that utilises its own game engine and editing suite (UnrealEd) in which the complex environments of the commercial game are made. Whilst this software is specifically created, or adapted from previous incarnations, for the use of the game developers it is also supplied to general public as part of the software game package. This is to encourage the development of brand loyalty to the game by supporting the Mod community attached to it. An extremely large and well-organised Internet community uses these resources to create modified versions of the game, releasing them as freeware to the community for peer appraisal – the most active of the fan sites is http://www.beyondunreal.com.

So there are a number of coincident parameters between the discussions of the philosophical aspects of digital culture in architecture, the software associated with the creation of game environments and the emerging theoretical culture on the nature of game-play. Architectural practices and schools regularly use 3DStudio Max for example to produce speculative work as part of their critical practice. These works tend to remain within that package, utilising the rendering capabilities of the package to produce sophisticated still images or animated fly-throughs of the building(s). These renderings currently tend to be very resource intensive, requiring specialist skill and dedicated hardware to be produced.

5. Our Work

At the Louis Laybourne Smith School of Architecture and Design and at the Spatial Information Architecture Laboratory at RMIT, we have currently been investigating the use of the Unreal Tournament game editor and engine in the exploration of architectural projects. At the most basic level, the level editor UnrealEd provides an environment within which designers can carve out a negotiable space, skin it in an appropriate texture, place digital objects within the space and tour around this environment in real time. The editor is extremely adept at reproducing texture and light effects in an internalised environment. With a little more experience, the designer can begin to create quite complex architectonic spaces with a variety of lighting and textural effects and even 'exterior' terrains that imitate the complex geometries of land-forms, vegetation and animated skies. However there are governing aspects of the game environment that tends to emphasise an economy of polygons. The frame-rate at which the processor is able to render scenes is directly proportional to the amount of complex polygonal faces it needs to surface and the lighting effects associated with them. For this reason, geometries that are composed of simple triangulations are more efficient than complex 3D surfaces. A square face has only 2 triangular polygons, whereas complex curves can have exponentially more.

This situation is somewhat alleviated by the creation of a category of pre-rendered objects (Static Meshes) that are skinned in an alternative program. This skin is then imported as a single texture. This situation, combined with the fact that game designers have traditionally not had an architectural background, tends to produce environments that have none of the spatial exploration or structural complexity, Figure 3, seen in contemporary architecture.

Figure 3. Terror-ain

Yet the opportunity exists for a creative use of this material. Not only for the immediate idea that it would be interesting to see how persons trained in the creation of architectural environments would utilise the medium, but also to see how more complex ideas on the nature of immersiveness within a digital medium might reflect a developing emergent identity for architecture. If we begin to develop these ideas in concert with thinking on the nature of digital and virtual experience, then the issue of how spaces, objects and surfaces are engaged with is significant.

In many respects there is an emerging public competency in negotiating digital space because of the ubiquity of PC games. Whether they are educational environments, adventure games, tactical games or first-person shooters, the relation between the tasks of the game and the manner in which environments are engaged with are structurally conjoined. The convention for exploring these spaces is often linear, or hub related. The player will be encouraged to follow an intuitive path, tightly scripted by the game designer, leading to the set pieces of game play. Generally speaking meandering is discouraged as it tends to affect the suspension of disbelief, the telepresence, critical to the immersive experience (Taylor, 2003). Yet anecdotal discussion of some games is full of just these forms of delinquent behaviour. The Cyan games *Myst* and *Riven* were noted for their (contemporarily) sophisticated landscapes and players would enjoy the effect of 'being' in the environment as much as the ludic aspects of the game play (mostly the solving of complex puzzles). This delinquency is crucial to the philosophical freedom of the medium as it grants the player the opportunity for rational action and free choice.

So the game engine is already coded as a performative environment in that it contains texture sets, static meshes, ambient sounds, sprites that are made up from the palette of the original game attributes. It is already, in the minds of many students, a place where you make game-like spaces as opposed to architectural spaces. It is arguable whether there is a necessary priority for either type of space or indeed whether they are as different a type of space as might be first assumed. But if contemporary architectural discourse on digital presence and the flow of information is engaged then fundamental questions regarding the architectural process are informative. These questions concern a number of issues that I can only briefly point to. The primal act of creation involves the separation of matter to make a void space that will become the theatre of actions; the first/third person perspective involves an ecology of care for the avatar in the created space; the practice of texturing is infinitely thin, even despite the illusionistic opportunities of bump-mapping on textures; the spectacle of events may be didactically controlled to point to something (or nothing); the scene may be triggered to invoke cut-scene segments that are fundamentally prophetic and/or textural; there is a gravitational physics for both player and objects that may be controlled; and finally, there is a normative component that de-emphasises the immanence of the fantastic.

6. From the Void

When making a game space the first condition that must be recognised is that the creation of a negative space must always precede the creation of an object. This is in direct contrast to most 3D modelling applications in which the object is the primary focus of construction, an exteriority that must be cored out to form the spaces of occupation, or must be part of an aggregation of objects that incidentally make a space. In this respect the game-space is already architectural in a fundamental fashion inasmuch as it proposes an interior without a meaningful exteriority. It is already a space of propinquities between objects, actions and events, quite coincidentally like the *khora* of classical antiquity. It is already the first part of the labyrinth, for every subsequent space is an interiorised connectivity. Even when creating significant external environments the idea of the infinite, Figure 4, is adumbrated by the limitations of the medium. In a traditional reading of the meaning of these spaces there is an immanent experience of the sublime as a vast interior – more Piranesi than Casper David Friedrich.

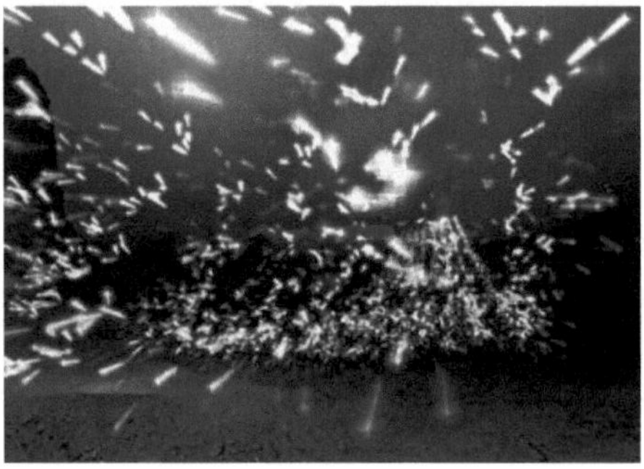

Figure 4. Two towers

7. The First Person Perspective

Without even considering the issues surrounding the nature of vision and the manner in which perspective appropriates and constructs our experience, the first person perspective possible within the game-engine environment is significant. It allows the viewer to move across any horizontal plane. It also allows the viewer to move in the vertical axis via the use of stairs and ramps. Immediately issues arise regarding the manner in which the phenomenology of sensate bodily experience occurs. Whilst we may be skeptical regarding the manner in which suspension of disbelief may occur in the immersive context of a game narrative, it is clear, in my belief that a desire to preserve the avatar presence occurs when confronted with places that may involve a dangerous fall, agoraphobic or claustrophobic situations. But as death is not the end in game-play, an ambivalent relationship develops between the self and the environment.

Further, if we are examine recent architectural discourse on the nature of post-Cartesian space, such as that famously of Henri Poincarre or latterly of Gilles Deleuze or Bernard Cache, the artificiality of the first-person perspective is immediately present – not simply as a defective representation of ontological presence – but as an artifice that is already outmoded. If architecture has relied on perspectival representation to simultaneously be a mode of representation and a vehicle for further critical scrutiny, the realisation that vision is a far more fragmentary and collagistic experience has significantly influenced the 'de-centering' of architectural theory. Much more can be said about the relationship between the desire for spectacle and the textuality of the medium in game culture, what is important is the nostalgia for outmoded forms of game-play. *Tetris*, *Space Invaders*, indeed any scroller game that de-ontologises presence in favour of the pleasures of geometry represents this.

This is a radically new set of questions for architectural theory: the illusion of freedom created through the démodé of camera perspective.

8. The Texture

Texturing, and the associated task of lighting, is again a fundamentally architectural practice for it attempts to approximate the haptic qualities of material whilst acknowledging the highly mediated manner in which this occurs. A textured object has the material applied equally across its designated polygons; it may then be adjusted in location and scale to create a more 'realistic' effect. The process of bumpmapping, creating a stereometric or Blinn effect in a texture to give the illusion of depth is not as sophisticated in UnrealEd as it is in 3d modelling packages, but there is alternatively a number of ways in which composite and animated textures can achieve the same effects.

Yet the process remains infinitely thin. Inasmuch as the interest in the fold of the surface (Rajchmann 1992), again a Deleuzian influence, represents an implicated spatiality – it is a spatiality of the surface that presents the material texturing as a simulacra of some Real texture from either empirical sources, or from work done in Photoshop. Yet though it is, in part, the ability of the texture to approximate 'reality' that helps to affirm the telepresence of the scene, the more effective textures tend to be robustly haptic in their visual effect. Flat, or subtle, textures tend to disappear under most simple lighting effects.

9. Movers

Within environments, it is possible to key-frame the movement of items to respond to any number of triggers – from player proximity to the effects of other components of the level. Using the Matinee function there are the further possibilities of creating complex camera movements associated with both animate and inanimate objects. Scripting this is a fundamentally cinematic process.

Figure 5. Home

So the environment is never fully created until the opportunity to present simple functional operations is taken up – from an opening door or window to more complex ballets of ghostly operations driven by the unseen hand of the architect/programmer. The idea of a *Deus ex Machina* is implicit in these events, presenting a logic for the transformation of the repetitive functional parameters of a map without this logic being necessarily explicit. Why does one door return to its original state whilst another stays open? Each movement seems to act as a didactic sign for the player, like the analogical universe of medieval culture in which there is an assumption that actions occur for reasons that may eventually be theologically explicable. The process of deriving and representing architectural experience, Figure 5, through the tools of animation questions the very idea of how time and temporality function within the architectural project.

For architecture this is a new level of control, for it may no longer be assumed that elements of the functionality of a building, its inherent repetitiveness, are a matter of simple alterity (Benjamin 2000). If an environment is animated, or one can suggest – has *anima*, then its definition as a functional presence, a place that will always work in a certain fashion, is significantly more complex.

10. The Cinematic Pause

Game play has instinctively modelled part of its narratival structure on the insertion of cinematic segments that aid the ongoing storyline, give the player a moment of respite, or summarise events to date (including resolving the arcs of the major protagonists – as with conventional cinema structure). What might be made of this for the specifically architectural environment remains to be seen, for it allows the insertion of different modalities of experience for the first/third person agent. It is unusual to be able to transform the phenomenologically attentive 'player' into the passive spectator of a spectacle and then re-place them in the environment with a possibly different ecology of risk, trust, care and danger. In essence it can act as a critical voice, a parallel text on the nature of exploration, or habitation, or the melancholy of the ruin, etc.

11. Physics

Of course part of the process of verisimilitude between the real world and the virtual turns on the manner in which random acts of physical expression are translated into events. The current leader in this area is *Half-Life 2* whose physics engine allows for incredibly real responses to force by objects – barrels fall, roll and float, mattresses slump, timber splinters and breaks. In all of these applications there is the possibility for amending the properties of objects. The degree of friction between an object and a surface may be modified, the buoyancy or pattern of action and reaction may be adjusted to make objects bounce in a counter-intuitive fashion, their pitch and yaw can be adjusted to make the laws of the entropy of energy seem unreal.

Obviously, in a fashion similar to that of the movers, this is an interesting challenge to architectural theory. It is as if a narcotic element may be introduced to dissociate the player from another aspect of their contact with real-world expectations.

12. The Normal

Fundamentally though, for all of the opportunities for creating wildly nomadic, transitive and surreal worlds, the medium works most effectively at the moment when it is merely showing the inflection of this change. The tension between an environment whose abstraction is immanent but never explicitly rendered and our experience of the everyday world is crucial. In some fashion we borrow this pattern from our understanding of fictional or counter-factual worlds. They are sensible (that is, seems to refer to something explicable) when they are at some measure real. Any of the visionary city/social-scapes of recent film science-fiction from *Solaris* to *Gattaca* to *Existenz* rely as heavily on the normalcy of the place as the desire to fetishize the differences.

13. Parting Thoughts – God Mode

The architectural opportunities of the 3d game engine are quite profound – for the structural opportunities they offer for re-presenting the world are massive. Principally though, these opportunities are meaningless without a coeval process of thinking-through of the implications of the medium. Architecture has a long, critical history of reflexive study of its mode of presentation. This is no different a circumstance. It is only the emergent breadth of events that are now part of digital worlds that makes one think that a fundamental shift is occurring in the spectrum of architectural knowledge. Whilst there is a long history of visionary thinking in architecture from, Alberti's *Hypnerotomachia* onwards, the ability to script morphologies that are utterly novel is unique to the medium.

The paper has attempted to open a number of questions: Why has architectural theory in relation to digital culture struggled to describe the manner in which the highly idiosyncratic forms have come about? And, in fact, are their differences only cosmetic? In this circumstance, if we look at the use of game-engine software, the questions about how it might be architectural are very interesting. First it provides a first-person perspective that seems to privilege a renaissance world-view. Yet this optical mastery is undermined by the freedom with which the 'world' under the gaze may be manipulated/coded to achieve remarkable experiences. And in fact the tools by which a recognisable world might be made: form, light, texture, movement are the same medium for making a profound and unsettling estrangement. Surely this is a core task of architecture.

References

Benjamin, A: 2000, *Architectural Philosophy*, Chapter 1, 'Time, Function and Alterity', Athlone Press, London.

Cache, B: 1995, *Earth Moves: The Furnishing of Territories*, The MIT Press, Cambridge, MA.

Frasca, G: 2003, Ludologists love stories, too: notes from a debate that never took place, *Proceedings of the 2003 Digital Games Research Conference (DIGRA).*

Jackson, M: 2003, *Diagram of the Fold – The Actuality of the Virtual in Architecture*, unpublished manuscript, ZKM (Centre for Art & Media Technology) University of Karlsruhe.

Maher, ML, Bilda, Z and Marchant, D: 2005, Comparing Collaborative Design Behavior In Remote Sketching and 3D Virtual Worlds, *Proceedings of International Workshop on Human Behaviour in Designing, Melbourne*, Victoria, Australia, Key Centre of Design Computing and Cognition, University of Sydney, pp. 3-26.

Perez-Gomez, A and Pelletier, L: 1997: *Architectural Representation and the Perspective Hinge*, MIT Press, Cambridge, MA, pp. 371-395.

Perrella, S (ed): 1998, *Hypersurface Architecture*, AD, Academy Editions, London.

Rosenman MA, Smith G, Ding L, Marchant D and Maher ML: 2005, Multidisciplinary Design in Virtual Worlds, *in* B Martens and A Brown (eds) *Computer Aided Architectural Design Futures 2005*, Springer, Dordrecht, Netherlands, pp. 433-442.

Wardrip-Fruin, N and Mountfort, N (eds): 2003, *The New Media Reader*, The MIT Press, Cambridge, MA.

Rajchmann, J: 1992, Perplications: On the Space and Time of Rebstock Park, *Unfolding Frankfurt*, Ernst and Sohn, Frankfurt, p. 36.

Taylor, L: 2003, When Seams Fall Apart, Video Game Space and the Player, *Game Studies*, **3**(2): http://www.gamestudies.org/0302/taylor/.

SPACENSING

A new method sensitizing users and their interactive environments

STEFAN ZEDLACHER
Graz University of Technology, Austria

Abstract. In this article we introduce the research on finding solutions using a 3D motion capture system for architectural design purpose by sensitizing a physical space and its virtual counterpart for user interaction and human motion input. We separate this use in four major steps to get a deeper understanding about the processes of space perception and space constitution in architectural (design) tasks. With detailed information about the manner of movement and the structured workflow it is possible to get new insights into space interaction. Furthermore *spacensing* provides a toolbox for users to investigate virtual space conditions as well as it allows to draw out conclusions on space sociological assumptions.

1. Introduction

"The connection between virtual and "grounded" spaces is not formed by technology, but by the body." (Löw 2001)

Several applications in the architectural research and the design process are concerned with the movement of bodies in (virtual) spaces (Hirschberg et al. 2006). There is also research within the body and its sociological importance in the perception of space (Krämer 2002). Using the advanced capabilities of optical 3D Motion Capturing Systems to take a closer look to human movement can provide new insights about these topics.

Spacensing (the word is a combination of space and sense) deals with the question how do movement-based interactive applications, that are common in architecture, affect the traditional, subjective space sensation and the architectural workflow. It describes an interactive, progressive space app-lication, which tracks movements, converts them to a model, characterizes actions and simulates alternatives that could be visualized to the user. Intuitively drawing in space based on natural human movement as part of the design process or transferring invisible datascapes into physical

A Dong, A Vande Moere & JS Gero (eds), CAADFutures'07, 211–222.

areas are practical applications of spacensing in architecture. In addition, the use of intelligent areas that pre-calculate the behavior of their users is to be examined.

3D Motion Capturing Systems offer a deep view into the nature of movements and permit conclusions on medical, ergonomic or economic conditions. Dealing with this advantage, spacensing is a workflow, bringing together motion tracking, analyzing and simulating motion data, to interact with architectural space by overlapping physical areas with virtual spaces. Peoples movement in specific areas releases a cybernetic computer model, which interprets the kinematic data from the system. It recognizes patterns and conditions from human movement and tries to simulate a possible behavior. The results of the computation are visually returned to the user, who reacts through his ongoing movement with the environment and starts interacting in that way.

Before describing the system in detail, we should have a particular look at the Sociology of Cyberspace.

2. Sociology of Cyberspace

Martina Löw (2001) describes two fundamental processes with which people generally constitute areas: the Spacing, which Löw defines as the relational arrangement of things in space, and their synthesis, the ability to link these things to a specific sense of space. The question we address in our research is, whether these definitions, which are used in space sociology with reference to physical space, also apply to augmented and virtual realities?

Therefore, we have to widen this space-sociological definition by the conception of Cyberspace. Löw takes the term of Cyberspace in consideration but underlying the classification by Featherstone and Burrows (1995). According to this classification, Cyberspace can be divided into Gibsonian Cyberspace, Barlowian Cyberspace and Virtual Reality.

Accumulated experiences and research suggest, that these distinctions can no longer be maintained. Cyberspace is not just a technology and its areas of application are not purely simulations, instead they are virtualized. This means that inside those areas, behaviors and actions get the quality, being a real experience inside a shapeable environment. In other words: "… that for cybernetic sociofacts they have the real experience quality of a designable topography." (Thiedecke 2004). Sociofacts is a translation of the german word Soziofakte that describes in general the observation of behaviors and actions. The question to be examined is: Which are the underlying regulations of virtualized connotations and how do the users constitute them in the cyber-areas? The transition to Cyberspace accomplishes, where a fundamental change in sensual perspective happens. This leads to a socio-technical representation of the imaginable (what describes the german term Vermöglichung) and appears on every, even partially virtual environment. (Thiedecke 2005). Interpreting Cyberspace according to Gibson (1984) as an area constituted of information that has been abstracted from any technical equipment makes it easier to understand every action or behavior inside this areas as cybernetic sociofact or digitized manners. Cyberspace, as the sensual scope of socio-technical enabled expectations (Thiedecke 2005) generates, provokes and reproduces cybernetic sociofacts. A method to address and connect these so called cybernetic sociofacts, in a virtualized area like our media laboratory, is represented by spacensing.

To get an imagination of the cybernetic sociofacts, we conceived the constitution of virtual spaces through four necessary steps, which are constructed on one to other. These steps are: tracking, analyzing, simulating and interacting. They are described in the following section. The fundamental idea consists of: Synchronizing the movement in physical areas with the movement in their virtual counterparts, extending this virtual area with individual components and finally designing these add-ons with customized "brushes". These "brushes" are virtual tools, generated as a simulation from previous movement analysis. Both, full body data, which deforms a volume in a specific relation, and rigid body data, which draws lines, models objects or produces particles, are applied.

Figure 1. Shows a visualization of full body interaction between users, a virtual volume and the physical area (the media laboratory where spacensing is installed)

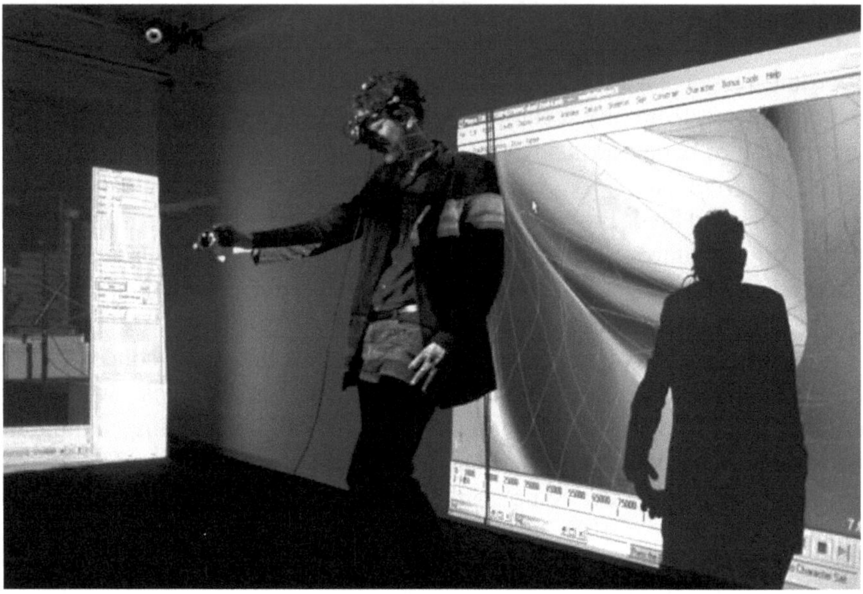

Figure 2. Physical interaction using spacensing to reshape a virtual designed furniture

3. How *spacensing* Works

3.1. THE FRAMEWORK

A lot of CAVE environments, where high-end technology is built onto existing rooms, can seamlessly perform 100% cyberspaces. Unlike them, *spacensing* is designed for a media laboratory, which integrates high-end technology with architectural space conditions. Tasks like: lessons, discussions, presentations or experiments should be furthermore possible in both, the virtual and the real part of the laboratory. The lab is a space-playground with *spacensing* as one of its necessary gadgets to bring together the highly evolved equipment with unexperienced users. Those users should work with the environment without detailed background information about the technical issues. Instead of learning new software and new application elements they should be able to operate with their bodily expressions and create input by natural movement.

The borders between virtual and physical areas start to dissolve by integrating the digital working environment as an overlay to a physical workplace. Through observations of variances in the movement we detect the cybernetic sociofacts.

3.2. TRACKING

The connection of movement to inverse kinematic skeletons *(joint angle)* or simple markers (*pose to pose* distance calculation) digitizes data from the nature of movement (ergonomics, speed, gesturing, mimic art, anatomy, motoricity, bio mechanics, economics …) in realtime.

Usually motion capture data is illustrated as dots (markers and joints) or lines (bones) in a graphical 3D environment (which represents the physical tracking volume). Beside this graphical output, there is a huge numerical output in several different file formats, e.g. comma separated csv-file format or Vicons v-file format. It's also possible to stream this data in realtime through TCP (tarsus server) or UDP (open sound control) which makes the data available for a lot of different multimedia or 3D applications like Maya, Motionbuilder, Processing, MaxMSP or pure data (PD).

Beside full body motion tracking, which is used to define brushes through analyzing this data (this process is explained in the next section), it is important to have a corresponding handle for partial body tracking, e.g. one arm, the head or some separate multiple objects like hands and feet. This is necessary because it's not possible to build a full body setup for only one particular movement. The parameterization process described by Guodong Liu et al. (2006a), which reduces a full body marker setup to a set of six principal markers, appears as a useful combination between these two, at the moment separated, tracking methods.

3.3. ANALYZING

The motion data sets are analyzed in order to assign them one or more characteristics (parameterization). Research within the range of *human motion databases* (Guodong Liu 2006b) can be extensively used here.

An eminent aspect during data analysis is not only the precise reconstruction of movement but also the attempt to find an abstraction layer, which allows an interpretation of the data without knowing the actual motion. The abstraction layer is also necessary because we are not able to handle the large amount of data in realtime. This exemplifies the metaphor of the *spacense*, which, like every system that works with sensors, must accomplish an individual level of abstraction for the interpretation of data coming from its senses (in our case the marker data coming from the VICON system). This leads us to the decision to define a virtual tool (the "brushes") out of the whole data coming from each person, which can be used as a multiplier in further (inter-)actions assigned with this person. It is important to understand, that according to the particular movement of each person individual tools are generated from the whole toolbox provided by the system.

At this point, the question of which data should be used for the first examination to build up some basic "brushes" remains. We were looking for datasets that are not representing typical human movement, what could be estimated from architectural design input. What we found was a dancer expressing emotional conditions, flux and motion intensity through her performance. Given an adjective, she tried to express this in her dancing. It is important to say that there is no need for an objective data analysis because the interaction only happens with specific users with their specific "brushes". This seems suitable because there is also research in imaginable and improvisatory space concepts through the correspondence between dance and architecture by William Forsythe (Maar 2006).

Figure 3. The dancer performing live inside the tracking area

Searching for the right abstraction layer we found a very interesting approach handling motion data like rendered textures (see Figure 4). The *Motion Texture* method (Pashley et al. 2005) combines concluded mocap sequences out of an existing database to one continuous new sequence. If you have one movement, a person standing up from a chair, and a second movement when the same person starts walking, motion texture merges the two original scenes by the use of *textons*. Processing colored images out of the original data, *textons* combine them to one procedural texture. This new texture is translated into the missing movement between the two source movements. Using colored images to visualize motion data also has the potential to simply focus on the major processes while losing no information. Progressing this method, we expressed the datasets by generating barcode-like images, finding out that we can reduce even complex movements to a barcode pattern and some filter values. The software we used here was Processing 1.0 (BETA) (Fry and Reas 2005).

Figure 4. The picture shows a motion texture from the dance performance. The first row shows rotations, the second one translations of all joints. The 51 sub-rows in each of the six rows (each sub-row with one pixel height) represent the Rotation/Translation along one axis (X, Y and Z) of one joint (form pelvis to the hands and foots). The grey-scale and the b/w rows show the same data in a different scale (the point of interest has been increased)

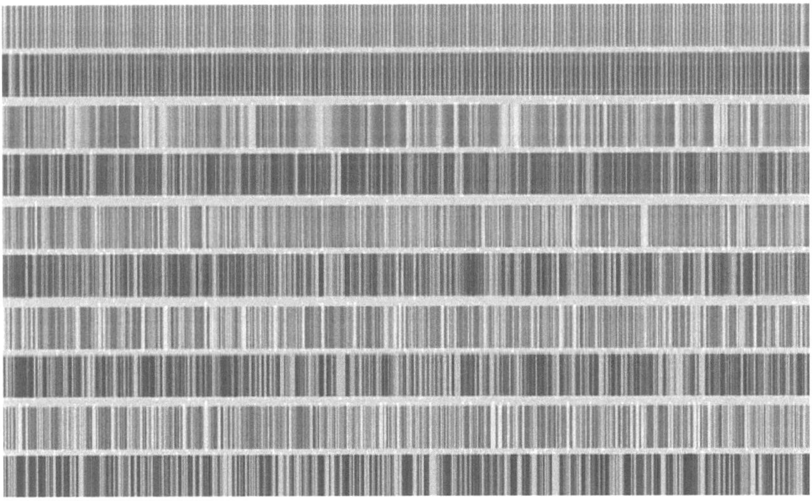

Figure 5. This picture represents the interpretation of the amount of movement into a barcode image. As you can see in the top pair of rows, the speed of the movement is indicated by the transition from red to yellow respectively from blue to cyan color. Less movement produces a wider transition. In the next pairs we reduced the colors by increasing the amount of motion that is necessary to cause a change (shifting the point of activation)

Figure 4 shows three pairs of rows, each pair representing the same motion. The upper row in each pair consists of 51 sub-rows (the pixel rows). Each of this sub rows represents the Rotation along one Axis (X, Y and Z) of one joint. We used a setup with 17 joints from the pelvis to the feet and the hands according to the Human RTKM v.2 model from VICON. The lower row of each pair represents the Translation along each Axis from each of the same 17 joints. The color of each pixel indicates the intensity of motion where green is neutral, violet represents a negative maximum and red a positive maximum of movement. The output of greyscaled (row 3 and 4) and black/white (row 5 and 6) colored pixel was necessary because small amount of movement cannot be seen very clearly in colored mode. But, as you can see on the right hand of rows 2, 4 and 6 (which show the same Translation), a difference emerges when switching in greyscaled or black/white mode. We call this method "shifting the point of interest".

The next step trying to visualize complex movement data in a simple, readable form is presented in Figure 5. In this picture the red rows representing the Rotation and the blue rows the Translation. But there are no longer joint movements along the three Axes that are coloring pixels, instead the amount of movement of all joints together produces a fade to yellow in case of Rotation and cyan in case of Translation. This gives, as you can see in the first pair of rows on top of the image, a clear view of the amount of movement. Here, a reduction in coloring the pixels (starting from 255 steps in the top rows and ending at two steps, red and yellow respectively blue and cyan, at the bottom pair of rows) does not decrease the information. We call this translation: "shifting the point of activation".

With these and other abstraction layers it is possible to diversify the huge amount of data into simple, legible images with some variables (primarily the start condition and the range between minimum and maximum values). These parameterized images are representing detailed movement information beyond the X, Y and Z position of an object, namely speed, acceleration, ergonomics, economics, motoricity or biomechanics. With these parameters it is also possible to do a reverse engineering, starting with a barcode image file, applying the variable parameters to it and attaching this to the setup condition (a full body skeleton or a certain amount of rigid bodies). These are the required ingredients for the simulation.

3.4. SIMULATION

After tracking and analyzing, *spacensing* must now estimate possibilities, expectations and developments. At this time, there are two possibilities trying to simulate a future behavior based on previous input. On the one hand we try to find a rhythm of rules (*cellular automata*) based on pattern recognition in certain movements from previous inputs. On the other hand we train a neural network algorithm with previous inputs. Both methods seem to fit for this task, although neural network algorithms are more precise, but pattern recognition needs less data and is therefore faster.

There is also a third method given to the participants. Alternatively to the two algorithmic simulations, they could decide to get a three dimensional output-file of their previous tracking sessions to generate an individual simulation out of their datasets. The files were generated with some basic setup brushes (coming from the first examination with the dancer), which draw simple curves or objects. The simulations were based on dynamic solvers for rigid bodies or particle fields. This part, like the interaction, was done in Maya.

As the results of the computations are passed on to the user, they evoke a change in behavior. Since this was not a component of the original simulation, a further simulation is needed. Interaction between space and users happens.

3.5. INTERACTION

By the interpretation of *spacensing* as the "eyes and ears" of an area and the collected data as information, new methods of space communication are to be tested. The focus lies on what's between the physical space and its virtual representation. Also the "grounded" (according to Martina Löw) and the individual conception of space, which is in fact based on human movement (Förster 1993; Debord 1958), are to be explored. Trough the possibility to interpret the digital sensation ("eyes" and "ears") and the resulting adaptation of the input for the human senses, the "in between" emerges.

At the moment *spacensing* is in the state of collecting data for further investigations. The setup, which is described in this paper, is finished and a first workshop was done with it. Exploring new design methods within a three dimensional environment, the students used *spacensing* for drawing directly onto space. Onward, they built cybernetic adaptive fittings while researching for their own particular design method (results can be seen at www.formotions.com). These fittings are a combination of the customized "brushes" and the architectural intervention the students designed for their virtual areas. Observations during this workshop revealed some specific qualities and some tasks for future work:

- Simple tasks like pushing or pulling objects, deforming a single volume or handling one specific particle emitter with gravity are much more handy than complex scenes.
- Most of the movements have slow motion with a unique flow. Unlike dancers who are used in expressing emotions through their

movement, the students have a very reduced "body language" which results in decreasing the bandwidth of their possibilities.

- Through the loss of all other senses except the visual sense (the perception of the virtual environment happens with a HMD (*head mounted display*), we observed an impairment in the beginning. Later it led however to a quality of the virtual area because it made it made it easier for the students to concentrate on the design task.
- There is a difference between gesture and movement input, which is currently not taken into account.
- Also the alternative working with borderless or unscaled virtual environments was not investigated.

In contradiction to previous works in this area, for example with the unreal game engine (Engeli 2005), the students this time broke through the imaginary wall that separates the virtual environment from the physical space. Working in a familiar surrounding, they accepted the existence of an invisible volume that could only be entered through their files, which were created in a piece of software they knew and used in other courses. Unlike usual practice, where the students spend most of the time behind a computer monitor with a mouse as a "pencil", spacensing puts them into a physical area with a virtual overlay and they use their natural body as an input device.

4. Conclusion

Currently, mediated architectural environments are in a state of evolution. With *spacensing*, we recommend a workflow that is both – an operating system for hybrid environments and an observation device for cybernetic space cognition. The question whether *spacensing* is research or an artistic project can be answered clearly. Like the architectural design process in general consists of research, experience, practice and intuition, *spacensing* ends up as a workflow built from scientific research for architectural and artistic use. The first utilization in a student workshop evinced that *spacensing* is a research tool to think with rather than an art performance tool though it could be used for.

The constitution of space happens as individual process inside the users. Therefore collective space perception goes along with communication (exchange of information) between individuals (Förster 1993). Rescission, redefinition and extension of physical conditions with digital information give the opportunity to rewrite the individual space syntax inside virtual environments. In this context *spacensing* allows us to take along the particular movement (as integral part of the space experience) into virtual environments.

Under these aspects it is clear that we need both parts of this system to address (cybernetic) sociofacts: An interface, which must be as simple as possible, and a scaleable observation framework, which is as flexible and descriptive like *spacensing*. All this happens without restricting the individual design process and with the possibility to develop further on personal design tools.

5. Related and Future Work

After utilizing the environment the first time with students in a workshop, the next step is to work with the dancers who produced the first datasets for generating the motion texture files. This has also a correspondence to the work of Paul Kaiser (2000) and Klaus Obermaier (2004). This is necessary to get a deeper understanding of expressing emotions through movement and will result in more particular "brushes" for the three dimensional design tools. Also it will work out differences between gesture and movement input.

The development of the cyber carpet as a part of the cyberwalk project (2005) and the up coming question of "what is beyond the use as immersive virtual reality environments" also relates to this work. Finally research on handling human motion databases (Guodong Liu 2006a/b) and the motion texture (Pashley 2005) is an important aspect of this work.

Acknowledgements

A special thank goes to the staff and the students of the formotions workshop (www.formotions.com) at the Institute of Architecture and Media, Graz University of Technology, and to Lucy Lungley, the dancer who provided most of the first datasets.

References

Cyberwalk: 2005, EU STREP Project FP6-511092, http://www.cyberwalk-project.org

Debord, G: 1958, Theory of the derive, *International Situationiste #2*, pp. 19-23.

Engeli, M: 2005, Noble dollhouses, violent shooter games: Reality, abstraction and shifting perspectives, *Altered States: transformations of perception, place, and performance*, Planetary Collegium, Liquid Press, University of Plymouth, Plymouth, UK. Retrieved from http://iam.tugraz.at/dollhouse/docs/ASCR2005_Maia_Engeli.pdf.

Förster, HV: 1993, *Wissen und Gewissen*, Suhrkamp Verlag, Frankfurt am Main.

Fry, B and Reas, C: 2005. Processing 1.0 (BETA). http://www.processing.org.

Guodong, L et al.: 2006b, A System for Analyzing and Indexing Human-Motion Databases, *SI3D 2006: Proceedings of the 2005 ACM SIGMOD international conference on Management of data*, Baltimore, Maryland, pp. 924-926.

Guodong, L et al.: 2006a, Human motion estimation from a reduced marker set, *SI3D '06: Proceedings of the 2006 symposium on Interactive 3D graphics and games*, pp. 35-42.

Gibson, W: 1984, *Neuromancer*, Harper Collins, London.

Hirschberg, U et al.: 2006, 3D Motion Tracking in Architecture – Turning Movement into Form – Emerging Uses of a New Technology, *Communicating Space(s) 24th eCAADe Conference Proceedings*, Volos, Greece, pp. 114-121.

Kaiser, P and Eshkar, S: 2000, Biped – digital projections for the state of Merce Cunningham.

Krämer, S: 2002, Verschwindet der Körper? *in* R Maresch and N Werber (eds), *Raum Wissen Macht*, Suhrkamp Verlag, Frankfurt am Main, pp. 49-68.

Löw, Martina: 2001, *Raumsoziologie.* Suhrkamp Verlag, Frankfurt am Main.

Maar, K: 2006, Korrespondenzen zwischen Tanz und Architektur *in* Geiger A, Hennecke S, Kempf C (eds), Imaginäre Architekturen, Reimer Verlag, Berlin, pp. 219-235.

Obermaier, K: 2004, Apparition *in* G Stocker and C Schöpf (eds), *Timeshift – Ars Electronica 2004.* Hatje Cantz Verlag, Ostfildern-Ruit, pp. 314-318.

Thiedecke, U (ed): 2004, *Soziologie des Cyberspace - Medien, Strukturen und Semantiken*, VS Verlag, Wiesbaden.

Featherstone, M and Burrows, R: 1995, *Cyberspace/Cyberbodies/Cyberpunk* – Cultures of Technological Embodiment. Sage Publications Ltd., London.

Pashley, H, Hays, JH and Liu, Y.: 2007, *2D Motion Texture*, Technical Report CMU-RI-TR-07-09, Robotics Institute, Carnegie Mellon University.

PUPPETEERING ARCHITECTURE

Experimenting with 3D gestural design interfaces

URS HIRSCHBERG, MARTIN FRÜHWIRTH
AND STEFAN ZEDLACHER
Graz University of Technology, Austria

Abstract. This paper documents and analyzes a set of experimental prototype applications for interaction with 3D modeling software through body movements. The documented applications are the result of two workshops dedicated to exploring the potential of 3D motion tracking technology in architectural design. The larger issue the work addresses is how one can create tools that allow us to bring our intuition and our talent for 'craft' into the digital design process and in how far tapping into the expressive powers of our body movements may provide new possibilities in this respect.

1. Introduction

It has often been pointed out that current CAAD systems are particularly weak in supporting the early stages of design (Knight et al. 2005; Gross 1996; Richens 1992). Among the most important (and perhaps most obvious) conclusions most researchers in this field came to is the need to make the interface as intuitive as possible, ideally to make it "disappear" altogether.

The goal put forward in many such projects was to come to a mode of interaction similar in ease as the traditional sketching. Sketching by some researchers is taken literally as the two-dimensional activity it is when one uses a pen or pencil on paper. A number of programs for conceptual design provide sophisticated sketch-recognition capabilities that enhance the sketching process (Schweikhardt and Gross 1998). Another branch of research takes the notion of sketching less literally. Their aim is to provide 3D modeling capabilities that can be used as simply and intuitively as a pencil without actually resorting to a pen as the input device (Kurmann 1995; Pratini 2001). Nevertheless, both approaches emphasize our capability to express ourselves through continuous (mouse-, resp. pencil-)

A Dong, A Vande Moere & JS Gero (eds), CAADFutures'07, 223–234.

movement rather than through typing keys on a keyboard or clicking buttons on a computer screen.

We may infer that an underlying premise of choosing the more fluid type of movements in the mentioned examples is that it allows us to interact with the computer in a more direct or more intuitive way. This notion can be taken further by exploring gestural interaction. Whereas in the sketching or mouse-movement paradigm the free movements are still limited to a plane, in gestural interaction, they can happen in space.

This paper documents and analyzes a set of experimental prototype applications for interaction with 3D modeling software through body movements. The documented applications are the result of two workshops dedicated to exploring the potential of 3D motion tracking technology in architectural design. The first workshop was conducted at our institute with a group of architecture students during one week in June 2006, the second with a different group in the winter semester 2006/07.

The larger issue the work addresses is how we can create tools that allow us to bring our intuition into the design process and in how far tapping into the expressive powers of our body movements might provide new possibilities in this respect.

2. Giving Form

> The apprehension and giving of form is a dynamic process, rather than a static code; giving form gives works their meaning. Of course the givers of form are the hands. […] Through the hand, workmanship involves execution, and expression involves workmanship. (McCullough 1996, p 8)

Computers are thought of as tools for the mind, rather than the hands (McCullough 1996, p. 17). But ever since graphical user interfaces were introduced, this has started to change. The notion that operating a computer has something to do with craft, as McCullough writes, is not outlandish. In fact it makes perfect sense. Homo faber, the species that makes things, has evolved to refine their talent for craft. And while manual labor is currently mostly thought of as a job that is not well paid, in the context of information technology manual labor can also be seen as a particularly rich and precise way of expressing ourselves and thus potentially transferring this rich information to a computer.

Current developments in computer interfaces, resp. in consumer electronics, certainly point in that direction: touch screens, the tablet PC, the Palm organizer, Apple's forthcoming iPhone – all replace the traditional buttons by smooth, continuous surfaces for user input. Conceptually the advantages are clear: the smooth surface that also doubles as a screen has much greater flexibility for user input. It can be used to process continuous strokes rather than just individual clicks, making it possible for the user to make more nuanced, personal input, such as handwritten notes or sketches.

Actually touch screens have been around for a long time and pen input, in the form of the light pen, was already used by the very first CAD pioneers (Sutherland 1963) and thus by far predates the mouse as an input device. But until recently these input technologies were confined to niche markets. One can only speculate about why they took so long in becoming more widespread. The main reason is probably that for the great majority of computer applications, mouse and keyboard are perfectly sufficient input devices. The average computer user has little need for the more nuanced and direct types of input. Therefore the market share of touch and sketch technologies has traditionally been marginal. And because in computing technologies it takes large numbers to drive down cost, they remained rather expensive.

Now it seems that this is starting to change. Quite possibly this change has been brought about by the sophistication of graphical user interfaces (GUI). Fluid transitions between different states of the screen have long been proven to make it easier for users to maintain a mental map of the screen content in their minds (Card et al. 1999, p. 30). More and more, today's interactive applications and graphical user interfaces are respecting this fact. Shunned as mere 'eye candy' by some purists, the popularity of these effects probably reflects a desire of our perceptual apparatus to see things behave in an analogue, life-like fashion. When there is 'life on the screen' (Turkle 1997), when interface elements resemble physical objects rather than abstract information as we manipulate them, we seem to enjoy dealing with them more. It is only natural, then, that there is also a desire to reciprocate these fluid graphical effects of the GUI on the input side. Thus the renewed interest in tablet or pen input doesn't come out of the blue. It is the logical consequence of our increasingly object oriented GUI metaphors. Current technological developments in this area, such as multi-touch interfaces (which are also advertised as part of the above mentioned fothcoming Apple iPhone) show this growing interest in more natural ways of human computer interaction and offer fascinating glimpses into unprecedented ways of working with computers (Han 2005).

As a perhaps unintended consequence of this quest for natural interaction, craft is back. The computer is more and more turning into a tool for both the mind and the hand.

If our analysis is correct we are currently witnessing a technology long in the making that is finally becoming mainstream and giving craft an unexpected comeback. But we can also look further into the future. Tablet and touch screen interfaces are a step towards more fluid interaction, but the development does not have to stop there. Our evolved bodily skills are not limited to sketching. Humans are good at doing things in three dimensions. To really take advantage of these skills our user interfaces have to be fully three dimensional as well. Arguably this is especially true for the three dimensional activity of giving form.

3. Background: Motion Tracking Technologies

In order to create three dimensional user interfaces and thereby bridge the gap between physical and virtual environments one needs to perform some sort of tracking of our body in space. Several technologies for tracking have been developed, including magnetic, mechanical, acoustic, inertial, optical and hybrid tracking (Bowman 2004). Among these, optical tracking systems currently reach the highest level of precision. This explains their widespread use in character animation as well as in medical applications. In both fields, sub-millimeter accuracy is needed to achieve the level of nuance and detail that has become standard practice.

The biggest disadvantage of optical systems is the problem with occlusion that can only be countered with a high redundancy of cameras, leading to the other major disadvantage: the rather high cost of the hardware. Another problem is that in order to track well, the field of vision of the cameras should be free of glare and reflections, limiting the types of environments such set-ups can be used in. Nevertheless, today's state of the art systems are typically rather simple and hassle-free to set up and use.

Besides speed and precision, their main advantage over most of the other mentioned technologies is that the user can be completely untethered from the computer, moving and behaving naturally (except for the markers they have to wear). For this reason optical motion tracking has been used in a number of artistic projects with dancers (Kaiser 2002). In the projects presented in this paper, a six camera VICON 3D motion tracking system was used in connection with the modeling and animation software Maya.

4. The Workshops

As we have described elsewhere (Hirschberg 2006) 3D motion tracking can be put to different uses in architecture. In the workshops described in this paper the goal was to find novel ways how one can interact with respectively give form to a virtual model. In the first one, which took place in June 2006, the topic of puppeteering was used. The second one was titled Formotion and addressed the topic of form through motion head-on.

4.1. PUPPETEERING ARCHITECTURE

When looking for new ways to apply a technology it is easy to get trapped in conventional ways of thinking. It is one thing to declare that giving form should happen in three dimensions and quite another to come up with concrete ideas of how this could be done in a meaningful way. In order to stay away from the common notions of computer aided design tools such as coordinate systems or object snap, the analogy to puppetry was chosen as a playful approach that put more emphasis on narrative than on the creation of form. This proved to be successful as many of the gestural interfaces the students produced contain rather novel interactive features.

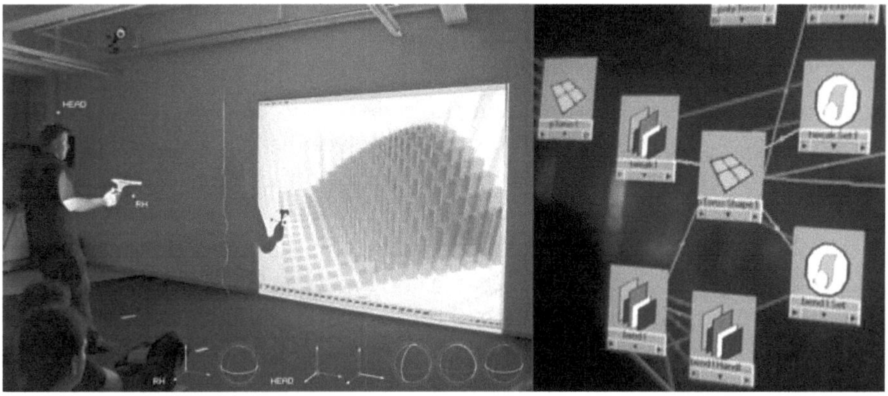

Figure 1. Project Student A: Interacting with a field of green cubes in different modes. Main control with object in right hand, switching of modes and adjusting parameters with head gestures (nodding, shaking); right: Linking of parameters and objects in the Maya hypergraph interface

Figure 2. Project Student A: sequence of interactions in different modes, switching of modes is controlled by nodding or shaking head

Technically the students developed their applications on the basis of an existing real-time interface between the VICON 3D motion tracking system and the modeling and animation software Maya, making use of the MEL scripting language.

The reference to puppeteering was used in the workshop as a way to give the work of the students a certain inspiration and direction while at the same time opening them up to new ways of conceiving of the interaction with a computer. The analogy was also appropriate as most students used just one object with markers to control their model, tying the X, Y, Z coordinates and the three angles by which the object's position is defined in space to various functions or properties in the modeling system.

Puppeteers can be seen as giving form to the movements and the interactions between the puppets they control. While puppetry per se has very little in common with the way architects tend to design (or for that matter sketch) spaces, what interested us was its narrative dimension. To control their puppets a puppeteer makes highly artificial and awkward movements, yet they are held together by the narrative of the play the puppets enact. Just so we wanted the students to steer clear of conventional approaches that tend to focus on individual gestures that trigger individual actions but rather focus on the overall sequence of events and the drama the movements create. Their final presentation was labeled as a performance rather than a presentation of their project. In fact it was only then that we brought the question into the discussion whether they thought that their puppeteering interface could also be used as a way to construct form.

4.2. RESULTS OF THE PUPPETEERING WORKSHOP

The workshop was designed as an open experiment. Figures 1 through 4 give some impression of the work produced. Some of the students' performances were very entertaining, though not everything worked as planned. Thus the above mentioned element of craft was clearly present: things happen live, one has to act at a certain moment, the skill of the operator was in some cases as important as the application.

Some interesting ideas the students came up with:

Mode Switching: Many projects support switching between different modes of interaction by some extreme movement: a high z-coordinate, so the operator would reach up high with their marker object, or an extreme angle, so they would turn the marker object upside down. In one project the switching was triggered by nodding or shaking of the head. This was meant to prevent unintentional mode-switches and usually worked reliably.

Two Marker Objects: Some students used two marker objects in parallel, thus potentially controlling twelve parameters at the same time. While interesting in their complexity, these projects were more confusing for an unexperienced user. Even when the second object was only used to control the interaction mode of the first one or the camera view, handling two marker objects at once still demanded a lot of concentration and was not exactly intuitive for first time users.

Accompaniment: The performance idea was taken literally by many students in that they chose some music as accompaniment. One student went even further in that he set his project performance both to a music score and to a keyframe animation. Thus the modeling environment to which he controlled his object was changing along with, yet independently of his actions. In a sense he had replaced the intentional mode-switching with a continuous loop of modes that merged into another.

When the projects were discussed as ways to design form rather than as virtual puppeteering environments, new questions and ideas came up. Rather than being permanently linked to a parameter with one's body, many

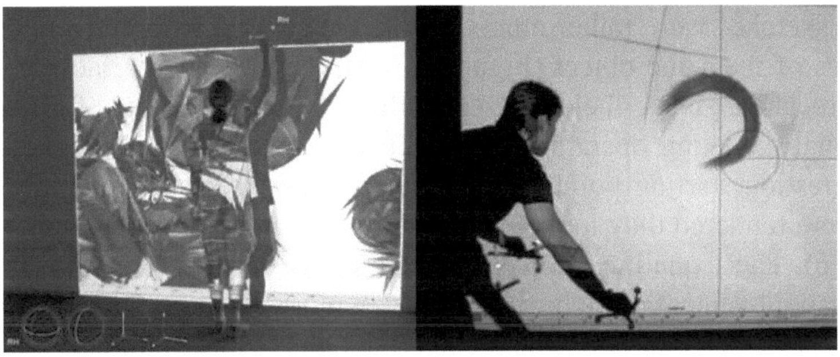

Figure 3. (left) Student B: controlling spin, size and edginess of space flowers; (right) Student C: The fight with the flying mustache – a dramatic confrontation

Figure 4. Student D: controlling a particle field with two hands. Student E: watering virtual flowers with one hand

expressed a desire to be able to grab and release objects, and thus to be able to move around the scene without influencing it.

Most students felt that controlling many parameters at once would be something that one would get better at with practice. But at this point nobody thought it would make sense to spend too much time learning to better work with their interaction patterns. They felt that in order to get people to practice with them, the logic of the 3D motion interface should be more forthcoming and intuitive to begin with.

4.3. FORMOTIONS

The title of the second workshop describes rather well what it was about: formotion can be read as the short version of form through motion, or formation by motion. The main difference to the first workshop was that students could use a head mounted display during their interaction with the virtual model. As a warm-up assignment, they were asked to draw a piece of furniture into space (Figure 5). As could have been expected, the resulting spatial sketches were rather clumsy. When compared with conventional 2D sketches of the same object (Figure 5, left), they revealed a lack of finesse and precision. Nevertheless, when they were processed further with additional modeling operations, these clumsy space drawings turned out to be interesting starting points and revealed some interesting qualities. Once they were rendered they looked very interesting and unique. (Figure 5, right; Figure 6). These qualities, however, had more to do with the intrinsic beauty of human movement (which we explored in more depth in: Hirschberg 2006) than with the fact that they were meant to be pieces of furniture.

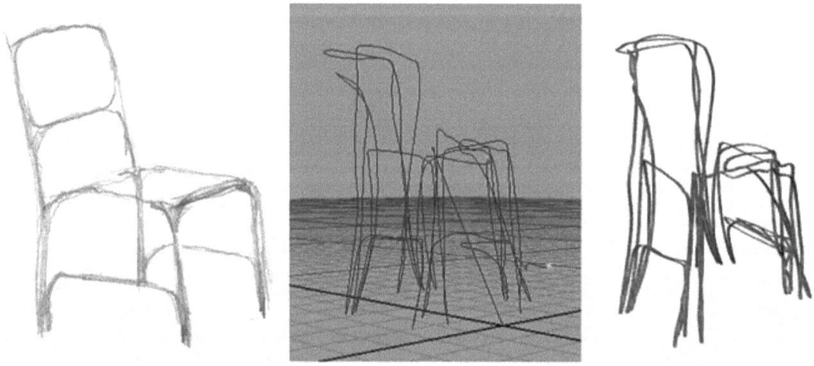

Figure 5. Freehand sketching into space. As a way to get to know the system, students tried to sketch a chair in space. Here shown as a handsketch (left) in the Maya modeling environment (middle) and as a rendering (right)

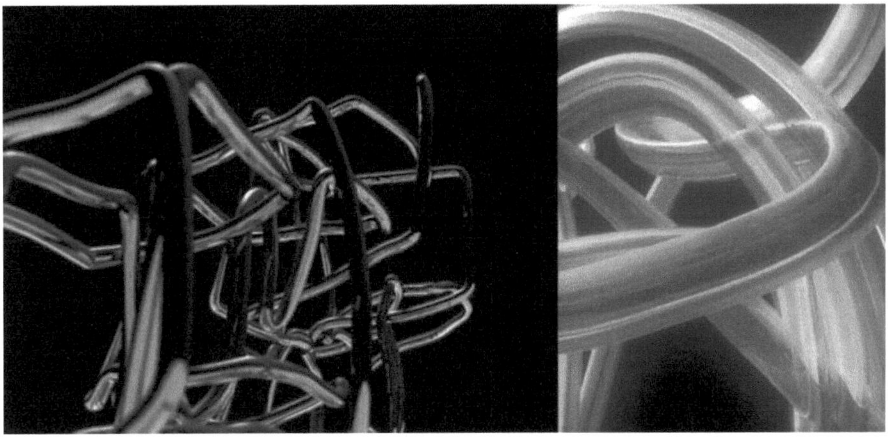

Figure 6. The space drawings of the furniture objects were developed further in Maya and revealed some surprising aesthetic qualities

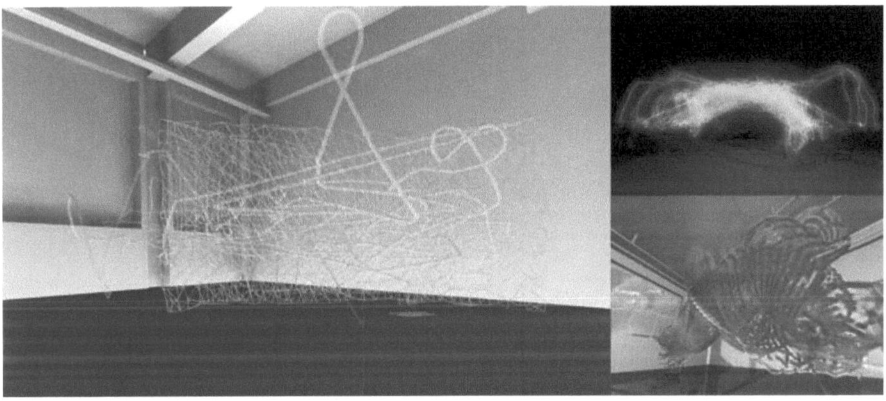

Figure 7. Augmented daydreaming: Using the virtual model of our lab as the setting, students had to come up with a scenario of how they could interact constructively with a virtual model

4.4. BEYOND SKETCHING

Some sort of sketching in space is probably the most obvious initial idea one might have about a 3d interface for a design tool. But despite their quirky esthetic qualities, the chair sketches suggest that, when operating in space, sketching might actually not be the most successful metaphor. This echoed some of the desires expressed at the end of the puppeteering workshop: that it wasn't nice to be permanently linked with a model. The ideas the students came up with instead were often inspired by less refined movements: pushing and pulling, blowing… It turned out that the dynamics engine of Maya provides some very effective modes of interaction, that the students experimented with in their Formotion projects.

One idea put forward by the teachers was to conceive of the role of the computer in these projects as enabling 'Augmented Daydreaming'. The immersive feeling of being able to physically walk around a virtual model and the possibility to interact with it in the soft and indirect ways the dynamics engine allows really brought out this feeling in the students. Of course it is very difficult to describe or convey the nature of such immersive, interactive experiences with static images. Yet they do give an idea of the variety of the works produced (Figure 7).

Beside the dreaminess, some projects also featured real inventions. One student differentiated between pushing and pulling by turning his hands around, thereby triggering the force field attached to his hand's position to change direction (Figure 8). This turned out to be very effective and was also immediately understandable for other users who picked up on it almost instantly.

Figure 8. Student G created an environment to move around boxes in space, differentiating between pushing and pulling by turning his hands 180 degrees, which proved to be a very successful gestural metaphor that people picked up easily

One student worked on spheres with a wind field, effectively shaping a soft, ephemeral object with a virtual blow dryer (Figure 9). There is something quirky about operating a virtual blow dryer, but as a way to define large, curvy shapes it seemed to be very practical. It reminded one of experiments in wind channels that are done in car design, with much less overhead, of course.

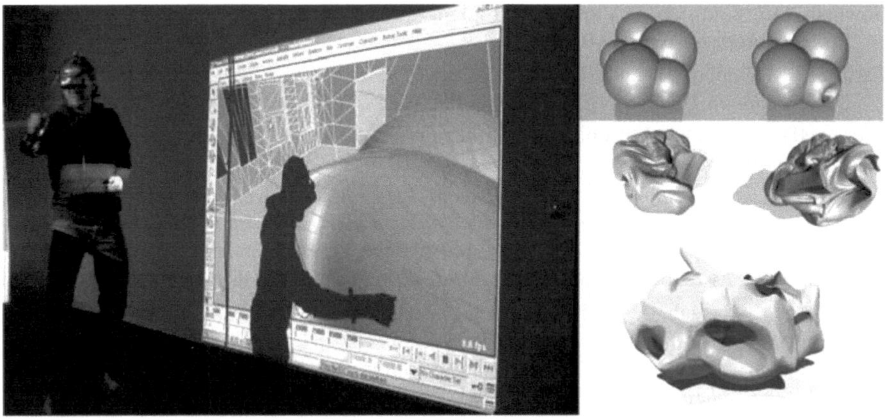

Figure 9. Student F shaping a soft, ephemeral object with a virtual blowdryer. On the right are different stages of the interaction: the initial arrangement of spheres, intermediate and final stages of different sessions

5. Conclusions

In this paper we described two workshops that explored 3D gestural interaction with virtual models, making use of an advanced optical tracking system. Our investigations are based on the assumption that the current trend towards continuous movement as input in human computer interaction will yield more intuitive interfaces and that eventually such interfaces will not be confined to a surface but take full advantage of our bodies' ability to move in space. The goal of the workshops was to experiment with these technical possibilities and thereby come to a clearer idea of how such gestural interfaces might eventually work.

Given the 'indirect' approach and the limited time of the workshops, the projects presented in this paper are obviously not meant to be understood as fully fledged gestural design tools. Nevertheless they provide some valuable insights. They show that by linking our movements with a modeling environment in intricate ways it is well possible to control many parameters at once, but that it is difficult to make this control intuitive. They also demonstrate how craft may become an important aspect of digital design again. They particularly seem to confirm the trend towards physical based behavior as a successful interaction metaphor for design: using a virtual blowdryer to shape an object was more successful than drawing an object with a line in space. In this way, the experiments we described are indicative of the potential of gestural interaction in design and provide ample reasons why this area should be explored further.

References

Bowman, DA, Kruijff E, LaViola, JJ and Poupyrev I: 2004, *3D user interfaces: Theory and Practice*, Addison Wesley, Boston.

Card, SK, Mackinlay, JD and Shneiderman, B: 1999, *Readings in Information Visualization. Using Vision to Think,* Morgan Kaufman Publishers, Academic Press, San Diego.

Gross, MD: 1996, The electronic cocktail napkin – working with diagrams, *Design Studies* **17**(1): 53-69.

Han, J: 2006, *demonstrates—for the first time publicly—his intuitive, "interface-free," touch-driven computer screen, which can be manipulated intuitively with the fingertips, and responds to varying levels of pressure*. Recorded at the TED conference in February 2006 in Monterey, CA. Retrieved from http://www.ted.com/tedtalks/tedtalksplayer.cfm?key=j_han.

Hirschberg, U, Sayegh, A, Frühwirth, M and Zedlacher, S: 2006, *3D Motion Tracking in Architecture: Turning Movement into Form – Emerging Uses of a New Technology* in V Bourdakis and D Charitos (eds), *Communicating Space(s), Proceedings of the 24th ECAADE Conference*, Volos, pp. 114-121.

Kaiser, P: 2002, Frequently Pondered Questions, *in* J Mitoma (ed), *Envisioning Dance on Film and Video*, Routledge, London, pp. 108-113.

Knight, M, Dokonal W, Brown A and Hannibal C: 2005, *Contemporary Digital Techniques in the Early Stages of Design, CAADFutures2005*, Vienna, pp. 165-174.

Kurmann, D: 1995, Sculptor – A Tool for Intuitive Architectural Design, *Sixth International Conference on Computer-Aided Architectural Design Futures*, Singapore, pp. 323-330.

McCullough, M: 1996, *Abstracting craft: the practiced digital hand,* MIT Press, Cambridge.

Pratini, E: 2001, New Approaches to 3D Gestural Modeling – The 3D SketchMaker Project, *Architectural Information Management [19th eCAADe Conference Proceedings]*, Helsinki, pp. 466-471.

Richens, P: 1992, The Next Ten Years, *in* F Penz (ed), *Computers in Architecture*, Longman, Harlow, Essex, England.

Schweikhardt, E and Gross, M: 1998, Digital Clay: Deriving Digital Models from Freehand Sketches, *Digital Design Studios: Do Computers Make a Difference? ACADIA Conference Proceedings*, Québec, pp. 202-211

Sutherland, I: 1963, *Sketchpad: A man-machine graphical communication system*, PhD Thesis, Massachusetts Institute of Technology. Retrieved from http://www.cl.cam.ac.uk/techreports/UCAM-CL-TR-574.pdf.

Turkle, S: 1997, Life on the Screen: Identity in the Age of the Internet, Touchstone, New York.

BECOMING LOGICAL

PARAMETRIC DESIGNING IN ARCHITECTURE

A parametric design studio

MARC AUREL SCHNABEL
University of Sydney, Australia

Abstract. Parametric design techniques offer obvious advantages for engineering and manufacturing processes, now architects emerge to apply these methods in their creation of design suggesting solutions at an earlier stage of the process. Through the coupling of architectural design with parametric modelling methods, the paper presents novel techniques that enhance architects' contribution to building processes based on parametric design creation. This allows a deeper comprehension of the design objectives and aids designers in their decisions to find solutions.

1. Parameters in Design Studios

Architectural design studios are an essential learning experience for architectural students. Their traditions and proceedings are well established. These studios are, additionally, informed and supplemented by courses and seminars, which can feed into their learning outcomes. Studios go beyond pure skill training and require reflection upon, and the creation of, knowledge. There can be, however, a gap between skills training and the application of knowledge within the studio context. At the final presentation of the work, students my not be able to identify how they arrived to their solution and what were the individual contributors that inform about the design.

This tension is also apparent in digital media courses. These present the underlying concepts of architectural design using digital communication tools, but also have to provide training in software skills and other technical subjects (Kvan 2004a). The integration of digital media courses into design studio curricula often fails, because the compound acquisition of skills prevents a deep exploration of design and the theoretical aspects involved. Participants can employ digital media tools within a studio context only long

A Dong, A Vande Moere & JS Gero (eds), CAADFutures'07, 237–250.

after they have learned subject matters and acquired proficiency in their skills. By then, however, the studio may consider these skills no longer valid.

A dilemma of semester-based teaching is that students reach their highest level of skills and experience at the end of a term, after which they leave for their break and are therefore unable to apply their knowledge immediately. At the beginning of the next following term, however, the knowledge and skills they had gained earlier are likely to be either inactive or not employed, and learning foci may have shifted to other aims.

The architectural design studio presented here addressed these issues by integrating the learning experience from the beginning by focusing on parameters that create or inform about the design. The objective of this 'parametric designing' was to allow participants to understand the impact each step and variable has on the design and follow the impact it has onto the project. Participants developed and communicated their understanding of architectural design parameters by utilising their skills training within the design-studio environment. Because of this, students began to think about design problems in different ways.

The studio explored design by basing it on parameters. In order to build up a philosophy around parametric dependencies and relationships, the participants used digital tools that allowed them to create and express their designs. With these tools, users can develop expertise to engage creatively in design. Typically, architects employ such tools only for visualisations, or after the designs are completed, in order to feed them into the construction and manufacturing processes.

Parametric applications have inherited two crucial elements. These are that all entities start with a point in space and allow the study of architectural conditions in a three-dimensional environment, rather than the commonly used two-dimensional or layering techniques. And that the underlying concept of parametric modelling is based on data, variables, and their relationship to other entities, which can then respond to variations of input data.

Participants were able to employ digital media skills early in the studio experience and expand on their understanding and communication of design issues from there. The studio built upon design studios where participants explored design methods and tools beyond their original definitions and perceived limits (Schnabel et al. 2004).

2. Parameters in Architecture

The exploration of the relationship between human beings and the natural world, and the subsequent implications of interactions between them, has deep roots in our social and cultural understanding of society. Cities, therefore, are direct reflections of their inhabitants, as their architectural expressions directly influence the living conditions of their people. In recent practice, architects have designed and described buildings through the means of master plans, or descriptions of picture-perfect, complete cities in which change was not part of the picture. A few, however, have tried different approaches to communicate architecture.

In their design for Beijing's Soho Shang-Du buildings, LAB Architecture Studio translated planning codes into series of parametric design rules (Figure 1). As a result, the outcome both complies with and confounds the rigid regulations (Davidson, 2006). In other words the architects did not prescribe a fixed gestalt, but on a set of rules and instructions that inform about and can generate the desired outcome. This allows a reaction on a variety of site-specific variables that can be modified according to the need.

Figure 1. Soho Shang Du, Beijing, by LAB Architects 2002

A design studio project at the Technical University of Eindhoven employed a similar methodology. Students responded to functionalism and economic cost-effectiveness of production processes in Sao Paulo's favela neighbourhoods by creating parameters from building blocks as well as architectural and urban contexts (Vanderfeesten and de Vries, 2005). This resulted in design a set of design proposals that can react to changing condition of the favela without loosing the influence of the architects design guidelines.

In the 1960s and early 1970s, Archigram already presented a similar idea. Reacting against the permanence of houses in what it called the "Plug-in City" (Figure 2), it proposed ever-changing units adaptable to different social and economic conditions (Karakiewicz 2004A). Despite that this design proposal did not develop any further than its conceptual stage, it contrasts the common design practice that Le Corbusier describes as non-intelligent building machines. These machines cannot think, and are therefore unable to adapt to change.

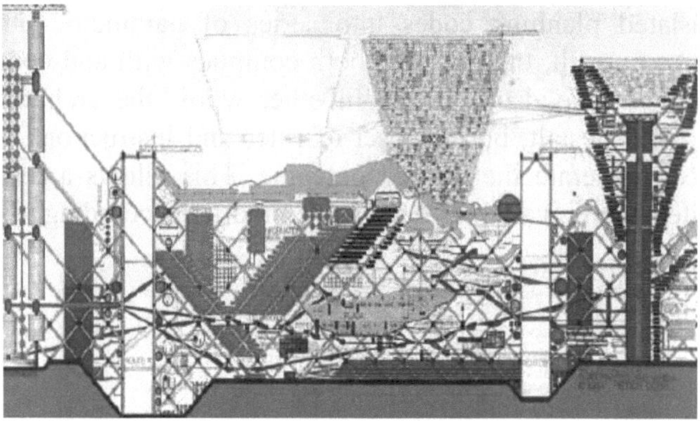

Figure 2. Archigram's Plug-In City 1962-1964

Interestingly, Pieter Bruegel painted in the sixteenth century a representation of the Tower of Babel as building that is constantly redefining its needs, as it grows larger and more complex (Figure 3). The painting depicts a tower piercing the clouds, showing all the problems then associated with cities, buildings and life within and the constant change and reaction to new situations during the process of building.

Figure 3. Pieter Bruegel (1525/30-1569) *Tower of Babel* at Kunsthistorisches Museum, Vienna

These samples illustrate the constant need for architecture to adapt and react to a variety of parameters that are driven by its use and context.

The gap between the architectural design conceptions and the translation of these designs into the real built environment can be addressed differently by an intersection of process and outcome. Parametric design techniques suggest controllable and adaptable solutions at an earlier stage of the process that react to the given situations and the outcomes.

3. Parametric Architectural Design Studio

A building or architecture in general can be expressed and specified in a variety of ways. Commonly, drawings describe geometric properties that can explain, depict, and guide the construction of buildings or streets. Alternatively, performance specifications can describe observed behaviours. It is also possible to describe properties as relationships between entities. Spreadsheets, for instance, specify the value of each cell as the result of calculations involving other cell entries.

These calculations or descriptions do not have to be explicit. Responsive materials change their properties in reaction to the conditions around them. A thermostat senses air temperature and controls the flow of electric current, and hence the temperature of the air supplied. Using such techniques, artists have created reactive sculptures and architects have made sentient spaces that react to their occupants or other relevant factors. Streetlights turn on if light levels fall below a threshold; traffic flow can be regulated according to need; walls can move as users change location.

Links to a variety of data can be established and subsequently serve as the bases to generate geometric forms using parametric design tools. When designing spaces, it is usual to collect some data of the type of architectural qualities desired. These are then, for example, translated into master plans, which are themselves specific spatial descriptions. Performance requirements for spaces can then be written, linking the description of the architecture to experiential, financial, environmental, or other factors (Picon 1997).

Design studios mimic the typical working processes of the architectural profession and are the essential learning experience for architects. However, little or no research exists that examines or validates the claim that the framing of design creation using parametric methods enhances the process (Schnabel et al. 2004). This studio, therefore, couples parametric methodologies within the creation of architectural design, ultimately reframing the question and proposing new answers and methods of design thinking.

Participants in this study solved a typical architectural design problem using applications that focused on the parametric dependencies of spatial perception, fabrication, and form finding. Their creation and exchange of ideas followed the rules of a design studio within a cyclical design-exploration paradigm (Schnabel and Kvan 2002). This design-cycle had the framing of the design question at its centre (Gao and Kvan 2004), while taking full advantage of available building information modelling technologies to explore it. This approach tested the limitations set by conventional, design-only methods. The cognitive aspects of the design creation and its relationship to parametric design methods operated as an influential factor for understanding the perception, framing, and creation of spatial knowledge within architectural design.

The studio then explored the design processes by using sets of variables and series of relations to question, create, and define the form and function of the resulting designs. Thus, it examined interaction techniques between the design intent, its framing of the design problem, and its subsequent creation, while at the same time establishing a connection to building information models. Participants engaged in a collaborative architectural design studio involving the creation and fabrication of architectural spaces. This formed the basis for a transfer of knowledge to the larger context of the profession and building industries (Riese and Simmons 2004).

The studio took a distinctive neighbourhood within the urban context of Sydney as its base of exploration. Within this suburb, a mix of residential, public and commercial buildings can be found: a medium dense area offering a variety of architectural languages.

Driven by a fast growing population, an architectural strategy that steers further development was sought. Sydney's scale, its growth through immigration and the need for new housing have an impact on its inhabitants' sense of place and sense of community. Earlier urban planning did not anticipate the changes that arose over years of population growth. A new strategy for development could address these issues, creating a new identity for the place and the city itself (Forrest et al. 2002).

The design studio examined a site with typical characteristics and architectural requirements. Located at the upper riverbanks of the Parramatta River, next to parkland, cultural, office and residential buildings, the site offered a great challenge for an architectural proposal. River, city, work and living had to be addressed and responded to.

4. Parameters of the Design Studio

To allow the students both to acquire skills and training within their studio and to apply this knowledge to their design, the studio had an integrated digital media component that addressed parametric modelling in architectural design. The studio was one of the required design studios of the postgraduate architectural programme at the University of Sydney.

Two groups of each fifteen students elected to join this studio, which was supervised by two design teachers and one architectural consultant in digital media. The studio was structured into four phases that related to and built upon each other. The aim was to acquire and integrate parametric design knowledge and to use it as the base of the design creation of their architectural proposal. This resulted that the final design could be modified and manipulated based on the parameters and their dependencies. This allowed a deeper understanding of the design process and outcome as well as the reaction of the proposal with the various influences of the environment.

4.1. CREATION OF PARAMETERS

The project's first component included the collection and understanding of data that arrived from the site. In order not to overcomplicate the issues, the tutors asked the students during this first stage to limit themselves to investigating of two parameters. This allowed focusing on the selection of the hierarchical parameters that the students believed would influence their building proposal or their site's perception the most.

The parameters they chose informed them about the variables of their guiding design rules and provided them a description based on dependencies and interconnected relationships of relevant information. The chosen parameters helped the students to understand their design what impact certain variables may have on a design strategy. This component concluded after two weeks with presentations of data, parameters, and individual interpretations of the site.

4.2. LEARNING OF PARAMETERS

The programme's second component focused on the understanding and creation of parametric concepts and the acquisition of design-application skills that allow rule-based three-dimensional design. Participants were trained intensively during studio time in the use of Digital Project ™ (2004). This software allows users not only to create three-dimensional models, but also to establish rules, create parameters and their dependencies on a variety of entities.

Parametric functions require a different understanding of the conceptual approaches to design. Creating rules and dependencies, which then create the design, involved the students in a higher level of problem framing and definition of the concept of design. It allowed the visualisation and modelling of highly complex forms that may result from non-traditional design data, such as noise data or spatial requirements.

The students used their own parametric and rule-based design analyses from the first component and subsequently studied the use and operation of the software, the creation of rules, and parametric and generative design.

During this phase, they used the time allocated to the design studio to establish a basic understanding of the software in its relationship to the design intent developed during the first phase. After three weeks of interactive digital media training, the students reached an advanced level of skills that enabled them to use the parametric software as a tool for the creation of their own designs.

4.3. DESIGNING OF PARAMETERS

The programme's third component, scheduled for seven weeks, concentrated on design creation, reflection, and the communication of architectural design proposals. Using the data of the first component and the skills of the second, the students then started to establish and visualise their designs in three-dimensional forms that created spatial expressions of their findings and explorations.

Due to the emphasis onto parameters, the studio was in particular interested in describing a building form by creating dependencies of parameters that defined the relationship of data to architectural expressions. With the use of a parametric modeller, it was easy to create geometric entities, relate these solids and voids. This method made it obvious to learn about the design and explore alternatives by manipulating the parameters, variables and rules.

4.4. MERGING OF PARAMETERS

The programme's concluding component brought together the various aspects and results of the earlier three modules. Within two weeks, the students merged their individual designs into larger cluster files. This synthesis created compound descriptions and dependencies that were highly complex and interrelated, yet both the content as well as the tool allowed seamless communication to a larger audience by using describing the rules and parameters. This phase created a design with shared authorship of all participants and allowed the students to study and understand the complexity and the interrelationships of architectural designing that they normally would have been unable to perceive immediately. The change of a single variable modified the whole design. Participants understood therefore the complex dependencies that one variable has in a large building and the impact in can have on the design.

5. Parametric Design Solutions

The students had already acquired the highest level of skills in using a specific tool within the first half of the semester. This enabled them to employ the tool as an amplifier to generate their design. Subsequently, they were not limited by their knowledge or level of skills in order to be able to create their designs.

The students produced a variety of individual design proposals as well as one large design-cluster. They created rules and parameters that allowed complex and interrelating designs to emerge. These representations, however, could not be communicated using traditional architectural design methods or tools.

For example, one proposal related street lighting, neon-signs and display-windows with human activity around the building site (Figure 4). These parameters provided the engaging surface for the building mass. Subsequently they controlled the use, orientation and appearance of the building. The author took references to Japanese inner cities, where innovative ways of spaces are created by the means of lights, advertising and projections. Void, volume and density is controlled and created by the rhythm and intensity of lights. The student transferred this concept into parameters, which redefined the spatial understanding of the site and used these variables to create an architectural proposal.

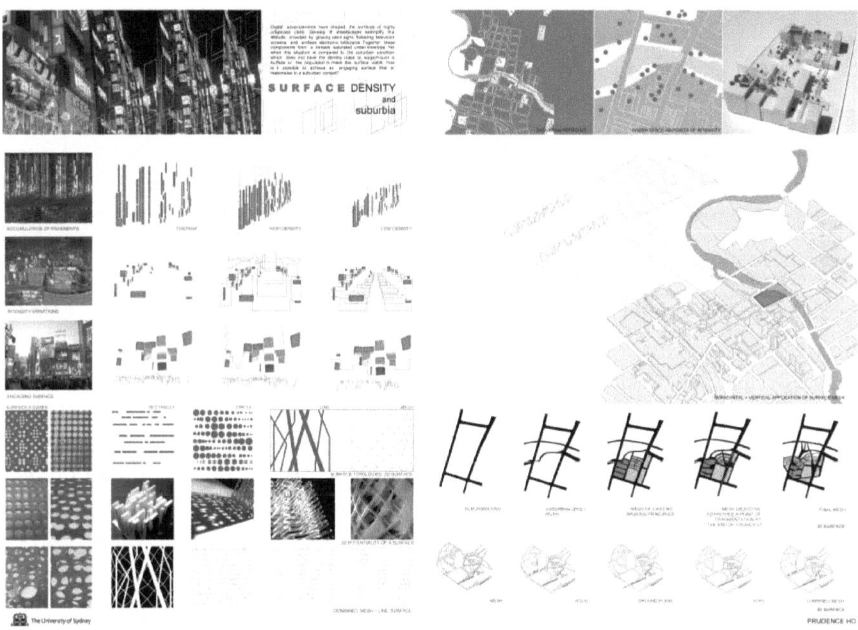

Figure 4. Prudence Ho: landscapes

Another solution explored biological growth models based on Lindenmayer's system fields (Figure 5). It explores the possibilities that a topological approach to designing with a parametric tool will yield an emergent architecture that is governed by a bottom-up hierarchy. Topological forms created a variety of physical and programmatic instantiations. The author had however, difficulties to translate the theoretical aspects of his parametric design studies into a buildable and inhabitable form. He acknowledged that he would require more time to become fluent with this novel approach to design. Therefore, he presented his work in two stages, the theoretical and the practical. Figure 5 illustrates the process of analysis and theory on the left side and the translation into a workable build form on the right.

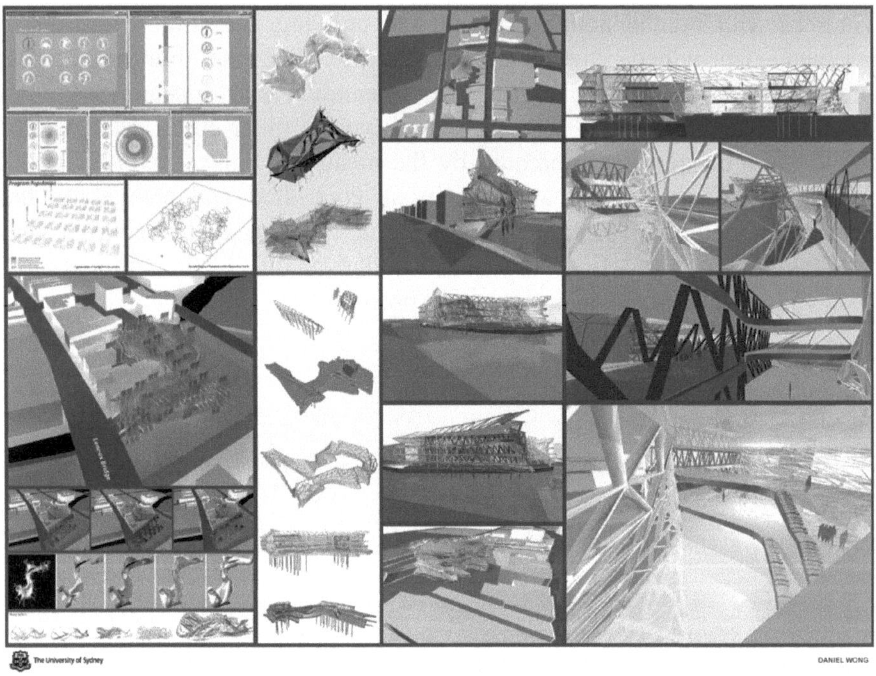

Figure 5. Daniel Wong: Western Sydney Virtual Offices

Other results used parameters that related to the relationships between people and attraction to spaces with responsive structures. Students created self-opening canopies that reacted to people activities, ferry schedules, weather conditions and the possibilities to collect rainwater to provide a comfortable environment in all conditions.

In the studio's fourth component, the students presented in-depth clusters of multifaceted architectural design proposals for the site. They demonstrated a high level of thinking processes resulting in the generation of compound rules and dependencies that finally create the architectural design schemes. Each student contributed simultaneously to create a variety of design proposals. The participants gained a high level of expertise with digital parametric tools as part of their development at the studio, and used this knowledge to design parametrically. The outcome clearly showed that thinking, learning and creating within parametric designing requires a novel and deeper understanding of the overall design goal and its anticipated outcome. This differs from design that deals with one problem at a time, regardless of its dependencies. The studio allowed participants to learn about designing and problem framing. They were able to theorise and reflect on design creation for this and other design tasks.

6. Discussion

With the development of various digital tools, designing in layers became popular, allowing architects to deal with problems that are more complex, with each different layer playing an equally important role. It allowed dealing with problems one at a time. Problems that are more complex were divided into separate issues and dealt with one by one. Parametric design opens up a novel set of opportunities. It enables architects to study causes of problems and their relationships to, and dependencies on, other elements directly.

This shift of design thinking and creation allows for spaces that accommodate change, diversity, and varied human activities without specifying particular functions. Additionally, such designs can provide for unpredictable events in connection with an overall architectural framework. Architecture can respond to unplanned changes and their resulting consequences. The outcomes of this design studio show that parametric dependencies allow still for a level of ambiguity that is required in creative processes.

One objective of the studio was to frame an intellectual research question that created links to data to generate form. The more interesting outcomes result from the ability to redefine and reframe the problems themselves by stepping out of preconceptions based on experience and exploring sets of unpredictable answers.

Preconceptions based on experience influenced previous methods of architectural design. Diagramming is an attempt by architects to allow for the reinterpretation of defined problems. In a certain way, parametric design tools do similar things, yet they act at a higher level of the problem framing. The establishment of meta-rules has instituted a form of problem framing that demands the reference of one problem or parameter with other ones.

The examples of the parametric design studio illustrate how non-linear design processes and the re-representation of ideas can lead to architectural expressions that differ from conventional approaches to design due to their different nature of design creation. The exploration of the gestalt can enhance the understanding of spatial issues and lead to meaningful and responsive architectural descriptions. Despite three-dimensional representations of an architectural space being only a medium through which to aid in the understanding and communication of spatial arrangements, the designers' comprehension of complex spatial qualities was enhanced by the re-representation by a parametric medium. The novel aspect of this studio work was the engagement of the process of translation itself as a creative act.

7. Conclusions

The parametric design studio presented in this paper addressed computational concepts of architectural designing that influence the recent development of architectural production. This studio exercise explored innovative methods of architectural expression, form finding, and communication, developing unconventional solutions. It coupled the studio-learning environment with an in-depth digital media assignment in order to close the gap between acquisition of skills and the reflection of knowledge, as well as to explore new avenues of framing and integrating compound design issues.

The use of digital parametric tools allowed the participants to design within an environment based on rules and generative descriptions. This amplified their design understanding and learning outcomes. The students connected their knowledge with their ambition to create their own design proposals.

The synthesis of all individual projects removed the students from individual ownership of their designs, but allowed them to reflect on both their own and their colleagues' designs as a complete cluster of contributions (Kvan 2004b). This related to earlier research into design studios based on the same principle, in which media were applied outside their normal pre-described purposes, and innovative design methods were deployed by interplaying digital media and design explorations (Schnabel et al. 2004).

With the employment of parametric software that allowed students to experience the dependencies and rules of the various individual contributions spatially, as well as the overall common proposals, the design could be communicated using physical and digital models and representations. The generated design data could then be linked in a variety of ways to extract or generate new geometric forms and understandings. These descriptions could then be used directly in the manufacture of objects by means of, for example, digitally controlled devices (Seichter and Schnabel, 2005).

Each of the components was an essential part of the design creation. They addressed and expressed certain aspects of the process. A holistic discussion about design, form, function, and development was established, which is significant not only within architectural education, but also in all other dialogues involving spatial representations. Following the tradition of artists and designers, participants have pushed creativity to new definitions of both their designs themselves and of their cultural contexts.

Acknowledgements

The author expresses gratitude to all the participants of the Open Design Studio at the Faculty of Architecture, Design and Planning at the University of Sydney, for their contributions and enthusiasm during 2006/07, and to Justyna Karakiewicz for her support and advice. Financial aid came from Research and Development Scheme of the University of Sydney.

References

Davidson, P: 2006, The Regular Complex in *NSK Wolfram Science Conference*, Washington, DC, 16-18 June, http://www.wolframscience.com/conference/2006/presentations/davidson.html.

Digital Project™: 2004, Gehry Technologies, 12541-A Beatrice Street, Los Angeles, California, USA, http://www.gehrytechnologies.com.

Forrest, R, La Grange, A and Yip, N-m: 2002, Neighbourhood in a High Rise, High Density City: Some Observations on Contemporary Hong Kong, *in* ESRC Centre for Neighbourhood Research ESRC Centre for Neighbourhood Research, http://www.bristol.ac.uk/sps/cnrpaperspdf/cnr2pap.pdf

Gao, S and Kvan, T: 2004, An Analysis of Problem Framing in Multiple Settings, *in* J Gero (ed) *Design Computing and Cognition '04*, Kluwer Academic Publishers, Dordrecht, pp. 117-134.

Karakiewicz, J: 2004A, City as a Megastructure, *in* M Jenks (ed), *Future Forms for Sustainable Cities* Oxford University Press, Oxford.

Karakiewicz, J: 2004B, Sustainable High-Density Environment *in* N Marchettini, CA Brebbia, E Tiezzi and LC Wdahwa (eds), *The Sustainable City III*, WIT Press, Siena, pp. 21-30.

Kvan, T: 2004b, Collaborative Design: What Is It?, *Automation in Construction* **9**(4): 409-415.

Kvan, T: 2004a, Reasons to Stop Teaching CAAD *in* M-L Chiu (ed), *Digital Design Education*, Garden City Publishing, Taipei, Taiwan, pp. 66-81.

Picon, A: 1997, Les Annales De La Recherche Urbaine, *Le Temps du cyborg dans la ville territoire*, **77**, 72-77.

Riese, M and Simmons M: 2004, The Glass Office - SCL Office and Showroom in Brisbane, Australia, *Fabrication: Examining the Digital Practice of Architecture*, ACADIA & AIA Technology in Architectural Practice Knowledge Community, Cambridge, Ontario, pp. 28-33.

Schnabel, MA and Kvan, T: 2002, Design, Communication & Collaboration in Immersive Virtual Environments, *International Journal of Design Computing (IJDC)*, Special Issue on Designing Virtual Worlds, **4**, www.arch.usyd.edu.au/kcdc/journal/vol4/schnabel

Schnabel, MA, Kvan, T, Kuan, SKS and Li, W: 2004, 3D Crossover: Exploring - Objets Digitalise, *International Journal of Architectural Computing (IJAC)* **2**(4): 475-490.

Seichter, H and Schnabel, MA: 2005, Digital and Tangible Sensation: An Augmented Reality Urban Design Studio, *in* A Bhatt (ed), *Tenth International Conference on Computer Aided Architectural Design Research in Asia*, CAADRIA, New Delhi, India, pp. 193-202.

Vanderfeesten, E and de Vries, B: 2005, Confection for the Masses in a Parametric Design of a Modular Favela Structure, *in* K Oosterhuis and L Feirass (eds), *Game Set and Match II*, Episode Publishers, Rotterdam, pp. 306-312.

SPATIAL SIMILARITY METRICS

Graph theoretic distance measurement and floor plan abstraction

THOMAS GRASL AND ATHANASSIOS ECONOMOU
Georgia Institute of Technology, USA

Abstract. Comparing space allocation programs computationally is a resource intensive task. This paper introduces a method which reduces the complexity of floor plan graphs to facilitate the problem. In a first first step the nodes are labeled according to a laid out classification scheme. This in its own right reduces the complexity of the comparison by introducing more diversity among the nodes. Subsequently the graph can be coarsened in several steps based on the category information. This does not only further reduce the necessary computation, but can also offer a visualization of and additional insight into the essential structure of the space allocation program at hand.

1. Introduction

Analyzing architectural composition and concluding on the expected performance has always called for systematic and reproducible methods. The translation of the architectural plan into a less ambiguous representation in form of a graph was the first step in creating a whole toolbox of methods following this ambition (March and Steadman 1974). Not only do graphs represent architectural layouts in a lean and computable manner, one can also take advantage of proven methods from a broad area of research in graph and network theory.

The computational and algorithmic complexity of many methods in these areas has often restricted their use for applications in the field of architecture. New algorithmic and electronic developments are however continuously extending the possibilities in this area of research.

The work presented in this paper modifies the graph theoretic methods of multilevel graph manipulation (Karypis and Kumar 1995) and error-tolerant graph matching (Bunke and Allermann 1983) to analyze buildings with complex space allocation programs. The corpus of buildings, that is used

A Dong, A Vande Moere & JS Gero (eds), CAADFutures'07, 251–263.

here to test the methodology and the application, consists of the federal Courthouses built since 1990. These buildings are complex structures, conceived as sorting machines, which are organized around explicit functional requirements.

The wider research project on the description and evaluation of new federal Courthouses has been supported by the GSA and the US Courts. The specific work presented here utilizes a graph representation of the courthouse plans to arrive at a distance measure for space allocation programs. Subsequently the intention is to expand the work into the foundations of a systematic theory on the typology of federal Courthouses.

Section 2 introduces the collection of methods used to arrive at the similarity metric. The problem of deriving the graph from the plan is discussed and an approach to facilitate computation through node labeling is introduced. The background to both the graph collapsing and the distance metric are explained before finally stepping through the implemented algorithm.

Section 3 briefly discusses the real world application for analyzing courthouses. This work is currently in progress and advancements are made continuously. Some findings from the first iterations are however discussed and more is soon to follow.

Finally, the infamous future work section describes some work currently being implemented and also an extended set of possibilities left open for the time being.

2. Method

The following section discusses how to arrive at the distance measure between two space allocation programs. Once the graph is created a method to collapse adjacent and similar nodes is introduced to enable comparison of the graph on various levels of coarseness, thereby enabling distance measures which are not dominated by minor differences in spatial composition, but which capture essential typological similarity. All graph computations are illustrated on the simple pictorial example shown in Figure 1, a floor plan taken from the work on Palladio by Stiny and Mitchell (1978).

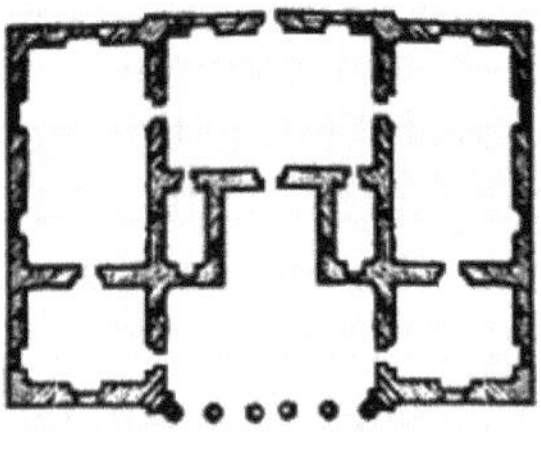

Figure 1. A floor plan in the Palladian style (Stiny and Mitchell)

2.1. DERIVING THE GRAPH

In order to represent floor plans as graphs the method described by Steadman (1976) was adopted. Generally it can be said that areas are mapped to nodes and relations between these areas are mapped to edges.

Any part of the floor plan may be considered to be an area represented in the graph (Figure 2); typically areas are defined by clearly denoted boundaries in the representation of the floor plan. It must however be realized that, the recognition of areas is not always a trivial task; if clear boundaries are not present it is often a matter of interpretation. Where does the entrance hall end and the corridor begin? A set of rules must be defined for each research project in order to resolve such issues consistently. Several methods to resolve this dilemma have been proposed, the most frequently adopted solution being the convex partition (Berg et al. 2000; Hillier et al. 1984).

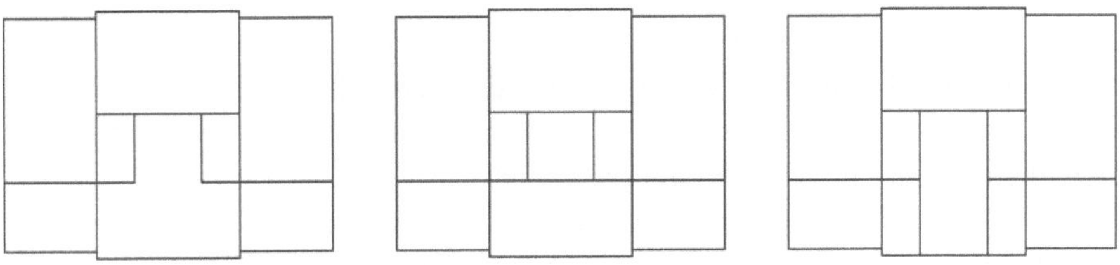

(a) (b) (c)

Figure 2. Alternative diagrammatic representations of the floor plan of figure 1. a) 8 areas b) 9 areas; c) 10 areas

Any relation between areas may be considered as a relation represented in the graph; adjacency (Figure 3-c) is the most frequently represented relationship. Steadman describes adjacency as sharing some length of wall in common.

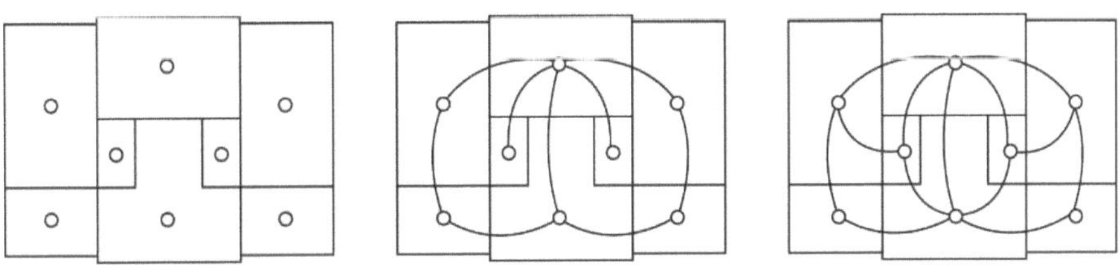

(a) (b) (c)

Figure 3. Alternative graph representations of the diagram of figure 2(a). a) Null graph; b) Accessibility graph; c) Adjacency graph. All graphs depict relations of areas within the plan and not with its carrier space

Thereby, whether the complete set of adjacencies or only a subset thereof is used is a matter of interpretation and will most likely be dictated by the nature of the problem being investigated. One may be interested only in adjacencies which additionally allow for circulation (Figure 3-b), or on the extreme, in no relations at all (Figure 3-a).

The increasing use of building information models, and hence appropriate space information, will lead to future projects which allow for automated graph generation. This of course does not eliminate the necessity to follow conventions; it merely shifts the responsibility to the creator of the building information model.

2.2. AREA CATEGORIZATION

Each node is assigned a category label which is compiled from a combination of access level, area function and unique identification. The root element to which all nodes are assigned is the generic area category. Subsequently nodes are divided according to their affiliation to the various subcategories (Figure 4). The first level represents the access zones, which can be seen as top level separator of the various user flows. Airport terminals may distinguish between public, passenger, staff and secure zones, whereas hospitals may chose to differ between staff, patient and public areas. Other building typologies may be categorized in similar ways.

The second and third levels of category are based on functional distinctions and should be configured in such a way as to allow grouping of similar areas. It will later become evident, that the sooner a differentiation between two adjacent areas occurs, the less likely it is that these areas will ever unite and the greater the impact will be on the similarity measure.

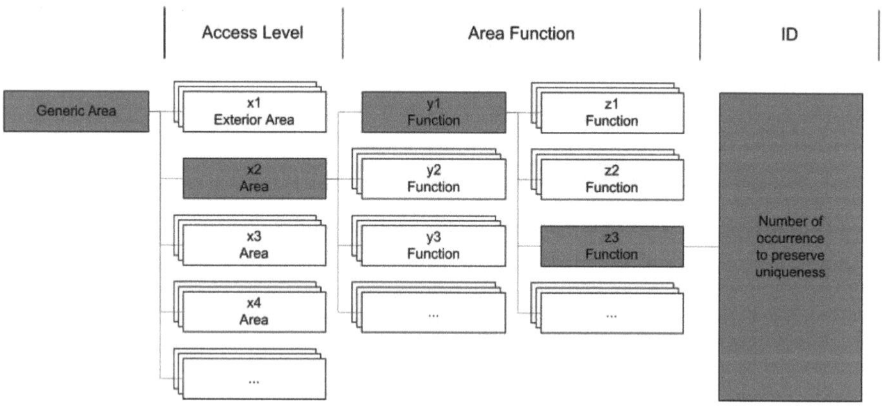

Figure 4. General structure of a category tree. The numbers of columns and rows of the data structure can be increased as desired

Finally, in order to systematically distinguish between two areas even if they belong to the same category, a unique identifier is added as last element. Whether a global or local identifier is used is not of importance.

The example described above uses a four level category tree, it is however possible to extend the depth of the tree arbitrarily to better represent the typology at hand. Especially the description of the functional category may well require more than two levels.

Several standards of area categorization, such as ANSI-BOMA, E1836-01 and ISO 9836 exist, should either of these fulfill the requirements of the typology at hand it is advisable to implement these.

2.3. GRAPH COLLAPSING

Simplifying graphs before executing expensive calculations is a technique finding increasing use in the field of computer science. The most prominent example being multilevel graph partitioning (Karypis and Kumar 1995), a graph partitioning approach which iteratively coarsens a graph to a computationally feasible size before performing the partitioning operation. The intermediate result is then brought back to the original graph, back-tracking the coarsening steps and refining the result in the process. In such a way good results are achieved even for the un-coarsened, original graph, while computation is kept at a manageable level.

While collapsing a graph necessarily information is reduced, hence the method of collapsing depends entirely on the feature of the graph which should be sustained. In most cases the subtracted information can be stored in a separate data-structure in order to be reintegrated in a later step. Shortest path algorithms often prune cul-de-sac branches and leafs to simplify the search, should the source or target node be amongst the pruned nodes the relevant information is added from a look-up table.

The approach taken here is to collapse an edge e into a hyper-node w, if its incident nodes u and v belong to the same category (Figure 5-a). This may be done on several levels of coarseness, by varying the depth of required equality (Figure 5-b). The first step may be to require identical categories on three levels, then only the first two levels could be taken into consideration and finally it would suffice if the nodes belong to the same access level group.

Moderately complex space allocation programs may comprise 200-300 individual areas. Not only is it computationally expensive to perform comparisons on such graphs, it also includes the danger that the resulting value is dominated by topological noise and fails to capture the essential aspects of the buildings. Differently placed support areas such as closets and storage areas may distort the similarity of the overall typologies. It is of

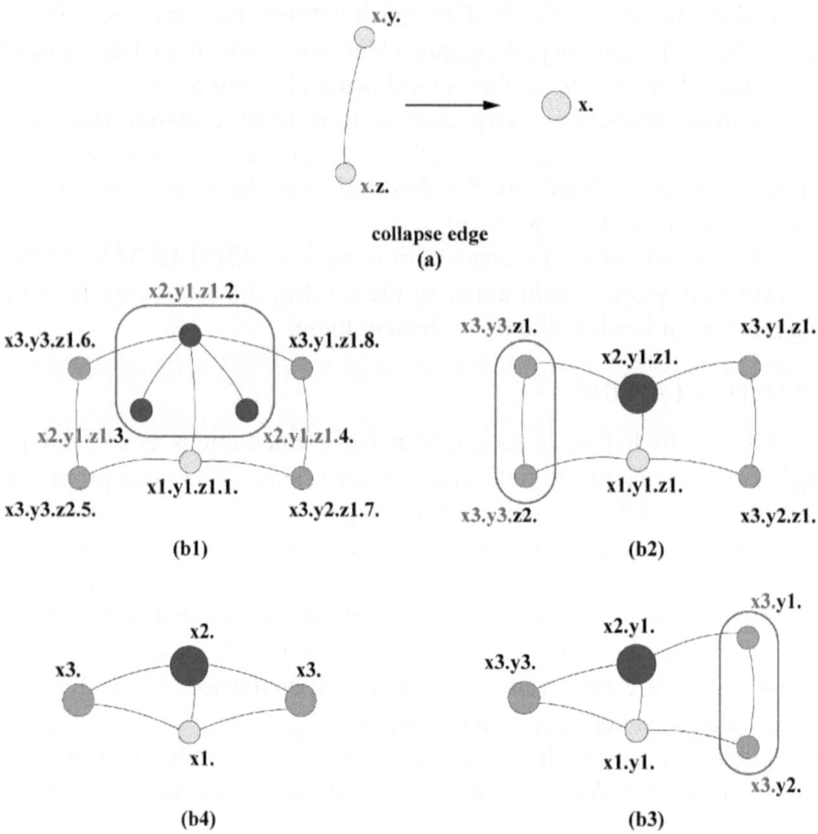

Figure 5. The collapse edge operation (a): The two nodes u→ x.y and v→ x.z collapse to a node w→x if u and v belong in the same category x. The new node w is represented with an area equal to the sum of the areas of the subsumed nodes. The application to a derivation: (b1) the original graph, (b2) graph collapsed to level 3, (b3) graph collapsed to level 2, (b4) graph collapsed to level 1

course a matter of interest at which level one engages with an analysis, one must however be aware that there are computational limits.

2.4. DISTANCE METRIC

The problem of finding a distance metric to compare two graphs for similarity has been of especial interest in the field of pattern recognition (Neuhaus and Bunke 2004). In architecture Conroy and Kirsan (2005) introduced graph matching to analyze genotypic differences in Greek and Turkish Cypriot housing.

The general approach is to define a set of operations to modify graphs and assign each a penalty cost. In order to compare two graphs $G = (V_G, E_G)$

and $H = (V_H, E_H)$ one graph is transformed into the other using these operations. The cost of the resulting mapping $m: H \rightarrow G$ equals the sum of the costs of its operations. The distance is then derived from the mapping which yields the least penalty cost. This distance metric strongly resembles the Levenshtein distance for string comparison.

In order to maintain relative algorithmic simplicity it was decided to restrict the set of operations to the most basic. Therefore four modification operations are defined (Figure 6), the insertion and the deletion of an edge and the insertion and deletion of a node. The associated costs are c_{IE}, c_{DE}, c_{IN}, c_{DN} respectively and can be adapted at will.

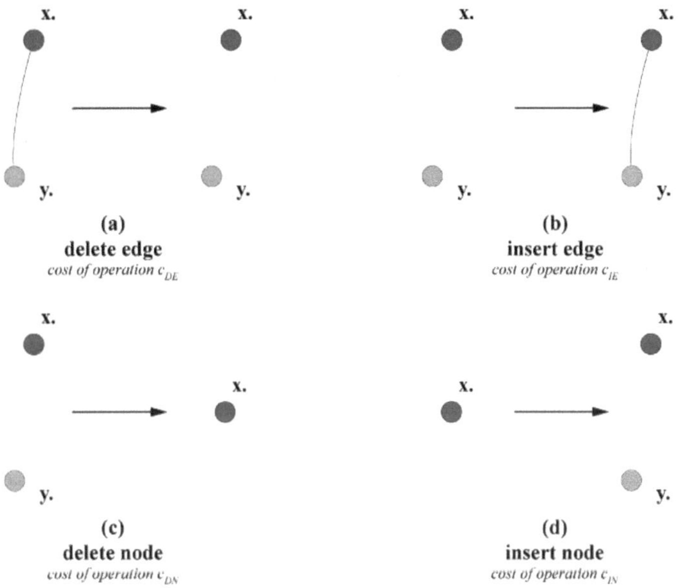

Figure 6. Modification operations; The four basic operations (a) delete edge, (b) insert edge, (c) delete node and (d) insert node

Further modification operations, such as node re-labeling or complex substitutions, are not included as these are essentially high level operations, which can be replaced by a combination of low level operations, thus once a solution is found the recorded set of operations may be analyzed and replaced by high level operations if required.

2.5. ALGORITHM

The algorithm used to arrive at the edit distance is essentially a graph search algorithm, which returns the shortest path between two nodes. The graph being searched is assembled at run-time; each node represents a mapping $m_i: H \rightarrow G_i$ and each edge stands for a performed modification operation or a newly mapped node. The start node is the empty mapping m_0: $H \rightarrow H$, while the target node is the correct mapping m_t: $H \rightarrow G$.

Once a node is visited all its unvisited neighbors are examined, their costs *f(x)* are calculated and the nodes are added to a priority queue, which is sorted by the cost *f(x)*. Initially the queue contains only the start node. Subsequently each step examines the first element of the queue until a solution is found with a total cost *f(x)* smaller than or equal to the total cost of the next node in the queue.

Generating the neighbor nodes at run-time requires taking an unmapped node from graph *G*, selecting all possible solutions in *H*, that is all unmapped nodes of equal category, and spawning a new branch for each. Additionally, one branch representing the insertion of a new node is spawned.

In cost based path finding the already covered path from the initial node to the current node is assigned a cost *g(x)*, in the case of graph matching this is the sum of all the cost of the operations used so far

$$g(x) = c_{IN}|V_I| + c_{DN}|V_D| + c_{IE}|E_I| + c_{DE}|E_D| \tag{1}$$

where V_I, V_D, E_I, E_D are the sets of inserted and deleted nodes and edges respectively.

In order to perform efficiently it is desirable to minimize the number of nodes visited by the search; this can best be done by giving the algorithm a sense of direction. Hence, while selecting a node to expand next, nodes closer to the target should be favored over ones still further away. In order to do this a best-case heuristic *h(x)* must be found to estimate the remaining distance to the target mapping. Since a best case heuristic is required one must assume, that all remaining unmapped nodes and edges of *H* can be mapped directly to *G*. Hence, the cost factor lies in the difference between unmapped elements of *H* and *G*, plus the cost of mapping the remaining elements. It follows that

$$\begin{aligned} h(x) &= c_{xN}\left\| V_G| - |V_H| + |V_D| - |V_I| \right\| \\ &+ c_{xE}\left\| E_G| - |E_H| + |E_D| - |E_I| \right\| \end{aligned} \tag{2}$$

where

$$c_{xN} = \begin{cases} c_{IN}, & if\ (|V_G| - |V_H| + |V_D| - |V_I|) \geq 0 \\ c_{DN}, & otherwise. \end{cases} \tag{3}$$

$$c_{xE} = \begin{cases} c_{IE}, & \text{if } \left(\left|E_G\right| - \left|E_H\right| + \left|E_D\right| - \left|E_I\right|\right) \geq 0 \\ c_{DE}, & \text{otherwise.} \end{cases} \tag{4}$$

Thus the minimal cost function *f(x)* for a node *x* is:

$$f(x) = g(x) + h(x) \tag{5}$$

Combining the cost of the covered path with the estimated cost of the residual path in such a way is known as the A* algorithm (Dechter and Pearl 1985).

3. Application

Part of a GSA funded project is the systematic analysis of federal courthouses. Within this larger framework graph distance analysis was implemented as a tool to describe similarities and eventually arrive at a set of courthouse typologies.

While the work is still in progress and additionally the secure nature of the project further restrict the possibility to depict detailed information some general findings can be shared.

3.1. COURTHOUSE SPECIFIC SETTINGS

The complete area classification table for federal Courthouses implemented in this work is based on the integration of various existing sources such as the courthouse design guide (GSA 1997). For the purpose of this analysis the federal Courthouses are organized into four discrete zones with respect to access requirements. The public zone includes all the areas accessible to the general public along with attorneys, clients, witnesses and jurors. The private zone includes all the functions that have a restricted access and are used by particular courthouse users such as judges, jurors, and employees. The secure zone is provided for the movement and holding of defendants in custody; it includes horizontal and vertical secure circulation systems as well as holding areas. The interface zone comprises the courtroom and its associated areas; it is here that the public, private, and secure zones interact.

One additional zone is defined as carrier space; it essentially represents all exterior spaces and is used to define entrances, windows and orientations. Access to secure areas is strictly monitored, these are the areas reserved for the inmates. And finally the courtroom as only interface where agents from all other access levels are brought together is represented as a separate access level.

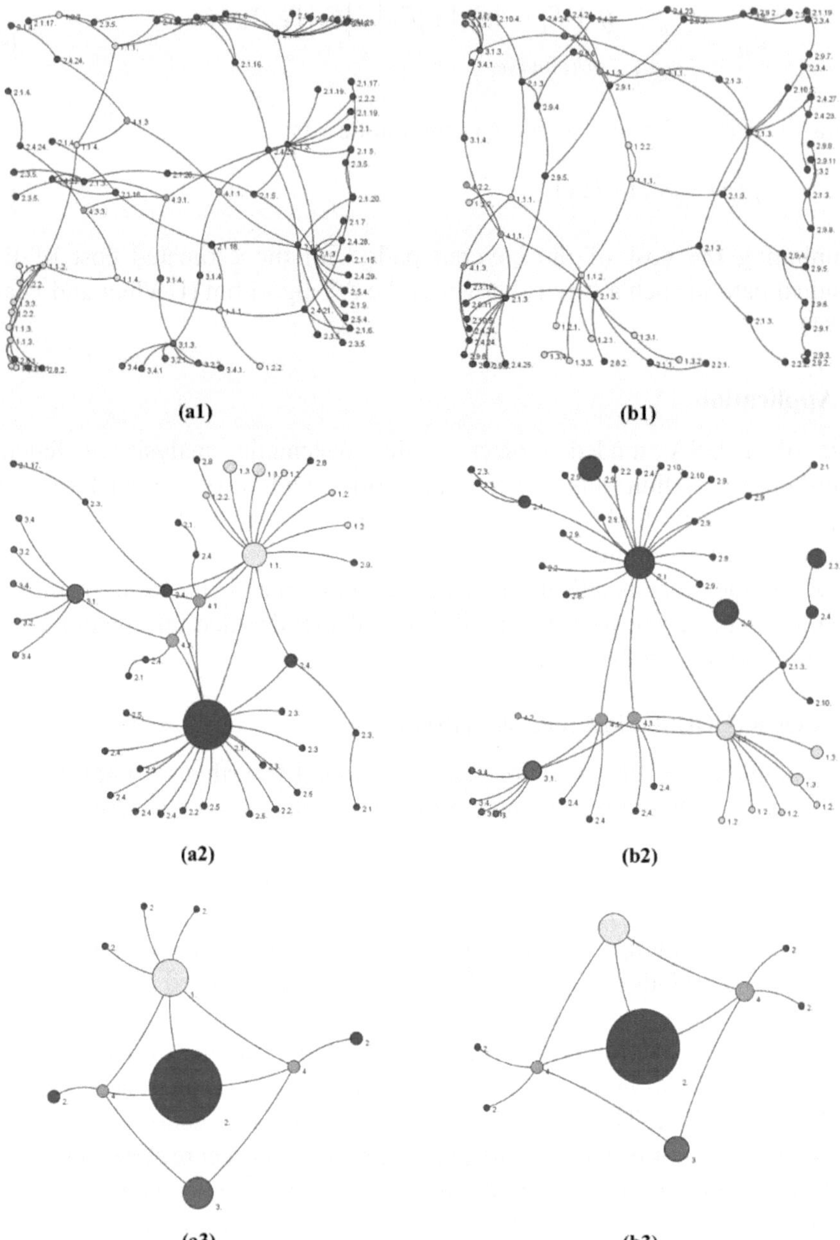

Figure 7. Two courtroom floors with approx. 80 nodes each; (a1) and (b1) show the un-collapsed graphs; (a2) and (b2) are collapsed to level 2; (a3) and (b3) are collapsed to level 1; at this level they have an edit distance of 6

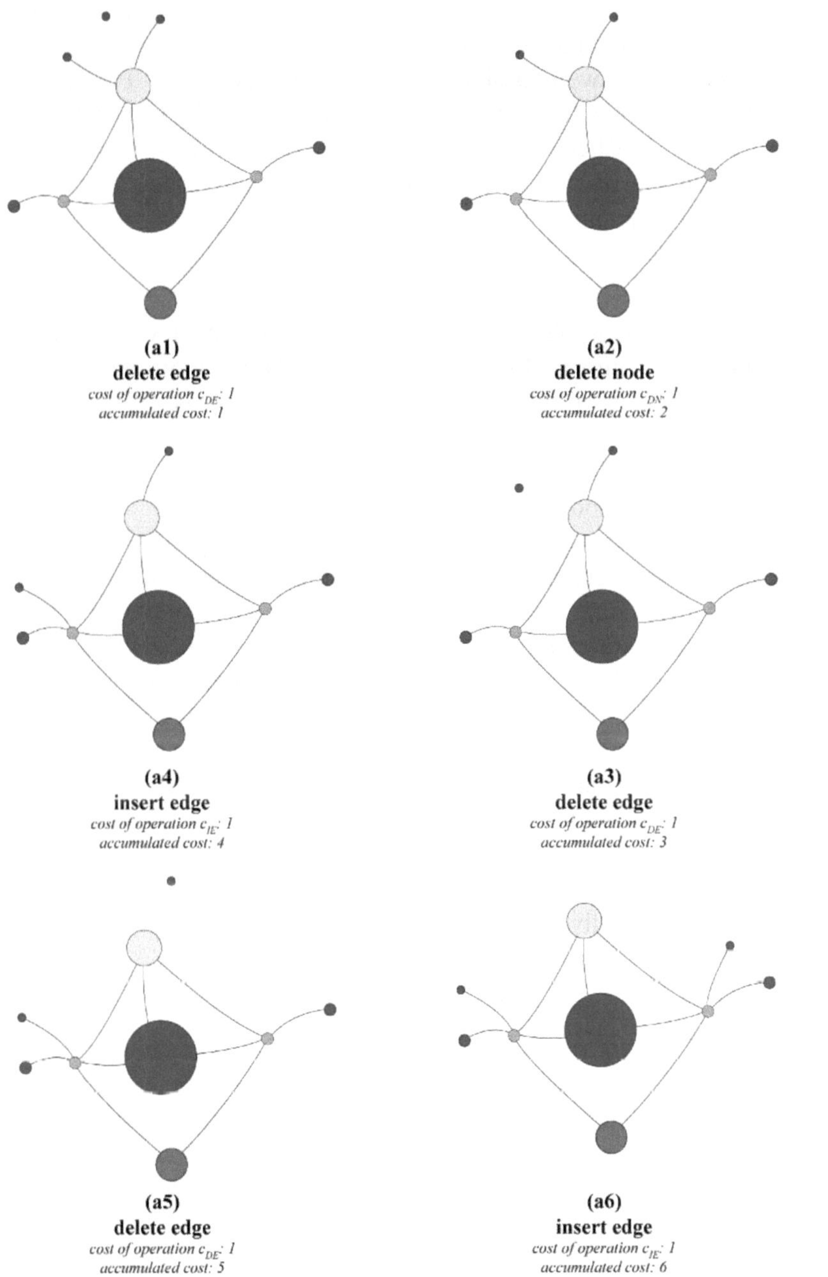

Figure 8. The six steps required to transform the source graph (Figure 7-a3) into the target graph (Figure 7-b3). Since every operation is assigned a cost of 1 the accumulated cost is 6

AQ: Please Figure 8 cit in text.

Area functions are also based on the courthouse design guide (1997) and require two levels in the category tree.

All operations were assigned a uniform cost of 1. Frequently edge operations are assigned a lesser penalty value than node operations; this may sometimes be justified by the nature of the system being abstracted by the graph. In the course of this application it was felt that equal costs best reflect the lean approach taken so far.

3.2. DISCUSSION

When collapsing graphs to the second, intermediate level numerous star configurations occurred (Figures 7-a2 and 7-b2), these are mainly collapsed circulation areas surrounded by other functional areas. A higher level of detail, i.e. more classification levels, and a differentiation of circulation areas by assigning them to the various functional classes would yield more meaningful hyper-nodes.

It is felt that the weight of a hyper-node, the number of collapsed nodes it represents, should somehow be reflected in the distance metric. This could be done by evaluating the difference while mapping a node onto another.

Calculations are extremely taxing on memory; some of the un-collapsed floor plans could not be compared at all. If these calculations remain incomputable despite future improvements, some form of approximation or at least of defining boundaries must be devised.

In addition to making distance measurements feasible, collapsed graph representations seem to also give a good visual representation of the essence of a floor plan. An algorithm to lay out the graph, while supporting this aspect would be helpful, since momentarily the nodes must frequently be repositioned manually.

4. Future Work

There is still ample room for optimizing the algorithm. Additional methods of minimizing the search area must be implemented. One could for example, favor categories with less member-nodes over categories with more when selecting the next node to map, this will reduce the initial complexity of the search tree and reduce the branches spawned before a solution is found.

For large graphs approximations based on the coarser results could be devised, perhaps by recursively calculating the distance of graphs within the hyper-nodes.

Finally, there is still additional need for the construction of architectural meaning emerging from these computations. The major thesis of this work, that graph distance metrics can provide additional insight into the essential structure of given typologies of buildings, will only be tested once these computations with graphs align with computations with spaces to cast light on the study of architectural structure.

Acknowledgements

This research was supported by the General Service Administration (GSA), more specifically by the Office of the Chief Architect. We would like to particularly thank the Center for Courthouse Programs for their invaluable help and architectural insight on the features and complexities of these buildings.

References

Administrative Office of the U.S. Courts: 1997, *U.S. Courts Design Guide.*

de Berg, M, van Kreveld, M, Overmars, M and Schwarzkopf, O: 2000, *Computational Geometry. Algorithms and Applications*, Springer, Berlin.

Bunke, H and Allermann, G: 1983, Inexact graph matching for structural pattern recognition, *Pattern Recognition Letters* **1**(4): 245-253.

Conroy, R and Kirsan, C: 2005, Graph Isomorphism and Genotypical Houses, *in* A van Nes (ed) *Proceedings of the 5th Space Syntax Symposium Vol. 2*, Techne Press, Delft, pp. 15-28.

Dechter, R and Pearl, J: 1985, Generalized best-first search strategies and the optimality of A*, *Journal of the ACM* **32**(3): 505-536.

Hillier, B, Hanson, J and Peponis, J: 1984, What do we mean by building function?, *in* J Powell and I Cooper (eds), *Designing for building utilization*, Spon, London, pp. 61-72.

Karypis, G and Kumar, V: 1995, Analysis of Multilevel Graph Partitioning, *Proceedings of the IEEE/ACM SC'95 Conference*, p. 29.

March, L and Steadman, P: 1974, *The Geometry of Environment: An Introduction to Spatial Organization in Design,* The MIT Press, Cambridge.

Neuhaus, M and Bunke, H: 2004, An Error-Tolerant Approximate Matching Algorithm for Attributed Planar Graphs and Its Application to Fingerprint Classification, *in* A Fred, T Caelli, RPW Duin, A Campilho, and D de Ridder (eds), *Structural, Syntactic, and Statistical Pattern Recognition, Proc. Joint IAPR Int. Workshops SSPR and SPR*, Springer, Berlin, pp. 180–189.

Steadman, P: 1976, Graph-theoretic representation of architectural arrangement, *in* L March (eds), *The Architecture of Form*, Cambridge University Press, Cambridge, pp. 94-115.

Stiny, G and Mitchell, W: 1978, The Palladian Grammar, *Environment and Planning B: Planning and Design* **5**: 5-18.

A PARAMETRIC REPRESENTATION OF RULED SURFACES

ELENA PROUSALIDOU AND SEAN HANNA
University College London, United Kingdom

Abstract. This paper proposes a simple parametric system to generate an almost complete set of ruled surfaces that may be used to describe building geometry. The major classes of regular, named ruled surfaces can be generated from a limited set of curves. Each of these is shown to be reducible to a transformation of a single standard curve, a helix, and therefore represented by a limited set of six parameters. Six extra parameters can position each surface on a global coordinate system. The representation is designed to be flexible enough to represent both planar and curvilinear forms, producing a description of form from minimal data.

1. Introduction

Generative digital techniques attempt to exploit the power of information technology as a direct tool to represent and generate architectural forms. Demonstrative approaches in this new field of design techniques are *parametric* and *evolutionary* design, often used in combination. Their common feature is the design of the end product as an instance of a class of possible solutions. Another similarity they share is the description of the product by a series of parameters that take on different values. These values can either be input by the designer, in the first case, or be evolved by a program, in the latter. Parametric and generative representations of buildings, whether based on orthogonal (March and Steadman 1971; Rosenman and Gero 1999; Steadman and Waddoups 2000; Steadman 2001) or curvilinear (DeCOi 2000) geometry, are powerful by virtue of their ability to capture a high degree of variation in a few numerical values.

This paper proposes a parametric representation of ruled surfaces that uses a minimal set of variables to represent a wide variety of surfaces, including those most commonly used in architecture. A serial composition of the surfaces can be applied in the representation of building geometry.

A Dong, A Vande Moere & JS Gero (eds), CAADFutures'07, 265–278.

1.1. ARCHITECTURAL STRUCTURES AS NUMERICAL SYSTEMS

Configuration of built forms as represented by Lionel March in his isomorphic Boolean approach (March 1972) and Philip Steadman in his archetypal building (Steadman 1998) are indicative early attempts to represent architecture using a numerical description of form. Both use binary encoding that corresponds to a matrix of cuboids. Although they do achieve a compact representation of rectangular forms, the underlying relations of the building elements are restricted to proximity and vertical/horizontal packing.

1.2. REPRESENTATIONS IN EVOLUTIONARY DESIGN

Representation of form in strings is widely applied in Evolutionary Design techniques where the generative process operates with various parameters encoded into string-like structures.

Approaches focused on orthogonal spatial configurations, such as the learning approach developed by John Gero and the hierarchical growth approach developed by Mike Rosenman (Rosenman and Gero 1999) or the procedure proposed by Jackson (Jackson 2002), use genes to represent simple design actions as production rules or drawing instructions which when executed result in shapes or produce parts of design solutions (Bentley 1999).

Representations of 3dimensional form are often based on modular assemblies of primitive forms, such as the Reptile system proposed by Frazer (Frazer 1995), 'clipped stretched cuboids' developed by Peter Bentley and Jonathan Wakefield (Bentley 1999a), Form Grow by Stephen Todd and William Latham (1999) or the production of objects represented through the insertion of spheres at the isospatial grid as proposed by Paul Coates, Terence Broughton and Helen Jackson (Coates Broughton and Jackson 1999).

While these modules are quite simple, a parametric description of form may be created that is flexible enough to represent complex curves and surfaces. This is aptly demonstrated by Burry's extended application of parametric techniques on the analysis of the ruled surfaces used by Antonio Gaudi. He applies parametric design software at the Sagrada Familia with the intention "to remodel and resolve the use of these surfaces into a measurable interpretation that can be used to advance the building work", a form of rationalisation useful in design (Burry et al. 2001).

The proposed model incorporates Burry's work, and presents a simple surface description that may be used in evolutionary design and other parametric approaches. It can be evaluated by the numbers of parameters needed and the range of forms it is capable of representing.

2. Ruled Surfaces

A ruled surface can be generated by the motion of a line in space, similar to the way a curve can be generated by the motion of a point. A 3D surface is called ruled if through each of its points passes at least one line that lies entirely on that surface.

Simple to define and construct at a local level, ruled surfaces are able to describe high levels of form complexity, especially by their intersections when assembled (Burry 2003). Ruled surfaces have been extensively applied to architecture, with their potential exploited by new technological means. The Paramorph (DeCOi 2000) is an example.

2.1. ARCHITECTURAL STRUCTURES

Traditionally the plane, cylindrical and conical surfaces have been of the broadest use in architecture, and their familiarity often obscures their definition as ruled. The hyperboloid and the hyperbolic paraboloid are the most typical examples of more complex ruled surfaces, followed by the helicoid and, recently, the moebius strip. Construction of new structural systems using hyperboloids and hyperbolic paraboloids was first accomplished by Vladimir Shukhov, at the end of 19th century (English 2005). The doubly-curved surfaces were formed of a lattice of straight iron bars. Gaudi extended the application of ruled surfaces by using three surfaces that could be constructed at his time: hyperbolic paraboloid, helicoid and hyperboloid, all generated through straight lines. The entire design of the nave in the Sagrada Familia is an assembly of these three geometries (Burry 1993). These forms were extensively used by Felix Candela, and Le Corbusier's attraction to them is demonstrated by Philips Pavillion.

2.2. SPECIAL FEATURES

The most important feature of ruled surfaces in respect to design is their simplicity of construction relative to their striking shape. Burry (1993) emphasizes their ability to facilitate construction: "Any of these surfaces can be simply enough described as the points of origin and termination of an appropriate number of straight lines." Furthermore, the components of a larger whole can be carved independently off-site and then be assembled to form the final composition.

3. Development of the Parametric Representation

The most familiar way of constructing the surfaces in CAD packages is using lines that join corresponding points between two algebraic curves. In mathematical terms, however, the most common way of describing the surfaces is using a straight line moving along a curve with the direction given by another curve.

A surface is called a *ruled surface*, if it has a C^2-parametrization of the following kind (Kühnel 2002):

$$f(u, v) = b(u) + v\,X(u) \tag{1}$$

where b is a (differentiable, but not necessarily regular) curve and X is a vector field along b which vanishes nowhere.

The v-lines (with constant u) are Euclidean lines in space. They are called generators or rulings of the surface and can be intuitively understood as the various positions of the generating line L, the movement of which depends on one parameter.

The construction of a surface requires two parameterised curves, i.e. the base curve and the director curve. The base curve b (or directrix) of the surface is the curve along which runs the straight line. The line extends in the direction given by the director curve d, which may be visualised as a vector field (a given sequence of unit vectors that varies continuously) on b. Mathematical equations for the two curves can be expressed as position vectors.

The parametric function of the helix expressed in vector form is:

$$[a\cos(t), b\sin(t), ct] \tag{2}$$

Simple transformations of the helix result in a set of the curves needed to generate ruled surfaces. If the z vector component is suppressed the curve is degenerated to a circle. If the x vector component is suppressed the curve is degenerated to the parametric sine function. If the x and y vector components are suppressed the curve is degenerated to a line.

TABLE 1. Curves represented as Vectors of trigonometric functions

	HELIX	[acos(t), bsin(t), ct]
	CIRCLE	[acos(t), bsin(t), 0]
	SINE	[0, bsin(t), ct]
	LINE	[0, 0, ct]

TABLE 2. Ruled surfaces

	LINE	CIRCLE	HELIX	SINE
LINE				
CIRCLE	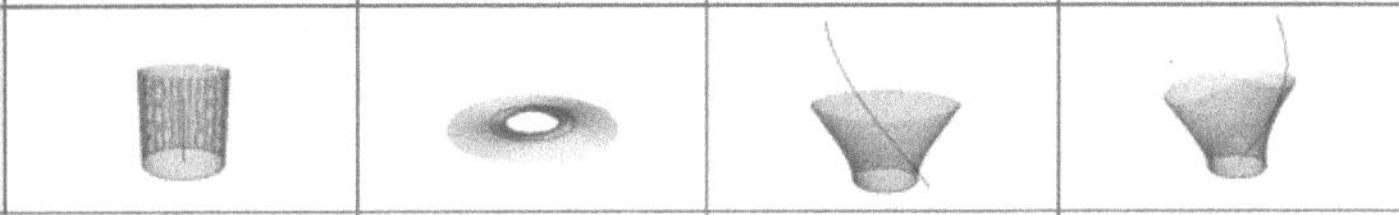			
HELIX	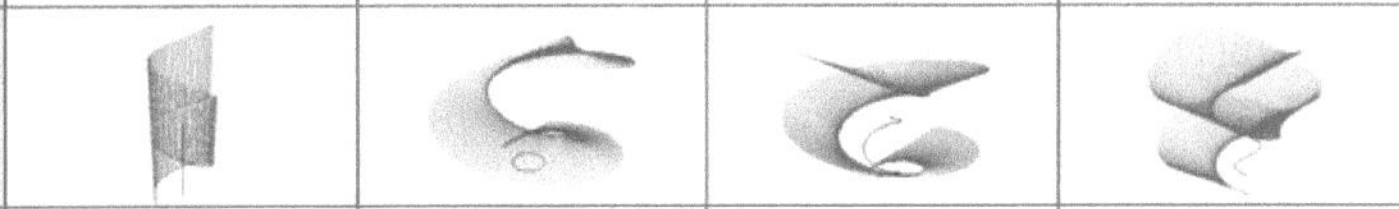			
SINE	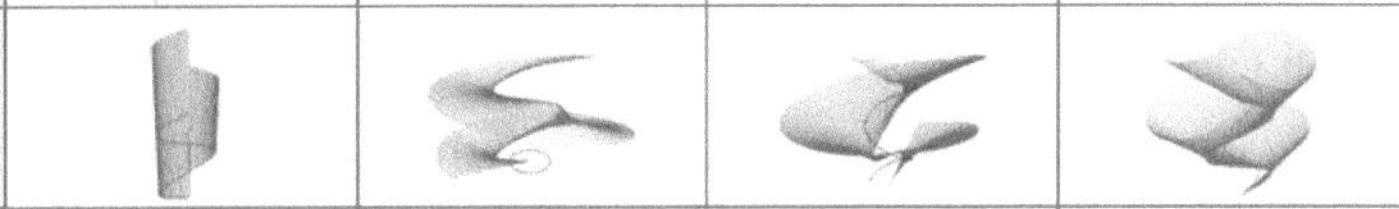			
LINE				
CIRCLE	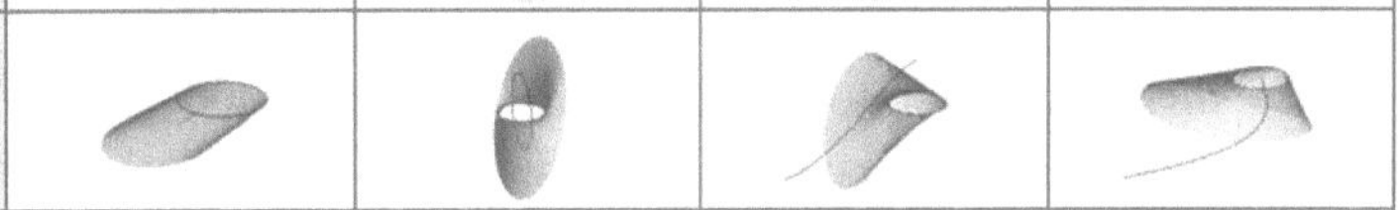			
HELIX	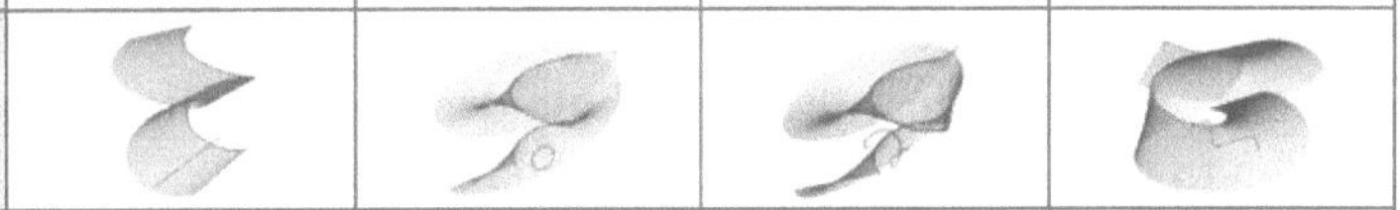			
SINE	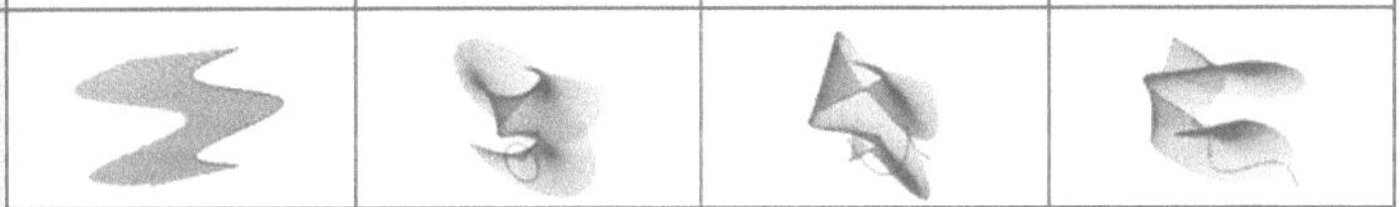			
LINE				
CIRCLE				
HELIX	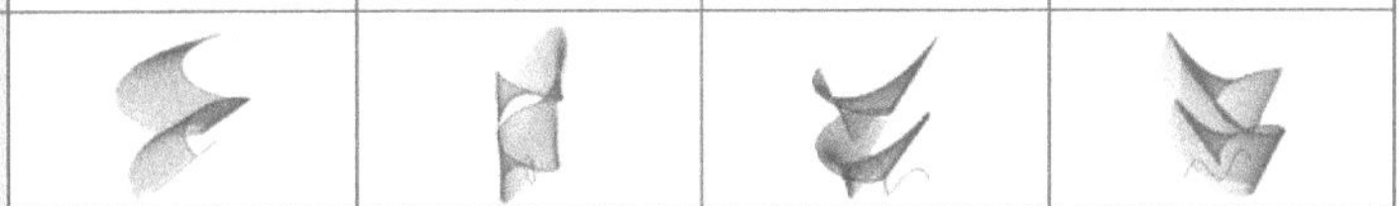			
SINE	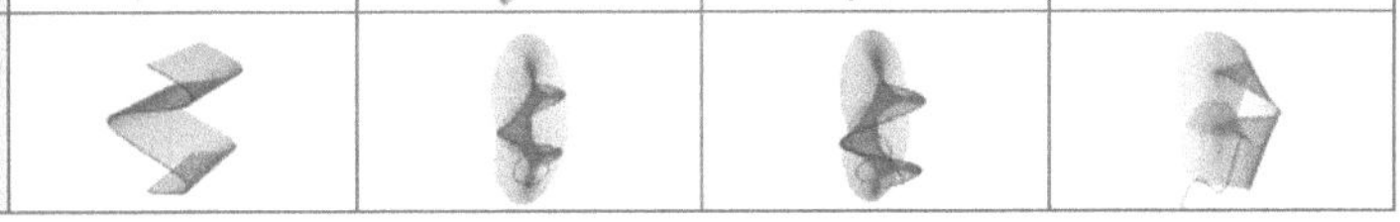			

The combination of these four curves as base and director respectively generates sixteen types of ruled surfaces. The rotation of one curve around the axes generates thirty two extra surfaces (sixteen for each rotation). Each surface of a structure can be expressed using six parameters: three for the base (a_b, b_b, c_b) and three for the director curve (a_d, b_d, c_d).

The plane and other surfaces require two curves along different axes. If the base curve is defined as mentioned above, the director curve should be defined either as

$$[b_d\sin(t),\ c_d t,\ a_d\cos(t)] \tag{3}$$

or

$$[c_d t,\ a_d\cos(t),\ b_d\sin(t)] \tag{4}$$

The procedure that was followed was the addition of an extra value in the x component of the director vector so that it becomes

$$[a_d\cos(t)+ d_d t,\ b_d\sin(t),\ c_d t\ ] \tag{5}$$

where parameter d_d is applied for rotating one curve before generating the surface.

The surfaces generated in this way are presented in Table 2. The base curve is constantly oriented along the Z axis while the director curve is oriented along axes X, Y and Z. Among these forty eight surfaces the plane, the cone, the cylinder, the hyperboloid and the helicoid are included, in addition to the commonly used sinusoidal surface.

When all n surfaces that form an architectural composition are indexed, a 13×n matrix can represent a building.

$$\begin{bmatrix} a_{b1} & b_{b1} & c_{b1} & a_{d1} & b_{d1} & c_{d1} & d_{d1} & t_{x1} & t_{y1} & t_{z1} & r_{x1} & r_{y1} & r_{z1} \\ a_{b2} & b_{b2} & c_{b2} & a_{d2} & b_{d2} & c_{d2} & d_{d2} & t_{x2} & t_{y2} & t_{z2} & r_{x2} & r_{y2} & r_{z2} \\ a_{b3} & b_{b3} & c_{b3} & a_{d3} & b_{d3} & c_{d3} & d_{d3} & t_{x3} & t_{y3} & t_{z3} & r_{x3} & r_{y3} & r_{z3} \\ & & & & & & \cdots & & & & & & \\ & & & & & & \cdots & & & & & & \\ a_{bn} & b_{bn} & c_{bn} & a_{dn} & b_{dn} & c_{dn} & d_{dn} & t_{xn} & t_{yn} & t_{zn} & r_{xn} & r_{yn} & r_{zn} \end{bmatrix}$$

Where:

α_b, b_b, c_b: parameters of base curve [acos(t), bsin(t), ct] and

α_d, b_d, c_d, d_d: parameters of director curve [acos(t)+ dt, bsin(t), ct]

t_x: translation of surface around X axis

t_y: translation of surface around Y axis

t_z: translation of surface around Z axis

r_x: rotation of surface around Z axis

r_y: rotation of surface around Z axis
r_z: rotation of surface around Z axis

3.1. HYPERBOLIC PARABOLOID

The above strategy represents many of the regular types of ruled surfaces, but the construction of the commonly used hyperbolic paraboloid requires the use of another type of curve, the parabola, which can not be produced by a linear transformation of the helix. Its function is expressed by the position vector

$$[t, 0, t^2] \tag{6}$$

and thus requires one additional, quadratic parameter e_d. The program was modified by adjusting the general function for the director curve:

$$[a_d\cos(t)+ d_d t,\ b_d\sin(t),\ c_d t+e_d t^2] \tag{7}$$

To represent this extra class of surfaces this single extra parameter was added to the vector's components.

4. Applying the Representation

The representation was implemented in a Processing program created to draw multiple surfaces. This receives a series of parameters for each surface as input by the user and draws an assembly of surfaces that represent the building.

Specifically, for each surface the program receives the parameters a_b, b_b, c_b and a_d, b_d, c_d, d_d as input and executes the algorithm as follows:
At each step:

1. increment parameter t by a constant number
2. calculate base and director curve vectors for value t and draw a point with coordinates defined by each vector
3. join consecutive points to draw two curves
4. calculate slope of director curve by subtracting successive values for each vector component.
5. normalise slope vector
6. draw a line of fixed length starting from the point on the base curve and has its direction defined by the slope of the director curve, i.e a ruling.

This iterative process is repeated for every point of the base curve. A new line is generated for each value of parameter *t*. The assembly of those lines compose the surface. In order to draw the assembly of many surfaces as a unified whole the code was modified to include the surface as a class, so that multiple instances can be created simultaneously. As long as the values of the parameters for each surface vary, the instances created display a wide variety of forms.

The program employs six more variables to define the transformation matrices (t_x, t_y, t_z, r_x, r_y, r_z) and some additional global variables such as the increment of value t, and the line length, which can either be fixed or modified by the user. These allow precise control of the relation between surfaces. Once the surfaces are assembled together, their intersections can be computed based on the properties of the rulings.

4.1. REPRESENTATION OF REAL BUILDINGS

The performance and efficiency of the system was tested by constructing concise, parametric descriptions for a series of existing structures, ranging in form from Calatrava's Bodegas Ysios and Bofill's El Prat Control Tower to Mies' Seagram Building.

The values of the parameters are presented in 13×n matrices, with the exception of the hyperbolic paraboloid assembly. The matrices vary in size: they are 13×n where n is the number of surfaces. Active parameters of each surface take a real or integer number value, otherwise they are set to 0.

The traffic control tower of El Prat combines cylindrical and conical surfaces with a hyperboloid. Values of the matrix are presented in more detail in Table 3. The effect of changing a single value in the matrix is demonstrated in Figure 2.

$$\left[\begin{array}{ccc|cccc|ccc|ccc}
\boxed{0} & 170 & 170 & 0 & 0 & 0 & 10 & 0 & 0 & 0 & 0 & 0 & 0 \\
0 & 200 & 200 & 0 & 0 & \boxed{0} & 10 & 0 & 0 & 20 & 0 & 0 & 0 \\
0 & 60 & 60 & 3 & 0 & 0 & 0 & 0 & 0 & 360 & 0 & 0 & 0 \\
0 & 30 & 30 & 0 & 0 & 200 & 200 & 0 & 0 & 50 & 0 & 0 & 0 \\
0 & \boxed{20} & 20 & 0 & 0 & 0 & 10 & 0 & 0 & 0 & 0 & 0 & 0 \\
0 & 30 & 30 & 0 & 1 & 1 & 6 & 0 & 0 & 65 & 0 & 0 & 0 \\
0 & 30 & 30 & 0 & 1 & 1 & -6 & 0 & 0 & 65 & 0 & 0 & 0 \\
0 & 53 & 53 & 3 & 0 & 0 & 0 & 0 & 0 & 410 & 0 & 0 & 0
\end{array}\right]$$

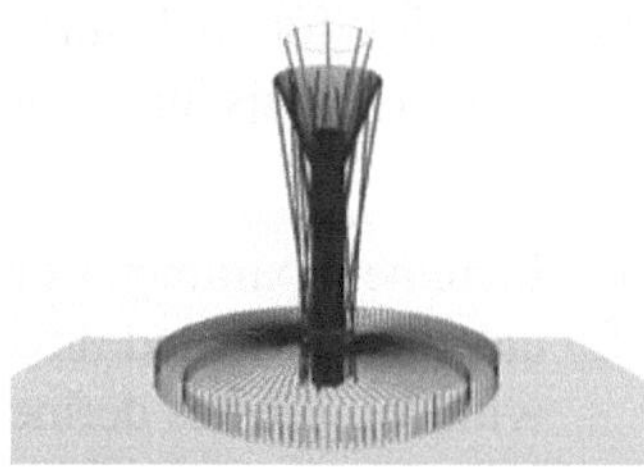

Figure 1. Traffic Control Tower-El Prat

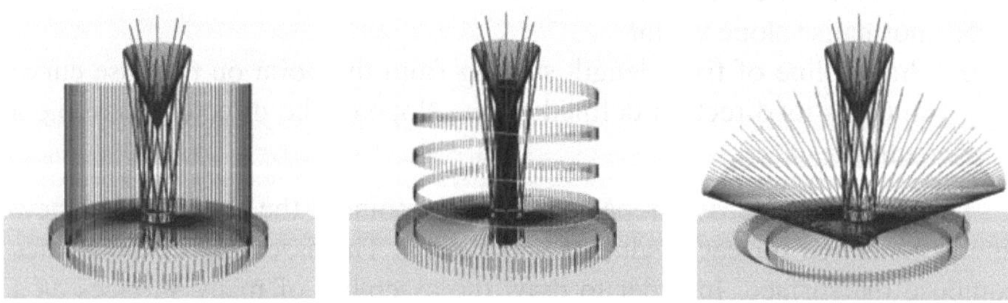

Figure 2. Variations of form by changing a value in the matrix

TABLE 3. Values of El Prat-matrix in detail

ROW	BASE CURVE parameters trig. function	DIRECTOR CURVE parameters trig. function	RULED SURFACE	TRANSLATION axis units
1	0,170,170	0,0,0,10	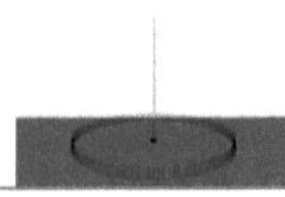	0,0,0
	[0,170cost,170sint]	[0,0,10t]		-
	circle	line		-
2	0,200,200	0,0,0,10	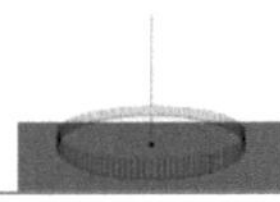	0,0,20
	[0,200cost,200sint]	[0,0,10t]		Z
	circle	line		20
3	0,60,60	3,0,0,0	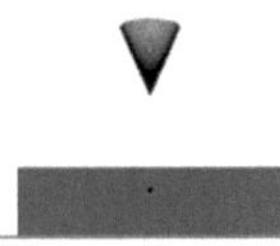	0,0,360
	[0,60cost,60sint]	[3t,0,0]		Z
	circle	line		360
4	0,30,30	0,0,200,200	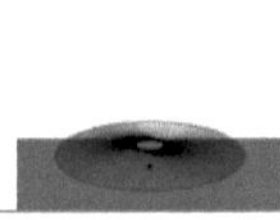	0,0,50
	[0,30cost,30sint]	[200cost,200sint,0]		Z
	circle	circle		50
5	0,20,20	0,0,0,10	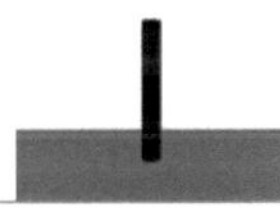	0,0,0
	[0,20cost,20sint]	[0,0,10t]		-
	circle	line		-
6	0,30,30	0,1,1,6	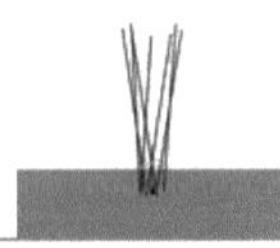	0,0,65
	[0,30cost,30sint]	[cost,sint,6t]		Z
	circle	helix		65
7	0,30,30	0,1,1,-6	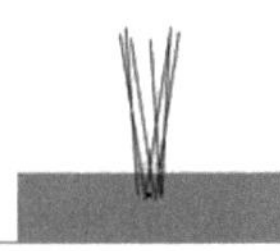	0,0,65
	[0,30cost,30sint]	[cost,sint,-6t]		Z
	circle	helix		65
8	0,53,53	3,0,0,0	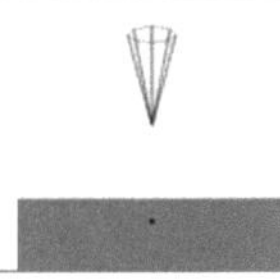	0,0,410
	[0,53cost,53sint]	[3t,0,0]		Z
	circle	line		410

In the case of Bodegas Ysios, the load bearing walls trace a sinusoidal shape and the roof is a ruled surface wave, which combines concave and convex surfaces as it evolves along the longitudinal axis.

$$\begin{bmatrix} 0 & 5 & 20 & 100 & 0 & 0 & 0 & -50 & 55 & -410 & 0 & PI/2 & 0 \\ 0 & 5 & 20 & 100 & 0 & 0 & 0 & -50 & -55 & -410 & 0 & PI/2 & 0 \\ 0 & 0 & 20 & 10 & 0 & 0 & 0 & 50 & 410 & -55 & PI/2 & 0 & PI/2 \\ 0 & 0 & 20 & 10 & 0 & 0 & 0 & 50 & -410 & -55 & PI/2 & 0 & PI/2 \\ 0 & 40 & 20 & 150 & 0 & 0 & 0 & -70 & 50 & -25 & 0 & PI/2 & -PI/8 \\ 0 & 0 & 21 & 20 & 0 & 6 & 0 & 0 & 90 & -425 & PI/2 & PI/2 & 0 \end{bmatrix}$$

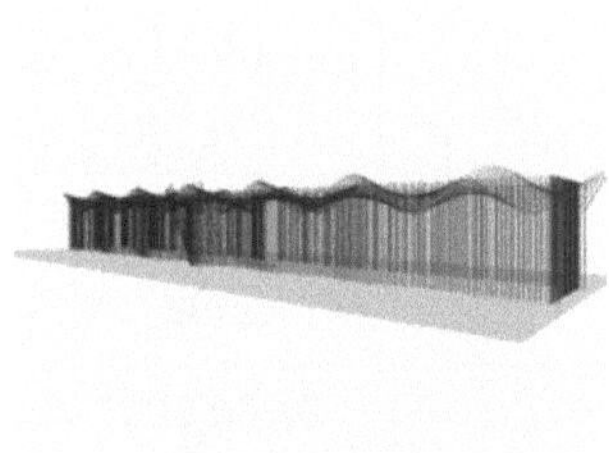

Figure 3. Bodegas Ysios

Palace of Assembly is a more complex composition of different surfaces: hyperboloid, planes, cylindrical surface in addition to a pyramid.

$$\begin{bmatrix} 45 & 45 & 0 & 0 & 2 & 2 & 5 & 0 & 0 & 180 & 0 & 0 & 0 \\ 0 & 0 & 20 & 10 & 0 & 0 & 0 & 0 & 170 & 0 & 0 & 0 & 0 \\ 0 & 0 & 20 & 10 & 0 & 0 & 0 & 0 & -170 & 0 & 0 & 0 & PI/2 \\ 0 & 0 & 20 & 10 & 0 & 0 & 0 & 0 & -170 & 0 & 0 & 0 & 0 \\ 0 & 0 & 20 & 10 & 0 & 0 & 0 & 0 & 170 & 0 & 0 & 0 & PI/2 \\ 170 & 0 & 0 & 0 & 0 & 0 & 40 & 0 & 157 & 0 & PI/2 & 0 & 0 \\ 0 & 0 & 20 & 10 & 0 & 0 & 0 & -240 & 145 & 0 & 0 & 0 & 0 \\ 0 & 0 & 20 & 10 & 0 & 0 & 0 & -240 & 95 & 0 & 0 & 0 & 0 \\ 0 & 0 & 20 & 10 & 0 & 0 & 0 & -240 & 45 & 0 & 0 & 0 & 0 \\ 0 & 0 & 20 & 10 & 0 & 0 & 0 & -240 & -5 & 0 & 0 & 0 & 0 \\ 0 & 0 & 20 & 10 & 0 & 0 & 0 & -240 & -55 & 0 & 0 & 0 & 0 \\ 0 & 0 & 20 & 10 & 0 & 0 & 0 & -240 & -105 & 0 & 0 & 0 & 0 \\ 0 & 0 & 20 & 10 & 0 & 0 & 0 & -240 & -155 & 0 & 0 & 0 & 0 \\ 30 & 20 & 0 & 0 & 0 & 0 & 10 & -240 & -100 & 0 & -PI/2 & 0 & 0 \\ 0 & 0 & 20 & 10 & 0 & 0 & 0 & 0 & -120 & 110 & 0 & -PI/6 & PI/2 \\ 0 & 0 & 20 & 10 & 0 & 0 & 0 & 0 & -120 & 110 & -PI/6 & 0 & 0 \\ 0 & 0 & 20 & 10 & 0 & 0 & 0 & 0 & 120 & 110 & 0 & PI/6 & PI/2 \\ 0 & 0 & 20 & 10 & 0 & 0 & 0 & 0 & 120 & 110 & PI/6 & 0 & 0 \end{bmatrix}$$

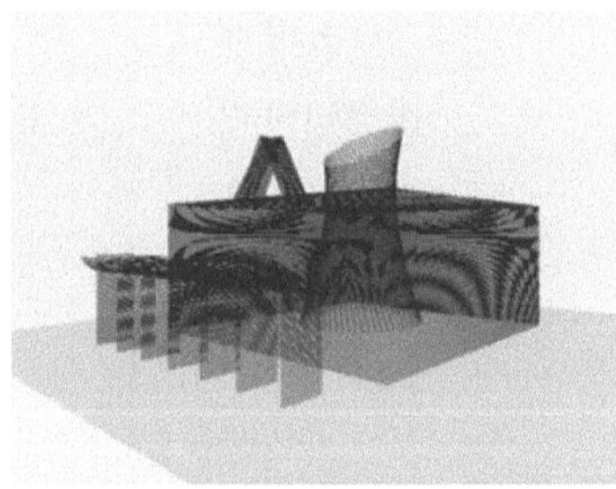

Figure 4. Palace of Assembly

Los Manantiales provides an illustrative sample of an assembly of hyperbolic paraboloids rotated around a central point. It was selected to test the extended version of the program.

$$\begin{bmatrix} 0 & 0 & 50 & -40 & 180 & 0 & 0 & -100 & 10 & 0 & -350 & 0 & PI/8 & 0 & 0 \\ 0 & 0 & 50 & -40 & 180 & 0 & 0 & -100 & 10 & 0 & -350 & 0 & PI/8 & 0 & PI/4 \\ 0 & 0 & 50 & -40 & 180 & 0 & 0 & -100 & 10 & 0 & -350 & 0 & PI/8 & 0 & 2*PI/4 \\ 0 & 0 & 50 & -40 & 180 & 0 & 0 & -100 & 10 & 0 & -350 & 0 & PI/8 & 0 & 3*PI/4 \\ 0 & 0 & 50 & -40 & 180 & 0 & 0 & -100 & 10 & 0 & -350 & 0 & PI/8 & 0 & 4*PI/4 \\ 0 & 0 & 50 & -40 & 180 & 0 & 0 & -100 & 10 & 0 & -350 & 0 & PI/8 & 0 & 5*PI/4 \\ 0 & 0 & 50 & -40 & 180 & 0 & 0 & -100 & 10 & 0 & -350 & 0 & PI/8 & 0 & 6*PI/4 \\ 0 & 0 & 50 & -40 & 180 & 0 & 0 & -100 & 10 & 0 & -350 & 0 & PI/8 & 0 & 7*PI/4 \end{bmatrix}$$

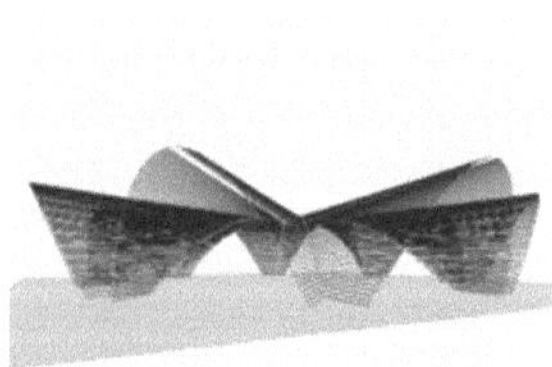

Figure 5. Los Manantiales

The Seagram Building is composed of planar surfaces. It was selected for a comparison to the representation proposed by L. March.

$$\begin{bmatrix}
40 & 0 & 0 & 0 & 0 & 0 & 10 & 0 & 0 & 0 & 0 & 0 & 0 \\
40 & 0 & 0 & 0 & 0 & 0 & 10 & 0 & 40 & 0 & 0 & 0 & 0 \\
18 & 0 & 0 & 0 & 0 & 0 & 10 & 0 & 56 & 0 & 0 & 0 & 0 \\
44 & 0 & 0 & 0 & 0 & 0 & 10 & 0 & 56 & 0 & 0 & 0 & 0 \\
44 & 0 & 0 & 0 & 0 & 0 & 10 & -25 & 84 & 0 & 0 & 0 & 0 \\
44 & 0 & 0 & 0 & 0 & 0 & 10 & 0 & 84 & 0 & 0 & 0 & 0 \\
20 & 0 & 0 & 0 & 0 & 0 & 10 & 20 & 39.8 & 0 & 0 & 0 & PI/2 \\
20 & 0 & 0 & 0 & 0 & 0 & 10 & 20 & -39.8 & 0 & 0 & 0 & PI/2 \\
10 & 0 & 0 & 0 & 0 & 0 & 10 & 46 & 17.91 & 0 & 0 & 0 & PI/2 \\
10 & 0 & 0 & 0 & 0 & 0 & 10 & 46 & -17.91 & 0 & 0 & 0 & PI/2 \\
20 & 0 & 0 & 0 & 0 & 0 & 10 & 64 & 17.91 & 0 & 0 & 0 & PI/2 \\
20 & 0 & 0 & 0 & 0 & 0 & 10 & 64 & -17.91 & 0 & 0 & 0 & PI/2 \\
20 & 0 & 0 & 0 & 0 & 0 & 10 & 64 & 43.79 & 0 & 0 & 0 & PI/2 \\
20 & 0 & 0 & 0 & 0 & 0 & 10 & 64 & -43.79 & 0 & 0 & 0 & PI/2
\end{bmatrix}$$

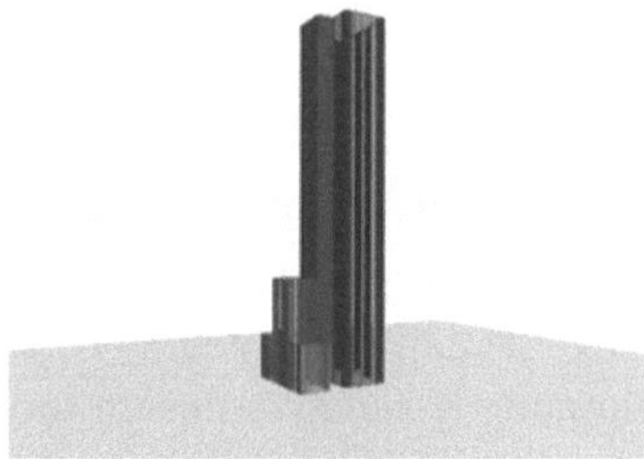

Figure 6. Seagram Building

5. Discussion

5.1. GENERAL CHARACTERISTICS OF THE SYSTEM

The parametric representation provides significant information in the matrix of values. Looking at the matrix, information can be instantly acquired about the type of surfaces that compose the structure (planar or curvilinear), the number of different types, various height levels, existence of repeated elements, relation between the locations of elements etc. Also some values, possibly signifying common features, can be directly read.

By expressing a structure as a series of values that correspond to a special configuration of elements, the designer can instantly create multiple variations of form presented as three-dimensional models. The user interacts by altering values. The model can be modified a limitless amount of times while always maintaining relations between parts. Embedding rules and constrains in the representation, in the form of parameters transforms the otherwise "passive" representation into an active "one" (Kalay 2004). It has been observed from the results that small changes in values can lead to unexpected changes of form. Thus experimenting with random values can lead to interesting creations that may provoke the designer's creativity.

The use of a limited number of variables renders the representation highly flexible. Elements can be assembled in an unlimited number of ways. Moreover it is efficient in terms of speed and simplicity. Embedding rules and relations between elements of the system makes it very easy to understand, manipulate and use. With no special effort a three-dimensional model can be produced simply by entering a number of values.

5.2. LIMITATIONS

The intention of using minimal data restricts the application of the parametric representation. It is not applicable to structures that are composed either of ruled surfaces swept along a free form curve, such as DeCOi's Paramorph, or of free form surfaces, such as the Guggenheim Museum in Bilbao.

5.3. FURTHER WORK

Apart from further development of the representation to include free form curves, it can be integrated with 3D CAD/modelling software as an exploratory generative design tool. Another general development can be the implementation of constraints that connect one surface to the other such as parallelism, perpendicularity and tangency. If the representation is used as a generative design method, constraints such as surface continuity would be useful to ensure that all designs make sense geometrically, or to reach objectives such as structural stability. Constraints can also be specified as conditional relations. Incorporating conditional expressions might extend the interest of the method.

The parametric representation may also be implemented in search techniques. The proposed representation would be integrated in a genetic algorithm by mapping the parameters that describe a surface to a genotype, the alleles of which would correspond to the set of values. An initial set of rules and constraints responding to a given problem and specification of fitness criteria is required, by which a fitness test would evaluate how close the values are to a given example or criterion. Such a process could be used to find a rational ruled surface definition resembling any given form, as in the building representations in section 4, and serve as a point of departure for further design exploration. Alternatively, an analysis of solar shading, structural performance or other properties could be performed on the model and the form optimised to solve a specific design problem.

6. Conclusions

Creating a parametric representation involves choosing the right parameters and establishing connections between them. In this case it has been based on relations between elements that are both simple and economic: the variations produced by the transformation of the helix. This economy of parameters results in a model that is powerful in that it requires very little numeric data to describe a large range of possible forms.

The number of parameters needed (the fewer the better) and the range of forms capable of being represented (the more the better) are the evaluation criteria for the method. In terms of representation, this minimises redundancy in the data required. In terms of search (e.g. genetic algorithm), it reduces the dimensionality of the search space and therefore simplifies the process.

The rich spectrum of produced forms, including planar and a significant number of curvilinear forms, do describe the geometry of a large number of buildings and because of the achieved parameterisation of the various generating curves in a single model, the number of parameters needed is reduced. The more familiar method of joining two boundary curves by line segments has the advantage of allowing any freeform ruled surfaces to be defined, but the majority of curves used in actual buildings are rational curves defined by the proposed method, and for these the parameterisation is minimal.

For buildings consisting of ruled surfaces, a significant amount of information about the form can be encoded in the matrix of values. Having a limited number of variables increases flexibility of representation.

Using surfaces composed of straight lines as building blocks of the system may simplify static calculations as well as the actual construction. The model implicitly offers indications of the structure and its behaviour.

Minimal encoding based on numerical parameters could benefit greatly from employing constraints or links between design elements, something that can be easily achieved in this model because it is mathematically explicit. Constraints are a part of implementation to follow depending on how the model is to be used.

The resulting implementation allows an interactive manipulation of the model by changing parameters. Multiple variations of the model can be rapidly produced so that design exploration is performed by selection of optimal variations. The procedure is simple, developed for a limited number of parameters, user-friendly and efficient in terms of speed. Apart from the integration of the representation in 3D modelling software, encoding structures in this way makes possible its integration in evolutionary design techniques, such as genetic algorithms.

It has been demonstrated how a simple parametric system based on relations of elements and using limited amount of data can be developed as a useful design tool. It can sufficiently represent a wide variety of forms efficiently and with few variables.

Acknowledgements

The authors would like to thank Chiron Mottram for his assistance in the development of the Processing program and his comments.

References

Bentley, P: 1999, An Introduction to Evolutionary Design by Computers, *in* P Bentley (ed), *Evolutionary design by Computers*, Morgan Kaufmann, San Francisco, pp. 1-73.

Bentley, P: 1999a, From Coffee Tables to Hospitals: Generic Evolutionary Design, *in* P Bentley (ed), *Evolutionary design by Computers*, Morgan Kaufmann, San Francisco, pp. 405-423.

Burry, M: 1993, *Expiatory Church of the Sagrada Família*, Phaidon Press, London.

Burry, M: 2003, Between Intuition and Process: Parametric Design and Rapid Prototyping, *in* B Kolarevic (ed), *Architecture in the Digital Age- Design and Manufacturing*, Spon Press, New York, pp. 147-162.

Burry, M, Burry J, Dunlop, GM and Maher A: Drawing Together Euclidean and Topological Threads, *SIRC 2001 – The 13th Annual Colloquium of the Spatial Information Research Centre*, University of Otago, Dunedin, New Zealand.

Coates, P, Broughton, T and Jackson, H: 1999, Exploring Three-Dimensional Design Worlds using Lindenmayer Systems and Genetic Programming, *in* P. Bentley (ed) *Evolutionary design by computers*, Morgan Kaufmann, San Francisco, pp. 324-341.

DeCOi: 2000, Technological Latency: from Autoplastic to Alloplastic, *Digital Creativity* 11 (3): 131-143.

English, EC: 2005, Vladimir Shukhov and the Invention of Hyperboloid Structures, *Metropolis & Beyond: Proceedings of the 2005 Structures Congress and the 2005 Forensic Engineering Symposium*, New York.

Frazer, J: 1995, *An Evolutionary Architecture*, Architectural Association Publications London.

Jackson, H: 2002, Toward a Symbiotic Coevolutionary Approach to Architecture, *in* P Bentley and W Corne (eds), *Creative evolutionary systems*, Morgan Kaufmann, San Francisco, pp. 299-312.

Kalay, YE: 2004, *Architecture's New Media: Principles, Theories, and Methods of Computer-Aided Design*, MIT Press, Cambridge.

Kühnel, W: 2002, *Differential Geometry: Curves - Surfaces – Manifolds*, AMS, Rhode Island.

March, L: 1972, *A Boolean description of a class of built forms*, Cambridge University Press, Cambridge.

March, L and Steadman, P: 1971, *The Geometry of the Environment*, RIBA Publications, London.

O'Neill, B: 1966, *Elementary Differential Geometry*, Academic Press New York.

Rosenman, M and Gero, J: 1999, Evolving Designs by Generating Useful Complex Gene Structures, *in* P Bentley (ed), *Evolutionary design by Computers*, Morgan Kaufmann, San Francisco, pp. 345-364.

Steadman, P: 1998, Sketch for an archetypal building, *Environment and Planning B: Planning and Design, 25th Anniversary Issue*, pp. 92-105.

Steadman, P: 2001, Binary encoding of a Class of Rectangular Built-Forms, *Proceedings, 3rd International Space Syntax Symposium*, Atlanta.

Steadman, P and Waddoups, L: 2000, A Catalogue of Built Forms, using a Binary Representation. *Proceedings 5th International Conference on Design and Decision Support Systems in Architecture*, Nijkerk, The Netherlands, pp. 353-373.

Todd, S and Latham, W: 1999, The Mutation and Growth of Art by Computers, *in* P Bentley (ed), *Evolutionary design by Computers*, Morgan Kaufmann, San Francisco, pp. 221-250.

MANAGING CONTINGENCY IN PARAMETRIC MODELS THROUGH IMPLICIT RELATIONAL MODELING

DAVIS MARQUES AND ROBERT WOODBURY
Simon Fraser University, Canada

Abstract. Modeling and maintaining relationships in a parametric model compounds the work of the designer. When major changes in design direction take place, the work invested in the modeled relations is often lost. We contend that an implicit relational modeling approach provides for loosely coupled relations between the 'parts' of a design and mitigates the loss of work that occurs when changes take place. In our implemented system, implicit relations participate in a pattern of interaction known as the Dynamic Proxy.

1. Managing Contingency and Change

Designs are contingent upon the contexts in which they arise. (Akin, 2000) When a Designer creates a design, she does so in light of her current understanding of what is to be accomplished and the opportunities available to her at that time. Changes to the context prompt the Designer to update or create new designs in order to regain the persuasiveness of her proposals. Similarly, Designers reflect on prior design work and search for design opportunities, then create new designs to reflect their changing goals.

Contingency and change challenge parametric modeling. Not only does the task of modeling relationships increase the complexity of designing but, when changes in design direction take place, the work invested in the modeled relations is lost, further compounding the problem. In the systems approach to organizational management forwarded by Russell L. Ackoff, the performance of a system and its capacity to deal with change are improved when emphasis is placed on *managing the interactions of the parts* rather than on managing the parts themselves. (Ackoff, 2000) We take his argument as instructive for our research in parametric modeling.

In the following, we discuss the process of establishing relationships in a parametric model, characterize the differences between explicit and implicit relations, and report on two recent studies we have conducted in implicit relational modeling.

A Dong, A Vande Moere & JS Gero (eds), CAADFutures'07, 279–288.

2. Explicit and Implicit Relations

Selection is the first step in the process of establishing relationships among objects in a CAD model. Typically, a Designer will establish a relation by using a mouse or keyboard to select two or more existing objects in the model, then apply a function to generate a relation between those objects. What results is an *explicit* relationship that binds one particular object or property to another. The system subsequently maintains the relation between the objects. Explicit relational modeling offers precise control and short execution time. However, if one of the related objects is deleted or changed, the work invested in the modeled relationship may be lost. Similarly, if the relationship itself requires changing, the Designer must visit each object in question, unbind it from other objects, then modify or establish new relations as required. As the size of the model increases and as the complexity of relations grows, changes to the model require increasing investments of time and effort to execute and therefore represent a significant increase in labor over a traditional modeling approach.

Selections may also be defined by other means, such as rules or procedures. In this case, instead of manually selecting the objects to be related, the Designer may define a rule that describes the basis by which relations should be made. When objects in the model satisfy the rule, the computer automatically establishes a relation. Likewise, when those objects no longer satisfy the relational criteria, the computer removes the relation. We characterize this as an *implicit* relational modeling approach, in the sense that the actually formed relations are an implied consequence of the rules expressed and the current configuration of objects.

While both explicit and implicit approaches result in relationships, important differences occur. In an explicit modeling approach, the selection event occurs only once and therefore the objects in the relation must exist in advance of the selection event. In an implicit modeling approach, objects are not required to exist in advance of the user defined selection rule; selection occurs whenever changes in the model trigger a need to update the selection set, and therefore the relations are always up to date. In this way, an implicit approach may reduce the effort of establishing relationships, particularly in situations where a large number of objects are involved. However, this increased expedience may come at the cost of reduced control and significantly increased execution time.

Existing parametric modeling systems provide limited forms of implicit relational modeling. In GenerativeComponents, for example, a Designer could create two objects – a single point (A) at the origin, and a collection of points (B) at some other location – and write a function that generates a line from A to each point in B. When the Designer adds to or removes a point from B, the change prompts the function to update the collection of lines.

The generated lines are created on the basis of the rule encoded in the function – 'from A to each element of B'. The relation between A and B is explicit in the sense that it is hard coded into the function. But, the relation between A and the elements of B is implicit in the sense that as the elements of B change, the corresponding relations will always be updated.

Our contention is that the extant facilities for implicit relational modeling are impoverished in comparison to those provided to form explicit relations. By developing facilities for specifying implicit relations, Designer action may be amplified.

3. Studies in Modeling Dynamic Relations

Contingency and change motivate our research. Design is characterized by a process of change and development. Systems that can automatically establish and maintain relationships in a parametric model will do much to enhance Designer action and reduce the loss of work that takes place when changes occur.

Our research began with experiments in object selection, using 'Bentley Systems' GenerativeComponents as a working environment. Therein, we developed a tool called the *Rule Based Selector* to evaluate means of selecting objects using rules rather than manual operations. Encountering limitations in the working environment, we developed our own test bed CAD system and proceeded to extend our prior work. We developed a computing object called *Behavior* to enact selections dynamically in the environment, and an interface called *IContext* to enable queries about objects in the parametric model. We observed that Behaviors exhibit a pattern of interaction known as the *Dynamic Proxy*. We describe these experiments below.

3.1. RULE BASED SELECTOR

Selection, as we have described, is the first step in establishing relations between objects in a model. The *Rule Based Selector* enables Designers to dynamically select objects in a model using rules rather than manual operations. It has been developed as a GenerativeComponents "Feature" object, written in C# for the GenerativeComponents API.

In GenerativeComponents, designs are represented by a symbolic graph that models the process by which geometry and relationships are generated in the application. Nodes in the symbolic graph are operators, and links are relations between the nodes. To employ the *Rule Based Selector*, Figure 1, the Designer creates an instance of it in the symbolic graph. The Selector takes one or more selection rule statements and an existing object collection as input, then returns references to a subset of the input collection as output. Input rules are entered through the Property Editor.

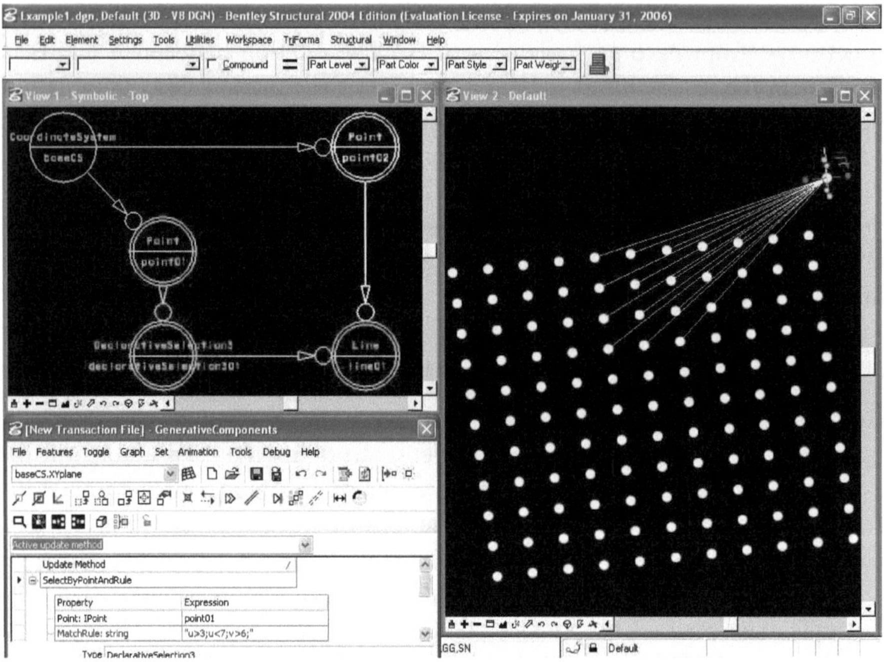

Figure 1. Rule Based Selector in GenerativeComponents. The interface provides three distinct views of the model (clockwise from the top left): a) symbolic graph, b) model view, and c) property editor

Five selection rules are available in the Selector: Exact Match, Range, Nearest Neighbor, Half Space, and Distance. Rules can match against three basic object properties: spatial coordinates (`x,y,z`), surface coordinates (`u,v,d`), and index in a collection (`i,j,k`). Exact Match takes an explicit location or collection index and returns only those objects that exactly match the specified location or index. Range Match takes an explicit location or collection index and returns all objects that fall inside the lower and upper range bounds, inclusively. Nearest Neighbor takes an explicit location for a point in space and finds the nearest elements in the input collection to that point. Half Space takes a plane, or two vectors that designate a half space, and returns all elements in the positive half of the space, inclusive of the boundary. Finally, Distance takes a point or collection as an input set, and a positive distance value and returns those elements of the input set which are equal to or less than the distance away. The result sets from each rule statement can then be further operated upon using logical operators `AND`, `OR`, and `NOT`. If the designer provides improper selection rules or input objects, or if the result is logically null, the Selector returns an empty set. Rules are specified using a functional syntax. For example, `Px(1.0,1.0,1.0)` uses the Exact Match rule to select an object that is at coordinates 1.0,1.0,1.0.

Wildcards may also be entered to create broad matches. For example, `Px(*,1.0,1.0)` selects objects with any x coordinate value, and y and z coordinates of 1.0.

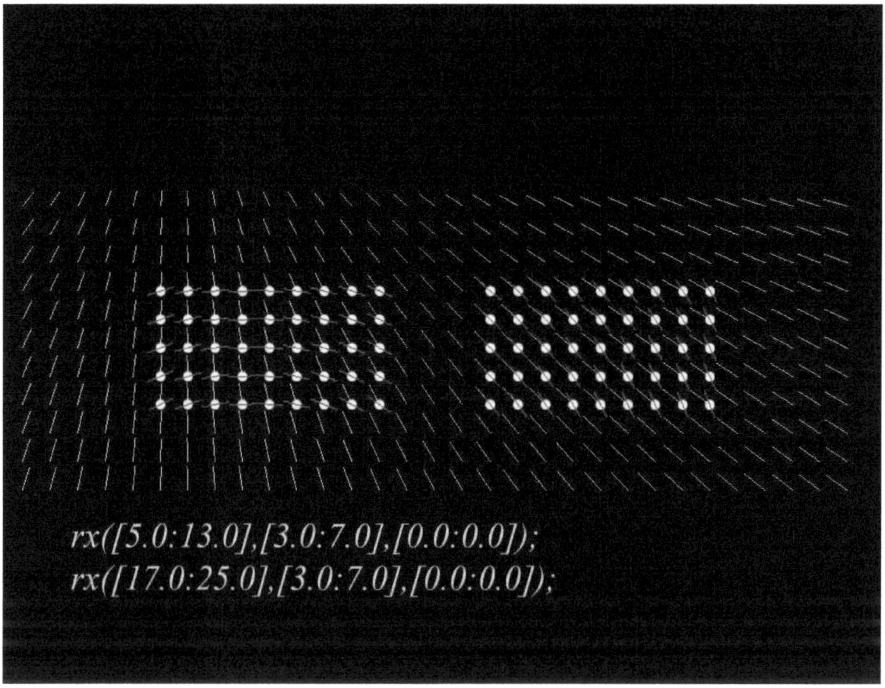

Figure 2. Selection rules can be used to make complex object selections with relatively little work. Here, the Rule Based Selector is employed to select two subregions of a grid of points. The large dots represent the selected points; the statements at the bottom of the image are the corresponding selection rules

In developing the *Rule Based Selector*, three areas for further development became apparent. First, Generative Components provided limited facilities for making queries of the model. Selector could effectively ask questions of its input node in the symbolic graph but, could not query the entire collection of objects that comprised the model, for example. Therefore, providing an interface in the environment to provide much broader querying facilities would aid the process of automating selection. Second, our functional selection syntax, while concise, greatly limited the properties that Designers could match against. Declarative selection languages such as Structured Query Language (SQL), for example, provide a better model for enacting selections against arbitrary object properties based on logical criteria. Third, selection is only the first step in the process of establishing a relation. Once a selection has been made, some action is still required to instantiate the relation.

3.2. BEHAVIOR AND ICONTEXT

Reflecting on our experiences with development of the *Rule Based Selector*, it became apparent that we needed to have access to the details of the modeling system in order to advance our research further. Consequently, we created our own rudimentary, propagation-based parametric modeler, called Federation, to give us an open test environment for our work. Federation is loosely modeled after Generative Components, and is implemented in the Java programming language. In Federation, we conceive of the parametric model as a system of interacting parts; the interactions of parts realize designs. Like Generative Components, a symbolic graph models the process by which parts are realized and interactions occur. Federation data models comprise three fundamental entities: *Assembly*, *Behavior* and *Scenario*. Assemblies are parametric objects. Behaviors are computational entities that assist the Designer in managing contingent relations between parametric objects. Scenarios are particular configurations of parametric objects and relations, constituting a design. Our immediate research goal was to devise an interface for making queries about objects in the parametric model, improve our selection rule syntax, and couple selection with an action in order to complete the process of establishing relationships.

Behaviors are computational entities that assist the Designer in managing contingent relations between objects in a parametric model. *Behavior* instances are comprised of two parts: a selection statement that defines objects and conditions of interest, and a *Context* that the *Behavior* observes for those objects and conditions. The selection statement is specified in a SQL-like language, and takes the following form:

```
SELECT [Target] FROM [Context] WHERE [Conditions]
[Post-selection commands]
```

The statement comprises four parts: target, context, conditions and post-selection commands. Statements always begins with the `SELECT` keyword, followed by the selection target. The selection target is the set of potential candidate objects for matching, and is either `*`, to designate any or all objects in a particular *Context*, `[Object Name]` to specify a particular named target, or `[Object Name].*` to designate any or all properties of a particular named object. Object names in Federation must be valid Java identifiers. Following the target is the `FROM` keyword, and a named *Context*. A *Context* is an object that contains other objects, and is identified by a unique name. Selection conditions begin with the `WHERE` keyword, and are followed by one or more Designer specified logical criteria. Currently implemented logical operators include equality (=), greater-than (>), less-than(<), inequality (`!=`). Operators produce result sets that can be operated on with `AND`, `OR` and `NOT` logical operators. Our current implementation includes only the `AND` operator. Post-selection commands are used to order, filter, and otherwise modify the result sets following identification of matching objects. For example, a command named `LIMIT` may be used to limit the number of matching objects in the result set. No post-selection commands are currently implemented in the current version. An example of a complete selection statement is as follows:

```
SELECT * FROM MyModel WHERE x>3.0 AND Color='RED'
OR name='GridLine01' LIMIT 1
```

The selection statement is decomposed into a parse tree and examined upon assignment to the *Behavior*. For the *Behavior* to be able to operate, the statement must not only be syntactically valid, but the specified *Context* to which it refers must both exist and be an observable object; that is, an object that extends the Java Observable class. The *Behavior* in turn implements the *Observer* interface. If the *Context* is valid, the *Behavior* observes it for changes. When a change occurs, the *Context* signals the *Behavior* through the update method of its *Observer* interface. If either condition is false, the *Behavior* produces an empty result set.

Queries of a *Context* are made through the *IContext* interface. The interface provides methods to get the list of elements that are members of the *Context*, and to lookup objects by name. Selections are made, or, in other words, target objects are located, by searching through the list of elements in the *Context*. Object properties are examined through reflection against the conditions held in the parse tree. When a match is encountered, it is added to a target list stored in the *Behavior*. The target list is updated each time a change occurs in the *Context*, or when the selection statement is changed.

Like Generative Components, relations in Federation can then be instantiated by objects in the symbolic graph that take the target list from the *Behavior* and use them as input to some other operation.

3.2.1. Dynamic Proxy Pattern

Christopher Alexander is credited with having introduced the notion of *design pattern*. A design pattern is quite simply a recurring relationship or interaction. The object-oriented software community has taken up the notion of design patterns as an outgrowth of object-oriented design techniques, and through the recognition of many recurring and useful interaction patterns among common software objects. We observe that Behaviors participate in a pattern of interaction known as the *Dynamic Proxy*. The *Dynamic Proxy* combines the *Observer* and *Proxy* patterns.

Figure 3. Observer pattern. The Observer monitors the Observable object for changes. It does so by telling the Observable object that it is interested in it. When a change occurs in the Observable object, it sends a message to all registered observers. The observers receive the update message through their Observer interface

The *Observer* pattern is comprised of two participants: an *Observable* object and an *Observer* that monitors that object for changes. The *Observable* object implements a method that enables the *Observer* to register its interest in that object. When a change occurs in the *Observable* object, it sends a message to all the registered *Observers* notifying them of the change. The *Observer* in turn implements an interface that enables it to receive messages from the *Observable* object. When the *Observer* receives a change notification message from the *Observable* object, it can then take action based on the nature of the change.

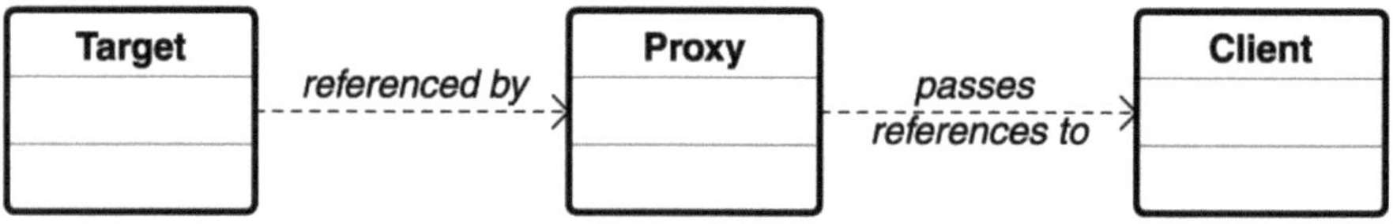

Figure 4. Proxy Pattern. The Proxy acts as a surrogate for the Target, or aids the Client by simplifying or hiding details of how the Target object is acquired

The *Proxy* pattern is comprised of three participants: Target, Proxy, and Client. The Target is an object of interest to another object we call the Client. The Proxy is an intermediary object that acts as a surrogate for the target, or otherwise hides the details of how the Target is created or acquired.

A *Dynamic Proxy* is a Proxy that monitors the *Context* or Target for changes and, when they occur, updates its relation with the Target and Client automatically. By changes, we suggest that either the object or objects that

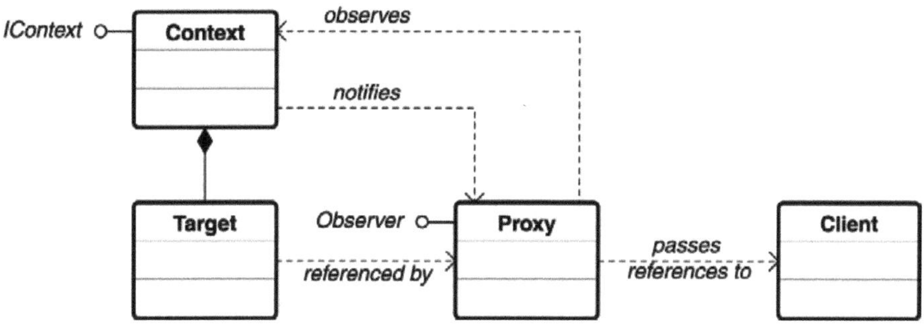

Figure 5. The Dynamic Proxy pattern. In federation, behavior plays the role of the proxy and monitors the context for changes. When changes occur, it searches the context for objects of interest to the client. References to the set of matching target objects are then passed on to the client

are the Target themselves change, or the state of the Target changes. Behaviors participate in the *Dynamic Proxy* pattern in our application.

We describe the *Dynamic Proxy* pattern here as comprising four participants: Context, Target, Proxy and Client. Figure 5 illustrates this interaction pattern. The Context is a collection of objects. The Target comprises one or more objects in the Context that match some criteria of interest to the Client. The Client registers its interest in the Target by way of the *Dynamic Proxy*. The Proxy, implemented by Behaviors in our application, observes the Context for changes. When a change occurs in the Context, the Proxy is signaled to update. If the Target changes, the Proxy informs the Client of the update and relays the new Target set to it. The Client may then retrieve the Target set from the Proxy, and use those objects for furthcr computation.

4. Future Research

We contend that implicit relational modeling provides for loosely coupled relations between parts, and serves the purpose of mitigating the loss of work when changes take place. The rule based approach to selection is an example of managing the interaction of parts. The *Dynamic Proxy* pattern elucidates the interactions of objects around the act of selection.

A number of avenues for future development present themselves. First, we recognize that when multiple Behaviors are instantiated in a single *Context*, search overhead becomes significant and highly redundant. An apparent means of increasing performance is to centralize the search process by having Behaviors register their targets with the *IContext*. The *IContext* in turn would index elements in the *Context* based on registered queries, group registered queries into a hierarchy of search conditions, and signal Behaviors when objects pertaining to their queries have changed. In this way, redundancy could be diminished and search speed increased. Second, more work needs to be done to investigate the connection between the act of selecting objects for relations and the act of establishing those relations. This is part of our current study. Finally, we recognize that there is potential to build implicit selection into manual interactions with the system. Selecting a source object and then selecting a target object while holding a modifier key could be used to automatically generate an implicit relation based on the target object name, for example. Or, selecting multiple target objects could prompt the system to make inferences about the common properties of the target set, and present the Designer with a palette of conditions from which to build the relation.

References

Ackoff, RL: 1999, *Recreating the Corporation, A Design of Organizations for the 21st Century,* Oxford University Press, New York.

Aish, R and Woodbury, R: 2005, Multi-Level Interaction in Parametric Design, *in* A Butz et al. (eds), *Smart Graphics 2005*, LNCS 3638, pp. 151-162.

Akin, O: 2001, Variants in Design Cognition, in C. Eastman et al. (eds) Design Knowing and Learning: Cognition in Design Education, Elsevier.

Alexander, C: 1979, *The Timeless Way of Building*, Oxford University Press, New York.

Cooper, JW: 2000, *Java Design Patterns: A Tutorial*, Addison-Wesley Professional, Reading, MA.

Marques, D and Woodbury, R: 2006, Using Rule Based Selection to Support Change in Parametric CAD Models, *in* A Butz et al. (eds), *SmartGraphics 2006*, LNCS 4073, pp. 230-235.

BEING SUPPORTIVE

EARLY ARCHITECTURAL DESIGN AND BIM

HANNU PENTTILÄ
Helsinki University of Technology, Finland

Abstract. This paper examines the meaning of information and communication technology (ICT) for architectural design in early design project phases, with a particular interest in building information modelling (BIM). Contemporary digital design environment, research context and objectives are first clarified, followed by the presentation and analysis of a few BIM-related projects. A key finding is that the architectural working environment, the design methods and the designer's roles have changed in the contemporary project context. Furthermore, other methods and tools are needed in addition to BIM in the early project phases, because it can not solve all required design aspects. [The presentation is part of the author's post-graduate studies in architectural BIM].

1. Background

1.1. CHANGES IN THE DIGITAL DESIGN ENVIRONMENT

It has recently been noticed that several changes within the domain of architectural design have been strongly affected by information and communication technologies (ICT).

The working environment of building designers as well as most of the core activities in the AEC-sector became digitalized during the 1990s (Samuelson 2002). In the Scandinavian construction sector, roughly 70-80% of drawings are currently produced digitally. A Nordic IT-barometer scanning the ICT-status was first published in 1998, then again in 2002 and a third survey is currently in progress, and is due to publish follow-up information in spring 2007.

Despite the tools and technology, the widening spectrum of requirements posed by our society has accelerated these changes in the professional environment. All these prevailing changes together are currently re-forming the contemporary profile of the architectural profession. New professional

A Dong, A Vande Moere & JS Gero (eds), CAADFutures'07, 291–302.

roles have also emerged within the architectural practice, in particular the ICT leaders, coordinators and managers (Penttilä 2006).

A positive sign is that the central designers' professional organizations (Bucher 2003; Eastman 2006) as well as other bodies in the construction field have noticed and reacted to these changes in the working environment, which are likely to expand with an accelerating pace in the future.

1.2. THE ADVENT OF BIM

It has been claimed that Building Information Modelling (BIM) has become one of the major trends in contemporary AEC-field information technology (Froese 2003) and will continue to do so in the near future. BIM is an integrated digital framework that forms the information management basis for all building project collaboration over the lifespan of the building in the design-construction-maintenance -chain. Recently, BIM-based methods have started to expand to design and construction practice. Active efforts towards BIM have been recognized at least in USA, Finland, Norway, Japan, Denmark, Germany, Australia and Singapore.

BIM has so far been mainly tested and piloted in component-based detailed design phases, where one selected design proposal is selected to be developed further. Beyond design, active fields for BIM-piloting have also been construction planning and actual construction phases. Even if the addressed and proposed advantages of using BIM derive from the earliest project phases, model-based design methods have not yet been used so much in the early project phases nor in early architectural design. Although the benefits of BIM in the management requirements of the early project phases have been addressed (Kiviniemi 2005), there are still no proper software tools to manage project objectives or requirements in the model-oriented design environment.

The major recent technical cross-platform data exchange standard in BIM applications is IFC (Industrial Foundation Classes). But despite IFC's ever-widening distribution, there have also been some drawbacks in the pilot projects in recent years. The criticisms have not been targeted so much towards the standard itself nor its structure but rather the IFC's actual promotion and the insufficient development activities (Kiviniemi 2006). Nevertheless, it seems that IFC will quite obviously be developed and used in the near future as the independent data exchange tool together with other software specific formats such as DWG and ArchiCAD's PLN.

Criticism has also recently been raised towards BIM from a theoretical aspect. It has been questioned whether top-down-oriented and "centrally controlled" data management approaches, which follow a single modelling method – such as BIM – really can be a proper platform for comprehensive architectural design data management (Kalay 2006). The nature and essence of the architectural information environment is heterogeneous, and hence rich and complex information structures should also be taken into account (Tuncer et al. 2001).

2. The Research Effort

2.1. THE RESEARCH CONTEXT AND LINKS TO RELATED RESEARCH

There is certainly a long research tradition in the design theory and design methods community within architecture (Groat 2002). The wide topic of *architectural design* can be seen as a design context issue as well as a qualitative issue. Design can also be seen as a more pragmatic design practice issue, dealing with the design activities, work and processing (Cuff 1992). The latter praxis-approach is closer to the research scope of the present on-going study.

The main research contexts of this work are *architectural ICT*, computer-aided design (CAD) as well as computer-aided architectural design (CAAD). This work is also related conceptually to several other design-related research domains. The most obvious context, *BIM-related research*, can be regarded as another major research trend.

Building information modelling has been under research within construction and design fields since the 1980s (Eastman 1999), but information modelling research in other industry areas such as product design, ship building, automotive & aviation engineering are still valid fields to include within the overall context. Model-based information management has much more extensive use in automotive design and naval architecture than in construction, and hence knowledge gained from these will definitely have an influence on some future trends, bringing forward solutions to architecture as well. Model-related issues and so-called simulation-based design (SBD) have been an active research area within naval architecture (Baum et al. 1997; Chang et al. 1998).

CAD and BIM have a strong research connection with software engineering. Within the building design context, one object-oriented software platform to test BIM in educational and research environment was the Building Design Advisor (BDA) during the late 1990s (Papamichael 1999). Despite the object-oriented approach, such topics as CAD-automation, design content analysis, design collaboration and agent-based design (Beetz et al. 2004) have been essential in design data integration. Currently active BIM-related research topics include, for instance, multiple model environments and BIM-model servers, which will possibly offer some solutions also for early design dilemmas.

Since the 1990s economy-oriented leadership and business management have affected the expansion of the design management research domain. Changes in business processes as well as the status of the architectural profession within construction have come to mean that architectural design is a sector which has to be managed, and hence the field requires also leadership actions (Otter and Prins 2002). Within the context of leadership, economic and organizational changes, an enthusiastic research domain in the management of change appeared the mid-1990s (Kotter 1996).

General design theory within civil and mechanical engineering and systems science has tackled the essential question of collaborative design and it has also been discussed within architecture (Haymaker 2000). Design requirements management, which has been a domain in systematic engineering and product-oriented design, has just recently emerged as a question in building projects information processes (Kiviniemi 2005).

To summarize the present research context, architectural design and construction field related ICT and BIM is a multi-disciplinary research area, where several adjoining and loosely related research domains form the actual research context, and where also non-traditionally architecture related domains have to be studied as well.

2.2. AIMS AND OBJECTIVES

The aim of my research (in the doctoral thesis) is to analyze and validate the possibilities of the widespread use of ICT in early architectural design, in project planning, in design proposals and their evaluation. Since the concept of BIM has recently raised hopes and aspirations, the changing effects of ICT- and BIM-based methods will be at the centre of the scope of the research.

Most important architectural design ideas and project principles are created in the earliest phases of architectural design. Fundamental design decisions are also made in the early project phases. Despite the designers' reputation and known references, another critical aspect in early design and even earlier designer approval, is the ability to generate and present design ideas and project proposals. Nevertheless, currently developing model-based design methods, such as BIM, seem to require very detailed component-based building modelling, methods, which usually are used only in the later design phases.

2.3. DESCRIPTION OF THE RESEARCH METHOD

A study of the literature dealing with contemporary architectural ICT and BIM has been made, as well as a few empirical case-studies. The next planned major research step is to undertake interviews to collect early design-related material from the Finnish AEC-field.

From the collected material (literature, case-studies and interviews) a comprehensive description of ICT and BIM within early architectural design will be presented in the form of a hypothetical framework or "model". Finally, the created framework and findings will be evaluated and validated.

Research categories for this work are applied research and information transfer from research to design and the construction field practice.

2.4. EXPECTATIONS OF THE FINAL RESULTS OF THE RESEARCH

The research will clarify the content and management of early architectural design related issues, in order to fit early design activities better within the contemporary digital design and construction chain.

Rather new topics, such as requirements management and modelling (Kiviniemi 2005), design management and client-related communication are regarded as essential and important for early architectural design; hence the role of ICT should be discussed in this context.

This work will also help in analyzing the dualism between architectural design and ICT, between "computer-aided" and "design". The dualism is characteristic of architectural ICT: on the one hand, the semantics of the most essential design content – the most traditional architectural virtue – and, on the other hand, the more pragmatic syntax of ICT-tools and methods in representing and managing the design content.

3. The Early Architectural Design Framework

Contemporary architects have to be, in accordance with their professional tradition, skilful designers who concentrate on design content, form-giving and overall design quality issues. But beyond the design work, architects today also have to be communicative leaders and project managers, who can coordinate and guide pragmatic design work. In the current ICT-dominated working environments, architects have also to master a wide variety of technical skills; i.e. to be ICT-specialists.

3.1. CLASSIFICATIONS

Since building projects vary a lot in regard to their organizational and owner structures, the project volumes and objectives as well as their design content, they have to be classified by their ICT-structure and information content. A usable classification basis has been put forward, for instance, in Anders Ekholm's paper "A conceptual framework for classification of construction works" (Ekholm 1996) and in ISO's classification of information in the construction industry (ISO 1994). But beyond the classification on the conceptual level, a more pragmatic classification has to be performed (i.e. project-owner based, size based, housing, building renovation, etc.) in order to properly fit the ICT-methods to the actual project context.

3.2. NEEDS AND OBJECTIVES FOR INFORMATION MODELLING

An important task before launching any building project is to define the project's information management objectives and aims, and to answer the question of *why* ICT or even BIM will be used in the project. Together with the defined objectives, also the pragmatic information management methods and tools have to be defined precisely.

3.3. INFORMATION EXCHANGE NEEDS

Derived from project objectives, all considerable data exchange needs in all project phases should be estimated before the project commences. Typical early project data exchange requirements are, for instance:

- information delivery to clients and project management
- the public sector's and authorities' information requirements and needs
- coordinated data exchange to later detailed design phases
- integrated information delivery within the design team (collaboration)

Especially in BIM-projects, proper information structuring, starting from the earliest project phases, has been crucially important to avoid later data format or structural modifications which will always cause unnecessary losses in information content.

A very pragmatic solution for the project's data exchange needs and definitions can be a list of agreed file formats and versions (DOC, DWG, IFC, etc.) as well as methods to be used (email, project web, etc.).

3.4. EARLY DESIGN MODEL CONTENT REQUIREMENTS

Since early design always has to be based on poorly structured, vague and fuzzy information, assumptions, best possible guesses or even illusions, the early architectural design information management context has to be as versatile and flexible as possible.

The ICT tools and methods for early architectural design have some general but important requirements. Characteristic of ICT in the early design phases is that all methods and tools have to be "supportive" for the design work as well as for decision making. Since early design data is by nature cumulative, the methods have to be easily modifiable. Because of the extensive variety of possible source information, the tools have to be very "responsive" to receive in the beginning almost whatever information.

4. Motivating Case Examples – An Empirical Approach

Three BIM-related case studies are presented briefly in order to describe the nature of early architectural design and its relation with ICT, CAD and BIM.

All presented cases are still on-going projects where the author has had a noticeable contribution.

4.1. BIM GUIDELINES AND STRUCTURAL LIBRARIES

The National Finnish Pro IT -guidelines for BIM were first written in 2004 and they were updated in 2005-2006. Two of them have already been published and the rest are currently in the process of being published by the Finnish Building Information Group. (The publications are being published in Finnish only, but there are plans to translate also a report in English in the near future).

TABLE 1. Finnish Pro IT building information modelling publications

	published	publishing plan
General BIM guidelines	2006	
Architectural design BIM-guidelines	2006	
Structural design BIM-guidelines		2007
Technical design BIM guidelines (HVAC, etc.)		2007
Project guidelines for a BIM-project		2007

Together with these reports, a set of structural building components have also been developed to form a proposed future platform for integrated design and production. The main idea has been to collect, approve and publish around 200 typical layered structural type structures, such as slab-, wall- and roof-types in digital form, which then could be used in BIM-based applications. The structural libraries will be published:

- as part of Building Information's so-called RT-building files (paper & CD)
- in CAD-systems' starting templates (Revit and ArchiCAD)

Figure 1. Finnish Pro IT structural type library, 2005

Pro IT has been accomplished as a committee work, with several active participants. The author, together with his company, has contributed as an editor in four of the above-mentioned reports as well as the structural type library.

The BIM-related research work and the recent pragmatic application and piloting phase together have formed a common understanding about a "desired BIM future" in Finland, where the whole process chain from building design through to production and maintenance could be managed and run in a well-structured and software-independent project environment.

The BIM-related activities are currently instructed with software-related and technical guidelines, but also some company level strategic and integrated instructions are available. The general objective for guidelines has changed from application-oriented guidance towards more operative steering procedures.

One important area, which needs further effort, is the juridical aspect of design and construction. Contracts and agreements between project participants concerning processes, operations and activities are currently based on [design] documents, even if they are done with CAD. The slow but indispensable evolution from document-oriented design towards model-oriented design still requires much rethinking and adjustments in regard to most parts of the building project chain. Recently most major project organizations and key players in the national AEC-field have produced their own objectives and strategies for modelling, which means that also the written and economic agreements will in the near future fit better to the BIM-context.

4.2. BIM IN RENOVATION DESIGN

Senate Properties, the largest real estate owner of state facilities in Finland, announced in December 2006 that after 1.10.2007 they will require design content to be delivered in IFC-format (Senate Properties 2006).

So far BIM activities have concentrated mainly on new buildings, and hence, Senate Properties launched a project to study BIM in the context of renovation of culturally-valuable facilities. Currently 55% of the total volume of construction in Finland is concerned with renovation projects. This research study was carried out by ArkIT, HUT's digital architecture team, and the work is due to be documented during spring 2007.

The main focus of this effort has been the different aspects of model-based renovation as it concerns the facility owners, project managers and renovation designers. In renovation design, especially in culturally-valuable facilities, all existing project inventory and status information should be easily accessible, usable and also digitally referable in order to support design decisions in all project phases.

In addition to presenting the various available information management, 3D-modelling and measuring methods such as 3D-laser scanning, the concept of an inventory model has been elaborated. Scattered inventory information has to be collectable and storable in well-structured formats through the whole renovation process.

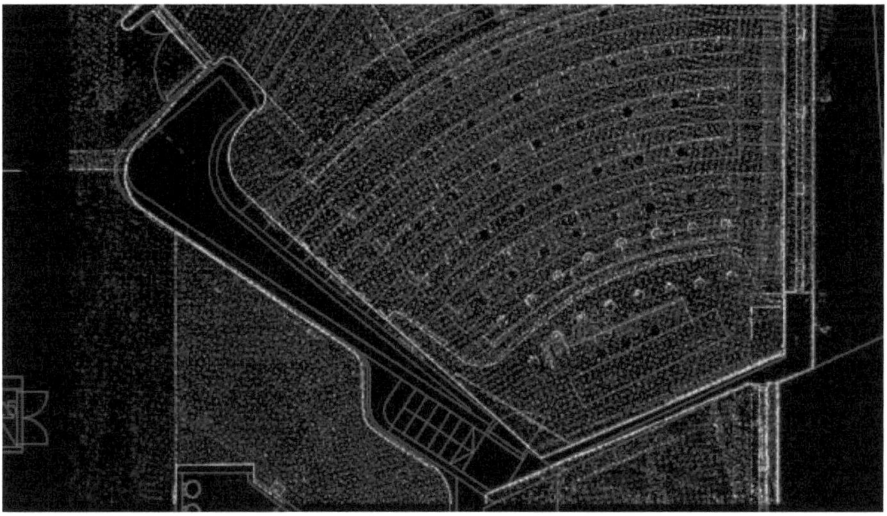

Figure 2. Example of inventory data from HUT's Department of Architecture building. Integrating the architect's original drawings (Alvar Aalto, 1961), digital inventory drawings (1994) and contemporary 3D-laser scanning data (2006)

One key finding has been the confirmed observation that renovation-related early design has to tolerate, accept and manage versatile material, which could hardly not be integrated into a single 3D or BIM-environment. Typical examples of existing content are photographs (paper and digital), written specifications, old drawings (paper and scanned) but also phone calls, agreements, approvals and decisions of various kinds. This may be the major difference, which deposes renovation design from considering designing new buildings.

4.3. A PRELIMINARY DESIGN MODEL STUDY IN COST ESTIMATION

The final case-study to be presented is the most technical, and it describes how a BIM-model can be connected to an existing CAD-tool.

Klara.biz is a PC-based single user cost-estimation software product for small- and medium-sized user organizations. The author has been responsible for the software platform and programming with relational database tools. Klara has been published in Finnish since 2001.

In the cost-estimation process, the most essential core information of design quantities is first transferred to Klara, either in a structured quantity file or, more traditionally, by hand. Data exchange from CAD-systems is done in a simple file format, but the possibility of also including an IFC-module within Klara, has been studied. The first part of the actual cost estimation is to link the quantity data to Klara's product library which should be harmonized with the CAD-systems equivalent libraries.

In the cost estimation process it is first essential to discover the cost components, which are not included in the CAD-based quantities. Typical examples are builder-related general costs, site-related costs and such technical systems which have not yet been designed. The cost manager continues, then, to adjust, fine tune and specify the cost components and finally confirms that all needed and relevant cost-related items have been included and are based on realistic foundations within the project.

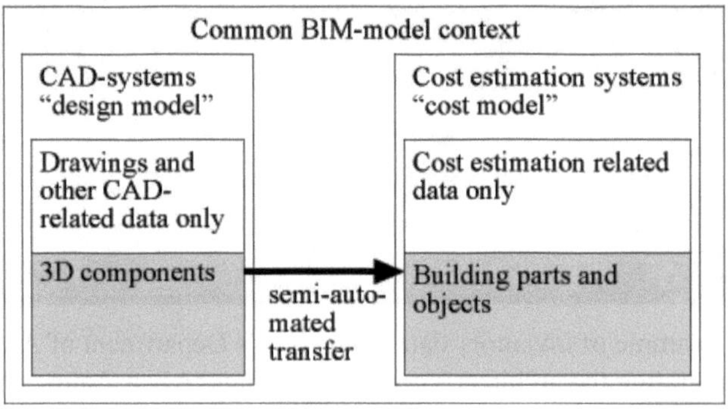

Figure 3. Diagram of CAD and cost-estimation data contents in relation to BIM

If the design proposal is represented in 2D CAD-drawings, the cost components are created in Klara-software by hand, but if the design proposal is modelled with 3D-components, some 50-60% of the total costs can be related to the building geometry, and hence that data can be transferred automatically to Klara.

Accurate cost estimation requires special building economics expertise, but more general understanding of building costs can be grasped with less experience. Hence, rough design-related building costs could be included even in architects' common knowledge, though economics is not the designer's core area of competence. Evaluative cost estimations – e.g. what is expensive and what may be cheaper? – can be semi-automatically calculated with contemporary software tools.

Cost-based content analysis in early design phases can offer valuable information for clients and managers, if the cost simulations are easy and quick to produce. Combined with other simulations and analysis – such as visual, functional, or thermal aspects – the project leaders can acquire a better and more comprehensive understanding of the project in a more extensive context already in the early and schematic phases of the project.

5. Conclusion

The work in the case-studies has been a question of re-defining and fine-tuning the BIM concept in terms of the way it has been of help in distributing the wider understanding of the model-based concepts and their meaning in design and construction practice.

The larger a building project is, the more potential it has to be a BIM project. For instance, well-structured and well-defined housing projects by one major developer have been effective for such modelling. The most successful BIM projects have had clear project objectives and a single major client/developer.

The need to coordinate interactively the complicated design contents of various disciplines, even with regard to long-term objectives in terms of lifecycle, has also been one feature (often a desired one) in the categorization of BIM projects. There is usually no urgent need to integrate information in small projects, but small projects may still well be valuable for learning and piloting building model-based activities.

The BIM concept is currently seen as one possible and promising working and data exchange method which enables wide cross-platform interaction and a possibility for life-long project data management. Nevertheless, BIM should not be seen as the one and only design method for an architectural designer in the early phases of a project. BIM is rather a method to be used, if and when interactive data exchange is required in later project phases.

BIM has been developed and so far also piloted mainly in detailed design and technical construction phases. For the early design context BIM is still a recommended entry point but one which needs further investigation, especially when further knowledge in the building project information chain is the desired objective in the information logistics of the construction field.

References

Baum, SJ; Ramakrishnan, R: 1997, Applying 3D Product Modeling Technology to Shipbuilding, *Marine Technology and SNAME News* **34**(1): 56-65.

Beetz, J, van Leeuwen, J and de Vries, B: 2004, Towards a Multi Agent System for the Support of Collaborative Design, *in* JP Van Leeuwen and HJP Timmermans (eds), *Developments in Design & Decision Support Systems in Architecture and Urban Planning*, Eindhoven University of Technology, Eindhoven, pp. 269-280.

Bucher, C (ed): 2003, Architect's Profile – Professional Practise, reference document, ACE, Architect's Council of Europe. Retrieved May 10, 2006 from http://www.ace-cae.org/Public/content/EN/pos/pro/prof001.html.

Chang, KH, Choi, KK, Wang, J, Tsai, C-S and Hardee, E: 1998, A Multilevel Product Model for Simulation-Based Design of Mechanical Systems, *Concurrent Engineering* **6**(2): 131-144.

Cuff, D: 1992, *Architecture. The Story of Practise*, MIT Press, Cambridge, MA.

Eastman, C: 2006; Report of Integrated Practice – University and Industry Research in Support of BIM, American Institute of Architects AIA. Retrieved March 20, 2007 from http://www.aia.org/.

Eastman, C: 1999, *Building product models. Computer environments supporting design and construction*, CRC Press, Boca-Raton, FL.

Ekholm A: 1996, A conceptual framework for classification of construction works, *Journal of Information Technology in Construction ITcon* **1**: pp. 25-50. Retrieved from http://www.itcon.org/1996/2.

Froese T: 2003, Future directions for IFC-based interoperability, *Journal of Information Technology in Construction ITcon* 8: 231-246. Retrieved from http://www.itcon.org/2003/17.

Groat, L and Wang, D: 2002, *Architectural Research Methods*, John Wiley & Sons, Chichester.

ISO Technical Report 14177, Classification of information in the construction industry. Retrieved January 16, 2007 from http://www.iso.org.

Kalay, YE: 2006, The impact of information technology on design methods, products and practices, *Design Studies* **27**(3): 357-380.

Kiviniemi, A: 2006, Ten years of IFC-development – Why are we not yet there?, *Building on IT – Joint International Conference on Computing and Decision Making in Civil and Building Engineering, ISCCBE, ASCE and CIB-W78 & CIB-W102*, Universite du Quebec, Montreal, Canada.

Kiviniemi, A: 2005, Requirements Management Interface to Building Product Models, CIFE Technical Report #161, Stanford University.

Kotter, JP: 1996, *Leading Change*, Harvard Business School Press, Boston, MA.

Nordic Information Society Statistics 2002, Nordic Council of Ministers, Yliopistopaino, Helsinki.

den Otter, A and Prins M: 2002, Design Management Within the Digital Design Team, *ECAM* **9**(3): 162-173.

Papamichael, K: 1999, Application of information technologies in building design decisions, *Building Research & Information* **27**(1): 20-34.

Penttilä, H: 2006, The effects of information and communication technology on architectural profession, ECPPM – eWork and eBusiness, Valencia, Spain, 13-15 September 2006 *in* M Martinez and R Scherer (eds), *Architecture, Engineering and Construction*, pp. 615-622.

Penttilä, H: 2005, The State of the Art of Finnish Building Product Modelling Methodology, *in* B Martens and A Brown (eds), *Computer Aided Architectural Design Futures*, Springer Verlag, Wien, pp. 225-239.

Samuelson O: 2002, IT-Barometer 2000 – The Use of IT in the Nordic Construction Industry, *Journal of Information Technology in Construction ITcon* **7**: 1-26. Retrieved from http://www.itcon.org/2002/1.

Senate Properties, Senate Properties' product modelling requirements 2007. Retrieved January 15, 2007 from http://www.senaatti.fi/document.asp?siteID=2&docID=517.

Tunçer, B, Stouffs, R and Sariyildiz, S: 2001, Rich Information Structures, *in* H Penttilä (ed), *Architectural Information Management 19th eCAADe Conference Proceedings*, Helsinki, pp. 30-35.

DEVELOPING A FRAMEWORK FOR LINKING DESIGN INTELLIGENCE FROM MULTIPLE PROFESSIONS IN THE AEC INDUSTRY

DOMINIK HOLZER, YAMIN TENGONO
RMIT, Australia

and

STEVEN DOWNING
Arup, Australia

Abstract. The research presented in this paper addresses the issue of bridging conceptual differences between the theories and practice of various disciplines in the AEC industry. The authors propose an application logic that works as a framework in assisting the evaluation process of multidisciplinary design. Parametric design templates assist in channeling and integrating information generated during the design process.

1. Introduction

The authors of this paper draw from experience in practice as well as academic discourse. They illustrate the development of a collaborative design framework which is extending the capabilities of a basic model which has previously been developed in the professional organisation (Arup) they are currently embedded in. It is assessed if synergies can be found between the proposed framework and existing efforts in the field – in particular the Building Information Model (BIM) through the application of Industry Foundation Classes (IFCs). The questions raised in this paper are of serious concern for building practice as well as building up epistemological knowledge in the field.

1.1. COMBINED PROFESSIONAL/ACADEMIC RESEARCH

It has shown highly beneficial in the conception of this paper that the authors are part of a team of professionals and researchers from architectural, IT/engineering and computer science background. Next to their commitment

A Dong, A Vande Moere & JS Gero (eds), CAADFutures'07, 303–316.

within academia, they are associated with a large multi-disciplinary design firm, which is acting on a global level. By working in this collaborative environment, the authors have been able to conduct applied research in order to bridge the gap between experimental academic discourse and requirements from everyday practice.

Due to the nature of the AEC industry, where teams reconfigure on a project-basis, few systems are in place to help transfer knowledge gained on projects across disciplines to foster systemic innovations. (Taylor and Levitt 2004) Professional organisations often face difficulties in developing procedural as well as organisational memory from the projects they carry out for building up epistemological knowledge in practice (Acha, Gann and Salter 2005). Preliminary outcomes of the research undertaken by the authors suggest that being in the centre of often contradicting layers of interest from different parties is not an easy position to be in, but it is at this cusp where the most challenging issues get raised.

1.2. RESEARCH AIM

One problem identified by the multidisciplinary organisation the authors are embedded in, is the insufficient interfacing capability of digital tools within the company and across their industry partners. As described in the 2006 *Report on integrated practice* of the American Institute of Architects (AIA), feedback from specialists to the designers in the AEC industry only occurs *at discrete points with varying frequency* (Bedrick and Rinella 2006) which causes delays and discontinuities in the workflow and consequently is responsible for coordination errors and the necessity to rework. Current specialist software tools of the individual professions in the AEC industry are not well suited for facilitating collaborative design, planning and construction (Kannengiesser and Gero 2004). An integrated workflow is depending on data exchange formats and capabilities of communicating design intelligence in a clearly understandable fashion across teams for feedback and evaluation purposes. (Chaszar 2003)

In response to the requirements mentioned above, the authors have focussed their investigation on the development of a domain independent framework for linking information through an application logic that allows for exchange of design intelligence by profession specific modules.

2. Research Interviews

The development of the application logic has been preceded by a series of research interviews which have been conducted by the authors within Arup to ensure that the objectives of the framework are informed by the requirements of practice. The interviews address the current problems and future expectations of practitioners in various fields of the AEC industry in regard to interoperability and the sharing of design intelligence. A representative cross-section of specialists has been chosen as interviewees, ranging from drafters, expert designers, team leaders, program developers and directors at Arup. The interviews were structured in three parts:

In the first part, practitioners were asked to comment on their design-deliverables and in particular elaborate on those tasks which appeared most repetitive and time-consuming to them.

– The more junior interviewees within Arup see their 'deliverability' mostly affected by with time- (and cost) pressure of getting information 'out' in the most streamlined fashion possible, while those in leading position understand a quest for broader collaboration across the AEC industry as the main potential of the integration of digital tools
– 70% of all interviewees refer to accommodating changes made by other parties as the most time-consuming part of their work, it is criticised that distinct applications require their own datasets.

The second part of questions dealt with the tools the practitioners were using and possible future requirements. In particular the integration of digital tools in the work-process and their data-interfacing-capability was investigated.

– Answers derived in this question give an indication that the practitioners are increasingly relying on 3D model information to produce their design output. In this regard a better integration of information within and across disciplines is mentioned as the main concern in order to get more intelligence out of the 3D model.
– It is acknowledged by all practitioners that increased interoperability of tools has to go hand in hand with a better dialogue with other parties involved. Only if the roles and contributions of others are understood, the knowledge transfer can be matched with according data-interfaces.

The third part of the interviews the practitioners were asked to comment about roles they would imagine an interoperability framework could perform in order to substantially foster collaborative design processes beyond the sharing of data.

– In response to the point made in section two, 30% of the interviewees state that it would be fundamental to the framework to implement a section that allows various users from the AEC industry to gain better understanding about the rules others are applying to finding their design solution.
– Addressing project specificity, some of the practitioners argue that the framework would have to be something that can be tweaked for different projects as requirements change from case to case
– In particular the more senior practitioners are critical about implications within the framework which aim at the automation of design. They argue that flexibility needs to be maintained so that expert input can occur at any time to avoid 'black box' scenarios.

– Those interviewees with an IT background and those being more technically inclined, point out that the framework should accommodate different plugin-modules to break things down into logical sub-schemas and to represent the profession-specific input of various user-groups.

Lessons learned in the evaluation process of the interviews have shown that the framework is expected to be open for change and individual adaptation from project to project. The users' capability of customising individual modules for interaction will be a necessary quality of the framework as well as transparent definition of rules for finding design solutions.

3. Linking Building Performance to Design Optimisation

3.1. INTERACTION AND AUTOMATION

The research team has investigated methods which assist in the creation of an iterative process where informed decisions can be made by professionals on the basis of performance aspects of the design. Methods for fostering the automation of geometry updates, data transfer, design analysis and code-checking of design were explored.

3.1.1. Decision Support

Previous investigations (Mueller 2006) illustrate that automated processes facilitated by computational means need to be integrated carefully with conventional (non computational) work methods as they can lead to *black box* results where team members have little insight in how any particular result was generated. When using automated processes in design optimisation, it often is crucial to understand how certain results were derived (how they evolved) for rapid interpretation and consequent design decision making (Baldock 2004). If a project team has access to automation routines at any point in the design process, members of that team can guide the direction of the optimisation to propose alternative design solutions. At the same time such methods enable the recording of *information trails* for showing how design decisions impact long term goals (Onuma 2006).

3.1.2. Parametric Geometry and Design Updates

In order to allow for designers to engage in an iterative process between performance analysis, optimisation and design decision making, the time factor is of high importance. The more immediate results can be communicated across a team, the better the information-flow and the collaborative capabilities. In this context, changes need to be adopted quickly and integrated into a flexible geometrical setup on the spot without requiring lengthy redraws. In the 2006 AIA *Report on integrated practice*

Eastman describes how parametric modelling enables to integrate and encapsulate the combined expertise of individuals into a design tool (Eastman 2006). Instead of working on a fixed geometrical template, parametric models allow incorporating various design intentions that *persist over geometric variations* (Schelden 2006).

Depending on the level of resolution required and the type of parameters chosen, parametric modelling offers manifold possibilities for addressing a range of issues at different levels of precision from the design ideation phase up to construction. In this context Aish speaks of parametric design as a way to *progress from intuition to precision*. (Aish 2005)

Once an initial desired form is agreed, it may be encoded within a parametric model and used to generate geometry through evolutionary means. Examples of this are present in the research undertaken by combining *EifForm* and *Custom Objects*, where a generative design tool is integrated with a parametric design environment to generate an array of possible solutions for a complex structure. (Shea, Aish and Gourtovaial 2003). An open source platform for collaboration which is taking reference to this principle is presented by the 'Open Source Architecture' group with the 'Hylomorphic' project. The *modes of operation* proposed for the project include the translation of knowledge into exchangeable data, the filtering of information into specific parameters for an architectural object and an iterative evaluation process (Sprecher, Chandler and Neuman 2006)

Recent approaches to standardise the exchange of parametric models and product data as described in the ISO 10303 Standard of the Exchange of Product Model Data (STEP) have shown that the attempt to do so is difficult even with the domain of exchanging between parametrically capable software, and within a single discipline due to accuracy problems and differences in modelling methodology (Eastman 1999) (Pratt and Kim 2006).

4. Precedence From Within the Profession

The authors have taken into consideration existing investigations that have been undertaken by members of the professional organisation within which the authors are embedded. A previously developed Collaborative Design Framework (basic CDF) has successfully been applied within the organisation while working on a stadium project. The research team has analysed the basic CDF in regard to its content, its relevance to the research undertaken by the team, and possible changes/alterations to better fit the objectives of the team.

4.1. THE BASIC CDF

The basic CDF is a Windows based (VB.Net) application which has been developed to interact with CATIA/Digital Project as a parametric modelling engine and Oasys GSA as a structural analysis engine. It contains a number of inbuilt modules for checking and optimising of a structural design.

First, the CDF requires a parametric model-template to be created in CATIA with careful adherence to a predefined naming-scheme for the elements in the CATIA model. A series of attributes required for structural design are then applied to the model by importing these attributes from a spreadsheet (using the element names as identifiers in the spreadsheet). These attributes include such data as design loadings, design conditions for any particular element/node and appropriate checks to be applied to that element.

Once the CATIA model has been built, the basic CDF application interacts with it through a COM (Component Object Model) interface to extract that information and a structural engineering analysis model can be created using that geometry and the associated attributes. The structural analysis model is built in GSA which too can export results to the basic CDF through a COM interface. Using CATIA and the basic CDF application to generate the structural analysis model in this method allows the engineer to quickly re-create an analysis model whenever the defining geometry in CATIA is modified (within the parameters and constraints defined by the parametric model).

Once the analysis model has been built and analysed it can be run through a series of inbuilt modules for checking and optimising the design. The final output of this is a structure whereby all elements have been sized and optimised as per the targets set in the optimisation module.

The basic CDF stores its data on disk using a 'serialisation' technique to write a binary file which is only readable by the basic CDF application.

4.2. LESSONS LEARNED

As an application built to support a particular project, the creators of the basic CDF have not been able to fully explore the universal potential of the framework due to time restrictions. Any multi-disciplinary functionality was not investigated.

Chief amongst the improvements that the creators of the basic CDF were forced to omit was the ability for outcomes of the analysis and design (such as member sizes) to be properly transferred back to the CATIA/Digital Project model, which meant that the documentation process is 'divorced' from the design analysis model.

Use of the basic CDF also highlighted a number of shortcomings when interacting with 3rd party applications through COM. This includes such processes as recursively querying the application for related data, when the relationships between that data can be reconstructed within the controlling application. It was also determined that the basic CDF was able to extract information from a CATIA 'Assembly' which are an aggregation of a number of CATIA design files (Parts). This enabled multiple members of the design team to connect several CATIA Parts in a robust manner.

The authors of this paper scrutinised the underlying source code in order determine if it could be made less project and domain specific or open to linking with other parametric/3d modelling software and other analysis software. Due to the rich OOP (Object Orientated Programming) class structure used during the development of the basic CDF, the authors believe there is great potential for generalising this basic CDF.

The data storage used by the basic CDF was seen as a weak both by both the original developers and the authors of this paper, although for different reasons. It was agreed among the authors of this paper to investigate Industry Foundation Classes (IFC) compatibility which would increase the ability to export static data to other applications, although the range of data capable of being exported is limited by the capabilities of the IFC format.

5. Extending the Basic Collaborative Design Framework

Based on the lessons learned from analysing the basic CDF and the aforementioned interviews the authors of this paper are currently developing an extended Collaborative Design Framework. The authors have scrutinised the current structure of the basic CDF to make it less project and domain specific and more open for interfacing design intelligence from multiple disciplines in the AEC industry.

The conception of the extended framework was informed by three insights resulting from project based work in practice as well as investigations from with the academy: The first insight suggested that one single generic tool can not facilitate a sensible integration of all possible design requirements, but that it would have to be an open, documented and extensible data structure without the requirement of expert programming skills. (Chaszar 2003) The second insight implies that a basic understanding of the production of code is about to become an integrative part of design culture and that designers will increasingly become more active in the development of small, tailor made scripts of code to fit project specific requirements of their design. (Silver 2006) The third insight addresses the situatedness of decision making based on observations and interpretations of results derived in an iterative process (Kannengiesser and Gero 2004). Rules need to be established to regulate trade-offs between the contributing parties and consequently add to the procedural memory and systemic knowledge within a project.

Four strategies have been developed by the authors in consideration of their previous investigation.

5.1. ECDF MODULAR FRAMEWORK

To satisfy the adaptation-requirement mentioned in the research interviews, a modular framework strategy has been developed by the authors which provides a balance between the required per-project flexibility and the desire to reduce unnecessary 'redevelopment' for each project. It is responsible for maintaining the data schema between different roles and hereby is acting as a bridge to connect between them (Figure 1). The framework supports a series of module roles which describe in the following:

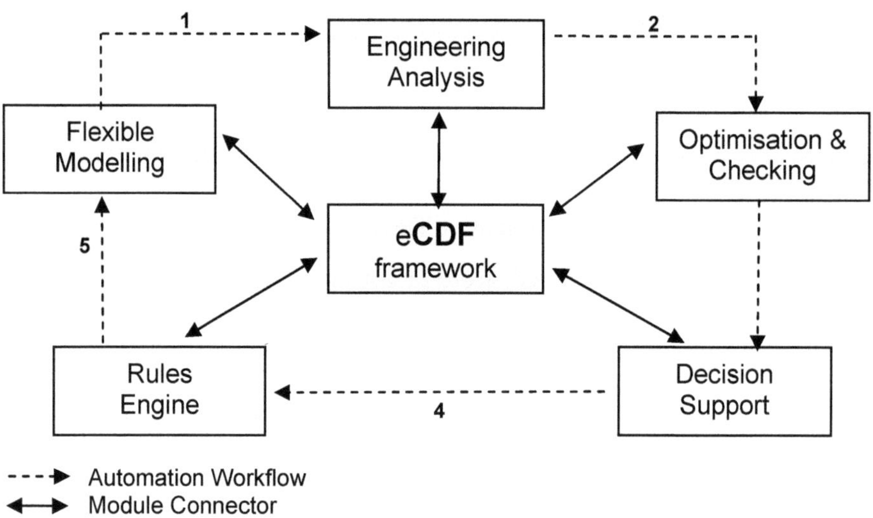

Figure 1. eCDF modular framework

5.1.1. Flexible Modelling Role

A design model is built either by flexible or generative geometry modelling. A static configuration of this geometry can then be extracted by application specific modules (acting in the flexible modelling role). Care should be taken to use a sensible naming convention as this will aid in the future identification of each element in the model.

5.1.2. Engineering Analysis Role

Within the engineering analysis module, the geometry and extra analysis attributes are used by different application specific modules (acting in the engineering analysis role). These may include structural, acoustic, mechanical, daylight-evaluation properties (or more) depending of the project-specific requirements.

5.1.3. Optimisation and Design Code Checking Role

The geometric model may also be passed through a material optimisation module (acting in the optimisation role) to minimise the material usage. The completed and analysed model may then be processed by a design checking module (acting in the design check role) so that the design produced conforms to applicable design codes. Both of these modules may initially be project specific, but over time generic modules can be derived.

5.1.4. Rule Engine Role

When the framework is running in 'automated' mode, the rule engine module will extract relevant data and use that as a bases for evaluating a series of user defined rules, the outcomes of which may be used to modify the initial design model and allowing the system to recompute the new model until the desired model according to the rule is found. Rule weight could also be assigned to help guide the important principals of the design. The weighting has to be done by the designer or the design team after several sub-optimal solutions are proposed by an automated process. In this way the 'rule engine' becomes a negotiation environment for different design disciplines to encode the ways the wish to modify a design under given conditions, and the acceptable boundary conditions for that design. Combined with a decision support module that graphically displays the results of these optimisation attempts, it allows AEC designers to evaluate the objective design performance alongside the subjective design appearance.

5.1.5. Decision Support Role

Once an optimised and compliant design has been found, this (and any other less-than-optimal designs) is passed to a decision support module. Using the module, a graphical display and comparison graph are created which allows design partners to review the relative merits of the proposed designs.

5.2. INFORMATION STORAGE STRATEGY

The authors have investigated various exchange formats such as STEP, IFC, IGES and other expedient project-specific data formats using Excel, Access or text files. The development of an extensible information schema is seen as one central element to the creation of the framework which supports the necessary project adaptation.

Research undertaken to this point suggests that the information schema must be able to support a superset of the information required by any tool acting as part of the framework, so that all the relevant information is available at every step during the design process. The information schema must be capable of containing the geometry, analysis requirements and analysis results for a particular design instance and when automation/optimisation is considered, the schema must be capable of coordinating and comparing multiple instances of these same data sets. When automation capabilities of the framework are being used, automation management information is stored in the schema, not just the information being manipulated by the process.

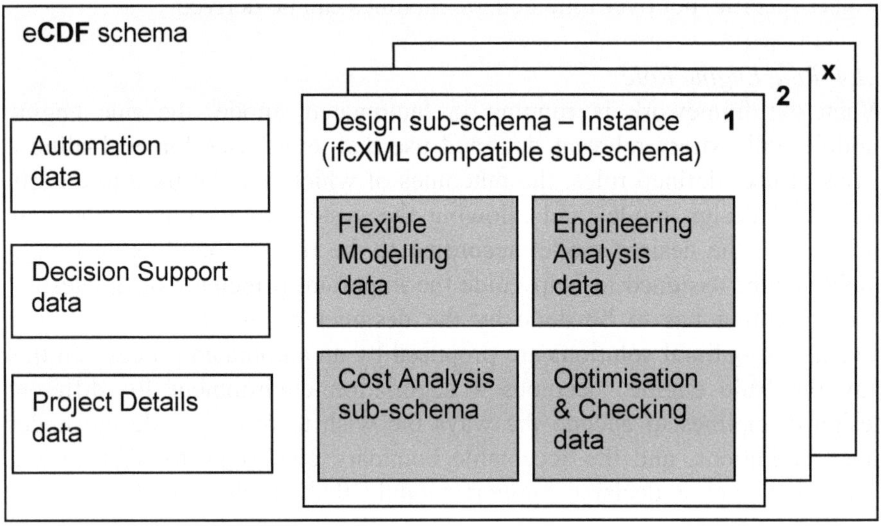

Figure 2. eCDF information structure

In order to support this, the overall eCDF schema is broken down into a number of sections which target particular roles supported by the framework. As shown in Figure 2, the main sections are Automation, Decision support, Project details and Design. The Decision Support section contains data used and captured by the Decision Support module, such as any analysis results extracted for use by the Rule Engine. The Automation section is primarily used by the eCDF controller application to store data required to construct the rules used by the Rules Engine and data pertaining to any automated processing, such as which particular plugins are used. The Project Details section contains information about the project, such as the source files that were used.

The Design sub-schema contains the information about geometry, analysis requirements and analysis results for a particular design instance. There may be multiple instances of the Design sub-schema, and this sub-schema is used by the Flexible Modelling, Engineering Analysis and Optimisation and Code Checking roles. The Design sub-schema also forms the basis of the data model used by the framework and the plugins fulfilling those roles, meaning that translation between the eCDF data model, and any application specific data models, only happens within that plugin. When introducing a new application to the framework, this limits the extent of changes required to only the plugin which interacts with the new application.

The data is stored in XML (eXtensible Markup Language) format which as a widely supported format offers well documented, strict syntax combining machine readability and (to a lesser degree) human readability. This in turn lowers the barriers for the primary developers using the framework who will be AEC designers, rather than professional software developers. It also offers related technologies such as XQuery to assist in the data management and XSLT (eXstensible Stylesheet Language Transformations) to enable transformation of the data into other text based file-formats. It is recognised that the XML format does suffer some weaknesses and limitations, such as it is a verbose format and is a hierarchical document based model.

5.3. FRAMEWORK FLEXIBILITY

To accommodate the required per-project flexibility, the framework was design with openness and pluggability in mind. This flexibility is allowed for in three ways:

1. Plug-in module: Framework roles will be paired with a suitable 'interface definitions' for the functionality which is required to support that role. Using these interface-definitions, a plug-in module can be written which either provides that functionality or allows the framework to interact with 3rd party software to provide that functionality.
2. Open data structure: The data schema allows for some extensibility and flexibility of the data and is stored in an industry standard XML Schema Definition format. Therefore, it is possible to write 'macros' or 'plug-ins' that run within 3rd party software (rather than within the framework) and can directly read and write the data used by the framework.
3. Rule engine: An embedded rules engine allows users to encode optimisation rules without needing to write a framework for processing the rules. If that proves unacceptable, the rules engine is itself a pluggable module and can be replaced.

5.4. STANDARDS COMPLIANCE

5.4.1. Information Schema Compliance

The International Alliance for Interoperability (IAI) was founded in 1994 and is developing a non-proprietary, multi-disciplinary data-exchange system based on the 'building product model' (Eastman 1999) (Malkawi

2004). The data-exchange system, known as Industry Foundation Classes (IFC), consists of object-based descriptions of building parts and their interrelation.

The authors acknowledge the value of IFCs as strong partner in augmenting the feasibility of the proposed framework and their possible compatibility-interfaces were examined. On the one hand the requirements for the application logic do differ from those of the IFCs while at the same time the extensive IFC structure does not provide enough flexibility to encompass all the data required by the framework. The IFC format does provide a good starting point for the requirement of an open, extensible data format as it includes the concept of "property sets" which allow for user defined data to be attached to any particular object within the schema.

The current data structure strategy is the use of a variant of the IFC schema in its XML format as the Design sub-schema within the larger CDF schema. (ifcXML - http://www.iai-international.org/Model/IfcXML2.htm). Although this format is less compact than the EXPRESS based IFC format, the XML based format allows developers to extend the schema as required, and still retain IFC compatibility by using XSLT transformations to convert the extended ifcXML back to pure ifcXML.

The eCDF data schema differs from the IFC schema in two significant ways. Firstly, the IFC schema is a published industry standard, and, as such, must be a stable, well-considered data format. The IFC format is still actively being drawn up, and it has been proven that even where IFC explicitly supports analytical data requirements for a particular design discipline, some data requirements may still be missing (Wan, Chen and Tiong 2004). As identified during the research interviews, 'flexibility' is a prime attribute of the framework, allowing end users to extend from the IFC data format when required. Using Structural Engineering optimisation as an example, investigation of the data formats used in the 'basic CDF' show that these extensions include new entities such as 'Profile Group' (a grouping of structural profiles, e.g. a group of IfcProfileDef's) or new attributes such as 'Target Utilisation' (a target value applied to each element to guide the optimization process).

Secondly, the eCDF schema must be capable of supporting multiple instances of similar designs (i.e. multiple instances of the 'Design' sub-schema), whereas the IFC format has been designed to contain a single instance of a design. By storing the results of multiple design options, the eCDF Decision Support module is capable of showing those options in a multi-disciplinary format, increasing the ability of designers to communicate design intelligence across discipline boundaries, and collaboratively explore the ramifications of design choices.

5.4.2. Compliance with Industry Practice

Since the bulk of design software used by the AEC industry is software running on the Windows® platform, this 'Collaborative Design Framework' is implemented using Visual Basic.Net (or other ".Net" compliant languages). This allows the framework to interact with other design software using .Net interoperability methods or COM. This provides AEC designers who may be familiar with scripting, and are generally not professional software developers, an easy transition into being able to modify or develop modules for the framework.

6. Conclusions

The research presented in this paper illustrates the development of a collaborative design framework based on project-based investigations in practice, requirements from expert in the AEC industry and supported by academic research in the field. Our investigation has shown that such a framework needs to be designed to separate the requirements for project-specific adaptation from the core unchanging concepts of workflow interaction and the conceptual tasks the software tools of individual domains within the AEC industry perform. This is achieved by structuring the framework to accept modifiable plug-ins to provide a link to the tool which will perform any particular task.

Setting up the framework around a central controlling application allows the system to provide automation capabilities, which combined with a situated rules engine provide practitioners with the option to more easily perform multi-criteria, multi-discipline optimisation. Central to this is the use of a parametric, associative modelling tool, which is driven by the rules engine during an optimisation process. A user interface facilitating decision support through knowledge visualisation is built into the framework to allow for conditioning and finetuning of the rules engine. Compliance to current IFC standards can be achieved by using a variant of the IFC schema in its XML format.

Acknowledgements

The authors would hereby like to acknowledge the contribution of Prof. Mark Burry, Andrew Maher and Anitra Nelson from RMIT University, as well as Richard Hough from Arup Australia in the conception of this paper. We would further like to thank all members of staff from Arup Australia who have volunteered to participate in the interviews which are referred to in this paper and which make a substantial contribution to our research.

References

Acha,VI, Gann, DA, and Salter, AM: 2005, Episodic innovation: R&D strategies for project-based environments, *Industry and Innovation* **12**(2): 255-281.

Aish, RO: 2005 From Intuition to Precision, Digital Design: The Quest for New Paradigms, *23rd eCAADe Conference Proceedings*, Lisbon, Portugal, pp. 10-14.

Baldock RO: 2004 *Structural System Optimisation Techniques for the Building Industry*, Cambridge University Engineering Department Report.

Bedrick, JI and Rinella, TO: 2006, Technology, process, improvement, and culture change,

AIA Report on integrated practice. Retrieved January 11, 2007 from http://www.aia.org/SiteObjects/files/8_Bedrick%20Rinella.pdf.

Chaszar, AN: 2003, Bridging the Gap with Collaborative Design Programs, *Architectural Design* **73**(5): 112-18.

Eastman, CH: 1999, *Building Product Models: Computer Environments Supporting Design and Construction,* CRC Press, Boca Raton, Florida.

Eastman, CH: 2006 University and industry research in support of BIM, *AIA Report on integrated practice*. Retrieved November 12, 2006 from http://www.aia.org/SiteObjects/files/2_Eastman.pdf.

Kannengiesser, UD and Gero, JO: 2004 Using Agents in the Exchange of Product Data, *in* M Bramer and V Devedzic (eds), *Artificial Intelligence Applications and Innovations*, Kluwer, Dordrecht, pp. 129-140.

Malkawi, AM: 2004, Performance Simulation: Research and Tools, *in* B Kolarevic and AM Malkawi (eds), *Performative Architecture: Beyond Instrumentality*, Spon Press, New York, pp. 85-94.

Mueller, VO: 2006, Integrating Digital and Non-digital Design Work, *Blurring the Lines: Computer-Aided Design and Manufacturing in Contemporary Architecture*, Academy Press, pp. 38-46.

Onuma, KI: 2006, The twenty-first century practitioner: Transformed by process not software, *AIA Report on integrated practice*. Retrieved December 4, 2006 from http://www.aia.org/SiteObjects/files/6_Onuma.pdf.

Pratt, MI and Kim, JU: 2006, Experience in the exchange of procedural shape models using ISO 10303 (STEP) *Proceedings of the 2006 ACM symposium on Solid and physical modeling,* Cardiff, pp. 229-238.

Shelden, DE: 2006, Tectonics, Economics and the Reconfiguration of Practice: The Case for Process Change by Digital Means, *in* M Silver (ed), *Programming Cultures*, *Architecture, Art and Science in the Age of Software Development*, John Wiley & Sons, London, pp. 82-88.

Silver, MI: 2006, Towards a Programming Culture in Design Arts, *in* M Silver (ed), *Programming Cultures*, *Architecture, Art and Science in the Age of Software Development*, John Wiley & Sons, London, pp. 5-11.

Sprecher, AA, Chandler AH and Neumann, ER: 2006, Critical Practice: Protocol for a Fused Technology, *in* C Hight and C Perry (eds), *Collective Intelligence in Design*, John Wiley & Sons, London pp. 31-35.

Taylor, JO and Levitt, RA: 2004, Understanding and Managing Systemic Innovation in Project-based Industries, *in* DP Slevin, DI Cleland and JK Pinto (eds), *Innovations: Project management research*, Project Management Institute, Newtown Square, Pennsylvania, pp. 83-99.

Wan, C, Chen, P and Tiong, R: 2004, Assessment of IFC's for Structural analysis domain, *Electronic Journal of Information Technology in Construction*. Retrieved March 2, 2007 from http://www.itcon.org/cgi-bin/works/Show?2004_5.

DESIGN COLLABORATION USING IFC

A case study of thermal analysis

JOHN MITCHELL, JUSTIN WONG AND JIM PLUME
University of New South Wales, Australia

Abstract. This paper reports a study that has been undertaken as part of an on-going project to examine the capacity of building information modelling (BIM) techniques to support collaborative design in the building industry. In particular, our premise is that effective design collaboration relies on the ability to exchange BIM data in a robust way using an open information standard such as IFC. The focus of this present work has been on the processes involved in design collaboration between architects and engineers responsible for advising on thermal performance issues. We begin by looking at the kinds of data that needs to be exchanged to support such collaboration. We then test the exchange using a pilot project model and finally review the capacity of the IFC standard to support such processes.

1. Introduction

As the demand for sustainability increases, building energy simulation has become an effective means to evaluate different design options and is seen as preferable to other less rigorous methods. However, the uptake of such practice is hindered by the way in which information is exchanged and the time consuming process of defining building geometry. To date, 2D drawings remain the normal mode of information exchange between architects and engineers, requiring the preparation of a text-based input file for building energy simulation. The extraction process is often error prone: Bazjanac (2001) makes the point that about 80% of the time spent preparing input files is devoted to defining and debugging building geometry.

In order to better understand the information exchange process, we have carried out a thermal analysis study on a well-constructed building model with three facade options using a thermal analysis tool known as Riuska. This has permitted us to examine in more detail the processes involved

A Dong, A Vande Moere & JS Gero (eds), CAADFutures'07, 317–329.

in architect/thermal analysis engineer collaboration. In particular, we examined the following questions: what data is needed in the design concept model (or more precisely, in the IFC export) for thermal analysis calculation; what additional information must be provided by the thermal engineer; what modifications in this snapshot of the model could be manipulated by the engineer to improve performance; what data or revised design suggestions are currently returned; and how this might be improved in the future.

There is now a growing awareness of the efforts, over the past decade, of the International Alliance for Interoperability (IAI) to develop a model schema that supports a semantically rich representation of a building for use during the life cycle design and management of a project (IAI 2007). The schema promotes information sharing between design disciplines. In addition to the need for a common data format that enables different design disciplines to share information, effective design collaboration requires members of the design team to understand the pathway by which information flows.

Since this project commenced, the IAI has published tools that permit the reliable definition and use of building component properties, allowing us to add and manipulate component property and performance data more easily and reliably. Furthermore, an IFC process methodology has been developed (known as the Information Delivery Manual, IDM) that permits the specification of exchange requirements (ER) and allows computer based methods to validate source model data for successful process interaction (IDM 2007).

2. Project Outline

Most of the earlier IFC demonstration pilot projects (Kam et al. 2003; Kam and Fisher 2004) focused on the capacity of the IFC model schema to support thermal analysis during the final stage of the design process, that is, when all major decisions had already been made. As a result, thermal analysis was mostly concerned with designing an HVAC system to suit the design, rather than to inform an understanding of environmental performance and positively influencing design decisions. In addition, Lam et al. (2006) have highlighted the need for further study in the distinction of architectural spaces and thermal zones to support thermal simulation. To the knowledge of the authors, none of that previous work has focused on the direct interaction between architect and engineer while investigating the capacity of the IFC model schema to support thermal analysis in the schematic/conceptual design stages.

In this paper, we begin by describing the project model and the tools used to carry out this investigation. We then discuss our findings under three broad headings. We begin by examining the information that must be provided to the thermal engineer, beginning with the concept of process modelling and its importance in articulating information needed for reliable exchange. The next section discusses the results of the thermal analysis, and issues to do with reliability and appropriateness of the data sourced from the architect's model. The last section examines how the thermal engineer's results are communicated back to the designer and the possibilities for design suggestions from a thermal engineer.

As an extension to some previous work (Plume ad Mitchell 2007), a pilot building project was selected to test the robustness of the semantic representation in support of thermal analysis. The building model consisted of a three storey office building situated in Sydney. Since the acquisition of building geometry was seen as one of the main barriers to the uptake of building energy simulation, it was the objective of the project to explore the process and test the efficiency of transferring building geometry using IFC. Our aim was to demonstrate that an IFC compliant building energy simulation tool is capable of evaluating the thermal performance of different façade options and shading strategies more efficiently than conventional methods.

Since we wanted to quantify the difference that certain cladding solutions would make and optimise a chosen design, we developed three façade options with a constant plan layout: a traditional framed "ribbon" window, a curtain wall and a "punched" wall using terra-cotta external tiles. Figure 1 illustrates the curtain wall solution with a horizontal shading device.

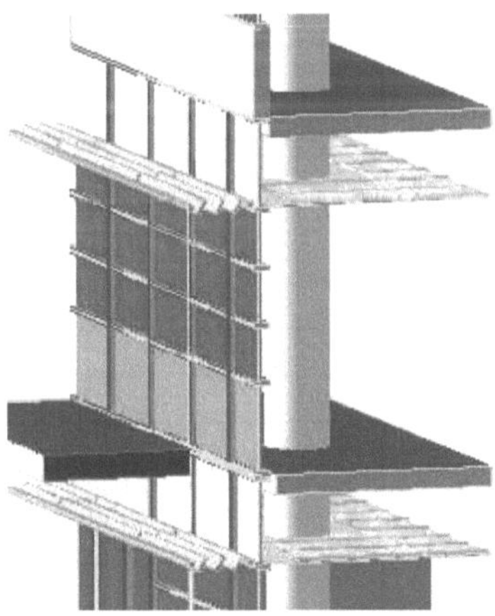

Figure 1. Curtain wall option with a horizontal shading device

The two IFC compliant tools used in this work were ArchiCAD (Graphisoft 2007) for architectural model building and Riuska (Olof Granlund, 2007) for thermal analysis. It should be noted that although we have used ArchiCAD and Riuska, they are chosen as exemplars of an IFC compliant BIM modeller and thermal analysis tool respectively, so that we may understand, critique and improve generic processes for building performance simulation and measurement.

The window elements were chosen from the standard ArchiCAD library parts as shown in Table 1. Table 2 shows the material properties of all the elements in the model.

TABLE 1. Project Model, Key Building Elements

Façade	Description	Library Part	Wall construction
Option 1	Ribbon	W Ribbon.gsm	cavity brick
Option 2	Curtain wall	W Curtain Wall Straight.gsm	external frame, masonry inner leaf at dado
Option 3	Punched	Vent Window.gsm	cavity brick

TABLE 2. Project Model – Building Element properties

Façade	Window type	Thickness (mm)	U-value	SHGC	WWR
Option 1	Single glazing tinted glass	6	5.02	0.73	0.67
Option 2	Stopsol SuperSilver green + low e	10	1.69	0.33	0.5
Option 3	Stopsol SuperSilver green + low e	10	1.69	0.33	0.3
Option 1	External wall	300	0.85		
	Surface Materials	15			
	Brick (Solid)	110			
	Air Gap	50			
	Brick (Solid)	110			
	Surface Materials	15			
Option 2	Curtain Wall	108	0.63		
	Air Gap	50			
	Mineral Wool 1	50			
	Steel sheet	2			
	Glass Crown (Soda Lime)	6			
Option 3	Austral terraCADE	216	1.4		
	Surface Materials	15			
	Brick (Solid)	140			
	Steel sheet	46			
	Bitumen	15			

3. Information Exchange – Architect to Thermal Engineer

What information does the analyst need to simulate thermal performance and how do we specify this in a robust way? We first introduce the concept of process modelling and the IAI's IDM developments, and then identify the specific data required by the thermal engineer.

3.1. PROCESS MODELLING

A process model allows each discipline to develop a thorough understanding of the interaction and flow of information occurring between disciplines. Failure to recognise the importance of the model exchange process will result in missing, incomplete or irrelevant data, the latter typically causing large, cumbersome files for IFC export (Fisher and Kam 2004). Therefore, it is critical for the design team to develop or agree a process model prior to project commencement.

Based on such a process model, both Figure 2 and Figure 3 show an overall and a specific process model respectively. Figure 2 is a process model developed as part of the ifcMBOMB project (Stephens et al. 2005). It informs both the architect and engineer, as a member of a design team, about their respective roles in relation to the whole design and construction phases of facility development.

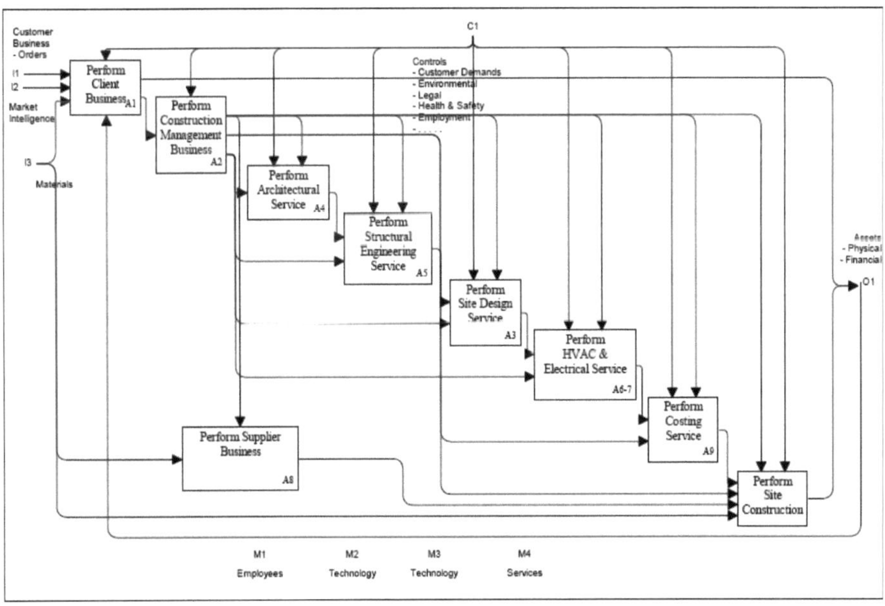

Figure 2. Process model

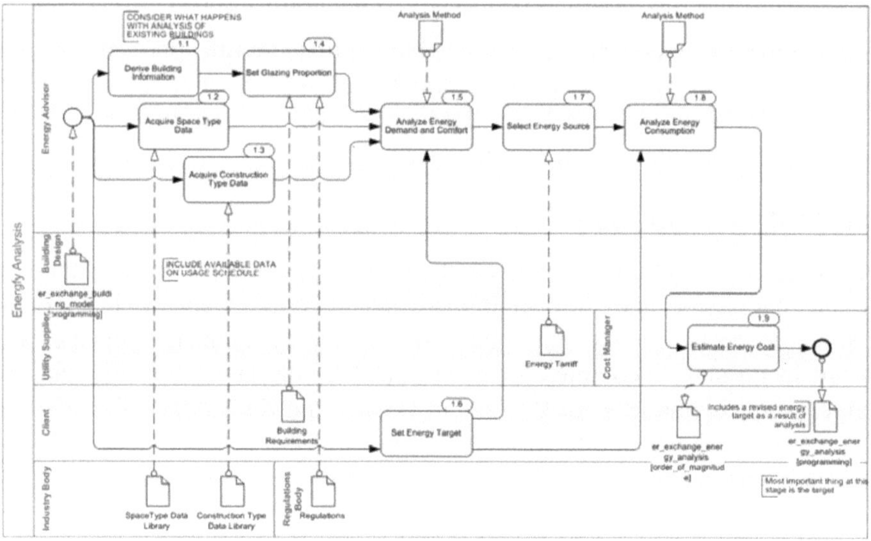

Figure 3. Process model for Energy Analysis

On the other hand, Figure 3 defines for the architect information that is required for the thermal analyst. The example shown is one of a draft set of process definitions prepared by the IAI Nordic Chapter's Information Delivery Manual project (Espedokken et al. 2006).

3.2. INPUT DATA REQUIRED FOR THERMAL ANALYSIS

Based on the process map outline in IDM for Energy Analysis, (IDM 2005) the list of input data for thermal analysis is shown in Table 3.

TABLE 3. List of input data for thermal analysis

Item	Description
1	Building layout including the layout and configuration of spaces
2	Building construction including the energy performance of all construction elements including walls, floors, roofs/ceilings, windows, doors and the like
3	Building usage including functional use and occupancy of spaces
4	Conditioning systems including lighting, HVAC, etc.
5	Utility rates provided by the user,
6	Weather data.

Item 1 is the 3D geometry of all building elements and spaces. All this data is currently interpreted by Riuska from the IFC export generated by the BIM modelling application. Items 2, 3 and 5 are assigned default values in

Riuska but are editable using information from either Riuska's internal database, building material references (e.g. the CIBSE Product Catalogue), created by the user, or with values confirmed by ad hoc agreement with the architect. Item 4 (as specified in the IDM draft) we take to mean other building services system loads that may impact on thermal analysis. Items 2-5 are not currently taken by Riuska from the IFC model. Item 6 would be sufficiently identified by a geographic *location* and *orientation*, but neither is currently supported (or to our knowledge, agreed by the IAI Implementer Support Group).

The architect's building model should thus reflect these exchange requirements specified by the process models and the understanding of input requirements for the thermal analyst. In ArchiCAD, this data is typically collected in a specific layer combination so that it can be exported as IFC data without other extraneous information. In the emerging IDM methodology, where a model is envisaged to be hosted in an IFC model server, the IDM definition can be used as a filter to more robustly and automatically check for data completeness and quality.

The architect, with a defined data scope, can now export the relevant IFC file for the engineer's analysis. Typically, a user who follows the requirements of thermal analysis is able to generate an IFC export with a file size that is orders less than the master model.

4. Analysis

This section reports upon the IFC import into Riuska, examining in detail aspects that determine accuracy and reliability, and then discusses the results of the three model façade options.

4.1. RIUSKA IMPORT

As shown in Figure 4, Riuska is efficient in handling building geometry as well as spatial information. This capability eliminates the need to spend time creating building geometry for thermal analysis. Not only did the building geometry import successfully, the engineer can also obtain information about spaces (rooms) as well as the height of each storey relative to the datum. Missing, however, is the building orientation, a vital aspect of thermal loads.

Given that item 1 in Table 3 represents the bulk of the input data required, it becomes relatively easy to get Riuska to simulate design day thermal performance and annual energy consumption.

The potential advantage of using an IFC compliant thermal analysis application such as Riuska is the ability to evaluate different design options and then communicate results with other disciplines, but how reliable is the data and the results? The next sub-sections examine key aspects of the modelling.

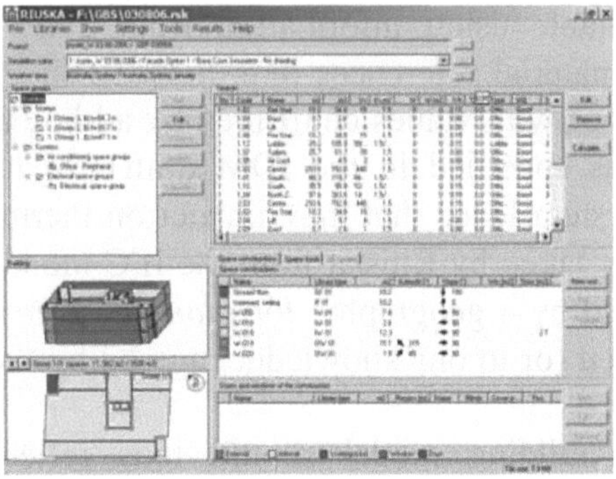

Figure 4. IFC import into Riuska

4.1.1. Accuracy of Semantics and Geometry

One of the issues encountered during the project is the difference in the semantic representation of objects. For instance, the glazing choice in Façade Option 2 was a *curtain wall* with a wall-to-window ratio of 0.67. A problem arose when the IFC export was generated, because the curtain wall was modelled as an ArchiCAD *object* with an overall area that included both vision glass and spandrel. However, common practice in the thermal engineering disciplines is to represent it as a window mounted on a *glass wall* where the window area is that of the vision glass. The incompatibility in representation materially affects the thermal performance calculation.

4.1.2. Shading

A good shading strategy can reduce the energy consumption of the building significantly. At present, the IFC model does not include the typing of a *shading* element. Consequently shading conditions are handled in Riuska's own shading interface which is manually entered by the thermal analyst. We are also unclear as to the analysis of surfaces shaded by the building itself.

4.1.3. Thermal Zones

Definition of thermal zones is another issue encountered during the project. Very often, architectural spaces are mistaken for thermal zones; indeed it implies prior understanding by the designers as to the thermal configuration. In some instances, thermal zones can be defined as a collection of architectural spaces of similar function during final design stage where the functionality of all spaces has been determined.

However, this concept is not always applicable during the conceptual design stage where, for example, the thermal zones in a commercial building depend upon the building orientation and its solar access. A typical approach, at this stage, would be to define perimeter zones where the effect of solar penetration is most significant and a core zone where the solar influence on the conditioned load is minimal.

Shortcomings of Riuska in this aspect are the lack of creation and editing options for zoning information, restricted modelling of isolated spaces and the inability to include an "airwall" or virtual boundary as the perimeter surface to a functional space. At present, this data must be added using the BIM tool (in our case, ArchiCAD), though one could argue that it really should be entered by the thermal engineer using their application.

4.1.4. Material Properties

Even though the specification of material properties of building elements is supported by the IFC model schema, such data is not used during the import. This is primarily due to the lack (until very recently) of a method to uniquely identify building element properties. These have many national variations and there is a lack of a universal database where material information can be readily obtained. In order to simplify the process, Riuska assigns a default value and configuration for each of the building carcass elements. It is then up to the engineer to specify precise performances for the purpose of the analysis.

4.2. THERMAL ANALYSIS RESULTS

Exploiting Riuska's database, parametric runs can also be created to investigate the effect of alternate material glazing properties or shading strategies on energy consumption and environmental system loads. This method was used to investigate the three façade options.

4.2.1. Energy Consumption

Figure 5 shows the breakdown in energy consumption between different design options. The breakdown allows the analyst to have a better understanding of the impact of the design change. Thus, instead of spending time fixing the building geometry, the engineer can do more value added analysis such as understanding the sensitivity of material performance, geometry, shading, and orientation.

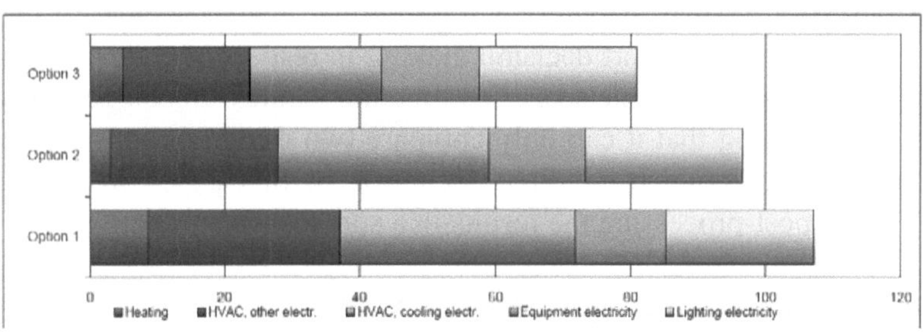

Figure 5. Comparison of energy consumption between options

4.2.2. Energy Cost

Figure 6 breaks down the cost of energy consumption between different design options. Results of this nature facilitate the decision process upstream. The architect can then review their design priorities accordingly.

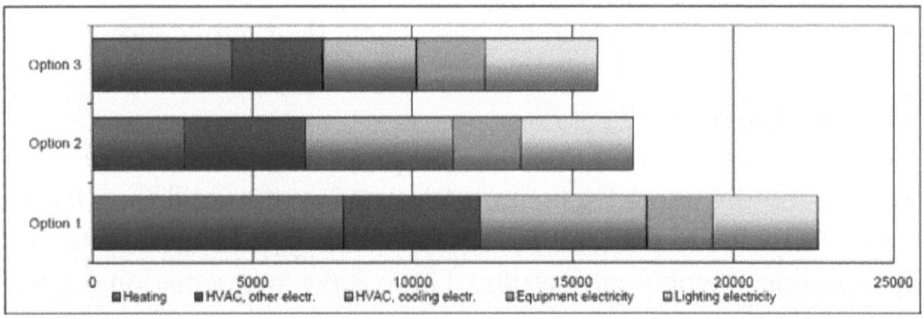

Figure 6. Comparison of energy cost between options

4.2.3. Design Day Air Flow Rate

This type of result (Figure 7) provides very useful information to the downstream HVAC engineer for duct design and fan selection. It allows them to have a better understanding of the range of air flow rate he is expected to work with while evaluating the different design options.

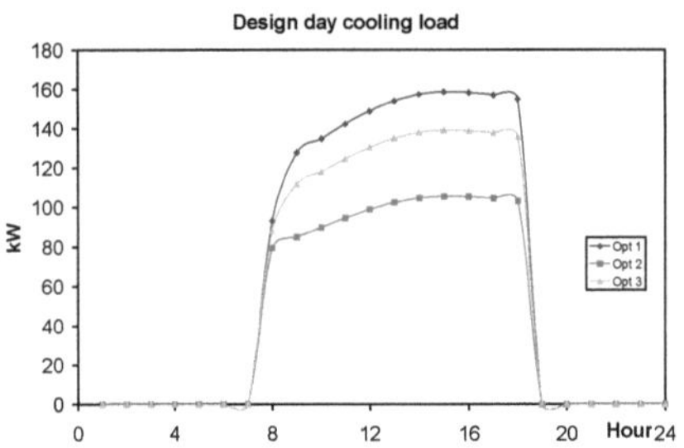

Figure 7. Design day air flow rate

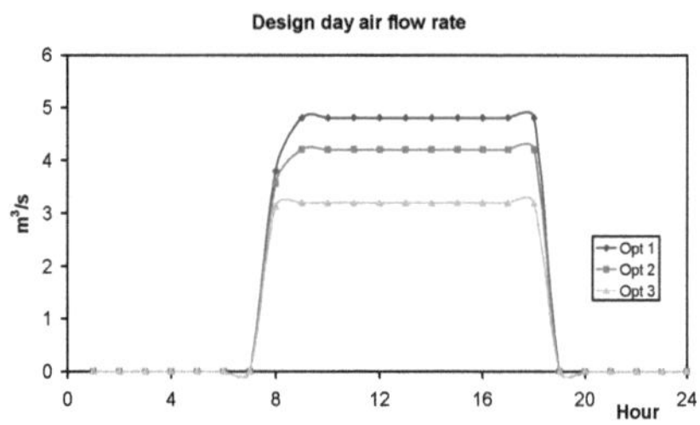

Figure 8. Design day cooling load

4.2.4. Design Day Cooling Load

Using the result shown in Figure 8, the thermal analyst is able to provide more information to support decision making in respect of code compliance. Given that Riuska's multiple scenarios function is one of its biggest benefits, it is a little limiting that it can only compare two design options at any one time: the figures comparing three scenarios in this paper were actually produced by post-processing the results in a spreadsheet application.

5. Information Exchange – Engineer to Architect

All too often the project schedule and other business factors restrict the exploration of design alternatives that lead to innovative solutions, better human comfort, etc. How can the results of thermal analysis be communicated with the architect and project team and what options can be identified by the engineer for alternative solutions? The following sections investigate these issues.

5.1. SYSTEM PERFORMANCE RESULTS

It has been an objective of the IFC model to support a comprehensive range of design performance measures. By re-importing the revised Riuska IFC export into ArchiCAD, the performance results are attached. This demonstrates IFC's capacity to store information for downstream use and helps the architect understand the thermal performance consequences of his design. Exchanging this updated model with the HVAC engineer provides rich integrated data to support the design of plant and distribution systems.

The IFC model supports the documentation of thermal performance of each *thermal zone*, *space*, *storey* and *building*. However, only *Pset_SpaceThermalRequirements* is implemented at present. Riuska exports *cooling dry bulb temperature heating dry bulb temperature*, *ventilation air flow rate* and *exhaust air flow rate*, back into the IFC file. A study of the IFC model schema reveals that IFC is capable of documenting more information than those mentioned above. A number of possible Psets have been developed for data related to *ifcSpaces* and *HVAC* systems (IAI 2007) that could have been exploited at the analysis phase.

5.2. DESIGN MODIFICATION FEEDBACK

The examples above demonstrate the capacity to determine loads and measure the performance of a design proposal, but also to assess alternate material and configuration improvements. To date, these are limited to changing the properties or configuration of existing elements in the model, rather than allowing for the introduction of new or re-positioned elements.

We envisage an extension of this where the thermal engineer suggests ideas for improving thermal performance. The suggestions range from those based on the above, i.e. different material or shading parameters, through to modification of an element's geometry (eg. width and height of a window, re-orientation of a building, and reconfiguration of spaces and related thermal zones). As this requires a design decision by the author of the model, the "suggestions" could be carried by Psets that are recognised by parametric tools in the receiving system.

In a model server environment model versioning is already operational, and such data would be the base of several building options based on the thermal engineer's design scenarios.

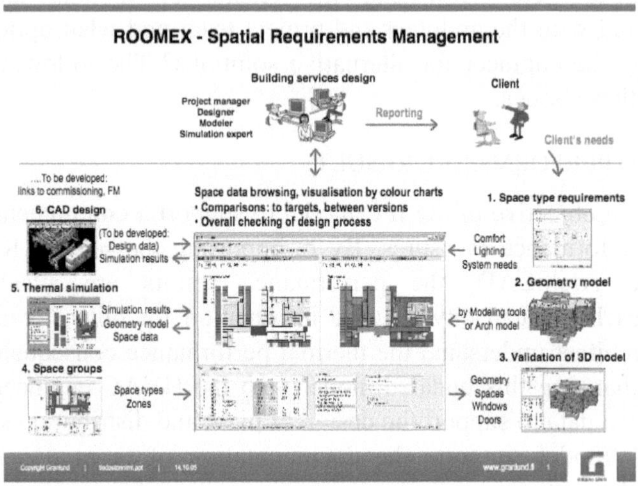

Figure 9. The Olof Granlund Oy vision for collaborative thermal analysis support (used by permission)

After our project completed Olof Granlund Oy published their vision for an enhanced tool for thermal simulation (see Figure 9 above). ROOMEX allows the successive imports of revised or evolving architectural models and tracks changes to the model, categorises them for rapid appraisal, and manages the many interactions (client needs, model validation, thermal zone types and editing, multiple simulations and support for downstream processes) in an integrated fashion. This development shows a maturity in the analytical processes, and will be very interesting to work with.

6. Conclusion

With respect to our project objectives we were encouraged by the results. The multiple scenarios we analyzed were handled efficiently by Riuska and we could compare performances to inform a specific design option. Overall, we obtained very efficient import based on IFC exchange, though it is yet, far from a "seamless" translation. The IFC model supports powerful design collaboration and, with good modeling practice, streamlines information exchange and management. The architect and thermal analyst are able to focus on adding value to the project by evaluating alternative strategies for energy efficient buildings.

A range of issues were identified: weaknesses in the IFC model; difficulties with modelling building elements; the collective inability to support shading devices; in Riuska, there is the lack of editing for thermal zones, the absence of humidity data or the lack of user selection of thermal model data to be returned to the master model (Haug et al. 2006). These are important, and often subtle, issues that do not diminish the model based approach but require resolution for more accurate and efficient processes. They will be the base of our continuing work.

Acknowledgements

Our thanks to Olof Granlund Oy, Helsinki and Graphisoft Australia for their considerable and continuous support for this project and teaching resources at the FBE, UNSW. We also thank P C Thomas of Team Catalyst, Sydney for his professional assistance.

References

Bazjanac, V, Crawley, DB: 1997, The Implementation of Industry Foundation Classes in Simulation Tools for the Building Industry, *in Building Simulation 1997, Proceedings of the International Conference*, Prague, Vol. 1: 125-132.

Bazjanac, V: 2001, Acquisition of Building Geometry in the Simulation of Energy Performance, *in* R Lamberts et al. (eds), *Building Simulation 2001, Proceedings of the International Conference., Rio de Janeiro*, 1: 305-311.

Espedokken, K et al.: 2006, Energy Analysis A-Process Maps. Retrieved May 30, 2006 from http://idm.buildingsmart.no/confluence/display/IDM/Energy+Analysis+%28PM%29.

Graphisoft: 2007, Graphisoft web site, http://www.graphisoft.com.au.

Haug, D, et al. 2006, R&D project no 11251 Pilot Project, Tromsø University College (HITOS) for testing IFC, Statsbygg, Oslo.

IAI: 2007, International Alliance for Interoperability, http://www.iai-international.org

IDM: 2005, Information Delivery Manual, Using IFC to Build SMART, J Wix (ed), http://www.iai.no/idm/learningpackage/idm_home.htm.

Kam, C, Fischer, M, Hänninen, R, Karjalainen, A and Laitinen, J: 2003, The product model and Fourth Dimension project, *ITcon*, **8**: 137-166.

Kam, C, Fischer, M: 2004, Capitalizing on early project decision-making opportunities to improve facility design, construction, and life-cycle performance—POP, PM4D, and decision dashboard approaches, *Automation in Construction*, No. 13: 53-65

Karola, A, Lahtela, H, Hänninen, R, Hitchcock, RJ, Chen, Q, Dajka, S and Hagström, K: 2002, BSPro COM-Server - Interoperability between software tools using industry foundation classes, *Energy and Buildings*, **34**: 901-907.

Lam, KP, Wong, NH, Shen, LJ, Mahdavi, A, Leong, E, Solihin, W, Au, KS and Kang, Z: 2006, Mapping of industry building product model for detailed thermal simulation and analysis, *Advances in Engineering Software*, **37**: 133-145.

Olof Granlund: 2007, Olof Grunland web site http://www.granlund.fi

Plume, J & Mitchell, J: 2007, Collaborative Design using a Shared IFC Building Model – Learning from Experience. *Automation in Construction*, **16**: 28-36.

Stephens, J, et al.: 2005, ifc-mBomb, Life Cycle Data for Buildings: Opportunities for the IFC Model-Based Operations and Maintenance, IAI UK Ltd, April 2005.

STRETCHING THE TROUSERS TOO FAR?

Convening societal and ICT development in the architectural and engineering practice

ANITA MOUM, TORE HAUGEN
Norwegian University of Science and Technology, Norway

and

CHRISTIAN KOCH
Technical University of Denmark, Denmark

Abstract. The publicly and privately funded national R&D program 'Digital Construction' was initiated in 2003 in order to establish a common platform for interchanging digital information and to stimulate digital integration in the Danish building industry. This paper explores the relation between visions, strategies and tools formulated in the 'Digital Construction' program, and the first experiences made from implementing the 3D work method part of the program in an ongoing building project. The discussions in the paper are placed in the complex field between choosing strategies for integrating information and communication technologies on national level, and the effects of these strategies on real life building projects.

1. Introduction

Information and communication technologies (ICT) are for good reason heavily linked to future prosperity and growth in a range of European countries. However, the Architecture-Engineering-Construction (AEC) industry has been slow in turning the potential of ICT and CAD into increased efficiency and quality (Gann 2000; Wikforss 2003), and the productivity status in the AEC-industry described in the Latham report in 1994 (Latham 1994), still gives raise to concerns. Based on this context, several international and national initiatives for integrating ICT in the AEC-industry have emerged. In Denmark the national research and development (R&D) program "Det Digitale Byggeri" (Digital Construction), co-funded by public and private sources, was initiated in 2003, in order to establish a

A Dong, A Vande Moere & JS Gero (eds), CAADFutures'07, 331–344.

common platform for interchanging digital information and to stimulate digital integration in the Danish AEC-industry (EBST 2005). The R&D program ended in March 2007.

This paper explores the relationship between the expectations, strategies and tools formulated in the 'Digital Construction' program and the benefits and challenges experienced from implementing and using 3D object models in practice. Are the trousers stretched too far regarding the convening of societal and ICT development in the architectural and engineering practice? The analysis will be based on an ongoing evaluation of this R&D program and the first experiences made from implementing a part of the program in the building design process of the new Icelandic National Concert and Conference Centre in Reykjavik (CCC-project). The discussion points on the challenges from convening societal and ICT development in the architectural and engineering practice.

2. Method

The discussions and analysis regarding the 'Digital Construction' program are based on the results from a qualitative process evaluation. Initiated by EBST (The National Agency for Enterprise and Construction, a Danish public body within the resort of the ministry of Economy and Business), the evaluation started in the winter of 2004. Seeing the Danish 'Digital Construction' program from a process evaluation point of view gives the possibility to evaluate the dynamic development of the program (Van de Ven 1999; Patton 1990, 1998). The process evaluation has been documented in four intervention and status notes of the program's progress (Koch and Haugen 2006). The process evaluation is based on an array of methods: interviews, participant observation and desk research. Just above forty interviews have been carried out, comprising biannual interviews with project managers from EBST and project managers representing the various active development consortia within the program, the surrounding learning network etc. The exploration of the experiences made from implementing 'Digital Construction' in the CCC-project build on the first findings from a qualitative case study of the project (Yin 2003). Around 12 semi-structured interviews (Kvale 1997) have been carried out in 2006 with architects and engineers involved in building design and management. Documentary analysis and observation of design meetings are further sources of the empirical data. The brief glimpses into other national and international initiatives for integrating ICT in the AEC-industry are based on interviews with key actors involved.

A research framework has been developed and applied for supporting the exploration of the ICT impact on the architectural design process (Moum 2006). The framework is based on the suggestion of three levels; a macro-level (AEC-industry), a meso-level (the design team in the CCC-project) and a micro-level (the individual architect/engineer). The discussion part of the paper is placed in the dynamic relation between these levels: between initiatives and strategies emerging on a national level (macro-level), the pro-processes within the project team (meso-level) and the individual experiences from ICT usage (micro-level). The framework focuses furthermore on four central design process aspects: generation of design solutions, communication, evaluation of design solutions and decision-making.

The authors recognize that through using an Icelandic building project as a case of the implementation of the Danish national program, the exploration is limited to the internal part of the design process. A full evaluation would encompass the interactions also with external actors, such as the Danish state acting as client. Nevertheless, the CCC-project's organizational structure, complexity, architectural ambitions and economical and management related aspects, makes it an exceptional project. Thus, the authors consider the project to be an interesting case for exploring not only technological, but also some non- technological challenges and benefits from of 'Digital Construction' in architectural and engineering practice.

3. R&D Efforts Integrating ICT and 3D CAD

The International Alliance of Interoperability (IAI) was founded with the aim of promulgating interoperability and efficient information exchange between different ICT systems (International Alliance of Interoperability 2006). IAI is the key actor behind the development of the file exchange format IFC (Industry Foundation Classes) to ensure a system-independent exchange of information between all actors in the whole life cycle of the building. The program of the international IAI conferences from the last two years indicates a focus change from being technology development oriented to becoming implementation oriented. Consequently, IAI introduced the new brand "BuildingSMART" in June 2005.

The Finnish Vera Technology Programme became a central player in IAI's efforts regarding the development of IFC as an international product model standard (VERA 2006). The program made Finland one of the leading countries developing ICT for the AEC/FM industry. Five years later, after this program came to an end, the Confederation of the Finnish Construction industries initiated the ProIT-project Product Model Data in the Construction Process (ProIT 2006), which focused on developing strategies for implementing 3D product models. The program was based on a joint effort between research and the building industry. Guidelines for architectural and engineering design were developed, and 3D product modeling was trialled in several pilot-projects.

Powerful players in the Norwegian AEC-industry have recognized the potential of introducing information exchange with IFC-based 3D object models throughout the value chain of the building process. The Norwegian BuildingSMART project is a joint venture of actors from both industry and research, and comprises several research and development projects. They include international projects (BuildingSMART - Nordic Chapter 2006) such as the IFD-project (Information Framework for Dictionaries), the IDM-project (Information Delivery Manuals), and electronic submissions to planning authorities. This last project is based on the experiences from Singapore, where they issued the CORENET in 2002 as a public e-submission system (CORENET e-Information System 2006). One of the implementation arenas for the BuildingSmart technology is the ongoing Norwegian pilot building project Tromsø University College, also called the HITOS-project (Statsbygg 2006). The public client Statsbygg (The Directorate of Public Construction and Property) requires and supports the implementation of IFC-based 3D object modeling by connecting a R&D project to the building project, based on a close collaboration between the design team, the software vendors and the Norwegian BuildingSMART.

Finnish promoters of the ProIT project, emphasized that Finland can harvest from the benefit of being a small country (ProIT information DVD "Product modeling as the basis for construction process", released 2005). Compared to many other larger countries, it is easier to gather the driving forces and to work together in implementing new technology. This situation has probably been a good starting point also for the R&D initiatives in Norway, and as we shall se later, for the Danish 'Digital Construction' program. In contrast, combining forces in the German AEC-industry is understood as far more challenging by its German promoters (interview with leader of the German BuildingSMART chapter). Some of the reasons for this situation are probably the complex and fragmented societal, political and business related structures of the country and the "bad times" in the German AEC-industry since the mid nineties. Generally, an essential target of the international BuildingSMART's and the German chapter's efforts are the players in the AEC-industry with the power and ability to implement the standards and technologies developed.

These are only selected examples from some European countries, not representing a complete picture of all worth mentioning international or national initiatives. The intention is to give the reader a brief glimpse into some trends as a "backdrop" for the further exploration of the Danish R&D program. Nevertheless, the authors interpret the Danish R&D program as strongly embedded in and characterized by the Danish institutional set up. A limitation of the present contribution is that the characteristics of this embedding and how it impacts on the program is not (yet) further developed.

A possible reference for investigating these aspects is Bang et al. (2001) in Manseau and Seaden (2001).

4. 'Digital Construction': A Public R&D Program in Denmark

A central feature of the 'Digital Construction' program is the belief in the client-power of the state. It is hoped that through a targeted development program the Danish state can set a standard for digitalized tendering, design, classification of building data, project webs and managing facilities. Three major professional state clients were envisioned to be central drivers in the program process. These three state clients of buildings cooperated with the consortia established in the program. The assumption was that the construction sector actors will engage in developing a basis for a future legislated digital interaction with the public clients. Another main idea of the program has been to adopt existing and developed generic software packages and configure those to support the developed guidelines and standards. The program has been taking a consensual approach in combining forces and mobilizing AEC-industry players, who were believed to be best able to drive and develop new methods and procedures to be used by the industry in the future. The establishment of proper and consensus based strategies for implementing the solutions agreed upon in practice, was an essential issue in the program. Based on this background, three main strategies have been defined (EBST 2005):

1. To provide a **digital foundation**for standards and methods to assure that all players in the construction business are "speaking the same digital language"
2. To establish a set of law-regulating **client demands,** which were issued by 01.01.2007 in public building projects
3. To build up a "**Best Practice**" base - a compilation of experiences of real life projects demonstrating how the integration of digital solutions in real life projects can enhance efficiency in the working process

In support of area "3," the program encompassed an effort to evaluate and communicate best practice experiences for implementing and operating ICT in construction. The consortium responsible for this part of the program featured a handful of the largest players amongst contractors and consulting engineers. The project ran into a number of problems; importantly it turned out to be very difficult to find best practice examples. In December 2006, the "best-practice" base of 'Digital Construction' included 17 cases, whereof 5 deal with 3D-issues, 4 with project web, and the rest with e-learning, commissioning, e-mail standard and other smaller ICT-issues. This base represents mainly cases with a limited scope, focusing on smaller parts of the building process. The cases are derived from the developmental work within Digital Construction of experimental character rather than well-documented "best practice", as also noted by the program itself ('Digital Construction' public website 2006).

4.1. THE DIGITAL FOUNDATION

Over the spring of 2004, the digital foundation part of "Digital Construction" was divided into four project proposals:

- Classification
- 3D work methods
- Logistics and Process
- Building Items Chart (not followed up)

This collection of projects reflects a delicate balance of interests. Object orientation has been "secured" space through the 3D work method project. Whereas positions of more pragmatic type as well as interests in favor of a "document-view" are secured space within classification. Moreover, logistics and process represents an area that contractors are interested in. Broad participation was assured at workshops and was obtained in the sense that more representatives from contractors than initially was mobilized. The design was challenged both internally and externally by website debate and in the program council. In May and June 2004 several elements were taken out in order to meet the overall budget. The remaining three projects (the first three bullet points) stabilized and all commenced before September 2004. As of 2007, the new classification has been developed and is now under scrutiny by external experts. The 3D work methods was finalized by summer 2006, with extensive material available on the public website and used in the case below. The results of the logistics and process- project was a proposal for the use of so-called "production-cards" a tool for detailed scheduling at the building site, inspired by last planner/lean construction ideas.

4.2. THE 3D WORK METHOD PROJECT

The 3D work method project is intended to match the building processes and technologies known today, and mirrors the general visions of the 'Digital Construction' program. An important issue in the development of the 3D work method was to ensure that the established manuals allow new and innovative collaboration scenarios and the implementation of future CAD technology. Around 35 companies representing different interests in the industry have participated. The joint efforts in the 3D work method project have resulted in a 3D CAD manual built upon four parts: (http://www.detdigitalebyggeri.dk):

- 3D work method (description of concept)
- 3D CAD manual (practical guidelines for building up the 3D model)

- Layer and Object structures
- 3D CAD project agreement.

The four manuals aim to specify a common working method for all parties in planning and construction to support the building-up, exchange, and re-use of the 3D models throughout all phases of the process (bips 2006). Further aims formulated in the concept are (examples): work process optimization and improved collaboration, improved quality and consistency of project material, clear definition of responsibility through common work method principles, improved communication through visually understandable 3D models, and automation of sub-processes.

The key idea of the 3D work method project is that each discipline shall build up, maintain and importantly, be responsible for their 3D discipline-specific object model. All necessary changes/editing shall be undertaken in these discipline models. The discipline-specific model is also the basis for generating 2D drawings and quantity take-offs. The exchange of the models between the disciplines is to be based on IFC or another appropriate file exchange format. The 3D work method manual furthermore suggests building up the 3D models according to seven information levels according to the increasing need for concretization. The 3D work method proposes in the next step to gather these discipline models into a common project model. The decision to which extent a common model shall be integrated and used in a building project depends on the project specific technical and financial possibilities to be clarified in the CAD agreement. From January 2007, the 3D work method project has been implemented as guidelines together with the client demands, requiring the compulsory use of 3D object models in public building projects with building costs exceeding 40 millions Danish kroner (5,3 mill. Euro). (EBST 2005)

5. The National Icelandic Concert and Conference Centre in Reykjavik

The National Icelandic Concert and Conference Centre (CCC), Figure 1, located in the harbor of Reykjavik, is a prestigious public-partnership project

Figure 1. Left: The CCC-project. Right: 3D visualization of quasi-brick-façade. (Courtesy: Henning Larsen Architects)

aiming to make Reykjavik visible in the international landscape of architectural and cultural high-lights.

5.1. THE ROLE OF THE 3D OBJECT MODEL IN THE CCC-PROJECT

The CCC-project is one of the first ongoing large-scale building projects in Denmark attempting to work with and exchange 3D object models. The interdisciplinary use of 3D object models is expected to play an important role in supporting the development of the complex design solutions and in the smoothing of interactions between the actors and the processes. Following the 3D work method manuals, each discipline has been building up their own discipline model using the software most appropriate for their specific needs (Figure 2). Each discipline can directly upload the model files from other disciplines as external references. A CAD operator gathers the different discipline models into a common model, which they use for making clash-detections for generating visualization files (Figure 3, left).

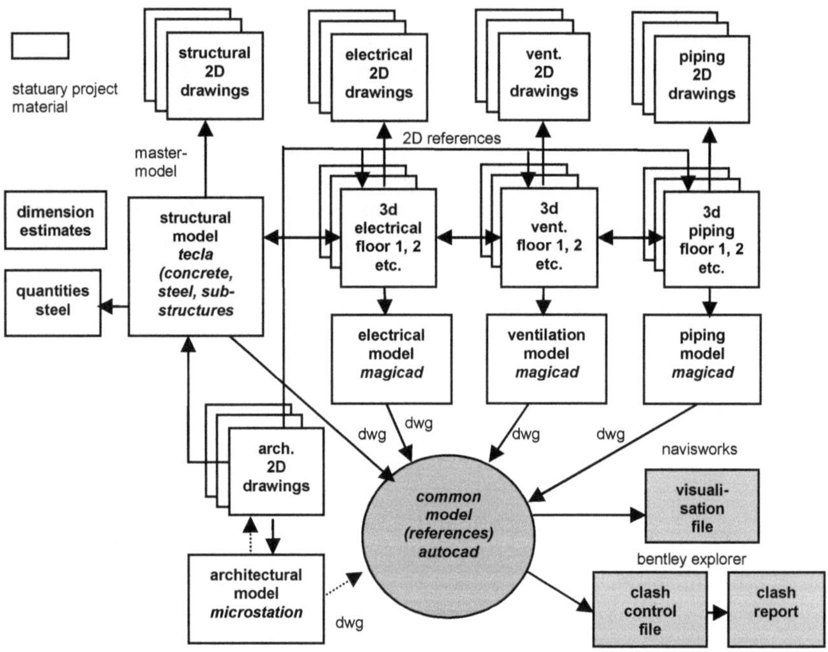

Figure 2. Overview ICT system CCC-project

An important issue which influences the interdisciplinary use of the 3D object model and the data-exchange between the architects and the engineers is that the architects are still mainly working with 2D CAD. 3D object models are only used in limited parts of the project, for instance in developing the complex building envelops and the quasi-brick façade. According to the architects' project manager, the risks connected to the implementation of a totally new CAD-technology into such a large and complex building project were considered as too high. However, the architectural company agreed to build up a "test" 3D object model as an "add-on" to the actual 2D project material in order to collect experiences and test out the potential. The first upload of the architectural 3D object model into the common model was possible summer 2006, toward the end of the design proposal phase. Generally, the importance of the 3D object model for the architectural design team has increased since the start of the project. In Autumn 2006, the architectural company was considering to generate parts of the 2D project material directly from the 3D object model in the detailed design phase.

To work with 3D object models is not yet an issue for the contractor partly because the contractor is an Icelandic company and thus not directly part of the target group of 'Digital Construction.' This also mirrors the situation in the program generally, where the architects and engineers were the most active players. Thus, the implementation and use of the 3D working method of 'Digital Construction' in this project is limited to the design group. The statuary documents of the project are traditional 2D drawings (partly generated from the discipline models).

5.2. EXPERIENCES FROM IMPLEMENTATION AND USE: EXAMPLES

Until a kick-off meeting where the 3D work method concept was presented within the engineering company, the project participants were overwhelmed and skeptical as they were confronted with the decision to implement interdisciplinary use of 3D object models in the project. According to the project manager of the engineering disciplines, the clarity of the concept regarding responsibilities and discipline models increased the acceptance among the project group actors.

The 3D object model has until autumn 2006 been playing its main role in supporting geometrical development, coordination and space management internally in the design team. Several interview respondents in the engineering company pointed out the improved understanding and control of the building geometry and geometrical relations between the different disciplines as substantial benefits. Clashes and failures could be recognized and solved earlier. The 3D visualizations have also been helpful in order to achieve a shared understanding regarding the needs and the intentions of each discipline. An interview respondent involved in the architectural façade group pointed out that developing and communicating the complex building envelope would have been nearly impossible without using a 3D model for solution generation, communication and evaluation (Figure 1, right). The 3D model has also contributed to improved communication of project intentions to actors outside the design team. In Autumn 2006, the engineering company presented and demonstrated their visualization file of the common model and the possibilities for easy 3D navigation. According to the project manager from the engineering company, this was a success and a breakthrough in communicating the very complex interplay between the different contributions in a visual and easy understandable way to project participants who had difficulties in interpreting traditional 2D drawings. Still, in most cases, the 3D object model has not been used directly or real-time in meeting situations.

Regarding other possible 3D model related aims and activities defined in the 3D work method concept, simulations based on the 3D model have not yet been carried out. Neither have quantity-take offs been automatically generated. An exception is the engineering group developing the steel constructions. They seem to utilize more fully the possibilities of their discipline 3D model. According to one of the interview respondents involved in the international IAI, the domain of steel construction is generally in a leading position regarding software development and use.

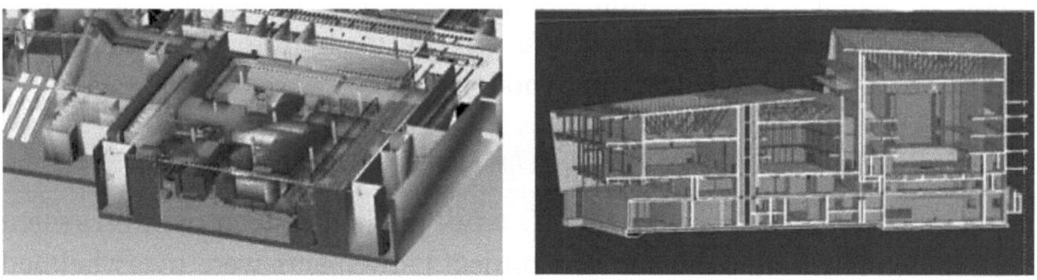

Figure 3. Left: view of the common model. Right: visualization of structural systems, with the façade "reference shells". (Courtesy: Rambøll Danmark A/S)

It soon also became clear that the seven information levels defined in the 3D work method project were difficult to handle in practice. Generally, the level of detail in the different 3D discipline models seems to depend on, for instance, the starting point of modeling, the software capacity, the skills of the user and not at least that the delivery to the contractor should mainly be based on traditional 2D drawings and details. The architects developing the building envelope soon realized that modeling the complete façades into detail would not only exceed the capacity of both the software and the user, but it would also be inefficient due to data exchange with the engineers. Thus, the architects established simplified "reference shells" of the façade, which are implemented in the discipline models and in the common model (Figure 3, right).

Several technical problems have emerged throughout the planning. The different software programs do not in all areas address the needs of the disciplines or the actual complexity of the processes. Through a narrow collaboration between the software vendors and the users of the software in the project, some of the most crucial problems are solved one by one. The main non-technical challenge in the project seems to be the different ambitions and possibilities of the architectural and the engineering company due to the use of the 3D object model. This situation has made the interdisciplinary coordination and the exchange of data between the architect and the engineer a challenging issue. An example from the exchange of data between the architects and the structural engineers in the summer of 2006 illustrates the challenges. The basis for the structural model would normally be the geometrical 3D "master-model" of the architect. In this case, the structural engineers had to build up a geometric model based on the architectural 2D drawings (Figure 2). Complete digital 2D drawings from the structural 3D model were not generated until the end of the design proposal, since the generation of 2D drawings from the structural model is a time consuming issue. The architects had to "transform" hand-sketches from the structural engineers into their architectural 2D drawings. Hence, both the architects and the structural engineers felt they had to do more work than necessary due to insufficient information delivery from "the other side."

Here an organizational aspect is additionally intensifying this challenge. Within the engineering company, the engineers normally have no CAD skills. They develop the concepts and systems based on hand drawings. Skilled CAD operators build up the 3D model. Although some few of the younger engineers are skilled within 3D CAD, indicating a generation shift, to change this situation will, according to the manager of the engineering disciplines, take time. In addition, building up CAD skills and competences is also a question of educational and organizational policies and strategies, both inside and outside the company. Within the architectural company, all architects are mastering 2D CAD. According to the manager of the architectural group, this is clearly the aim regarding 3D object modeling. However, until autumn 2006, there were few architects with such skills. Lastly, it seems to be a general challenge to implement new technology within the limited time and financial frames of this ongoing and very complex building project. Nevertheless, there is awareness among the actors that not all the aims defined in the 3D work method concept can be fulfilled in the CCC-project.

6. Stretching the Trousers Too Far?

During the development of the 'Digital Construction' implementation strategies, it has been criticized that implementing existing ICT-systems in the AEC-industry is a conservative rather than forward looking approach. There have been efforts within the 3D part of the program to develop and implement ICT concepts based on more advanced technology, where all participants work with "common core data" throughout all stages of the building project. This project stagnated due to several issues such as implementation problems in practice and coordination issues within the program. However, there is much activity and effort within research at architectural schools, universities and applied science units to develop more innovative concepts and technologies. A weighty argument for the chosen level of ambition was that only aiming for the "low hanging fruits" could be a proper match to the actual status of the industry. The first experiences from implementing the 3D work method concept into the CCC-project indicate powerful benefits of the technology, but there are still many challenges to be handled before all aims and visions can be turned into reality. There are several points to be mentioned, which impact the situation.

First, the initiative for introducing and testing out the 3D work method concept and 3D object models in the CCC-project came form the engineering company. It was not a client demand, not to mention that the client is not a representative of the Danish state as the program envisions. Thus, the 3D work method until now only has been implemented in the design team. In addition, neither extra time nor financial means have been made available for the implementation. The engineers and architects have to carry the risk of negative consequences. Moreover, the shortcomings of the technology are make the handling of the 3D object models complicated and time-consuming. Finally, most of the actors in the design team do not have previous experiences and skills working with 3D object models.

When transplanting the 3D work methods to Danish AEC-industry as part of 'Digital Construction' a number of training and support measures are set up in the socalled Implementation network (Implementeringsnetværket 2007). It is interesting to compare the situation in this project with the Norwegian pilot-project mentioned earlier in the paper. In the HITOS project the client demanded and supported the testing of new technology. Implementing the new technology was a part of the contract. The design team was already trained in building up information rich 3D object models although not in exchanging information or merging them into a common model.

The question how far the trousers can be stretched regarding the implementation of a national based ICT platform into real life projects seems to depend on an array of issues placed on different levels. Based on the analyses in this paper, at least three issues can be mentioned: the impact power of the initiator for integrating 3D CAD in the whole life cycle of the building project; the potential of the technology to address the actual needs inherited in the project processes; and the readiness and skills of the project participants, both regarding the use of the technology and in adapting new working methods and processes.

7. Conclusions

The explorations and discussions in this paper are placed in the complex and iterative field between strategies for integrating ICT on national level. R&D programs on macro-level, such as the 'Digital Construction', could contribute to bridging the gap between research and practice through convening societal and ICT development in the building practice and the focus on implementation. The experiences in Denmark indicate that the involvement of public clients is a possible strategy for integrating ICT in the AEC-industry. However, the tightrope act between developing proper strategies and deciding an appropriate level of ambition on the one hand, and the actual readiness of the industry for ICT integration on the other, is challenging. The balance requires a broad understanding of the mechanisms and relations on many levels in practice. Process evaluations and multi-level explorations of practice could contribute to such an understanding.

From January 2007, the Danish state provides a stronger push toward the integration of ICT and 3D object modeling in the Danish AEC-industry. Thus, in Denmark as also for instance in Norway and Finland, powerful players have brought the snowball to roll. The first experiences made in Denmark could be an important contribution to the crucial discussions about strategies and aims for a pro-active ICT integration within the trinity of architectural and engineering design: research, practice and education.

This paper has explored only a limited part of this large scale and complex R&D program. As this paper is written, the first Danish public clients are now providing projects where the Digital Construction program results are used in full scale. More than 50 projects are underway. The Danish 'Implementation Network' (Implementeringsnetværket 2007) shall ensure and support the further implementation of the program and its solutions after the R&D program ended in March 2007. The trousers might be stretched, but reinforcements are on their way.

Acknowledgements

The authors would hereby like to thank all interview respondent and contact persons involved in the R&D programs and building projects described and explored in this paper.

References

Bang H, Bonke S and Clausen L: 2001, Innovation in the Danish Construction Sector: the role of policy instruments, *in* G Seaden and A Manseau (eds), *Innovation in Construction - an International review of Public Policies*, Spon Press, London.

bips: 2006, 3D arbejdsmetode 2006, Det Digitale Byggeri. Retrieved December 2006 from http://www.detdigitalebyggeri.dk.

BuildingSMART: n.d., Nordic Chapter. Retrieved December 2006 from http://www.buildingsmart.no/.

CORENET e-Information System: n.d., Singapore Government, Building & Construction Authority. Retrieved December 2006 from http://www.corenet.gov.sg/einfo/index.asp? currentState=SHOW_INTRO.

Det Digitale Byggeri ('Digital Construction'): n.d. Retrieved December 2006 from http://www.detdigitalebyggeri.dk.

EBST: 2006, December, Bekendtgørelse om krav til anvendelse af Informations- og Kommunikationsteknologi i byggeri. Retrieved December 2006, from Det Digitale Byggeri Web site: http://detdigitalebyggeri.dk/component/option,com_docman/ Itemid,110/ task, cat_view/ gid,58/

EBST: 2005, March, ICT takes a big leap forward in the construction sector. Retrieved December 2006, from Det Digitale Byggeri Web site: http://www.detdigitalebyggeri.dk

Gann, DM: 2000, *Building innovation -complex constructs in a changing world*, Thomas Telford, London, pp. 139-180.

Implementeringsnetværket: n.d., Det Digitale Byggeri. Retrieved March 2007 from http:// detdigitalebyggeri.dk/om-det-digitale-byggeri/om-implementeringsnetvaerket_3.html.

International Alliance for Interoperability: n.d. Retrieved December 2006 from http:// www.iai-international.org/.

Koch, C and Haugen, T: 2006, Can the skipper ride the storm? The state as ICT-client in Danish construction, *in* D Bennett, B Clegg, A Greasley, and P Albores (eds), *Technology and Global Integration*, *Proceedings of Second EuroMOT Conference on "Technology and Global Integration"*, Aston Business School and IaMOT, Birmingham, pp. 368-375.

Kvale, S: 1997, *Det kvalitative forskningsintervju*, Gyldendal Akademisk, Oslo.

Latham, M: 1994, *Constructing the Team*, HMSO, London.

Moum, A: 2006, A framework for exploring the ICT impact on the architectural design process, *ITcon* **11**: 409-425.

Patton, MQ: 1990, *Qualitative Evaluation and Research Method*, Sage Publications, Newbury Park CA.

Patton, MQ: 1998, Discovering Process Use, *Evaluation* **4**(2): 225-33.

ProIT, Product Model Data in the Construction Process (n.d). Retrieved December 2006., from http://virtual.vtt.fi/proit_eng/indexe.htm.

Sjøgren, J: 2006, buildingSMART in norway - a Norwegian IFC story and lessons learnt. Retrieved December 2006 from http://coreweb.nhosp.no/buildingsmart.no/html/files/ 181006_Norwegian_buildingSMART_project.pdf.

Statsbygg, The Norwegian Agency of Public Construction and Property: 2006, REPORT: Experiences in development and use of a digital Building Information Model (BIM) according to IFC standards from the building project of Tromsø University College (HITOS) after completed Full Conceptual Design Phase. Retrieved December 2006 from ftp://ftp.buildingsmart.no/pub/ifcfiles/HITOS/HITOS_Reports.

Van de Ven, AH, Polley, D, Garud, R and Venkataraman, S: 1999, *The Innovation Journey*, Oxford University Press, New York.

VERA Technology Programme, TEKES, the National Technology Agency. Retrieved December 2006 from http://cic.vtt.fi/vera/english.htm.

Wikforss, Ö (ed): 2003, *Byggandets informationsteknologi - så används och utvecklas IT i byggandet*, Svensk byggtjänst, Stockholm.

Yin, RK: 2003, *Case Study Research - Design and Methods*, 3rd edition, Sage Publications, Beverly Hills, CA.

BEING VIRTUAL

URBAN GENERATOR

Agent-based simulation of urban dynamics

LUCA CANEPARO, MATTIA COLLO, ALFONSO MONTUORI
AND STEFANO PENSA
Politecnico di Torino, Italy

Abstract. The paper presents an ongoing project to interactively simulate urban and regional dynamics at the building scale. Urban Generator is a system for generating a large number of design solutions and for browsing, searching and structuring the high-dimensional space of the design solutions further to variable and customisable factors defined by the designer. The number of these factors is recognised as large; furthermore they are often ill-defined. Urban Generator does not model every factor; instead it supports the designer in defining the significant factors and their interconnections, then freely exploring the dimensions of the space of the design solutions generated by the system.

1. Introduction

Urban Generator is a challenging prospective for exploring the numerous and often interconnected factors that can affect the urban design potentially. The number of these factors is recognised large, furthermore they are often ill-defined, and can assume different meanings relating to the urban context. They often play in interrelated ways: "depending on how it is acted upon by other factors and how it reacts to them" (Jacobs 1961). Jane Jacobs (1961) also stated: «Cities happen to be problems in organized complexity, like the life sciences. They present "situations in which a half-dozen or even several dozen quantities are all varying simultaneously and in subtly interconnected ways." »

Urban Generator is not committed to model each and every factor; instead it supports the designer in defining the significant factors and their interconnections, and then freely exploring the dimensions of the space of the design solutions generated by the system.

A Dong, A Vande Moere & JS Gero (eds), CAADFutures'07, 347–360.

The dimensions of the solution space increase exponentially; thus the system is implementing strategies and tools for exploring the very large number of designs solutions generated (Garey and Johnson 1979). This approach substantially differs from an optimisation process wherein solution space is explored by an algorithm in order to recognise the solution best fitting the given criteria. With the proposed methodology, the designer can explore the high-dimensional space of the solutions, generated by the system according to the given constraints and criteria, in order to find the solution/s that best fit the implemented criteria but also further ones that the system is not considering, while the designer is. For instance, the designer can be considering aesthetic criteria or ones relating to the site or the milieu etc. These additional criteria possibly are not implemented in the system explicitly.

The paper presents strategies and technologies for searching the high-dimensional space of design solutions and for defining and presenting structures in the space of solutions. We do expect structures in the space of the solutions to be a promising methodology for more effectively supporting the designer in recognising the "neighbourhood" where s/he expects to be the design solutions, and then to explore this neighbourhood to evaluate the small variations in the constraints and criteria that defines them. Thus, the final aim of the generative system is not defining one, best fitting solution; rather the aim is to drive the designer towards one ore more "neighbourhoods" in the space of the design solutions where s/he can gather suggestions or directions in designs that otherwise s/he will possibly not have been considering.

2. Related Works

We are recognizing two main directions of research in CAAD dealing with our approach to urban design. The first puts forward tools for supporting the design process. The second generates designs of urban configurations.

To the first direction relates tools for the support of the various scales, models and disciplines in urban design. From the building scale, for instance models focusing on the simulation of the thermal performance of buildings. Bouchlaghem (1999) advances computer models not only for simulating the thermal performance of the building taking into account design variables related to the building's envelope and fabric, but also applies numerical optimization techniques to automatically determine the optimum design variables, which achieve the best thermal comfort conditions. The main optimization program is supported by a graphical model for the design. The models offer a valuable decision support system for designers at an early design state for the optimization of the passive thermal performance achieving optimum thermal comfort and savings in heating and cooling energy.

Development simulator is a decision making support system, which helps urban designers and architects, along with developers, city officials. It integrates two tools: a calculating tool and a form shaping tool. As a calculating tool, it helps designers do calculation, computation and estimation. Given criteria, it helps designers to search for the optimal result. As a form-making tool, it gives direction to building form driven by the results of calculation, computation and estimation. (Samiaji 2001)

An early contribution to the second direction of research is Hillier and Hanson's (1984) basic model of the evolution of urban configurations, where every plot is discretised on a bi-dimensional grid.

A further contribution comes from shape grammars, for instance Mayall and Hall's (2005) work, which uses a vocabulary of landscape object types and spatial syntax rules, and these can be used to generate scenes.

There is also an algorithmic design of architectural configurations, relating to the capability to rank different alternatives: Fuhrmann and Gotsman (2006) consider computing the merit of a given configuration of units, to generate configurations by "greedily adding and removing units with the aim of maximizing the merit of the resulting configuration, either in a planar or a spatial setting".

3. Urban Generator

Usually we pay attention to what happens between the design process in architecture with all its requirements and the strategies used by the designer to work into it. Certainly urban design incorporates complex factors which comprehend multiple principles, including visual representations, numerical data, mediations, analysis. Generally we have to compound the accomplishment of quantitative requirements: to fulfil the urban regulations and to satisfy the qualitative standards.

Urban Generator is a system for simulating different urban scenarios in relation to the uniqueness and constraints peculiar to a project or a site. These factors produce different configurations relied with typological and measurable inputs, and generate a large number of solutions.

For exploring the high-dimensional space of design solutions the system offers both tools for searching it and for structuring it (cf. 6. Value results. A cluster analysis of solutions).

3-D scenarios allow urban designers to explore the space of design solutions defined, for instance by typological, quantitative and performance factors. The simulation makes it possible also to structure the units in relation to different typologies (e.g. type and quantity). Thus we can explore the multiple simulations of scenarios to understand what happens to the system when we change the quantity of a specific typology for a site. Obviously this change affects the interrelated types. We can verify the impact of the sun irradiance on the buildings to estimate not only the cast shadows and the daylight illuminance, but also perceived qualitative aspects as daily solar and sky visibility access. Consequently the system evaluates the solar potential for each point of the plot depending on the shape, size and place of the buildings. Thus it is possible to evaluate the daylight comfort for each building and unit in relation with its neighbourhood (Cheng et al. 2006). Urban Generator is a hybrid system, software seamlessly integrating the generator of a large number of design solutions and the browser for searching and structuring the high-dimensional space of the design solutions, according to variable and customisable factors defined by the designer.

4. Typologies

We understand architectural typology as a methodology to express the designers' awareness of basically different design options, according to their understanding of their appropriateness to various desires and requirements, or also the combination of several diagrammatic representations and characters structured into recognisable pattern. (Van Leusen 1996).

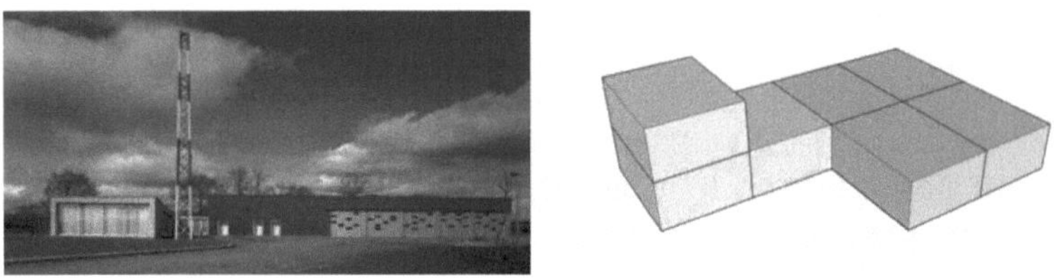

Figure 1. Road maintenance centre, Barré Architectes, Pleuguéneuc, France

We have been analysing different building typologies for exploring the rules that can gather their shape and dimension into recognisable patterns. This way we are able to define the common reference elements to formulate evolutionary and associative grammars for each typology (see Figure 1).

We presuppose buildings discretised on a grid, so in order to describe typologies we use unitary volume parameters as height, length and depth (the number of cells on the grid). Thus we defined grammars which the system has to meet for aggregating the cells.

5. Rules as Design Process: The Multi-Agent Model

Elementary the system consists of the representation of the plots, rules and typologies that describe the methodology for aggregating the units in buildings/s, and evaluation parameters.

After Hillier and Hanson (1984), we map the plots on a three-dimensional grid. For simplicity, we use a cubic grid (for instance, 1 by 1 by 1 m). On the other hand this simplification has demonstrated flexible enough to represent concave plots (e.g. in historical cities) or buildings with non Euclidean envelope.

We define rules as mandatory and non-violable set of constraints, which describe the urban regulations and the geometrical features of the plots. Besides we consider on the same rank the area covered by the building and the layout of the site fitting the requirements of the design. Combining these parameters we were able to address the development and the distribution of the units into building volume/s on the site. The space of the design solutions generated is directly related to the mandatory rules, e.g. from the urban regulations as maximum height, distance from other buildings, etc. Despite of a number of rules, the space of the design solutions is still high-dimensional.

The space of the design solutions is generated by a multi-agent model. Agent-based modelling offers a flexible way to study the behaviour of mathematical models. In agent-based models the time evolution of all the system emerges from the level of the agent's action and behaviour.

Agent-based modelling has demonstrated effective in economic, social and natural sciences, and design (Gero and Fujii 1999), especially when it is not possible to define an analytic solution to the problem.

We designed and implemented the multi-agent model in Java Swarm environment (Minar et al. 1996). The input to the multi-agent model is generated by the relationships between "local" actors (e.g. the owners of the land, dwellings etc.), "global" actors (investors, public decision-makers etc.) and their interactions (market, social, etc.). We can simulate different urban dynamics at the building scale considering as input the following factors:

1. Typology
2. Plot edge
3. Total building volume
4. Front and depth dimensions
5. Floor number and height
6. Number of buildings
7. Minimal distance between buildings
8. Minimal distance from the edge

The multi-agent model generates and evaluates the suitable solutions to the input problem which satisfy the hard constraints imposed by the input factors, considering as evaluation parameters the following:

a. Solar availability on building façade (irradiance performance)
b. Ratio between floor gross surface and open surface
c. Ratio between floor gross surface and façade surface
d. Ratio between floor gross surface and roofing surface
e. Construction cost
f. Land value

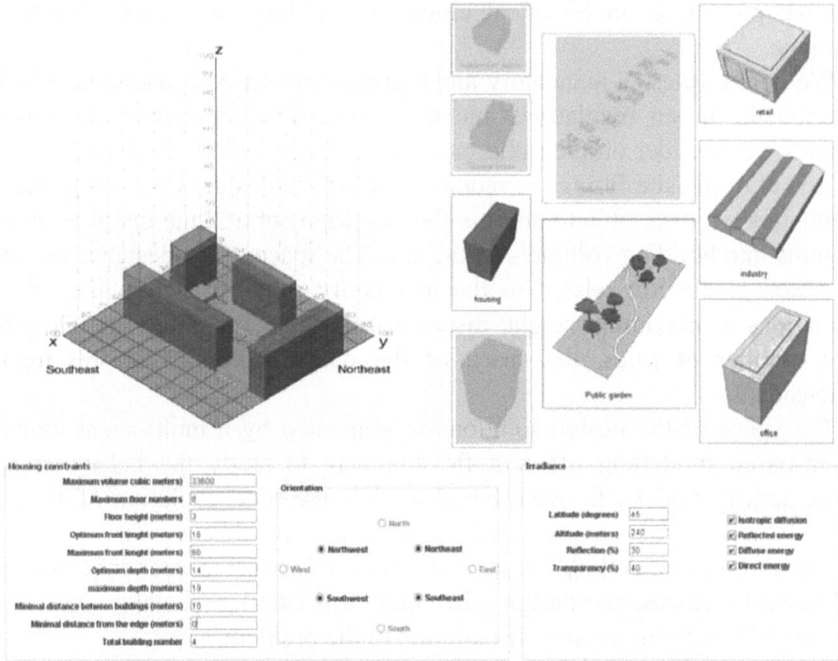

Figure 2. The graphic user interface of urban generator

We define a *building agent* for each building. Each building agent starts from a building with minimum, suitable layout and tries to optimize the layout adding new units-cells to the building. The starting seed location of building/s is random. We decided to use an exhaustive research strategy to exhaust the space of the design solutions, reducing pruning rules to a minimum. In this way we were able to generate a large number of initial, random seed solutions to explore unexpected solutions and relations between the units.

The building agent uses cellular automata (cf. next paragraph) to add cells to the building and communicates with the other agents in order to respect the hard constraints on distances between buildings. Since each building-agent can create a proper schedule, it is important that all of these activities are coordinated in a logical way. A top level agent schedules the action of each building-agent. The top level agent also manages the user interface, scheduling the updating of the graphical display (see Figure 2).

This multi-level integration of schedules is typical of Swarm based models, in which the simulation can indeed be thought of as a nested hierarchy of models, in which the schedules of each agent are merged into the schedule of next higher level (Johnson 1999).

The simulation proceeds in discrete time steps. As the simulation proceeds, the building agents update their state and report their state to the observer top-level agent. Auxiliary agents that facilitate the work of the building agents can be instantiated if more than one typology is present.

5.1. THE CELLULAR AUTOMATA

A cellular automaton is a collection of cells on a grid of specified shape whose state evolves through a number of discrete time steps according to a set of rules based on the states of neighbouring cells (Weisstein 1999).

Two of the most fundamental properties of a cellular automaton are the type of grid on which it is computed and the number of distinct states (usually represented with different colours) a cell may assume. We defined the cellular automata used by the building agents on Cartesian grids in 3 dimensions with binary cells representing the occupied/not occupied state. The user can decide the dimensions of each cell (for example front by depth by height = 1 m by 1 m by 3 m).

In addition to the grid on which a cellular automaton lives and the states its cells may assume, the neighbourhood over which cells affect one another must also be specified. In this case the most natural choice could seem the "nearest neighbours," in which only cells directly adjacent to a given cell may be affected at each time step. Instead, we decided to use the 3-d generalization of the von Neumann neighbourhood (a diamond-shaped neighbourhood, see Figure 3), because in this way the automata update algorithm was less computationally expensive than the nearest neighbours one and able to accomplish the requested task.

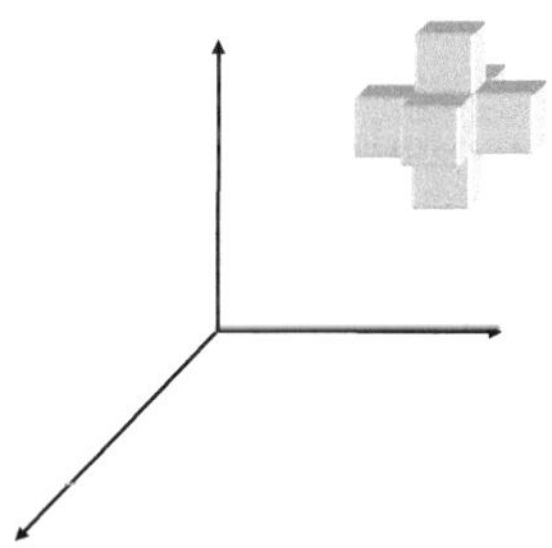

Figure 3. Three-dimensional von Neumann neighbourhood

For instance, we based the update rule for the "single family" typology on the relationship between the cost C and the building dimensions depth D and front F. Starting from this relationship a score S was assigned at each pair of values D and F by means of the following quadric in the 3-D space (depicted in Figure 4), i.e. the product of the score S_1 for D and the score S_2 for F:

$$S = S_1 \cdot S_2 = (a_1 \cdot D^2 + a_2 \cdot D + a_3) \cdot (\alpha_1 \cdot F^2 + \alpha_2 \cdot F + \alpha_3) \qquad (1)$$

We set the values of the coefficients (a_1, a_2, a_3) and (α_1, α_2, α_3) so that the scores S_1 and S_2 were both equal to 0 for D=8 m, D=14 m and F=5 m, F=9 m respectively, and both equal to 1 in the maximum (we assigned a dummy value v<0 to if S D<8 m or D>14 m or F<5 m or F>9 m).

The automata add a new cell in the position which maximizes the score. When the first floor of the building is completed the automata proceeds to complete the remaining floors. Each time a cell is added the building agent communicates to the top-level agent the new state of the automata. This process continues for each automaton until the total volume requested for the site is reached, as checked by the top level agent.

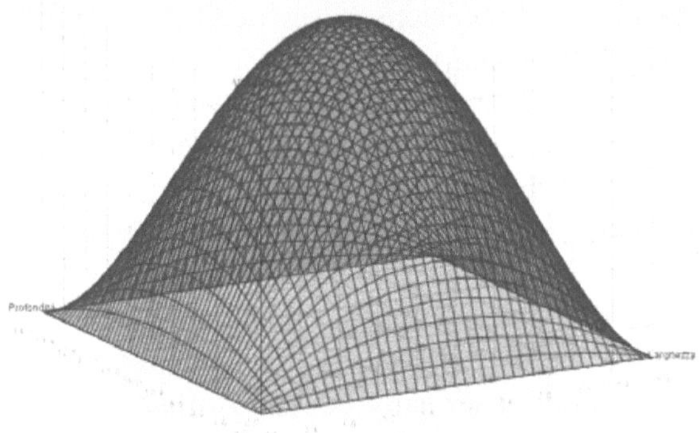

Figure 4. Construction cost function

6. Value Results: A Cluster Analysis of Solutions

The challenge is to design a formal solution which fulfils each normative requirement but also improves the qualitative standards. Measuring the idea of form and sustainability, as agreement with a regulated context, results being the balance among different aspects of a project in an urban milieu. These aspects are sometimes independent, sometimes interdependent and they have distinctive criteria of evaluation. They are related, so the increase of one's score determines the other's decrease.

It is important in the generative process that some constraints are stronger and more relevant than others, which means that the complexity of the factors can be structured and then reconciled with a hierarchy of decisions. Furthermore we must filtrate out the data because the dimensions of the space of the design solutions are high. If the space of the solutions is not ranked or structured, it demonstrates intractable and useless for the designer. We investigated the methodologies to rank and structure the space of the design solutions, setting relationships between urban regulations, sustainable practices, construction costs, and land values. We had to integrate the peculiar aspects of the various strategies to integrate the evaluation parameters with the normative constraints.

We created views on the high-dimensional space of the solutions to cluster different/alternative design scenarios, according to the designer's defined hierarchy in the factors. The clusters are defined homogeneous groups of design solutions in the view of the defined factors, e.g. solar availability on building façade (irradiance performance), ratio between floor gross surface and façade surface, ratio between floor gross surface and roofing surface etc. Cluster views demonstrated intuitive for a visual, prompt recognition of different groups/alternatives in design. The post-evaluation of the space of the design solution gives the system directions for generating further solutions, which can consider deeply the use of the plot or the density and distribution of the buildings on the site. At the same time, the designer can direct the guidelines of generation of the whole system in order to deepen the evaluation of these parameters.

The system implements further visualization techniques: 3-d scatter charts using glyphs and parallel coordinates.

Glyphs are a multi-variant analysis tool, which can be used as an effective way to represent the relationships between more than 3 variables in a single, comprehensible view. Besides the x, y and z axis the glyphs view uses the dimension of the glyphs (height, diameter, etc.) and its colour to allow rapid comparisons between the variables (see Figure 5).

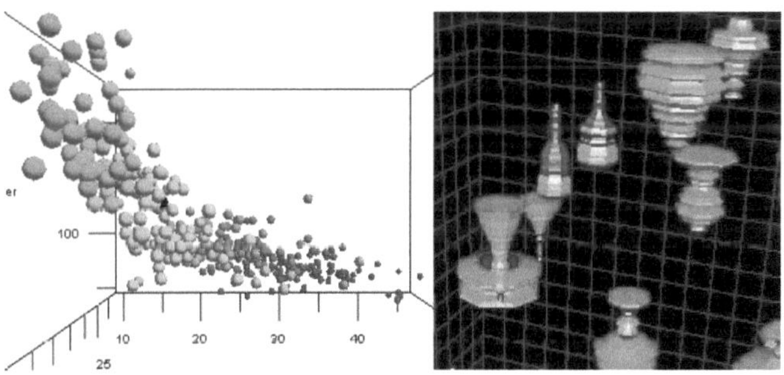

Figure 5. Glyphs

The resulting image would resemble a room of floating glyphs. The room could be rotated, and the relative size, shapes, positions, and colours of each glyph could be observed. In a single image, the use of glyphs allows a researcher to absorb a large quantity of information easily (Visual and Spatial Technology Centre).

Parallel coordinates were proposed by Alfred Inselberg (1984) as a new way to represent multidimensional information. A parallel coordinates visualisation assigns one vertical axis to each variable, and evenly spaces these axes horizontally (see Figure 6). This is in contrast to the traditional

Cartesian coordinates system where all axes are mutually perpendicular. By drawing the axes parallel to one another, one can represent data in much greater than three dimensions. Each variable is plotted on its own axis, and the values of the variables on adjacent axes are connected by straight lines. Thus, a point in an n-dimensional space becomes a polygonal line laid out across the n parallel axes with n-1 line segments connecting the n data values (Goel 1999).

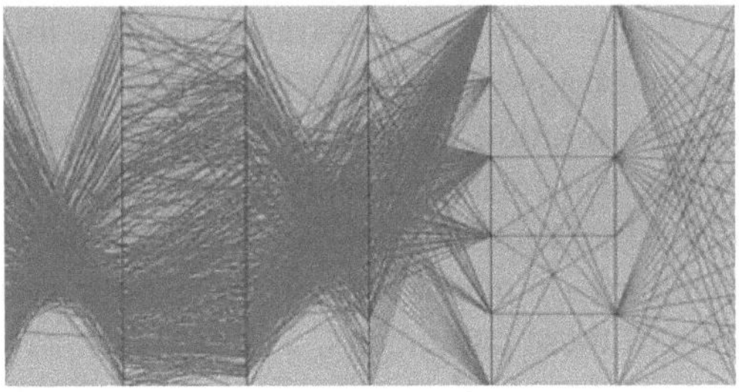

Figure 6. Parallel coordinates

Many such data points (in Euclidean space) will map to many of these polygonal lines in a parallel coordinate representation. Viewed as a whole, these many lines might well exhibit coherent patterns which could be associated with inherent correlation of the data points involved. In this way, the search for relations among the variables is transformed into a 2-D pattern recognition problem, and the variables become amenable to visualization.

7. Case Project: Mirafiori Area in Turin

We have experimented the methodology and platform in several case projects. Here we present a project at the urban scale: the possible evolution scenarios for the Fiat Mirafiori factory in Turin, Italy. The case project outlooks the reconversion of a portion of the factory, since the Fiat Company has dismissed a slice of about 310,000 m^2, of the total, huge area: about 3,000,000 m^2. In the historical evolution of the site, the considered industrial area has become an integral part of the urban milieu of Turin.

The Mirafiori project may become an opportunity for the city to explore a number of possible scenarios both on the expectations on the production models and on the perspectives for the metropolitan area inserted in a larger network of cities. Thus we consider the case project as the act of exploring advanced indications, representing them beforehand by next-decades scenarios. The aim of these scenarios is not foreseeing future urban morphologies and policies, but to expose factors that can contribute to the shaping of a large area: making these factors visible, so that the various actors involved or with responsibilities in the process can recognise and weight them.

The scenario making for this project has been a way of understanding the dynamics of the area and city, consequently trying to identifying the leading factors that can drive the dynamics. Figure 7 synthesises a set of the factors along two main axes: the horizontal axis represents the degrees of uncertainty between the demand-density for the area; the vertical axis represents the uncertain of the model of evolution (economic and social mainly) in the next decades, which involves not only the dynamics of industrial production, but also new opportunities to create places to live and to exert an influence on the very shape of the city.

The simulation of these scenarios with Urban Generator aims exploring: a) the hypotheses regarding the future use of the area, as the result of an open decision-making process, aimed to define a strategic plan for renewing the site (Spaziante 2006); b) the urban morphology as the subject of the scenario generation and evaluation, to support the designers', planners', decision-makers' and citizens' structuring and describing of the relations between the factors that shape the morphology at the urban scale.

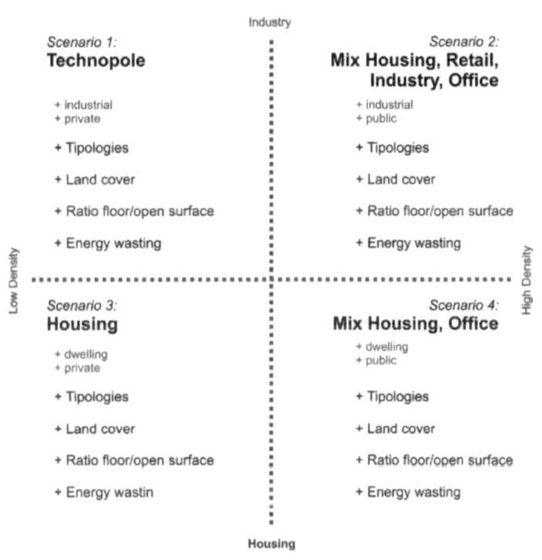

Figure 7. Matrix as a set of scenarios for the future

The simulations of the four scenarios with Urban Generator allow us making visible the relationships among alternative destinations, typologies, and variable volume, height, distance between buildings, plot edges etc. (cf. 5. Rules as design process: the multi-agent model).

Each scenario was implemented and simulated in Urban Generator to generate the respective space of the design solutions. Figures 8 and 9 illustrate a glyphs view on the high-dimensional spaces of the design solutions and the inputs to and outputs from Urban Generator for three scenarios: 2. Mix Housing, Retail, Industry, Office; 3. Housing; 4. Mix Housing, Office. Figure 2 presents Urban Generator simulating one block in the framework of scenario 2.

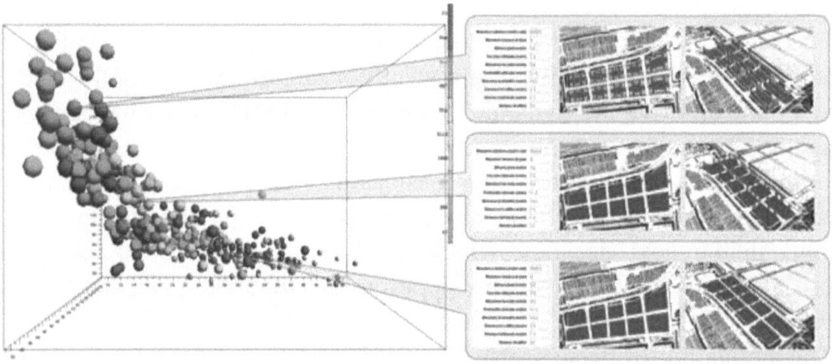

Figure 8. Glyphs view on three scenarios simulated with urban generator

8. Conclusions: Exploring Design Alternatives: A Tool for Decision Making

Urban Generator aims to support the early evaluation of alternative solutions from the initial phases of the urban design process. Especially the capability to rapidly generate alternatives is conceived to support design and planning practices, particularly during decision-making, because it can quickly represent alternatives and their interrelations (e.g. scenarios) into morphological, three-dimensional outcomes.

The capability to explore urban design in 3D models allows the designers and decision-makers to verify the process at the full extent: it demonstrates a powerful tool for widening the discussion and participation among designers, planners, decision-makers and citizens. According to our experience, often these meeting stuck the discussion into opposite positions that, in principle, can hardly find a balance. Instead the high-dimensional spaces of the design solutions of Urban Generator can be used to demonstrate that there is not a unique solution, instead there is a large space of alternative and visualising them is very useful to outline both the interrelation between the factors and the borders between the possible and the unsuitable.

Urban Generator can help visually estimating the morphological outcomes and interrelations in urban regulations. It can assist planners in verifying regulations not only from a quantitative point of view or a bi-dimensional one, instead from a full three-dimensional perspective. It has demonstrated useful in stressing and exploring the application of a regulation and also the interrelations among a specific regulation and further ones.

Last, but not least, the experimentations of Urban Generator in real projects has opened a plethora of issues. Just to mention the main ones, the typological representations have to be improved, as well as the interrelations

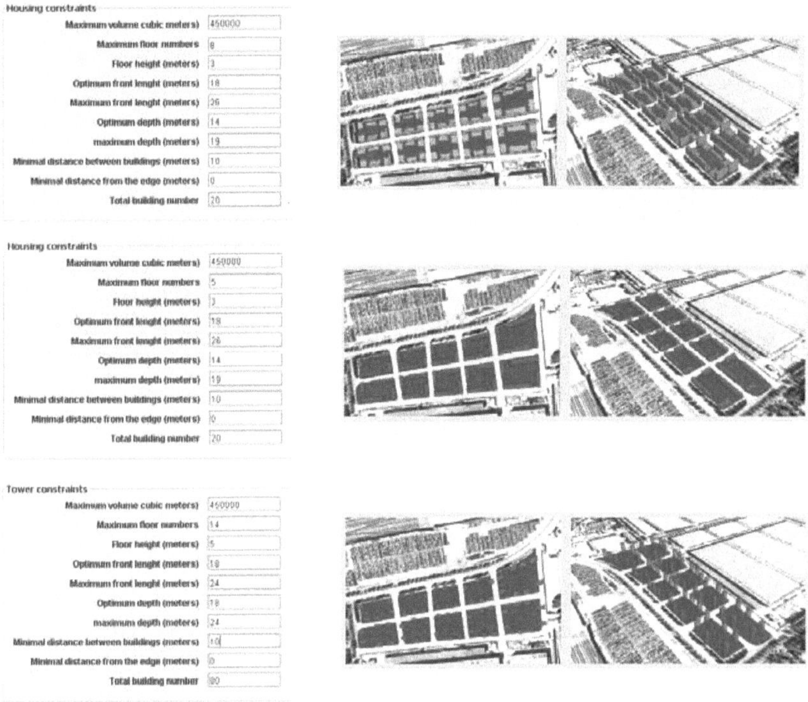

Figure 9. Scenarios 2, 3, and 4. Inputs to and outputs from urban generator

among different typologies in the same plot. Also the interrelations among different, adjacent plots considered simultaneously by the system have to be reconsidered. On the usability side, considered the prompt capability to generate vast amount of alternatives, the users-designers would really appreciate representation tools that will go beyond the structuring and visualising of one space of the design solutions, while they are requesting tools for comparing the interrelations/differences between variable factors and the resulting different spaces of the solutions.

Acknowledgements

This research is supported in part by the Politecnico di Torino Grant PTOL014234 and by the Ministry of University and Research Grant 2005088848. The conception and development of the platform is undertaking by an interdisciplinary group at High-Quality Laboratory – Territorial-Integrated Project, Politecnico di Torino, especially by Prof. Liliana Bazzanella, Prof. Franco Corsico, Prof. Matteo Robiglio, Prof. Lamberto Rondoni, Arch. Damiano Gardiman, Arch. Francesco Guerra, Arch. Elena Masala, Dr. Cinzia Mulas, Arch. Luigi Ponzio, and Arch. Giuseppe Roccasalva.

References

Bouchlaghem, N: 2000, Optimising the design of building envelopes for thermal performance, *Automation in Construction* **10**: 101–112

Cheng, V, Steemers, K, Montavon, M and Compagnon, R: 2006, *Urban Form, Density and Solar Potential*, PLEA2006 The 23rd Conference on Passive and Low Energy Architecture, 6-8 September 2006, Geneva, Switzerland.

Fuhrmann, O and Gotsman, C: 2006, On the algorithmic design of architectural configurations, *Environment and Planning B: Planning and Design* **33**(1) 131-140.

Garey, M and Johnson, D: 1979, *Computers and Intractability*, W.H. Freeman, San Francisco

Gero, JS and Fujii, H: 1999, A computational framework for concept formation for a situated design agent, *in* K. Hori and L. Candy (eds), *Proceedings Second International Workshop on Strategic Knowledge and Concept Formation..*, Iwate Prefectural University, Iwate, pp. 59-71.

Goel, A: 1999, *Visualization in Problem Solving Environments*, Master's thesis, Virginia Polytechnic Institute and State University, Blacksburg, VA.

Hillier, B and Hanson, J: 1984, *The social logic of space*, Cambridge University Press, New York.

Inselberg, A: 1984, Parallel Coordinates for Multi-dimensional Information Displays, *IEEE Proc. of Pecora Symp. Spatial Inform. Tech. for Remote Sensing*, pp. 312-324.

Jacobs, J: 1961, *The death and life of great American cities*, Random House, New York.

Johnson, P: 1999, *Swarm User Guide*, University of Kansas.

Mayall, K and Hall, GB: 2005, Landscape grammar 1: spatial grammar theory and landscape planning, *Environment and Planning B: Planning and Design* **32**(6) 895–920.

Minar, N, Burkhart, R, Langton, C and Askenazi, M: 1996, *The Swarm Simulation System: A Toolkit for Building Multi-agent Simulations*, Santa Fe Institute, Santa Fe, NM. Retrieved from http://www.santefe.edu/projects/swarm/.

Samiaji, D: *Development simulator: a tool for architects and urban designers*, MUD Thesis, University of Washington, Seattle, WA.

Spaziante, A: 2006, *Ricerca sul sito di Mirafiori, fase 1 – Linea C*, Technical Report LAQ-TIP, Politecnico di Torino.

Van Leusen, M: 1996, A typology of dwelling arrangements *Environment and Planning B: Planning and Design* **23**(2): 143–164.

Visual and Spatial Technology Centre, *Visualisation - a general introduction*, University of Birmingham, Birmingham, UK. Retrieved from http://www.vista.bham.ac.uk/avs-vis/Viz3DGlyphs.htm.

Weisstein, EW: 1999, *CRC Concise Encyclopedia of Mathematics*, CRC Press, Boca Raton, FL.

AVATAR EXPRESSION AGENT IN VIRTUAL ARCHITECTURE

JUMPHON LERTLAKKHANAKUL, SUN-HWIE HWANG
AND JIN-WON CHOI
Yonsei University, South Korea

Abstract. The lack of understanding of the character essence of avatars brings about limitations in interaction with their expressions. With the state-of-the art CAD standard and virtual reality, our approach is to explore the different paradigm of virtual architecture focusing on social interaction through avatars' gesture expression. The method to classify context-aware expression data model and to autonomously activate it in real-time along with users' communication is investigated. A domain of virtual office has been chosen as our study model based on our previous research. To achieve our goals, an avatar expression agent is developed based on our previous context-aware architectural simulation platform so called 'V-PlaceSims'. The output is delivered as a Web page with an ActiveX control embedded to simulate and to evaluate through the internet. As users communicate with one another using a text box, the avatar expression agent simultaneously detects the users' emotion by parsing the input texts to perform related gestures automatically. The result reveals a new convenience way to communicate with the other users with an enhancement in automated expression.

1. Introduction

Recently, research and studies about *functional virtual place* (Richens and Nitsche 2005) have revealed the new role and the new boundary of architecture changing the way we conceive it. Virtual architecture has been concerned as a place for functional activities. Many of those researches have suggested the significant of social interaction in the virtual environment. Perhaps, one of the most relevant issues is the concept of place that connects architecture to its context and makes it responsive to given needs (Kalay 2004-1). This distinguishes a place from a space by means of context and embodiment (Kalay 2004-2). Many researches have been done towards the same tendency by engaging avatars and context-aware ability into the virtual architecture.

A Dong, A Vande Moere & JS Gero (eds), CAADFutures'07, 361–372.

Nonetheless, the essential of avatar is not well concerned thus brings about limitation in interaction in terms of expression. Typical application using virtual reality (including virtual architecture) is that groups of people interact with one another through their shared interest in some simulated objectified process. The virtual reality in each case provides a scenario. In addition, the fundamental interaction is between each individual user and the environment. However, it was always found that the avatars' lack of expressiveness (as they were only able to turn and to move through the environment) impeded the development of significant social interaction between participants (Slater et al. 2000). In the domain of collaborative virtual environments, it has been pointed out that expression of avatar plays the key role to engage social interaction in shared virtual place (Liang et al. 2003). Nevertheless, the model for generating communicative behaviors in avatars has generally relied on explicit user input, such as key presses or menu selections (Vilhjálmsson 2004). For example, Second Life[1] provides an advanced expression module enabling their avatars express customized emotions. In fact, when people communicate face-to-face, they are not used to think about gesture production because it is something that happens spontaneously without conscious effort (Kendon 1990). An experiment by Cassell and Thorisson (1999) indicates envelope feedback is more important than emotional feedback for none-verbal behavior of avatar. Furthermore, Vilhjálmsson (2004) has suggested that avatars should also provide the basic nonverbal foundation autonomously for communication. Regardless of these studies, a framework that specifies the relationship between expression and context is missing. Such issue is becoming more critical as numbers of activity taken in the virtual world has gradually increased in various virtual places such as virtual museum, virtual classroom, virtual hotel etc. In fact, a user can perform different expressions for one emotion according to context in the real world. Likewise, such capability has not been realized and must be provided in current virtual architecture.

With the state-of-the art CAD standard, virtual reality and agent technology, our approach provides a better method to deliver social expression in virtual architecture, which is simpler, faster and more intuitive way. In this paper, we explore the different paradigm of virtual architecture focusing on social interaction through avatars' gesture expression. The method to classify context-aware expression data model and to autonomously activate it in real-time along with users' communication, thus, is investigated. A domain of virtual office has been chosen as our study model based on our previous research.

---

[1] http://secondlife.com/

To achieve our goals, all relationship among gestures, emotions and contexts have been listed and classified into an expression data schema at first. Second, context-aware emotion architecture is defined. Third, we captured all required motions in the collaboration with Motion Lab, Seoul National University. Fourth, all data have been converted into a database with Biovision Hierarchical data format and linked to avatar module developed by SpaceIllusion Inc.[2] Fifth, an avatar expression agent is developed in C++ environment based on our previous context-aware architectural simulation platform so called 'V-PlaceSims' (Lertlakkhanakul et al. 2006-2) . Finally, the output is delivered as a web page with an ActiveX control embedded to simulate and to evaluate through the internet.

2. Avatar and Emotion in Virtual Architecture

To elaborate our model as a new method, which enables social interaction in virtual architecture, it is necessary to understand about various related subjects including virtual architecture, avatar, emotion architecture and context-awareness. This section describes fundamental knowledge and state-of-the-art of such technologies to clarify our research position developed with a novel approach.

2.1. AVATAR IN VIRTUAL PLACE

The advent of Cyberspace has initiated new relationships among human, space and time. At the beginning, disembodiment and hyperlink architecture played a key role to constitute the virtual environment. While the Net disembodies human subjects, it can artificially embody these software go-betweens (Mitchell 1995). Such statement implies the needs for *human factors* because the Net is a territory for everyone. Regardless of an individual purpose, the root of interactions taking place in Cyberspace can be considered as communication between people. Here, what makes users perceive as if "being there" relies on their representation and interaction in such anti-spatial world. Various from two-dimensional icons used in typical Multi-User Domain (MUDs) to three-dimensional human figures founded in sophisticated online community, one can socially interact either with other virtual users or with one self by means of *avatar*, a graphics representation of one self. In fact, there is no limit number of one's avatar. At this point, what makes the distinction between simple and complex avatar relies on different type of metaphor. *Virtual place* (Kalay 2004), a paradigm shift in metaphor for virtual environment, constitutes an attempt to spatialize the anti-spatial and the data-oriented cyberspace. This, in turn, re-constructs

[2] http://www.spaceillusion.com/

familiar non-verbal communication by increasing the degree of reality into virtual environment including avatars as well as enhancing the social interaction and the sense of place.

So far, the majority of current research on social interaction in virtual place can be found in Collaborative Virtual Environments (CVEs). In addition, the research can be divided in to two groups. The first one explores possibilities of the architectural design in virtual environment. The examples for this group are Bartlett (Gavin 2001) and Virtual Office (Maher et al. 2000). Whereas, another group focuses on investigating the practical use of virtual architecture called *functional virtual architecture*. Virtual Statistics Class (Kalay et al. 2004), MUVEES[3], Oakland Blues (Kalay and Grabowicz 2006), DesignWorld (Maher et al. 2006) and CyberOne[4] belong to this group. Most of the mentioned projects are developed based on Activeworlds[5] and Second Life, commercial virtual environment platforms. Thus, communication and social interaction are handled by the platforms without any intervention from the researchers. The avatar exploited in such projects is bundled with abilities to express various gestures and emotions according to user's need. In Second life, users can even define their own customized gestures linked to trigger keywords. However, it requires inputting each trigger keyword separately from chatting dialog. In accordance with Kendon (1990), people autonomously use gestures along with their face-to-face communication. The behavior happens spontaneously without conscious effort. Recently, some scholars such as Vilhjálmsson (2004) propose the concept of *avatar agent* providing the basic nonverbal foundation autonomously for communication.

According to the gradually increasing number of Netizen[6], many of our common activities will take place in virtual places soon. It is not exaggerated to imagine people working at virtual workplaces, playing inside virtual theme parks and shopping at virtual market places in the coming future. We can see this trend through on-going vanguard projects mentioned above. Despite of diverse virtual spatial domains such as virtual classroom, virtual museum and virtual hotel, there is no empirical study about integration between emotion architecture and spatial context in functional virtual architecture. Such missing point is essential since one should be able to express an emotion in different expressions depending on context. For example, a student may have to raise his hand (unconsciously) to ask the teacher a question during a class. Such gesture may be not necessary if the

---

[3] http://www.gse.harvard.edu/~dedech/muvees/

[4] http://blogs.law.harvard.edu/cyberone/

[5] www.activeworlds.com

[6] A User of the internet, A Net "citizen."; www.answer.com/topic/netizen

student wants to ask the question right after the class while the teacher is still in the classroom. The method to enable such ability differentiates our context-aware emotion data model for avatar from the others as discussed in the next section.

3. Avatar Expression Agent

Maher and Gu (2002) distinguish a 'User-centered' approach from 'Place-centered' virtual architecture. By means of agent computation, their developed virtual user-centric architecture is dynamic and associated with the representation of users. The agent is a system that operates independently and rationally, seeking to achieve its goal by interacting with its environment. In such project, User-centered Virtual Architecture (UcVA) agent is created to manipulate the communication between users as well as to assist them how to design virtual space. In accordance with UcVA project, our research involves the development of user centric models for virtual architecture that builds on implementations of our previous research. However, our focus is to enable the virtual architecture to automate user expression according to the user's context. A multi-user environment is created using client-server technology. The system model comprises of three modules; client module, web application and server data module as shown in Figure 1. A user interacts with other users and the virtual environment through user interface layer provided in a client browser. Avatar expression agent and place agent running in the web application layer sense the ad-hoc context and commit changes to the virtual world. Details of the agent and the data model are explained in this section.

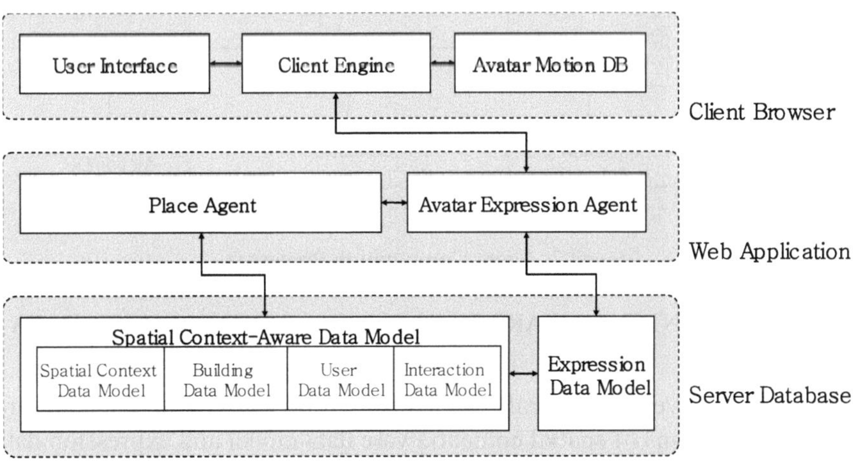

Figure 1. System diagram of collaborative virtual environment

3.1. PLACE AGENT AND AVATAR EXPRESSION AGENT

The feature to automate gestures according to current context is realized by two agent modules: *avatar expression agent* and *place agent* Our main computation processes for the agents are created based on UCVA Agent Model (Maher and Gu 2002). Agents are defined as 'Reactive' agents reasoned response to an expected event in the virtual world. Their main processes are sensation, perception and action. Figure 2 shows the agent computation process in details. Place agent takes care of context-aware reasoning including social event definition as well as spatial interaction control between users and the virtual space. It collects all context information for each space such as space type, number of user, current activity compared with social event definition to define current event for a single space. In contrast, avatar expression agent concerns user conversation. It can filter out trigger words or phrases linked to relevant user gesture according to current event. Finally, it commits expressions along with input conversation for each user.

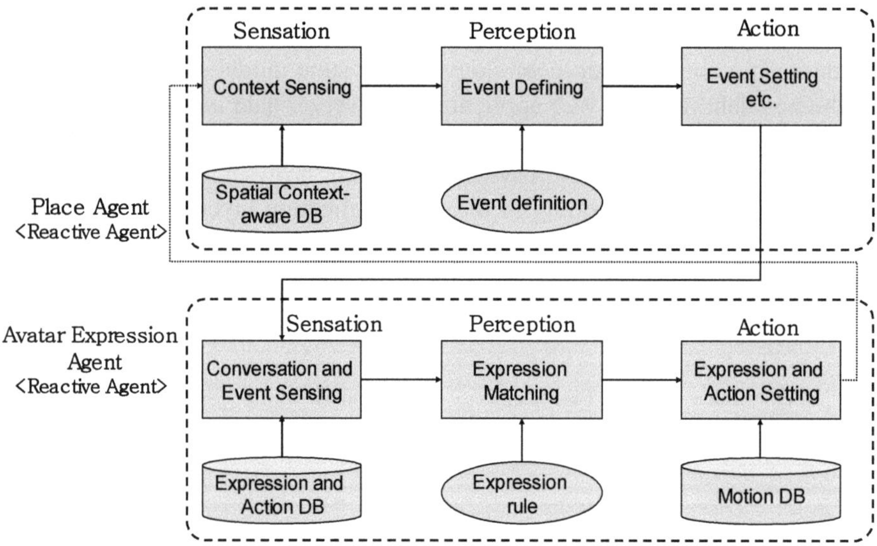

Figure 2. Agent Computation Processes

3.2. SPATIAL CONTEXT-AWARE DATA MODEL AND EXPRESSION DATA MODEL

On the lowest layer, the overall mechanisms of the virtual architecture are motivated by means of spatial context-aware data model and expression data model. Spatial context-aware data model comprises of building topology, spatial context, object, user and interaction data models. The data model is capable of storing semantic information and spatial context for smart architecture apart from geometric data. More details about the data models can be found in V-PlaceSims (Lertlakkhanakul et al. 2006).

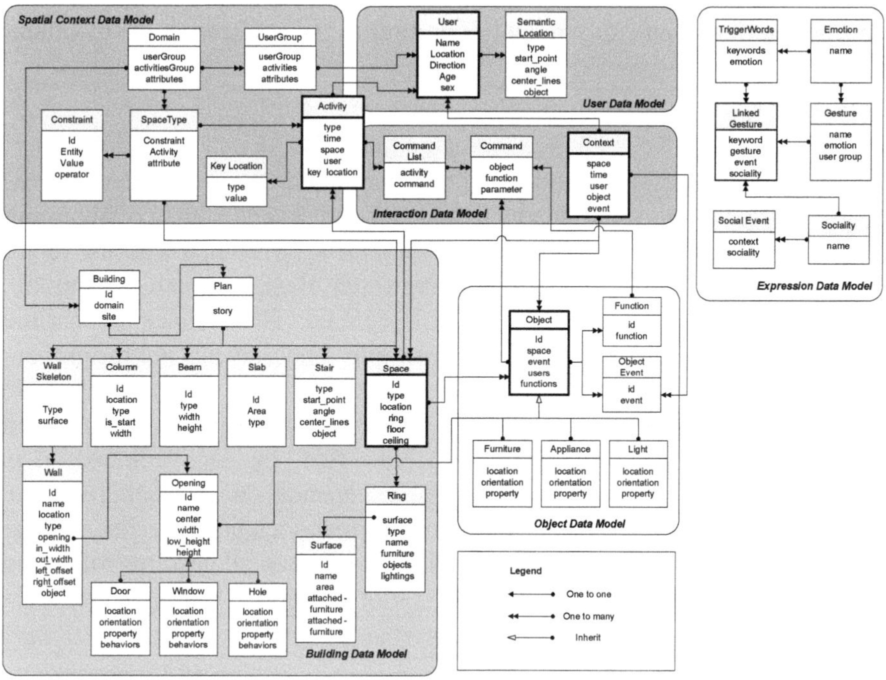

Figure 3. Spatial context-aware data model with expression data module

Our approach is to create the relation between gesture and social event using sociality information. Since a user can perform different gestures for one expression according to the current event. To enable context-aware expression data modeling, we append the mentioned data model with an expression data model. The holistic structure is shown in Figure 3. Among all member classes, *Linked gesture class* functions as a junction linking gesture class, emotion class, and sociality class to social event class. The data stored in the *event class* serves as a reasoning rule used by the avatar expression agent during the computation processes. *Gesture class* contains all avatar gestures and motion database. *TriggerWords class* embodies possible keywords input by user using a keyboard. All gestures and trigger keywords are classified following different emotions. Lastly, *sociality class* inscribes information to distinguish different gesture for disparate social value of an event, which is automated by the place agent in accordance with its predefined generative rule.

4. Implementation

To realize our framework, our existing on-line collaboration platform to simulate smart space so called ‘V-Placesims’ is modified by improving social interaction and agent computation. This section explains the implementation from study model definition to the application development in details.

4.1. STUDY MODEL

To demonstrate our idea, we defined our study model to a domain of virtual office. In the virtual office, there are a leader and several staffs collaborating regularly. The office space is composed of a meeting room, a working room, a common room and the leader’s working room. Based on such assumption, a set of social events generating rules is defined. The number of possible events is minimized to keep the system simple. Those events are discussion, party, chat, formal chat, rest and report. The details to define each event are shown in Table 1. Consequently, we categorize all possible gestures and their linked emotions and key words. Note that, for each emotion, it is possible to have more than one gesture depends on its sociality type. Currently, we concern only formal and informal sociality type for a social event to create our study model. In addition, we group all gestures following emotion architecture according to Elliot (1992). The gesture data classification can be found in Table 2.

TABLE 1. Social event data from the study model

Social Events	Space	User	Activities	Objects	Sociality
Discussion	meeting room	any	presentation	whiteboard	formal
Party	meeting room	any	dancing	audio	informal
Chat	any	between staffs	-	-	informal
Formal Chat	except leader room	between the leader and a staf	-	-	formal
Rest	common room	any	-	-	informal
Report	leader room	between the leader and staffs	-	-	formal

4.2. MOTION DATABASE AND AVATAR

Regarding the motion database creation, we captured some parts of the required motions according to the gesture data structure described in table 2 and Figure 4 in the collaboration with Motion Lab, Seoul National University. Then, all data have been converted into a motion database with Biovision Hierarchical data format and linked to an avatar skeleton. Until now, the implemented avatar figures are developed by SpaceIllusion Inc.

The avatars vary in age, sex, height, and style. Regardless of their cartoon-like appearance, they make the system become more user-friendly than typical behavior simulation tools.

TABLE 2. Expression data from the study model

Emotion Group	Emotion	Key phrases	Gestures (Sociality)
Well-being	joy	"wonderful", "splendid", "great"	"embrace"(f),"hula-hula"(i)
	distress	"sad"	"bow"(f), "cry"(i)
fortunes of others	happy for	"happy", "glad"	"rock back and forth"(i)
	gloating	-	-
	resentment	"I have a question"	"raise one's hand"(f),"sway one's head" (i)
	sorry	"sorry"	"bow"(f), "look down and around"(i)
Prospect based	hope	-	-
	fear	-	-
Confirmation	satisfation	"that's good", "that's right", "I got it"	"nod"(f),"shake one's hand"(i)
	relief	"getting better"	"nod"
	fears-confirmed	"not sure", "don't know", "don't	"shake one's head" (f),"headache"(i), "shrug"(i)
	dissappointment	"bad", "upset"	"shake one's head" (f), "fold one's arms"(i)
Attribution	pride	-	-
	admiration	-	-
	shame	-	-
	reproach	-	-
Attraction	liking	"I like", "beautiful"	"nod"
	disliking	"don't like" , "ugly"	"fold one's arms"(f),"shake one's head" (i)
Well-being/ attribution	gratitude	"thank you"	"nod"(f),"shake one's hand"(i)
	anger	-	-
	gratification	"lucky"	"nod"
	remorse	"forgive me"	"look down and around"(f), "swing one's leg"(i)
Attraction/attribution	love	"I love"	"nod"(f),"hula-hula"(i)
	hate	"I hate"	"fold one's arms"(f),"shake one's head" (i)

4.3. V-PLACESIMS RECONFIGURED

Finally, all processed are integrated and developed based on 'V-PlaceSims', our existing simulation tool. The virtual office space is created using PlaceMaker (Lertlakkhanakul et al. 2006). At the data model level, expression data model is added to the spatial context-aware data model as mentioned previously. Place agent and avatar expression agent is newly applied to the system. The development is mainly done in C++ environment. Eventually, the output is delivered as a web page with an ActiveX control embedded to simulate and to evaluate through the internet. The user interface of 'V-PlaceSims' is shown in Figure 5 (left).

At the moment, all communication between users is done through an input textbox located below the scene and an output callouts appeared above each avatar. Furthermore, two scenarios are demonstrated to verify the system model; chatting scenario and discussion scenario. As shown in Figure 5 (left), chatting scenario takes place in the common room between staffs. Thus, all gestures are automated in informal manners. In contrast, gestures in discussion scenario are generated using formal actions. Having entered the meeting room and started their conversation, staffs unconsciously commit a 'discussion' activity detected by the place agent. A brief comparison between gestures of both cases can be found in Figure 5 (right). While users are chatting and doing activities, the place agent traces a current event for each room. Then, the avatar expression agent of each user detects the defined event and finds its coherent gesture after analyzing the input keywords. All processes are evoked automatically without any users' interfere. In general, users can type, send their sentences and see the automated gestures displayed along with the conversation.

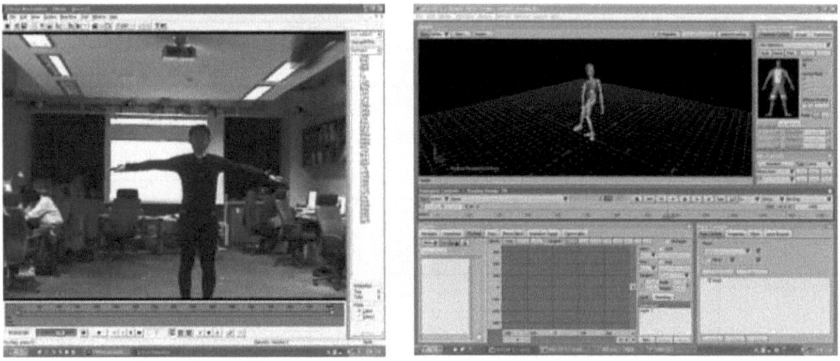

Figure 4. Motion capture (left), motion data creation (right)

Figure 5. Dialog in chatting scenario at the common room (left), automated gesture motions for informal sociality case (top-right), automated gesture motions for formal sociality case (bottom-right)

5. Conclusion

As users communicate with one another using a text box provided in the webpage, the avatar expression agent simultaneously detects users' emotion by parsing the input texts to perform related gestures automatically. The result reveals a new convenience way to communicate with the other users with an enhancement in automated expression. Moreover, by means of the context-aware capability, the agent can also perform appropriate gestures according to users' current situation. Thus, our research can establish the missing social expression part in virtual environment increasing the level of immersion toward functional virtual architecture.

Although, this paper only focuses on virtual office domain, it is, nevertheless, possible to apply the avatar expression agent to the other virtual architectural domain such as smart home, virtual classroom, virtual heritage, etc. Some problems arise during our research. Occasionally, automated gestures are chosen unexpectedly due to the simplification of using reactive agents for place agent and avatar expression agent. In fact, we believe that the solution is to apply more intelligent agent as reflective agents (Maher and Gero 2002) capable of learning ability to develop more complicated system. After all, this will not only dramatically enhance social interaction between virtual users but also elaborate new user activities in virtual architecture.

Acknowledgements

This research was partially supported by the MIC (Ministry of Information and Communication), Korea, under the ITRC (Information Technology Research Center) support program supervised by the IITA (Institute of Information Technology Assessment).

References

Cassell, J and Thorisson, KR: 1999, The Power of a Nod and a Glance: Envelope vs. emotional feedback in animated conversational agents, *Applied Artificial Intelligence* **13** (4-5), 519-539.

Eilliot, C: 1992, *A Process Model of Emotion in a Multi-agent System,* Ph.D. Thesis, Northwestern University, Evanston, Illinois.

Gavin, L: 2001, Online Learning in Multi-User Environments, *in* M Stellingwerff and J Verbeke (eds), *ACCOLADE - Architecture, Collaboration, Design*, Delft University Press, The Netherlands, pp. 59-64.

Kalay, YE: 2004, *Architecture's New Media*, The MIT Press, Cambridge, USA

Kalay, YE: 2004, Contextualization and Embodiment in Cyberspace, *Proceedings of CAADRIA 2004*, Seoul, pp. 5-14.

Kalay, YE and Grabowicz, P: 2006, Featured 3D Project: Oakland Blues, *Virtual Preservation of Seventh Street's 1950s Jazz Scene, 3DVisA Bulletin*, Issue 1.

Kalay, YE, Jeong, YW, Kim, SW and Lee, JW: 2004, Virtual Learning Environments, *Proceedings of CAADRIA 2004*, Seoul, pp. 871-890.

Kendon, A: 1990, *Conducting Interaction: Patterns of behavior in focused encounters*, Cambridge University Press, New York.

Liang, R, Chen, C, Pan, Z and Bu, J: 2003, Human Expressions Interaction between Avatar and Virtual World, *Proceedings of ICCSA 2003*, pp. 59-66.

Lertlakkhanakul, J, Kim, M, and Choi, JW: 2006, V-PlaceSims: A Web-based Simulation Platform for Pre-occupancy Evaluation of Smart Architecture, *IBPSA Australasia 2006*, pp. 66-72.

Maher, ML and Gu, N: 2002, Design Agents in Virtual Worlds - A User-Centred Virtual Architecture Agent, *in* JS Gero and FMT Brazier (eds), *Agents in Design 2002*, Key Centre of Design Computing and Cognition, University of Sydney, pp. 23-38.

Maher, ML, Rosenman, M, Merrick, K, Macindoe, O and Marchant, D: 2006, Designworld: an augmented 3D virtual world for multidisciplinary, collaborative design. *Proceedings of CAADRIA 2006*, pp. 133-142.

Maher, ML, Simoff, S, Gu, N and Lau, KH: 2000, Designing Virtual Architecture, *Proceedings of CAADRIA 2000*, pp. 481-490.

Mitchell, W: 1995, *City of Bits: space, place, and the infobahn*, The MIT Press, Cambridge, MA.

Richens, P and Nitsche M: 2005, Mindstage: Towards a Functional Virtual Architecture, *Proceedings of CAAD Futures 2005*, Vienna, pp. 331-340.

Slater, M, Howell, J, Steed, A, Pertaub, D-P and Gaurau, M: 2000, Acting in Virtual Reality. *Proceedings of the third international conference on collaborative virtual environments*, ACM press, New York, pp. 103-110.

Vilhjalmsson, H: 2004, Animating Conversation in Online Games, *in* M Rauterberg (ed), *Entertainment Computing ICEC 2004*, Lecture Notes in Computer Science 3166, Springer, pp. 139-150.

DOES COLOR HAVE WEAKER IMPACT ON HUMAN COGNITION THAN MATERIAL?

CHIU-SHUI CHAN
Iowa State University, USA

Abstract. This project intends to develop a method for using virtual reality (VR) to represent a built environment for simulating environmental influences on occupants. Objectives of the project were to explore: (1) what environmental stimuli would affect habitants' perception, and (2) what possible factors in the built environment would affect occupants' cognition. An office was selected as the subject of study. Methods were to create a number of digital models, each containing an embedded variable, and then test the impact of environmental influences on visual perception. Results obtained in this study indicate that materials have stronger impact to human perception than colors, and VR has great potential for design decision making and post-occupancy evaluation.

1. Information Impacts on Human Cognition

Based on major concepts from information-processing theory (Newell and Simon 1972) and verified by various research conducted in the field of neuroscience (Bear Connors and Paradiso 2001), the fundamental assumption of this research is that the human brain is constantly processing information (Singer 2007). It accepts information input from the environment and generates certain reactions as output. This sets up the basic premise of this research project.

A building houses human activities which could be affected by the quality of the building. An office building, for example, is a working environment that produces various sensory stimuli—light, sound, color, texture, temperature—to which occupants react on both conscious and subconscious levels. All this sensory information is intangible, but subtly influences human cognition and perception in ways that yield intellectual responses (Reed 1992). Because the mind experiences architecture through visual perception (Eberhard 2000), if good information is received and

A Dong, A Vande Moere & JS Gero (eds), CAADFutures'07, 373–386.

perceived, the response should be positive and productive. This study, therefore, posits that "the information generated in a space affects human cognitive performance and an effective workplace environment would provide positive stimuli to promote productive cognitive responses." Under this hypothesis, understanding what the occupants' actions and reactions are, as well as how and why they occur in a particular environment, would help designers to improve their designs (Wierenga Hase and Call 2004). This project intended to develop feasible methods to explore this idea.

2. Exploring Visual Information

Audio and visual information are the most immediately recognizable inputs in any given space. Visual information relates to images of objects perceived through forms, materials, and colors, whereas audio information consists of the sounds occurring in the environment. The appearance of objects and sounds in space are the major sources of sensory information for human cognition. This paper provides a set of experiments focusing on visual information and discusses findings in the context of an ongoing study of broader scope.

Typically, experiments for studying sensory impacts or causal effects in environments are conducted in physical buildings to observe results first-hand. However, if there are different experimental settings that must be changed sequentially for different tasks, it is too time-consuming to modify settings and too costly to run short experiments at different settings, especially if the task is complex and the settings are complicated. A virtual reality (VR) environment, however, is suitable for such circumstances. Virtual environments that can generate a high degree of presence are thought to be more effective and better suited to task performance (Slater 1994; Nunez and Blake 2001).

3. VR Representation for Visual Information

Virtual reality—a scientific, three-dimensional representation of objects displayed digitally—is an exciting new technology that offers a way to address many aspects of human behavior in a simulated environment (Thalmann and Thalmann 1994; Chan Hill and Cruz-Neira 1999; Chan Tong Dang and Qian 2003; Vince 2004). A virtual environment that allows an investigator to modify a model and immediately see the results is even better. A full-scale, immersive VR environment (e.g. three-sided or six-sided VR facility, see Figures 1 and 2) is superb, for it provides more direct information for studying impacts, as it yields a greater sense of presence (Chan and Weng 2005).

Figure 1. Three-sided VR facility

Figure 2. Six-sided VR facility

The concept of sense of presence relates to the sense of "being there" and the sensation of reality in the projected space. Three major conditions are used to judge the sense of presence created by a system: image quality, image size, and viewing distance (Lombard and Ditton 1997). In general, larger, higher-resolution images and close proximity between viewers and images yield a higher sense of presence, as they provide more reality, intimacy, involvement, and participation for the viewers with the environment. A full-scale immersive system thus serves the purposes even better, for it closely approximates actual size and distance with full-scale, high-resolution 3D objects generated in real time. Therefore, the immersive VR environment of three- or six-sided CAVEs may create a much more vivid sense of presence than other facilities with head-mounted or bench displays.

Following this line of thought, it is justifiable to say that experiments conducted in full-scale virtual environments are reasonable representations of the visual experiences obtained from real-world interactions. Therefore, applying VR technology as a study tool to represent a building and examine its design through perception is very appropriate (Patel Campion and Fernando 2002). Because visual perception provides us with more content and meaning than other senses, it more easily triggers the sense of presence.

4. Cognitive Processes in Human Perception

Perception occurs after the information presented in the environment has been attended and received. The perceived information is encoded in the visual register (visual buffer) in its original form. At this time, the mind performs pattern recognition and searches for stored knowledge associated with the pattern, to help decide appropriate actions to be taken (Anderson 1980). If the new input does not match any stored patterns—if the coding is different—then learning occurs. Consequently, decisions could be affected, actions could be changed, and results could be either strengthened or weakened. Therefore, the information provided by the living or working environment may exert a great deal of influence on cognitive processes which affects occupants' level of comfort in the environment. The possible information (environmental stimuli) includes materials and colors of artifacts in the space, which leads to the following hypotheses.

5. Theoretical Hypotheses

In building design, certain materials are used for certain components to meet certain structural requirements. Thus, the attributes and properties of materials should match with the typology of the building. If material use does not match building typology, then the perceived image is likely to elicit a certain cognitive response.

On the other hand, color is considered one of the most useful and powerful design tools to affect human emotions and perceptions. People respond to different colors in different ways, and these responses take place on a subconscious and emotional level. Birren (1978) defined two systems of color: warm and cool. Warm colors are those between red and yellow on the spectrum, whereas cool ones are between green and violet. Warm colors tend to stimulate the human organism. When human beings perceive warm colors, blood pressure, pulse rate, respiration, and perspiration accelerate and brain waves increase; feelings of restlessness and excitation may follow. There also is a noticeable muscular reaction (tension) and greater frequency of eye blinks. Conversely, cool colors are relaxing and retard bodily processes. Blood pressure and pulse rate are lower, skin response (perspiration) is less, and brain waves tend to decline.

Goldstein (1939) similarly found that red incites activity and is favorable for emotionally-determined actions; green induces a meditative mental state and creates an environment favorable to meticulousness. Red may be suited to produce the emotional state out of which ideas and action will emerge. Environmental colors have also been documented as affecting learning ability. A three-year experiment conducted on rooms painted light blue, yellow, yellow-green, and orange found that a variance of up to 12 points could be measured on standardized intelligence tests. Certain colors, including white, black, and brown, caused a drop in measured IQ. Researchers found that popular colors also stimulated alertness and creativity; white, black and brown playrooms made children less active. In advertising, this knowledge suggests that color evokes feelings or memories that encourage viewers to keep the goods on display. In hospitals, a green color scheme has been used to create a relaxing environment to help ease stress for patients.

Symbolically, each color has certain positive and negative meanings (Nolan 2002; see Table 1). But colors are subtle with great variations, and it is difficult to make clear-cut or absolute statements on their meanings. It is the same in perceiving materials. However, if there is a tool that could be used to systematically represent materials and scientifically control the variation of colors, then results of perception could be recorded for justifying the embedded value in color and material. Applying virtual reality as a study tool to understand how color and material affect human perception and reaction would serve the purposes and further demonstrate the application value of virtual reality.

TABLE 1. Positive and negative meanings of color

Color item	Positive meaning	Negative meaning
White	Clean, innocent, pure	Cold, empty, sterile
Red	Strong, brave, passionate	Dangerous, aggressive, domineering
Green	Natural, tranquil, relaxing	Cold, depressing, gloomy
Blue	Strong, trustworthy, authoritative	Jealous, inexperienced, greedy

Based on the biological findings of Birren and Goldstein, it is assumed that red (warm) colors in a space will stimulate and excite occupants, and blue (cold) color will have a calming effect on occupants. Thus, the second hypothesis assumed that cool (blue) color would generate more comfortable feelings in a stressful office environment than warm (red) color did. However, emotion might also have connections with previous experience stored in memory. Thus, from a cognitive psychology point of view, occupants' remembered experience and personal preference on colors might add an extra dimension to their reaction to environmental input. As such, emotion and personal experience would be different from person to person due to the individual differences. But, this second hypothesis applies primarily to studying the level of comfort elicited by color, and it is necessary to find a common denominator across individuals.

6. Methodology

The Adaptable Workspace Laboratory (AWL), an office environment located on the seventh floor of the US General Services Administration (GSA) headquarters in Washington, DC, was selected as the study subject for this project. The AWL encompasses 11,000 square feet and houses about four-dozen federal agency employees. This lab was designed and installed in 1999 by the General Services Administration, Carnegie Mellon University, and Oudens + Knoop Architects to turn the 85-year-old historic space into a modern office facility. Subsequently, the American Institute of Architects (AIA) has partnered with GSA to include neurological/cognitive research on how occupants react to their physical surroundings. This project is a part of those efforts.

Based on drawings provided by GSA and AIA (see Figure 3) and an on-site survey to determine accurate dimensions of each component, a digital master model of the AWL was developed (see Figure 4). In addition to applying similar methods to those used in reconstructing historical heritage and archaeology (Gaitatzes Christopoulos Roussou 2001; Zach Klaus Bauer Karner and Grabner 2001, Chan Dang Tong 2005), this high-resolution, realistic computer model inserted certain levels of detail, personal touches, and office supplies in the cubical to suggest the existence of occupants (see Figure 5).

Figure 3. Floor plan of the AWL

Figure 4. Master model of the AWL

Figure 5. Image of a cubical

Figure 6. Blue color on wall

Figure 7. Red color on the wall

After the master model was finished, four models, with identical geometry, were generated with changes in wall color. For instance, the wall color in Figure 6 is blue and red in Figure 7. The model in Figure 8 has blue painted from floor to ceiling and red is used similarly in Figure 9. The purpose is to study how colors actually impacted human perception.

Figure 8. Blue color on wall + ceiling

Figure 9. Red color on wall + ceiling

Figure 10. Three different materials used on all structural components

Figure 11. Three different materials for the partition walls only

Figures 10 and 11 show the changes in materials, including brown oak wood, dark cherry wood, and light marble. Traditional partition walls in an office environment were plastic with gray fabric. If material changes are made in a conventional space, occupants might not be able to accept the changes psychologically. If the changes are unconventional and dramatic, then the psychological reaction may be even stronger. Figure 10 shows the changes in materials on the partition walls plus structural frameworks to oak, cherry, and marble. Models in Figure 11 have only the partition walls

Figure 12. AWL model seen in the immersive VR environment

changed to oak, cherry, and marble. These models were converted to VR model format and displayed virtually afterward.

Thirty-one subjects participated in the experiment, which was held in the three-sided immersive VR facilities at Iowa State University (see Figure 12). Among them, eleven were architecture majors and twenty were non-architecture majors. Subjects were required to first view the master model, navigate through the entire space and memorize the scene. Afterward, they would view the remaining ten different models representing the changes in color and material, and rank their satisfaction at the end of each model. Scores range from zero to nine, with zero meaning the subject found the change very unsatisfactory and nine meaning it was very satisfactory. The experiment time was about one hour.

7. Experiment Results

In this experiment, subjects were divided into two groups—architecture majors and non-architecture majors. The experiments had ten treatments, categorizable into two major treatment groups of color and materials. The first four columns in Table 2 represent the color group, in which the names with "–all" represent the color painted on walls and ceilings. The last six columns describe the material group. The material names ending with "p" represent that these materials are used only on partition walls, while others are used on walls plus structural frames.

The average mean scores of each treatment are given in Table 2. Row one and two of the table are the average mean score of each treatment by subject group. Row three is the overall mean for each group. Row four is the "estimated" value of least squares means through the procedure for mixed (proc mixed) model method.

According to repeated measure ANOVA statistical analysis, the residuals are distributed normally, and there is no evidence of interaction between the treatments across the subject groups (P=0.8560). Thus, it is justifiable to compare the mean scores across treatments between the two subject groups. In comparing the differences between the two subject groups, the p-value for the architecture subjects' main effect is 0.9965. As such, it is indicated statistically that there are no differences between the average scores of the two subject groups in responding to the treatments.

In studying the significance of mean score of each treatment, the p-values for treatments are <0.0001 (standard deviation = 0.3221), which indicates that there are significant differences between at least two treatments. The score given in the last row of Table 2 shows the differences.

TABLE 2. Means of subject groups and grand means

	blue	red	blue-all	red-all	oak	cherry	marble	oak-p	cherry-p	marble-p
Arch	5.27	5.82	5.27	5.27	5.05	3.91	3.55	6.45	4.73	4.23
Non-arch	6.15	5.80	5.00	4.85	5.10	4.15	3.55	5.80	4.80	4.33
Grand-mean	5.84	5.81	5.10	5.00	5.08	4.07	3.55	6.03	4.77	4.29
Estimate	5.71	5.81	5.13	5.06	5.07	4.03	3.54	6.12	4.76	4.27

TABLE 3. T-value and p-value in comparing color pairs

10 models	Treatment	Treatment	T-value	P-value
Treatments	blue	red	-0.25	1.0000
Treatments	blue	blue-all	1.46	0.9169
Treatments	blue	red-all	1.64	0.8393
Treatments	red	blue-all	1.7	0.8098
Treatments	red	red-all	1.89	0.6965
Treatments	blue-all	red-all	0.19	1.0000

In order to test the effects within and between the color and material groups, pair wise comparisons were used for all treatments. In comparing the group differences among color and material groups, a contrast statement is used in SAS to test whether the average mean scores of treatments in color group is different from the average scores of treatments from material group. Results show the difference is significant ($p < 0.0001$, standard deviation = 0.1840). This indicates that some variables (treatments) in the material group are more significant than others (see Tables 3 and 4).

Regarding differences within color groups, the adjusted p-value using the Tudey-Kramer method is shown in Table 3. The p-values among the pairs of blue wall, red wall, blue wall-and-ceiling, red wall-and-ceiling were not significant (P values are greater than 0.05; standard deviation = 0.4022). This means that the color used in this experiment makes no significant differences to the subjects.

TABLE 4. T-value and p-value in comparing material pairs

10 models	Treatment	Treatment	T-value	P-value
Treatments	oak	cherry	2.61	0.2391
Treatments	oak	marble	3.82	0.0079
Treatments	oak	oak-p	-2.68	0.2198
Treatments	oak	cherry-p	0.76	0.9990
Treatments	oak	marble-p	1.97	0.6190
Treatments	cherry	marble	1.21	0.9729
Treatments	cherry	oak-p	-5.30	<0.0001
Treatments	cherry	cherry-p	-1.87	0.7279
Treatments	cherry	marble-p	-0.65	0.9998
Treatments	marble	oak-p	-6.52	<0.0001
Treatments	marble	cherry-p	-3.09	0.0834
Treatments	marble	marble-p	-1.87	0.7327
Treatments	oak-p	cherry-p	3.45	0.0273
Treatments	oak-p	marble-p	4.68	0.0003
Treatments	cherry-p	marble-p	1.23	0.9699

However, in comparing the mean score of materials, there are significant differences within the group. Especially, the oak wood used for the cubical partition walls (represented by oak-p) has the highest score received among the entire treatments. In other words, whenever the oak material used for partition walls (oak-p) is drawn from the data for comparison, their p-value is always significant except in comparing with the oak for partition-wall-and-frames (see Table 4). In this study, marble used on partition wall and frame received the lowest score of 3.54 ($p<.0001$, standard deviation = 0.3247), which is significant in this treatment.

8. Discussion

In this study, the purposes were to test and explore the environmental stimuli that would affect visual perception and to explore the factors that impact human cognition. The methods included: (1) developing a VR model representing a built environment, (2) sequentially changing the model to simulate various changes of the environment, (3) recording the reaction from viewers to verify the impacts, and (4) analyzing the data from comparing each variables to justify the significance of each impact. Through the analysis, it is very interesting to find out from data that material plays an important role in the visual perception of the environment. Oak wood (oak-p) is the popular element (mean score of 6.1273, standard deviation = 0.3221) that is welcomed by viewers followed by cherry (cherry-p, 4.7636, standard deviation = 0.3221) and marble (marble-p, 4.2761, standard deviation = 0.3221) regardless if viewers have trained design knowledge background to make judgment or not. In office design typology, the modern standardized material used for cubical partition is fabric. Marble is mostly used in grand scale of buildings or public buildings, which is also not a convention used in semi-private working spaces. Therefore, spaces having marble shown in partition walls and structure framework (represented as marble) are unusual, which is the reason why it is treated as uncomfortable environment with mean score of 3.6472 (standard deviation = 0.3247). Maybe there are other emotional factors attached to it, but, hypothesis one that "if the use of material does not match the building typology, then the perceived image would have some cognitive reactions" is confirmed in this round of study.

Regarding color factors, blue had the highest mean score (6.15, $p<0.0001$, standard deviation = 0.3838) among the four color treatments in the non-architecture group; but second highest in the architecture group. It also found that the models with blue ceilings (blue-all) had scores equal to or greater than red in the two subject groups (see Table 2). The higher scores on blue-all than on red-all group slightly proved the hypothesis two, even though the statistical analysis doesn't show significant p-value in comparing this pairs.

Another reason for the slight difference between the two colors could be explained as that color effects are always temporary (Birren 1978). Exposure to color does not cause reactions of any substantial duration. The reaction to color is similar to the reaction to alcohol, tobacco, coffee up to a short period and then down. In fact, if red is stimulating after a length of time bodily responses may fall below normal. But, this hypothesis addresses mainly, again, on studying the level of comfort agitate by colors. On the other hand, the applied statistical analysis treated subjects as random sample, which means that the subject pool participated in this study have no influence to larger sample pool. Thus, if the population size of subjects increases, the result might have changed accordingly.

It is not surprising that the differences among architectural group and non-architecture group were not statistically significant. This is due to the facts that: (1) the architecture pool is a small pool of eleven, and (2) five out of eleven in the architecture group were freshmen, who do not have enough training in architectural design at the time of participating the experiments for this to be a factor in their responses. It is assumed that trained designers would definitely have good design knowledge on color and better understanding on the use of material to fit special functional requirements in design.

Based on the data analyses on the series of VR experiments, two hypotheses were tested and slightly proved to some degree, which yielded two findings. The first one relates to the discovery of factors in the built environment. The factors affecting viewers' perception are materials and colors shown in artifacts in space. Material factors are statistically stronger than color in the effectiveness on visual perception. Viewers could perceive the existence of these environmental stimuli through the texture and color of materials on surfaces. Based on their previously stored visual memory, viewers would react to the perceived image and express their satisfactory level immediately. For instance, one subject in the architecture group who commented on color immediately noted that "the red color shown on ceiling is a strange look and presumably is not acceptable in a federal office building," which leads to the second study.

The second study relates to the factors in a built environment that would affect human cognition. These factors could be the design representation used by designers and the design knowledge owned by viewers. The design representation includes the common design convention applied in the profession and possibly the design knowledge that viewers have learnt previously. For instance, if there are unconventional design shown in the built environment, viewers would perceive the representation, do pattern recognition, search for design related knowledge in memory and respond the matching results back afterwards. If the perceived image does not match with the information stored in knowledge repertoire, then new information would fit into existing one (assimilation), or alter the existing one in order to accommodate new information (accommodation), or a new knowledge representation is created. That is why the design representation affects learning through perception; which changes the knowledge structure affecting human cognition.

9. Conclusions

This study is a long term study pursuing a larger scope on human cognition in space. The intentions on setting up the experiments were to be testing whether people with prior training in architecture respond differently to changes in materials and colors than people without such background. In order to collect more data for verifying this hypothesis, an advanced method of protocol analysis should be applied. In fact, protocol analysis had been applied to a couple of subjects, but, will be a part of future studies.

After all, the most amazing result in this study shows the value of applying virtual reality to simulate a physical environment. This study demonstrated that VR is a very good tool for building performance evaluation. If this study could get more subjects involved to increase the subject population size, it would improve the statistical significance to validate (confirm or refute) the concept and theory further, which will be the goal for future studies.

Acknowledgements

This project was funded by the General Services Administration and the American Institute of Architects from 2002 to 2005. Thanks go to YuNgok Lo and Qian Chen for digital modeling and Kerstin Hovland for development of algorithms. Eight figures shown in this paper were created by Qian Chen. Special thanks also go to Kevin Kampschroer, John Eberhard, John McRae, and Edward Jackson for their encouragement and support; and to the Virtual Reality Applications Center at Iowa State University for the use of the immersive three-sided virtual reality facilities.

References

Anderson, J: 1980, *Cognitive Psychology and its Implications*, W. H. Freeman Co, San Francisco, pp. 32-35.

Bear, MF Connors, BW and Paradiso MA: 2001, *Neuroscience: Exploring the Brain*, Lippincott, Baltimore.

Birren, F: 1978, *Color and human response: Aspects of light and color bearing on the reactions of living things and the welfare of human beings*, Van Nostrand Reinhold, New York, p. 34.

Chan, CS Dang, A and Tong, Z: 2005, A 3D model of the inner city of Beijing, *in* B Martens and A Brown (eds), *Proceedings of CAADFutures 2005*, pp. 63-72.

Chan, CS Hill, L and Cruz-Neira, C: 1999, Is it possible to design in full scale? A CAD tool *in* synthetic environment, *in* J Gu and Z Wei (eds), *Proceedings of CAADRIA 1999*, Shanghai Scientific and Technological Literature Publishing House, pp. 43-52.

Chan, CS Tong Z Dang A and Qian J: 2003, Virtual Reality modeling of traditional Chinese architecture, *in* H Thwaites (ed) *Hybrid Reality: Art, Technology and the Human Factor*, International Society on Virtual Systems and Multimedia, Montreal, pp. 13-22.

Chan, CS and Weng, CH: 2005, How real is the sense of presence in a virtual environment? *in* A Bhatt (ed), *Proceedings of CAADRIA 2005*, TVB School of Habitat Studies, New Delhi, pp. 188-197.

Eberhard, J: 2003, How the brain experiences architecture, *AIA Journal of Architecture* Spring, pp. 1-5.

Evans, H and Dumesnil, C: 1982, *An Invitation to Design*, New York: Macmillan Publishing, p. 43.

Gaitatzes, A Christopoulos, D Roussou, M: 2001, Reviving the past: Cultural heritage meets virtual reality, *in* D Arnold, A Chalmers and DW Fellner (eds), *Proceedings of the 2001 Conference on Virtual Reality, Archeology, and Cultural Heritage*, ACM Press, New York, NY, pp. 103-110.

Goldstein, K: 1939, *The Organism*, American Book Co., New York.

Lombard, M and Ditton, T: 1997, At the heart of it all: The concept of presence, *Journal of Computer-Mediated Communication* **3**(2), http://jcmc.indiana.edu/vol3/issue2/lombard.html.

Newell, A and Simon, H: 1972, *Human Problem Solving*, Prentice-Hall, Englewood Cliffs.

Nolan, K: 2003, *Color it Effective: How Color Influence User*, http://office.microsoft.com/en-us/assistance/HA010429371033.aspx.

Nunez, D and Blake, E: 2001, Cognitive presence as an unified concept of virtual reality effectiveness, *in* A Chalmers and V Lalioti (eds), *Proceedings of the 1st International Conference on Computer Graphics, Virtual Reality and Visualization*, ACM Press, New York, pp. 115-118.

Patel, NK Campion, SP and Fernando, T: 2002, Evaluating the use of virtual reality as a tool for briefing clients in architecture, *in* AD Williams (ed), *Proceedings of the Sixth International conference on Information Visualization*, IEEE, Los Alamitos, CA, pp. 657-663.

Reed, S: 1992, *Cognition: Theory and Applications*, Brooks/Cole, Pacific Grove, CA.

Singer, E: 2007, Raising Consciousness, *Technology Review* **110**(1): 50-54.

Slater, M: 1999, Measuring presence: A response to the Witmer and Singer presence questionnaire, *Presence* **8**(5), 560-565.

Thalmann, NM and Thalmann, D: 1994, Introduction: Creating artificial life in virtual reality, *in* NH Thalmann and D Thalmann (eds), *Artificial life and virtual reality*, John Wiley & Sons, New York, pp. 1-9.

Vince, J: 2004, *Introduction to virtual reality*, Springer, New York.

Wierenga, D Hase, B and Call, R: 2004, Evolutionary psychology and workplace design: Doing what comes naturally, *AIA Academic Journal,* http://www.aia.org/journal_aah.cfm.

Zach, C Klaus, A Bauer, J Karner, K and Grabner, M: 2001, Modeling and visualizing the cultural heritage data set of Graz. *in* D Arnold, A Chalmers and DW Fellner (eds), *Proceedings of the 2001 Conference on Virtual Reality, Archeology, and Cultural Heritage,* ACM Press, New York, pp. 219-226.

DESIGNING VIRTUAL WORLDS FOR 3D ELECTRONIC INSTITUTIONS

A distributed and heterogeneous multi-agent system

GREG SMITH, MARY LOU MAHER
University of Sydney, Australia

and

NING GU
University of Newcastle, Australia

Abstract. 3D Electronic Institutions (3DEI) are 3D virtual worlds that are dynamically designed in response to the users' needs and the rules of an electronic institution. Electronic institutions can be modelled as multi-agent systems inspired by analogous physical institutions. This paper describes coupling of a multi-user 3D virtual world to an electronic institution. The resulting 3DEI is a distributed and heterogeneous multi-agent system that provides the advantages of both with the organizational structures imposed by the electronic institutions and the spatial characteristics provided by 3D virtual worlds.

1. Introduction

Contemporary living is inseparable from digital information and the web. As a result, our holistic living environments have been gradually expanding to include internet environments. Complementing the physical world, these networked environments become unique online places where we work, learn, shop, get social and be entertained. Current designs of internet environments are largely influenced by and with metaphorical references to architecture, web design or computer programming. They are often hand crafted because we lack formal design methods. Our research develops and demonstrates a multi-agent system that provides a model for designing 3D virtual worlds that are inhabited by people and interact with electronic institutions.

A Dong, A Vande Moere & JS Gero (eds), CAADFutures'07, 387–400.

Electronic institutions can be modelled as multi-agent systems inspired by analogous physical institutions (Esteva et al. 2004). This paper describes coupling of a multi-user 3D virtual world to an electronic institution. The resulting 3DEI is a distributed and heterogeneous system that provides the advantages of both with the organizational structures imposed by the electronic institutions and the spatial characteristics provided by 3D virtual worlds. A 3DEI is a 3D virtual world that is dynamically designed in response to the users' needs and the rules of the electronic institution. After describing a model of a 3DEI, we describe a prototype implementation.

2. The 3D Electronic Institution

Virtual worlds are networked environments designed using the metaphor of architecture to support various activities online. This architecture metaphor provides a consistent and familiar base for designing the worlds and for virtual world occupants (commonly called citizens) to interact with the designed environments and with each other. Such multi-user virtual worlds are useful when it is prohibitive time-wise (such as for online meetings or remote surgery) or it is otherwise undesirable to travel (such as to avoid the hassle international air travel has become). With a virtual world we can access remote information, services and social interaction from where we are. They allow for anonymous interaction with others, for non-anonymous interaction with those that we would not otherwise meet, and can encourage design and interdisciplinary team collaboration (Rosenman et al. 2006). They let us experience or practice behaviours that would be hazardous or impossible, for whatever reason, in our world. A virtual world allows us to do things that we cannot do in the real world: fly, teleport, build and walk through building designs, explore non-3D-Euclidean worlds (imagine a virtualisation of Ian Stewart's "Flatterland") and so on.

Electronic institutions (Esteva 2003) are multi-agent systems inspired by analogous physical institutions like banks, travel agents, government organisations and academic institutes. We are interested here in facilitating behaviours of citizens that extend beyond the virtual world; in particular, to electronic institutions. Consider an example scenario: a virtual travel application. Some of the possible behaviours of virtual world citizens include:

- Chatting with others, for which a virtual world is ideal but for which an electronic institution is largely irrelevant
- Visiting virtual places like a virtual Lord Howe Island, for which a virtual world is ideal but for which an electronic institution is irrelevant

- Asking for information on trips, for which a virtual world is ideal and for which an electronic institution may or may not be useful depending on what information is to be supplied
- Purchasing flights, accommodation and goods, for which an electronic institution is suited and for which virtual world can be used but so can other web technologies.

The question is how to couple a multi-user 3D virtual world to an electronic institution. How do we facilitate a dynamic, interactive virtual world experience and at the same time keep citizens, resources and agents safe? There are 2 philosophies. The first is to prohibit everything not explicitly allowed: require that every agent ask a governor for permission to activate each action. An example of this would be a central bureaucracy called The Governor that controls citizen behaviour. If a citizen wants to buy bread they put in a request for bread purchasing rights to The Governor and if approved the citizen takes that approval along to a citizen or agent that has the corresponding bread sales approval. The second philosophy is to allow everything not explicitly prohibited: let agents and citizens activate actions autonomously but restrict them when they try to do specified prohibited things.

Consider an example scenario: a visit to an old fashioned bank that is in a physical building to withdraw money. The bank protects itself by having trained tellers that are able to access its resources (money, etc.) and follow the bank's rules. So a 3DEI that facilitates these same behaviours would need to somehow follow these rules. But only a part of the behaviour is explicitly in these rules. The structure of the bank building is equally important: barriers to encourage queuing, desk partitions that force the customer to use tellers to get to money, and so on. There are also behaviours of tellers and customers that are not and should not be in the rules, like walking into the building and straight back out again. The rules are just a protocol, not agent behaviours. When using an electronic bank, the protocols for the messages to and from the system that maintains the bank state (a database) enforce the rules. Other behaviours in the world need not be constrained.

We believe that a virtual world should be as open and unrestrictive as possible. It certainly shouldn't be more restrictive than the real world. So we tend towards the second philosophy, but how is this to be done? We place resources to be safeguarded under the protection of agents, and each agent provides services for possible use by others. Agents act autonomously and should only be stopped when their actions break a protocol rule. These rules can be designed using a protocol editor like Islander (Esteva 2003), or designed manually as is desired. The protocols could be used for agent learning, for a virtual world design grammar (see Section 3), or via a protocol server like AMELI (Esteva 2004).

So we want dynamic worlds that provide services to citizens related both to virtual and non-virtual worlds. A service is a request in an agent communication language (ACL) to an agent; the agent may be an avatar or other virtual world object we have assigned agency to, or may be a non-virtual world agent. There are three approaches to relationships between agents and services (Martin et al. 2004):

1. Agents use services: there are web services or otherwise servers in a client/server fashion, and agents make use of those services.
2. Services are agents: the only way to do anything is to send a request to an agent to do it for you.
3. Dynamic hybrid.

An example of approach 3 is semantic web descriptions of web services like WSDL, UDDI and SOAP, together with an agent factory to compose new agents as required by new service requests (Richards et al. 2004). In virtual world terms this extends naturally into launching sets of design grammar rules (Gu and Maher 2005) to change a world according to new requirements, but put as service requests that could also contain non-3D-design requirements.

In the prototype described below the design requirements derive partly from the formal description of an electronic institution. These formal descriptions provide a partial design specification for the design agents. Design considerations such as visual and spatial layout of objects and spaces, design constraints, and design styles are represented in the design grammars.

Not every agent is in a virtual world, and not every object in a virtual world has agency. In the Bank example, the carpet isn't an agent but there would be some agent from which we could request cleaning. The result is a heterogeneous system of virtual and non-virtual worlds, agents and services.

Not all users need to connect to an electronic institution via the virtual world. An authorised user should be able to write an external agent or web site that interacts with our virtual world or electronic institution. An example is using JADE[1] with an AMELI protocol server, meaning that authorised users could launch their own JADE agents to interact with both AMELI and the virtual world. Using an open agent framework such as this would also

[1] JADE is a Java implementation of the FIPA agent specifications that can be used as the communication layer for AMELI (Esteva 2004). The FIPA (fipa.org) is an IEEE standards organization that promotes and develops standards for inter-operable multi-agent systems.

provide a means for changing design grammars at runtime by representing designers by JADE agents.

Figure 1 shows an example institution agent that creates room agents. These agents communicate with the electronic institution to ensure that the users comply with the organizational structures and the institutional rules. The design agent society starts with design requirements from the electronic institution. The example in Figure 1 constitutes an institution agent and various room agents. These two different kinds of design agents taken together will dynamically design, modify and remove the 3D virtual world or a portion of the world as needed for the electronic institution.

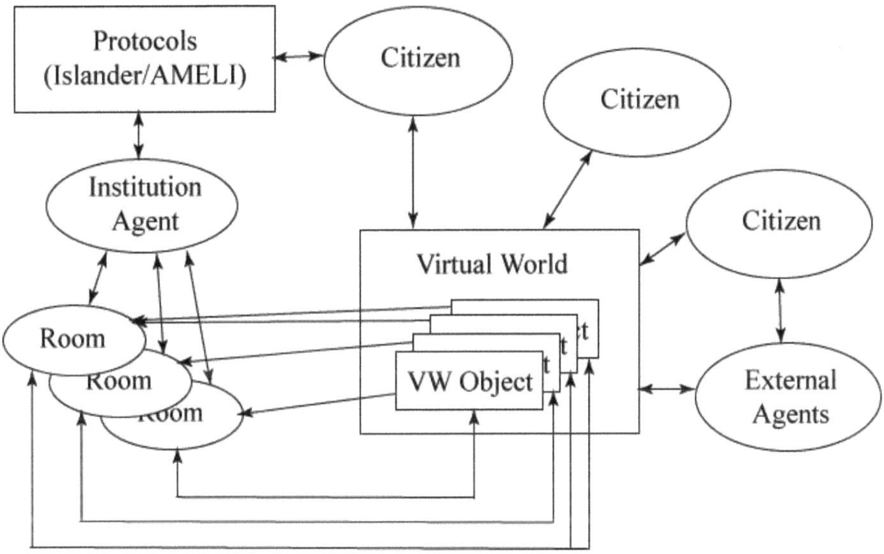

Figure 1. Society of agents for a 3DEI (arrows indicate direct and indirect interactions)

The institution agent in this example is the "mega" agent that is responsible for the 3D virtual world designs for the electronic institution and the creation of room agents. Initially, the institution agent applies its design grammar to generate a 3D virtual world design based on the design specifications of the electronic institution. The design will comprise a series of rooms. Each room has a specific purpose supporting certain intended online activities in the electronic institution. A room agent provides a kind of intelligent agency to a particular room in the designed 3D virtual world. Each room is therefore unique and maintains its own history of reasoning and changes. Once the 3DEI is established, a room agent will monitor the activities and changes in a room and make necessary changes to the room as needed, during the online session.

Design knowledge is represented as design grammars. Design grammars have been applied for describing and generating 3D virtual world designs. Design grammars for 3D virtual worlds are inspired by the notion of shape grammars (Stiny and Gips, 1972). The way that shape grammars function lies in the unique view of designs. A design generated by a shape grammar is viewed as "elements in relations" (Stiny, 1999). To apply a grammar for design generation is basically to change (add, subtract or replace) the "elements" and define or alter the "relations" among the "elements" via shape rule applications. In this manner, grammars can generate rather complex designs based on simple design elements. This view of designs is accordant with the object-oriented nature of virtual worlds. A virtual world design can be viewed as "objects in relations".

Most virtual worlds are object-oriented systems. They are among the examples designed using various commercial platforms, such as Active Worlds[2], Blaxxun Platform[3] and Virtools[4]. An object-oriented virtual world is constructed through the placement and configuration of objects. Each object can have an appearance of a 3D model in a virtual world, and together these models provide the visualisation of the environment. The objects then can be configured or programmed to have certain behaviours that allow the occupants to interact with the world and with each other. Therefore, a virtual world design basically comprises various objects in terms of the following two aspects (Gu and Maher 2003).

- Visually/spatially, via the use of architectural metaphors, the 3D models are composed to form an ambient environment which virtual world occupants can inhabit and where the intended activities can take place online.
- Functionally, selected objects are ascribed with behaviours to support the intended activities online. Therefore, interactions become possible.

Similar to the way shape grammars formalise designs in general, in designing virtual worlds design grammars describe various virtual world objects and their properties, define the relations among them, and generate virtual world designs based on these elements. This compositional characteristic of design generation makes design grammars an appropriate design formalism for virtual worlds.

The stylistic characterizations of the generated designs have also been defined in terms of visualization, navigation and interaction (Gu and Maher, 2005). A design grammar G comprises design rules R, an initial design D_i,

---

[2] http://www.activeworlds.com
[3] http://www.blaxxun.com
[4] http://www.virtools.com

and a final state of the design D_f: G = {R, D_i, D_f}. The basic components of a design grammar are design rules R. The general structure of a design grammar for 3DEI comprises four sets of design rules (Figure 2). These are layout rules R_a, object placement rules R_b, navigation rules R_c, and interaction rules R_d: R ={R_a, R_b, R_c, R_d}. Following the structure of the generative design grammar framework, virtual world design styles can be considered in terms of visualisation (layout of places and visual forms of virtual objects), navigation methods and interactions. They are three inseparable parts for providing an integral experience of 3D virtual worlds. This general structure of a design grammar is determined by the four design phases of virtual worlds.

- To layout virtual rooms for the 3DEI: each room is represented by a room agent and has a specific purpose supporting certain intended online activities in the institution.
- To configure the virtual room: each room is then configured with certain objects, which provide visual boundaries of the room and visual cues for supporting the intended online activities.
- To specify navigation methods: navigation in 3D virtual worlds can be facilitated to consider the use of way finding aids and hyperlinks, for assisting the users' movements from one room to another.
- To provide interactions: in general this is a process of ascribing behaviours to selected objects in each room, so that the users can interact with the 3DEI and with each other.

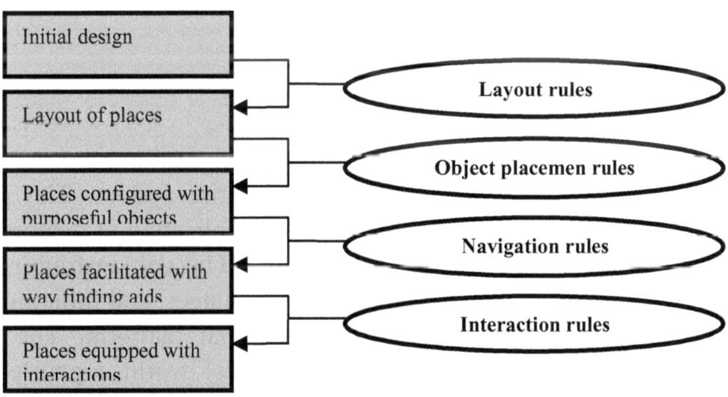

Figure 2. Structure of a design grammar for 3D virtual worlds (Gu and Maher 2005)

The basic components of a generative design grammar are design rules. The general structure of our design rules is a replacement rule, LHS → RHS, which specifies that when a left-hand-side pattern (LHS) is found in the design, it will be replaced by a right-hand-side pattern (RHS). The replacement of patterns is applied under a set of operations or spatial transformations. The patterns are labelled (the use of spatial labels and state labels) for controlling the rule applications. In our grammar, a design rule is defined as "LHO + sL → RHO" which specifies that when a left-hand-side object (LHO) is found in the virtual world, and the state labels sL are matched, the LHO will be replaced by a right-hand-side object (RHO). The term "object" used here can refer to virtual world object(s) including the 3D model(s) and/or object behaviour(s). The general structure of design rules implies that:

- State labels are singled out and expressed explicitly as sL in the structure. The use of state labels is essential to the application of generative design grammars as they direct the application to ensure that the generated design satisfies the institution agent's current design goals. Each design rule is associated with certain state labels representing specific design contexts that can relate to the institution agent's design goals. In order for a design rule to be fired, virtual world object(s) need to be found in the virtual world that match the LHO of the design rule, and the design contexts represented by the sL of the design rule need to be related to the institution agent's current design goals.
- The basic components of design rules are virtual world objects. They are not entirely visual/spatial and contain functional and behavioural information. For the interaction rules and parts of the navigation rules, the replacement of LHO with RHO is applied under a set of general transformations.

3. Prototyping

The ideas described above have been prototyped, trialling the various parts of 3DEI as described without building an entire system. The prototype scenario is the "World Trotter" travel agency application to demonstrate the use of the 3DEI model and the design grammar. This demonstration provides the basis for evaluating the advantages, disadvantages, and limitations of the implementation platform, and the 3DEI on that platform. The platform chosen was Second Life[5], a popular 3D virtual world supported by the typical client-server connection, which is most common to current virtual world platforms.

The institution is specified using Islander as the protocol illustrated in Figure 3. The "World Trotter" travel agency has the following "scenes": reception, booking room, hotel room, auction room, and shop. Based on

[5] http://www.secondlife.com

these scenes, the set of roles that users can play in each scene are determined. In this context a role defines a pattern of behaviour establishing the list of actions that the users are allow to perform. The "World Trotter" contains the following roles: customer, travel agent, auctioneer, receptionist and shop assistant.

The word "scene" comes from Islander. The electronic institution regulates "multiple, distinct, concurrent, interrelated, dialogic activities, each one involving different groups of agents playing different roles" (Esteva et al. 2004) through interaction protocols. Each interaction protocol is a directed graph whose nodes represent states of a dialogic interaction and arcs represent illocutions. Each protocol that connects any two scenes is unique. As shown in Figure 3, they are illustrated with specific symbols and annotated with different labels to distinguish from each other. While the word "scene" in common usage implies that entities that are serial and non-concurrent: a movie contains one scene, then another scene, and so on; there is nothing inherent in the interaction protocols that prevent an agent from engaging in multiple scenes concurrently (Esteva 2006), and the "allow everything not explicitly prohibited" principle means not unnecessarily constraining virtual world behaviours. For example, a student can sit in a lecture (scene A) while concurrently engaging in an online auction (scene B).

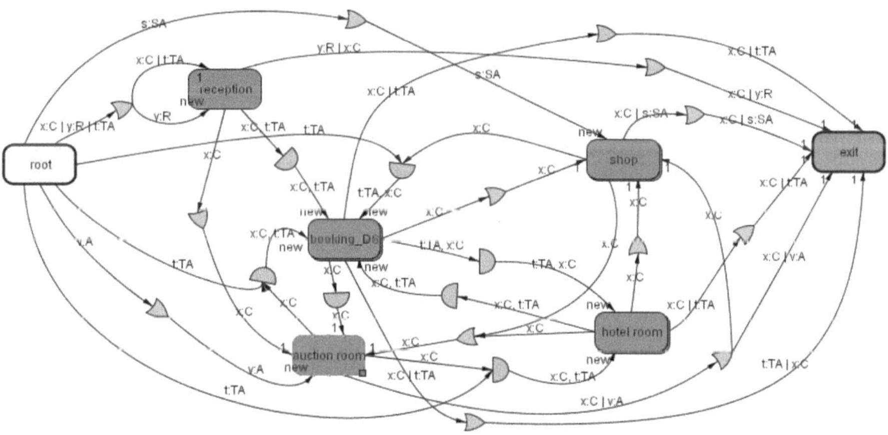

Figure 3. Performative structure of the "World Trotter" institution

These protocols are used to generate the design representations of the specified institution in the 3D virtual world. The institution agent applies its design grammars and transforms the design specification from the previous step into a 3D design in Second Life. In the prototype the "scenes" defined in the specifications become 3D rooms and arcs in the protocol graph(s) (in Figure 3) are transformed into doors between those rooms. Such design automation is achieved by adopting a computational approach using design grammars. Remember the "allow everything not explicitly prohibited" philosophy, though. One scene maps onto one room in the grammar for this prototype, but this is not necessarily the case. It is not necessary for virtual world rooms to be used at all providing some other appropriate metaphor replaces it. The design rules are selectively applied to generate suitable 3D designs for the institution as needed. This process provides a linkage that translates the "specification language" of the institution into the "design language" of 3D virtual worlds.

The prototype designer is implemented in Java and Jess[6]. The 3D virtual world platform selected for demonstration purpose is Second Life. Protocols in XML are parsed, firing Jess rules that implement the design grammar. The generated designs are stored in a design database whose format can be flexibly adapted to suit different 3D virtual world platforms for implementation. The database holds an assembly of 3D virtual world objects, each of which has a name and a set of object properties like primitive object shape, 3D location, 3D rotation and 3D extent. In a post-prototype implementation this may not be the case. The vision is of a distributed system of agents on an open, multi-agent platform such as is provided by JADE. In such a case the design agents would communicate at runtime with AMELI serving the protocols, and would communicate directly with virtual world agents like the institution agent of Figure 1.

The four sets of design rules: layout rules, object placement rules, navigation rules and interaction rules are written in Jess. According to Maher and Gu (2002), the design space in a 3D virtual world, that is, the space of alternatives from which components are selected and aggregated can have two major categories of elements:

- 3D models of virtual world objects to be part of the world.
- Behaviours of these objects that provide simple and aggregate behaviours of the world. In Second Life, object behaviours are realised using Linden Script Language[7] known as LSL. This scripting language follows the familiar syntax of C/Java.

These two categories of elements are represented as "facts" in Jess which can be use to describe and generate designs of 3DEI. The LHO and RHO of each design rule are made up of these Jess facts.

Figure 4 shows one of the generated designs. Our approach has a number of advantages. Changes to the specification or the runtime environment (the virtual world state, the electronic institution state or the state of an agents) can be addressed dynamically as needed through the grammar application by

---

[6] A forward chaining Rete engine written in Java.

[7] http://www.lslwiki.com

alternating the choices and order of the design rules during the application. Changes to the virtual world platform used will only require a re-mapping between the designed elements and basic primitives of the virtual world, without undergoing any major system changes.

Figure 4. A "World Trotter" travel agency design in second life

The institution agent activates actions through its various effectors so as to realize the design. Second Life is a proprietary platform that allows scripts to run on virtual world objects, but with constraints. Second Life has a centralised server farm and simpler clients. This necessitated running our agents outside of the world and communicating with the representations in the virtual world. But communication into and out of Second Life is restricted. XML remote procedure calls (XML-RPC) are implemented by the Second Life builders with prevention of denial of service attacks in mind. The result for project such as ours, however, has been the need for a pull-based architecture with polling to get information out of Second Life (Macindoe 2006). This is very slow. The Second Life implementation of HTTP requests has similarly been restricted.

4. Discussion

Electronic institutions are determined by three kinds of conventions (Bogdanovych et al. 2005):

- The communication language and ontology for agents to use.
- The kinds of activities that agents can participate in.
- The behaviours that agents are allowed.

While electronic institutions may do a good job of enforcing restrictions on agent activities and behaviours, they do not easily facilitate their use by human users. The use of 3D virtual worlds draws a close analogy between the virtual environments and the physical world, which enable people to better orientate and interact in the electronic institutions by applying knowledge and experiences that they have learnt and adopted from the physical organisations. Hence 3D electronic institutions are a method for enabling electronic institution activities by human users from within user-friendly virtual worlds.

From our experience in implementing the 3DEI, we have found that the realisation of a feasible 3DEI is limited by a number of factors. Firstly, current virtual worlds have limits on in-world agent computation and communication with external processes. Secondly, the agent models of electronic institutions are influenced and constrained by known examples of physical institutions.

The distributed, multi-agent nature of the system being described clearly makes agent communication essential. The deliberate constraints on communication between out of world agents with in world objects in Second Life hampers the current performance of the prototype, but these performance constraints are of Second Life not of 3DEIs in general. Our long term view is of a massively multi-agent system that still works successively as a multi-user virtual world. Understandably, the main concern of most 3D virtual world designers is the realistic rendering of the 3D world across networks of large numbers of users.

Some entities in a virtual world need non-static behaviours. Some Second Life objects will be scripted but most will not, and of those that are scripted only a few require agency. We can imagine an entirely agent-oriented virtual world, but would that be desirable? Probably not given what is required to realistically render a 3D world across a large, distributed community of users in real time. Wouldn't it be nice, though, if we could have all of the benefits of a multi-user world like Second Life but without the limits on computation and external communication. With such a platform, avatars and scripted objects without computation limits could communicate with external agents via a standardised and open agent platform like JADE. Adequate performance of a 3DEI requires a virtual world platform like Second Life that is also powerful enough for non-trivial agents to run inside its world and that has good external communications. Additionally, an effective 3DEI requires an agent standard such as the JADE implementation of the FIPA standard, with a directory service on agents such that agents can be added dynamically at runtime. Ultimately, we look forward to a virtual world that will allow plug-and-play agents into virtual and non-virtual agent societies.

The notion of dynamically designing and redesigning a virtual world according to institutional requirements is something we believe has promise. The development of dynamic designs of 3D virtual worlds would be particularly useful for large-scale 3DEIs with users who would be engaged in a wide variety of online activities. Further development of the prototype may lead to a generic system for customers to realise their 3DEIs that are ready for use, according to different specifications. The approach could be extended to personalising 3DEIs by dynamically designing and modifying them according to the needs of individuals. In other words, for each person in the institution, only those portions of the 3D virtual world relevant to their current activities would be designed and generated.

Further research into 3DEIs should further articulate the roles of agents such as the institution agent and the room agents, as well as consider the use of other design agents to enrich the current agent hierarchy. For this prototype we selected a particular metaphor: institutional architecture. This metaphor influenced the choice of institution and room agents but the model of a 3DEI does not assume this metaphor. Of particular interest are metaphors that do not unnecessarily require serial, non-concurrent access to protocol "scenes". The example grammar developed in this research was likewise influenced by the particular architecture metaphor chosen for the prototype. More examples of design grammars need to be developed to look at their usability in other 3DEIs, and a design grammar developed to automate or partly automate the process of grammar design and implementation.

5. Conclusion

The contribution of this paper to CAAD lies in a model of 3DEIs as 3D virtual worlds that are dynamically designed in response to the users' needs and the rules of the electronic institution. The formal description of an electronic institution provides a partial design specification for the design agents. Design considerations such as visual and spatial layout of objects and spaces, design constraints and styles are represented as design grammars. The dynamic design of 3D electronic institutions is an effective approach to designing and generating virtual environments as needed for supporting human activities online. This approach also provides solutions for practical issues such as instancing in large-scale multi-user networked environments.

Acknowledgements

This research was supported by a grant from the Australian Research Council. This paper was written while Mary Lou Maher was working at the National Science Foundation in the United States. Any opinion, findings and conclusions or recommendations expressed in this paper are those of the authors and do not necessarily reflect the views of the National Science Foundation.

References

Bogdanovych, A, Berger, H, Sierra and Simoff, S: 2005, Narrowing the Gap between Humans and Agents in E-Commerce: 3D Electronic Institutions, *Proceedings of the 6th International Conference on Electronic Commerce and Web Technologies*, Copenhagen, Denmark, pp. 128-137.

Esteva, M: 2003, Electronic Institutions: from Specification to Development, *IIIA Ph.D. Monography* (vol 19).

Esteva, M, Rosell, B, Rodriguez-Aguilar, JA and Arcos, JL: 2004, AMELI: An Agent-based Middleware for Electronic Institutions, *Proceedings of AAMAS'04*, pp. 237-242.

Esteva, M: 2006, *Electronic Institution Project*, Private e-mail communication, 13 September 2006.

Gu, N and Maher ML: 2005, Dynamic Designs of 3D Virtual Worlds Using Generative Design Agents, *Proceedings of Computer Aided Architectural Design Futures 2005*, Springer, Dordrecht, The Netherlands, pp. 239-248.

Gu, N and Maher, ML: 2003, A Grammar for the Dynamic Design of Virtual Architecture Using Rational Agents, *International Journal of Architectural Computing* **4**(1): 489-501.

Maher, ML and Gu, N: 2002, Virtual Worlds = Architectural Design + Computational Elements, *Proceedings of ANZAScA*, Deakin University, Australia, pp. 305-312.

Martin, D, Burstein, M, MacIlraith, S, and Sycara, K: 2004, OWL-S and Agent-Based Systems, *in* L Cavedon, Z Maamar, D Martin and B Boualem (eds), *Extending Web Services Technologies: The Use of Multi-Agent Approaches,* Springer, Berlin, pp. 53-79.

Macindoe, O. 2006, *Ideas for Development of Second Life Prototype*, Project report, 5th July 2006.

Richards, D, van Splunter, S and Brazier, FMT: 2004, Composing Web Services using an Agent Factory, *in* L Cavedon, Z Maamar, D Martin and B Boualem (eds), *Extending Web Services Technologies: The Use of Multi-Agent Approaches,* Springer, Berlin, pp. 229-252.

Rosenman, M, Merrick, K, Maher, ML and Marchant, D: 2006, DESIGNWORLD: A Multidisciplinary Collaborative Design Environment Using Agents in a Virtual World, *in* JS Gero (ed), *Design Computing and Cognition'06*, Springer, Dordrecht, The Netherlands, pp. 695-710.

Stiny G: 1999, Commentary: Shape, *Environment and Planning B: Planning and Design* 26: 7-14.

Stiny G: 1990, What Is a Design?, *Environment and Planning B: Planning and Design* 17: 97-103.

Stiny G, and Gips J: 1972, Shape Grammars and the Generative Specification of Painting and Sculpture, *Proceedings of Information Processing 71*, North Holland, Amsterdam, pp. 1460-1465.

BECOMING TOOLS

LOCAL NAVIGATION CAN REVEAL IMPLICIT RELATIONS

YINGJIE CHEN, ZHENYU QIAN AND ROBERT WOODBURY
Simon Fraser University, Canada

Abstract. This paper intends to analyze, compare, understand and explore the data relations among a collection, the collected items and user-created meaning appearing in different digital applications. Details of such relations are introduced and investigated with reference to several actual systems. In order to represent these three components in a way easy for users to interpret, navigate and interact, we introduce NEAR, a localized graph visualization tool to help people browse, understand and manipulate information in a digital architectural repository A•VI•RE.

1. Introduction

Through several distinctive use cases, we analyze the information seeking problems existing in different digital applications. In these systems, digital collections share a common form that includes the collection, the objects collected and the meaning of the collection. Relations between these three components are complicated. Some of the relations are obvious such as an object may be included by a collection. Others, such as *bibliographic coupling* and *co-citation*and are hidden under the surface. In this paper, we consider to use these relations as shortcuts for navigation design. After analyzing four use cases in actual systems, we review related theories and technology. In an architectural visual repository A•VI•RE, we present a visualization panel to prototype and evaluate our understanding of a more supportive navigation tool through visualizing and manipulating relations.

2. Several Use Cases

We start by considering four use cases selected from extant systems.

2.1. USE CASE 1: SEARCH FOR IMAGES IN THE IMAGE BANKS

A creative graphic designer requires large collection of raw images as antecedents and points of departure. Many public image banks such as DGL

A Dong, A Vande Moere & JS Gero (eds), CAADFutures'07, 403–416.

(digital graphic library of Microsoft), Flickr.com and Corbis.com provide image searching service. In these galleries, images are cataloged or tagged by keywords. Because of its multi-perspective nature, an image usually belongs to different catalogs or has multiple keywords. The rich cataloging system may help users to find as many related images as possible.

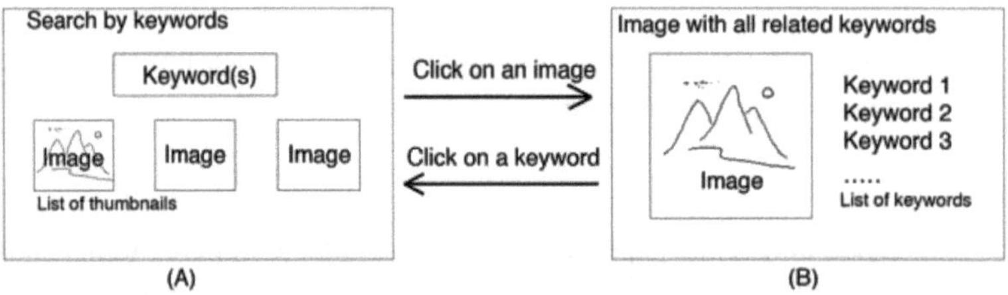

Figure 1. Scenarios of image searching in image banks

In many image gallery systems, users can search multiple keywords/tags at once to sort out the intersection of different collections (Figure A). Most of them also provide backlinks allowing users to read keywords related to the image (B). In the DGL and Corbis, when a user opens the window of one image, all related keywords would be listed (A→B). The user can click on any keyword to navigate to the whole collection of all the images tagged by this word (B→A). DGL only provides a clickable link from the keyword back to image list while Corbis allows users to select on multiple keywords at once. So in Corbis, the user can search for more similar works by selecting related keywords.

However, the searching task is still challenging since the user has to make several clicks and go through different webpages to get the result. Human's visual working memory is quite limited (with acquisition 3-4 chunks in 30 seconds). Also there is no easy way to find the difference or intersection of two sets of results, so it is hard to compare image features. The user usually has to open many windows and show all the potentially useful results on the desktop. Keyword and tagging system links related images together, but navigating through this net of words and looking for specific images is still an intricate task.

2.2. USE CASE 2: SEEKING ADVICE FOR NEW PRODUCTS

When a customer purchases a new product, he/she usually relies on expert reviews or others' experience to make the decision. Many websites provide a space for users to exchange opinions and post comments on products. Some websites also use such information for product recommendation.

Dpreview.com is a website providing digital camera reviews for photography fans. In the site, there are reviews from professional photographers and testing results in laboratories. Users can discuss different kinds of digital cameras and compare them in different forums as well. Generally these forums are grouped by brands and full of discussion threads. Famous brands (such as Nikon and Canon) of digital single-lens reflex (DSLR) camera introduce new products every year. Many new users come to this site to seek for advice from experts. Users usually have strong preferences for different brands. For example, in Canon forums, most discussions relate to Canon and in Nikon forums, most discussions relate to Nikon. To compare the cameras across models and brands, there are separate threads located in different forums. Some threads pay attention to technical data while others emphasize ergonomics and handling. Unavoidably, biases exist in many of the discussions. To gather a whole picture, the user has to shift across forums to find all the related threads. The user may use keyword search to help, but it is hard to gather all related discussion threads without bias.

While reading one discussion thread, the user may want to see the whole picture or focus the following topics: details of all the products discussed in the thread; any other threads also discussing products in the current thread; and any other forums on similar products. The current system does not provide such capability.

2.3. USE CASE 3: TRACE ACAEMIC RESEARCH PAPERS

In academia, researchers read and refer to others' publications frequently, building webs of citations. For a professional researcher, the following are important: citations in this paper, any paper citing this paper, and the originality of the idea. In citation index research the concepts of *bibliographic coupling* and *co-citation*are both essential in to finding similar papers or papers originating from the same idea but going in different directions.

In some online library systems such as Sage publication's digital library, a citation map is generated for every journal article. The map faithfully reflects all citation relations around this paper. The researcher can see connections between papers and read the idea flow. However, it is hard to get a clear overview as the number of cross links grows. It is also hard to recognize the strength of the relations among papers. Due to the incomplete collection of resources, the originality of a theory is a difficult task. The academic world still needs a more complete solution that can include and represent clearly relations of reference, citation, bibliographic coupling and co-citation.

2.4. USE CASE 4: EQUIP A CUSTOMIZED SYSTEM ONLINE

A functional system is usually a combination of several components. A digital SLR camera cannot work without lenses, memory card, battery reader and other supplements. To equip a HDTV, the customer also needs an AV receiver, speakers and cables. In e-commerce systems, although there are kit solutions provided, many users still want to make their own customized solutions. Novice users need, not only the technical data of equipments, but also accounts of other "experienced" users' solutions. In some e-commerce system, such as Amazon.com, collaborative filtering recommendation has been widely used. In forums or customer reviews, there are also many users discussing combinations of equipments, but there is still no simple and centralized channel through which the user can read others' customized combination as references.

3. Understand Local Browsing in the Use Cases

3.1. RELATIONS EXISTED IN THE USE CASES

Considering the above four use cases, there are three kinds of objects involved: collections, user's comments and products. Among these objects, the most basic relation is the *inclusion/reference* relation: images are cataloged under categories (or keywords/tags), discussion threads are grouped by forums, and products are referenced by discussion threads.

Being included is the reverse of inclusion. One object can be included into multiple collects. *Being included* also assigns multiple attributes to an object. In the digital world, *inclusion* (link) and *included-in* (back-link) form complex relations, which can be locally or globally transitive, symmetric reflexive, one-to-one, one-to-many, many-to-one and many-to-many. Some visualization technologies such as CZWEB (Collaud, Dill, Jones et al. 1995) have been developed to represent link and backlink relations between Internet nodes, treats the web as an information space and represents the complex link structure as a map.

Extending the relations of inclusion and included in, *co-citation* (Small 1973) and *bibliographic coupling* (Kessler 1963) relations can be found. If two papers refer to the same paper, they are bibliographically coupled. In contrast to bibliographic coupling, if two papers are cited together by the same paper, they are related by co-citation. Bibliographic coupling and co-citation pattern among research papers are importance in computing similarity of papers.

In digital space, bibliographic coupling and co-citation relations are very common. Two images could be co-cited by the same tag(s), and two products can be co-cited by the same discussion(s). On the other hand, similar to papers being bibliographically coupled by the same references, discussions can be coupled by talking about same product(s), and two customers' shopping carts can be coupled by having the same item(s).

3.2. SIMILARITY RANKING AND COLLABORATIVE FILTERING

Many applications require a measurement of similarity among objects. An obvious example is "find-similar-document" on the Web (Baeza-Yates and Ribeiro-Neto 1999). Co-citation and bibliographic coupling have been applied to cluster scientific papers according to topic or cluster web pages (Larson 1996). SimRank (Jeh and Widom 2002) developed mathematical equations to formalize the recursive notion of structural-context similarity and defined similarity scores in terms of these equations.

Collaborative filtering (CF) has been widely used in recommender systems including e-commerce systems such as Amazon.com (Linden, Smith and York 2003). In the process of decision making, people tend to make use of the advice of others who have made decisions earlier (Schotter and Sopher 2001). Based on building a database of preferences of users or an item-item matrix, CF is one of the most promising technologies for recommendation. In the use cases we studied above, CF algorithms could be applied to improve the system's usability and help people make decisions.

3.3. LOCAL BROWSING AND DIRECT MANIPULATION

Media present both themselves and the external events they depict to users. Users interact with a medium and so are indirectly interacting with the event. A good user interface should bring the user face-to-face with whatever is being manipulated and experienced. Principles of immediacy and direct manipulation (Shneiderman 1983) are essential. The intention of direct manipulation is to allow a user to directly manipulate objects presented to them, using actions that correspond at least loosely to the physical world. It involves continuous representation of objects of interest, rapid, reversible, incremental actions and feedback. With direct manipulation, users may learn more quickly, make fewer errors and operate more effectively.

Immediacy is the erasure of the gap between signifier and signified, such that a representation is perceived to be the thing itself. The desire for immediacy is the desire to get beyond the medium and get to the objects of representation themselves. An interactive system designer should attend to immediacy in at least three dimensions that are important for users experience: time, space and semantics (Ungar 1997). Temporal immediacy links cause and effect. Humans recognize causality without conscious effort only when the time between causally-related events (latency) is kept to a minimum. Spatial immediacy means that the physical distance between causally related events is kept to a minimum. Objects that are widely separated by space on the screen force the user to devote more conscious effort to link them. Semantic immediacy means the conceptual distance between semantically related pieces of information is kept to a minimum. In interactive interfaces, the conceptual distance between two pieces of information is represented by the number of operations such as mouse clicks.

With the address of direct manipulation and immediacy, a system with good usability should present all the related information in a simple, compact way.

3.4. EXAMPLES OF INFORMATION VISUALIZATION SYSTEMS

Information visualization is useful in visualizing objects and may help users understand them. We are interested in representing object relations and context as well as the objects themselves. Therefore, our focus is on representing the object and context, as well as reviewing the current theories, technologies and design projects.

3.4.1. Visualizing Large Image Database with Context

In most image database systems, image data are put into categories related to metadata and keywords. The result of a query in the image database systems is usually a set of images, displayed in an Image Browser or shown in a two-dimensional grid of thumbnails (Ogle and Stonebraker 1995). For document browsing, the Document Lens (Robertson and Mackinlay 1993) uses a focus+context technique to display the document of interest in detail while compressing the rest of the document space. Apart from giving an overview of the entire document/image space, recent projects such as Concentric Rings (Torres, Silva, Medeiros et al. 2003) and MoiréGraphs (Jankun-Kelly and Ma 2003) highlight the relations among documents/images. However, in their detailed examples, images are overlapped and relation lines are entangled with each other.

3.4.2. Compact Visualization with Rich Information

"Useful field of view" (UFOV) is a concept developed to define the size of the region (one to 15 degree) from which we can rapidly take in information (Ware 2004). When we are reading fine print, we can read only the words within the foveal view, but we can see the overall shape of a larger pattern at a single glance. Thread-Arcs email visualization is a novel interactive visualization technique designed to help people make use of threads found in emails (Kerr 2003). Thread-Arcs combine the chronology of messages with the branching tree structure of a conversational thread in a stable and compact visualization panel. The threads are visualized in a node-link graph. Message nodes are linearly distributed from left to right connected by arcs.

Thread Arcs also have an interaction to allow users to highlight and inspect thread and message attributes dynamically. By quickly scanning and interacting with Thread Arcs, people can see various attributes of conversations and find relevant messages at a glance. Thread Arcs thus are a good example of compact visualization with rich information.

To implement our understanding of supporting local browsing, we designed and implemented visualization tool on an architectural visual repository.

4. Local Browsing in a Visual Repository A•VI•RE

4.1. DATA STRUCTURE AND NAVIGATION ISSUES IN A•VI•RE

A•VI•RE (available at: http://www.avire.ca) is a generic repository for visual material related to cultural disciplines. A•VI•RE is designed to be an online space where different users (such as curators, exhibitors, critics and viewers) play together to create a large social entity. Users upload new resources, organize exhibitions, and annotate resources and exhibitions in the system. A•VI•RE began as an architecture visual repository hosting about 4000 architecture slides. There are three main types of objects in A•VI•RE, exhibition, annotation and resource. The information structure was designed according to following principles:

- A resource can be any type of digital work, such as an image, a multimedia file, a paper, or a webpage.
- An exhibition is a collection of exhibitions, annotations and resources.
- An annotation is a mixture of text and references to exhibitions, annotations and resources.
- One resource, annotation or exhibition can be referenced in multiple exhibitions.

Figure 2 demonstrates the data structure of A•VI•RE projects. In A•VI•RE, at the time of writing this paper (Jan 2007), on average each exhibition includes 30.8 resources and the standard deviation is 52. One exhibition has a maximum number of 179 resources. In contrast, on average each resource is included in 2.05 exhibitions, standard deviation 4.2, with a maximum number of one resource being included in 27 exhibitions.

Due to the rich content and flexible information structure, there exist some usability issues when users are browsing or searching in the system:

- It is hard to provide a contextual view of a resource from different perspectives.
- It is hard to see the sharing relations between exhibitions.

- It is possible to see a resource as referenced by multiple exhibitions and annotations and concepts across annotations, but hard to see the relations among annotations and exhibitions.
- It is hard to locate relevant resources, exhibitions and annotations. It is easy to search one resource or exhibition by key words, but searching for an unknown object with some related hints is still difficult due to the lack of information about the direct keywords or metadata.

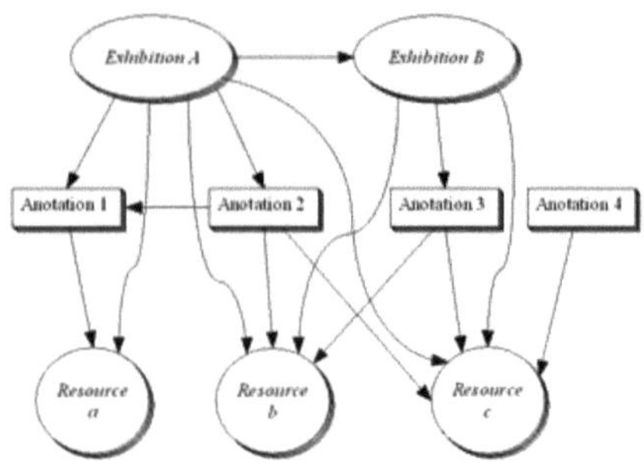

Figure 2. Data structure of objects in A•VI•RE (Chen 2007)

We believe a compact, small-scale, interactive visualization embedded into the interface of the A•VI•RE system can enhance the user's experience while browsing, navigating, understanding and using information in this generic multimedia repository.

4.2. KEY PROPERTIES AND QUALITIES FOR REPRESENTING A•VI•RE OBJECTS

As the first step to solve above issues, we propose a compact interactive visualization panel to help users visualize, analyze and navigate through A•VI•RE objects (Qian, Chen and Woodbury 2006). The panel's name is called "Navigating Exhibitions, Annotations and Resources" (NEAR). There are several key properties of A•VI•RE objects addressed in the design: *relations* among resources, exhibitions or annotations; *popularity* of an object, the object's *visitation status*, and *chronology* (evolution and creation sequence of idea).

The qualities of the visualization we considered most important were: compact, simple, preattentitive, responsive, recognizable and scalable to handle reasonable number of objects in a relatively small area. To achieve a successful solution, the development process for NEAR comprised three spiral cycles. Formative evaluation studies with small sets of users advised the next design cycle.

5. Design of NEAR Panel

There are three parts in the design: icons are used to represent the individual objects of exhibitions, annotations and resources. Graphs represent the relations among objects and the interaction helps users to explore and reveal deeper relations.

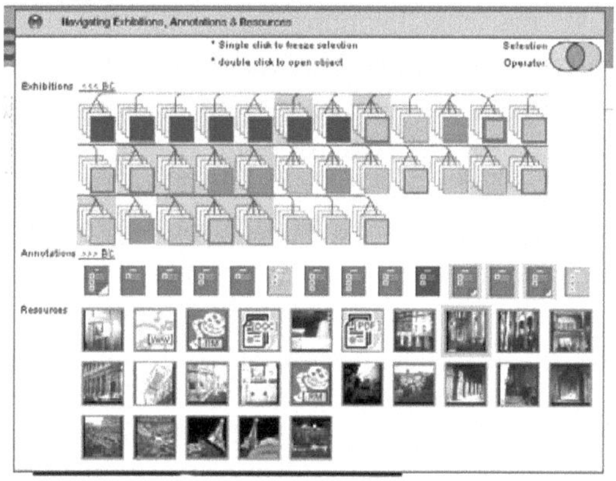

Figure 3. Screenshot of the NEAR panel in A•VI•RE

Figure 3 is an expanded exhibition-centered view showing: all resources referenced in the current exhibition, all exhibitions that are bibliographically coupled with the current exhibition, and all annotations that annotate any of the resources (the annotation does not necessarily belong to current exhibition). Individual objects of exhibitions, annotations and resources are represented by icons. Content-based thumbnails are used to represent resources to provide maximum preview where possible, otherwise type-based icons are used. The levels of bibliographic coupling with the current exhibition are indicated by the links on top of the exhibition icons.

5.1. ICONS FOR OBJECTS

In NEAR, icons are designed to visually represent individual objects. Attributes of the object (visitation status, popularity, size and content

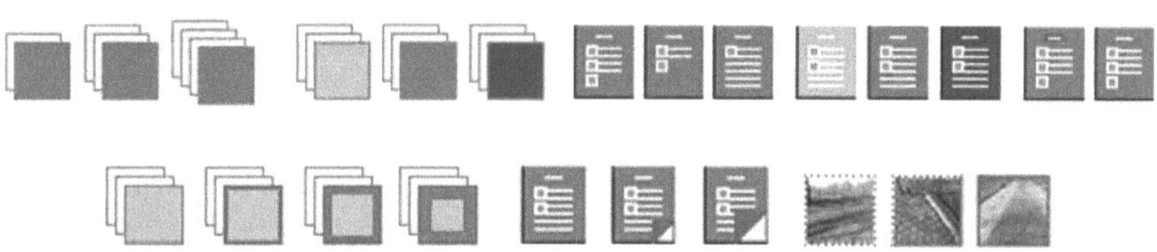

Figure 4. Examples of icons – exhibition icons, annotation icons and visitation status for all objects (Qian, Chen and Woodbury 2006)

arrangement etc.) are mapped to the features (or degrees of freedom) of the icons. Due to the limited capacity of human visual working memory, only three to four variations for each attribute are represented in the design.

5.2. LINKS OF HIDDEN RELATIONS

As demonstrated in Figure 2, co-citation and bibliographic coupling create crosslinks. To make the visualization planar, we use node-link graphs to represent the indirect relations, and hide the direct inclusion relations among exhibitions and resources. The direct relations only appear at the user's request by interaction. In NEAR, smooth continuous curves show the relations of co-citation and bibliographic coupling (Figure 5). Exhibitions, annotations and resources can be linked by such edges to represent bibliographic coupling and co-citation information when the user is focusing on different objects. The level of sharing is represented by the number of branches from the node. Since all the relations are counted toward the current object, it is important to show the "root" in the graph representing the current object. The exhibition icon with thick red borders indicates the current visit, and all edges from other icons bend toward the current icon to emphasize such root information again.

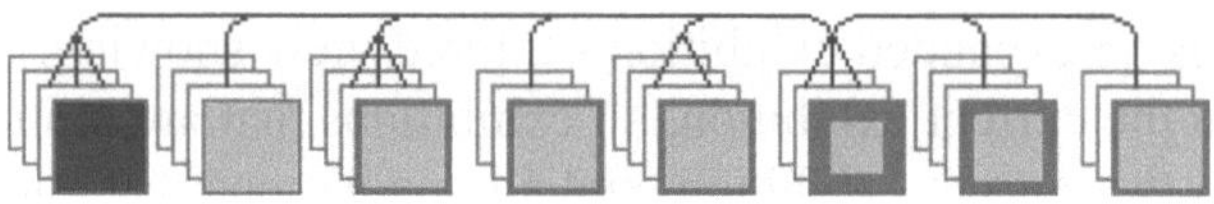

Figure 5. Bibliographic coupling relations between exhibitions
Branches on the top of icons show the levels of sharing resources

5.2.1. Interaction Design

The NEAR panel uses interactions to support local navigation in the hierarchy and citation graph of A•VI•RE. There are three kinds of interactions in NEAR: cursor over (brushing), click and double-click. Cursor over and click provides "filter" related objects by highlighting, and double-click leads users to view the details. Brushing by mouse over enables visual linking of components of heterogeneous complex objects dynamically and immediately. More importantly, brushing avoids link collision in the graph if large numbers of bibliographic coupling and co-citation relations exist within an exhibition.

Figure 6 shows an instance of how NEAR works. Moving the cursor over a resource will highlight all annotations and exhibitions that include the resource with red backgrounds, over an exhibition will highlight all the referenced resources and annotations, and over an annotation will highlight all quoted resources and related exhibitions. The user can freely move the mouse without changing the highlights. To avoid flicker, a click on the object will freeze the view. A click on an empty space re-activates the mouse-over effect. To support navigation, similar to desktop applications, double-clicking opens the document in the main window to display the full content of the object.

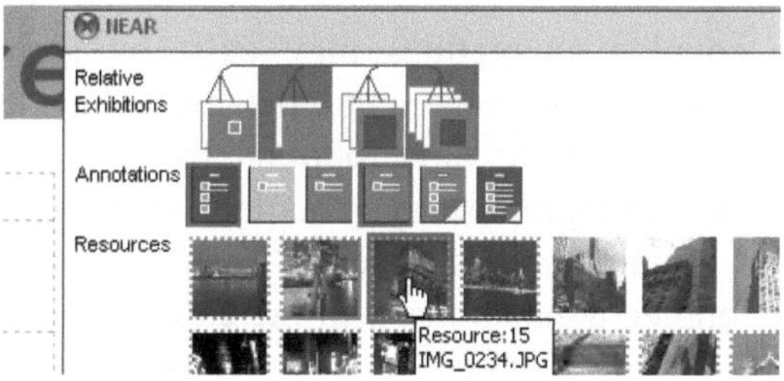

Figure 6. Screenshots of NEAR panel when the mouse cursor is over a resource

5.2.2. Views

Relations among A•VI•RE objects construct a general graph. When we focus on one specific object, objects linked to it could be of interest. These objects can either be similar to the current object, or be supplemental information.

Just like the name "NEAR", when a user focuses on a specific object, we want the NEAR panel to bring the related objects of the current selection "near" to the user. The NEAR panel provides three different views to reveal relations around each type of object when user focuses. Each view has two states: the simple state shows the direct relations (inclusion and annotation), and the advanced state has multiple (2~3) complex views to show co-citation and bibliographic coupling information.

The NEAR panel switches to the annotation-centric view when the user is reading an annotation. This view focuses on the current annotation, listing all related exhibitions, annotations and resources around the annotation.

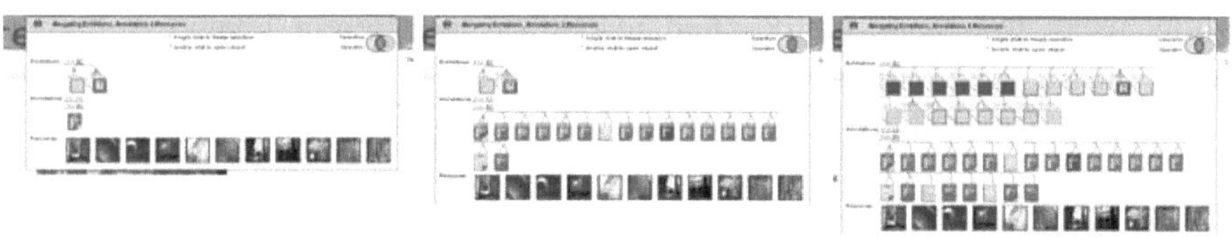

Figure 7. Annotation-centric views (left: simple view; middle: expand to show bibliographic coupled annotations; right: expand to show all)

The simple view of the annotation-centric view (Figure 7) provides the overview of the current annotation. The centre annotation icon shows the content arrangement of the annotation. The top exhibitions area shows all exhibitions that include the current annotation. All resources that have been annotated are listed on the bottom.

There are three views in the annotation panel's extended state due to an annotation's special position in the structure.

Since an annotation may include several resources and be included in several exhibitions, the following situations exist: exhibitions may bibliographically couple with the current annotation by resources; bibliographically coupled annotations may exist by including the same resources; and co-cited annotations may exist by being included the same exhibitions. Hence we provide three options for users to explore these relations: show all bibliographically coupled exhibitions with current annotations; show all annotations co-cited by the exhibitions; show all bibliographically coupled annotations with the current annotation. The three expanded views can be integrated with any combination. The user can choose to expand any two views or even three views together.

Exhibition centric view shows all related objects around the visiting exhibition, including annotations and resources referenced in the exhibition, and can be extended to show all bibliographically coupled exhibitions and annotations. The simple exhibition-centric view shows the most fundamental hierarchy structure of a current exhibition. Its annotations area lists all annotations and resources area lists all resources included. The expanded view shows all bibliographically coupled exhibitions. Also, annotations bibliographically coupled with current exhibitions can be expanded to be seen as well. Both in the simple view and expanded view, the resources area lists all resources under current exhibition.

The resource-centric view provides views from different aspects by showing all related exhibitions, annotations and similar resources. Resources can be co-cited by exhibitions and annotations. The strength of co-citation relations between two objects is determined by the number of parent objects citing these two objects together. The more objects co-cited by the two objects, the stronger the relation. Therefore we provide seven options to allow users to search for co-cited resources at different levels. A higher threshold of co-citing objects means the co-cited resources have stronger relationship (or similarity), but the user will see fewer of them.

5.2.3. Evaluation

Our design goal of NEAR is to have most of users understand the design (icons, graphs and interaction). We used evaluation to provide ideas for future improvement. We asked two groups of users to evaluate the current design. One group had three users who had participated in the design process to provide formative comments on the first two versions of NEAR. The other group has three novices who have never seen the interface before.

During the evaluation, we initially asked users to play with NEAR without any introduction and explanation and asked them to guess the meanings of each component: meanings of icon variations, the link graph, interaction and clickable links. After comparing the guessed meanings and our designed meanings, we found that experienced users grasp the semantic meanings faster than novices. We designed two rounds of experiments and assigned some small information seeking tasks for users to accomplish. In the first round, NEAR panel was disabled. Users were allowed to use NEAR in the second round. They found the panel gives them much useful information and shortened their navigation paths. Similar or relation objects are much easier to find. When focusing on one object the different views provide different levels of surrounding information based on their needs Generally, the feedback suggested that the NEAR approach maybe useful. We understand that it is only the starting point of an entire evaluation, acting as a short and nice pilot study. In the next stage of design, an extended evaluation would follow.

6. Conclusion

If we can apply the NEAR solution to the four use cases we discussed, maybe the distance between different pieces of information could be shortened, and their context objects could be better represented to users. In use case 1, a NEAR solution could allow the users to see connections among keywords, among images, and among keywords and images in one window. In use case 2, the user would be able to view all the discussion threads around one product, other products mention in these comments, and other discussion forums contain related discussions. Thus he/she could gain perspective and make a "smarter" choice. In case 3, the researcher can observe the idea flow though citations and references in a selected paper. In case 4, the customer may see how other people equip a whole system with the same product and their use review of the system before he/she makes the decision. The Internet has caused a flood of information, and what we most easily see is the information itself: the surface of the flood. Underneath and much more vast are the relations among the information elements. Our intention of NEAR is to reveal this underneath hidden information, bring this information close to user, and free the user from seeking information so that they can focus more on creative work. Although there is room for improvement, the user studies and our implementation show us our design approach has potential.

References

Baeza-Yates, R and Ribeiro-Neto, B: 1999, *Modern Information Retrieval*, Addison Wesley, Reading, Massachusetts.

Chen, YV: 2007, *Revealing Hidden Structure: Visualizing Bibliographic Coupling and Co-citation Relations in Multimedia Collections*, School of Interactive Arts and Technology, Simon Fraser University.

Collaud, G, Dill, J, Jones, C and Tan, P: 1995, A Distorted View Approach to Assisting Web Navigation, *Workshop on New Paradigms in Information Visualization and Manipulation* (in conjunction with 4th Int. Conf. on Information and Knowledge Management (CIKM'95). Baltimore, pp. 95-100.

Jankun-Kelly, TJ and Ma, K-L: 2003, MoireGraphs: Radial Focus+Context Visualization and Interaction for Graphs with Visual Nodes, *Proceedings of the 2003 IEEE Symposium on Information Visualization*, IEEE Computer Science Press, Seattle, Washington, pp. 59-66.

Jeh, G and Widom, J: 2002, SimRank: A measure of structural-context similarity, *Proceedings of the Eighth ACM SIGKDD International Conference on Knowledge Discovery and Data Mining*, Edmonton, Alberta, Canada, pp. 1-11.

Kerr, B: 2003, Thread Arcs: An Email Thread Visualization, *Proceedings of the 2003 IEEE Symposium on Information Visualization*, IEEE Computer Science Press, Seattle, Washington, pp. 211-218.

Kessler, MM: 1963, Bibliographic Coupling between Scientific Papers, *American Documentation* **12**: 10-25.

Larson, RR: 1996, Bibliometrics of the World-Wide Web: An Exploratory Analysis of the Intellectual Structure of Cyberspace, *Proceedings of the Annual Meeting of the American Society for Information Science*, Baltimore, Maryland, **33**: 71-78.

Linden, G, Smith, B and York, J: 2003, Amazon.com Recommendations, Item-to-Item Collaborative Filtering, Industry Report, *IEEE Internet Computing* **7**(1): 76-80.

Ogle, VE and Stonebraker, M: 1995, Chabot: Retrieval from Relational Database of Images, *IEEE Computer* **28**(9): 40-48.

Qian, CZ, Chen, VY and Woodbury, RF: 2006, NEAR: Visualizing Information Relations in a Multimedia Repository, *Smart Graphics, 6th International Symposium, SG2006*, Vancouver, Canada, pp. 236-241.

Robertson, GG and Mackinlay, JD: 1993, The Document Lens, *Proceedings of the ACM Symposium on User Interface Software and Technology (UIST93) Visualizing Information*, pp. 101-108.

Schotter, A and Sopher, B: 2001, *Advice and Behavior in Intergenerational Ultimatum Games: An Experimental Approach*, Department of Economics, New York University, New York

Shneiderman, B: 1983, Direct Manipulation: A step beyond programming languages, *IEEE Computer* **16**(8): 57-69.

Small, H: 1973, Co-citation in the scientific Literature: A New Measure of the Relationship between Two Documents, Journal of the American Society of Information Science **24**: 265-269.

Torres, RS, Silva, CG, Medeiros, CB and Rocha, HV: 2003, Visual Structures for Image Browsing, *CIKM'03*, New Orleans, Louisiana, pp. 49-55.

Ungar, D, Lieberman, Henry., Fry, Christopher: 1997, Debugging and the experience of immediacy, *Communications of the ACM* **40**: 38-43.

Ware, C: 2004, *Information Visualization: Perception for Design*, Morgan Kaufman, San Francisco, CA.

COMPUTER-AIDED DESIGN TOOLS THAT ADAPT

WEI PENG
CSIRO, Australia

and

JOHN S GERO
George Mason University, USA

Abstract. This paper describes an approach that enables a computer-aided design tool to learn conceptual knowledge as it is being used, and as a consequence adapts its behaviours to the changing environment. This allows the tool to improve the effectiveness of designers in their design tasks over time. Design experiments evaluate the effectiveness of this prototype system in recognizing optimization problems in heterogeneous design scenarios.

1. Introduction

The development of computer-aided design tools has moved from representation to knowledge encoding and support in knowledge-based systems. A large number of design knowledge systems have been prototyped or commercialized, such as OPTIMA (Balachandran 1988) and KNODES (Rutherford and Maver 1994). Designing is intrinsically dynamic and interactive, in the sense that designers reflect on their actions (Schön 1983) and often change the course of the developing design (Gero 1998). Many CAD researchers turned to building systems that can automatically learn to cope with this ill-structured problem. Machine learning techniques have been widely adopted in knowledge-based systems to provide knowledge acquisition, modification and generalization, for example ECOBWEB (Reich and Fenves 1991) and BRIDGER (Reich 1993). These systems treat knowledge as universally applicable context-free generalizations and descriptions (Reffat and Gero 2000), so that they can be reused in different circumstances. It is argued that there are disadvantages of a black-box, context-free learning machine (Lieberman and Selker 2000).

A Dong, A Vande Moere & JS Gero (eds), CAADFutures'07, 417–430.

A fundamental question is how to enhance design effectiveness using computer-aided tools. The effectiveness of a design process is often associated with the term "efficacy" when a design tool is applied in a design activity. The efficacy of the tool usually refers to the ability to produce a desired amount of a desired effect. To enhance the efficacy of a CAD tool, we need a mechanism to bring changes in the system that are adaptive, in the sense that these changes enable the system to tackle the same task or tasks drawn from the same population more successfully the next time (Simon 1983). A design tool that adapts based on its experience of its use is claimed to be effective (Gero 2003). This paper describes an approach that enables a computer-aided design tool to be built on an adaptive paradigm, so that a design tool can learn conceptual knowledge as it is being used, and as a consequence adapts its behaviours to the changing environment. We present a computational model that is founded on notions of situatedness from cognitive science and computational agency.

2. Situatedness and Adaptation

The concept of "situatedness" has been developed in different areas resulting in diverse terms, such as "situated action" (Suchman 1987) and "situated cognition" (Clancey 1997). Situatedness involves both the context and the observer's experiences and the interactions between them. It is inseparable from interactions in which knowledge is dynamically constructed. Situated cognition copes with the way humans construct their internal worlds via its interaction with the external world (Gero 2003). The notion of adaptation originates from the ability of a biological system to accommodate incremental changes and to react to unexpected events in its environment. Adaptation can be viewed as the system's capability of modifying its behaviours to its context and improving its performance over time (Boer and Canamero 1999). The adaptive behaviour results from the interaction between an agent and its environment (Beer 1997). In this paper, we present a situated agent-based design tool, which consists of an existing design tool, a situated agent and interactions between the agent and its environment. A situated agent is wrapped around the design tool, learns from and adapts to its interactions with the design environment. Adaptation enables the design tool to cope with situatedness in a dynamic design process (Gero and Peng 2004). The concepts about interactions are constructed and grounded into the agent's experiences. These experiences bias the agent's later memory construction when a similar situation is encountered. The constructive memory model embodies a mechanism whereby an agent learns new concepts.

2.1. SITUATED AGENTS

A situated agent is a software agent built on the notion of "situatedness". Adaptivity, the agent's capability to learn and improve with experience (Bradshaw 1996), is a salient feature of a situated agent. A constructive memory model (Gero 1999) serves as an operational utility that implements the idea of "situatedness" into agent architecture. Adaptive behaviours, in terms of reflexive, reactive and reflective behaviour (Maher and Gero 2002), can result from the multi-level processing and constraints imposed by a situated agent architecture. Experience is a general notion that comprises the knowledge or skill of some thing gained through direct involvements or activities. This paper represents experience as structures. They can be classified into three categories:

1. The sensory experience holds discrete symbolic labels for discerning sense-data. They are the built-in features for sensors. Each sensor captures a particular type of information. Once an environment stimulus is detected, the agent attaches an initial meaning to it, based on its sensory experience;
2. The perceptual experience captures historical representations of perceptual categories and their interrelationships, including entities, properties and entity–property relationships with degrees of beliefs;
3. The conceptual experience comprises the grounded invariants over the lower level perceptual experience. The conceptual experience explicitly states the regularities over the past observations of perceptual instances.

Situated agents can sense and put forward changes to the environment via sensors and effectors. Sensors gather environmental changes into data structures called sense-data. Sensation (S) is the process that transfers sense-data into multi-modal sensory experiences. This is through "push" and "pull" processes. A push process is a data-driven process in which changes from the external world trigger changes in the agent's internal world, for example, the agent's experience. A pull process is an expectation-driven process in which the agent updates the internal world according to the expectation-biased external changes (Gero and Fujii 2000; Gero and Kannengiesser 2006). The push and pull processes can occur at different levels of processing, for example, sensation, perception and conception. The pushed sense-data are also called exogenous sense-data (S_e). They are triggered by external environmental changes, that is, actions performed by designers in using the design tool. The pulled sense-data are intentionally collected during the agent's expectation-driven process. Sensory data (S_{e+a}) consist of two types of variables: the exogenous sense-data (S_e) and the autogenous sensory experience (S_a). S_a is created from matching the agent's exogenous sense-data (S_e) with the agent's sensory level experience. Sensory experience (S_{e+a}) are a combination of the agent's exogenous sense-data (S_e) and the related autogenous information (S_a). For instance, sense-data S_e is captured by sensors as a sequence of unlabelled events:

- S_e (t) = {...... "a mouse click on a certain text field", key stroke of "x", "y"......}.

Based on the lowest level of sensory experience, which holds modality information, the agent creates an autogenous variable (S_a) with its initial label for the S_e:

- S_a (t) = {"Label for the clicked text field"}.

Thus, sensory experience S_{e+a} can be created as:

- S_{e+a} (t) = {...... ["Label for the clicked test field" | Key strokes "x", "y"]......}

Perception (P) generates percepts based on the agent's sensory experiences. Percepts are intermediate data structures that are generated from mapping sensory data into categories. Sensory experience S_{e+a} is categorized to create initial percept (P_i) which can be used to generate a memory cue. The initial percept can be structured as a triplet "Percept (Object, Property, Values of properties)". It is expressed as:

- P_i (t) = Object {Property for the clicked test field, value of that property "xy"}

The perceptual object can be used to cue a memory of the agent's experience. A cue refers to a stimulus that can be used to activate the agent's experience to obtain a memory of that experience. It is generated from matching percepts with the agent's perceptual experience. A cue is subsequently assigned with an activation value to trigger responses from the agent's experience. The cueing function is implemented using experience activation (I_a) and reactivation (I_r), in which a memory cue is applied to the experience structure to get a response.

Conception is the process of categorizing perceptual sequences and chunks in order to form proto-concepts. A concept is regarded as a result of an interaction process in which meanings are attached to environmental stimuli. In order to illustrate a concept formation process, we use the term "proto-concept" to illustrate the intermediate state of a concept. A proto-concept is a knowledge structure that depicts the agent's interpretations and anticipations about its external and internal environment at a particular time. Conception consists of three basic functions: conceptual labeling (C_1), constructive learning (C_2) and induction (C_3). Conceptual labeling creates proto-concepts based on experiential responses to an environment cue. This includes deriving anticipations from these responses and identifying the target. Constructive learning allows the agent to accumulate lower level experiences. Induction can generalize abstractions from the lower level experience and is responsible for generating conceptual knowledge structures.

The hypothesizing process (H) generates a hypothesis from current learned proto-concepts. It is where reinterpretation takes place in allowing the agent to learn in a "trial and error" manner. A situated agent reinterprets its environment using hypotheses which are explanations that are deduced from its domain knowledge (usually conceptual). An agent needs to refocus on or construct a new proto-concept based on hypotheses. Validation (V_d) is the process in which the agent verifies its proto-concepts and hypotheses. It pulls information from the environment to observe whether the environment is changing as expected. A valid concept or experience will be grounded into experiences by incorporation or reinforcement.

The grounding process refers to the experiential grounding (Liew 2004). This reinforces the valid concepts or activated experience via changing the structures of the experience so that the likelihood of the grounded experience being activated in similar circumstances is increased. This is implemented by a grounding via weight adaptation process (W_a), which adjusts the weights of each excitatory connection of the valid concept of a Constructive Interactive Activation and Competition (CIAC) neural network (Peng and Gero 2006), which is an extension of IAC neural network (McClelland 1981), so that those nodes that fire together become more strongly connected.

2.2. ADAPTIVE BEHAVIOURS AND LEARNING MECHANISMS

The agent's reflexive behaviour occurs at a macroscopic level when the experiential response to current sensed data is sufficiently strong to reach a reflexive threshold. A sensory experience can affect action directly. In this circumstance, the agent reflexes to environment stimuli based solely on its experience without activation. In its reactive mode, an agent applies its perceptual experience to respond to an environment stimulus in a self-organized way. The perceptual experience, in terms of a habitual sequence of actions, is manifested as an initial concept. The agent reflects on its actions by drawing new sense-data from a lower level and hypothesizing a new concept. A situated agent reflexes, reacts or reflects corresponding to concepts constructed from its constructive memory model. "Situatedness" emphasizes the role of social relations and interactions in learning. An agent that is designed to be situated at a conceptual level can be implemented using various machine learners. The situated learning can be studied on the following two levels: 1. At a meta-level, learning refers to the concept formation process arising from a constructive memory model for a situated agent; 2. At a base-level, various concept formation composites can be modeled via various machine learners, for example, connectionist neural networks, inductive and analytical machine learning algorithms. The learning process is the process wherein the agent constructs new concepts, such that the agent's experiences (as structure) are reinterpreted, re-structured and constructed in the current context.

3. Situated Agent-based Design Optimization Tool

This research is presented within the design optimization domain. Many design optimization tools focus on gathering a variety of mathematical programming algorithms and providing the means for the user to access them to solve design problems.[1] Choosing a suitable optimizer becomes a bottleneck in a design optimization process. The recognition of appropriate optimization models is fundamental to design decision problems (Radford and Gero 1988). Some of the knowledge required for the recognition of an optimization problem can be expressed in terms of semantic relationships between design elements. An example of such knowledge is illustrated in Table 1. The application of this research to design optimization focuses on learning and adapting the knowledge of applying various optimization algorithms in different design contexts. For example, a designer working on optimizing a hospital layout may find that a certain optimizer is more efficient in solving the problem applied. As the same or other designers tackle a similar design problem, the same tool draws on its experience to construct memories of a design situation and anticipates the tool's potential use. It can offer help to designers in their interactions in designing even before they call for it.

TABLE 1. Knowledge in choosing an optimizer (after Radford and Gero (1988))

if	all the variables are of continuous type
and	all the constraints are linear
and	the objective function is linear
then	conclude that the model is linear programming
and	execute linear programming algorithm

We further discuss a scenario that depicts potential impacts of such a situated agent-based design tool in a design optimization process. Under normal circumstances, a designer uses a design optimization tool to define and solve a problem. No matter how many times he or she applies the same tool to address similar design problems the tool remains unchanged from its

[1] http://www-fp.mcs.anl.gov/otc/Guide/SoftwareGuide/.

use. The designer has to repeat each step each time. We suggest that there are potential benefits if design knowledge can be learned and become available for use without repeating the often demanding design optimization process (Radford and Gero 1988).

A design trajectory consists of a sequence of actions performed by a designer. It represents the procedure via which a design problem has been solved. An assumption here is that the system has already gained certain experiences in design optimization. This assumption is realistic from what we have seen in previous sections. For example, the knowledge of the optimality for the unconstrained quadratic programming problem may contain associative rules like:

- Hessian matrix (positive-definite) → Local-min achieved;
- Hessian matrix (indefinite) → Saddlepoint achieved.

When a designer is keying in a quadratic objective function, the system forms a concept derived from the constructed memory (assuming there exists a similar design optimization instance). According to the problem it recognizes, the system can present the anticipated steps to remind the designer. These include suggestions like (also shown in Figure 1 as "1", "2" and "3" of the concept formed from the system's reactive behaviour):

1. "may be a quadratic programming problem";
2. "may look at Hessian function and second-order of Hessian function to decide its type";
3. "may be a local minimum because Hessian matrix is positive-definite from the system's memory of a similar design instance, use medium-scale quadratic optimizer";

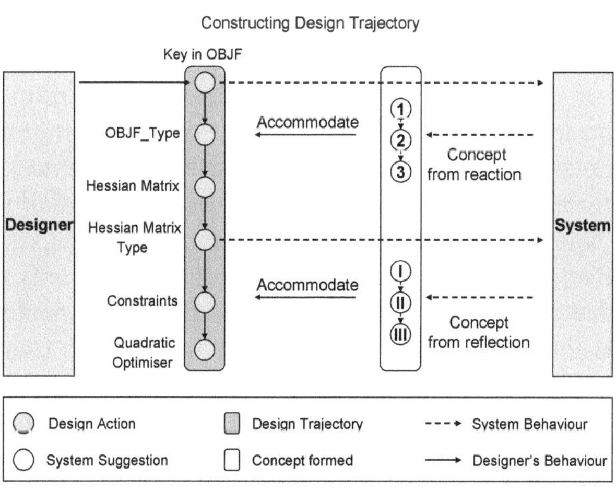

Figure 1. A scenario of constructing a design trajectory in interactions

This concept may guide the designer to focus his or her attention on the contextual information that is drawn from the system's experience on similar problems. This may reduce repetitions in solving a design problem. The system can then observe the designer's actions in deciding its subsequent moves. If the designer works out the Hessian matrix to be indefinite, the system can draw on the knowledge of the optimality to deduce a possible explanation (also shown in Figure 1 as "I", "II" and "III" of the concept formed from the system's reflective behaviour):

I. "may still be a quadratic programming problem";
II. "may be a saddle point because Hessian matrix is indefinite from the system's memory of a similar design instance, don't forget constraints if there are";
III. "may use large-scale quadratic optimizer".

In this way, the concept formed by the system can be infused into the designer's actions. A design trajectory can be constructed and modified in the interactions. As illustrated in Figure 1, the concepts formed from the system's reactive and reflective behaviour are accommodated into a designer's design trajectory. The tool that maintains such a predictive model based on valid anticipations may improve the efficacy of a design process through introducing the agent's experience in developing the design outcome. The efficacy of such a design tool can be measured through its correctness in recognizing a design optimization problem.

4. Design Optimization Experiments

The implemented prototype system is applied to assist the use of a design optimization tool (the Matlab Optimization Toolbox). Matlab Optimization Toolbox is a collection of functions that extend the capability of the MATLAB numeric computing environment. The toolbox includes routines for a variety of optimization classes, including unconstrained and constrained nonlinear minimization, quadratic and linear programming, and nonlinear optimization. It has been widely used by engineers in various domains. A situated agent learns knowledge from how Matlab is utilized by a designer in solving various optimization problems and uses the learned concepts to affect the tool's future use. This section presents a number of experiments that have been carried out on the implemented prototype system. The basic assumption for the experiments is that a user has already worked out the objective function and constraints; he or she uses a design tool to solve that problem. The purpose of the experiments is to evaluate the situated agent-based design tool through:

- examining whether the system can learn new concepts from interactions;
- investigating whether the implemented model can develop adaptive behaviours in different circumstances based on the knowledge structures it learned; and
- studying the characteristics of the agent's behaviours in various circumstances and evaluating the efficacy of the implemented prototype system.

4.1. EXPERIMENT RESULTS

This test (Test 1) focuses on observing and analyzing the agent's behaviours in heterogeneous design optimization scenarios. A sequence of 15 design scenarios is created and adopted. Each scenario represents a design task which is further composed of a number of design actions. For example, a typical design optimization task consists of a number of actions:

- defining objective function and identifying objective function type;
- defining design variables, variable types, design constraints and constraint types;
- typing in gradients of objective function and constraints, defining matrices, such as Hessian matrix and its type;
- selecting optimizers, submitting design problem or editing design problem; submitting feedback on agent's outputs.

The sequence of 15 tasks is represented as {L, Q, Q, L, NL, Q, NL, L, L, NL, Q, Q, L, L, L}, in which "Q", "L" and "NL" represent quadratic, linear and nonlinear design optimization problems respectively. The initial experience of the agent holds one instance of a design optimization scenario solved by a quadratic programming optimizer. The symbols in Table 2 represent these behaviours. According to data obtained from this test, we can further cluster the system's learning behaviour into three stages: Stages I, II and III. We use behaviour rate (B_r) to measure distributions of various behaviours in each stage. The behaviour rate (B_r) for each stage is defined as:

$$B_r = \frac{\textit{Numbers of a particular behaviour}}{\textit{Total numbers of behaviours in the stage}}$$

The B_r of a particular behaviour represents the frequency of this behaviour in the learning stage in which it occurs. The results of various B_r for the three stages are presented in Figures 2-4. Stage I consists of Tasks 1 to 5. No high-level experience or processes (C_3, H) are involved in this stage. The system reacts and learns via C_2 (constructive learning), as depicted in Figure 2.

TABLE 2. Symbols that represent various behaviours

Symbols	Behaviours $(B)_E$	Descriptions
C_1	Conception process 1 – conceptual labelling	Focusing on the target concept from the activated experience
C_2	Conception process 2 – conception via constructive learning	Creating perceptual experience from memory construction (constructive learning)
C_3	Conception process 3 – conception via inductive learning	Creating conceptual experience from generalization (inductive learning)
H	Hypothesizing	Deducing proto-concepts from hypotheses
I_a	CIAC neural network activation	Activating the perceptual experience structure (CIAC) to get response
I_r	CIAC neural network re-activation	Re-activating the perceptual experience structure (CIAC) to get response
P	Perception	Low-level behaviour in creating percepts and memory cue
R_{ex}	Reflexive experience response	Returning experience that reaches reflexive threshold (no reasoning and activation required)
S	Sensation	Low-level behaviour in creating sensory data
V_d	Validation	Comparing anticipation with environment changes
W_a	Weight adaptation	Reinforcing the experience when it is useful

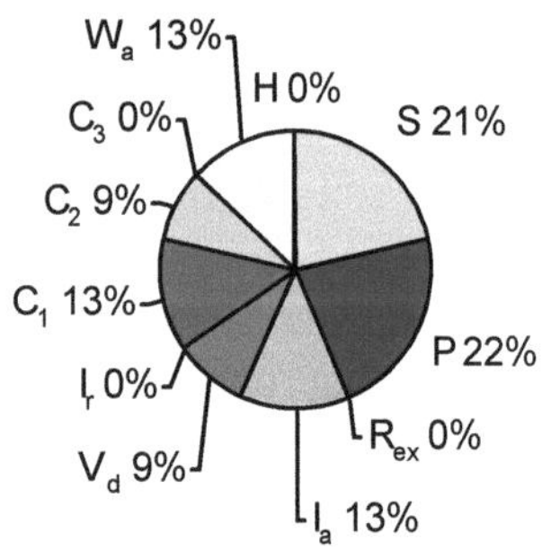

Figure 2. Agent behaviour in learning Stage I

In Stage II (tasks 6 to 12), high-level processes, such as reactivation (I_r), inductive learning (C_3) and hypothesizing (H) become dominant and the system is concentrated on reflection, Figure 3. In Stage III (tasks 13 to 15), the experience for a certain type of design optimization problem becomes highly grounded and the system commences its reflexive behaviour, as illustrated in Figure 4.

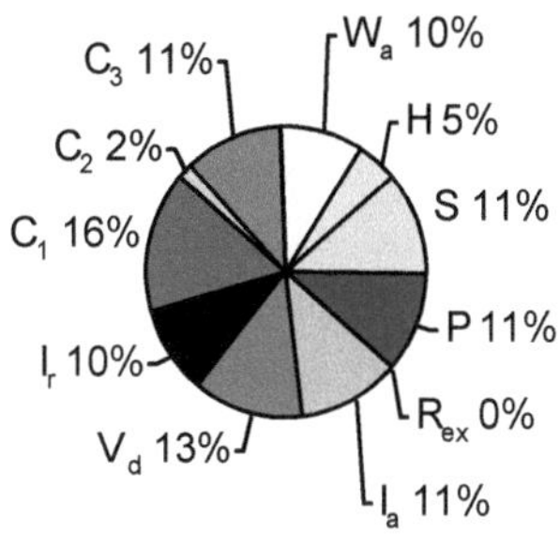

Figure 3. Agent behaviour in learning Stage II

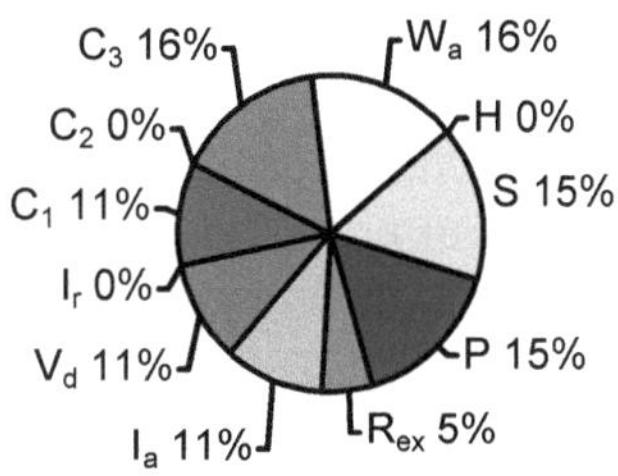

Figure 4. Agent behaviour in learning Stage III

A comparative study of these learning stages shows a higher percentage of C_2 (constructive learning) in Stage I (9%, compared with 2% for Stage II and 0% for Stage III). This means that the system is in the initial stage of learning – constructing new memories. There are no high-level behaviours (I_r, H, C_3) and much higher percentages of sensation (S) and perception (P) in the initial stage of learning (Stage I). The system's behaviours are more low-level oriented at this point, due to the lack of resources in generalization. With conceptual knowledge being formed at the beginning of Stage II, the system manifests a reflective behaviour in which it revisits its experience to reactivate and make hypotheses.

As illustrated in Figure 3, the agent's reflection-related behaviours, such as H and I_r contribute to 5% and 10% of its overall behaviours, compared to 0% in other stages. The salient feature for Stage III is that the system demonstrates a higher percentage of reflexive behaviour (5% against 0%) than those in the other two stages. Stages I, II and III are similar in reaction, validation and grounding related behaviours, such as I_a V_d and W_a, because the system has similar proportions of grounded reactive experience. This three-stage taxonomy can be explained by the internal structures created in the experiment. Conceptual knowledge is learned at task 6, which is the grounded commonality over the incrementally gathered perceptual experience (from the CIAC neural network). This concept enables the system to create hypotheses and therefore contributes to the system's reflective behaviour at Stage II. At the end of task 14, the experience for the linear optimization problem is so strong that it is on the threshold of producing the reflexive behaviour in Stage III.

4.2. A COMPARISON TEST

In this test, we investigate the performance of three systems: a static system, a reactive system and a situated system, in learning to recognize design optimization problems. The design scenario of Test 1 is adopted. A static system can only use the predefined knowledge to predict a design task. A reactive system can use *a priori*knowledge to respond to an environmental cue. It can also learn via constructive learning, provided it encounters a new design problem. A situated system not only employs its existing experience to react, it also reflects using the hypotheses created based on the accumulated conceptual knowledge. The performance is defined as the correctness of the system's response to an environmental cue, which predicts an interaction situation, and hence assists the applied design task. We use prediction success rate (P_s) to measure the overall performance of a system in this test:

$$P_s = \frac{Number\ of\ correct\ predictions}{Total\ numbers\ of\ predictions\ in\ the\ test}$$

The prediction success rate corresponds to the percentage of correctly predicted examples over total test examples. Based on the results measured from this test, we can calculate prediction success rates for each system. A situated system produces a prediction success rate of *0.80*, followed by the rates of *0.67* for the reactive system and *0.33* for the static system respectively. We conjecture the reason for this is the ability of a situated system to generalize across observations and subsequently to deduce explanations for environmental changes. It is also noted that the agent uses the conceptual knowledge to hypothesize and reflect from Task 10, thus providing better performance from that point.

5. Conclusion

Experimental results show that the implemented system can learn new concepts through its use in interactions in design optimization. Another finding is that the agent can develop adaptive knowledge structures through constructing a memory, during which the agent coordinates the system's experience and environmental context in a situated manner. The system exhibits adaptive behaviours to this end. Compared to a static system based on pre-defined knowledge and a reactive agent which learns by the constructive learning, this situated agent-based design interaction tool performs better. In summary, the approach plays potential roles in enhancing design effectiveness through introducing mechanisms that enable a computer-aided design tool to adapt based on its experience of its use in a dynamic design process. The framework developed here may also lay foundations for future research into adaptive and personalized design tools.

Acknowledgements

This work was supported by a CRC-CI Scholarship, a University of Sydney Sesqui R&D grant and partly carried out at the Tasmanian ICT Centre which is jointly funded by the Australian Government through the Intelligent Island Program and the CSIRO. The Intelligent Island Program is administered by the Tasmanian Department of Economic Department.

References

Balachandran, MB: 1988, *A Model for Knowledge-Based Design Optimization*, PhD Thesis, University of Sydney, Sydney.

Beer, RD: 1997, The dynamics of adaptive behaviour: A research program, *Robotics and Autonomous Systems* **20**: 257-289.

Boer, B and Canamero, D: 1999, Situated learning in autonomous agents, *in* J Joan Bliss, R Saljo and P Light (eds), *Learning Sites: Social and Technological Resources for Learning*, Pergamon, Amsterdam, pp. 236-248.

Bradshaw, J (ed.): 1996, *Software Agents,* MIT Press, Cambridge.

Clancey, W: 1997, *Situated Cognition: On Human Knowledge and Computer Representations,* Cambridge University Press, Cambridge.

Gero, JS: 1998, Conceptual designing as a sequence of situated acts, *in* I Smith (eds), *Artificial Intelligence in Structural Engineering*, Springer, Berlin, pp. 165-177.

Gero, JS: 1999, Constructive memory in design thinking, *Design Thinking Research Symposium: Design Representation,* MIT, Cambridge, pp. 29-35.

Gero, JS: 2003, Design tools as situated agents that adapt to their use, *in* W Dokonal and U Hirschberg (eds), *eCAADe21*, eCAADe, Graz University of Technology, pp. 177-180.

Gero, JS and Fujii, H: 2000, A computational framework for concept formation in a situated design agent, *Knowledge-Based Systems* **13**(6): 361-368.

Gero, JS and Kannengiesser, U: 2006, A framework for situated design optimization, *Design & Decision Support Systems 2006*, Springer-Verlag, Berlin, in press,

Gero, JS and Peng, W: 2004, A situated agent-based design assistant, *CAADRIA 2004*, Yonsei University Press, Korea, pp. 145-157.

Lieberman, H: 2001, Introduction, *in* H Lieberman (eds), *Your Wish is My Command: Programming by Example*, Morgan Kaufmann, San Francisco, pp. 1-7.

Liew, P-S: 2004, *A Constructive Memory System for Situated Design Agents*, University of Sydney, Sydney.

Maes, P: 1994, Agents that reduce work and information overload, *Communications of the ACM* **37**: 31-40.

Maher, ML and Gero, JS: 2002, Agent models of 3D virtual worlds, *ACADIA 2002: Thresholds,* California State Polytechnic University, Pomona, California State Polytechnic University, Pomona, pp. 127-138.

McClelland, JL: 1981, Retrieving general and specific information from stored knowledge of specifics, *Proceedings of the Third Annual Meeting of the Cognitive Science Society,* Erlbaum, Hillsdale, NJ, pp. 170-172.

Peng, W and Gero, J: 2006, Using a constructive interactive activation and competition neural network to construct a situated agent's experience, *PRICAI 2006: Trends in Artificial Intelligence, Ninth Pacific Rim International Conference on Artificial Intelligence*, Springer, Guilin, pp. 21-30.

Radford, AD and Gero, JS: 1988, *Design by Optimization in Architecture and Building,* Van Nostrand Reinhold, New York.

Reffat, R and Gero, JS: 2000, Computational situated learning in design, *in* JS Gero (eds), *Artificial Intelligence in Design'00,* Kluwer Academic Publishers, Dordrecht, pp. 589-610.

Reich, Y: 1993, The development of BRIDGER: A methodological study of research in the use of machine learning in design, *Artificial Intelligence in Engineering* **8**(3): 165-181.

Reich, Y and Fenves, S: 1991, The formation and use of abstract concepts in design, *in* D Fisher, M Pazzani and P Langley (eds), *Concept Formation: Knowledge and Experience in Unsupervised Learning*, Morgan Kaufmann, San Mateo, CA, pp. 323-353.

Rutherford, JH and Maver, TW: 1994, Knowledge-based design support, *in* G Carrara and YE Kalay (eds), *Knowledge-Based Computer-Aided Architectural Design*, Elsevier Science, Amsterdam, The Netherlands, pp. 243-267.

Schön, D: 1983, *The Reflective Practitioner: How Professionals Think in Action,* Basic Books, London.

Simon, HA: 1983, Why should machine learn, *Machine Learning: An Artificial Intelligence Approach,* Springer-Verlag, Berlin, pp. 25-37.

Suchman, LA: 1987, *Plans and Situated Actions: The problem of human-machine communication,* Cambridge University Press, Cambridge.

INTEGRATING ADVANCED SHADER TECHNOLOGY FOR REALISTIC ARCHITECTURAL VIRTUAL REALITY VISUALISATION

The impact of advanced shaders on real-time rendering performance

TAN BENG KIANG AND DANIEL HII JUN CHUNG
National University of Singapore, Singapore

Abstract. The gaming industry plays a pivotal role in creating real-time advanced shaders nowadays. With better and more affordable computer hardware, shaders are beginning to be used in other non-gaming softwares. The virtual reality visualization tools used by the architectural designers can benefit from this. This paper investigates the impact of real-time shaders on the performance of architectural virtual reality visualization of 3D models and provides a guide for architectural users to decide the optimal number of shaders to use based on the size of the model.

1. Introduction

Traditional shaders have been around for some time but the advanced ones or sometimes called programmable shaders are still in the process of development with new upgrades. They have been used heavily in 3D games with the help of the evolution of the new generation graphics processing unit (GPU). Since the introduction of the first consumer-level 3D hardware accelerated graphics card, the 3Dfx Voodoo in 1995, real-time 3D graphics have become a true reality (Sebastien 2004). By 1999, the ability to perform transform and lighting of vertices on the graphics accelerator becomes available, hence, advanced shaders were first used. (Möller 2002)

The beauty of advanced shaders is the ability to simulate how the material should look and behave as close as it is in the real world. Surface qualities such as reflection, refraction, specularity, glossiness, bumpiness and how these surfaces react to light and shadow real-time give them more realism than the traditional shaders. The traditional shaders such as the flat, Gouraud, Phong, Lambertian and Blinn lack the ability to constantly change in real-time. They merely help bring out the qualities of a material through a

A Dong, A Vande Moere & JS Gero (eds), CAADFutures'07, 431–443.

flat 2D texture which is basically fixed and dead. These make some materials like those with refraction, reflection and water movement not possible to be rendered real-time. Advance shaders are programmable because you can adjust how it changes through time as well as having repetitions. Therefore, it is much more versatile and flexible as well as ease of maintenance (Fernando 2004) compared to the traditional shaders. Therefore, they can produce stunningly realistic images (Lastra 1995).

Advanced shaders are at present still quite exclusive because they are meant to be designed for specific platforms or specific softwares only according to the alterations of the programmer. There is a fair amount of work to go into developing a communication layer that supports shaders (Fernando 2004). Therefore, the process of importing and exporting the advanced shaders from one software to another is quite restricted and limited for an architect who is not a programmer. They are constrained by the number of choices available in the shader library of the software. Even though there are softwares like AMD Inc./ATI RenderMonkey™ and nVidia® Corp. FX Composer™ in the market to help design and develop shaders, they still require programming skills to transfer them into other programs. They were meant for games in the first place and even games programmers have to accommodate the new architecture in these shaders for next generation games (Penflod 2002).

The availability of these shaders enables architects to use them for real-time architectural virtual reality visualization to increase the realism of materials which cannot be done with traditional shaders. This will definitely bring out the real design intentions to be communicated accurately as desired and avoid frustration of flat and fake rendering by traditional shaders' limitations. Audience viewing the presentation will also be able to make believe something closer to what it should be in real life. A good example will be a river being applied a water texture map versus a river being applied a water shader which we can control its wave speed, length, height, width, colour and intensity. In real-time visualization, that water will move naturally like how it should in real-life. We can apply a looped movie file of a river flowing but again it has very limited control for adjustment unlike what the advanced shaders can provide and when viewed from some angles you will definitely know that it is a flat movie file applied on a surface.

Advanced shaders are available under the OpenGL and DirectX API (Application Programming Interface). An API functions to communicate with the hardware to tell it which geometry to render and how it is rendered (Sebastien 2004). There are two main types of shaders, namely vertex and pixel shaders. In real-time rendering, vertex shaders manipulate geometry (vertices and their attributes) and pixel shaders manipulate rendered pixels (Luke 2006). Both work hand in hand to generate a shader. They give the developer a lot more freedom to do things that real-time applications have never experience before (Engel 2002). The Cg (C for Graphics) language is based on both the syntax and the philosophy of C language (Mark 2003). Its rendering is API independent and this allows it to operate under DirectX or OpenGL. Figure 1 illustrates the relationship of the most famous advanced shader languages in the market currently.

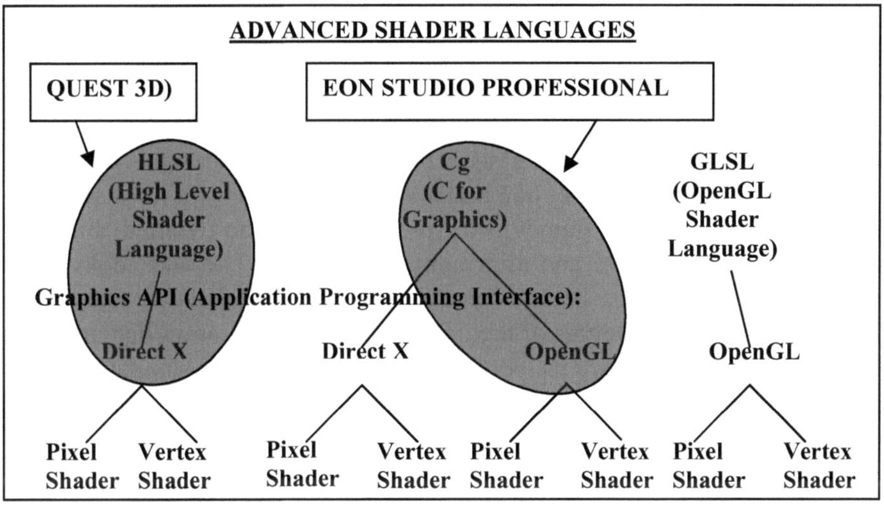

Figure 1. The advanced shader language hierarchy

We create and edit our models in Autodesk® 3ds Max® 8 before exporting to both platforms namely EON Reality Inc™ EON Studio (with EON Professional) Version 5.5.0 (Build 1134) Beta1 and Act-3D™ B.V. Quest3D™ 3.6 to run the architectural virtual reality visualization. The advanced shaders in Quest3D™ uses the DirectX graphics API (Application Programming Interface) written in HLSL (High Level Shader Language) while the ones in EON Studio (with EON Professional) uses the OpenGL graphics API written in Cg.

2. Objective

The research done so far on shaders are by computer graphics scientists who are interested to compare the efficiency of the different shader algorithms available, their memory usage, impact to frame rate, parallel or non-parallel units, unified or non-unified shader models (Moya 2005) and the possibility to optimise performance by having graphics hardware run a programmable graphics pipeline specifically (Proudfoot 2001). However, architects and architectural students are interested in applying shaders for realistic visualisation and for presentation to clients. Their concern is to do it with the least effort and in the shortest time. When creating 3D models and visualisation, models can get too complex and slow to navigate in real-time. It is often a painful trial and error method to get a model to have smooth navigation in real-time.

There is little research done on optimal shaders to use in an architecture model before real-time performance deteriorates. Thus, this paper aims to measure performance and establish a guide to help users predict beforehand the performance of real-time navigation for the model they have. It will help users plan their usage of shaders in a scene and plan how complex a model they could create.

To demonstrate the difference between a model with shaders and without, we applied metal and water Cg shaders on an unbuilt project – the Cloud Forest Biosphere designed by the architect, Geoffrey Bawa. The shaders are applied on the lake, the frames and truss system of the pyramid. Figure 2 shows the project before and after applying shaders. The lake looks more realistic and the trusses on the pyramid have more definition and depth. Table 1 shows the properties of them both and it clearly shows that applying Cg shaders will slow down the performance of the real-time simulation.

The experiment in this paper seeks to find out the extent of the impact of the Cg shaders on the performance of real-time rendering. Real-time

Figure 2. Cloud Forest Biosphere without and with shaders

TABLE 1. Cloud forest biosphere without and with Cg shaders

	Without Cg shader	With Cg shader
Frame Rate (fps)	12	7.1
Total Triangles	347,928	347,928
Triangles with Shaders	0	168,118
Amount of Shaders	0	2
Percentage Applied (%)	0	48.32
Texture Memory (Kb)	10528	11243
Vertex Memory (Kb)	6338	8794

rendering means maintaining continuous frame replacements at minimum 6 frames per second, where a sense of interactivity starts to grow (Möller 2002). This refresh rate is fast enough for our eyes not to detect the arrival of each frame to replace the one before. Lagging will be felt when a simulation runs below 6 frames per second. Thus, any rate above 6 is preferred and when shaders are applied, the aim is to have the frame rate maintained at above 6. In this paper we focus on the impact of Cg shaders. The performance of real-time rendering in the experiment is measured for frame rate, vertex memory and texture memory used.

3. Experiment

3.1. HARDWARE AND SOFTWARE

The experiment was conducted in a visualization lab with a 4.5m × 2.5m flat rear projection screen projected by 4 bright high-resolution projectors. We used a PC desktop machine that supports graphic application (Intel® Pentium® 4 Dual Xeon™ 3.2 GHz; 2GB system RAM; Leadtek 256MB nVidia® Quadro FX300G graphic accelerator card[1]; Microsoft® Windows® XP Professional Version 5.1.2600 Service Pack 2 Build 2600. The virtual reality software is EON Studio Professional running on OpenGL 2.0.[2]

3.2. SCOPE AND CONSTANTS

We acknowledged that many factors such as number of objects, triangles, textures, vertices, lights, particle systems, collision objects, and interactivity scripts can affect performance in VR visualization. Texture memory will be used heavily if there are numerous textures in the scene. All surfaces in the models used in the experiment are applied with standard DDS (DirectDraw Surface) format textures. This is the most efficient format and uses the least memory in comparison with common texture formats such as jpeg, png and targa (Tan & Hii 2007). Vertex memory will be used heavily if the there is a large number of vertices in the scene (vertex memory normally increases if triangles count increases). In an earlier research, we have identified three significant variables – triangle count, geometry count and number of textures and the extent they affect real-time navigation (Tan & Hii 2007). This paper focuses solely on the impact of advanced shaders in affecting

---

[1] The graphic card can generate 100 million triangles per second and 3.2 billion texels per second tested on a 3.2GHz Pentium® 4 system with driver release 60.60. (Nvidia 2007).

[2] EON Cg implementation is compiled against NVidia Cg Runtime version 1.2 with graphics cards with drivers that support ARB_fragment_program and ARB_vertex_program OpenGL extensions.

performance during VR visualization. In the experiment, all other variables remain constant and the only changing variable is the number of advance shader applied and the percentage of surfaces in a model applied with shaders. Nothing else was added or altered in the model and only mouse input is used in our system to interact with the scene visualized.

The models to be used for the experiment are of sizes and complexity that is of a real world architecture project. To establish what range of architecture projects to be used in the experiment, we compared our collection of 3D models of different scale architecture projects and of different geometric forms (see Figures 3 and 4).

1. Single storey office building - 85,240 triangles,
2. A fort with many single storey structures on a hilly terrain, Fort Serapong - 204,424 triangles,
3. 4 pyramidal structures with lake, contour and landscape, Bawa's Cloud Forest Biosphere - 347,928 triangles,
4. a 14-storey office building, Mahaweli - 988,368 triangles,
5. Chinese historical buildings in an ancient town, Chang'An Ming De - 2,296,030 triangles,
6. Urban scale site with many blocks of dormitories, Warren Hostel - 3,096,786 triangles

A 3D CAD model of a small building may consist of 50,000 triangles or 500,000 triangles depending on how detail the model is. Therefore, the size of projects in terms of floor area and volume is not a good measure of model size. We concluded that we should categorise model size in terms of number of triangles.

Figure 3. Fort Serapong and WarrenHostel

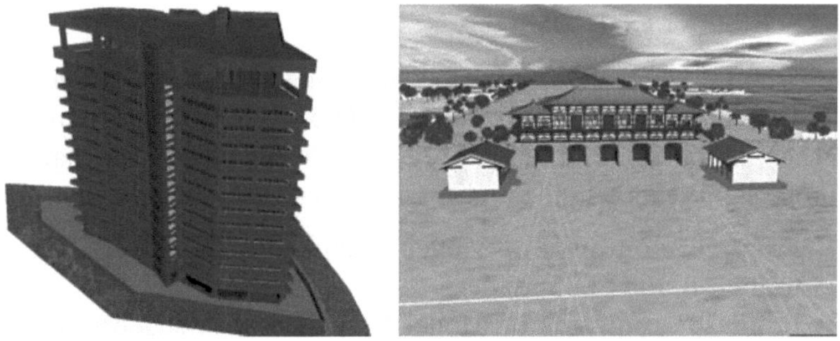

Figure 4. Mahaweli and Chang'an Ming De

The advanced shaders experiments were divided into the usage from 1 to 5 shaders per simulation run. For each simulation run, increasing percentage of the triangles in the scene were applied with shaders in increment of 5%, 10%, 20%, 50%, 80% and 100%. The corresponding frame rate, vertex and texture memory used were recorded. For fairness, we use the same model of Cloud Forest Biosphere so that it will be consistent. We added or subtracted model parts from it depending on the model size range required. We categorise model size in terms of number of triangles.

The range of model size is 10,000 to 2,000,000 triangles and 6 model sizes were used i.e. Model A (20,014 triangles), Model B (101,832 triangles), Model C (234,978 triangles), Model D (1,009,740 triangles), Model E (1,517,200 triangles) and Model F (2,021,360 triangles). From our collection of 3D models, we are confident that this range of models represents a good range of architectural projects from a simple building to an urban scale development. The intention is also to consider all the range of materials possible to be applied with advanced shaders. The five shaders used in the experiments are: 1. Chromatic Glass; 2. Fabric; 3. Granite; 4. Wood; and 5. Water.

4. Results

The experiment shows clearly that the advanced shaders will slow down the performance of the simulation as expected. If used extensively in huge scenes, they are resource intensive to render, consuming a lot of processing power. However, they are still quite reasonable in small to mid range architecture projects. For instance, in the experiment, all models with less than 1,000,000 triangles (for 1 to 5 shaders) meet a real-time performance of 6 frames per second. They start to impact the frame rate critically when the number of triangles is beyond 1,000,000. Below are the details.

4.1. EXPERIMENT OUTCOME

Table 2 shows the results from the experiments of the three larger models of Model D (1,009,740 triangles), Model E (1,517,200 triangles) and Model F (2,021,360 triangles). From the test results, we can clearly see that the frame rate drops significantly at the higher triangle counts shown below:

1. From 50% onwards of Model D applied with shaders (i.e. 504,870 triangles), for 1 to 5 shaders
2. From 20% onwards of Model E applied with shaders (i.e. 303,440 triangles), for 1 to 5 shaders
3. From 20% onwards of Model F applied with shaders (i.e. 404,272 triangles), for 1 to 5 shaders

TABLE 2. Simulations with frame rate below 6
The shader column represents the amount of triangles applied with it. The tex mem column represents texture memory and the Ver Mem column represents the vertex memory with both calculated in Kb

1 Shader				
Percent	Shader	Frame Rate	Tex Mem	Ver Mem
50%	504870	4.3	1184	9849
80%	807792	2.7	1568	13454
100%	1009740	2.2	1568	12233
20%	303440	4	256	30812
50%	758600	2.3	256	40965
80%	1213760	1.5	256	48475
100%	1517200	1.2	256	55836
20%	404272	4	640	25218
50%	1010680	1.9	640	30711
80%	1617088	1.2	640	45737
100%	2021360	0.95	640	53891

2 Shaders				
Percent	Shader	Frame Rate	Tex Mem	Ver Mem
50%	504870	4.4	1312	12901
80%	807792	2.6	1152	9349
100%	1009740	2.2	1184	15285
20%	303440	4.45	2304	29848
50%	758600	2.2	2304	40965
80%	1213760	1.45	2304	48475
100%	1517200	1.2	2304	56090
20%	404272	4.05	1152	25218
50%	1010680	2	1152	30711
80%	1617088	1.3	1152	45737
100%	2021360	1	1152	53891

3 Shaders				
Percent	Shader	Frame Rate	Tex Mem	Ver Mem
50%	504870	4.65	2029	13108
80%	807792	3.25	2029	15400
100%	1009740	2.7	1696	18336
20%	303440	4.8	3181	30051
50%	758600	2.7	3181	40965
80%	1213760	1.7	3181	48475
100%	1517200	1.4	3181	56090
20%	404272	4.15	2029	31043
50%	1010680	2.35	2029	30711
80%	1617088	1.6	2029	45737
100%	2021360	1.5	2029	53891

4 Shaders				
Percent	Shader	Frame Rate	Tex Mem	Ver Mem
80%	807792	4	2029	22651
100%	1009740	3.25	2029	24482
20%	303440	5.65	3181	30051
50%	758600	3.1	3181	40965
80%	1213760	2.2	3181	48475
100%	1517200	2	3181	56090
20%	404272	5	2029	30376
50%	1010680	2.5	2029	30711
80%	1617088	2	2029	45737
100%	2021360	1.45	2029	53891

5 Shaders				
Percent	Shader	Frame Rate	Tex Mem	Ver Mem
80%	807792	3.95	2029	22651
100%	1009740	3.4	2029	24482
20%	303440	5.75	3181	30051
50%	758600	3.25	3181	40965
80%	1213760	2.4	3181	48958
100%	1517200	2	2029	56090
20%	404272	5.25	2029	31709
50%	1010680	3	2029	30711
80%	1617088	1.95	2029	45274
100%	2021360	1.5	2029	53891

(light shading)	Model D (1,009,740 tri)
(medium shading)	Model E (1,517,200 tri)
(dark shading)	Model F (2,021,360 tri)

It is very clear that the frame rate does not change much with the increase in shaders from 1 to 5 shaders in the scene. Therefore, it is proven that if there are 5 shaders and less used in a scene, triangle count rather than shaders affects the performance most.

4.2. CORRELATIONS

A bivariate correlation, Table 3, is calculated to test the strength of the relationship between two variables without considering the interference from other variables that may cause the relationship between the two variables tested. From Table 3, we can see all the 7 variables are tested. The variables are:

1. percentagetri: percentage of triangles from 5-100%
2. framerate: frame rate during simulation
3. texmem: texture memory consumed
4. vermem: vertex memory consumed
5. shadertri: amount of triangles applied with triangles
6. shaderamount: the amount of shaders used from 1-5
7. modelsize: the size of the 6 models from Model A to Model F

TABLE 3. Correlations of all variables

Correlations

		percentagetri	framerate	texmem	vermem	shadertri	shaderamount	modelsize
percentagetri	Pearson Correlation	1	[redacted]					
	Sig. (2-tailed)		[redacted]					
	N	180	[redacted]					
framerate	Pearson Correlation	-.344**	1	[redacted]				
	Sig. (2-tailed)	.000		[redacted]				
	N	180	180	[redacted]				
texmem	Pearson Correlation	.037	-.101	1	[redacted]			
	Sig. (2-tailed)	.618	.177		[redacted]			
	N	180	180	180	[redacted]			
vermem	Pearson Correlation	.161*	-.513**	.041	1	.593**	[redacted]	
	Sig. (2-tailed)	.031	.000	.587		.000	[redacted]	
	N	180	180	180	180	180	[redacted]	
shadertri	Pearson Correlation	.561**	-.562**	.055	.593**	1	.000	[redacted]
	Sig. (2-tailed)	.000	.000	.461	.000		1.000	[redacted]
	N	180	180	180	180	180	180	[redacted]
shaderamount	Pearson Correlation	.000	-.021	.704**	-.057	.000	1	.000
	Sig. (2-tailed)	1.000	.785	.000	.445	1.000		1.000
	N	180	180	180	180	180	180	180
modelsize	Pearson Correlation	.000	-.754**	.083	.676**	.642**	.000	1
	Sig. (2-tailed)	1.000	.000	.268	.000	.000	1.000	
	N	180	180	180	180	180	180	180

**. Correlation is significant at the 0.01 level (2-tailed).

*. Correlation is significant at the 0.05 level (2-tailed).

From the results, we can see the correlation coefficient between frame rate and model size to be highest at -0.754. The second highest goes to the correlation coefficient between texture memory and shader amount at 0.704. Both are correlated at p-value of less than 0.01 which means they are statistically significant. They have strong negative and positive correlation respectively. This means the bigger the model size, the lower the frame rate. Another conclusion is that the more shaders we have in the scene, the more texture memory will be consumed.

4.3. ALL COMBINATIONS

We plot a graph (see Figure 5) to represent all 5 shaders. We took 6 readings (5, 10, 20, 50, 80, 100%) per model for all 6 models from 1 to 5 shaders. This means a total of 180 combinations. This is to get a general fit for all the shaders against the amount of triangles. The high R Square value of 0.901 in Table 4 confirms that the frame rate is highly correlated with the triangles count. On average, real-time navigation can still be maintained at the limit frame rate of 6fps for a model that has 342,195 triangles applied with up to 5 shaders.

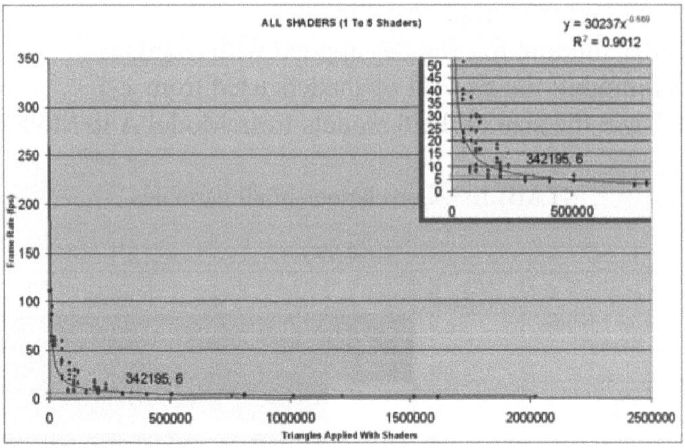

Figure 5. Frame rate against triangles count graph

TABLE 4. All combinations graph fit result

Model Summary and Parameter Estimates

Dependent Variable: framerate

	Model Summary					Parameter Estimates	
Equation	R Square	F	df1	df2	Sig.	Constant	b1
Power	.901	1624.095	1	178	.000	30237.381	-.669

The independent variable is actualtri.

4.4. EACH SHADER'S LIMIT

After that, we plot a graph for each shader amount to see the trend for every one of them separately. All the trend types are power graphs with R Square value of 0.8982 and above, which confirm that they fit the formula quite well. From there, we can find the limit of triangles count to be applied with shaders at frame rate of 6fps for 1 to 5 shaders, for instance, a model of 338,350 triangles can have 3 shaders applied 100% to it and still able to be maintain the threshold frame rate of 6fps in real-time (see Figure 6).

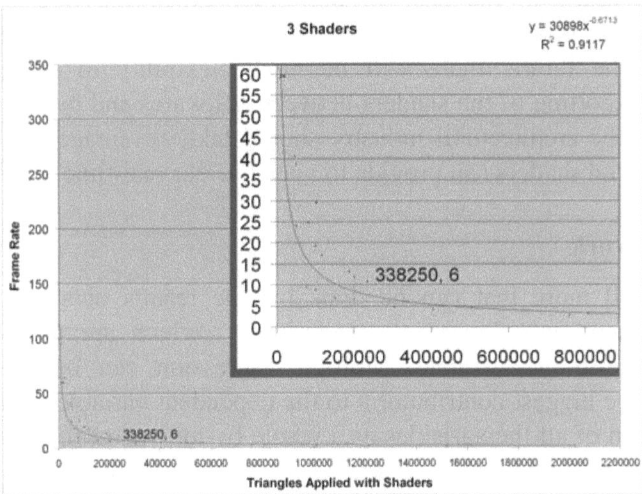

Figure 6. Frame rate against triangles count graph for 3 shaders

5. Conclusion

The results show clearly that the amount of triangles is the biggest factor in slowing down the frame rate and not the advanced shaders. This means that advanced shaders are not a burden to the simulation to the extent that we need to be extremely careful in using them. Three main conclusions are:

1. We can use shaders extensively (i.e. 100% of the model can be applied with shaders) for a model size range of up to 300,000 to 400,000 triangles before performance suffers (Figure 5).
2. The number of shaders (e.g. water, glass, etc) used in the scene will only affect the performance if more than 50% of a model of size up to 1,000,000 triangles is applied with shaders as shown in Table 2.
3. The number of shaders, up to 5 types in a scene, will not make much difference to the performance as shown clearly in Table 2 above.

The result serves as a guideline for architectural users who want to use shaders in their scenes. The table and graph (Table 2 and Figure 5) tell the users the impact shaders will have on the simulation from the number of shaders used, from the number of triangles (from small to big scale models) and from the percentage of the model being applied with shaders. All these data serve as a good reference for them to determine and plan the usage of advanced shaders in the scene. They can decide the right number of advanced shaders to use based on the size of the 3D model they have. And shaders can be more effectively and optimally applied in architecture VR visualizations.

Advanced shaders are here to stay and will be expected to get more popular in usage in the near future. Their capabilities are expected to improve constantly with the flourishing games market. The expectation is that in the future, there will be more flexibility of integrating and importing/exporting of the shaders between softwares and between different platforms. The architectural industry should take advantage of the realism these advanced shaders can provide to visualise our real-time scenes.

6. Future Work

There is still more that can be done for the results obtained. What we determined are only bivariate correlations – which are the relationship between one-to-one variable. Multiple regression can be calculated to determine the biggest contributor/s to the dependent variable (frame rate) in consideration of all the variables as a whole by looking at their coefficients. The formula of Y and the Xs generated can be used for users' calculations of the impact of each variable against frame rate. Apart from that, future experiments can be done further on the HLSL-DirectX API (Application Programming Interface) to see how the shaders perform. We can then compare the two interfaces and determine which is aesthetically more realistic and performs much better with shaders. We can identify the pros and cons from there so we can take advantage of the strengths and weaknesses of both platforms. The scope we covered is up to 5 shaders and within the capabilities of the hardware as well as the versions of software and the OpenGL version we currently have. More experiments can be done beyond that as the usage of advanced shaders become more common in the future especially in game engines.

Acknowledgements

The authors would like to thank Chew Chun Boon, Chris Hee Jee Kwang and Siow Ming Khang who contributed to the preparation and the completion of the experiments, Heng Chye Kiang, Stephen K. Wittkopf and John N. Miksic for permission to use the models.

References

Boeing, A: 2004, *The DirectX 8 Pixel Shader*: CFXweb. Retrieved 4 January 2007 from http://www.cfxweb.net/modules.php?name=News&file=print&sid=1305.

Engel, W: 2002, *Introduction to Shader Programming, Fundamentals of Vertex Shaders*: GameDev.net. Retrieved 2 January 2007 from the World Wide Web: http://www.gamedev.net/reference/articles/article1496.asp.

Fernando, R (ed): 2004, *GPU gems: programming techniques, tips, and tricks for real-time graphics*, Addison-Wesley, Boston, MA.

Haines, E: 2006, An Introductory Tour of Interactive Rendering, *near-final draft, 9/23/05, IEEE CG&A January/February 2006*, pp. 76-87.

Lastra, A, Molnar, S, Olano, M, Wang, Y: 1995, Real-time programmable shading, *Proceedings of the 1995 ACM Symposium on Interactive 3D Graphics,* pp. 59-66.

Luke, A: 2006, *3D games textures*, Elsevier Focal Press, Amsterdam; Boston.

Mark, WR, Glanville RS, Akeley, K, Kilgard, MJ: 2003, Cg: a system for programming graphics hardware in a C-like language, *Proceedings of ACM SIGGRAPH 2003*, pp. 896-907.

Moya, V, Gonzalez, C, Roca, J, Fernandez, A, Espasa, R: 2005, Shader Performance Analysis on a Modern GPU Architecture, *Proceedings of the 38th Annual IEEE/ACM International Symposium on Microarchitecture (MICRO'05)*, pp. 355-364.

Möller, T: 2002, *Real-time rendering*, AK Peters, Natick, Mass.

Nvidia: 2007, *Nvidia Quadro FX Product Comparison*. Retrieved 30 March 2007 from the World Wide Web: http://www.nvidia.com/object/IO_11761.html.

Olano, M, Akeley, K, Hart, J, Heidrich, W, McCool, M, Mitchell, J, Rost R: 2005, *SIGGRAPH Real-Time Shading Course 1 Notes*.

Proudfoot, K, Mark, WR, Tzvetkov, S and Hanrahan, P: 2001, A Real-Time Procedural Shading System for Programmable Graphics Hardware, *Proceedings of the ACM SIGGRAPH 28th Annual Conference on Computer Graphics and Interactive Techniques*, pp. 159-170.

Penfold, D: 2002, *Vertex Shaders and Pixel Shaders*: Tom's Hardware. Retrieved 2 January 2007 from http://www.tomshardware.com/2002/01/16/vertex_shaders_and_pixel_shaders.

Sebastien, SL: 2004, *Shaders for game programmers and artists*, Thomson/Course Technology, Boston, Mass.

Slater, M, Steed, A and Chrysanthou, Y: 2006, *Computer graphics and virtual environments: from realism to real-tome*, Addison Wesley, Harlow, England.

Tan, BK, Hii, JCD: 2007, *Optimising real-time virtual reality presentation*, CAADRIA 2007: Proceedings of the 12th International Conference on Computer-Aided Architectural Design Research in Asia, Southeast University, Nanjing, China, 19-22 April 2007.

Valient, M: 2001, *3D Engines in games – Introduction*. Retrieved April 2007 from http://pisa.ucsd.edu/cse125/2006/Papers/Introduction_to_3d_Game_Engines.pdf.

BECOMING FUTURISTIC

FROM PASSIVE TO PROACTIVE DESIGN ELEMENTS

Incorporating curious agents into intelligent rooms

MARY LOU MAHER
University of Sydney, Australia

KATHRYN MERRICK
University of Sydney and National ICT Australia, Australia

and

ROB SAUNDERS
University of Sydney, Australia

Abstract. Agent technology has been used as an organising mechanism for software systems that focus on modularity and autonomy. This paper presents two applications that explore the potential of combining agent technologies with physical building design elements to change the nature of the built environment from a passive space to one that proactively engages with its inhabitants. We focus on how these curious places sense the state of the environment and the activities of the humans in the environment and *enhance* the human experience, thus going beyond the concept of *supporting* human activities in traditional approaches to intelligent rooms.

1. Introduction

Agent technology provides a model for an autonomous reasoning entity that senses its environment and determines a response as an action on that environment. Agents have been used as an organising mechanism for software systems that focus on modularity and autonomy (Wooldridge and Jennings 1995). In this paper we go beyond software systems of agents and look at how agent technology can sense and effect physical building design elements, changing the nature of the built environment from a passive environment to one that proactively engages the environment and its

A Dong, A Vande Moere & JS Gero (eds), CAADFutures'07, 447–460.

inhabitants. We focus on how curious places that sense both the state of the environment and the activities of the humans in the environment can *enhance* the human experience, going beyond the concept of *supporting* human activities in traditional approaches to intelligent rooms.

Our basic approach builds on previous work in computational models of curiosity, novelty (Saunders 2001), motivation and learning (Merrick and Maher 2006) in agents. Artificial curiosity is modelled on Berlyne's psychological theory, which states that the most curious sensations are those that are moderately stimulating in terms of their similarity to previously encountered stimuli (Berlyne 1960).

2. Approaches to Intelligent Rooms

The concept of an intelligent room is a physical space for living or working that includes embedded computational power to facilitate or augment the actions of users of the environment as they perform their daily tasks. Intelligent rooms monitor the activities that take place within them using sensors and respond to sensations using effectors in order to exhibit intelligent behaviour and assist users. Sensors may include devices such as motion detectors or pressure pads while effectors may include devices such as lights, projectors or doors.

Research in intelligent rooms can be regarded as a sub-field of ubiquitous computing which aims to integrate computers seamlessly into everyday living. Brooks (1997) and Coen (1998) have argued that intelligent rooms should:

- Adapt to and be useful for ordinary everyday activities,
- Assist the user without requiring the user to attend to them,
- Have a high degree of interactivity,
- Be able to understand the context in which people are trying to use them and behave appropriately. (Kulkarni 2002)

An intelligent room is essentially, as Kulkarni (2002) suggests, an immobile robot. However, the design requirements of an intelligent room differ from those of normal robots in that they are oriented towards maintaining an internal space rather than exploring or manipulating an external environment.

Current agent based approaches to intelligent room design include MIT's intelligent room prototype e21, which facilitates activities via a system called ReBa (Hanssens et al 2002). ReBa is a context handling system that observes a user's actions via the reports of other agents connected to sensors in the room's multi-agent society and uses them to build a higher-level representation of the user's activity. Each activity – such as watching a movie or giving a presentation – has an associated software agent, called a behaviour agent. The behaviour agent responds to a user action and performs a reaction, such as turning on the lights when a user enters the room. Behaviours can form layers based on the order of user actions, acknowledging differences in context such as showing a presentation in a lecture setting versus showing one in an informal meeting. Although ReBa can infer context in this way, it cannot adapt to patterns of usage: to create an entirely new context, ReBa's behaviour agents must be reprogrammed to recognize the user's actions and take an appropriate reaction. It does not self-adapt to new usage patterns.

Other researchers have taken approaches to designing intelligent rooms that are not explicitly agent-based. Both the University of Illinois' Gaia Project (Roman et al. 2002) and Stanford University's Interactive Workspace Project (Johanson et al. 2002) have taken an operating systems approach, developing Active Spaces and Interactive Workspaces respectively, which focus on the role of the physical space as a platform for running applications rather than as a proactive facilitator: in these systems, actions are triggered by the user and behaviours are pre-programmed by the applications developer. Gaia's context service provides the tools for applications developers to create agent-based facilitating applications so the overall model is reactive rather than adaptive.

Our approach to an intelligent room uses an adaptive agent model (Maher et al. 2006). An agent is a system that perceives its environment through sensors and uses some characteristic reasoning process to generate actions using effectors. Agent models correspond well to intelligent rooms as both are described as having sensors for monitoring their environment and effectors for making changes to the environment. A variety of agent models have been developed with different characteristic reasoning processes for mapping sensor input to effector output. These range from simple rule-based reactive agents to complex cognitive agents that try to maintain and reason about an internal model of the world using planning or machine learning algorithms. This raises the question of what kind of agent model is most suitable as a basis for an intelligent room.

In this paper we present two applications that contribute to the development of models for proactive, intelligent rooms as a new kind of building design element. The first is a curious information display that observes the movement of people in the room and tries to attract their attention by learning different information display combinations. The second is a curious researcher that observes the content of the research presentations given in the room and generates its own research presentations that are interesting to the human researchers. From these applications we can draw some conclusions on the type of agent models that can become part of building design elements to transform the built environment from a passive space to a proactive place.

3. Curious Information Display

A curious information display augments physical places by attracting the interest of observers and selecting information to display by being curious and learning about the structure and content of the information it presents. Traditional information displays such as posters and billboards present a fixed image to observers. Recently, digital displays have become a popular means of presenting information. Digital displays allow the amount of information presented to be increased, often by attaching the display to a computer that changes the contents of the display automatically. The full power of a digital display has not yet been realised, with the most common scenario using a database of images and displaying images at random or in a predefined order. In this section we describe agent models that provide the infrastructure for a proactive information display, intended to attract and respond to the people in the room.

In scenarios where the display of digital information is more familiar, such as web-browsers, novel interaction algorithms have been developed to automatically personalise the digital space (Dieterich et al. 1993). Similarly, intelligent tutoring systems use artificial intelligence algorithms to tailor learning material to the individual needs of students (Graesser et al. 2001). Large digital information displays in public spaces have the same capacity for the use of novel techniques to improve the usefulness of the displays. However the public, multi-user nature of these displays calls for new algorithms to improve the ability of such displays to impart information.

This section introduces two models of curious information displays that display information about design, computing, agents, and curiosity. Information on these themes is obtained from a research image database, the

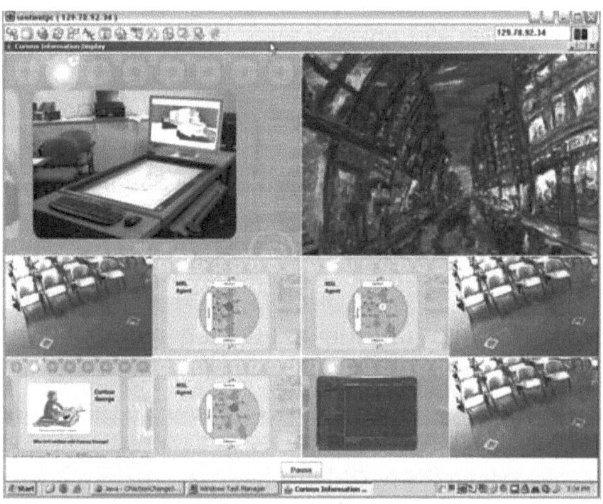

Figure 1. The curious information display

world-wide-web and live webcam images. The display is located in a research seminar room and uses a motivated reinforcement learning agent model (Merrick and Maher 2006) to detect and learn interesting events.

Our curious information display comprises a matrix of displayed information items (IIs). The source of the II may be a definition or an image from a database, an image from the web, or video from a webcam. Each item can be displayed in a 1×1, 2×2 or 4×4 cell as shown in Figure 1. Each cell is referenced as a leaf node and contains an II from one of the three sources based on one of the keywords design, computing, curiosity, or agent.

The curious information display agent is a motivated reinforcement learning agent. Its reasoning process is decomposed into four sub-processes: sensation, motivation, learning and activation, illustrated in Figure 2.

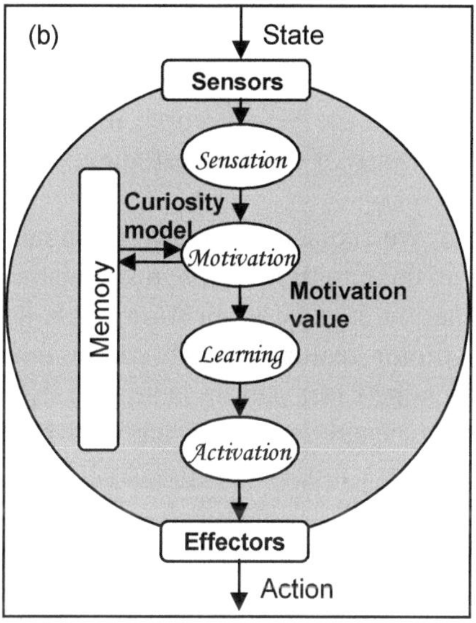

Figure 2. Motivated reinforcement learning agent model used to control the curious information display

The sensation process transforms raw data from the agent's sensors into structures to facilitate further reasoning. These include the observed state of the environment and the change or 'event' between the current and previous observed states. The motivation process reasons about the current observed state, events, and/or a representation of the set of all observed states encountered so far, to produce a motivation value which is used as an intrinsic reward signal for the learning process. The learning process performs a reinforcement learning update to incorporate the previous observed state, action and current rewards into a policy defining how the agent should act. Finally, the activation process selects an action to perform from the learned policy.

The role of the motivation process in motivated reinforcement learning is to provide an intrinsic reward signal to direct the learning process. Firstly, events and observed states are received from the sensation process. Next, a focus of attention structure is used to distinguish between different input stimuli. One or more characteristic motivation functions are then used to compute motivation values. These motivation values are combined using a reward function which computes a single intrinsic reward signal. This value and the observed state are then passed to the reinforcement learning process.

To create displays that are both interesting to their viewers and also interested in the structure and content of the information they display, we modify the Saunders (2001) model of interest to create an intrinsic motivation signal for motivated reinforcement learning. This model first computes the novelty of a stimulus from the environment using an Habituated Self-Organising Map (HSOM) as a focus of attention mechanism. The characteristic motivation functions are Stanley's model of habituation for computing novelty (Stanley 1976) and the Wundt curve for computing interest (Wundt 1910). The computed value of the interest function is used directly as the reward signal.

In this application, we replace the SOM component of the HSOM with K-means clustering as the attention focus mechanism. In environments such as the curious information display application where sequential stimuli share a large number of common features, SOMs can be dragged towards a corner of the state space when the same neuron is repeatedly selected as the winner. In K-Means clustering, a single neuron can move without deforming the entire network, making it a more appropriate attention focus mechanism in this application.

While the motivated reinforcement learning agent model is designed to be independent of any specific reinforcement learning algorithm, certain classes of reinforcement learning are more appropriate in intelligent room applications where learning is continuous rather than episodic. Temporal difference reinforcement learning algorithms such as SARSA (Rummery and Niranjan 1994) and Q-learning (Watkins and Dayan 1992) are the most appropriate in these settings as they do not require a model of the environment from which to learn and learning occurs after each action that is performed by the agent. As the curious information display has a large problem space we use Q-learning combined with neural network function approximation in the learning process in this application.

We implemented two types of curious information display using different aspects of our model of motivation that offer different capabilities. The first uses events to trigger intrinsic motivation while the second uses observed states.

3.1. A CURIOUS INFORMATION DISPLAY USING INTERESTING EVENTS

This curious information display extends static information displays by reasoning about the changes it can make in the structure and content of the IIs it displays and finding interesting patterns of behaviour to modify the structure and content. This aim of this type of display is to achieve sequences of actions that make interesting changes to the structure and content of information items being displayed. To facilitate this, the motivation process reasons about events in order to identify interesting changes in the display.

One weakness of this agent from a visual perspective is its tendency to favour simple behaviours of only one or two actions. The simplest technique for repeating most of the events in the environment is to cause the event, undo it, then repeat it. This 'shortest path' is naturally favoured by reinforcement learning. This phenomenon is a result of a state space with a moderate level of structure and complexity. There is enough complexity to continually stimulate the agent's motivation process to produce high reward and focus learning on new two-step changes, but not enough structure to motivate the emergence of more complex behaviours as has previously been possible in MRL agents in other environments (Merrick and Maher 2006). Further work is required to understand the impact of the state space structure on learning.

The key characteristic of this type of display is its ability to change rapidly between different configurations and different information content. This is because the MRL agent controlling the display is reasoning about events or changes in the display and is thus motivated to continue to change the layout and content of the display either to focus on an interesting change or to search for new changes that might be interesting. This type of curious information display could be useful as an ambient display device for information in pictorial or diagrammatic form which can be understood at a glance, rather than requiring reading. Changes in the display are eye-catching and the movement between different displays holds the viewers' attention by displaying related information.

3.2. A CURIOUS INFORMATION DISPLAY USING INTERESTING OBSERVED STATES

This curious information display extends static information displays by reasoning about the structure and content of the information items it displays and learning to maintain interesting displays. To achieve this, the motivation process reasons about observed states to identify interesting display states.

Observations show that this display appears to react much more quickly to high reward than the previous display. When high reward is encountered the agent freezes the display within an action or two and focuses on that configuration until reward is reduced and boredom triggers exploration.

In contrast to the previous display, this type of curious information display tends to maintain specific configurations of the display for longer periods of time. This type of curious information display could be useful for both diagrammatic and textual information which requires more time for the viewer to understand. Because this display naturally changes more slowly, sudden changes caused by change in the reward signal are highly noticeable.

4. Curious Research Space

Here we introduce the infrastructure for curious research spaces, which extend the intelligent room with agent technologies that actively contribute to research activities. In a curious research space, agents monitor digital research data produced by humans, such as documents and presentations. They extract keywords to model human data and identify relevant new data from documents on the world-wide-web, which is compared to the human research data model using a computational model of interest to select data to be presented. Interesting new data is then automatically formatted into a slide show presentation be presented at research group meetings.

Much research effort has been applied to the development of web-search engines to extract data from the world-wide-web given keywords, resulting in products such as the Google (www.google.com) and Yahoo! (www.yahoo.com) search engines and web-search clustering tools such as the Carrot2 clustering engine (http://demo.carrot2.org/demo-stable/main). Our curious research space makes use of these tools but extends existing technologies by integrating them into a physical environment. The keywords which trigger a search are extracted from research data generated by human activities in a physical space and the large amounts of data which result from a search are reduced and focused using computational models of interest to value search results. The curious research space also contributes to the field of automatic document generation, by using a grammar for producing slide shows automatically.

The agent environment is defined by the people and the research data presented in a single room. The room includes a computer with a database into which human researchers can enter the URL of research data they present at meetings or seminars. The room is also fitted with Bluetooth sensors to provide additional information for the database about the human researchers present when a particular research data item is presented. The agents, like human users, can update the database with new research items or access existing data already in the database. This setup is illustrated in Figure 3.

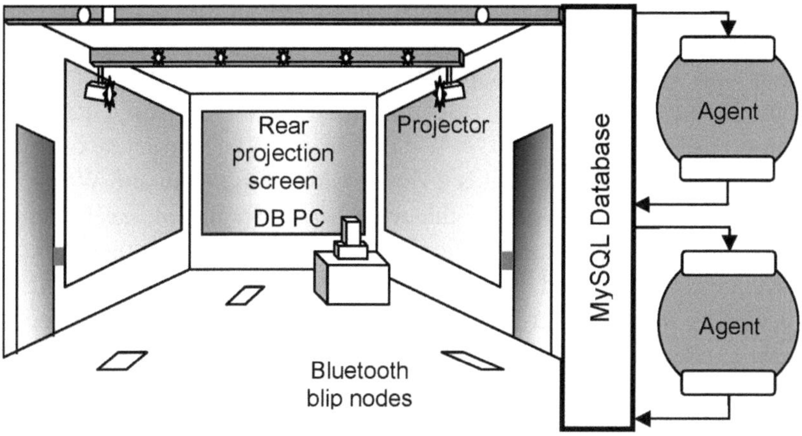

Figure 3. The curious research space agent society and its environment

Two types of agent models are incorporated into the curious research space: reflex agents and motivated agents. Reflex agents monitor their environment using sensors and reason about the environment using two characteristic processes: sensation and activation as shown in Figure 4(a). The sensation process transforms raw sensor data into structures for further reasoning. The activation process uses a set of rules to choose actions based on sensed data. Rules in reflex agents may be implemented in a number of different ways including as a sequence of programmed operations or as a set of if-then rules forming a grammar. We use both approaches for reflex agents in the curious research space: web-search agents use sequences of programmed operations while presentation agents use a grammar comprising rules for effective presentations. The agent architecture provides a uniform interface of sensors and effectors by which these different types of agent interact with a common environment.

Motivated agents incorporate a motivation process into a reflex agent framework as shown in Figure 4(b). The purpose of the motivation process is to influence the selection of actions through computational models of motivation such as interest, curiosity and novelty in order to facilitate more adaptive, emergent behaviour. Motivation is computed based on an agent's experiences, so, unlike standard reflex agents that exhibit the same behaviour in the same situations, motivated agents may exhibit different behaviour in the same situation based on their previous experiences in their environment. This is the key to their adaptive behaviour.

Curious research space agents can make use of two types of sensor and one effector. Different agents use different combinations of these sensors and effectors and use different reasoning processes to trigger effectors based on sensed data. Agents in the curious research space can sense two types of data from their environment: information about research data presented by humans and information about human presence in the physical space via Bluetooth information. The research data sensor senses URLs in the database, uses PDFbox (http://www.pdfbox.org/) to extract text from the referenced document and creates a word vector (Raghavan and Wong 1986). Word vectors contain a list of the words in a document, excluding stop-words like 'the' and 'and', together with a count of the number of occurrences of each word. The word vector, document title, URL and author are passed to the agent for further reasoning.For example, a word vector for the title of this section might look like:

<curious:1><research:1><space:1>

The Bluetooth sensor monitors human presence in the physical meeting room by monitoring the presence of Bluetooth devices. This allows agents to reason not only about research data, but about the people to whom it may be relevant.

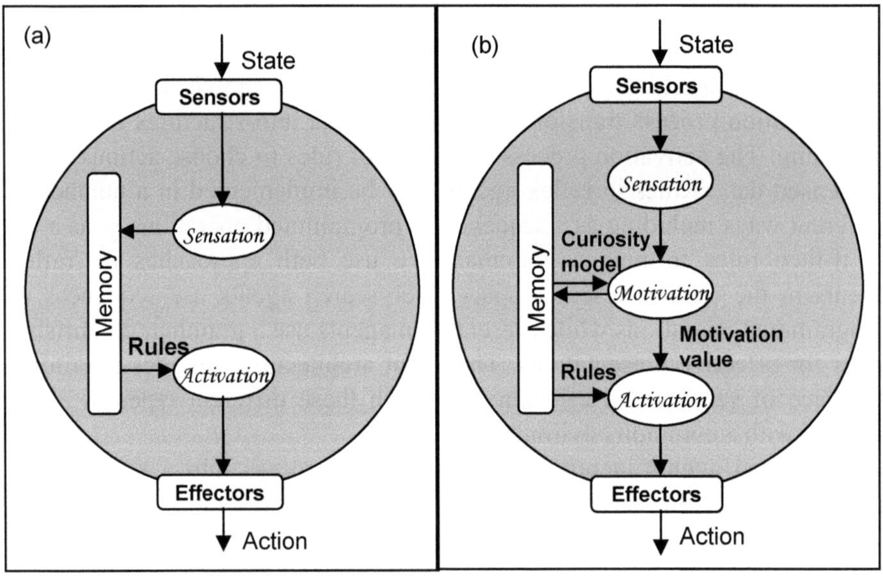

Figure 4. (a) Reflex agents and (b) motivated agents

4.1. WEB-SEARCH AGENTS

Web search agents are reflex agents that sense human research data and search for new, related data using existing web-search tools. They use research data sensors and research data effectors. The key difference between these agents and existing web-search tools is that key-words used in the search are extracted automatically from human research data associated with the physical environment. We have experimented with two different web-search agents using different approaches to key-word extraction and search. The first web-search agent, a simple search agent, uses the four most frequent words in the feature vector of each human research item sensed to trigger a search with the Yahoo! search engine. The second web-search agent uses the Carrot2 clustering engine to cluster human research data then uses the cluster headings to trigger a search with the Yahoo! search engine. The web-search agents modify the environment by inserting records into the research database. Only search results that are in pdf format are added to the database as an initial means of focusing the search results on files most likely to represent research papers.

4.2. RESEARCH ASSISTANT AGENTS

Research assistant agents are motivated agents that reason about data produced by both human researchers and search agents to identify research data produced by search agents which may be of interest to human researchers. Research assistant agents use research data sensors and Bluetooth sensors to monitor human research data and human presence when research data is added to the research database. They use research data effectors to add records to the database describing research items they computed to be highly novel. We have experimented with a number of different techniques for modelling the motivation component of these agents as a computational model of curiosity. The key idea of all of these techniques, illustrated in Figure 5, is to cluster or classify human research data using a machine learning or document classification algorithm.

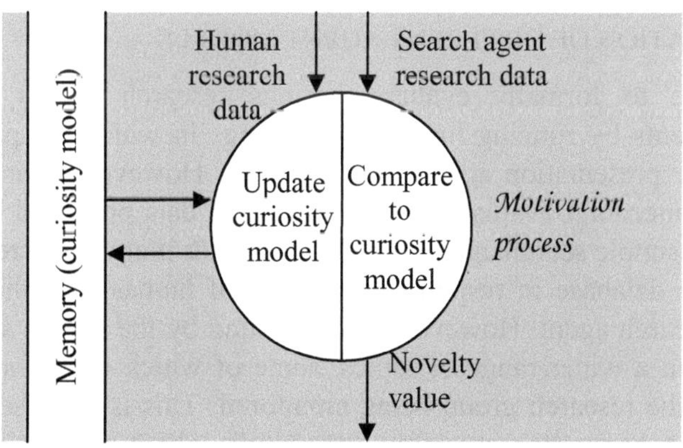

Figure 5. Modelling curiosity as novelty

Curiosity is modelled as novelty, with the novelty of research data found by search agents computed as the classification error if a search agent document were to be classified, without actually classifying those documents. That is, research data found by search agents does not contribute to the model of research data produced by humans, but is only compared to that model. We experimented with a variety of supervised and unsupervised learning approaches to document classification including K-Means clustering, KNN classification, Naïve-bayes classification and LSI clustering as the motivation component. These include both semantic and word vector based approaches to document classification.

4.3. PRESENTATION AGENTS

Presentation agents are reflex agents that monitor research data produced by research assistant agents and use grammars to produce new research data as presentations of data found by the research assistant agents. Presentation agents also monitor the physical space to determine which presentations to display based on presence information from the environment.

Presentation agents use a research data sensor and a research data effector. The grammars, which define the reasoning process of a presentation agent, describe principles for good presentation design and automate the production of presentations.

At present, we have implemented one presentation agent that produces slides by extracting keywords from interesting documents and laying them out as a single bullet list. We used the s5 slide show system (http://meyerweb.com/eric/tools/s5/) as a template for these slides. In future we hope to extend the techniques used to extract summary data from documents, to include full sentences and images. Likewise, we will continue to develop the layout grammar to extend to these cases.

4.4. EVALUATION OF DIFFERENT AGENT MODELS

We propose to formally evaluate curious research spaces comprising different agents by running lunchtime meetings in which the presentations produced by presentation agents are displayed. However, prior to this, we have some anecdotal evaluations of the research data produced by different agents. The simple search agent, for example, adds many more research data items to the database in response to a batch of human data than does the clustering search agent. However the data found by the simple search agent tends to span a wider range of topics, some of which do not appear to be relevant to the research group being monitored. This is because the simple search agent bases its search on key-words which do not capture the semantics of the document they represent. In contrast, the clustering search agent searches using cluster headings created after a semantic analysis of the human research data.

With respect to the research assistant agents, the K-Means and LSI based approaches to motivation appear to compute interest values which identify as interesting, sets of documents which conform most closely to a human assessment of the same data. KNN clustering does not achieve high enough resolution of interest values, particularly on small sets of human input data. Naïve-bayes as an approach to modelling motivation proved inappropriate as the confidence value produced by classification tends to be universally close to 1 so novelty is high for all documents.

Other approaches to modelling curiosity may also be possible. For example, curiosity can be modelled as interest by applying the Wundt curve to novelty values. In this model, interesting documents are those with a moderate degree of novelty. In this case, however, the question is raised as the values of novelty at which the Wundt curve should peak.

5. Conclusions

The development of motivated and learning agents as an infrastructure for proactive design elements promises to change the way in which we conceive of and design buildings and public spaces. Using sensors to observe the activities in the room and effectors to make changes in the visible aspects of the room opens the possibility of a room as a proactive environment that exhibits characteristics of curiosity. The applications described in this paper highlight some of the alternative computational models and the impact of using different models in different scenarios.

Acknowledgements

This research was supported by an Australian Research Council Discovery Grant titled "Curious Places: Agent-Mediated Self-Aware Worlds". This paper was written while Mary Lou Maher was working at the National Science Foundation in the United States. Any opinion, findings and conclusions or recommendations expressed in this chapter are those of the authors and do not necessarily reflect the views of the National Science Foundation.

References

Berlyne, DE: 1960, *Conflict, arousal and curiosity,* McGraw-Hill, New York.

Brooks, RA et al. 1997, The intelligent room project, *The Second International Cognitive Technology Conference* (CT'97), Aizu, pp. 271-279.

Coen, M: 1998, Design principles for intelligent environments, *The Fifteenth National/Tenth Conference on Artificial Intelligence/Innovative Applications of Artificial Intelligence*, Madison, Wisconsin, USA, pp. 547-554.

Dieterich, H, Malinowski, U, Khme, T and Schneider-Hufschmidt, M: 1993, State of the art in adaptive user interfaces. *in* M Schneider-Hufschmidt, T Khme and U Malinowski (eds), *Adaptive User Interfaces: Principlse and Practice*, North Holland, Amsterdam.

Graesser, A, VanLehn, K, Rose, C, Jordan, P. and Harter, D: 2001, Intelligent tutoring systems with conversational dialogue, *AI Magazine* **22**(4): 39-52.

Hanssens, N, Kulkarni, A, Tuchinda, R. and Horton, T: 2002, Building agent-based intelligent workspaces, *The Third International Conference on Internet Computing*, pp. 675-681.

Johanson, B, Fox, A and Winograd, T: 2002, The interactive workspaces project: experiences with ubiquitous computing rooms, *IEEE Pervasive Computing* **1**(2): 67-74.

Kulkarni, A: 2002, Design principles of a reactive behavioural system for the intelligent room. Bitstream: *The MIT Journal of EECS Student Research*: 1-5.

Merrick, K and Maher, ML: 2006, Motivated reinforcement learning for non-player characters in persistent computer game worlds, *International Conference on Advances in Computer Entertainment Technology*, CA, USA, pp. (electronic proceedings).

Raghavan, VV and Wong, SKM: 1986, A critical analysis of vector space model for information retrieval, *Journal of the American Society for Information Science* **37**(5): 279-87.

Roman, M et al. 2002, A middleware infrastructure for active spaces, *IEEE Pervasive Computing* **1**(4): 74-83.

Rummery, GA and Niranjan, M: 1994, *On-line q-learning using connectionist systems.* CUED/F-INFENG/TR 166, Cambridge University, Engineering Department.

Saunders, R: 2001, *Curious design agents and artificial creativity.* PhD Thesis, University of Sydney, Sydney.

Stanley, JC: 1976, Computer simulation of a model of habituation, *Nature* **261**: 146-148.

Watkins, C and Dayan, P: 1992, Q-learning, *Machine Learning* **8**(3): 279-292.

Wooldridge, M and Jennings, N: 1995, Intelligent agents: theory and practice, *The Knowledge Engineering Review* **10**(2): 115-152.

Wundt, W: 1910, *Principles of physiological psychology*, Macmillan, New York.

A FRAMEWORK FOR THE DESIGN OF KINETIC FAÇADES

JULES MOLONEY
University of Melbourne, Australia

Abstract. The particular requirements of kinetic façades are discussed in relation to a general model for future CAAD research – a 3D digital prototype based on (1) the concurrent evaluation of quantitative and qualitative performance over time (2) the calibration of geometry and physics to materiality and mechanics. Concurrent performance in the case of kinetic façades is determined by the dual role as environmental screens and the socio-cultural function as the public face of architecture. From these principles a framework is proposed that informs the conceptualisation of software that will address unique requirements – the design of façades as process systems that perform over a range of time scales.

1. Introduction

There has been interest for some time with 'intelligent' façades that can react to changing climatic conditions and user needs in order to improve functional performance (Wigginton 2002). Design of such environmental screens has concentrated on technical developments with little appreciation that façades are the public face of architecture. As well as providing comfortable enclosure, façades form the backdrop to urban spaces to help shape cultural identity and social behaviour, an issue that informed psychological studies in the 1960's and 70's (Norberg-Schulz 1971, Rapoport 1969). The socio-cultural performance of façades has re-emerged as part of contemporary discussions on the quality of the built environment (Leatherbarrow 2002). It has been argued that intelligent façade design based on techno-functional performance is socially inert and offers little cultural value (Anshuman 2005). By comparison a parallel form of kinetic façades – media screens – act as urban interfaces to information and allow engaging contemporary artworks (ag4, 2006). Intelligent façades and media screens are two examples of kinetic façades. The novel aspect to their design requirements is that they are temporal artifacts, or more correctly process systems, that are required to perform over time. These temporal

A Dong, A Vande Moere & JS Gero (eds), CAADFutures'07, 461–474.

requirements together with the need for architectural façades to perform to both environmental science and socio-cultural agendas suggest a holistic approach to CAAD tools is required. From this viewpoint, the research presented below addresses the question – how might design software be developed to accommodate the temporal, and the dual performance role of kinetic façades?

This paper is organised in two sections. The first places the design of kinetic façades in the wider context of CAAD at the early design stages. Through this overview and discussion a general model is proposed based on a performative 3D digital prototype. This research approach is in line with current thinking on new generations of CAAD that proposes an emphasis on support for creativity at the early stages of design (Reffat 2006). The general model described here is based on two principles: (1) the concurrent evaluation of quantitative and qualitative performance over time (2) the calibration of geometry and physics to materiality and mechanics. This generic approach is refined in section 2, which adopts a methodology from the discipline of information systems (IS) that proposes 3 research stages – conceptualisation, implementation and evaluation (Nunmaker 1991). Conceptualisation involves the identification of user needs and the development of design methods, theoretical models and system architectures. This section reports on the conceptual stage for the design of a CAAD system to support the requirements of kinetic façades. Within the IS research framework the conceptual stage generally does not involve implementation but some experiments and trial applications may be developed to illustrate the approach. Here we develop a theoretical model for a general system to support the design of kinetic façades and illustrate the concept via a particular example – the design and simulation of kinetic sunscreens for a tower building type. The requirement for the example sunscreen system is that it operates in relation to environmental and occupant needs, but also integrates the abstract display of information and the capacity to act as a large scale kinetic artwork.

2. The Function of a Digital Prototype in the Early Design Stages

2.1. CONCURRENT EVALUATION

When the term ‘performance’ is used within CAAD research the tendency is to regard this in relation to the legacy of design science – structural, environmental and planning performance from which comparative data can be produced to aid the decision making process. This continues the legacy of the early history of CAAD which is aligned with the re-definition of architectural education in scientific terms implemented in the 1960’s and ‘70’s after the 1956 RIBA Oxford conference (Glanville 1999).

Architectural design was rationalised as a series of quantifiable problems mapped against physical, environmental and sociological data and an analytical 'methods' approach to producing design solutions became prevalent. Within this scientific paradigm the foundations of CAAD were established and developed (Atkin 1986; Gero 1977; Maver 1970). The computer as a decision support tool was framed against architecture as design science and the challenge was to calculate solutions to design as a series of quantifiable problems.

While it is now acknowledged that architectural design must perform in an expanded field, in which performance in socio-cultural and aesthetic terms should be considered alongside functional performance, there is a lack of CAAD research that supports concurrent evaluation. The initial sticking point would appear to be around the issue of measure. Proportional systems or shape recognition techniques can be used to determine objective qualities, but this is based on an outdated gestalt model in which perception is explained in terms of neutral cognition of figure ground relationships. While there is still much more research to be undertaken within psychology, the current agenda is to consider perception a complex interplay between the full range of sensory inputs, memory and in the case of architecture the local cultural and environmental framing of the architectural design (Montagna 1995).

If objective measure is improbable, advances in design visualisation offer the potential for the simulation of designs in a photorealistic temporal context that enhances subjective evaluation prior to construction. We should be cautious in accepting the veracity of any simulation as they will never capture the full range or nuance of actual experience, but developments such as augmented reality (AR) show much promise. If combined with the graphical display of scientific performance, AR offers the potential for the concurrent evaluation of the quantitative and qualitative attributes of design options (Moloney 2006). The need for CAAD to consider performance in an expanded field in which the concurrent evaluation of environmental performance and performance in socio-cultural terms is possible would seem a logical and necessary development.

2.2. CALIBRATED PERFORMANCE

At a recent design workshop digital theorist and architect Greg Lynn raised the issue of closer correlation between design software and the constraints of fabrication (VC Lecture series, University of Auckland, 2004). He made the observation that architects who wish to engage with spline geometry often use software developed for product design. Other designers such as Lynn, who use animation as part of the conceptual design process, typically use software from the motion graphics industry. While such applications may be effective for small scale products or filmic effect, when the design outcomes have to cross over into the constrained world of architectural fabrication there is often a mismatch between the digital form and the reality of construction. By contrast previous analogue methods for designing non-standard geometry often have the constraints of construction embedded in the design tools. For example Ronchamp and other curvilinear designs by Le Corbusier were developed on the drawing board using the technique of ruled surface, an approach that has a direct correlation to construction techniques (Evans 1995). Another precedent outside architecture is the automotive industry where full scale physical prototypes were sculpted using tools calibrated to the curvature of metal stamping machines used to produce car bodies. The car shaper using analogue tools could work in an intuitive and creative manner, secure in the knowledge that the prototype shape could be translated to manufacture.

There would appear to be a gap in CAAD software for design applications that can be calibrated to in particular, the construction challenges of non standard geometry. While there are parametric libraries of window joinery and the like provided by manufacturers, these are not particularly useful at the early stages of design. In an earlier publication, we discussed the possibility of a CAAD interface that started from the basis of materials that incorporated physical constraints, such as minimum curvature or typical manufacturing dimensions. Rather then using abstract geometry, the designer would select materials that would then constrain geometry within the tolerances of the material and typical fabrication (Moloney 2003).

In the case considered here, the design of kinetic façades, the issue of correlating the design simulation to achievable construction is complicated by the kinetic requirement. The degree and speed of translation and rotations in the physical world are constrained by both the geometry of the components and the mechanics of the kinetic system. However in comparison to static façades we anticipate there will be a limited number of construction systems, which make the possibility of implementing physical calibration feasible. In addition there is a greater designer need, as in this emerging field the impact of the construction limitations is comparatively untested. Software that realistically simulates physical movement in relation to construction systems will facilitate a shift of emphasis – from the design of the components to designing the kinetics. This is new territory for architectural designers who will be required to think of performance and composition over time as opposed to the design of a static artefact. With static façade design, experienced design architects soon develop an intuitive understanding of materials and a personal vocabulary of geometry related to construction. This enables design at the early stage to occur using sketches and physical or computer massing models that operate as a form of notation that references previous experience. In effect the experienced designer intuitively calibrates the sketch design to a logic of construction. However with the design of kinetic façades the architect is removed from this mode of intuitive calibration as there are minimal examples of working systems to reference, nor is it probable that the designer can imagine the full range of kinetic outcomes. This is particularly so if the kinetic system interacts with weather patterns or human input that adds an additional level of complexity over that of static architectural composition.

2.3. NEW GENERATIONS OF CAAD RESEARCH

A recent journal article provides a useful summary of computing in architectural design and an approach to new generations of CAAD (Reffat 2006). The approach articulates a shift of emphasis from the design development stages to the early concept forming stage of design and proposes a research model for CAAD that has three aspects: Design occurs in a collaborative 3D virtual environment; this environment is intelligent utilising a software agent approach; the design aids are situated. The proposal here is aligned with this research approach, but at this stage the focus is on the development of the 3D environment rather then software agents or situated design. However rather then referring to the design media as a virtual environment we prefer to use the term digital prototype. Virtual is a loaded term that is perhaps now best returned to its role in philosophical discussion (Leach 1997).

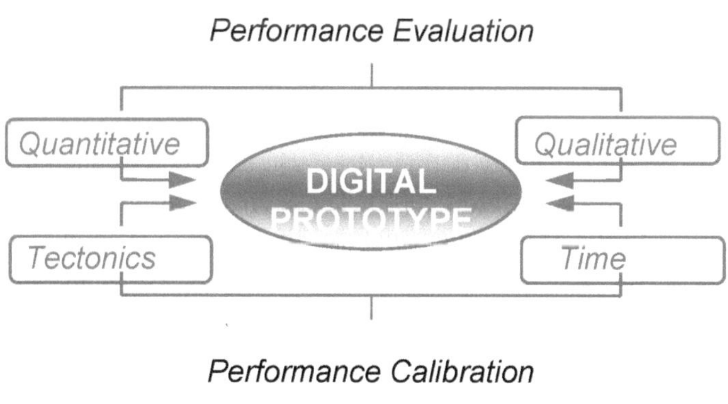

Figure 1. Requirements of a Digital Prototype

Figure 1 summarises the requirements of the digital prototype in reference to the principles discussed above – performance evaluation and performance calibration. The diagram articulates the requirements of a digital prototype that supports an inclusive and holistic approach to design and simulation during the early design stages. In summary: *performance evaluation* occurs in relation to an expanded field where the evaluation of *quantitative* data and *qualitative* experience is concurrent; *performance calibration* of the prototype constrains design options in regard to the reality of *tectonic* limits; the evaluation and calibration of the prototype is determined in relation to multiple viewpoints over a range of *time* scales.

3. Software Conceptualisation

The aim of this section is to refine the concept of the digital prototype above in relation to a particular case – the design and simulation of kinetic façades. Conceptualisation is the first of a three stage approach to research as established in the field of Information Systems (Nunmaker 1991). The methodology is useful for architectural researchers, as it allows the development of a theoretical model that can be handed over to those with programming expertise for the subsequent implementation and evaluation stages. Conceptualization is structured here around the identification of the likely user requirements, the articulation of a design methodology and the development of a theoretical model.

3.1. USER REQUIREMENTS

Who are the potential users and what are the range of requirements for this digital prototyping system? As outlined in the introduction there are currently two distinct groups – designers of intelligent and media façades.

3.1.1. Intelligent Façades

In the last twenty years advances in electronic control systems have progressed to where a building can be described as intelligent rather than responsive. A recent overview defines the basic criteria by which a building can be so considered (Wigginton 2002). These are (1) an input system, (2) a processing or control system which analyses this input , (3) an output system which reacts to the analysis of the input, (4) this response occurs with a consideration of time (5) learning ability (although earlier definitions of intelligence often do not include this last criteria). The idea that buildings should be some sort of intelligent entity separate from users has not surprisingly being subject to debate. There are a few examples which break the closed system of input/control/output to include the user in the monitoring and decision making process. The control system of the GSW headquarters building in Berlin makes recommendations to users about the selection of natural or mechanical ventilation by means of green or red lights on the window transoms. The user can decide to accept or override the recommendation from the control system. Such examples suggest a transition from the intelligent façade as an autonomous machine, to that in which the user engages with and is part of the decision making.

The definition of intelligent façades above provides a useful guide to the range of design decisions for functional performance. 1) *Input* methods need to be determined – what environmental data and user requirements are going to be monitored and how? 2) The *control* system to process the input data needs to be designed 3) The design of the *output* system – mechanical and/or electronic kinetic systems. In relation to qualitative performance requirements we can first consider the form of the output device. There are some recent systems that change the material properties of glass to affect light penetration and thermal performance. However, most environmental control systems are based on mechanical systems – louvers or fins of varying materials, profiles and proportions. There are two general tectonic approaches to mechanical systems: either to embed the kinetic component or fin within the composition of the façade thus minimizing aesthetic impact; or to design the shading or ventilation elements as a separate prosthetic device which serves the building. In either approach seldom are the mechanics of the device articulated with any great aesthetic attention, perhaps reflecting the typical separation between architect and environmental engineering consultants.

A notable exception that seldom finds its way into surveys of intelligent façades is the Arab institute in Paris designed by Jean Nouvel in 1988. The southern wall is protected from the sun by a 60 meter wall composed of multiple panels composed of variously dimensioned metallic diaphragms. These operate like a series of camera lenses, shrinking and widening in response to sensors in order to control the penetration of sun light into the building. Even when at rest the tectonic quality and detail of this wall is stunning, while the dappled light which results generates seductive internal spatial qualities. This iconic building sets a precedent for the integration of functional performance and aesthetic effect in kinetic façades. Besides the material form of the façade the type of movement and its control has a major effect, which suggests that the process control should also be examined in relation to qualitative performance. In the case of the Arab Institute the contraction expansion movement is purely reactive with each panel individually controlled by a local sensor. This gives an engaging albeit random dynamic to the façade. In contrast to this on/off reactive approach a central control system could for example 'orchestrate' patterns of movement over time within a functional performance threshold. The opportunity for embedding qualitative aspects within the operation of environmentally driven kinetics is an aspect that is seldom exploited.

3.1.2. Media Façades

Anders in his work on what he terms cybrid architecture suggests the needs of contemporary society have extended beyond that of a communal physical reality (Anders 2005). Media screens can be seen as early manifestations of architecture adapting to an information rich society and adding to its sphere of practice by mediating between physical and information space. As would be expected at these early stages the majority of such media screens take the form of large scale computer displays, using data projection or video walls on the façades of buildings. More recently light-emitting diodes (LED) have been utilized to turn whole buildings into a computer controllable image. A more low tech, but highly effective approach is the 'BIX', a 900 sq. m. light installation set behind the double curved acrylic surface of the Kunsthaus in Graz, Austria. Made up of standard circular fluorescent lamps, these act equivalent to pixels, each individually controlled by a central computer to enable the generation of low resolution imagery. Regardless of the time of day, or content, the tectonic quality of the BIX wall is engaging beyond that achieved by standard video screen technologies. Rather then been perceived as applied surface or screen, the display reads as building skin integrated into the constructional logic of the whole, and has a tectonic quality over and above its display function. Another example that falls between object and surface and operates at an urban scale is the D-tower, an art piece commissioned by the city of Doetinchem in the Netherlands. The D-tower consists of three parts: a website (accessible to everybody), a questionnaire (accessible to a hundred different people each year) and a 12 meter tower. All three parts are interactively related to each other, with the tower being internally lit with a mix of red green and blue light. Updated each night, the mix of color reflects responses to the questionnaires, which are intended to gauge the mood of the town in relation to a variety of issues. The tower is expected to stay in place for decades and has already added to a sense of social cohesiveness in this small provincial centre.

A primary problem with light based media walls is they are only marginally effective in day light. The Agesis Hyposurface is an example of an alternate approach, in which imagery is created through physical movement of architectural surface. Made up of triangulated metal plates driven by a bed of pneumatic pistons, dynamic 'terrains' are generated in real time. In this way imagery on a computer can be transferred to a three dimensional relief, the triangulated plates operating as 3D pixels. At the other end of the technical spectrum, artist Ned Kahn was commissioned to produce a wind veil for a non-descript parking building in the small town of Charlotte, USA. Any wind eddy is picked up by the 75mm reflective disks, generating an effect not unlike the quality of metallic fluid. This skin as installed is reactive only to wind, but suggests possibilities for low tech systems that have passive energy sources.

Returning to the digital prototype framework, we can summarise the requirements for designers in a similar manner to that of intelligent façades. Media screens may have a functional performance, the communication of information, but more often the emphasis is on qualitative performance – presenting information in a socially engaging and culturally enhancing manner. The extreme end of this qualitative function are those designed solely to an artistic agenda to operate as a public work of art. Despite this shift in emphasis, the same underlying *input-control-output* structure identified for intelligent façades can be applied to media screens. The input may be sampled environmental data, information networks, or human interaction. Media screens also require a processing unit and a method of display, which may be tectonic mechanical systems or electronic light systems.

3.2. DESIGN METHODOLOGY

Despite the different agendas of the designers of kinetic environmental systems and those designing cybrid interfaces to information embedded in building façades, the novel requirement in comparison to static façades is that both groups require the design of a process rather then an artifact. Where do the design decisions occur when considering the design of process for kinetic façades? The objective here is to identify the factors to be considered, rather then the prescription for any particular design approach. We propose a general methodology built on the input-control-output structure identified in the discussion of user requirements.

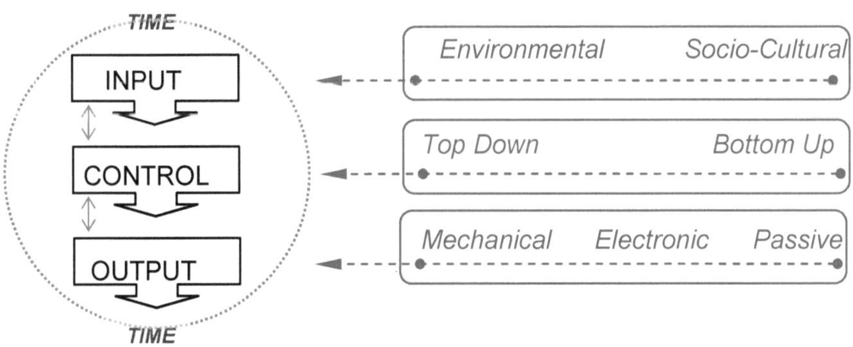

Figure 2. General Design Framework for Kinetic Façades

On the left side of Figure 2 are the three design stages, while on the right is the 'range' within which primary decisions are undertaken: for the input stage this is a broad distinction between environmental and socio cultural data/user interaction; for the control system we can distinguish between a bottom up or top down approach where the outcome is to varying degrees emergent or prescribed; while the output would be located within a range of mechanical, electronic and what we term passive or low energy systems. The aim of the diagram is to identify where design decisions are made and the general range of approaches that may be considered by the designer.

We would argue that the key design decisions occur at the process stage where the design of the control system can address qualitative as well as functional performance criteria. Here there may be an opportunity for auto-poesies in which design occurs at the level of determining the parameters or rules from which kinetics is emergent. Alternatively the personal aesthetic of the designer may be embedded in a similar manner to, for example, such proportional systems as used by Le Corbusier.

The diagram also foregrounds that all design stages – input, process and output – are made in relation to time. Designers of kinetic façades need to consider foremost that the design and simulation of performance needs to consider a range of time scales, from the micro to the macro. For example input may be processed to output in a real time response and/or be processed to create macro scale trends that affect kinetics that emerge over a longer time period.

3.3. THEORETICAL MODEL

We have outlined user requirements and identified a general design framework. The objective here is to develop a concept for design software to meet these unique requirements. This is based on the CAAD digital prototype developed in Section 1 where a key aspect is the calibration of performance to the geometry and physics of construction.

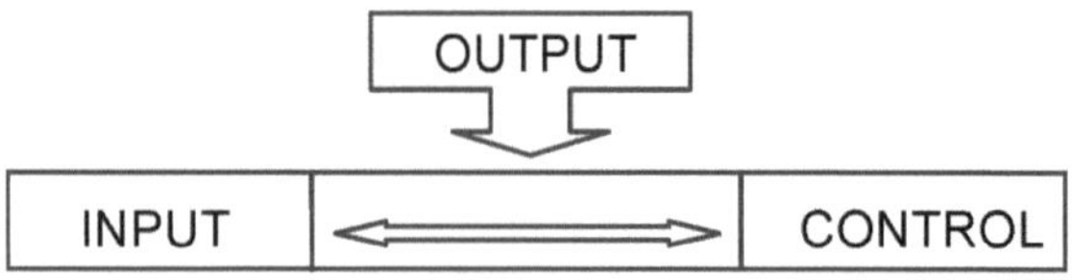

Figure 3. Revised design process for Calibrated Kinetic Façades

As illustrated in Figure 3, the starting premise is that the software architecture would reverse the input-control-output sequence and proceed from the basis of user choice of the output technology. It is proposed that the development of the software architecture would proceed first with the identification and design of a range of output mechanisms presented to the user as parametric libraries. These parametric library parts would consist of: associative geometry cognizant of standard component dimensions; materials; a range of kinetic parameters calibrated to typical mechanical, electronic or passive motor physics; fabrication options that are calibrated to fabrication logistics; and designer preference for detailing.

The second premise of the software architecture is the requirement for temporal visualization that allows concurrent evaluation of quantitative and qualitative performance across a range of time scales. This is in recognition that the novel design challenge for kinetic façades is that the outcome is a process system that can only be evaluated in relation to performance over time. Elsewhere we have developed an approach to temporal visualization based on screen based AR that allows real time animation and the simultaneous display of functional performance (Moloney 2007). This approach can be utilized here to provide a degree of photorealism to enhance the qualitative assessment of the design. Moreover it was proposed that the display of the functional performance should be displayed in graphics alongside the 3D visualization to allow the designer a broad brush and intuitive understanding of quantitative performance *as* the model is being interactively designed. As well as real time simulation it was proposed the AR environment should incorporate time-lapse approaches to allow a range of time scales to be considered.

We have outlined two aspects of the theoretical model – that user interaction starts from the choice and customization of a parametric library and secondly concurrent evaluation occurs in a screen based AR visualization system allowing real time animation, time lapse functionality and the display of functional performance data.

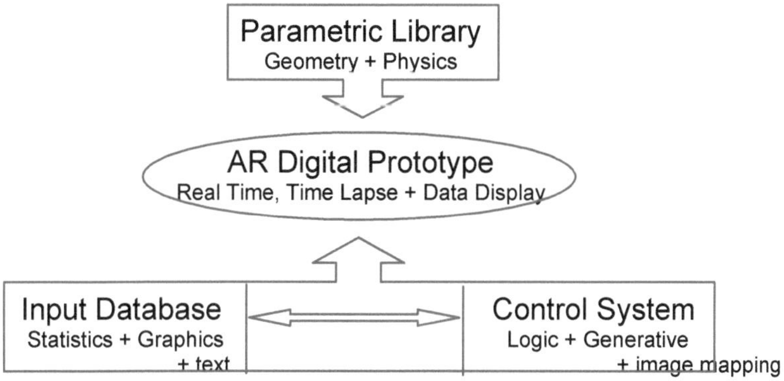

Figure 4. Software architecture for kinetic Façade Design

Figure 4 illustrates that once the parametric library has been customized by the user, performance within the AR environment is simulated by the design of the control system in relation to a database. For the design of a process over time the control system is where we argue the crucial decisions occur. We propose the software architecture of the control system module should allow a range of approaches: a generative 'engine' that maximises functional performance but also allows design preconceptions (Janssen 2006); a shape grammar approach that enables experimentation with proportional relationships over time (Stiny 1980); an image mapping module that allows translation of graphics to kinetics. Given this range, we anticipate the control system will require an interactive graphical user interface (GUI) and a scripting interface. The final component of the proposed architecture is a database that would allow users to evaluate the control system against the relevant input. In the case of intelligent façades this may be, for example, historical weather data collected over time that can allow a fine grained and localised testing of daily and seasonal variation. This data could be used to also project future longer term variation as a result of global trends in temperature and sunlight frequency. In the case of media façade the database can be linked to streaming input from information networks that would include data in graphical and text formats.

3.4. ILLUSTRATION OF APPROACH: ITERATION 1

Typically the IS Research method adopted here refines the software architecture conceptualization to a level of detail and then proceeds to collaboration with software engineers to implement a full working beta application and formal user trials. Given the novel aspects of kinetic façades and the lack of precedent, we have decided to implement initial tests or 'illustrations' of the model during the software conceptualization. These are to be undertaken in an iterative manner looking at a range of example case scenarios, and then reflecting on the outcomes in order to develop the theoretical model in more detail. The intent is not to develop full functionality but to enable preliminary evaluation of the design sequence – specification of the output via a parametric library, then design of the control system and evaluation of the outcome sampling input from a real time database. The first iteration examines the case of an external sunscreen system for a high rise building. Typically the control mechanism for such a system would be developed by a consultant in relation to a purely functional agenda. The intent of the trials is to test the premise of the concurrent evaluation of environmental performance and allow the design architect to experiment with the qualitative outcomes of the kinetics.

The design scenario for this first iteration is to develop an aesthetic quality to the kinetics as the control system evaluates the environmental data and operates the individual sunscreens. When the light levels are such that sun shading is not required the kinetic façade can be utilised as a media screen to communicate local and global information, or be made available for public art purposes. Figure 5(a) illustrates a parametric sunscreen component where the user can customize geometry including overall proportions, frame dimensions, materials, type of detailing. In addition there are physics parameters such as pivot points, rotation and/or translation speeds calibrated to typical drive mechanisms. Figure 5(b) and 5(c) illustrate two options for sun tracking where the sun angle is articulated as a slow moving 'wave' across the façade. The two options are differentiated by in this case by the rotational axis of the individual screens.

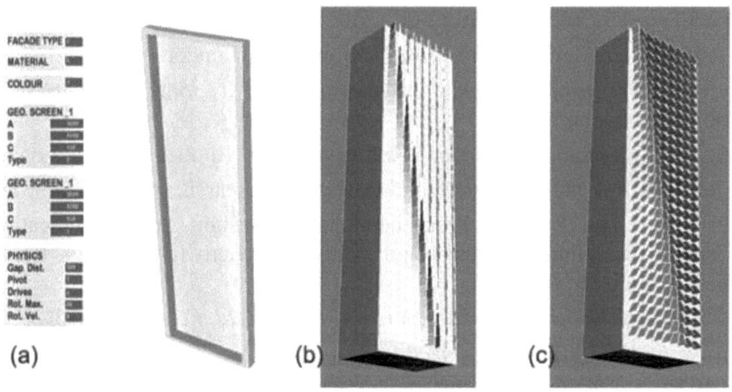

Figure 5. Illustration iteration 1 – screen grabs of parametric module and experimentations with kinetic control module

The examples illustrated here show a 'top down' design approach where the façade is conceived as a compositional whole mapping environmental change and articulating the edge condition and the overall chiaroscuro effect. Currently in development is a more bottom up design approach that simulates a scenario where occupants have the ability to affect the position of individual screens. In combination with a graphic display of environmental performance the intention is for the designer to be able to test the qualitative and quantitative impact of limiting the degree of occupant control.

4. Further Work

The intent of the illustration was to test the software architecture concepts in a similar manner to the reflection-in-action approach associated with architectural design (Schön 1983). Similar to a sketch, these preliminary moves clarify intentions and demonstrate the significance of the unique challenges of kinetic design. Iteration 1 will be further developed as indicated and this conceptualization stage will continue via a series of other iterations that explore a range of technologies and case scenarios. The objective is to use the iterative 'conceive- test via particular example – reflect' approach to ensure a well thought through architecture is established before a full software implementation.

References

ag4: 2006, *Media Façades*, Ralf Daab, Cologne.

Anders, P: 2005, Cybrid Principles: Guidelines for Merging Physical and Cyber Spaces, *International Journal of Design Computing,* 3, pp. 391-406.

Anshuman, S: 2005, Responsiveness and Social Expression; Seeking Human Embodiment in Intelligent Façades, *ACADIA*, pp. 12-23.

Atkin, O: 1986, *Psychology of Architectural Design*, Pion, London.

Evans, R: 1995, *The projective cast: architecture and its three geometries*, MIT Press, Cambridge, Massachusetts.

Gero, J (ed): 1977, *Computer Applications in Architecture*, Applied Science, London.

Glanville, R: 1999, Researching Design and Designing Research, *Design Issues,* **15**(2): 80-92.

Janssen, P: 2006, The Role of Preconceptions in Design: Some Implications for the Development of Computational Design Tools, *in* J Gero (ed), *Design Computing and Cognition '06*, pp. 365-384.

Leach, N: 1997, *Rethinking architecture: a reader in cultural theory*, Routledge, New York.

Leatherbarrow, DMM:2002, *Surface Architecture*, MIT Press, Cambridge, Mass.

Maver, T: 1970, A Theory of Architectural Design in which the Role of the Computer is Identified, *Building Science,* 4, pp. 199-207.

Moloney, J: 2006, Augmented Reality Visualisation of the Built Environment to Support Design Decision Making, *Information Visualization 2006*, pp. 687-692.

Moloney, J: 2007, Screen based augmented reality for architecture, *CAADRIA*, pp. (Publication pending).

Moloney, J, Issa, R: 2003, Materials in Architectural Design Education Software: A Case Study, *International Journal of Design Computing,* **1**: 46-58.

Montagna, C, Bonnes M, Secchiaroli, G: 1995, *Environmental Psychology: A Psycho-Social Introduction*, Sage, London.

Norberg-Schulz, C.:1971, *Existence, Space and Architecture*, Praeger, New York.

Nunmaker, J, Chen, M., and Purdin, TDM: 1991, Systems Development in Information Systems Research, *Journal of Management Information Systems,* **7**(3): 89-106.

Rapoport, A: 1969, *House Form and Culture*, Prentice-Hall, New Jersey.

Reffat, RA: 2006, Computing in architectural design: reflections and an approach to new generations of CAAD, *Electronic Journal of Information Technology in Construction,* **11**: 655-668.

Schön, DA: 1983, *The Reflective Practitioner*, Harper Collins, USA.

Stiny, G: 1980, Introduction to Shape and Shape Grammars, *Environment and Planning B* **7**: 359-367.

Wigginton, MHJ: 2002, *Intelligent Skins*, Butterworth-Heinemann, Oxford.

DESIGN SCIENCE LABS

Why architectural research needs laboratories for integrated and networked simulation

URS HIRSCHBERG
Graz University of Technology, Austria

and

MICHAEL STADLER
NINSIGHT Corporation, Austria

Abstract. The ever increasing complexity of architectural projects demands efficient tools to assist within their associated design processes. We present an infrastructure initiative to tackle these challenges with Design Science Labs that are heavily rooted on simulation techniques in various academic fields. The merits of these techniques are discussed under the prospect of research and teaching experience as well as practical applicability. For an increased benefit, strong interoperability between these simulation techniques is desirable, but still not easily achievable. The infrastructure initiative aims to build smooth bridges between these fields and to gain additional architectural design space from their interaction.

1. Introduction

This paper describes an infrastructure initiative of our university aimed at setting up a network of research laboratorics that cnablc thc intcgration of state of the art simulation methods into the architectural design process. The basic premise of the initiative is that the architectural profession needs to start thinking big in its approach to research and to scientific methods.

While traditionally architects were content with studio space as their working environments, we argue that it's time architects take to developing their design work in close collaboration with specialized research laboratories. Given the complexity architecture inherently possesses and the ever increasing societal demands new constructions need to fulfill, architects

A Dong, A Vande Moere & JS Gero (eds), CAADFutures'07, 475–488.

have no other choice but to become very professional about their working methods. The close coordination and integration of various types of simulation methods into the design process is a key aspect of this. In fact, the collaborative interdisciplinary teamwork from the earliest stages of design has long become standard in international competitions. Yet, despite occasional examples of the contrary, adequate laboratories that would allow to conduct and research similar design strategies in academia are still largely missing in most architecture schools.

An inspiration for this integration of scientific processes into the design practice is Buckminster Fuller, who coined the term design science, defining it as "*the effective application of the principles of science to the conscious design of our total environment in order to help make the Earth's finite resources meet the needs of all humanity without disrupting the ecological processes of the planet.*"

The integration of simulation methods into the design process has been a constant subject of CAAD research over the past 30 years at least (Augenbroe and Winkelmann 1991; Chaisuparasmikul 2006; Flemming and Mahdavi 1993; Mahdavi et al. 1997; Maver 1988). While advances in physical based simulation methods have improved dramatically in certain fields, leading to entirely new subdomains in building design, the integration of these specialized domains into the design process is still unsatisfactory, despite the fact that the notion of building performance and energy efficiency are currently getting a lot of public attention (Cody 2005). The initiative put forward here differs from earlier work in that it puts its focus not so much on the development of unified standards and more coherent or more powerful software packages, but on establishing smooth collaborative processes between the individual laboratories. Furthermore the labs are based on a notion of performativity that goes beyond physically based digital simulation to reflect also the cultural and social aspects of design (Kolarevic and Malkawi 2005; Hauser 2005). Thus we believe that the issue is best addressed by networking spaces and people, not just by developing new software (although that remains an important part of it).

The rationale for this undertaking as well as the outline of its implementation is described in the following sections. Since simulation is a central part of the present project, we provide three general arguments how the architectural practice may take advantage of it in Section 2. The most useful fields of application are particularized in Section 3. The relationship between digital and analogue simulations as our approach in the design science labs concept, as well as a brief description of the individual laboratory setups is discussed in Section 4. Our proposed approach to achieve interdisciplinary connections and exchange mechanisms between these labs is outlined in Section 5.

2. Why Simulation in Architecture?

The simulation of a process means to synthesize a model that incorporates most of the characteristics of the original process. There are several reasons why simulation is important for architects.

- *Enhancement of creativity*: The creation of new and original solutions to a given problem is an iterative process. It depends inherently on the feedback that comes from the actual exploring of successive development stages. Building physical realizations of each design step is expensive and cumbersome. With simulation, new solutions to existing problems can be explored without having to spend money for physical realizations of any intermediate development stage. Furthermore, the feedback parameters may be difficult to obtain by hand (e.g. energy consumption, sociological quality, structural cost,…). With simulation, these project descriptors are readily available and the designer can learn from the outcome, which may in turn lead to improved solutions.
- *Building safety*: Building regulations may preclude certain architectural forms due to their inherent dangers. For example, fire regulations may prohibit open office spaces connected to an atrium, because the smoke may flow into the atrium and render fire exits unusable, which may be located there. However, with simulation, the flow of smoke becomes accurately predictable and hence it can be shown if an architectural form provides enough safety for its users.
- *Optimization* is an algorithmic enhancement to the design process, made possible via simulation. In the present context it can be useful in one of two aspects: (a) finding solutions which nobody may have come up with before and (b) allowing a design process to be guided by physical principles.

The *first* aspect is associated with genetic search strategies. As a suitable mathematical analogy, complex architectural problems can be described as a multi-parameter and non-convex problem. Although mathematically not simple, standard algorithms are available for this of problem. Then, in conjunction with a simulation, genetic search algorithms can help to find architectural solutions that were not investigated before for various reasons.

The *second* aspect of optimization is associated primarily with 'Topology Optimization'. It helps to initiate an automatic design process that leads to structures which resemble natural load bearing structures like human cortial bones (for further details, see Sec. 3.5).

3. Important Fields of Simulation

3.1. LIGHTING

Lighting simulation has always been of interest for architects because it allows to create certain moods, which can not be designed just by the organization of the building structure. One of the first simulation tools was 'Radiance', which allows for quite realistic estimation of the lighting results. It achieves its results by using a hybrid approach of Monte-Carlo and deterministic raytracing. Thereby, the calculation of light transport is divided into three main parts: the direct component, the specular indirect component, and the diffuse indirect component (which became later known as the 'radiosity'-method). Although this leads to good results for many standard situations, it fails for a number of special cases, e.g. heliostats or parabolic light fixtures.

On the other side, an armada of accelerated rendering software was developed, that built solely on raytracing. Although it proved much faster, pure raytracing ignores diffuse reflections. Many workarounds were developed but none of them yielded physically accurate lighting results.

Some time ago, an algorithm called 'Metropolis Light Transport' method was developed (Veach and Guibas 1997). It provides un-biased, hence physically accurate results and is implemented in the commercial renderer 'Maxwell'. Hence, both Maxwell and Radiance represent useful tools for realistic lighting simulations.

3.2. FLUID DYNAMICS

Fluid dynamics can be subdivided into hydro- and aero-dynamics (dealing with the flow of water and air, respectively). Both fields are relevant for architectural projects (Chen and Srebric 2000). Hydrodynamic applications are, for example, the development of projects in a flooding area. Another application is the analysis of the flow of rain water over the free form surface of a building. The outcome can be used for technical reasons or to make an aesthetic statement.

Sample applications for aerodynamic analyses are: the structural integrity due to wind loads, the production of sounds from vibration of façade elements, the reaction of moving elements to wind as well as energetic aspects such as ventilation.

To summarize, fluid dynamics allows us to analyze the interaction between an architectural project and the fluids around it. Previously, this analysis was carried out in wind channels which were expensive to operate. Nowadays, in many areas, the use of wind channels has been superseded by 'Computational Fluid Dynamics' (CFD). Thereby, the flow is simulated via the solution of the Navier Stokes Equation on a mesh of finite elements.

Although the method demands a lot of CPU time, it is much more affordable than wind channels. An additional advantage is that the digital architectural model is directly amenable to automatic optimization.

The major software players in this field are 'CFX', 'Fluent' and 'Star-CD'. However, they have a steep learning curve and require a broad fluid dynamical background. Hence, we have developed an in-house application that utilizes a standard-CFD-core and a graphical user interface that is tailored to the needs of our architectural practice and teaching requirements (see Figure 1).

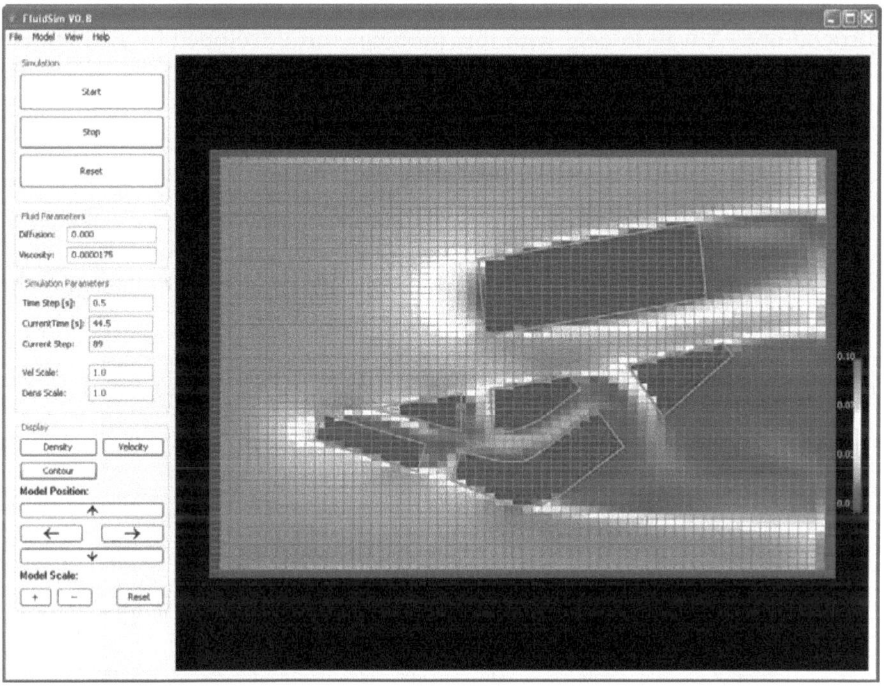

Figure 1. Computational Fluid Dynamics (CFD) application used for teaching. It shows the wind velocity distribution around clustered office buildings

3.3. BUILDING ENERGY SIMULATION

Due to rising energy prices, the accurate management of the energy consumption of buildings has received major interest in recent years. In several countries even the legislation demands certain energetic criteria to be satisfied, before a project can be built.

Another important application tightly related to building energy simulation is the control of the micro climate in buildings. This becomes increasingly important for large rooms such as open office spaces or atria.

Especially in a high atrium, the temperature gradient from floor to floor is a natural phenomenon, but may be undesirable. The simulation and control of this effect is possible with the appropriate tools.

One of the most widely used tools in this field is 'EnergyPLUS', developed by the Lawrence Berkeley National Lab (Crawley et al. 2000). It is based on its predecessors DOE-2 and BLAST, which both have been verified over a long time on many large scale projects. Another application, more in use for climate control, is the software 'HevaComp'.

3.4. SOCIOLOGICAL ANALYSIS

The prediction of the sociological impacts of architecture is likely the most difficult one. A way to deal with this problem was developed by Bill Hillier. It is the well known 'Space-Syntax', which represents a scientific methodology to assess certain sociological aspects of architectural spaces (Hillier 1997). The method is currently used with great success to design spaces which reduce the crime rate, offer great communication qualities as well as many other aspects.

One major drawback of the method is that it is currently only available in 2D. Hence, for city topographies built on hills (e.g. San Francisco), the

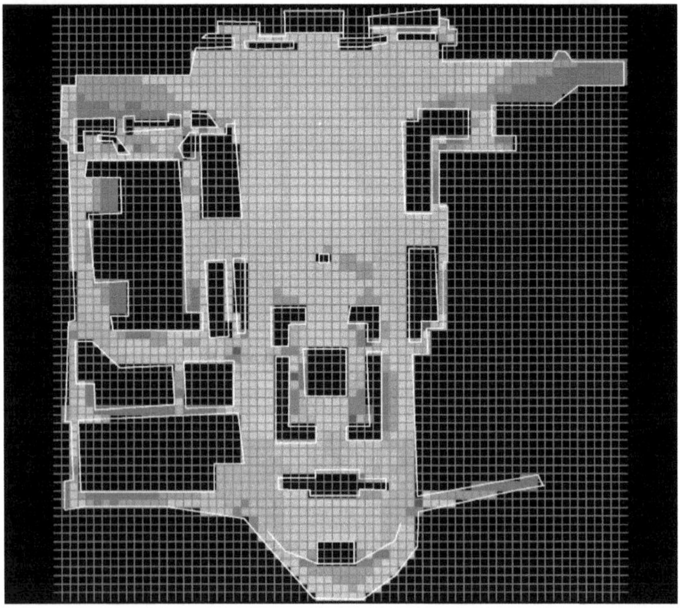

Figure 2. Sample results of the sociological analysis of 'Tiananmen Square' (Place of heavenly peace, Beijing, China). A specially designed Space-Syntax analysis teaching software was utilized

actual sightline differs significantly from the sightline in a 2D-projection. The specially designed teaching software we are using (see Figure 2) can consider arbitrary 3D topographies.

3.5. STRUCTURAL AND TOPOLOGICAL ANALYSIS

The analysis of structural integrity was probably for a long time the most important one in architecture. Elementary statics are idealizations or simplifications of the real structure. These methods were used until the rise of the 'Finite-Element-Method'. It helps to solve any physical problem up to a certain precision, which solely depends on the discretization (grid size). Consequently, it allowed the secure construction of many free form shapes that could simply not be analyzed with elementary statics methods.

Another very important aspect of structural analysis is known as 'Topology Optimization': in conjunction with an evolutionary optimization method, the structural analysis can be used to guide a design process that leads to optimal load bearing structures (Wang M.Y. et al. 2003). The resulting structures resemble human cortical bone or other natural load bearing structures. They offer the best possible trade off between structural integrity and mass.

In general, topology optimization is mathematically very complex and the available commercial codes (e.g. 'Tosca') have a steep learning curve. Hence, for teaching and in-house-use, we have developed an application that hides much of the complexity but delivers an excellent quality of structures (see Figure 3).

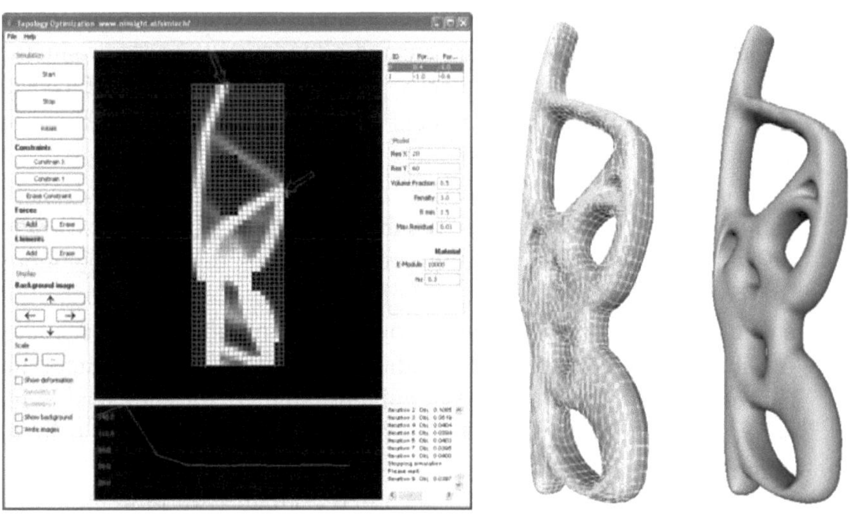

Figure 3. Teaching application used for topological optimization (left). A given set of boundary conditions (loads, constraints, material parameters) leads to an optimal load bearing structure (right)

4. Design Science Labs

4.1. DIGITAL VS. PHYSICAL MODELS AND ENVIRONMENTS

In Section 3 we outlined the most useful fields of application for simulation methods in architecture. Common to all methods mentioned in that section is that when the necessary software and the appropriate project data is available, they can be carried out on standard computers. Thus, the outline in Section 3 is based on the tacit assumption that simulation in architecture is equivalent to digital simulation. Given the widespread availability of computers in architecture schools, one might question the need for dedicated laboratories. As a matter of fact, the notion that digital simulation is the future and that the integration of the different simulation methods and domains will happen naturally in software rather than in a laboratory space is a basic premise of many research approaches about architectural simulation.

In this section we challenge this notion. Simulation in architecture cannot and should not be limited to digital methods. Rather, a broader, more holistic approach to simulation must take physical models as well as digital models into account.

The main reasons for this are the following:

- *Tactility of physical models*: To this day physical models are seen as important ways to explore the architectural qualities of unbuilt projects. Despite the advances in computer graphics and the easy availability of realistic renderings and walkthrough simulations one has become accustomed to, physical models have not disappeared from the architecture studio. On the contrary: digital tools such as 3D printers and laser cutters have created a tendency towards producing physical models more frequently and of higher quality. Physical models can be immediately understood, they give a reliable sense of scale and they have tactile qualities no digital model can possess.
- *Physiological effects of light*: As mentioned above, physical based simulation of light leads to reliable data about light density and distribution and can also reliably predict the look of lighting solutions for both natural and artificial light. But they are not capable of sufficiently exploring the physiological and psychological reactions of humans to certain light conditions. Therefore these important aspects of lighting design can only be studied through tests with actual lighting fixtures at 1:1 scale. These physical tests help to complement the results we get from digital simulation.
- *The psychology of human movement*: We know very little about the intricate ways how people's movements in the spaces architects design for them are influenced by how they are designed. When the human interaction with work spaces or living spaces needs to be

assessed in more detail (because of safety hazards, space limitations or simply because novel solutions are tried out) common ergonomic standards or guidelines often are not sufficient. Especially if such assessments are not seen as purely biomechanical, but try to take the psychological aspects of human movements into account, they can only reliably be done by tracking the physical movement of a human body. Tracking systems such as the one we installed in our media lab enable this type of simulations. Furthermore they can be used to experiment with gestural interaction in Virtual or Augmented Reality.

- *New materials*: For new types of materials, often times sufficient data for digital simulations are not available. Simulating their behavior in real world applications thus requires that physical prototypes be built and tested. One of our labs is set up to specifically explore these topics, which are currently gaining greater importance in architecture (e.g. smart and responsive materials, see Addington and Schodek 2005).

As the above examples illustrate, there are many instances where analogue and digital technology must be combined in order to achieve a holistic simulation. This need for both digital and analogue methods is a central aspect of the approach we took in conceiving the design science labs initiative.

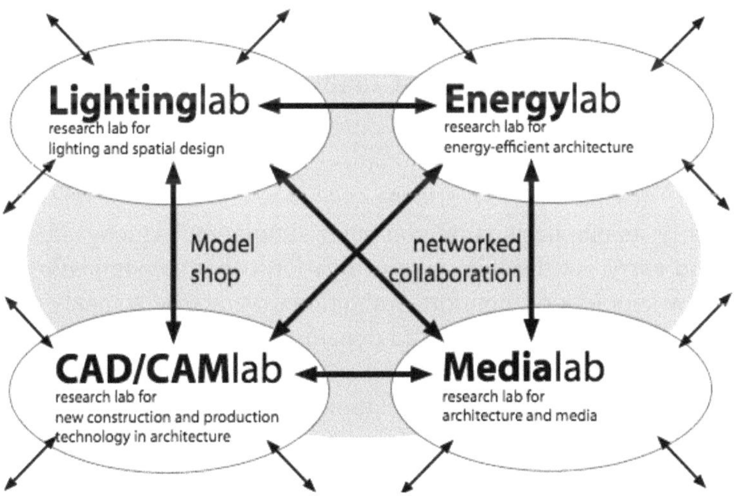

Figure 4. Diagram of the four labs realized as part of the first stage of the TU Graz Design Science Labs initiative

4.2. DESIGN SCIENCE LABS, FIRST STAGE

In its first stage of development the Design Science Labs (DSL) initiative comprises four labs: an energy lab, a lighting lab, a CAD/CAM lab and a media lab. All four are networked and share computing resources as well as facilities for creating physical and digital models.

Not all of the labs are situated in the same building, which on the one hand is not ideal as it limits personal interaction between the lab staff. On the other hand the separation led us to setting up and promoting digital communication methods. These will be addressed in the next section. Based on these modes of communication the future development of the DSL initiative can happen independent of the spatial constraints of any single existing building. The openness of the networked communication also allows for future growth: a structures lab, an urbanism lab and a landscape lab are planned for the next stage of development.

4.3. CAD/CAM LAB

The CAD/CAM lab is divided in two parts: it contains equipment to study the experimental use of new materials (such as foams, smart materials, textile concrete reinforcements etc.) in architecture. The other part is essentially a research database in which the results of these experiments are systematically gathered to be able to share it with partners inside and outside our university. The CAD/CAM lab is the brains behind our extended model shop. Besides standard analogue machinery for building architectural models and 1:1 prototypes the model shop contains various Computer Aided Manufacturing facilities, such as a CNC milling machine, a 3D printer, laser cutters.

4.4. ENERGY LAB

Methodically its emphasis is on computer simulation. Among others it will be set up to carry out the following evaluations: thermal simulations, multi-zone airflow simulations, comfort-evaluations, weather-data analysis, energy simulations, 3D Computational fluid dynamics, shadow studies, daylight and artificial light simulations. The lab is also equipped with various sensors and measuring devices to validate computational results in situ.

4.5. LIGHTING LAB

The lighting lab is situated in a very large (110m^2) and tall (8m) dark space, set up to explore the effect of light colors ranging within the spectrum of daylight. It supports the use of state of the art technology for dynamic lighting control using the DMX protocol and a variety of peripheral media and software. The setup provides a wide variety of spots that can be easily rearranged with a small crane. From a control-booth the physical simulations can be done in parallel with digital simulations on a virtual model. The lighting lab is situated next to the faculty's model shop, which makes it convenient to study the lighting properties of physical models and to study the interrelations of light and material.

4.6. MEDIA LAB

The media lab is an environment for simulating the augmentation of space with digital media. It contains an optical tracking system and an openly programmable set of sensors and advanced input and output devices (such as a head mounted display, high definition projectors and tablet screens) by which the lab's space can be turned into a reactive environment. Three main types of investigations are supported: The precise tracking of human movement as a way to simulate patterns of usage and action of a (virtual) space; gestural interaction with different media as a way to simulate new types of spatial user interfaces and hybrid environments; and immersive modeling to explore multisensory ways of creating and interacting with architectural form.

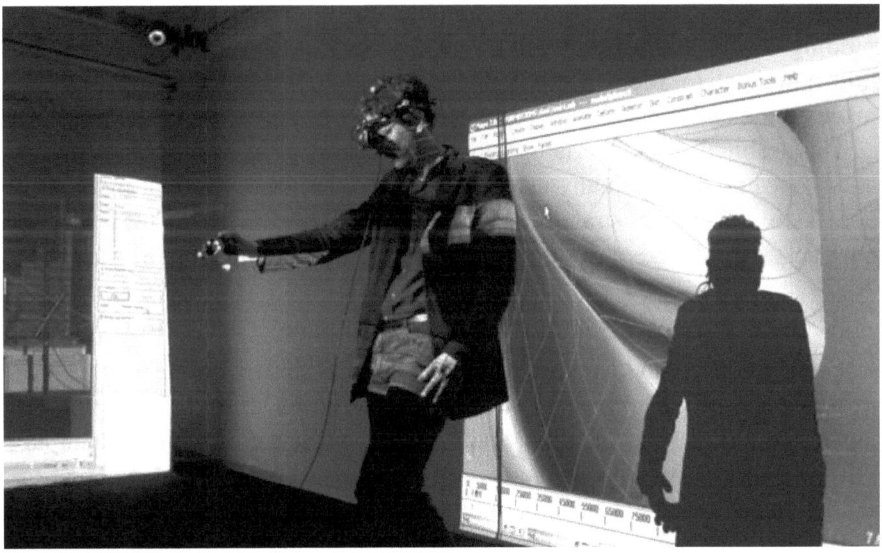

Figure 5. Media Lab for Augmented Architecture. The Lab contains an optical 3D Tracking System and an openly programmable set of sensors and advanced input and output devices (such as a head mounted display, high definition projectors and tablet screens)

5. Networking of the Labs

Usually, it is difficult to transfer data from one simulation application to another one. The reason is that the process is equivalent to transferring the problem from one physical idealization to another one. For example, for a lighting simulation, the thickness of the wall is irrelevant, while for an energetic simulation it is most relevant. One way to overcome these problems is to use a common building model that can incorporate all possible physical domains. Similar strategies are used with great success in mechanical engineering practice. However, for architectural applications, such a strategy does not yet exist.

In the case of the Design Science Labs initiative, this problem is made even more complex by the mix of digital and analogue procedures that are employed. If combining the different abstractions into one comprehensive model in the digital realm appears to be difficult, the hybrid analogue/digital nature of the approach taken in our labs makes it impossible. So what do we refer to if we call the labs networked?

5.1. PRAGMATISM

Finding a one-size-fits-all format suitable for the description of a common building model might be possible one day, but for the time being it seems more practical to adopt a more pragmatic strategy that tries to adjust the means to the ends.

The problem of course is to know beforehand which simulations do and which ones do not yield any useful results. So the idea we adopt in the DSL labs is to develop a strategy for finding and documenting best practice approaches for different design tasks and to share these among the labs.

5.2. ONLINE ENVIRONMENT: BEST PRACTICE AND PEOPLE

Software licenses and computing resources are shared online in the local area network of our university. Obviously the new Design Science labs are networked in this sense. On top of that, a web-presence of all individual labs will be established that includes information about the current set-up, regulations, user manuals etc. – all of this, of course, is just common sense.

Beyond that, we are planning to set up an online database on which all users can save and document their simulation work. Based on experiences we have gained using our online environments for creative collaboration in teaching we hope to be able to set up an environment common between all four labs in which students share and discuss their simulation work. Over time this database will become a case base new users can turn to in order to see what's been done before and what's possible with the different methods and means available in the labs. Furthermore these online environments can be analyzed to derive best-practice models for different tasks based on user preferences and experiences. Especially when people work on their projects in more than one lab in parallel, the synergies between different types of simulations will become manifest.

In the end one of the strongest arguments for setting up actual laboratories, spaces that people go to for special types of investigations, rather than just providing specialized software, is not only the physical infrastructure needed for some simulations. It's also the specialized expertise of people that one can find in those spaces. The online database will make it easier to find experts based on the prior work they have done. But the labs are the places where these experts can get together, where the knowledge and expertise about these topics that are so important to architecture can be developed.

6. Conclusion

> "[...] With an inventory of available resources in hand, the next step for a designer is to use it well. Comprehensive anticipatory design science demands maximum overall efficiency with the least cost to society and ecology. Being comprehensive is a direction that implies extensive, omnidirectional research. [...] The goal is to optimize, rather than compromise." Buckminster Fuller (quoted from Baldwin 1996, p.62)

In this paper we gave an overview over the Design Science Labs, a recent infrastructure initiative at our university. Its goal is to make scientific simulation methods an integral part of architectural design processes. We argued that, while this has been a topic in CAAD research for a long time, and is currently getting a lot of public attention in international competitions, the topic has not been taken on by architecture schools in as big a way as it would deserve. By establishing laboratories for different distinct types of simulations which are set up to support a mix of analogue and digital methods as necessary, and by providing online support for creating a pool of best practice examples, the goal is to identify best practice approaches and to build up a network of experts and synergies between the individual labs.

At the time of this writing, only two of the planned four labs are in operation, while two more are scheduled to open next month. Nevertheless the initiative has already stirred a lot of enthusiasm and our faculty is likely to get funding for setting up the mentioned additional labs. Thus we will come closer to an environment that can foster a comprehensive anticipatory approach to architectural design. To what degree the synergies between the labs we anticipate will come about and how big the impact of the new facilities will be on design studio rather than just on research remains to be seen.

References

Addington, M and Schodek, DL: 2005, Smart Materials and Technologies for the architecture and design professions, Elsevier, New York.

Augenbroe, G and Winkelmann, F: 1991, Integration of Simulation into the Building Design Process, *in* JA Clarke, JW Mitchell, and RC Van de Perre (eds), *Proceedings, Building Simulation '91 IBPSA Conference*, pp. 367-374.

Baldwin, J: 1996, Bucky Works - Buckminster Fuller's Ideas for Today, John Wiley Sons, New York.

Chaisuparasmikul, P: 2006, Bidirectional Interoperability Between CAD and Energy Performance Simulation Through Virtual Model System Framework, *Synthetic Landscapes [Proceedings of the 25th Annual Conference of the Association for Computer-Aided Design in Architecture]*, pp. 232-250.

Chen, Q and Srebric, J: 2000, Application of CFD tools for indoor and outdoor environment design, *International Journal on Architectural Science* **1**(1): 14-29.

Crawley, DB, Lawrie, LK, Pedersen, CO and Winkelmann, FC: 2000, EnergyPLUS: Energy simulation program, *ASHRAE Journal* **42**: 49-56.

Cody, B: 2005, Form Follows Energy in GAM02 Design Science in Architecture, Springer, New York, pp. 28-41.

Flemming, U and Mahdavi, A: 1993, Simultaneous Form Generation and Performance Evaluation: A "Two-Way" Inference Approach, *Proceedings of CAAD Futures '93*, Pittsburgh, pp. 161-173.

Fuller, RB: Retrieved from http://www.anticipation.info/texte/buckminster/www.bfi.org/.

Hauser, S: 2005, The Knowledge of Architecture – An Essay in GAM02 Design Science in Architecture, Springer, New York, pp. 21-27.

Hillier, B: 1999, Space is the Machine: A Configurational Theory of Architecture, Cambridge Univsersity Press, Cambridge.

Kolarevic, B and Malkawi, AM (eds): 2005, *Performative Architecture. Beyond Instrumentality,* Spon Press, New York and London.

Mahdavi, A, Mathew, P and Wong, NH: 1997, A Homology-Based Mapping Approach to Concurrent Multi-Domain Performance Evaluation, *CAADRIA '97 [Proceedings of the Second Conference on Computer Aided Architectural Design Research in Asia/ISBN 957-575-057-8]*, pp. 237-246.

Maver, T: 1988, Software Tools for the Technical Evaluation of Design Alternatives, *Proceedings of CAAD Futures '87*, Eindhoven, Netherlands, pp. 47-58.

Veach, E and Guibas, LJ: 1997, Metropolis Light Transport, *SIGGRAPH' 97 Proceedings*, Addison-Wesley, pp. 65-76.

Wang, MY, Wang, X and Guo, D: 2003, A level set method for structural topology optimization, *Comput. Methods Appl. Mech. Engrg.* **192**: 227-246.

MORPHOSIS

A responsive membrane

NANCY DINIZ
University College London, United Kingdom

CESAR BRANCO
Augmented Architectures, Portugal

MIGUEL SALES DIAS
ADETTI/ISCTE and Microsoft Portugal, Portugal

and

ALASDAIR TURNER
University College London, UK

Abstract. In this paper, we introduce *Morphosis*: A Responsive Membrane, which physically responds to movement, light and sound interacting spatially and temporally with the environment and their inhabitants. The fundamental hypothesis is to create architectural systems as living, evolving materials. The dynamic of the material is produced by dozens of actuators made by Shape Memory Alloys (SMAs) and LED's which react in real time to change the behavior of the membrane. The system is controlled by a genetic algorithm in an attempt to develop a technological approach to performance skins that possess adaptive and evolutionary personality relative to changing phenomena of the environment of buildings.

1. Introduction

We consider that digital technology and kinetic structures should be implanted in the physical materials of architecture. As part of our ongoing research we developed a prototype interface titled *Morphosis* (Figures 5-6) a reconfigurable and visual system, based in our previous work (Diniz 2006),

A Dong, A Vande Moere & JS Gero (eds), CAADFutures'07, 489–498.

and inspired by the manner in which an organism, or any of its parts, evolve and change form in a short lapse of time, triggered by some combination of external stimuli in the ever changing surrounding environment. This paper proposes the *Morphosis* prototype as a model that is suitable for execution of a responsive architecture material and that enables the development of transformable architectural surfaces that have the ability to act in a responsive way, thus communicating and constantly reshaping our perception. The paper is structured as follows. In the Section 2, we examine related work in the artistic and architectural domains, focusing in the investigations in kinetic surfaces and aiming at understanding the objectives and design processes, proposed by their creators. In Sections 3 and 4, we describe the *Morphosis* prototype: its objectives, system design and implementation. In the later sections, the outcome results (Section 5) and future work directions (Section 6) are discussed.

2. Related Work

A direct relation between the human activity and the manifestation of surfaces; in this fusion between body and machine has been demonstrated by numerous systems which act as physical networks of a digital information landscape. Highly influenced by cybernetic thinkers, including Norbert Wiener (Wiener 1967), John von Neumann (von Neumann 1966), and Gordon Pask (Pask 1969) during the 1960's and 1970's, architects were encouraged to think of buildings as feedback systems rather static objects. Later, John Frazer at the Architectural Association (between the end of the 1980's and beginning of the 1990's) created a whole new lexicon towards an evolutionary architecture with many experimental projects with his students (Frazer 1995). He investigated fundamental form-generating processes, paralleling a wider scientific search for a theory of "morphogenesis" in the natural world. Gordon Pask describes it like this: "The role of the architect, I think, is not so much to design a building as to catalyze it; to act that they may evolve" (Frazer 1995).

Cedric Price was one of the first architects who actually formulated this model into a project becoming famous on the radicalism of his un-built ideas. His project, "The Fun Palace", although never built, was one of his most influential projects to a generation of architects. The idea central to Price's practice was the belief that through the correct use of new technology the public could have unprecedented control over their environment, resulting in a building which could be responsive to visitors' needs and the many activities intended to take place there. The building constitutes an open framework into which modular, pre-fabricated elements can be inserted and removed as required according to need. For Price, time was the fourth spatial dimension: length, width and height being the other three.

Kas Oosterhuis (1995) published the article "*Liquid Architecture*" describing the design of a pair of buildings known as the "*Salt-Water*" and "*Fresh-water*" pavilions, respectively designed by his firm Oosterhuis and the architectural firm Nox. These buildings incorporated numerous electronic sensors into their designs to gather information about both interior and exterior changes. Although the changes were mere virtual projections, the incorporation of computer sensing and display technology in the design of the buildings was a touchstone in the architectural discourse of computationally enhanced environments in which the building is loosely defined as an *Interface*.

Mark Goulthourpe's system "*Aegis Hypo-Surface*" built in 2001 is perhaps the world's first interactive wall. The piece is a triangle metallic surface that has potential to deform physically in response to electronic stimuli from the environment (movement, sound, light, etc). Driven by a bed of 896 pneumatic pistons, the effects are generated as real-time calculations. This project has potential for information to literally translate into form, it offers an entirely new medium, digitally dynamic yet materially tactile. Any digital input (microphone, keyboard, movement sensor) can trigger any physical output (a wave or pattern or word). In this *Aegis* has potential beyond that of a screen to being a fully 'architectural' (i.e. social, physical) interface, where activity (sound, movement, etc) translates into form (Leach 2002).

Very recently a variety of designers using shape memory alloys as actuators in kinetic architecture and computer-controlled projects allowed form to represent dynamic change in original ways ranging from aesthetic like "Implant Matrix" to functional approaches like "Pixel Skin".

"*Implant Matrix*" is described by the authors as "A network of mechanisms that reacts to human occupants as erotic prey". It represents an interactive geotextile similar to a natural system and aesthetically it displays a very sensual and delicate appeal. The piece is composed of "purpose programmed micro-controlled sensors and actuators that provide a mechanical response to user stimuli". Implant Matrix is organized as a lightweight large organic array of shape memory alloy arrays, sensors and distributed microprocessors that open and close as people touch the matrix to achieve a responding performance producing waves of motion. The matrix is capable of mechanical empathy, it responds to human presence with "subtle grasping and sucking motions" (Beesley 2006).

"*Pixel Skin*" (Anshuman 2004) is a heterogeneous smart surface that could be used to generate low resolution images, low refresh rate videos or graphical patterns. The interactive facade uses shape memory alloys to actuate each of the 4 triangular panels. Depending on the opening coefficient each set of 4 panels acts as a pixel (255 states between fully open to fully closed). The simulation controls the pattern type in response to live weather prediction for the day. This project deals with finding a solution to contemporary architectural surfaces; where conventional windows have to compromise between providing a natural light source and climate protection versus facilitating advertising and information display.

3. Objectives

The *Morphosis* prototype, borrows its design logic from ubiquitous electronic technology, artificial life, robotics, and human computer interaction (HCI) models as integral components of the design system, Figure 1. Its objectives are to explore the potential of architecture to communicate, respond and perform for its inhabitants. *Morphosis* aims also at developing an affordable artifact that combines architecture in form and function; and proposes a selected mix of technologies as a way to really augment the physical capabilities of architecture, by sensing the environment and responding to stimulus and analog inputs, and by evolving and achieving a symbiotic behavior, that are characteristics of the natural environment.

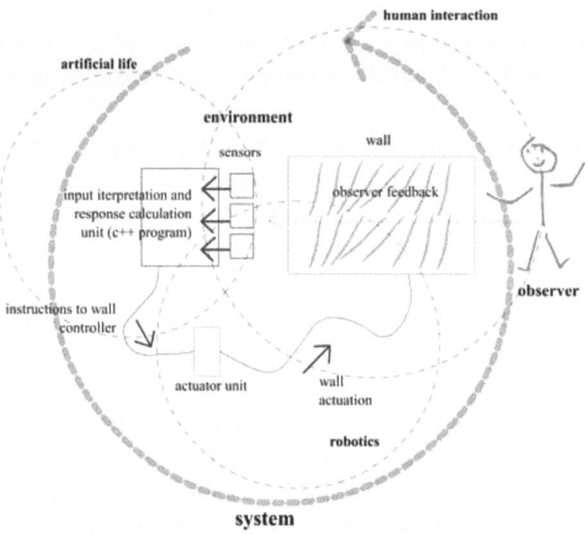

Figure 1. Morphosis Design Control Logic

3.1. A FUNCTIONAL RESPONSIVE SKIN

The abundance of sensing devices now available means that designers have a whole range of new possibilities for adaptive systems. We sought after to develop a smart structure that is light, strong and able of make extensive shape changes that minimizes the consumption of energy. Complex building structures now incorporate sensors, displays, and a range of mechanical functions. Many of our actions trigger automatic responses in our environment. Buildings contain innumerable sensors already, which detect temperature, humidity, light, fire and many other parameters relevant to the operation of the facility and the safety and comfort of their occupants. Sensing devices are becoming ubiquitous. The manufacture of these sensing devices for high volume commercial use has provided access to artists and scientists who want to create interactive systems responding to movement, light, touch, heat, acceleration, and position. Because these devices are increasingly inexpensive, it becomes possible to use them in experiments without commercial purposes. We have followed this approach in the *Morphosis* system design.

4. System Description and Design

The *Morphosis* system, Figure 2, consists of a physical structure with an embedded dynamic kinetic membrane, measuring 0.8 meters tall by 0.5 meters wide. Its objective is to create a human sized, sensitive, interactive (Figure 7) and multimodal, scalable structure that can be used as an architectural material. After analyzing the background work and presenting a critical review of the state-of-the-art, we introduce the system design of our prototype (Figure 5 and 6). This comprises a tactile and visual wall using an array of individual shape memory alloys (SMA), to actuate electric “muscles” that are anchored to an elastic skin, controlled by a microprocessor. For each muscle wire, we attach a LED that lights proportionally to the strength applied by the muscle. A stressed muscle will make an illuminated bump on the skin; a relaxed muscle will leave the skin dark at its neutral position. Additionally, this LED matrix can also constitute a low resolution image display, to transmit messages or design patterns.

Figure 2. Morphosis conceptual design depicted as a virtual prototype

4.1. TECHNICAL HARDWARE/SOFTWARE IMPLEMENTATION

The scheme behind the project requires a computer controlling an array of physical levers in real time. To make this possible the computer has to physically connect the Flexinol® SMA, and control the electrical power going through it at any given time (Figure 3 and 4). The chosen interface was the Phidget 64 LED controller that connects to the computer USB port. A C++ library is supplied so it is possible to write a C++ program to drive each individual LED (in 256 different intensities). This program can read the sensor inputs (web cam, vibration sensor, ambient light sensor) and decide which LEDs output to activate and thus the corresponding lever. A key component of the system software, detailed in Section 5, is the Genetic Algorithm.

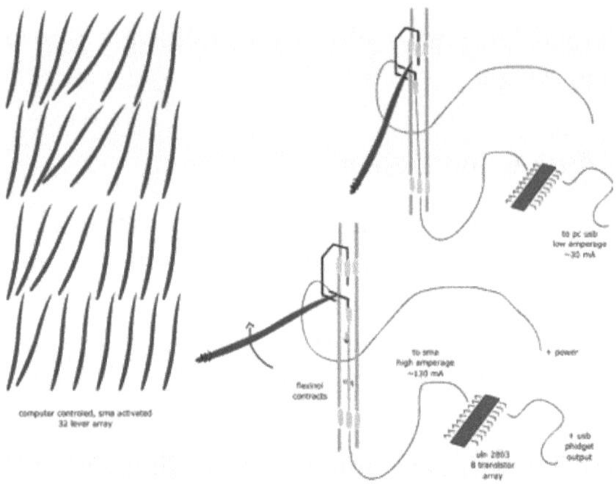

Figure 3. Views of the levers setup.

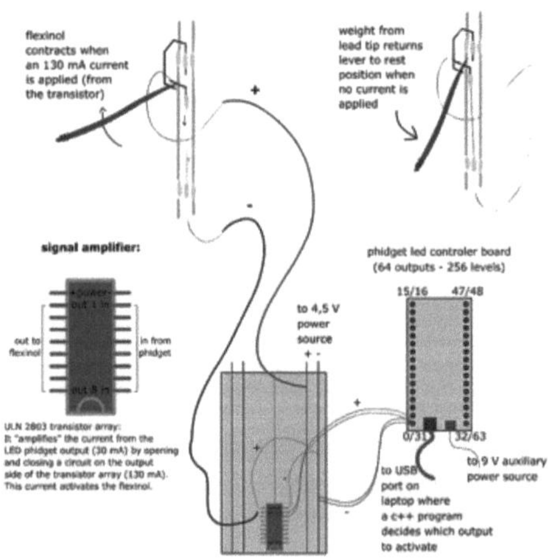

Figure 4. Diagram of Morphosis hardware setup

The system software, written in C++, launches an individual thread for each LED output. These are activated in power bursts, with the following characteristics: 2000 ms to activate the Flexinol®, plus 10 sequences of power (100 ms)/no power (200 ms) to maintain the Flexinol® contracted.

When the lever is to return to its default configuration, no power is applied and the lead weight at the tip of the lever, under the influence of gravity, brings the Flexinol® to the rest position.

Figure 5. Morphosis prototype without membrane and its SMA levers

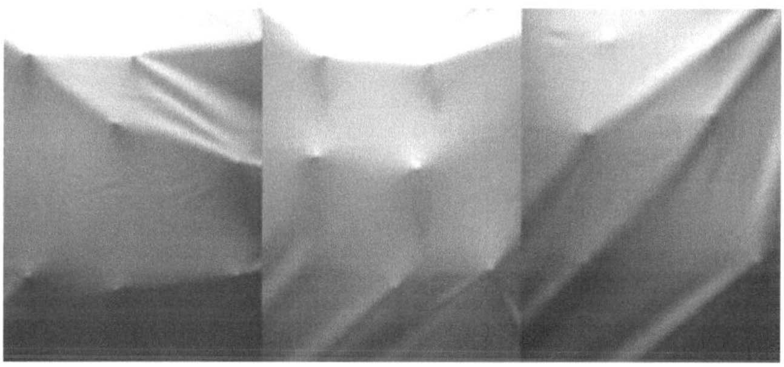

Figure 6. Morphosis prototype with a latex membrane and its actuated systems changing its shape. This prototype was produced by the authors in January 2007

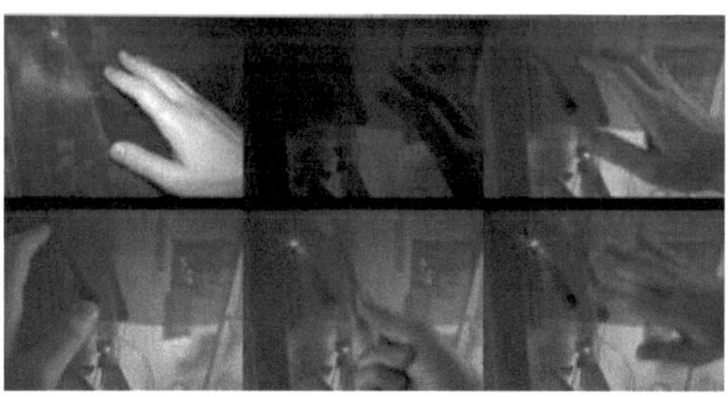

Figure 7. Changes in shape and lighting through proximity interactions by a user. The prototype was produced by the authors in August 2006

4.2. REAL-TIME DESIGN PROCESS

In this project most of the design process in non-CAD. The geometric form is crafted in the traditional model-making *modus operandi*. Form is fabricated with steel, latex, PVC, wires, and electronics are embedded within it, catalyzing material response to the external inputs. This way, a "performance based design" takes place, promoting a design approach which integrates form, structure and behavior as equal elements of the design process as a whole.

In our system, the process used of mounting surface modules connected to a computer via a standard, off the shelf USB controller, allows for the repetition and assemblage of several wall modules with no significant extra cost. This also brings the advantage of controlling several walls in an integrated fashion, sharing inputs and responding as a single structure.

Interlocked *Morphosis* modules could begin to design and export behaviors (wall/lever configurations) to structures (with variations from the simple rest form), depending on multiple variables: the time of day, temperature, ambient light levels, exceptional events and human response to it. Therefore, the modules have "memory, processing power and connection to the network" enabling a designer to give indications not only spatially but also temporally. Effectively, authors are designing systems in space and in time, hence in 4 dimensions.

5. Results and Discussion: Morphosis in Use

5.1. A STEP TOWARDS PHYSICAL AUGMENTED-ARCHITECTURE

We have developed *Morphosis*, in part, to investigate how the learning qualities of a material could be used to improve communication between buildings and its inhabitants.
The prototype behavior is the result of a complex system composed by sensors, actuators and a Genetic Algorithm (GA) component. From the literature, we know that GA is computational technique that roughly simulates biologic genetics (Mitchell 1998). A GA involves a "genotype" which is a string of code specifying a "phenotype".

In *Morphosis*, our "phenotype" is the shape of the membrane and the behavior of the levers and LED's. The input actions of the users and the environment are inputs for the genetic variations. Three input devices inform the computer of the status of the surrounding environment: a vibration sensor, a proximity sensor and a light sensor. These sensors are unobtrusively included in the wall and "feel" the environment informing the wall:

- Whether loud music is playing or someone is walking, for example, on a wooden floor (vibration sensor).
- If there is a rapid change in the ambient light levels (light sensor).
- If someone approaches the wall in a touching distance (proximity sensor).

These inputs change the behavior of the *Morphosis* in shape, trigger motion and light and can create random patterns on the surface, making the wall a responsive part of space, a lighting element, a functional architectural element and a performance piece.

The wall should respond to empathy and repulsion of the people present around the wall: their needs being coded as a measure of how a spectator is keeping herself/himself near the wall and their dislikes being coded as an evaluation of how a spectator is approaching the wall and leaving soon after. A wide range of possible phenotypes can be generated, and are evaluated for their "fitness", based on some formally specified criteria. The wall begins its learning phase, by running a random set of behaviors (raising and lowering levers to form patterns), and will try to adapt its effect sequences to get the maximum "empathy" responses. The wall also registers the environment with the aid of the vibration and light sensors, to detect which environment variables and effects are most liked. This way the wall tries to maximize the enjoyment of the people around it at all times and conditions. We think this kind of functionality may be included in outdoors as well as indoors structures, combining a structural functionality (facades, walls, lighting) with an artistic and empathic purpose.

The programmed GA works like this:

There are 3 different types of wall behaviors (effects): (1) Horizontal waves (left to right and right to left); (2) Vertical waves (top to bottom and bottom to top); (3) Random bumps.

There are 2 types of human responses to the wall:

- Empathy: the human approaches the wall and stays close (< 100 cm) to the wall for 2 minutes or more
- Dislike: the human approaches the wall and leaves the proximity of the wall, close to the wall (< 100 cm) for less than 2 minutes

The behaviors are randomly triggered and the wall waits for someone to approach the wall (detected by the proximity sensor or a web cam). The computer will register the particular effect combination being displayed at the times a viewer likes or dislikes it, and the circumstances (environment): time of day, luminosity and activity around the wall (measured by the vibration sensor). The wall will then try to exhibit the behaviors most liked at any given environmental conditions.

6. Future Work and Conclusions

The concepts described in this paper result from work carried out by the authors to build a functional and responsive surface (measuring 0.7 meters tall by 0.6 meters wide), actuated by shape memory alloys. Each actuator is controlled by a mixture of distributed, embedded, digital, and analog circuitry. Our prototype development was both satisfying and awe-inspiring; testing upon the aesthetic possibilities and technical opportunities of our model has allowed us to conceptualize more fully functional applications. Nevertheless, much more work, formal testing and usability evaluation with a set of selected subjects, following international standards, remains to be done.

One of the interesting developments is to make the surface more sensitive to the sound level, by introducing a Genetic Algorithm to make the wall react to undesirable sound conditions, and by re-arranging it in order to reduce the ambient noise; this is achievable using the computer microphone. As an example, a set-up like this could be used as an active feature in public spaces where low sound levels are required. A spiked wall could soften the ambient noise in large empty halls. Such spikes could be produced with the bumps made by the handles. In another example, when in situations of crowded spaces, the wall could fallback to other behaviors.

We will soon be extending the work to produce, test and evaluate a large-scale structure (measuring 1.4 meters tall by 2 meters wide). The prototype will be built from aluminum, rubber and steel components making it more robust and efficient. From its conception, *Morphosis* was intended to be a scalable multimodal material to be used on an architectural scale, rather than just "yet another interactive device", that could transmit meaning through functional and visual movement. For the future results we envisage not only incorporating interactivity within the physical nature of the material with performance and aesthetic nature, but also adding levels of functionality for Architecture purposes.

References

Anshuman, S and Kumar, B: 2004, Architecture and HCI: a review of trends towards an integrative approach to designing responsive space, *International Journal of IT in Architecture, Engineering and Construction* **2**(4): 273-284.

Beesley, P, Hirosue, S and Ruxton, J: 2006, *Toward Responsive Architectures: Subtle Technologies*, Riverside Architectural Press, Toronto.

Diniz, N and Branco, C: 2006, An Interactive membrane: Envisioning Physically Mutable Materials for Architecture, *in* JS Gero (ed) *Design Computing and Cognition '06* [Poster abstracts edition].

Oosterhuis, K: 1995, Liquid Architecture, *Archis* **11**.

Frazer, JH: 1995, *An Evolutionary Architecture*, Architectural Association, London.

Leach, N: 2002, *Designing for a digital world*, Wiley Academy Press, London.

Mitchell, M: 1998, *An Introduction to Genetic Algorithms*, The MIT Press, Cambridge.

Pask, G: 1969, The Architectural relevance of Cybernetics, *Architectural Design* **7**(6): 494-496.

von Neumann, J: 1966, *Theory of Self-Reproducing Automata,* University of Illinois Press, Urbana.

Wiener, N: 1967, *Cybernetics: Control and Communication in Animal and Machine*, The MIT Press, Cambridge.

BECOMING DETERMINABLE

MEASURING HUMAN BEHAVIOUR USING A HEAD-CAVE

CHENGYU SUN
Tongji University, PR. China

and

BAUKE DE VRIES, JAN DIJKSTRA
Eindhoven University of Technology, The Netherlands

Abstract. In this research funded by NSFC (50408038), an agent-based simulation model is developed for the human evacuation behaviour determined by a list of so-called architectural clues in the environment. A research method is introduced with an application for one of these clue types called Doorway. A six-variable model and a related set of virtual scenes were constructed and implemented in a Head-CAVE system, in which 102 subjects were tested as in an evacuation game. With the binary logit regression analysis a utility function is estimated indicating how these variables affect human choice on any pair of doorways in a scene. Evidence was found that the distance from the decision point to the doorway is not always the most important factor as it is assumed in the other evacuation models.

1. Introduction

As many mega cities in China, Shanghai is entering a period of booming underground space development, Figure 1, in the next 20 years. As the government planned, the subway system will increase from 82 km to more than 400 km by the year 2010, and the daily passengers will increase from 1.3 million to 6 million. With the big step of the underground space development, the security problem on how the public space evacuates people in an emergency is coming to the surface.

Building performance research with regard to hazard situations resulted in simulation models of human movements. These models are based on social force methods (e.g. Helbing et al. 2000) and cellular automata methods (e.g. Nishinari et al. 2004).

A Dong, A Vande Moere & JS Gero (eds), CAADFutures'07, 501–511.

Figure 1. The crowded underground space in Shanghai

Performance-based evaluation methods together with some commercial evacuation simulation models for underground space design were introduced to the government of China. However, due to the limited background knowledge, most of the evaluation models were found too complex to be used by architects. Actually these models are used by the experts in the fire security department to check the evacuation problems in the most critical situations.

In this research an agent-based simulation model is developed for the behaviour of humans determined by the public architectural space of the underground environment. All the other factors investigated in the existing models such as fire, smoke, toxic gases, alarm, signalling, etc. (Kuligowski and Peacock 2005) are excluded from this model. The focus is on architectural clues that drive the movement through the space. A set of experiments in virtual architectural spaces is designed and implemented with the assumption that "If a setting works well under normal conditions, it will have a better chance of working well in emergency conditions." (Arthur and Passini 1992)

The outline of the paper is as follows: First we will describe the list of architectural clues and the related evacuation strategies. Next the research method is explained, followed by the analyses of the data. We will finish with preliminary conclusions and outlooks.

2. Architectural-based Model for Underground Space Evacuation (AMUSE)

From previous research (Sun and Vries 2006) a list of so-called architectural clue types was deduced, namely Outdoors, Exits, Stairs, Slopes, Escalator, Raised Ceilings, Columns and Doorways. Based on these architectural clue types, 3 evacuation strategies are introduced ordered in a priority from high to low.

Strategy I. *Go to the safety*

Any architectural clue indicating itself as a safety termination of the evacuation such as Outdoors and Exits in the subject's view will be picked as a target to approach.

Strategy II. *Go to the higher floor*

Any architectural clue indicating itself useful to get the subject closer to the ground level such as Stair, Escalator, Slope in the subject's view will be picked as a target to approach.

Strategy III. *Try the more likely*

Any architectural clue indicating that it might lead to a probable way out such as Columns/Doorways leading to other spaces with lower/higher Ceilings in the subject's view will be picked as a target to approach.

The assumption is that from the set of architectural clues in sight, the human selects the one with the highest priority and performs a related strategy (Lawson 2001). If there are several clues with the same priority, for example three Exits in the same view, the subject has to pick the most probable one by a choice mechanism through pair wise comparison. In Table 1, we summarized how the architectural clue types are divided into three groups for the three strategies.

TABLE 1. Evacuation strategies and Architectural Clue Types

Evacuation Strategy	Architectural Clue Type
Go to the safety	Outdoors
	Exits
Go to the higher floor	Stairs
	Slopes
	Escalator
Try the more likely	Doorways with or without various Ceiling
	Columns

The agent uses its vision to perceive the environment and recognize the above clues in the 3-dimensional space to support the decision making during the evacuation simulation. The pixel-based recognition algorithm of the clues in the agent's vision will be presented in another publication. In the following section the research method is described to determine the decision-making parameters that lead to the selection of a specific evacuation strategy.

3. Research Method

The agent interpretation method raises a lot of questions, such as: are the priorities right, what about the preference between architectural clues with the same priority and finally, does the interpretation leads to valid behaviour of the agents? In this paper we will focus on the second question and on one priority level, namely the Strategy III 'Try the more likely', because the research methodology here is basic to the rest of the research project.

For all types of Doorways in Strategy III the following variables and corresponding attributes are defined (see Figure 2):

Distance from the entrance to observation point, defined as **D**, assumption is that a longer distance decreases the importance;

Width of the doorway, defined as **W**, assumption is that a wider doorway increases the importance;

Height of the doorway, defined as **H**, assumption is that a higher doorway increases the preference;

Angle between the direction of the view direction and the doorway, defined as **A1**,assumption is that a narrower angle increases the importance;

Angle between the direction of the view direction and the doorway axis, defined as **A2**, assumption is that a narrower angle increases the importance;

Besides the above variables, the left-right preference will be considered as another variable **LR**, assumption is that there is a cultural determined importance.

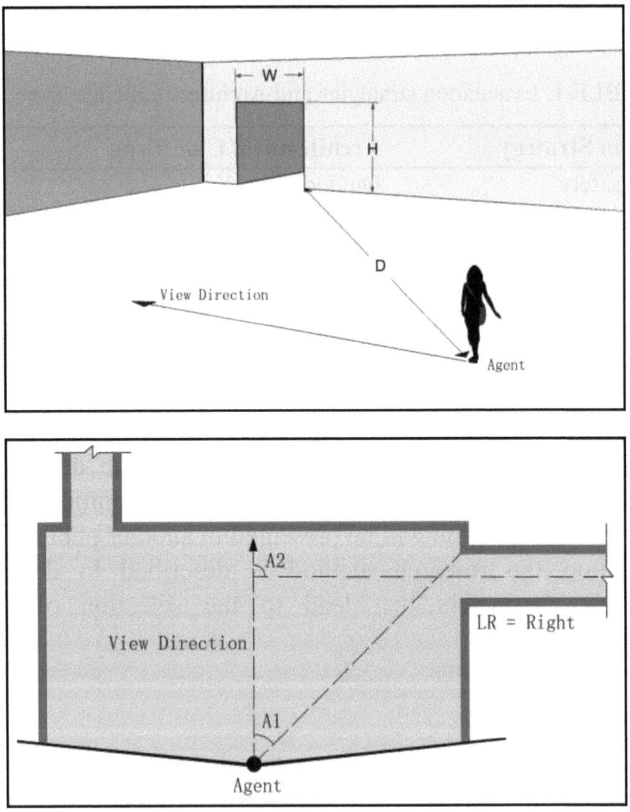

Figure 2. The definition of the variables of doorway

A statistic choice model Binary Logit is chosen to measure the relative importance of attributes influencing subject's choices. Hereby, subject's responses on choices are observed in hypothetical situations designed under controlled experiments in such a way as to satisfy the assumptions of statistical choice models.

To maximize statistical efficiency, attribute profiles and choice sets are constructed according to the principles underlying the design of statistical experiments. The main objective is to determine the contribution of predictor variables (attribute levels) to the overall preference or satisfaction. In the case of the choice task, in addition to estimating the utility function, the goal is to estimate the parameters of the choice model. In the Binary Logit model it is assumed that the probability that an individual will choose alternative a_i of the two alternatives from the choice set C is given by Equation 1.

$$p(a_i \mid C) = \frac{\exp[U(a_i)]}{\sum_{j=1}^{2} \exp[U(a_j)]} = \frac{\exp(x_i \beta)}{\sum_{j=1}^{2} \exp(x_j \beta)} \quad (1)$$

Where:

$p(a_i \mid C)$ is the probability that choice alternative a_i is chosen from set C;

$U(a_i) = \beta_0 + \beta_1 D + \beta_2 W + \beta_3 H + \beta_4 A1 + \beta_4 A2 + \beta_5 LR$

β_0 is a constant, β_i is the parameter for every variable.

In the experiment, choice sets of two alternatives are recorded. One alternative is chosen, the other not. Therefore, $p(a_i \mid C) = 1$ if alternative a_i is chosen otherwise $p(a_i \mid C) = 0$. The sample of the recorded dataset is shown in Table 2.

TABLE 2. A sample of the recorded choice for one scene in the experiment

Scene ID	p	*D*	*W*	*H*	A1	A2	LR
00024	0	0	1	1	0	1	0
00024	1	1	0	0	1	0	1
Etc.							

4. Experiment

From previous experiments we learned that the scenes with a wide angle view presented on a flat screen have a big distortion on the subject's depth perception, which plays an important role in the measurement of the human behaviour (Sun, de Vries and Dijkstra 2007). There are precedents of research on human behavior in built environment done in virtual environment. To provide the subjects with a nearly 170 degree view (Turner and Penn 2002), such experiments generally use CAVE systems (Achten, Jessurun, and de Vries 2004). In this research, the authors built a Head-CAVE system with three LCDs, as shown in Figure 3.

Figure 3. The Head-CAVE system

In this experiment, two scene sets (A and B) were prepared, each set containing 32 scenes, each with two doorways, but with different attributes values, see Table 3.

TABLE 3. The two scene sets

Scene Set A

Scene ID	Left Doorway						Right Doorway				
	A1	**A2**	**W**	**D**	**H**		**A1**	**A2**	**W**	**D**	**H**
1	5	0	2.5	30	3		30	45	5	45	4
2	30	45	5	45	4		5	0	2.5	30	3
...	...	...	...	...	...		...	...	...	...	...
31	5	45	5	45	4		30	0	2.5	30	3
32	30	0	2.5	30	3		5	45	5	45	4

Scene Set B

Scene ID	Left Doorway						Right Doorway				
	A1	**A2**	**W**	**D**	**H**		**A1**	**A2**	**W**	**D**	**H**
1	5	0	2.5	30	3		55	90	7.5	60	5
2	55	90	7.5	60	5		5	0	2.5	30	3
...	...	...	...	...	...		...	...	...	...	...
31	5	90	7.5	60	5		55	0	2.5	60	3
32	55	0	2.5	30	3		5	90	7.5	45	5

The subjects observed two doorway options in every scene according to the above table through the T-window as showed in Figure 4. All the choices were recorded in the format indicated in Table 2.

Figure 4. The scene with two doorway options through the HEAD-CAVE

Altogether 102 subjects took part in the evacuation experiment, which was designed to be something like a first person shooting game, such as DOOM. Each subject can see a timer on the screen and hear from his earphone a heartbeat as well as an alarm urging him to evacuate. In the Head-CAVE system, the subject is faced with scenes from the two sets of experiments by random. He is required to imagine himself in an underground space and to get out of there as soon as possible by choosing either the left or the right doorway in each scene. He is also required to act on instinct. The subject who escapes the building in the least time wins. Every subject experiences all 64 scenes in one experiment. From the experiment we found that under the effect of the sound, the timer, and the dramatic game, the subjects were all rather absorbed in the experiment.

5. Analyses

In each scene there were only two escape options, a single choice of a subject brings about two statistical samples, each concerning one doorway. Each sample contains one dependent variable (**p**) and six independent variables (**D, W, H, A1, A2, LR**), also see Table 2. When a doorway is chosen, **p** is recorded as 1, or else 0. When the left doorway is chosen, LR is recorded as 1, or else 0. For weighting comparison, the smaller values of the other five independent variables are recorded as 0, and the larger as 1. Thus, for D, W, H, A1, A2 two distinct values were used. The experiment was conducted with two scene Sets. In Scene Set A the ratio of the distances from the two doorways to observer equaled to 1:1.5; whereas in Scene Set B, when the ratio of distances rose to 1:2. Binary Logistic Regression (forward

Stepwise LR) in the SPSS was applied to analyze the results. The most significant variables (Sig. equals 0.000), are shown in Table 4, from which we can conclude that in a model of the six variables mentioned, A1, W, D are the three main factors that effect the inducement of a doorway in evacuation.

TABLE 4. The result of Binary Logit analyses
(B=β from equation (1), S.E.=Standard Error, Wald=$(B/S.E.)^2$, df= degrees of freedom)

Scene Set A

		B	S.E.	Wald	df	Sig.	Exp(B)
Step 1(a)	A1	-.352	.057	38.060	1	.000	.703
	W	2.058	.059	1236.418	1	.000	7.834
	D	-.992	.058	288.605	1	.000	.371
	Constant	-.357	.054	44.392	1	.000	.700

Scene Set B

		B	S.E.	Wald	df	Sig.	Exp(B)
Step 1(a)	A1	-.779	.057	188.635	1	.000	.459
	W	1.564	.058	722.204	1	.000	4.776
	D	-1.472	.058	641.336	1	.000	.229
	Constant	.344	.053	41.480	1	.000	1.410

From the experiment we observed: In Scene Set A, the main variables that effect induced evacuation behavior and their weights in order are: W (2.058), D (-.992), A1 (-.352); In Scene Set B: W (1.564), D (-1.472), A1 (-.779). A positive weight means that the larger variable value the higher chance the doorway being chosen, while a negative weight means the larger value the less chance. From the data above, the we found that the result of the two sets of scenes indicates the same main factors (W, D, A1), although the weights of the factors vary as the variable values change.

6. Preliminary Conclusion

From the results of experiment above, we conclude that the assumption in other existing evacuation models that people evacuate to the nearest doorway is inaccurate, or at least tenable only under certain circumstances. We discovered that, in the experiment of Scene Set A, the width of the doorways had a crucial effect on the observer's decision (with a weight twice that of the distance and making up 60% of the total weight); whereas in the experiment of Scene Set B, the effectiveness of the width and distance of doorways became rather the same (their weights close, each 26% of the total weight). From this trend, we deduced that when the ratio of the distances from the two doorways to observer is higher than 1:2, the weight of the distance will continue increasing while the weight of width will fall, which means that the distance of the doorway from the observer will play a crucial part in effecting the evacuation behavior. Therefore, only then the "nearest-doorway assumption" is tenable.

This conclusion can be used to modify the judgment on the pedestrian flow made by architects in designing a plan. It is obvious that when the ratio of the distances from the two doorways to the evacuees is lower than 1:2 the architect can guide evacuation by widening one of the entrances, as show in Figure 5. Otherwise, the misusing of the "nearest-distance assumption" and neglect of the significance of the width of the doorways can cause problems in evacuation, as shown in Figure 6.

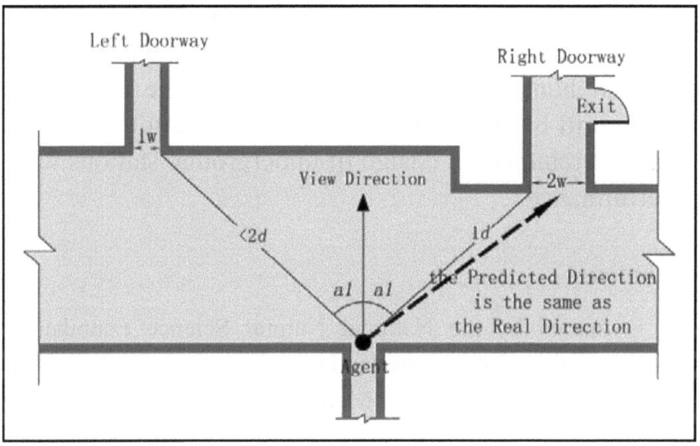

Figure 5. Correct prediction considering on the width factor

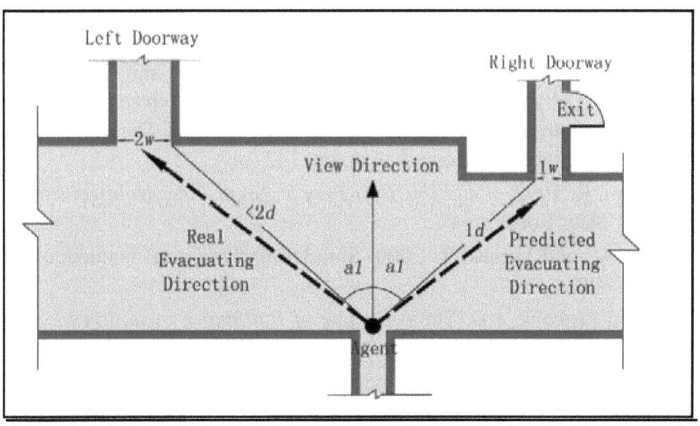

Figure 6. Wrong prediction ignoring the width factor

7. Summary and Outlook

In this paper, a Head-CAVE-based experiment on measuring the human's evacuation behavior in front of two doorway options was introduced. The research method has proven that a doorway-oriented evacuation decision model can be constructed through Binary Logistic Regression. According to the preliminary model the nearest-doorway assumption in other evacuation models is questionable in some circumstances. Moreover, the relative critical value of the distances' ratio is discovered.

The next step in this research project is to conduct experiments for the other architectural clues, using the same methodology. After that a digital model of a complete underground space will be constructed including all architectural clues. The movement pattern of the agents in the simulation model AMUSE, based on architectural clue guidance, will be compared with real movement of humans in a Virtual model of the underground space. Finally AMUSE will be integrated into a CAD system to support architects in analyzing their architectural design of underground stations with regard to evacuation performance.

Acknowledgements

This research is funded by the National Natural Science Foundation of China (NSFC) and supported by the Netherlands Organisation for Scientific Research (NWO) and the National Laboratory of Modern Technology in Urban Planning and Design, Tongji University.

References

Achten, HH, Jessurun, AJ and de Vries, B: 2004, The Desk-Cave - A Low-Cost Versatile Virtual Reality Design and Research Setup Between Desktop and CAVE, *in* B Ruediger, B Tournay and H Orbaek (eds), *Proceedings of the 22nd International Conference on Education and Research in Computer Aided Architectural Design in Europe,* Royal Danish Academy of Fine Arts, Copenhagen, pp. 142-147.

Arthur, P and Passini, R: 1992, *WAYFINDING People, Signs, and Architecture,* McGraw-Hill Book Company, New York.

Helbing, D, Farkas, IJ and Vicsek, T: 2000, Simulating dynamical features of escape panic, *Nature* **407**: 487-490.

Kuligowski, ED and Peacock, RD: 2005, *Review of Building Evacuation Models*, NIST TN 1471, NIST Technical Note 1471.

Lawson, B: 2001, *Language of space,* Architectural Press, Oxford.

Nishinari, K, Kirchner A, Namazi, A and Schadschneider, A: 2004, Extended floor field CA model for evacuation dynamics, *IEICE Transactions on Information and Systems* **E87-D** (4): 726-732.

Sun, CY and de Vries, B: 2006, An Architecture-Based Model for Underground Space Evacuation, *in* W Borutzky, A Orsoni, R Zobel (eds), *Proceedings of the 20-th European Conference on Modelling and Simulation ECMS 2006*, Bonn, pp. 578-583.

Sun, CY, de Vries, B and Dijkstra, J: 2007, A Research method on human behaviour induced by architectural clues in public underground spaces *in Proceedings of CAADRIA 2007*, Nanjin. (forthcoming)

Turner, A and Penn, A: 2002, Encoding natural movement as an agent-based system: an investigation into human pedestrian behaviour in the built environment, *Environment and Planning B: Planning and Design* **29**: 473-490.

AUTOMATIC PRODUCT COLOR DESIGN USING GENETIC SEARCHING

HUNG-CHENG TSAI
Nanhua University, Taiwan

CHIA-YOUNG HUNG
National Cheng Kung University, Taiwan

and

FEI-KUNG HUNG
WuFeng Institute of Technology, Taiwan

Abstract. Color plays a key role in determining a consumer's response to a product appearance. A gray-theory-based linguistic evaluation method and a color-harmony-based aesthetic evaluation method are combined in this study to diagnose appropriate product-color schemes. Accordingly, this study develops a RGB-based quantitative aesthetic and linguistic measurement scheme to evaluate the image perception of a particular product-color scheme. In an inverse process, genetic algorithms are applied to search for the near-optimal color combination which satisfies the designer's specified product-color linguistic evaluation goal and achieves a high degree of color harmony.

1. Introduction

The functions of most products surrounding us in our daily lives are now mature. For products with similar functions, the style of the product becomes an important factor in a consumer's decision-making process when deciding which particular product to purchase. The consumer's perception of the product's style is generally induced by a combination of the product's color and its form. It is wasteful and expensive for an enterprise to attempt to design the wide variety of product forms which would be required to meet the needs of each individual consumer. Traditional products with their specific color matches fail to satisfy the vast range of consumer's needs

A Dong, A Vande Moere & JS Gero (eds), CAADFutures'07, 513–524.

However, enterprises can vary the color matches of product's individual components in order to generate a wide variety of product image perceptions. In this way, one product from a single fixed mold can be extended to numerous color series to meet the consumers' needs Generally, a designer carries out the color planning element of the product design based upon his or her individual experience, artistic sense, and subjective view, but this is not objective enough and very inefficient. If the designer possessed the facility to access a powerful tool to evaluate the product image sensations induced for designed color matches of a product, he or she could quickly display the appropriate product colors on a PC-based monitor during the conceptual design period. Additionally, the development of information and internet technology enables designers to browse real-time rendered 3D models with the simulated colors. For a single color product, it is feasible to predict the mental perception of its image using a color-image database. However, predicting the overall image evaluation is much more complicated if the product comprises a variety of differently-colored components. Therefore, this study develops a gray system method of evaluating the relationship between the color matches of a product and the consumer's perception of its overall image.

Previous studies of color-image perception focused mainly on the image evaluation of single-color products. For example, Hsiao (1994) applied fuzzy set theory to select the most suitable color for a car from a range of specified colors. In a later study (Hsiao 1995), the same author proposed a systematic method for product-color design based on the Munsell color system. Choo and Kim (2003) investigated the color effect in fashion fabric products using Munsell and PCCS color notations for the color variables. Nowadays, color designs based on the CIE color system can be easily rendered on 3-D CAD models in the color planning stage of product design. However, the color image models traditionally employed in such applications are generally based on the colors of the object rather than on the three primary colors of light (i.e. red, green and blue). Ou et al. (2004) established color emotion and color preference models for single colors using the CIELAB color space. In a study investigating the evaluation of images comprising multiple colors in the interior design field, Shen et al. (1996) proposed a linguistic-based evaluation model specified in terms of color harmony based on the CIE system. Meanwhile, the current author applied gray system theory (Deng 1987) to develop a systematic method for evaluating the overall image perception of a product comprising components of different colors defined using RGB parameters (Hsiao and Tsai 2004).

The color-image studies outlined above considered the image evaluation of products with predefined color combinations. However, comparatively little attention has been paid to the inverse case, in which the aim is to identify the color combination which satisfies a specified color image evaluation requirement. Linguistic image-oriented auto-searching schemes for optimal color combinations must be supervised by appropriate color harmony theories since if such supervision is not applied, the search results are liable to be dull and uncoordinated even if the color combination is close to the specified linguistic evaluation goal.

The evaluation of aesthetics on a quantitative basis was originally considered by Birkhoff (1933). Subsequently, Moon and Spencer (1944a, 1944b, 1944c) applied Birkhoff's theory of aesthetic measurement to the problem of color harmony based on the Munsell system. This study also combines a color-harmony-based aesthetic measurement method with the gray-theory-based linguistic evaluation method to evaluate the image sensations induced by different color combinations. In the proposed approach, the Munsell-based color parameters of the aesthetic measurement scheme are transformed into RGB parameters such that the evaluation results can be integrated with a CAD system. Subsequently, genetic algorithms (Goldberg 1989) are employed to identify the near-optimal color combination which matches the specified image requirements expressed in terms of linguistic and aesthetic measures.

Unlike conventional problem-solving techniques, genetic algorithms converge towards the optimal solution from multiple directions. In the current application, the chromosomes produced during the population-based search method of the genetic algorithm represent the color-design candidates produced in a brainstorming process. Although optimal solutions generally exist for most engineering problems, it is frequently difficult to identify these solutions at the conceptual design stage. In most cases, a near-optimal solution represents the best solution which can reasonably be hoped for. However, in the current application, by carefully defining the color evaluation algorithms employed by the genetic algorithm, the designer can increase the likelihood of the final solution closely approximating the optimal solution.

In the proposed approach, color parameters are either input to the image prediction sub-system or output from the color-combination search sub-system. Meanwhile, the predicted/desired image evaluation is output from the image prediction sub-system and input to the color-combination search sub-system. Using the proposed design system, the designer is able not only to determine the likely consumer reaction to any color scheme proposed for a product, but can also search for an ideal (near-optimal) color-combination which will likely satisfy the desired product-color perception. The customized interfaces of the proposed system are integrated with the I-DEAS system to enable the designer to view 3-D colored models rendered with the assigned input color parameters or to search for suitable color schemes which satisfy a particular set of image evaluation targets.

2. Outline of the Implementation Methods

2.1. PRODUCT COLOR EVALUATION

The color planning stage of a baby walker design activity is used as an example to demonstrate the procedure adopted in this present study. A rendered 3-D model of the constructed walker is shown in Figure 1. The design model procedure comprises the following steps:

- Select an objective product as the subject and construct its 3D CAD model for investigation purposes.
- Analyze the color categories of the model's various components.
- Use the RGB color system to establish basic color samples which can be presented on the rendered 3-D model.
- Design questionnaires to establish the relationships between a set of basic color samples and their corresponding image evaluation words.
- Establish the gray clustering algorithms to evaluate the overall image perception of multi-colored products.
- Construct a Back-Propagation Neural network (BPN) to evaluate the total image perception of the multi-colored product.
- Compare the Root Mean Square Error (RMSE) values of the results of the gray theory model and the BPN model with the experimentally-verified target results.
- Construct a consultative program and an interface for color planning purposes.

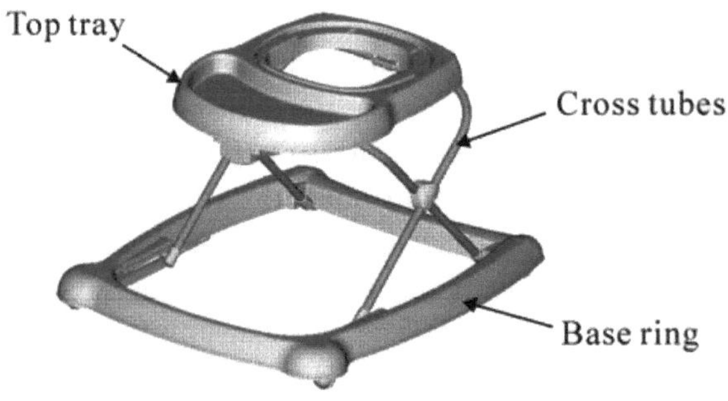

Figure 1. A rendered 3-D model of the constructed walker

2.2. LINGUISTIC AND AESTHETIC IMAGE-BASED GENETIC SEARCHING

This study integrates the aesthetic measurement method, gray theory and genetic algorithms to develop a computer-aided automatic product color image prediction and color-combination search system. The proposed system comprises two fundamental mechanisms, namely: (1) a linguistic and aesthetic color image prediction function based on gray theory and Moon and Spencers' aesthetic measurement method, respectively, and (2) a search function for optimal two-color combinations based on genetic algorithms. The basic concepts of these two functions, and the interrelationships between them, are illustrated in Figure 2. The linguistic and aesthetic image prediction function enables the likely consumer reaction to a product color image to be predicted for any given set of input color parameter values. Meanwhile, the color combination search function performs essentially the inverse operation, i.e. given a set of image perception requirements, this function searches automatically for the near-optimal color combination which satisfies these requirements. Gray theory is employed to establish the relationship between the linguistic image evaluation and the color parameters, and the aesthetic measurement method is applied to evaluate the aesthetic degree of the color combination in terms of its color harmony. During the search procedure, genetic algorithms are used to perform an evolutional search for elite color combinations, with the suitability (fitness) of each candidate solution being evaluated by the linguistic and aesthetic image prediction function.

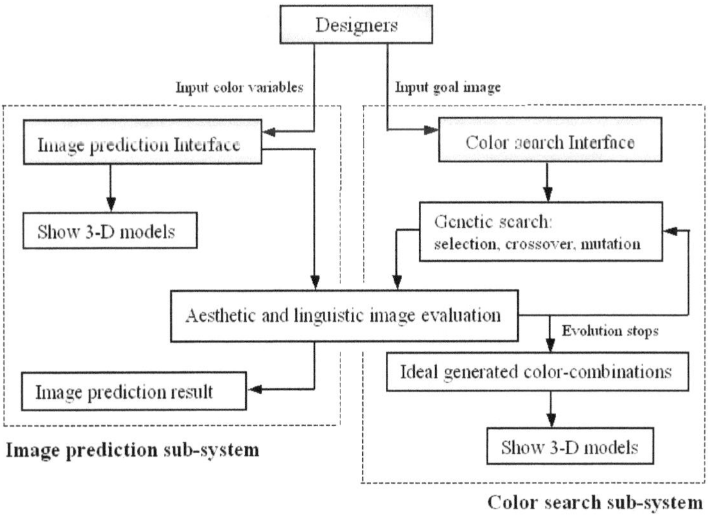

Figure 2. Basic concepts of automated image prediction and color search mechanism

This case study verified the effectiveness of the automatic color design system by considering the case of the color design of a thermos flask. The detailed procedures involved in implementing the color system are described below.

- Construct 3-D model of thermos flask with two-color appearance (Figure 3).
- Carry out product-color linguistic and aesthetic image evaluation experiments.
- Establish evaluation model for linguistic image measurement mechanism.
- Establish evaluation model for aesthetic image measurement mechanism.
- Demonstrate reliability of proposed color evaluation model by performing further image experiments.
- Establish genetic algorithm-based product color combination search model.
- Construct operational system for linguistic and aesthetic image prediction and color-combination search.
  - Interface for product-color image evaluation
  - Interface for product-color search

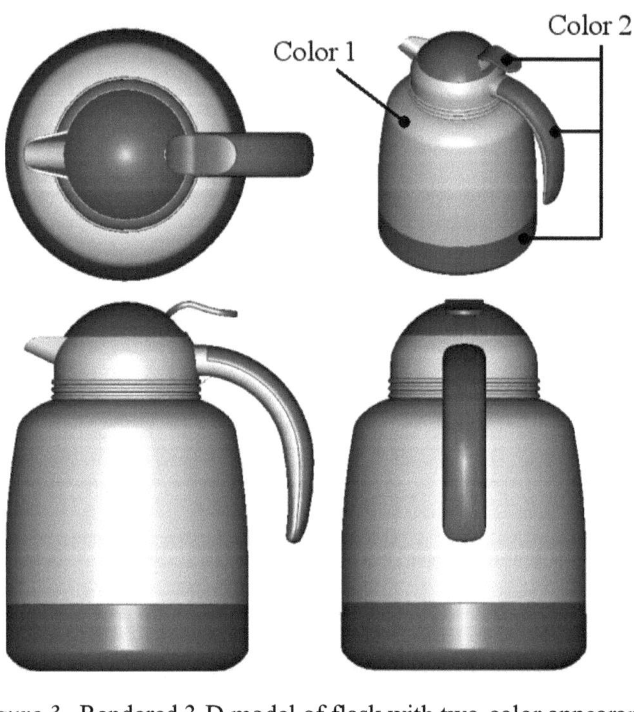

Figure 3. Rendered 3-D model of flask with two-color appearance

3. Case Studies

3.1. EXAMPLE I FOR PRODUCT COLOR EVALUATION

A color design interface based upon the gray algorithm is constructed for the baby walker design. For the user's convenience, the operating interface can be accessed via the VBOI component included within the I-DEAS software. The RGB-parameter setting and image evaluation window is shown in Figure 4. The RGB values for individual color groups are entered into the system, and then the 'Evaluate' button is pressed to calculate the three corresponding linguistic membership grades. Simultaneously, the color-rendered model is automatically shown on the VRML browser, Cosmo Player (Figure 5). Consequently, not only can the designer obtain the color evaluation information, but he or she can also browse the rendered dynamic 3-D model using the planned colors.

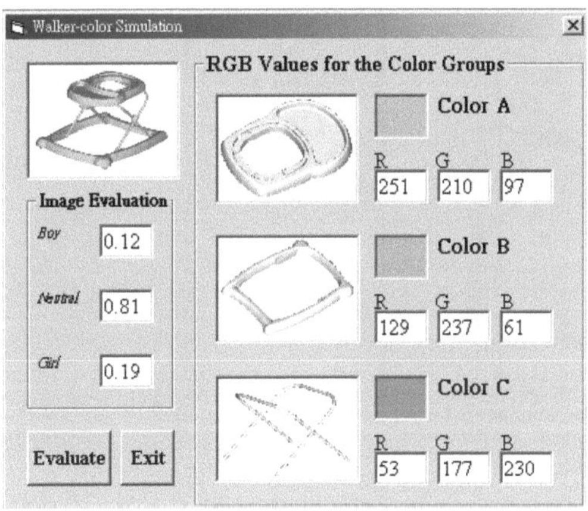

Figure 4. The RGB-parameter setting and image evaluation window

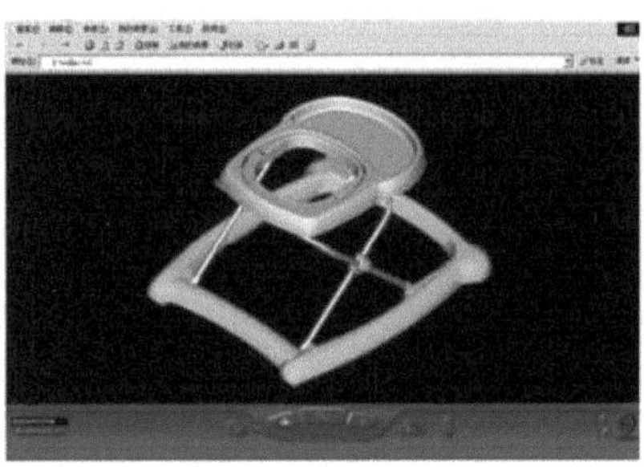

Figure 5. The rendered 3-D model of example I displayed on the cosmo player

3.2. EXAMPLE II FOR LINGUISTIC AND AESTHETIC EVALUATIONS

This example considers the image evaluation prediction of a thermos flask with assigned color parameters. In the interface shown in Figure 6, the RGB color parameters are specified as: Color 1 (56, 83,148) and Color 2 (144, 165, 214). Clicking the "3-D Color Simulation" button reveals the 3-D model rendered with the corresponding colors (see Figure 7). Alternatively, clicking the "Image Evaluation" button displays the predicted image evaluation window shown in Figure 8. In this example, it is found that the predicted linguistic and aesthetic evaluations of the two-colored flask are 0.61 and 0.92, respectively.

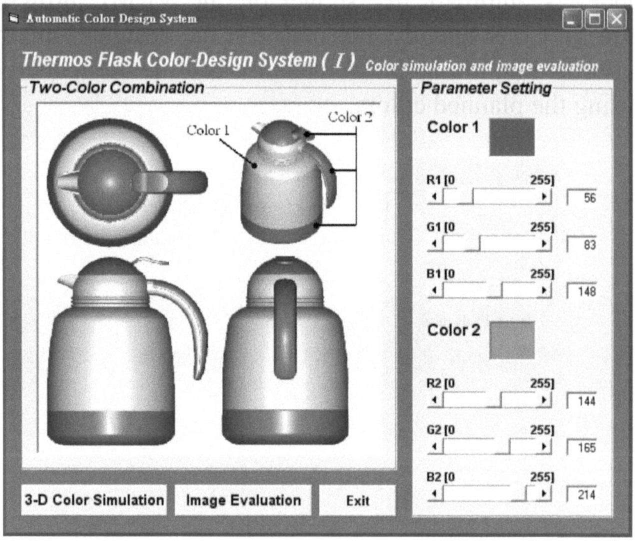

Figure 6. Interface for constructing 3-D model and performing color-image prediction

Figure 7. 3-D VRML file presented on Cosmo Player

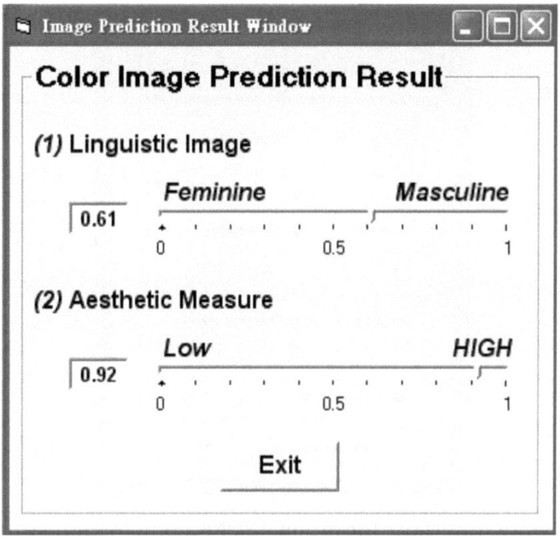

Figure 8. Color-image prediction window

3.3. EXAMPLE III FOR IDEAL COLOR COMBINATION SEARCHING

In this example, the designer specifies targets for the linguistic and aesthetic properties of the two-colored flask, and then uses the design system to search for an appropriate two-color combination. Using the interface shown in Figure 9, the designer specifies a target linguistic evaluation (feminine–masculine) of 0.2, a linguistic weight of 0.5, an aesthetic weight of 0.5, and 100 iterations in the search routine. Note that the latter setting implies that the optimization system will execute the fitness function evaluation process 1000 times since the population size is set by default to 10.

Figure 10 shows the trends of the fitness of the candidate solutions over the evolution of the search process and indicates the corresponding variations of the linguistic and aesthetic evaluations. It can be seen that as the generation number increases, the linguistic and aesthetic evaluations vary irregularly in order to maximize the fitness value, i.e. to obtain a color combination which increasingly fits the goal image. Figure 11 indicates the best-fitted color combinations at the 1st, 20th, 40th, 60th, 80th and 100th generations, respectively. The final search results are presented in the window shown in Figure 12. As shown, the window indicates both the actual and the target linguistic and aesthetic evaluation ratings, the RGB parameters for the two best-fitted colors, and the overall fitness of the final two-color design. Clicking, the "3-D Color Simulation", the designer is presented with a 3-D image of the flask rendered in the best-fitted color combination.

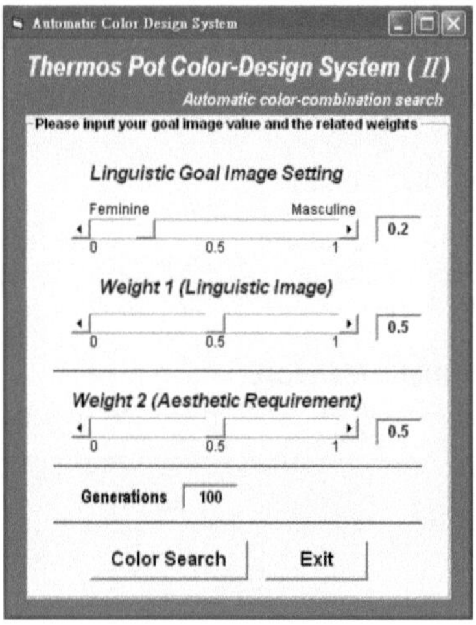

Figure 9. Interface for product color combination search

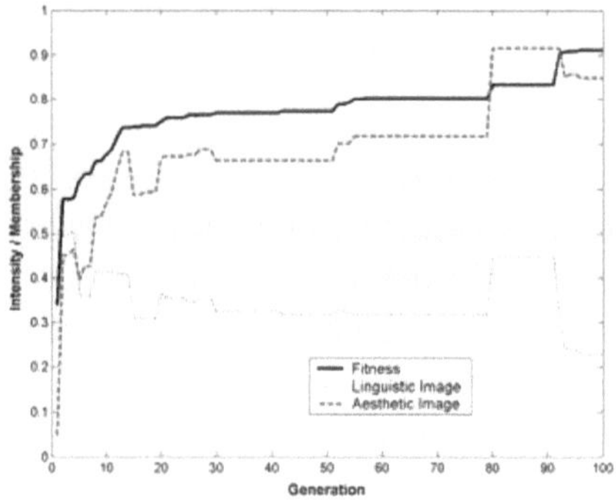

Figure 10. Trends of fitness function and image evaluation ratings during search process

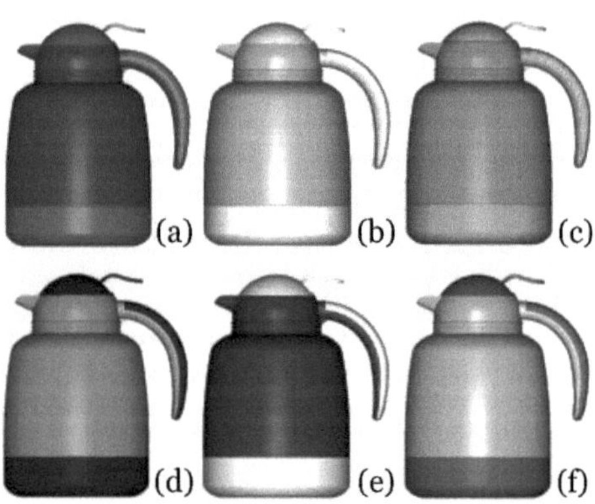

Figure 11. Color evolution: best-fitted color combinations at: (a) initial, (b) 20th, (c) 40th, (d) 60th, (e) 80th and (f) 100th generation

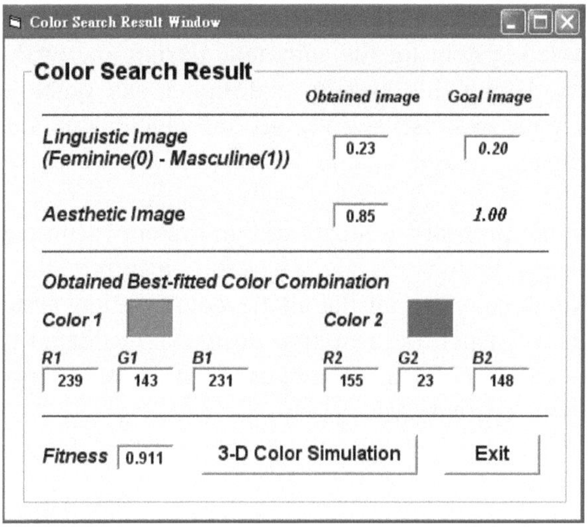

Figure 12. Search-result window presenting evolved color variables of best-fitted colors and corresponding image data

4. Conclusion

In the conceptual product design stage, designers tend to carry out their color-planning activities based on general stereotypes and their previous design experience. A consumer's mental perception of a product is commonly described by some adjectival image words. However, most products comprise several groups of components, each with different colors, and hence it is not easy to use the results of single color experiments to predict their overall image evaluation. In this research, the algorithms, constructed in quantitative measures of the gray system model, help to establish the relationship between multi-colored products and their images. Further, developing a color-searching method capable of automatically generating a large number of diverse color-combination schemes and then identifying the most appropriate color design is of considerable benefit.

However, if such schemes fail to take account of the color-harmony properties of the color design when searching for the optimal color combination, there is a high likelihood that the final color scheme will be aesthetically displeasing to the human eye. Consequently, this study has developed an automatic design method based on the principles of aesthetic measurement, gray theory and genetic algorithms to generate and evaluate color-design candidates. Although the prediction performance of this system regarding the aesthetic properties of the color design is not as high as that for the linguistic properties of the design, the system is nevertheless capable of evolving color-design candidates with a high degree of aesthetic appeal.

The design method presented in this study makes possible the creation of a PC- or web-based system for the automatic design and evaluation of two-colored products. Using this system, a designer can quickly establish an optimal color scheme to satisfy a given set of image evaluation goals, or can obtain the predicted image evaluation results for a set of input color parameters.

Additionally, the present automatic design system is limited to two-color designs and a single linguistic scale. Therefore, a future study will address the feasibility of developing an automatic color design system for multi-colored products, in which the resulting design is evaluated using multiple linguistic scales and a color-harmony scale with a more robust reliability than that used in the current case.

Acknowledgements

The authors gratefully acknowledge the support provided to this study by the National Science Council of Taiwan under grant NSC94-2213-E-343-001.

References

Birkhoff, GD: 1933, *Aesthetic measure*, Harvard University Press, Cambridge, Massachusetts.

Choo, S and Kim, Y: 2003, Effect of color on fashion fabric image, *Color Research and Application* **28**(3): 221-226.

Deng, JL: 1987, *Essential topics on gray system: theory and applications*, Huazhong University of Science and Technology Press, Wuhan, China.

Goldberg, DE: 1989, *Genetic algorithms in searchingoptimization and machine learning* , Addison-Wesley, Massachusetts.

Hsiao, SW: 1994, Fuzzy set theory on car-color design, *Color Research and Application* **19**(3): 202-213.

Hsiao, SW: 1995, A systematic method for color planning in product design, *Color Research and Application* **20**(3): 191-205.

Hsiao, SW and Tsai, HC: 2004, Use of Gray System Theory in product-color planning, *Color Research and Application* **29**(3): 222-231.

Moon, P and Spencer, DE: 1944a, Aesthetic measure applied to color harmony, *Journal of the Optical Society of America* **34**(4): 234-242.

Moon, P and Spencer, DE: 1944b, Geometric formulation of classical color harmony, *Journal of the Optical Society of America* **34**(1): 46-59.

Moon, P and Spencer, DE: 1944c, Area in color harmony, *Journal of the Optical Society of America* **34**(2): 93-103.

Ou, LC, Luo, MR, Woodcock, A and Wright, A: 2004, A study of colour Emotion and colour preference. Part I: colour emotions for single colours, *Color Research and Application* **29**(3): 232-240.

Shen, YC, Chen, YS and Hsu, WH: 1996, Quantitative evaluation of color harmony via linguistic-based image scale for interior design, *Color Research and Application* **21**(5): 353-374.

INTERPRETING ARCHITECTURAL SPACE THROUGH CAMERA MOVEMENT

WEI YAN AND WEILING HE
Texas A&M University, USA

Abstract. This paper examines how camera movement interprets architectural space and describes a navigation system that is designed to facilitate real time path planning and control of camera movement. The navigation system also allows people to save and retrieve walkthrough paths and thus enables different interpretations of the space by different observers to coexist in the same space. With case studies, we demonstrate that whether a space appears intelligible or unintelligible may be manipulated in the way how the space is interpreted through camera movement.

1. Introduction

In studying architectural space, walking through the space inherits a tremendous difference from looking at a model of the space. In the former case, space embodies experience, while, in the latter case, space becomes an object to be looked at from outside. Moreover, experiences within a space vary widely depending on how the space is walked through or looked at, although certain obvious attributes of the space remain. For example, the Barcelona Pavilion by Mies van der Rohe would appear to be composed of linear wall elements no matter how the space is perceived. However, whether the space appears confusing or not depends on how the space is experienced. The experience of space is similar to the performance of a music score. While the score determines the structure and components of a piece of music how the music is played would lead to different versions of musical interpretations, some of which can be extremely unlike in terms of how the music sounds. Same in the spatial interpretation of architectural space, although certain elements are so strong that they almost lead to identical experience, some are much dependent on how the space is walked through and looked at. The same space may have various, if not opposite, renditions. We call this phenomenon spatial interpretation through camera movement.

A Dong, A Vande Moere & JS Gero (eds), CAADFutures'07, 525–539.

Experiments have been done in using digital models with virtual cameras and recording the walkthrough into video clips to study the spaces, e.g. a John Hejduk's un-built project, the Diamond Museum (He 2006). In that experiment, individual walkthrough animations were made in order to use camera movement as a tool to test architectural concepts in space. Hejduk's original argument of how the diamond space becomes flat was examined. The method of using camera movement to test architectural ideas was convincing.

To further explore the research of interpreting architectural space through camera movement, an architecture-specific navigation system is desired. Ideally, it would allow interactive walkthrough in a space for richer experiences than that obtained through video, and more importantly, enable different interpretations of the space by different observers to coexist in the same space. Our recently developed architecture specific navigation system is used for this further exploration of interpreting architectural spaces. The system has the following features that facilitate the exploration. It integrates a perspective view and a map view. In the perspective view, route knowledge enables navigation from point to point using landmarks, and is based on an egocentric reference frame. In the map view, survey knowledge enables interactive and efficient planning of journeys, and is based on an exocentric reference frame. The observers' paths with related information, including coordinates and viewing directions, can be saved in real-time over a network and can be loaded and replayed later by other observers. That way, observers can experience the same walkthrough made by any other observer, e.g. the space's designer who wants to present the design through his/her preferred paths. This enables different interpretations of the space by different observers to coexist in the same space.

With the help of the new system, a series of experiments are conducted to test the spatial quality of intelligibility versus unintelligibility. By intelligibility we mean the quality of being able to let the viewer anticipate what to expect in space. The notion of spatial experience anticipation has been used in the study of virtual environment simulation processes (Kardos 1995). However, the problem of how to use variables to manipulate the extent of anticipation is less studied. Barcelona Pavilion, which is commonly regarded intelligible space, is compared to the Diamond Museum, which is commonly regarded unintelligible space. By manipulating the camera angles and paths, the space of Barcelona Pavilion appears unintelligible while the Diamond Museum appears intelligible. We pushed the study of the interpretation of architectural space to an extreme that a space may appear the opposite to its objective architectural characters. In the paper, we describe the implementation of the navigation system and demonstrate its application in examining and proving the subjectivity of spatial cognition.

The results of this research can be applied to design studio teaching for analyzing and interpreting designed spaces through camera movement, which utilizes an architecture specific navigation system.

2. Camera Movement in Architectural Space

A camera is a spatial device that interprets the embodiment of space. It not only indicates a hypothetical observer's position within the space but also implies how the observer looks at the space. Therefore, a camera is more than a viewing instrument. It is an extension of the observer's body and hence an experiential instrument. To set up a camera is to unavoidably give answers to the many questions related to the observer's body in space. Is he/she moving fast? Is he/she taking swinging steps? How close is he/she to the boundary of space? Is he/she taking the center of the space or almost touching the walls? In other words, technical parameters of a camera bear variables as to an observer's embodiment of space.

The spatial experience documented by a camera is personal by definition. Subjectivity comes in play whenever there is a choice of camera movement although some personal experience may appear more objective than others. For example, a continuous shot at eye level may look more objective than a continuous shot of a worm's eye view. A continuous shot in which the camera keeps on the same level and in the same direction may appear more objective than a shot with camera rotations. However, no matter how objective the shot may look the route of the camera is a complete subjective choice. Therefore, to examine a space, one has to determine a route first.

2.1. ROUTE

A space embeds certain attributes, some of which can be quantified while some can only be qualified. Taking a route in a space is in fact crossing areas with various attributes. A route not only implies which areas are shown and which are not, or the sequence in which individual areas of a space appear but also, more importantly, implies if certain spatial attributes are shown, if so, in what way.

2.2. CAMERA ANGLE

At each point of the route, a camera may take various shots with different settings, such as distance, focal length of lens, camera height, camera pan and zoom. These settings compose a camera angle. These technical factors indicate experiential aspects of space.

2.2.1. Distance and Focal Length of Lens

The distance of seeing is how far a camera is to the subject, which determines if the texture or the structure of the subject will be perceived. Looking closely at the subject tends to foreground its texture, an extremely local attribute of space. Looking from a distance at the subject, the relationship among parts of the subject becomes obvious. A wide focal length of lens may compromise the local view resulted in a close distance. By using a wide angle focal length, the camera view is no longer about the texture of an object but about how one object is related to another.

2.2.2. Camera Height and Subject Angle

Camera heights differ dramatically how space appears in a photo or a movie. Normally, an eye-level shot is less dynamic than other camera heights, such as a high angle, a low angle, or tilted "Dutch" angles, and thus less interesting in terms of the composition of each individual image. However an eye-level shot is the closest to a normal view of a observer in space among all camera heights. A high angle or a low angle shot limits what can be seen through the camera while tilted "Dutch" angles aggressively challenge the normal orientation of gravity.

Besides camera height, subject angle also plays an important role in depicting a space. Subject angle determines the appearance of flatness or depth of a space. Whenever an object presents only a single surface to the camera it appears to be flat. When the object presents two or more surfaces to the camera its depth becomes apparent.

2.2.3. A Pan or Dolly Shot

A pan or dolly shot happens when a camera itself rotates. If a camera revolves along horizontal or vertical axes, which is to follow the orientation system defined by gravity, the pan or dolly shots help extend the limited view of a still shot. For example, by using a horizontal pan shot, the camera may provide a wider view of space. The observer may see not only what in front of him/her but also what behind him/her so that an overall understanding of the space starts to form in the observer's mind. In real life, a pan or dolly shot is to look around.

2.2.4. A Zoom Shot

A zoom shot depicts space across distance. For example, when zooming in, the camera captures an overall view first and gradually changes to a close-up view. The camera or the hypothetical observer from the camera does not travel across the space to achieve the change of views. What has been changed in the zooming process is the subject that the camera depicts.

Therefore, the indication of a zoom shot is the change of focus of the observer.

2.3. DURATION AND TRAVEL SPEED

Along the route, a camera may travel in various speed and duration. The appearance of space may be different in a time dimension. They indicate how long the observer stares in the same direction, how frequently the observer changes views, how fast the observer relocate him/herself in space. Whether a space appears intelligible or not may be resulted in by whether enough time is given for the spectator to capture and understand the visual information through camera.

3. Navigation and Camera Control System

For the purpose of interpreting architectural space through camera movement, we examined the current available tools and found the problems of current camera control and navigation systems, such as: (1) Difficulty in path finding makes users often get lost because of the nature of complex environments and the lack of cues for path finding. (2) Excessive freedom of movement makes users difficult to have natural paths as in the real world, e.g. users often bump into walls or make unnatural sharp turns. (3) Designers or users of virtual spaces often have preferred paths for others to visit in order to present their design or interests, but they have no control of where others will go, unless the paths can be stored and retrieved in real time.

3.1. PREVIOUS WORK AND NEW SOLUTION

Previous research work has addressed some of these issues separately, e.g. adding global maps in addition to local views (Elvins et al. 1998; Fukatsu et al. 1998) or adding various landmarks (Darken et al. 1996; Vinson 1999) to help path finding; using the "river analogy" (Galyean 1995) or "StyleCam" (Burtnyk, et al. 2002) to guide users and enable users to deviate from the guided paths. However, each of these methods alone cannot provide a satisfactory solution, e.g. adding maps or landmarks cannot solve the natural path and the guided tour problems; the "river analogy" or "StyleCam" does not provide map knowledge thus users are still lacking context for path finding and lacking capability for path planning. Also, none of them addresses the problems of real-time path saving and retrieving. A more recent and closely related work was the Architectural Cinematographer (Calderón et al. 2006). The focus of the work was to apply cinematic principles to explore architectural design in real-time virtual environments, but not to address all the above problems. It is our purpose to address the above important problems comprehensively with an easy-to-use user interface. Our solution includes the following aspects:

1. It integrates a perspective view and an interactive map. In the perspective view, Route Knowledge (Edward and Hand 1997) enables navigation from point to point using landmarks, and is based on an egocentric reference frame. In the map, Survey Knowledge (Edward and Hand 1997) enables efficient planning of journeys, and is based on an exocentric reference frame.

2. Employing a 2D map, the system enables users to draw paths and improves path planning in a Web-based environment. In addition, the system can generate natural paths with a curve-fitting algorithm. It also can indicate users' position and orientation on the map.

3. Path control is merged into users' interactive walkthrough seamlessly and intuitively. Users take a walkthrough by following the pre-defined paths and by simultaneously and interactively controlling their orientation in a control panel. The walkthrough is partially guided by the pre-defined paths and partially controlled by users' real-time input. This integrates and balances freedom and control in walkthrough.

4. Further more, the paths with related information, including coordinates and orientations, can be saved in real-time over a network by a user and can be loaded and replayed later by other users. That way, users can experience the same walkthrough made by any other user, e.g. the space's designer who wants to present the design through his/her preferred paths.

3.2. USER INTERFACE OF THE SYSTEM

Our system consists of a 3D perspective view that allows users to walk through, a 2D map view that enables users to draw paths and see their locations and directions, and a control panel that allows users to control their camera parameters, e.g. turning left, right, up or down, increasing or decreasing the field of view (FOV), and increasing or decreasing travel speed, during the journey in real time. The system is implemented through embedding VRML and Java in a web page. A user can first set up the height of the camera in the web page and load a VRML 3D model and its 2D rendering of the top view for creating the user interface of the navigation system. The navigation interface consists of a VRML browser for the perspective view and a Java applet for both the map and the control panel. The communication between VRML and Java is achieved through EAI (External Authoring Interface). The viewpoint in the perspective view is controlled by a path planned in the map view. The control panel controls the camera parameters and results in view change in the perspective view and camera location and orientation changes in the map view. Paths with related

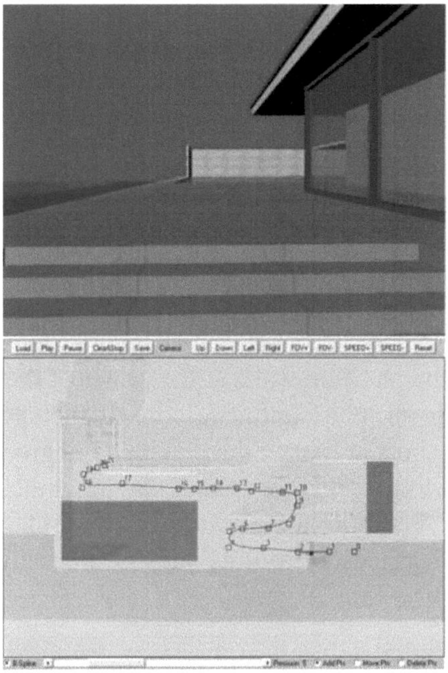

Figure 1. User interface of the navigation system. Top: perspective view; Middle: control panel; Bottom: 2D map with paths and the indicator of the camera location and orientation (Sample VRML source model of the Barcelona Pavilion: Emdanat 1999)

information, e.g. coordinates, can be saved by a user and can be loaded and replayed later by other users (Figure 1).

For path planning, the map enables users to click and create control points of a path. We applied B-Spline algorithm to curve-fit the initial paths (polylines) using a user's input as control points. In addition to creating paths, the user can also load pre-recorded paths. Once a path has been created or loaded, the user can start the walkthrough. During walkthrough the user can use the control panel to change the viewing direction, the field of view, and the travel speed while following the path.

4. Experiments: Exchanging Roles between the Barcelona Pavilion and the Diamond Museum

A series of experiments are conducted to test both our navigation system and our hypothesis: camera movement can interpret space in a subjective manner. We choose the Diamond Museum by John Hejduk (Hejduk 1985) and the Barcelona Pavilion by Mies van der Rohe (Sola-Morales 1993) as two samples for comparison.

Although both being modern architecture with free-standing walls, the space of the Diamond Museum and the space of the Barcelona Pavilion appear to be different in terms of intelligibility. However, through manipulation of camera movement the intelligible may become unintelligible and vice versa.

4.1. AT THE CENTER

It is widely accepted that because of the open plan the space of the Barcelona Pavilion is clear (intelligible) rather than confusing (unintelligible). As opposed to the Barcelona Pavilion, the Diamond Museum is much bigger in scale. In addition, the partition walls at the center of the Diamond Museum are curvilinear, which forms a confusing core of the space.

Two identical pan shots at the eye-level with 45 degree FOV are set at the centers of both buildings. On one hand, having much less partitioning elements, Barcelona Pavilion appears to be the interplay among solid surfaces, transparent surfaces as well as gaps between them (Figure 2, first row).

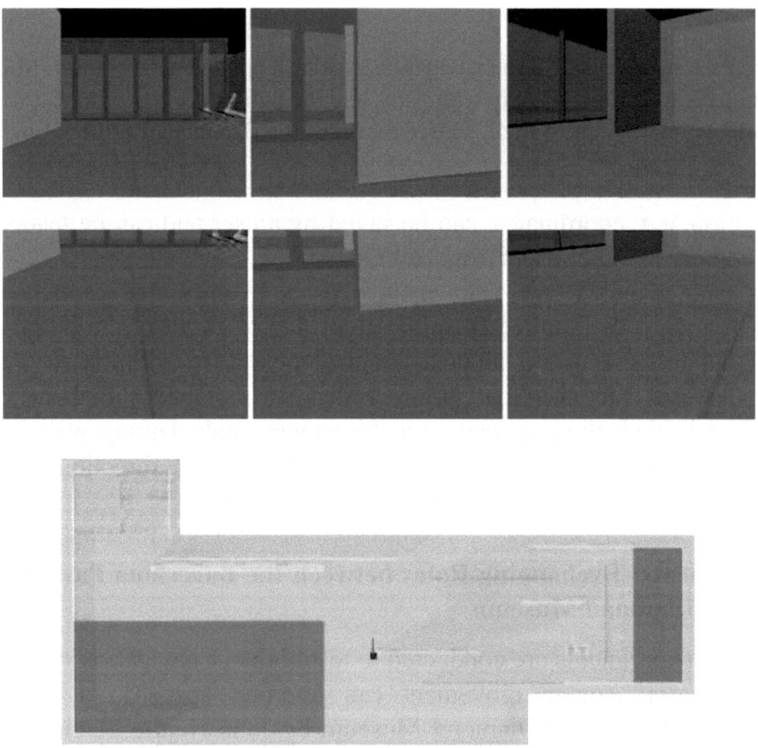

Figure 2. Center views of the Barcelona Pavilion. First and second rows: screenshots of the perspective views; Third row: map view

Turning the camera downwards, the space of the Barcelona Pavilion becomes confusing. Only the floor surface and a small part of the vertical surfaces are captured in the camera. Comparing this shot and the original shot at the center of the Diamond Museum, it is hard to conclude which space is clearer to understand than the other. The more limited the view is the more confusing the interpretation of the space is (Figure 2, second row).

The straight edges of the surfaces perfectly match the observer's expectation. A coordinate system is easily formed in the observer's mind. On the other hand, at the center of the Diamond Museum, one is surrounded by curved walls so that his/her orientation is completely lost. Therefore, by the first comparison, the space of the Barcelona Pavilion is more intelligible than that of the Diamond Museum. (Figure 3)

Figure 3. Center views of the Diamond Museum. First row: screenshots of the perspective views; Second row: map view

4.2. ON THE PERIPHERY

Interestingly, the shot at the periphery of the Diamond Museum seems to be more intelligible than that at the periphery of the Barcelona Pavilion. Along the periphery of the Diamond Museum, the observer is set in a logical system with straight lines that are clear and definite on one side of his/her body while a complex with straight and curvilinear elements on the other. This situation is consistent throughout the route on the diamond shaped periphery (Figure 4). In the case of the Barcelona Pavilion, an eye-level shot is taken along the accessible edge of the building. The direction of the camera is always forward with 45 degree FOV. Throughout the path, there is not much visual consistency. In other words, the observer cannot predict what to be seen through the camera (Figure 5, first row). The space of the periphery of the Diamond Museum appears more intelligible than that of the Barcelona Pavilion.

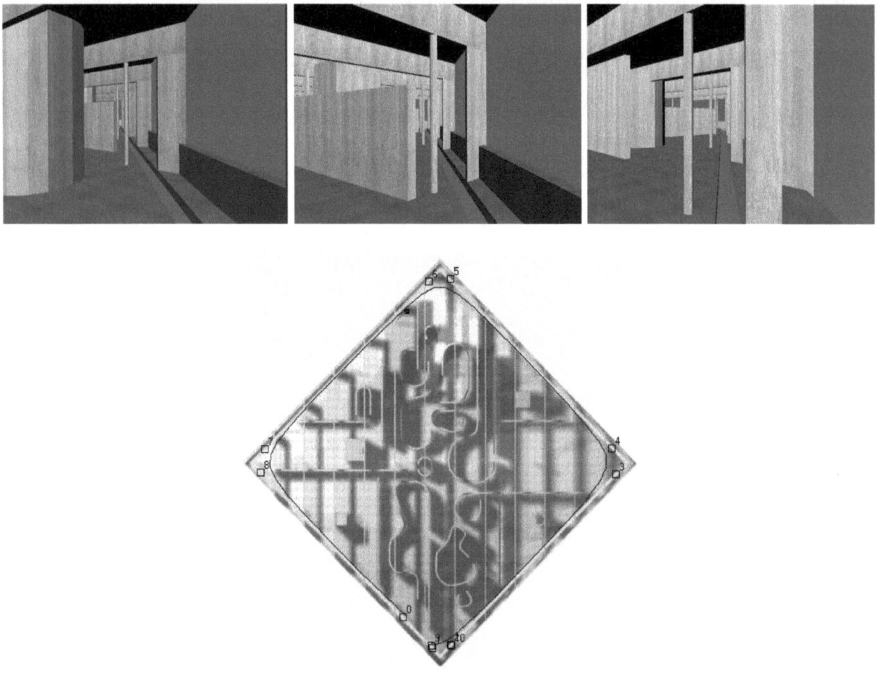

Figure 4. Views at the periphery of the Diamond Museum. Top: Perspective views Bottom: Route in map view

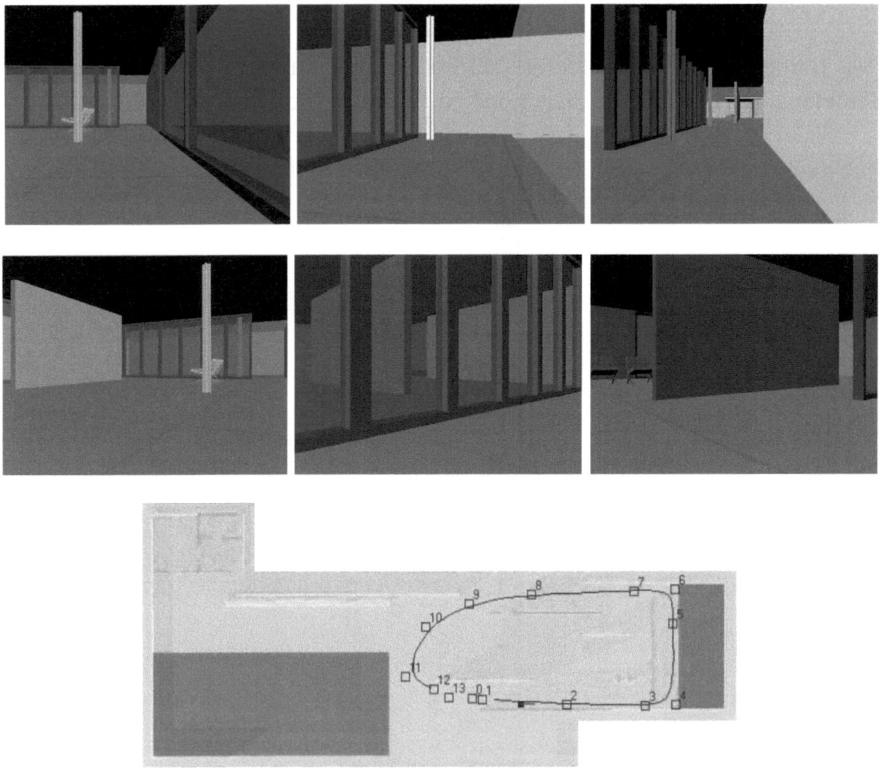

Figure 5. Views at the periphery of the Barcelona Pavilion. First Row: Camera shooting forward; Second Row: Camera shooting the consistent reference of the wall; Bottom: Route in map view

The appearance of the Barcelona Pavilion can be changed through one single camera setup. We turn the target of the camera towards the wall at the center of the space and take the same route again. The wall becomes the consistent reference of the space. The local visual changes in the space are related to the unchanging visual element, the wall, and thus can be understood in relation to the wall. The space becomes easier to comprehend (Figure 5, second row).

4.3. CROSSING THE SPACE

Two routes across the space are set both in the Diamond Museum and the Barcelona Pavilion. In the Diamond Museum, the camera is set at eye-level

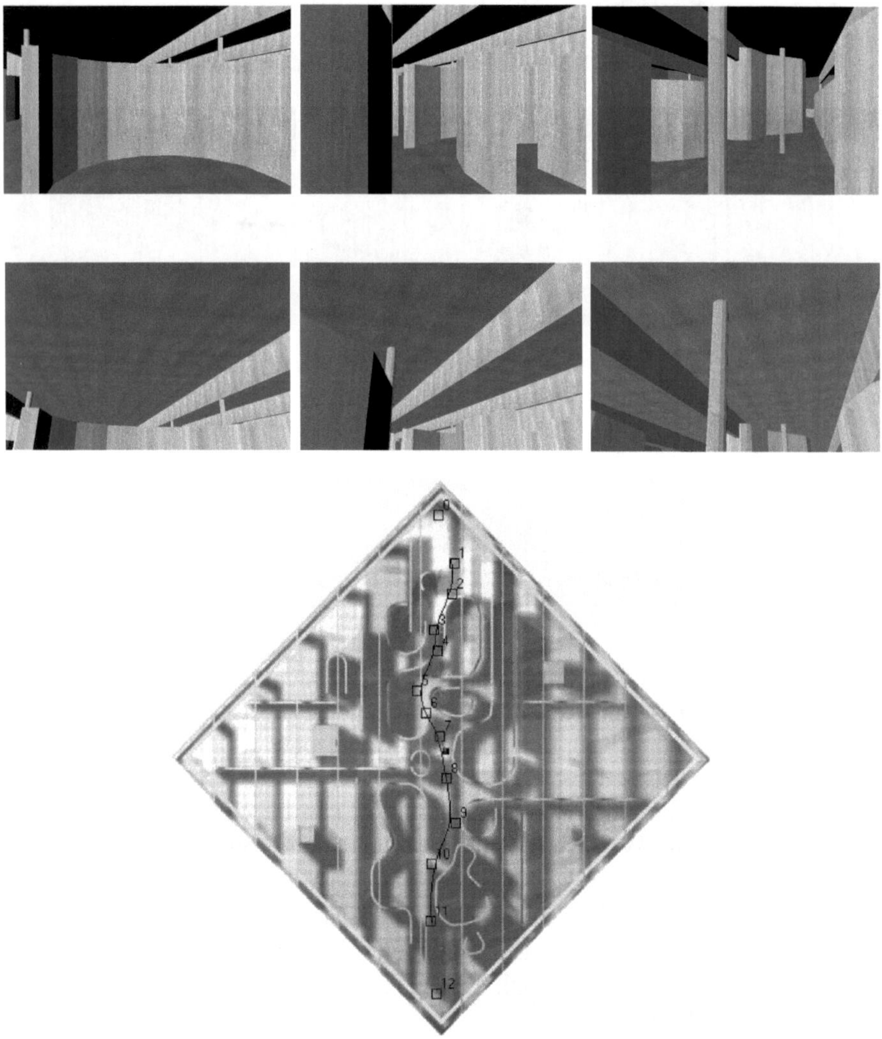

Figure 6. Views across the Diamond Museum. First Row: Camera shooting forward; Second Row: Camera shooting upward; Bottom: Route in map view

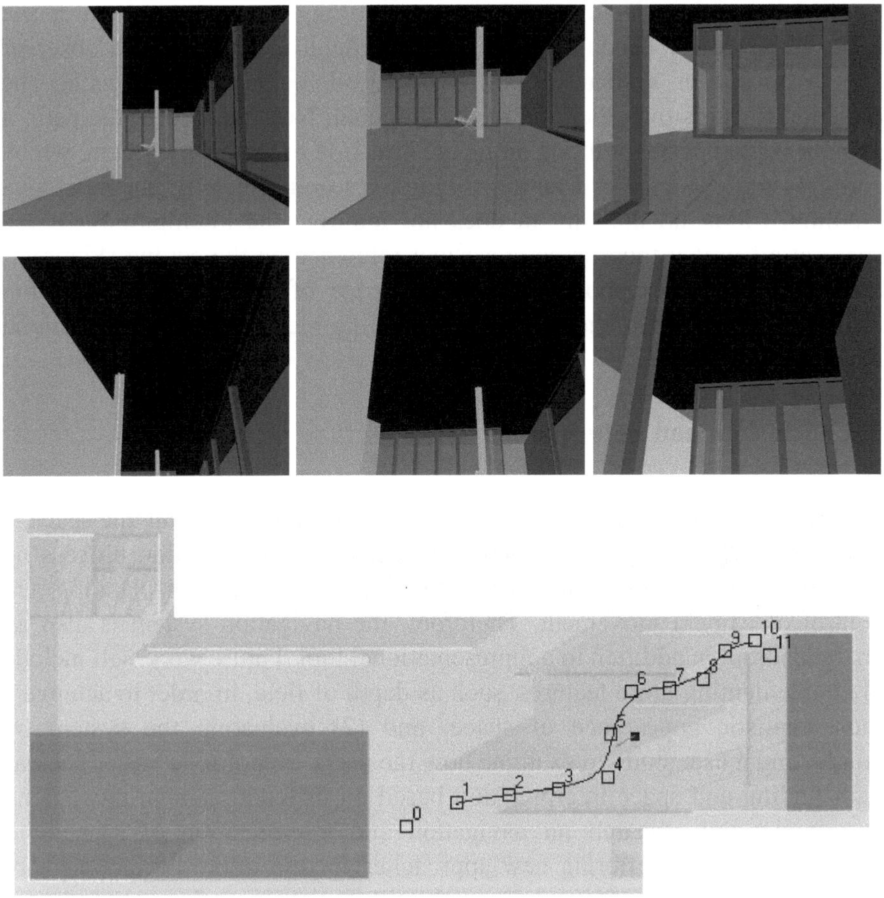

Figure 7. Views across the Barcelona Pavilion. First Row: Camera shooting forward; Second Row: Camera shooting upward; Bottom: Route in map view

horizontally targeting forward. Moving along the path, the observer is always surrounded by curved walls, except near the ends of the path. These walls force the view to meander around rather than shooting in a consistent direction. The frequent curved turns cause the observer to lose his/her orientation (Figure 6, first row). In the Barcelona Pavilion, similar situation occurs although there are no curved walls. Both spaces appear confusing (Figure 7, first row).

However, in the Diamond Museum, by tilting the camera upwards the space immediately becomes intelligible. Through the camera, the observer sees a consistent system of beams overhead, a way of suggesting the direction towards the other end of the diagonal. Near the end of the path, a straight wall appears, pointing along the direction of the beam system, which confirms the expected orientation (Figure 6, second row). In the Barcelona Pavilion, tilting up the camera does not improve the intelligibility of the space at all in that there is no consistent reference on the ceiling (Figure 7, second row). The supposed intelligible space of the Barcelona Pavilion changes its role with the supposed unintelligible space of the Diamond Museum.

5. Conclusions and Future Work

By using camera movement, we demonstrate that whether a space appears intelligible or unintelligible may be manipulated in the way how the space is interpreted. Our navigation system can assist the interpretation process by providing a proper user interface to facilitate real time path planning and control of camera movement. Therefore, the navigation system is also an analytical tool in addition to a representational tool. Future work will include (1) implementing more features, such as depth of field, in order to achieve a more realistic appearance of space; and (2) evaluating the system by conducting a user study to examine how the users' response to issues such as path-finding and space interpretation based on different camera movement. We expect our research on navigation and interpretation of space will ultimately assist in offering new approaches for the future development of architecture-specific 3D viewers and will assist in architectural design presentation and analyses that employ Virtual Reality technology.

References

Burtnyk, N, Khan, A, Fitzmaurice, G, Balakrishnan, R, and Kurtenbach, G: 2002, StyleCam: Interactive Stylized 3D Navigation using Integrated Spatial & Temporal Controls, *ACM CHI Letters* **4**(2): 101-110.

Calderón C, Worley N, and Nyman K: 2006, Spatial cinematic mediation in real-time architectural walkthroughs, *ITcon* **11**: 343-360, http://www.itcon.org/2006/25.

Darken, R, and Sibert, J: 1996, Wayfinding strategies and behaviours in large virtual worlds. *ACM CHI'96 Conference on Human Factors in Computing Systems*, pp. 142-149.

Edwards, J and Hand, C: 1997, MaPS: Movement And Planning Support For Navigation In An Immersive VRML Browser, *VRML '97: Proceedings of the second symposium on Virtual reality modeling language*, ACM Press, New York, pp. 65-ff.

Elvins, T, Nadeau, D, Schul, R, and Kirsh, D: 1998, Worldlets: 3D thumbnails for 3D browsing, *ACM CHI'98 Conf. on Human Factors in Computing Systems*, ACM Press, New York, pp. 163-170.

Emdanat, S: 1999, http://www-personal.umich.edu/~emdanat/vr-projects/Barcelona/. Last accessed January 14 2007.

Fukatsu, S, Kitamura, Y, Masaki, T, and Kishino, F: 1998, Intuitive control of bird's eye overview images for navigation in an enormous virtual environment, *ACM VRST'98 Symposium on Virtual Reality Software and Technology,* ACM Press, New York, pp. 67-76.

Galyean, TA: 1995, Guided navigation of virtual environments, *ACM I3D'95 Symposium on Interactive 3D Graphics*, ACM Press, New York, pp. 103-104.

He, W: 2006, Flatness through Camera: The Implications of Camera Movement in the Digital Reconstruction of Diamond Museum, Synthetic Landscapes, *in* G Luhan, P Anzalone, M Cabrinha and C Clarke (eds), *Proceedings of the 25th Annual Conference of the Association for Computer-Aided Design in Architecture (ACADIA)*, Louisville, Kentucky, pp. 270-277.

Hejduk, J: 1985, *Mask of Medusa: Works 1947 – 1983*, Rizzoli Press, New York.

Kardos, P: 1995, The Role of Spatial Experience Anticipation in Architectural Education and Urban Design, *Proceedings 2nd EAEA-Conference,* European Architectural Endoscopy Association, Tampere, pp. 21-24.

Sola-Morales, I, Cirici, C, and Ramos, F: 1993, *Mies van der Rohe: Barcelona Pavilion,* G. Gili, Barcelona.

A NOVEL ROOM RE-LAYOUT DESIGN TOOL FOR PREPAREDNESS OF EARTHQUAKE DISASTER USING REAL-TIME PHYSICS SIMULATION AND FORCE- FEEDBACK INTERFACE

Proposition of adopting real-time physics simulation for architectural design verification process

JAEHO RYU AND RYUZO OHNO
Tokyo Institute of Technology, Japan

Abstract. The virtual reality (VR) generated by computer graphics (CG) has developed very rapidly in accordance with the rapid improvement of computer hardware and CG algorithms. Not only visual still images but also the representation of the behavior of virtual objects has became possible owing to real-time physics simulation, which can provide a high sense of presence to users. Adopting the real-time physics simulation and the force-feedback interface to the architectural design process in VR could make it more realistic by providing a sense of virtual objects such as the weight of the mass, tactile sensation, and interaction between virtual objects and users. As a pilot application of real-time physics simulation and the force-feedback interface in the architectural field, we are developing an educational VR system for earthquake disaster preparedness through a room re-layout design process.

1. Introduction

1.1. VIRTUAL REALITY IN ARCHITECTURAL DESIGN AND EVALUATION

Nowadays, the use of VR technology has spread quickly to many fields of industry including architectural design, because VR technology generated from Computer Graphics (CG) has been extensively developed in accordance with the rapid development of hardware and CG algorithms. From HMD (head-mounted display) to CAVE (cave automatic virtual environment) (Cruz-Neira et al. 1993), the visualization and presentation ability of VR technology is a great merit, compared with other representation tools, in several aspects, such as economic cost, high realism, and easy

A Dong, A Vande Moere & JS Gero (eds), CAADFutures'07, 541–554.

modification of data. Many researchers have been attempting to create a new application of VR technology in the design field utilizing of these merits. In particular, in the architectural field, there are already some VR applications as the design-support tools that help the designer explore the results of the design process and stimulate the design idea by constructing and modifying models in virtual environments at various scales (Hill et al. 1999; Leigh and Johnson 1996).

Not only visual presentation but also representation of the behaviors of virtual objects employing real-time physics simulation has become possible, which can provide a high sense of presence in the virtual world. The adoption of a force-feedback interface in the interior design process, which enables the designer to change the position of furniture directly and intuitively, has already been introduced in previous research (Ryu et al. 2004). In this paper, we show that adding the realistic behaviors of virtual objects supplies a different dimension of the sense of presence to the application. The potential advantages of using real-time physics simulation is the capability not only to show a realistic scene in VR space but also to help the user carry out a realistic design process in VR by feeling the real sense of virtual objects, such as the weight of the mass and the interaction between objects, using a force-feedback interface. As the first prototype of the application of real-time physics simulation for architectural design, we are developing an educational and room re-layout design tool for earthquake disaster preparedness.

1.2. EARTHQUAKE SIMULATOR FOR ENVIRONMENTAL HAZARD PREPARATION

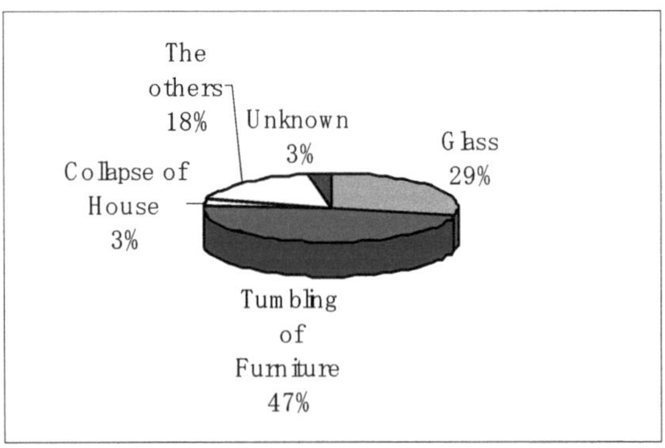

Figure 1. Causes of injury in the 1995 Kobe earthquake

In Japan, the probability of the occurrence of an earthquake is relatively high compared with other countries because the geological location of the country is near a seismogenetic area. Thus, there are many researches about the earthquake preparedness education (Masuda et al. 1988; Takimoto et al. 1999). Major cities in Japan, such as Tokyo and Kobe, make great efforts to inform the citizens of the risk of earthquake disaster through several disaster education facilities. These facilities play a central role in the disaster education system that provides various kinds of learning and training. First, we surveyed these facilities to devise some guidelines for the development of a tool for earthquake disaster education using VR technology. The survey targets included the several representative facilities in Tokyo and the Human Renovation Institute in Kobe.

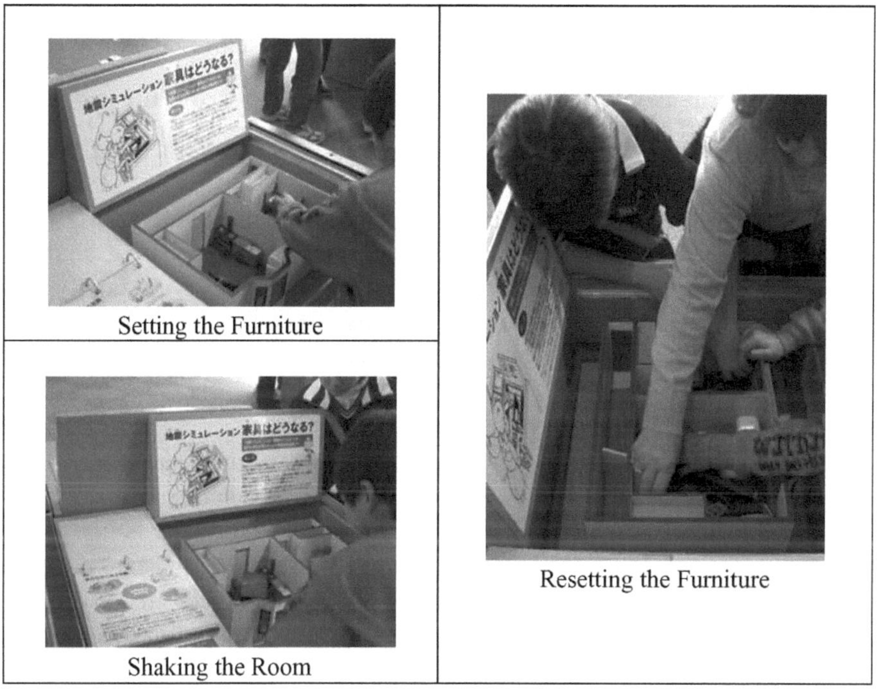

Figure 2. Real-object tool for verifying the collapse of furniture during an earthquake at the disaster reduction and human renovation institution in Kobe

Earthquake disaster preparedness education on earthquake is particularly important because damage due to earthquake can be considerately reduced if daily preparedness is properly conducted. Since earthquakes usually occur suddenly without warning time to react, daily preparedness in the event of earthquakes is more important than for other types of disaster. For example, the statistical analysis of the causes of injury people in the 1995 Kobe earthquake (Figure 1) reveals tumbling furniture in the house to be prominent reasons, which could be prevented by daily carefulness or by applying knowledge gained through disaster awareness education programs

(AIJ 1996), such as avoiding putting tall furniture in bedrooms or fixing them to walls using metal supports. The disaster education program using VR tools will facilitate understanding by the educatee, which will lead to the mitigation of damage due to disaster.

As a room re-layout design tool for earthquake disaster preparedness using real-time physics simulation we are developing a prototype VR tool using the physics simulation engine, PhysX (formerly called NovodeX), which is a partly open library for noncommercial use. This system will employ the real-time physics simulation instead of a real-object simulation tool such as the earthquake disaster preparedness education tool shown in Figure 2.

2. Improving the Effectiveness of Disaster Education Program

Adopting new media in education, for example the Internet and visual materials such as movies and CG animations, is a very effective method for young students because they are easy to understand and to access. The survey by Shaw et al. revealed a high degree of preparedness of students who had received active education through conversation with family and community education. This result exemplifies the effectiveness of spontaneous and active participation in disaster preparedness education (Shaw et al. 2004).

According to Rohrmann, there are three stages in a socio-psychological model of the risk communication process: *Risk (Re)-Appraisal → Decision for Preventative Action → Risk-reducing Behavior* (Rohrmann 2000). Of these three stages, the final *Risk-reducing Behavior* stage is the most important stage for reducing the damage from environmental hazards as well as natural disasters. To encourage the educatee to reach the last stage, effective media are required to provide the proper information. Rohrmann also mentioned that practical experience might not be sufficient to ensure satisfactory results. Rather, a comprehensive theoretical framework is needed to guide risk communication efforts.

After surveying the disaster education facilities and interviewing some managers of the exhibition, we have figured out these facts: (1) visual content is useful and effective for disaster education, (2) there is a need for portability of the VR system to reach more students who cannot visit the facilities for reasons, such as long distance, economic cost, and time, (3) interactive content is necessary to maintain the interest of the student, and will lead to more effective results of disaster education. In order to carry out effective disaster education, the continued interest of and intuitive understanding by the participant are essential. The VR technology is suitable because the three-dimensional computer graphics presentation will satisfy the above requirements. There is a previous report of the effectiveness of using VR for training process (Bliss and Tidwell 1997).

2.1. PORTABILITY OF EDUCATION TOOL FOR BROAD DISASTER EDUCATION

One of the requests for effective earthquake disaster education is visual content for easy understanding. To show visual content, a special system for displaying graphic becomes necessary. Usually, such a system is heavy and fixed in one place because it is difficult to move and re-install the structure in other places. Therefore, the educatee must come to the location of the equipment, which is one of the obstacles to achieving high accessibility by students. A potable VR system will be a solution to this kind of problem. Also, a portable of VR system can broaden the number of participants who receive disaster education.

2.2. CONTENTS OF EDUCATION TOOL (DETAILED AND EXECUTABLE INSTRUCTION FOR INDIVIDUAL)

Another request for effective disaster education is interactive, interesting and intuitive contents to acquire long-continuing concern. To satisfy this requirement, the interactive VR system can be effective in this aspect because there has been considerable progress in computer graphics regarding reality and real-time physical simulation. Also, adding multi-modal interfaces for interaction, such as locomotion (navigation), haptic (grasping & force) interface, and motion tracker, to the VR system could render it a highly effective composite system (Buoguila et al. 1997). The realization of a high sense of presence and intuitive physics simulation with rich interaction will help to improve the education program. This paper includes the framework for developing a portable VR system. For the development of several interfaces, we are planning to collaborate with the computer department laboratory in our university for the near future.

3. Real-Time Physics Simulation in VR

3.1. REAL-TIME PHYSICS SIMULATION

In the virtual world, the realistic movement of objects has been required in order to provide viewers with a high sense of presence. Before the availability of real-time physics simulation, precalculated animated sequences were used to show the realistic behavior of objects in the virtual world. One of the obstacles to using the real-time physics simulation in VR was the long calculation time required to attain the results, which was too long time to display a smooth motion scene on the computer.

In the real-time physics simulation, the physics engine simplifies the calculation and lowers the accuracy so that it can render the scene at an appropriate rate for composing a continuously moving image. Recently, real-time physics simulation has come to be adopted for constructing the VR world and for game applications owing to the rapid progress in both the physics simulation algorithms and the hardware. The realization of the proper object movement in VR space improves the sense of presence of the viewer. There is one concern that the physics engine for real-time rendering of earthquake disaster is insufficient to predict the precise behaviors of virtual objects. However, realizing such precise behavior is not the aim of this application. The goal of this application is to stimulate the students to think about their room environment when an earthquake disaster occurs. We place priority on interaction and interest to achieve effectiveness disaster education. The current real-time physics engine is sufficient to show the realistic movements of virtual objects. Furthermore, they are rapidly attaining the preciseness of physics simulation.

There are open source physics engine such as ODE (Open Dynamic Engine), Bullet, and OPAL, and commercial engines such as Havok, and PhysX (formerly called NovodeX). There is even a proposal to use the Physics Processing Unit (PPU) from AEGIA PhysX, such as CPU (Central Processing Unit) and GPU (Graphics Processing Unit), to support the calculations in physics simulation. In our research, we have chosen the PhysX physics engine because of the stability of simulation and the availability of many support documents that are helpful in making a new code for our system. Using the real-time physics simulation, we can attain the physics-based VR environments that provide us with a higher sense of presence than do conventional ones.

3.2. FORCE-FEEDBACK INTERFACE FOR INTERACTION

We are also planning to use SPIDAR, a wire based force-feedback interface, to enable the user to directly manipulate the furniture in a VR room (Ishi and Sato 1994). SPIDAR is an original force-feedback interface that was developed in the Precision and Intelligence (P&I) Laboratory, Tokyo Institute of Technology. The merits of using this force-feedback interface are easy calibration and relatively light weight equipment.

The integration of SPIDAR to our system is in the near future in collaboration with the P&I Laboratory. This device will reinforce the feeling of immersion of user, through the sense of touch and force-feedback, in the virtual space. Finally, the user will be able to touch and manipulate objects in the virtual space via force-feedback interaction.

4. Room Re-layout Design Tool for Earthquake Disaster Preparation

In our prototype room re-layout design tool, the user can control the furniture in a virtual room and change its layout using the pop-up menu or force-feedback interface (using SPIDAR in the near future). After arranging the furniture in their room, they can verify the degree of danger of their room in the event if an earthquake, which will enable them to devise a new safer layout of their furniture.

The purpose of this system is to prompt users to reconsider the status of their room by simulating the effect of an earthquake. After setting the furniture, users can verify the extent of the damage caused by an ill layout of furniture in the room, as shown in Figure 3. For example, a tall bookshelf will tumble over a wide area and hence one must avoid placing it near a bed or sofa. Furthermore, the placement of heavy furniture, such as television and sculptures, must be avoided in high places or near sitting and sleeping areas.

The system can represent the situation during an earthquake through visual display and sound effects. This system can be operated in a stand-alone computer or an immersive three-sided screen system that can be taken to various places as needed. Verifying the damage due to earthquake disaster will induce students to communicate with each other, and think about the risk of their room layout, and improve their room environment. This will mitigate the actual damage caused by a real earthquake.

At the present stage, we are planning to carry out the education program for children using our original Portable VR system. We also plan to investigate the effectiveness of education itself and of using VR tool compared with other education media such as text or picture.

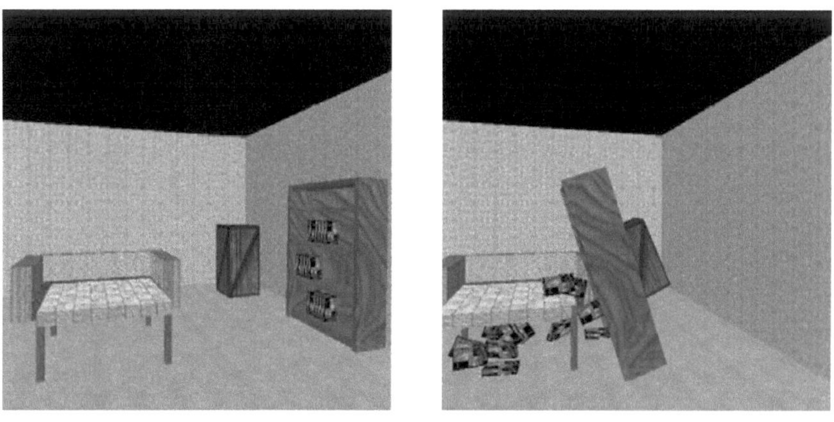

Figure 3. Image of room before and after an earthquake produced by the real-time earthquake simulator

The users reproduce the furniture layout of their room. The furniture can be set using a keyboard. Input using the keyboard and mouse is illustrated in Figure 4. The user can change the position of furniture using the pop-up menu on the screen. This is a very familiar way of manipulating images on the screen for users who regularly operate a computer.

Another method is the use of a haptic interface to manipulate the virtual furniture. The prototype application of using wire based haptic interface, Big-SPIDAR, for manipulating objects was proposed in a previous study (Ryu et al. 2004). Now, we are at the stage of preparing the sole use for this system from the former study.

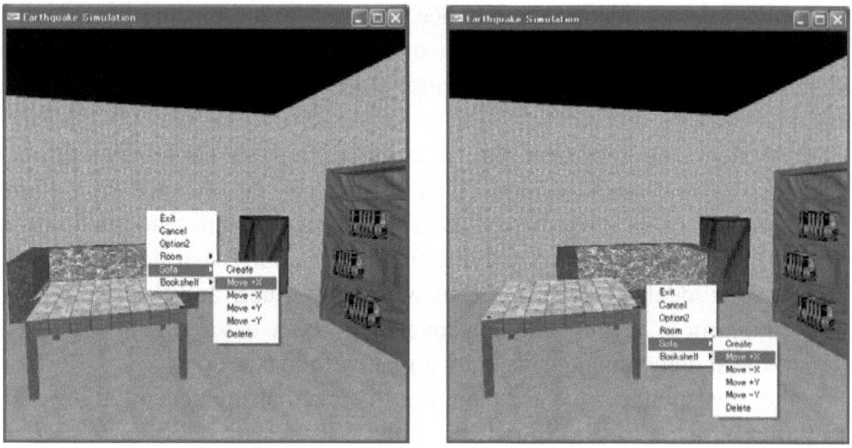

Figure 4. Using keyboard and mouse input to arrange the furniture layout

5. Development of Portable VR System

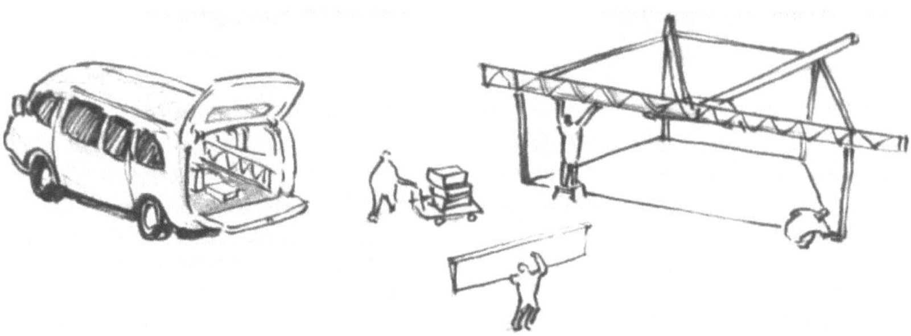

Figure 5. Concept of portable VR system (assembly and disassembly)

There have been many proposals of immersive VR systems, such as CAVE, CABIN (Hirose et al. 1998), D-vision (Ryu et al. 2004) and Smart Projectors (Bimber et al. 2005). However, it is rather difficult problem to transport the system and to realize the proper VR space for the viewer under various room conditions or even in an open space such as a public plaza.

In order to provide earthquake disaster education with a high sense of presence, we have designed a portable human-scale immersive VR system composed of three screens of 2.0 meter (width) × 1.8 meter (height) for the room re-layout design tool.

We focused on two main points in the development of the new portable VR system, portability and compactness, because we are assuming that there will be a need to install the system even in a small room. This system is the embodiment of the result of interviews that showed the need for the portability of the VR system in order to enhance the effectiveness of the education for children through the virtual experience of a disaster situation.

We have tried to achieve the portability of the system by simplifying the structure, electrical connections, and device carrier, and by reduction of the large frame parts, into on assembly of small parts, which is convenient when changing the location of installation.

5.1. THE CONFIGURATION OF PORTABLE VR

The portable VR system involves two main functions for producing the virtual experience of an earthquake disaster. The first function is to present the CG image that is generated in real-time by the rendering computer to synchronize the three computers to produce one whole image over a viewing angle 120 degrees on the three joined screens. The second function is to present the high-quality movie file on the wide screen using three projectors.

The total resolution of combined three screens is about 3000 pixels X 1000 pixels, because three projectors each have SXGA resolution (1280 X 1024). The total resolution is similar to that of a high-definition video image, 1920 X 1080. The displayed image is monoscopic in this system. The ideal viewing point is approximately 2.2 meters from the central screen in a seated position, as shown in Figure 6. In our application, the users remain in a fixed position, which eliminates need for head tracking to achieve the correct user perspective view.

The three rendering computers that control each projector are connected through a Gigabit Ethernet network. The broad band of the network enables fast data traffic to project the image onto the screen.

The rendering computer machines are normal PCs that have a high-speed CPU, a graphic card, and the AEGIA PhysX processor (physics processing unit) to accelerate the calculation of the physics simulation.

5.2. STRUCTURAL FRAME FOR PORTABLE VR

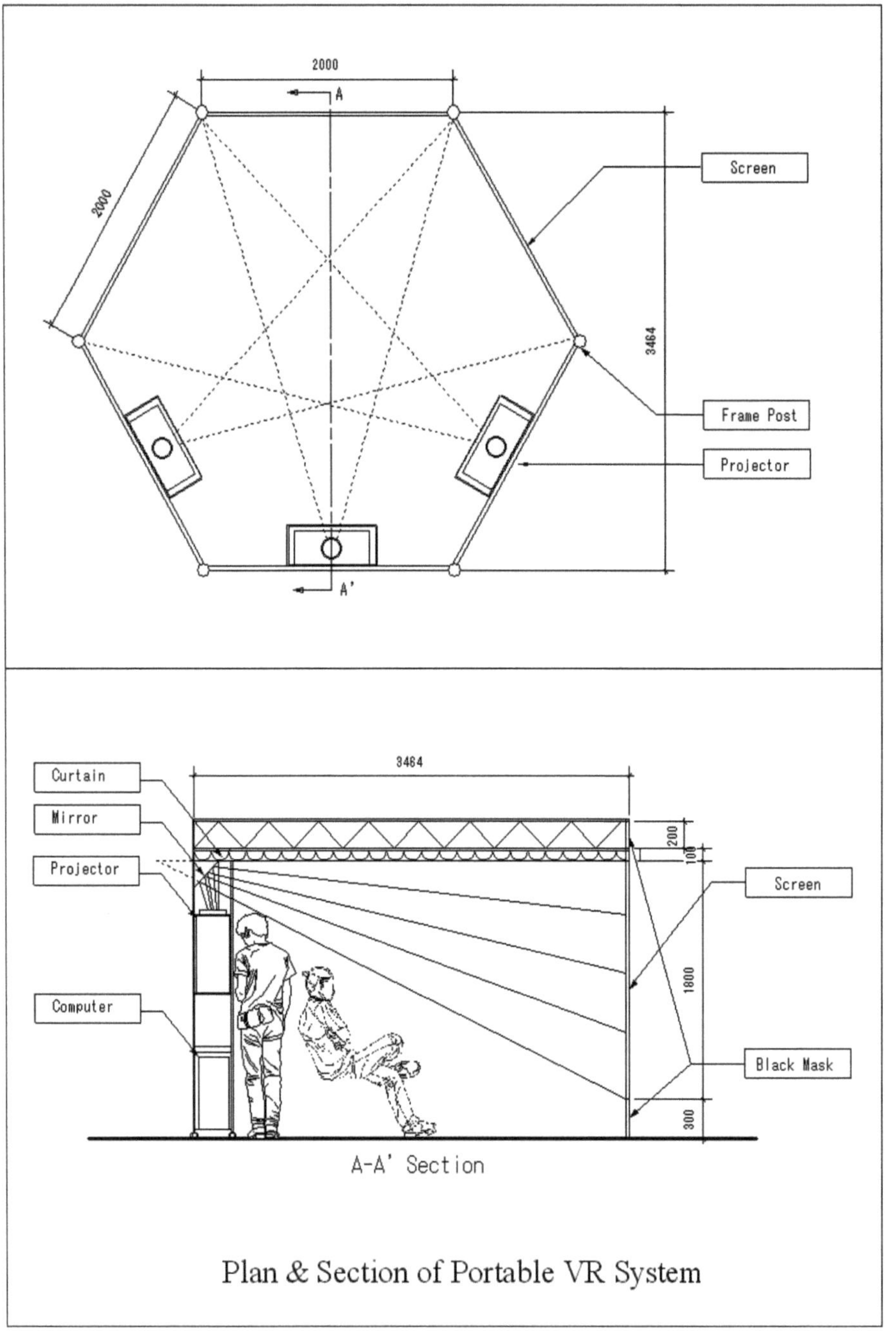

Figure 6. Plan of portable VR system

The hexagonal shape of the frame was devised to support the three projectors and the three screens with easy assembly process. Also, the hexagonal shape is structurally stable and has efficient space occupancy. The adoption of the front projection method within the hexagonal frame saves on space.

In order to avoid creating shadows of viewers inside of system, mirrors were used to heighten the reflection point of projection and shorten the horizontal throwing distance. The system can be installed in a 5 meter × 7 meter space including the computer-related hardware and electric power cables, because of the simplification of the parts to be assembled. Not only is the required room space of the assembled system frame small, but also, the space occupied by the set of disassembled parts is also small enough to fit into a mini van that has a 3.0 meter × 1.3 meter × 1.5 meter cargo volume.

Assembly and disassembly each requires only a couple of hours and is not an obstacle to the transport of the system. Figures 6 and 7 show the concept of the hexagonal system frame and the projection method of using mirrors. Figure 8 and 9 show the computer cluster and three projectors of front projection using mirrors for live-action movie and CG presentation. The calculated maximum number of people who can watch the screen at one time is 15 persons.

Figure 7. Image of portable VR system

Figure 8. Computer cluster for live-action movie and CG presentation

Figure 9. Three projectors of front projection using mirrors

6. Conclusion

We have developed a novel room re-layout design tool for earthquake disaster preparedness using real-time physics simulation on the basis of a survey of several disaster education facilities in Kobe and Tokyo. We have also proposed the use of the force-feedback interface for direct manipulation of the virtual furniture, which is currently being developed. The visual presentation and high sense of presence are expected to yield the merits of easy understanding and continued interest than with compared with text presentation.

The use of real-time physics simulation as an architectural design support tool is a new concept of CAAD. Furthermore, adding the force-feedback interface to the real-time physics simulation would produce innovative effects in various points. In the role of a sensor in the design process, the conventional CAD has no function to connect the sensory feeling and the design process but merely alleviates drawing task. The physics simulation and force-feedback haptic interface could provide a connection between the human sensor and the design process. This attempt will enhance the design support ability of CAAD for the realization of a high sense of presence.

In the future work, we are planning to combine the force-feedback interface, SPIDAR-G, with our portable VR system in collaboration with the computer department laboratory. We will also conduct some fundamental experiments to prove the effectiveness of our system.

References

Architectural Institute of Japan: 1996, *Report of Damage Occurring Inside of Houses at Hanshin-Awaji Great Earthquake*, AIJ (Japanese).

Bimber, O, Emmerling, A, and Klemmer, T: 2005, Embedded Entertainment with Smart Projectors, *IEEE Computer* **38**(1): 56-63.

Bliss, JP and Tidwell, PD: 1997, The Effectiveness of Virtual Reality for Administering Spatial Navigation Training to Firefighters, *Presence* **6**(1): 73-86.

Buoguila, L, Cai, Y, and Sato, M: 1997, New Haptic Device For Human Scale Virtual Environment: Scaleable-SPIDAR, *ICAT'97*, Tokyo, pp. 93-98.

Cruz-Neira, C, Sandin D, and DeFanti, T: 1993, Surround-Screen Projection-Based Virtual Reality: The Design and Implementation of the CAVE, *Proceedings of ACM SIGGRAPH'93*, pp. 135–142.

Hill II, LC, Chan, C-S, and Cruz-Neira, C: 1999, Virtual Architecture Design Tool (VADeT), *Third International Immersive Projection Technology Workshop (IPT 1999).*

Hirose, M, Ogi, T, Ishiwata, S, and Yamada, T: 1998, Development and Evaluation of Immersive Multiscreen Display "CABIN", *The transactions of the Institute of Electronics, Information and Communication Engineers D-II* **J81**(5): 888-896.

Ishii, M and Sato, M: 1994, A 3D Spatial Interface Device Using Tensed Strings, Presence: *Teleoperators and Virtual Environments* **3**(1): 81-86.

Leigh, J, Johnson, A, Vasilakis, C, and DeFanti, T: 1996 Multi-perspective Collaborative Design in Persistent Networked Virtual Environment. *Proceedings of IEEE Virtual Reality Annual International Symposium'96*, pp. 253–260.

Masuda, H, Midorikawa, S, Miki, C, and Ohmachi, T: 1988, Formative Process of Consciousness of Earthquake Preparedness and Evaluation of Effects of Earthquake Education, Journals of the Japan Society of Civil Engineers **398**(I-10): 359-365. (Japanese)

Rohrmann, B: 2000, A socio-psychological Model for Analyzing Risk Communication Process, *The Australasian Journal of Disaster and Trauma Studies*, **2000-2**, http://www.massey.ac.nz/~trauma/issues/2000-2/rohrmann.htm.

Ryu, J, Hasegawa S, Hashimoto N, and Sato M: 2004, Multi-Projection Display System for Architectural Design Evaluation, *The 9th Conference on Computer-Aided Architectural Design Research in Asia (CAADIRA)*, pp. 901-910.

Shaw, R, Shiwaku, K, and Kobayashi, H: 2004, Study on New System of Earthquake Disaster Education at High School (-analysis of factors affecting awareness in questionnaire survey targeted for high school students-), *Journal of Environment Engineer AIJ*, **585**: 69-74 (Japanese).

Takimoto, K, and Miura, F: 1999, Development of Earthquake Preparedness Education Software for an Elementary and Junior High School Students and Its Evaluation, *Journals of the Japan Society of Civil Engineers* **619**(I-47): 155-167 (Japanese).

http://www.dri.ne.jp/index.html: Disaster Reduction and Human Renovation Institution of Kobe City.

http://www.disastereducation.org: The National Disaster Education Coalition (NDEC) of USA.

http://www.tfd.metro.tokyo.jp/ts/museum.htm: Fire Museum of Japan & Disaster preparedness Center.

http://www.uni-weimar.de/medien/ar/sARc/index.htm.

BEING CREATIVE

IDEA HITCHHIKING IN THE IDEA ASSOCIATION PROCESS

Exploring the transformation process of design ideas during the conceptual design stage

IH-CHENG LAI
Chaoyang University of Technology, Taiwan

Abstract. Idea association is an important behavior to generate diverse ideas during the conceptual design stage. In the idea association process, the designer links and generates related ideas in conjunction with other participants by idea hitchhiking. By looking for combinations, more novel and useful ideas are found. For understanding how ideas are hitchhiked and combined, we apply a computational tool called DIM and conduct a design experiment to approach this research. Through the analysis of the generated graph-like structure (called idea map), some observations are found and discussed in this paper.

1. Introduction

Design is an interactive endeavor involving the evolution of ideas between two or more participants in discussion, especially during the conceptual design stage. *Idea association* is an important behavior for generating diverse ideas through the dynamic exchange of varied knowledge possessed by the participants (Osborn, 1963). During the design process, designers first apply idea association to generate ideas, which then inspire other participants to generate other ideas by building on other ideas (or *idea hitchhiking*). By looking for combinations, more novel and useful ideas are found (Lugt, 2000). These ideas will serve as leads to development of possible design alternatives or solutions towards diverse problems (Petrovic, 1997; Lai, 2005). Therefore, idea association can be regarded as the first step to trigger the interaction among the participants.

Since ancient times idea association has been considered an important technique in linking internal human thought with the external living environment (Rapaport, 1974). In the design domain, idea association focuses on the process of "linking" among distributed knowledge (Lai, 2005;

A Dong, A Vande Moere & JS Gero (eds), CAADFutures'07, 557–570.

Lai and Chang, 2006). By linking the designer's long-term memory internally and the various participants' knowledge externally, diverse design ideas can be generated. In the linking process, idea hitchhiking is an important guideline to link and generate new ideas in conjunction with other participants' ideas that have been generated (Osborn, 1963).

Therefore, idea hitchhiking focuses on the transformation process of design ideas. This transformation process, which one idea leads to another idea, depends on their relationships. Goldschmidt (1995) and Lugt (2000) indicate that the relationships among generated ideas play an important role in the idea association process. They call such relationships as *design move* and *linking* respectively. In the computational domain, such transformation process implies the transformation among the design states.

2. Transformation Process within Idea Hitchhiking

According to our pilot studies, there are two levels of transformation process within idea hitchhiking: idea level and participant level (Figure 1). The three principles of idea association provide the transformation of design states of ideas through reminding in the idea level. The three principles (including *similarity*, *contrast* and *contiguity*) are originally identified by the Ancient Greeks. In the participant level, role-playing supports the transformation of design states of participants through communication. Through the two levels of transformation process, designers seek combinations among the hitchhiked ideas in order to develop possible design solutions.

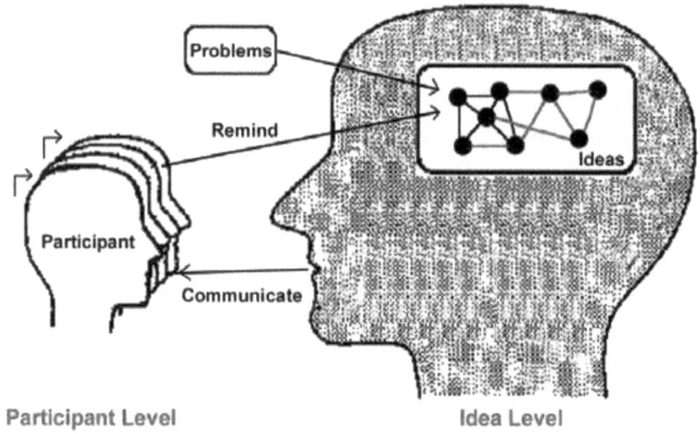

Figure 1. Two levels of transformation process: participants and ideas

Ideas need to be somewhat related to the task at hand and they need to provide some kind of a solution (Lugt, 2000). Thus an idea can be considered as a solution for solving a specific problem within a given task. For solving the design problems, designers are used to decomposing a design into several architectural elements and using the attributes of these elements as keys to search for relevant ideas within a particular design case (Maher et al. 1995). They also are unique in their capacity to use symbols to represent the meaning of ideas and to construct relationships between ideas that explain how things appear or function.

2.1. USING THREE PRINCIPLES OF IDEA ASSOCIATION

As mentioned before, the three principles of idea association: similarity, contrast and contiguity, are used to link ideas (Lai, 2005). Similarity principle links ideas with similar attributes; conversely, contrast principle links different ideas based on their dissimilarity. The reasoning relationship between different ideas can be linked using the contiguity principle. However, these principles can differ according to the context and type of ideas that are exchanged.

In the idea association process, designers apply the similarity principle to remind design ideas with ‘similar’ solutions. However, the contiguity principle can be applied to find the same solutions for ideas with different design problems. Because designers often describe design concepts using conceptual vocabulary (Oxman, 1994), contrasting conceptual vocabulary can be used to remind contrasting design ideas, such as public and private, solid and void, linear and center, etc. These three principles, which embody the different relationships among the ideas, provide the mechanism of transformation process of design ideas.

2.2. USING ROLE-PLAYING

Idea association involved dynamic action and reaction of the participants’ internal and external knowledge through communication. In the idea association process, designers always play the different roles and then utilize the different principles described above to connect and generate diverse ideas. For example, when designing a house, designers sometimes play the role of the client to link conceived ideas with a real-life situation, before slipping back into their primary role of designer and exploring further design possibilities suggested by the experience.

There are two kinds of interactions within the role-playing: internal interaction and external interaction. In the internal interaction, each participant plays different roles and uses different principles to link ideas to the long-term memory. To generate ideas in conjunction with those of other participants, each designer interacts with the other participants as well as the external design situation in the external interaction. This interaction also directly encourages the designer to play different roles and use different principles to link their ideas. The two interactions follow a sequentially ordered process for exchanging information.

2.3. SEEKING COMBINATIONS

Through the two levels of transformation process within idea hitchhiking, the hitchhiked ideas provide designers the guideline to look for combinations. Therefore, more novel and useful ideas are found. These ideas will serve as leads to development of possible design alternatives or solutions towards diverse problems. Simultaneously, most ideas can be improved upon by modifying their attributes. In our previous design experiment (Lai, 2005), a designer combined three related ideas to develop a design alternative for solving the circulation problem in a brainstorm meeting. The three ideas are "floating space", "elevator entrance" and "courtyard" which are inspired from the design cases of Villa Savoye by Le Corbusier, Maison a Bordeaux designed by Rem Koolhaas and the traditional Taiwanese row house respectively (Figure 2).

Due to the characteristics of the transformation process (such as reflection, correlation and confliction), it is hard to understand how design ideas are hitchhiked and combined in the real design situation. Therefore, this paper adopts a computational tool called DIM (Dynamic Idea Maps) to understand the mechanisms within the transformation process as well as find some computational advantages for supporting idea hitchhiking under real design situations.

Figure 2. An idea sketch inspired from three design cases

3. DIM: A Design Tool for Representing the Transformation Process of Design Ideas

DIM proposed by Lai and Chang (2006), which applies the mechanisms of case based reasoning (CBR) and software agent (agent), is a computer-support system for supporting the distributed linking in the idea association process. Through linking distributed and related ideas automatically, a graph-like structure (called *idea map*) of nodes (ideas) and arcs (links) is generated (Figure 3). The idea map, which represents the transformation process of ideas and their relationships, help us approach this research. Its components and technologies are described in the following sections.

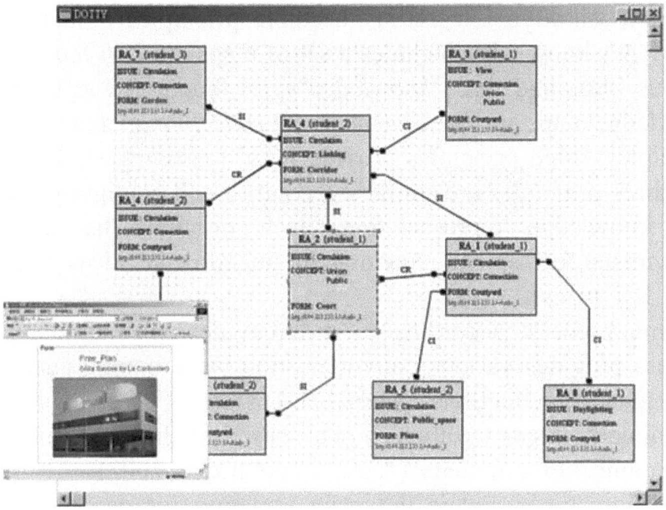

Figure 3. A generated idea map

3.1. DIM COMPONENTS

DIM includes two kinds of components: agent entities and design knowledge. Agent entities are assigned to different sub-tasks that are decomposed from a specific design task. According to different design situations, these agent entities collaborate to generate design ideas and links. There are five types of agent entities: role agent (RA), user agent (UA), director agent (DA), stage agent (StA) and scene agent (ScA). Each RA has the reasoning skill and memory to link and generate ideas. The ScA controls the list of RAs and time duration in each scene. StA is in charge of storing the design outcomes. UA and DA are regarded as the user interfaces that provide human designers to interact each other in the DIM environment. Through the DA or the UA, participants (human designers) can individually load different RAs to play (linking and generating ideas) in sequential scenes which are controlled by ScAs. The design outcome (an idea map) in each scene is automatically stored in the StA's repository.

Three kinds of design knowledge support the behaviors within agent entities mentioned above. They are *knowledge*, *principles* and *linking process*. Knowledge represents design ideas and memory organization within agent entities. Principles provide the capability to allow agent entities to link diverse ideas dynamically. Through linking process in the internal and external interactions, these agent entities can interact various design situations dynamically. The details are described as follows:

1. Knowledge: In DIM, ICF (issue, concept and form) schemata proposed by (Oxman, 1994) mainly represent knowledge within RAs' long-term

memory. Through integrating the three principles of idea association, each RA's knowledge includes a set of maps: an *ICF map* for installing various ideas and three *knowledge maps* functioned as dictionary. The knowledge maps are the *issue map*, the *concept map* and the *form map*.

2. Principles: three principles provide RAs' reasoning skills to link ideas. The three principles are similarity, contrast and contiguity. Based on the ICF knowledge representation, each principle has an individual mechanism for textual matching to link diverse ideas within various RAs' ICF maps.
3. Linking process: according to different design situation, the linking process provides various communication ways among agent entities in two kinds of interactions: internal and external. These agent entities can dynamically interact with each other based on the mechanisms of Agent Communication Language (ACL) (Wooldridge, 2002).

In addition, the *script* is the main structure for describing sequential events including the list of RAs, the acting of RAs, performing time duration and so on. Through the sequential events, the agent entities interact dynamically each other in different design situations.

3.2. DIM TECHNOLOGIES

The multi-agent environment of DIM is implemented on top of JADE (Java Agent Development Framework) (JADE, 2005) with JESS (Java Expert System Shell) (JESS, 2005) as the reasoning engine inside the agents. The ACL among these agents is based on the FIPA (Foundation for Intelligent Physical Agents) communication language (FIPA, 1999). In DIM, each UA (including DA) has an individual FIPA platform to control these agents. These FIPA platforms are communicated by using the HTTP message transport protocol to exchange ideas emanating from different geographical locations.

4. Design Experiment

The design experiment was held in a computer laboratory (Figure 4). In the experiment, we chose three architecture students (fourth grade) as participants to keep the group process simple and observable. They were $Student_{1}$, $Student_{2}$, and $Student_{3}$. We expected the group members to be very fluent in the idea association process. They were accustomed to working together. All participants with similar design domain knowledge were familiar with the DIM environment.

Figure 4. The design environment

The purpose of this meeting was to develop design strategies for the spatial organization of a single-family row house by generating ideas during the conceptual design stage. The duration time of the meeting was 10 minutes. The addressed design problem was daylight. Besides, the three participants were asked to insert three additional role agents (RAs) to help in the design task. Three RAs inserted by $Student_{\_1}$ are RA_1, RA_2 and RA_3. Three RAs inserted by $Student_{\_2}$ are RA_4, RA_5 and RA_6. Three RAs inserted by $Student_{\_3}$ are RA_7, RA_8 and RA_9.

In DIM, a design task of linking ideas is called *play*. A play includes three steps: initializing a play, editing a script, and directing a play. Each step has its individual window for participants to input related information. Additionally, only DA can edit the script of the design knowledge of ScAs and StA. In the play, $Student_{\_1}$ is the DA. $Student_{\_2}$ and $Student_{\_3}$ are UAs. The order of generating ideas is $Student_{\_1}$, $Student_{\_2}$, and $Student_{\_3}$.

4.1. INITIALIZING A PLAY

There are two steps in the initialing play: loading agents and linking agent platforms. In the step of loading agents, each participant loaded his agents that will join this play by inputting the agents' AIDs (agent identities) and their Java class paths. For example, $Student_{\_1}$ should load and input the information of a StA, a ScA and three RAs. In the step of linking agent platforms, the three participants added remote agent platforms of other participants. Through HTTP message transport protocol, they exchanged ideas emanating from their JADE agent platforms. These agents in the

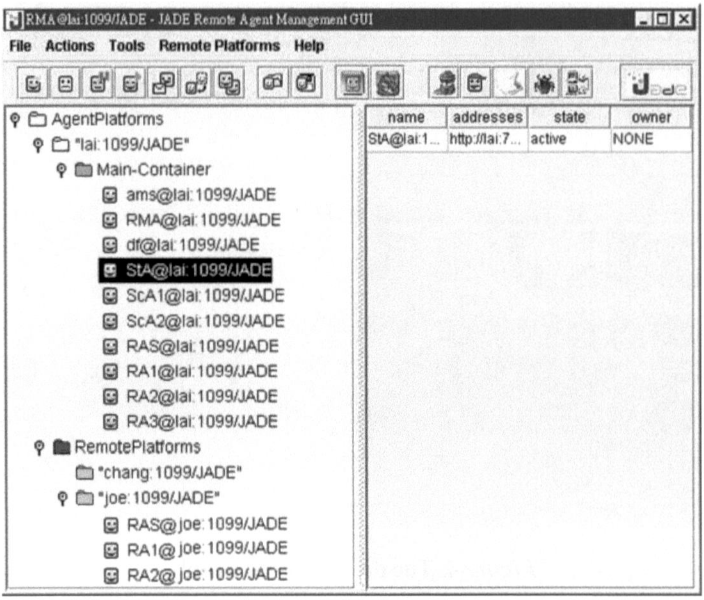

Figure 5. Agent management GUI

different JADE agent platforms can be visualized and controlled through the Agent Management GUI (Figure 5).

4.2. EDITING A SCRIPT

After loading agents and linking agent platforms, Student$_{_1}$ should input the design knowledge of StA and ScA through the Script Editor GUI (Figure 6). Student$_{_1}$ first input the AID of StA (StA@lai:1099/JADE) in the Receivers slot. He also input the information in the Content slot. The information included the design task (row_house), the design problem (daylight) and the duration time (10) (seen in Figure 6). In the same slots of the Script Editor GUI, Student$_{_1}$ then input the AID of ScA and the ScA's information including the design problem, the duration time, the number of RAs and RAs' skills (similarity, contrast or contiguity).

4.3. DIRECTING A PLAY

After Student$_{_1}$ finished editing the script, Student$_{_1}$, Student$_{_2}$, and Student$_{_3}$ started to generate design ideas. Student$_{_1}$ first input the information in the Content slot in the Script Editor GUI. The information included issue, concept, form, RAs' AIDs and types of principles. Then, DIM automatically generated an idea and a link that connected into the original idea map (seen in Figure 3). According to the order of generating ideas, other participants followed the same way as Student$_{_1}$ to generate ideas and links within the

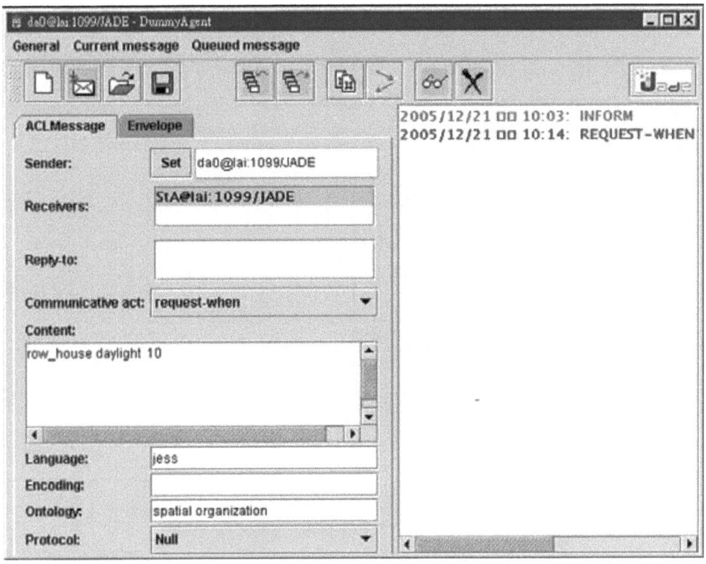

Figure 6. Script editor GUI

duration time. When the time (10 minutes) was up, DIM automatically terminated the play. The outcome of the play is shown in Figure 7.

5. Analysis and Observations

In the generated idea map (Figure 7), each box as an idea includes four kinds of information. They are the AID of RA that generates this idea and the ICF (issue, concept and form) value within this idea. Each arc (or link) between the two boxes represents a kind of relationships including similarity (SI), contrast (CR) or contiguity (CI). For example, the idea (in the right bottom corner) is generated by RA_8. The value of ICF is daylight, interaction and hole, and cutting wall and URL which can be hyperlinked to a specific design case (seen in Figure 3). This idea has three links (SI) which connect to other three ideas generated by other RAs (RA_5, RA_1, RA_1).

In order to understand the mechanism of the transformation process, participants used the generated idea map to seek combinations. Each participant was asked to develop two more design alternatives for solving the problem of daylight in 20 minutes by drawing idea sketches (Figure 8). According to their design alternatives, they should individually frame the range of the selected ideas and their relationships (dotted-line area in Figure 7) in this idea map. In the framed range, the ideas and different types of links are labeled and numbered for our analysis. The meeting process was also recorded on videotape to complement insufficient information of the analysis.

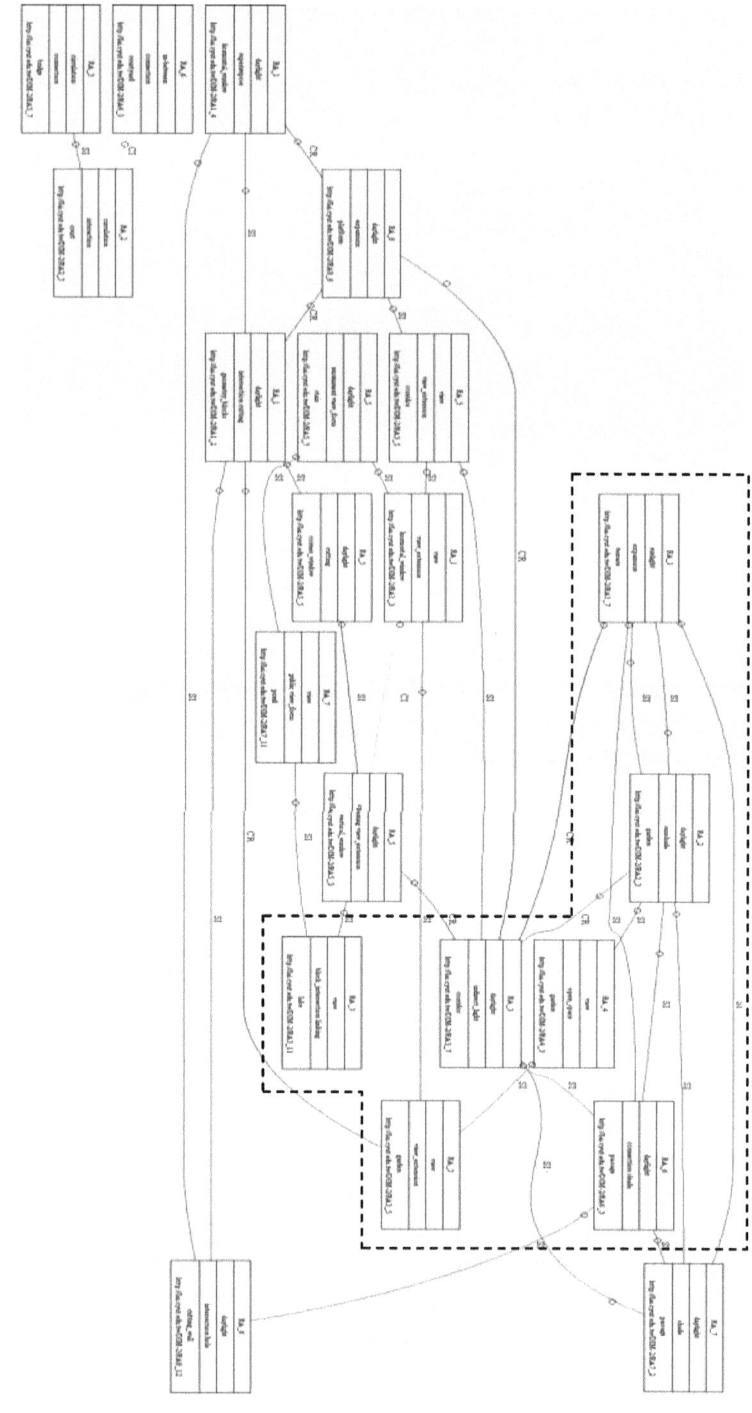

Figure 7. The generated idea map and the framed range (dotted-line area)

Figure 8. An idea sketch by Student$_{_1}$

5.1. ANALYSIS

In this experiment, the participants generated an idea map including 21 ideas and 34 links (seen in Figure 7). Within the 21 ideas, there were three new design problems (issues) and 18 new design solutions (concept and form). The three new design problems were circulation, view and ventilation. Within the 34 links, there were 21 similarity links, 9 contrast links and 4 contiguity links.

Based on the idea map, Student$_{_1}$,, Student$_{_2}$, and Student$_{_3}$ developed three, two and three design alternatives respectively through seeking combinations. The number of ideas and links (including different principles of links) within the framed range of design alternatives are shown in Table 1. In the Table 1, the Case 1 developed by Student$_{_1}$ composes of 5 ideas and 5 links including 3 similarity links, 1 contrast link and 1 contiguity link. Through the analysis, some observations are found as described in the following section.

TABLE 1. The number of ideas and links in different design alternatives

Participants	Student$_{_1}$			Student$_{_2}$		Student$_{_3}$		
Design alternatives	Case1	Case2	Case3	Case1	Case2	Case1	Case2	Case3
Ideas	5	5	5	4	5	7	6	7
Links	5	4	4	4	4	6	6	7
Similarity	3	3	2	2	2	5	5	5
Contrast	1	1	2	2	2	1	1	2
Contiguity	1	0	0	0	0	0	0	0

The transformation process of idea hitchhiking is also related to the transformation of design problems. While the contiguity link is applied to find different design problems with same solutions, the analysis also quantifies the links within the ideas that has the contiguity link. The purpose is to understand how the designers decide the priority of the design problems. The number of the different types of links within the different design problems is shown in Table 2. In Table 2, the circulation problem has 5 links including 3 similarity links, 1 contrast link and 1 contiguity link. All participants selected the circulation problem as the first priority for problem solving in the next scene.

TABLE 2. The number of different types of links within the three design problems

Problems	Circulation	View	Ventilation
Links	5	3	2
Similarity	3	2	0
Contrast	1	0	1
Contiguity	1	1	1
Participants	Student$_{_1}$, Student$_{_2}$, Student$_{_3}$	No	No

5.2. OBSERVATIONS

The three principles of idea association and role-playing provide the effective mechanisms for the transformation process within idea hitchhiking. Thus, correlated ideas and their relationships can be generated reflectively. When the designer does not agree with other participants' ideas, he/she can dynamically change the roles or principles to solve such design *confliction.* Another important lesson we learned is *consonance.* The ideas with most consonance with others will be selected as a candidate (called *key idea*). The key idea provides an important start point for participants to search (including depth search and breadth search) for other alternative ideas to seek combinations. Besides, several mechanisms of ideas hitchhiking are found as described below.

- Based on the consonance, the combined ideas are below 7 ideas. The number seems to reflect the limitation of working memory, which is proposed by Miller (1956). Besides, these combined ideas mostly compose of more links than other ideas that are not combined.
- Three types of principles have the different functions for transforming ideas. The similarity link and the contrast link offer an important guideline for seeking combinations. The contiguity link provides the indication for participants to decide the priority of design problems.
- The transformation process of idea hitchhiking can be re-used and integrated with the new transformation process. The combined transformation process gives participants another alternative for seeking combinations.

In addition, some computational advantages that support idea hitchhiking under real design situations are found in DIM environment. They are 1) to provide three means for collaboration, including human-to-human, human-to-machine and machine-to-machine; 2) to automatically connect blocked linking processes of idea association and 3) to dynamically add the design knowledge to further the agents' learning.

6. Conclusion

Idea hitchhiking focuses on the transformation process of ideas and their relationships during the conceptual design stage. There are two levels of transformation process within idea hitchhiking: idea level and the participant level. Through the two levels of transformation process, designers seek combinations among the hitchhiked ideas in order to develop possible design solutions toward the problems. DIM provides an effective design tool to understand the mechanisms of the transformation process.

Through the design experiment, some mechanisms (such as design confliction and consonance) within the idea hitchhiking and the computational advantages of DIM are found and discussed in Section 5.2. There is a drawback from our design experiment. It is the information visualization with the complexness of the maps when they come to be real uses.

The research will provide an essential prerequisite of preparation for supporting distributed linking process of idea association in any creative problem solving meetings. Participants (human or computers) can hitchhike and combine related design ideas to serve as leads to development of possible design alternatives without the barriers of geographic limitations and different time zones.

References

FIPA: 1999, Specification part 2-Agent communication language

Goldschmidt, G: 1995, The designer as a team of one, *Design Studies*, 16(2), pp. 189-209

JADE: 2005, http://jade.tilab.com/

JESS: 2005, http://herzberg.ca.sandia.gov/jess/

Lai, IC: 2005, Dynamic Idea-Maps: A Framework for Linking Ideas with Cases during Brainstorming, *International Journal of Architectural Computing*, 4(3), pp. 429-447.

Lai, IC and Chang, TW: 2006, A Distributed Linking System for Supporting Idea Association in the Conceptual Design Stage, *Design Studies*, **27**(6), pp. 685-710

Van der Lugt, R: 2000, Developing a graphic tool for creative problem solving in design groups, *Design Studies*, **21**(5), 505-522

Maher, ML, Balachandran MB and Zhang DM:1995, *Cased-Based Reasoning in Design,* Lawrence Erlbaum Associates, Mahwah, N.J.

Miller, GA: 1956, The magical number seven, plus or minus two: Some limits on our capacity for processing information, *The Psychological Review*, **63**, pp. 81-97

Osborn, AF: 1963, *Applied Imagination: Principles and Procedures ofcreative thinking* , Charles Scribner, New York.

Oxman, RE: 1994, Precedents in Design: a computational model for the organization of precedent knowledge, *Design Studies*, **15**(2), pp.117-134.

Rapaport, D: 1974, *The History of the Concept of Association of Ideas*, International Universities Inc., New York.

Petrovic, IK: 1997, Computer Design Agents in a Brainstorming Session, *eCAADe'97*, Vienna.

Wooldridge, M:2002, *An Introduction to MultiAgent Systems*, John Wiley & Sons Ltd., Chichester.

HOW TO IMPROVE CREATIVITY

Can designers improve their design creativity by using conventional and digital media simultaneously?

ZI-RU CHEN
National Chiao Tung University, Taiwan

Abstract. From previous works, we know that the distinguishing characteristics of design media cause different influence on design creativity. However, the cognitive research about the application of conceptual sketches design by integrating both conventional and digital media simultaneously is absent. In this research, we would like to discuss that can it inspire more creative works if designers use conventional and digital media simultaneously as sketching media to generate conceptual sketches. The results show that using conventional and digital media simultaneously comparing with only using individual media can help arouse creative thinking, cognitive activity and design outcome in the stage of conceptual sketches design. The findings may suggest that the integration of various design media provides one feasible ways to inspire creativity, which can apply to the design training of creativity on education and to the designer's practical operation, but initiates more possibility of new media to assist design.

1. Introduction

1.1. CREATIVITY AND DESIGN CREATIVITY

Making variations on a theme is the crux of creativity (Minsky 1987). Creativity is to break former rules, and then make unexpected and valuable things and ideas (Gero 1996). In 1960's, Getzels and Csikszentmihalyi (1976) presented an important concept, which was the preliminary phase of discovering or devising problem, to added a new phase before Helmholtz's cumulative phase. As a result of the accumulation of previous research, we derive a rough structure of creating process, which is inspiration, accumulation, incubation, heuristic, and verification. Liu (2001) and Lynn's mentioned that someone has to concentrate on some system unceasingly, and

A Dong, A Vande Moere & JS Gero (eds), CAADFutures'07, 571–583.

then creativity might just occur until he mastered the main points of the system.

However, Csikszentmihalyi (1988) thought *creativity* could not be only defined by itself, but must be generally consider “field”, “domain”, and “person”. He brought up the concept of social/cultural creativity. Later, Liu (2000) combined the model of social/cultural creativity with personal creativity from Simon’s problem-solving view (Newell, Shaw and Simon 1962), and then presented a dual generate-and-test model of creativity. Nevertheless, the research mainly discusses the relationship of creativity between personal and design media and therefore does not extend to think about the relation of society and culture.

Creativity is always interested in many fields. Particularly, creativity and design creativity have many interpretations (Boden 1991; Gero and Maher 1993; Kim 1990; Sternberg 1988). The design process is generally thought five stages, analysis, concept design, preliminary design, fine design, and production. Among the process, the stage of concept design is the behavior of conception of bringing up temporal solutions (Jones 1992). The Behavioral and Gestalt school take the mental careers of this stage as “black box” (Rowe 1987).

1.2. THE SIGNIFICANCE OF CONVENTIONAL AND DIGITAL MEDIA IN THE PROCESS OF CONCEPTUAL SKETCHES

In the early conceptual design process, designers use large number of sketches and drawings (Purcell and Gero 1998). Furthermore, the sketch as a design tool can inspire the designer while increasing the creativity of the designer’s work (Goldschmidt 1994). Mitchell (1993) also indicated the image recognize of sketches behavior was the main origin of creativity. Design thinking is viewed as a creative thinking process that transforms designers’ mind to its corresponding visual image (Nagai et al. 2003). The sketches were the start of creativity inspiration (Tversky 1999). Therefore, the drawing process of sketches included a lot of creative thinking and process, and previous work showed that the freehand sketches by conventional media have been believed to play an important role in processes of the creative design thinking (Goldschmidt 1991; Schön and Wiggins 1992; Goel 1995; Suwa et al. 1997; Verstijnen et al. 1998). Most of these studies have used freehand sketches as a media to analyze the design activity. Also, digital sketching as a media can be studied, as there is little research on comparing the traditional versus digital media (Bilda and Demirkan 2003).

Many studies have verified that using conventional media in the conceptual sketches arouse creativity (Goldschmidt 1991; Schön and Wiggins 1992; Goel 1995; Suwa et al. 1998). Furthermore, with the emergence of digital media recently, there are more and more researches an increasing number of studies have investigated on the influence on creativity of digital media. After computer media stepped in to design activity, computer-aided-design made a lot of changes in all the design process. Recently, many design-based studied of creativity have investigated to the field of design operations and attempted to identify the possibility of combining creative activities with computer use (Gero and Maher 1993; Mitchell 1993; Gero 1995, 1996; Boden 1998). Consequently, digital media have been utilized to apply creative activities, which generated the unexpected discovery in early design processes (Boden 1998; Chen 2001; Gero and Maher 1992; Mitchell 1993). Additionally, Mitchell (2003) believed that there was the absolute correlation existed between media and and creativity, and that the tools used are important to art and design. Furthermore, Mitchell also argued that digital science and creativity can make up for deficiencies in human being's creative thinking. Most of previous research determined that conventional and digital media influence design creativity. Therefore, this study attempts to understand design creativity phenomena using conventional and digital media.

2. Problem and Objective

This study first investigated the design behavior of practical designers familiar with both conventional and computer media. These designers utilize conventional and digital media simultaneously when producing conceptual sketches. Interestingly, designers are unaware of the correlation between creative thinking and design media in this process and don't pay close attention to it. Why designers choose two types of the media simultaneously when sketching conceptual processes, and then whether they can inspire more creative idea by using conventional and digital media simultaneously.

Different design media have different affects on design creativity; however, because of different research problem and objective, previous works only discussed that the effect of the individual media on design creativity (e.g., Chen 2001; Coyne and Subrahmanian 1993; Goldschmidt 1991, Goel 1995; Liu 2001; Mitchell 1993; Verstijnen et al. 1998). Therefore, the author feels like adding to discuss using two types of the media simultaneously in the design process, and this study investigates whether it could inspire increased creativity when designers use conventional and digital media simultaneously as sketching media to generate conceptual sketches? This study also examines some phenomenon of combining both conventional and digital media on design creativities in the conceptual sketches and compares them with that when using an individual media. If designers using conventional and digital media simultaneously during conceptual processes have more creative ideas than only using one media of them, it would follow that using diversified media can help enhance design creativity.

3. Methodology and Steps

Cross (1999) brought up for almost forty years the kinds of methods for researching the nature of design thinking that have been used have included *interviews with designers*, *observations and case studies*, *protocol studies*, *reflection and theorizing*, and *simulation trials*, and then interviews with designers, observations and case studies, and protocol studies all are suited to the interaction of designers and design tasks. The research mainly discusses the relationship of creativity between design media and conceptual sketches. However, when designers drew sketches by using design media at the concept generation stage of the design process, they don't usually take care of the conventional or digital media in hand. Therefore, if designers are expected to perceive and present explicitly the relationship of media and creativity, it may some of the following difficulties.

- In the design process, an expert designer's eyes, hands, and brain interact frequently himself and he usually takes no notice of his design tools in hand. Most of time he unconsciously changes a suitable design media for his drawing. Because designers commonly don't think more about the issue of design media in the design process, the author maybe not get multi-aspect and deep answers by directly interviewing with designers.
- When designers choose conventional media, digital media or both of them at the concept generation stage of the design process, the reason may be the convenience of situations at that time or the suitability of the design case. However, most of time designers themselves never think about the issue. If asking them to separate into three kinds of situations and to discuss them, it may make confuse and then can't reflect the problems correctly.
- Expert designers almost think the inspiration of creativity is affected by designers themselves. They usually are not conscious of the influence of design media on creativity, even not identify with it. So if to discuss the relationship of media and creativity with designers, the author may get unreal answers.

Because of previous phenomena, the author needed to design an experiment situation in order to get objective data. The author arranged a design task. Different participants individually finished the same task with different design media, and later proceed with a brief interview based on the previous design process. The research mainly observed the influence of creativity on conventional and digital media. Because the sketches in the concept generation stage are the most important and creative stage (Purcell and Gero 1998; Goldschmidt 1994), the research concentrates the data on the stage of conceptual sketches to collect and analyze. The use of sketches is mainly at the early concept generation stage of the design process; therefore, the research defines sketches as all the conceptual drawings before deciding the final case.

The research consists of two parts. The part one also includes two stages. At stage one, there are three experiments in a protocol analysis of retrospective reports. Three participants individually worked on a design task while drawing sketches by skilled in conventional media, digital media, and both conventional and digital media simultaneously as design tools. At stage two, the author interviews the designers based on the precious process of experiments. After these three experiments are completed, the second part is the analysis of the reported verbal data and visual image from the stage of conceptual sketches during the design task. The data is discussed with two aspects, creative thinking processes and design results. Before the experiments, the warm-up experiments should be accomplished to prove that the chosen subjects are suitable for the experiments.

3.1. EXPERIMENTS

The most typical method for analyzing subjects' cognitive processes is and has been concurrent thinking-aloud verbal reports (Ericsson and Simon 1993). The method is extensively applied to the research of design activities. However, previous works indicated that talking aloud may adversely interfere with participants' perceptions during their sketching activities (Ericsson and Simon 1993; Lloyd 1995; Suwa and Tversky 1997). Edwards (1986) also mentioned that there are two cognitive modes in human's brain, the L-mode of vocabulary and the R-mode of vision. If people draw and talk at the time, there will be conflict between L-mode and R-mode. So they can't work simultaneously. Therefore, participants were not asked to report concurrently what was going on in their minds, nor were they interrupted by the experimenter during the design task. Their sketching activity was videotaped and the author did not participate in it. Following the design task was the report task which watched their own videotape. Participants were asked to remember and report what they were thinking as they drew each portion of each sketch.

The object of research results expected to suit to all novice designers and students in design schools in order to be the reference of design training of creativity. The study selected participants are from a pool of designers with creative potential, and are not generally acknowledged as creative designers in the world. Thus, all of the participants have already been awarded some design prizes.

In the design task, each participant worked on designing a logo of theater and concert hall through successive for 45 min. The logo included National Theater and Concert Hall of Chinese and English name and presented the human characteristic of performing arts in Taiwan. Because Logo design is the groundwork for various field of design and not the fixed rules and criterions, it is very suitable for the subject of conceptual thinking. It can also be applied extensively later.

3.1.1. The Preparation of Pre-experiment

Due to the difference of design discipline, experience, and background, each participant showed various creative thinking and ideas. In order to reduce the diversity, the author chose ten pieces of the most general but different pictures which were related to the design task and then the pictures would be the start of each participant's conceptual thinking. After participants received the same visual stimulants, immediately they worked on designing the task by using different media.

3.1.2. Experiment One: Conventional Media

The experiment is with respect to the behavior that designers generate sketches while using conventional media in the concept generation stage. It is done according to the traditional sketching method, not concerning about computers. The objective is to discuss the creative thinking of designers generating concepts in his traditional way.

1. Subject A: An expert designer is one who has an excellent ability to generate conceptual sketches using conventional media, and has more than three years of design-based education.
2. Topic: The logo of National Theater and Concert Hall.
3. Tools: Papers, pens, rubbers and rules.
4. Process: Subject A was asked to generate 8-10 idea sketched fitted the demand of the experiment and then selected 2-3 satisfied conceptual ideas and say why.

After the experiment, Subject A was asked a brief interview about his sketches. After experiment one finished, the cognitive behavior of the designer while using conventional media generating concepts was studied.

3.1.3. Experiment Two: Digital Media

The experiment is with respect to the behavior that designers generate sketches while using digital media in the concept generation stage. It is done according to the computer-aided sketching method, not concerning with the conventional media. The objective is to discuss the creative thinking of designers generating concepts in the computer-aided aspect.

1. Subject B: An expert designer is one who has an excellent ability to generate conceptual sketches using digital media, and has more than three years of design-based education.
2. Topic: the same as Experiment one.
3. Tools: Hardware (Pentium D computer, 19inch monitor, keyboard, and mouse), Software (Illustrator CS2).
4. Process: The same as Experiment one.

3.1.4. *Experiment Three: Conventional Media and Digital Media*

1. Subject C: An expert designer is one who has an excellent ability to generate conceptual sketches using both conventional media and digital media, and has more than three years of design-based education.
2. Topic: the same as Experiment one.
3. Tools: Conventional media: papers, pens, rubbers and rules; Digital media: hardware (Pentium D computer, 19inch monitor, keyboard, mouse, and scanner), software (Illustrator CS2).
4. Process: the same as Experiment one.

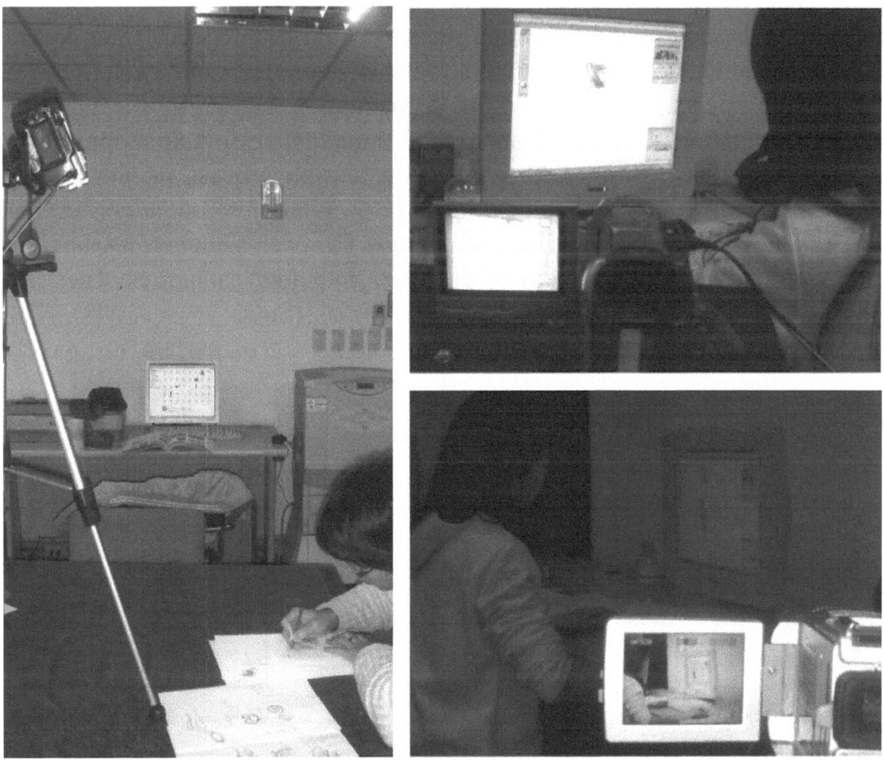

Figure 1. The process of experiment one and experiment two

3.2. BRIEF INTERVIEWS

After a participant finished the first stage, the author interviewed with him at once. There are two parts in the interviews. In part one, according to the used design media of the design task, the participants would discuss it more deeply. In part two, according to each sketch in sequence, the participants of experiment one and experiment two would try to compare with the difference between the use of original media and the added other type of media; and further, the participants of experiment three would try to think what different from only using one of both the media.

3.3. ANALYSIS

After these three experiments are completed, the second part of the method was the analysis of the results from those experiments. The major analytical source was the retrospective data, and the supporting data was the verbal data of the interviews that subjects were asked after the experiments. The verbal protocols of the retrospective data were the main target of my analysis.

A conceptual sketch of the entire design process in one experiment is regarded as a section and then each section would be encoded. After coded, each encoded data of sections are put together to integrate and compare with three experiments. The method of segmentation based on the shift of subject's intention, of the contents of their thoughts, or of their action (Suwa et al. 1998, 2000). Furthermore, the entire design process includes many blocks of contiguous segments. Suwa (1997) brought up a concept of 'dependency chunk'. Each block is a *chunk*. For each segment, it would be simply coded cognitive actions of designers into four categories. They are physical, perceptual, functional and conceptual (Suwa et al. 1998). The entire process of analysis is briefly showed in Figure 2.

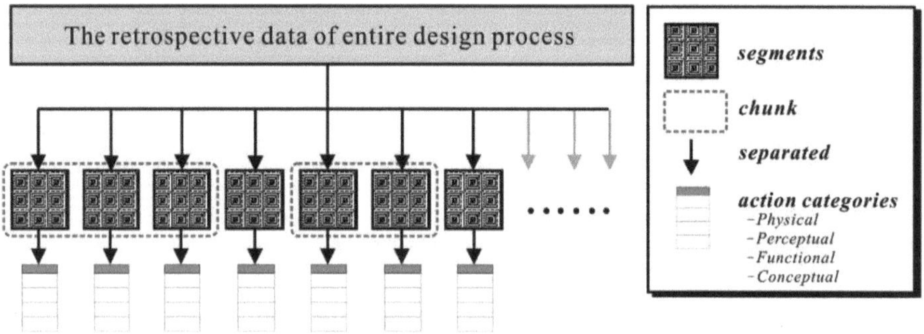

Figure 2. The process of analysis

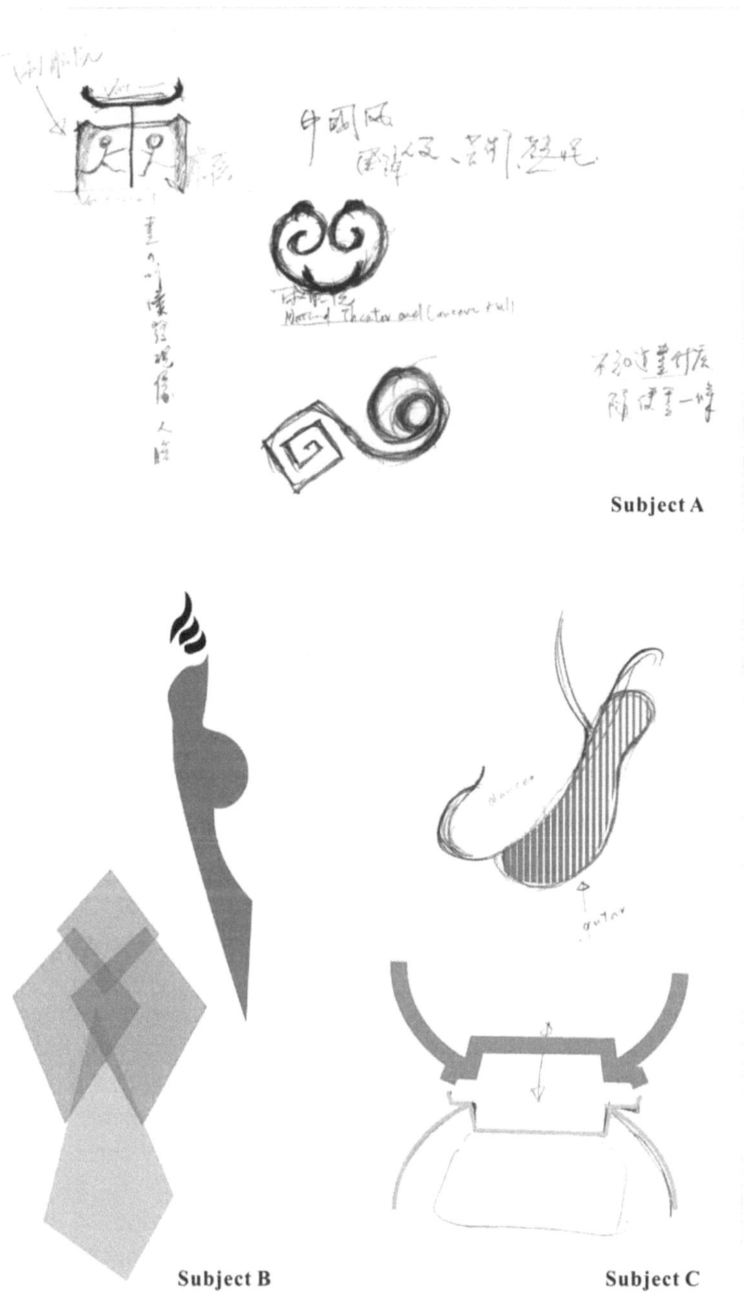

Figure 3. The satisfied conceptual sketches selected by three participants

4. Results

This paragraph mainly discusses some phenomena associated with the design processes of the three participants' and their sketches during the early conceptual design phase. In the aspect of the design process, there are two parts. First, it has more *instants* when using conventional and digital media simultaneously than when just using either conventional or digital media. It is perceived that using conventional and digital media together generates more complex design thinking in the shift of cognitive actions of designers. In conceptual actions, the difference in numbers of *instants* for using conventional and digital media simultaneously and one of them is small. However, the contexts of conceptual actions in experiment three covers both contexts of experiment one by using conventional media and experiment two by using digital media. Second, for experiment three, when the participant changed from one media to the other, the participant could continue thinking about new possibilities and solutions based on existing conceptual drawings. Consequently, it would obtain the longer *chunks* than experiment one and experiment two; furthermore, there are some different styles before and after changes of media. In other words, when using conventional and digital media simultaneously, the designers would think more deeply and the creative thinking would be more flexibility. It would widen the thinking space. Therefore, after changing media, designers could refresh the old conceptual ideas which originally were ceased thinking or could not be thought.

In the aspect of the design results, in the experiment one, the freehand sketches had more ambiguous part and conventional media were easy to be noted. Ambiguous and vaguely defined properties of the design sketches came was recognized as a major influence on the creative process (Liu 1998). By using sketches and notes, the designers could arouse creative thinking. This is because of the characteristics of conventional media. In the experiment two, the designer could easily paint colors, and then consider color combinations. Furthermore, he could start to consider the possibility of overlapping colors; however, the sketches developed using digital media lacked the ambiguous characteristics. In the experiment three, the designer considered the conceptual ideas more deeply than in the other two experiments and continued thinking about others due to owing both properties of the conventional and digital media to operate. The latter sketches would be influenced by the former, such that the former sketches using both conventional and digital media owned two design styles and then affect the latter ones which were not likely to stimulate in the experiment one and two.

The experimental results demonstrate that using conventional and digital media simultaneously, as comparing with using only one media, helps arouse creative thinking and cognitive activity and improves the design outcome in the stage of conceptual sketches design. Particularly, the interaction between two media promotes cognitive thinking to the broader field and find more complex mode of design thinking. The combination of conventional and digital design media not only provides diverse experiential association, but also has more opportunities than individual media to generate creative results. Therefore, the integrating design media may stimulate design creativity in the stage of generating concepts.

Designers can get diverse conceptual ideas and be guided into gradational thinking by using both media simultaneously. Designers generate two different results that can be combined when designing with the two media, thereby promoting creative thinking. All of them can help arouse creativity.

5. Conclusions

The objective of this research was to verify the hypothesis that using conventional and digital media simultaneously can improve designers' design creativity during the early conceptual design phase. However, the process of the experiment three identified the shift between conventional and digital media which mirrors the transformation from analog to digital data. That is time-consuming and inconvenient. Moreover, the research investigated the relationship between personal creativity and design media, but did not extend to discuss the relationship between society and culture. Using conventional and digital media simultaneously to improve designers' design creativity may be insufficient for obtaining socio-creativity results. To produce the socio-creativity must be integrated with numerous elements and efforts and then just will be possible to make it. Even though it is, the results of the research suggest a capable method for promoting design creativity. Furthermore, because only one invited participant using one media, study results are limited by insufficient sampling. This is one of the limitations in the research. If it can be applied in practical and observed quantitatively in the future, we can discuss the results further.

The research found that when using conventional and digital media in combination, designers can get more creative ideas during the stage of conceptual thinking than when just using conventional or digital media. These findings suggest that integrating various design media is one feasible method of inspiring creativity, and can be applied to the design training of creativity on education and to the designer's practical operation. Additionally, in the application of Computer-Aided Design, we have known digital media brought a new face in the world, and have stimulated the creative design thinking, especially during the stage of conceptual thinking. However, the use time of conventional media is longer than that of computer media. In the past, designers only used conventional media, but their creative ideas have never brought to an end. Computer and conventional media have different advantages. If we can integrate these two media, we may be able to find some creative integrated idea or provide a new opportunity to initiates more possibility of new media to assist design. That supply a new way in the development of CAAD. Research into creativity can create a way to improve creativity forward and might help understand *what creativity is*.

Acknowledgements

The author would like to express my sincere gratitude to Prof. Aleppo for his comprehensive help and guidance and especially three participants for the experiments. Also, I am so grateful to my friends in NCTU for all that they had done and my family for their support.

References

Bilda Z and Demirkan H: 2003, An insight on designers' sketching activities in traditional versus digital media, *Design Studies* **24**(1): 27-50.

Boden, M: 1991, *The Creative Mind, Myths and Mechanisms*, Wiedenfeld and Nicholson, London.

Boden, MA: 1998, Creativity and artificial intelligence, *Artificial Intelligence* **103**(1-2): 347-356.

Chen, SC: 2001, The Role of Design Creativity in Computer Media, *The 19th eCAADe conference*, Helsinki, Finland, pp. 226-231.

Cross, N: 1999, Natural intelligence in design, *Design Studies* **20**(1): 25-39.

Csikszentmihalyi, M: 1988, Society, Culture, and Person: A systems view of creativity, *in* RJ Sternberg (ed), *The Nature of Creativity*, Cambridge University Press, Cambridge, pp. 325-339.

Edwards, B: 1986, *Drawing on the Artist Within*, J.P. Tarcher, Los Angeles.

Ericsson, KA and Simon, HA: 1993, Protocol analysis: verbal reports as data, MIT Press, Cambridge.

Getzels, JW and Csikszentmihalyi, M: 1976, *The Creative Vision: A Longitudinal Study of Problem Finding in Art* John Wiley & Sons, New York.

Gero, JS: 1996, Computers and creative design, *in* M Tan and R Teh (eds), *The Global Design Studio*, National University of Singapore, Singapore, pp. 11-19.

Gero, JS: 1996, Creativity, emergence and evolution in design: concepts and framework, *Knowledge-Based Systems* **9**(7): 435-448.

Gero, JS and Maher, M.L: 1992, Mutation and analogy to support creativity in computer-aided design, *in* GN Schmitt (ed), *CAAD Futures '91*, Vieweg, Wiesbaden, pp. 261-270.

Gero, JS and Maher, ML (eds): 1993, *Modeling Creativity and Knowledge-Based Creative Design*, Lawrence Erlbaum, Hillsdale, NJ.

Goel V: 1995, *Sketches of Thought*, MIT Press, Cambridge, MA.

Goldschmidt, G: 1991, The dialectics of sketching, *Creativity Research Journal* **4**(2): 123-143.

Goldschmidt, G: 1994, On visual design thinking: the vis kids of architecture, *Design Studies* **15**(2): 158-174.

Jones, JC (ed): 1992, Design methods, *VNR*, New York.

Kim, SH: 1990, *Essence of Creativity*, Oxford University Press, New York.

Liu, YT: 1998, Where should architecture go in the computer era, *Dialogue* **9**: 31-33.

Liu, YT: 2000, Creativity or novelty?: Cognitive-computational versus social-cultural, *Design Studies* **21**(3): 261-276.

Liu, YT: 2002, Digital Creativity: Conversations with Peter Eisenman, Greg Lynn and William Mitchell, *in* YT Liu (ed), *Defining Digital Architecture: 2001 FEIDAD Award*, Birkhäuser, Basel, Switzerland, pp. 18-25.

Lloyd, P: 1995, Can concurrent verbalization reveal design cognition, *Design Studies* **16**(2): 237-259.

Minsky, ML: 1987, The Society of Mind, *William Heinemann Ltd*, London.

Mitchell, WJ: 1993, A computational view of design creativity, *in* JS Gero and ML Maher (eds), *Modeling creativity and knowledge-based creative design*, Erlbaum Press, Hillsdale, NJ, pp. 25-42.

Mitchell, WJ: 2003, Beyond Productivity: Information Technology, Innovation, and Creativity, National Research Council, Washington, D. C.

Nagai, Y., Candy, L. and Edmonds, E. A.: 2003, Representations of Design Thinking- A Review of Recent Studies, *Journal of the Asian Design International Conference*, Vol.1, Index No. 341 Asian Society for the Science of Design, pp. 1-9, Tsukuba, Japan.

Newell, A, Shaw, JC and Simon, HA: 1962, The Process of Creative Thinking, *in* H Gruber, G Terrell and M Wertheimer (eds), *Contemporary Approaches to Creative Thinking, Atherton Press*, New York, pp. 63-119.

Purcell, AT and Gero, JS: 1998, Drawings and the design process: A review of protocol studies in design and other disciplines and related research in cognitive psychology, *Design Studies* **19**(4): 389-430.

Rowe, PG: 1987, Design Thinking, *MIT Press*, Cambridge, MA.

Schön, DA and Wiggins, G: 1992, Kinds of seeing and their function in designing, *Design Studies* **13**(2): 135-156.

Sternberg, R (ed): 1988, *The Nature of Creativity*, Cambridge University Press, Cambridge.

Suwa, M and Tversky, B: 1997, What do architects and students perceive in their design sketches? A protocol analysis, *Design Studies* **18**(4): 385-403.

Suwa, M, Purcell, T and Gero, JS: 1998, Macroscopic analysis of design processes based on a scheme for coding designers' cognitive actions, *Design Studies* **19**(4): 455-483.

Suwa, M, Gero, J and Purcell, T: 2000, Unexpected discoveries and S-invention of design requirements-important vehicles for a design process, *Design Studies*, **21**(6): 539-568.

Tversky, B: 1999: What does drawing reveal about thinking?, *in* JS Gero and B Tversky, (eds), *Visual and Spatial Reasoning in Design*, Key Centre of Design Computing and Cognition, University of Sydney, Sydney, pp. 93-101.

Verstijnen, IM, Hennessey, JM, Leeuwen, C, van Hamel, R and Goldschmidt, G: 1998, Sketching and creative discovery, *Design Studies* **19**(4): 519-546.

ENABLEMENT OR RESTRICTION?

On supporting others in making (sense of things)

THOMAS FISCHER
The Hong Kong Polytechnic University, Hong Kong and RMIT, Australia

Abstract. In this paper I present and reflect upon a five-year investigation of *designing digital tools for designing* in the area of architectural space grid structures. I understand design as a novelty and knowledge generating conversational process as described by Pask (see Scott 2001) and Glanville (2000). Furthermore, I regard making design tools as a design task in itself, rendering this paper a reflection on *designing for designing*. This paper gives a report on observations I made during the toolmaking study, and subsequently contextualizes these observations using second-order cybernetic theory. This reflection focuses on different relationships between observers and systems, on conditions under which observers construct knowledge and on limits of supporting others in this activity.

1. Background

Embarking on a study of digital toolmaking for design five years ago, I assumed the challenges of the subject to be primarily technical ones and aimed to tackle them accordingly. Chiefly inspired by the use of genetic algorithms in design (see Frazer 1995, pp. 57 ff.), I assumed, without being aware of it, that digital design tools could be made, offered to designers and then be picked up and applied in a way similar to the way hammers, screwdrivers or bulldozers are. In studying digital tools for designing, I initially also assumed that the tools themselves should be of primary interest, for example in order to improve their performance. But as other's studies on toolmaking and tool use in primates and children demonstrate (see Baber 2003, pp. 27-39), the qualities of the tools are not necessarily the most pertinent focus of the study. The focus should also be on us and our relationships with our tools and with our environments. The study outlined here has thus become a journey away from the technically focused

A Dong, A Vande Moere & JS Gero (eds), CAADFutures'07, 585–598.

development of digital design tools towards a reflection of the conditions under which designers make design tools to help themselves and others in making things. Having initially studied second-order cybernetic theories of design, it was only with this change of focus that I found these theories increasingly meaningful and relatable. This brief summary of key milestones in the study and their subsequent framing within some concepts of second-order cybernetic theory retraces and comments on the above-mentioned change. I emphasize some aspects of design and knowledge generation that arose as central insights such as the drawing of distinctions and of analogies, the distinction between digital and analog and the notions of pre and post rationalization. This paper follows the rough sequence of events as they occurred in the study. Observations made during the study are then reflected upon, drawing on second-order cybernetic theory. The paper concludes with remarks that may be interesting to those who are investigating or developing digital tools for designing, and to those who wish to support others in knowledge construction in general.

2. Practice: Toolmaking for Designing Space Grid Structures

The toolmaking study started off driven by a personal curiosity in natural form-finding as well as by a fascination with other designers' interest in natural form-finding processes such as those described in Thompson's (1992) "On Growth and Form". This fascination coincided with an increase in the impact of digital tools in advanced architectural practice (Kolarevic 2003) and with an interest in applying genetic algorithms to design as discussed by Frazer (1995). Regarding digital toolmaking for design as a primarily technical challenge, I approached this study in the way basic research is usually approached and commenced without attaching it to applied design projects. Due to the generic way in which it relates to design, I chose form-finding by tessellating space into grid structures as the task for which to provide tool support. This approach is based on translating packed polyhedra into grid structures by interpreting elements of grid topologies as building components such as struts and nodes (Fischer 2007a, pp. 46-47).

2.1. CELLULAR DEVELOPMENT

In the field of computer-aided design research, biologically inspired genetic algorithms have been applied as a technique for generating design variants (see Frazer 1995). In biology, developmental and evolutionary studies have recently been merged into a unified field (Goodman and Coughlin 2000) dubbed "evo-devo" in recognition of their interrelatedness in the expression of biological form. The lack of a developmental counterpart to genetic algorithm-based computer-aided design offered a starting point for the investigation of the possibility of toolmaking for a new design approach based on cellular development. Inspired by the way in which higher organisms are observed to express their tissues and organs from coded lineages of cells, I co-developed a new tool to translate user-coded digital zygotes into tissues of differentiated forms for design purposes (Fischer and Fischer 2003b). The tool, named *Zellkalkül*, was intended to allow the evaluation of the new method and to be passed on to others for application in design. It provides the user with a virtual space in which cellular tissues can develop from single initial zygotes. Cells pack closely to form tissues and can be visually represented as packed spheres, rhombic dodecahedra or as octet truss space grids. Each cell can be programmed and is able to program other cells to act as autonomous computers performing functions similar to the principles of natural cellular development. Test applications of the tool included re-modeling of the shape of Frazer's (1974) *Reptile* enclosure as well as known biological development processes, namely differentiation in the eye-disk of the fruit fly and the development of nematode embryos (Fischer et al. 2002). Producing previously known patterns, the outcomes of these exercises had little to do with novelty generation. Other, less deterministic exercises produced interesting looking "complex" patterns that, however, did not address a specific applied design project. At this point I decided to explore alternative strategies to identify possible uses of the tool.

2.2. PROGRAMMING TEACHING

As one of these alternative strategies *Zellkalkül* was applied in introducing scripting to design students without prior computer programming skills (see Fischer 2002). This educational application of the tool with its limited representational capabilities was expected to be useful for quick experiments as its constrains formal exploration, thus offering a very "controllable" design space. The tool served as a means to teach basic coding skills and as an environment to experiment with the generation of patterns of different degrees of complexity in three dimensions. Making use of only a limited set of the tool's capabilities, students requested additional features to be incorporated during the course of the subject, such as time and date functions to allow more varied results. The rhombo-dodecahedral cellular packing geometry of *Zellkalkül* is based on close-packed spheres and is not perfectly Cartesian, which posed some challenges to the visual readability of generated tissues. A more comprehensible cubic packing logic might have been more helpful in this context. Despite the possibility to execute cellular code scripts in parallel, the students focused entirely on sequential programming, that is, on scenarios in which only one single cell (usually the initial zygote) executes its code to control larger sets of other, passive cells. This choice of an "outside-in" perspective effectively contradicts the intentions underlying the tool. The students succeeded in generating unforeseen cellular patterns. Due to the limitations I encountered before, they did not use the tool for the intention-driven generation of anything of design relevance outside of the tool.

2.3. SUBWAY CONSTRUCTION

The next attempt to propose a use for the tool was to develop strategies for massively-parallel and decentrally controlled automated construction (see Fischer et al. 2003b). This approach was inspired by previous work in the fields of automated self-assembly and motion planning in swarms of robots (Yim et al. 1997), which happen to share the same rhombo-dodecahedral packing geometry as the cells in *Zellkalkül*. Yim at al. present a motion planning strategy for the self-assembly of cellular robotic compounds. It is based on centralized planning and parallel robotic motion. In reference to the underground growth of plant roots, I envisioned that cellular robotic units could "grow" structures such as subway systems without the need for centralized control. The process should not follow a precisely defined blueprint. Rather, it should aim to fulfill given requirements in a variety of possible ways. Simulating scenarios of this kind was hampered by limitations of available computing power but much more so by apparent principal challenges. Programming of massively parallel maneuvers from a central initial perspective was much more easily envisioned than put into practice. The pragmatic solution chosen in response to this problem was similar to the approach previously used by the students mentioned above. I programmed the zygote with a data structure corresponding to the intended cellular compound and to simply place cells at their target locations as opposed to instructing them in less deterministic ways to autonomously find their way. The result was not a simulation of the envisioned process but an illustration of preconceived outcomes.

2.4. PARAMETRIC SURFACE GEOMETRY

The third strategy addressed *Zellkalkül's* shortcomings with respect to its formal representational capabilities. The basic cellular units assemble into structures that are geometrically largely constrained to the system's packing geometry and produce jagged assemblies. This renders the modeling of most intended surface geometries effectively impossible and was hence seen as another obstruction to applying the tool in designing. The focus of this study therefore moved towards a search for geometrical strategies to support more flexible and detailed representations of form (Fischer et al. 2003b). At the core of this objective lies a dilemma between irregular visual appearance and the need for regularly structured coded control. Individual cells need the capacity to change their polyhedral shape while the number of each cell's neighboring positions, as determined by the underlying grid structure, must remain constant to allow unambiguous scripting control. Seven potential approaches were identified (Fischer et al. 2003a, pp. 442-443), only one of which was found to offer a practical response to the above-mentioned dilemma without involving parametric mapping onto secondary geometric shapes or involving very large numbers of cells. In this approach, all faces of the rhombo-dodecahedral cell representations are split into two triangles, allowing parametric movement of cellular vertex points as well as straightforward data output for rapid prototyping purposes. The resulting flexibility of cellular shapes was seen in analogy to the irregular geometric assemblies observed in natural cellular tissues. However, not all parts of the grid topology permit for parametric manipulation equally. Six of the fourteen vertices of each dodecahedron are parametrically over-constrained and require a geometrically awkward workaround. As mentioned before, the programming of intended developmental processes from the "inside-out" viewpoints of a digital zygote and its descendants is a challenging task for the user of the tool. This task was now further complicated by requiring yet more differentiated control to be exerted from this difficult perspective.

2.5. BEIJING NATIONAL SWIMMING CENTRE

At this point it was taken that the conventional pattern of making generic tools for problems with known solution strategies is not likely to contribute to applied design. Hence, I sought involvement in design projects. The first such project offering itself was the space grid design for the Beijing National Swimming Centre (PTW, ARUP, CSCEC). The structure was required to satisfy the contradicting criteria of cost-efficient regularity in manufacturing and construction and visual irregularity resembling liquid foam contained in a box shape. Posing a challenge with no known solution strategy, this project gave the toolmaking study a "moving target" to relate to. The primary challenge moved away from software development technicalities towards finding possible strategies, adapting tool and outcome scenarios accordingly and evaluating them. Notably, this challenge and approaches to solving it moved temporally ahead of the toolmaking process. Only once a candidate strategy was identified did tool development start. The aspect of the design process that is concerned with making irregular shapes buildable by efficient means is referred to as geometry rationalization. The rationalization approach taken by ARUP, the engineers for the project, was based on a foam structure previously presented in response to the so-called Kelvin Problem (Weaire and Phelan 1994). This approach initially promised a high degree of efficiency (Bosse 2004), which later had to be largely renounced when the structure was cropped to form planar exterior and interior walls. Investigating geometry rationalization, which is usually characterized as

Pre- or post-rationalization, a third approach referred to as co-rationalization, arose in conversations with experts in the field. Before identifying new solutions in response to the Beijing project, I studied the rhombo-dodecahedral grid used in *Zellkalkül* as a potential solution for this project. The result is an irregular octet-truss derivation reported in Fischer (2005), which does however not circumscribe convex polyhedra as required for the structure to resemble liquid foam.

2.6. SELF-SUPPORTING, VISUALLY IRREGULAR FAÇADE SYSTEM

The basic topology of that approach, however, offered itself as a starting point for another applied project, which required a semi-permeable, self-supporting free-form façade. Based on previously developed code and geometry it was possible within a short time frame to resolve the packed dodecahedra into a system of folded sheet metal units, which could be assembled into semi-permeable structures of irregular appearance. Software development followed preceding strategic ideas and served purposes of evaluation, increased productivity and illustration to communicate possible outcomes. In contrast to previous work undertaken in this study from a toolmaker's perspective, I assumed the designer's perspective. I did not aim to support anybody else designing but myself. I provided design proposals for and in parallel to the project engineers, who, after testing tens of their own ideas received my proposals very positively.

2.7. GRID TOPOLOGY DESIGN

Searching for more appropriate solutions to the Beijing problem that have irregular appearances, allow cost-effective rationalization and resemble liquid foam, toolmaking was pursued with less priority. Much of the investigation now focused on non-digital strategies and I engaged more in conceptual design using sketching or just thinking as my main methods of enquiry. Another approach was to use existing tools others have made, mainly for computing convex hulls and minimal surfaces. This led to some new ideas based on systematic combination of convex polyhedra and on "evolving" three-dimensional Voronoi diagrams to approximate liquid foam geometry. These ideas are reported in sections 2.1 and 2.2 of Fischer (2007a). The idea involving combination of convex polyhedra considers configurational laws before a grid topology is assembled while the idea involving existing tools for minimal surface computation is based on generating an irregular grid topology first and then modifying it so as to conform to configurational laws. This reinforced my interest in the different approaches of pre- and post-rationalization and also in co-rationalization, which experts in the field sometimes refer to as "embedded rationale". Pre-rationalization describes a process in which the compositional system is defined before it is used in the actual design process. Post-rationalization takes a designed form and imposes a compositional system onto it retroactively. Co-rationalization is described as a process in which the compositional system is defined alongside and through the process of designing a form. This seems to indicate a new quality in design rationalization. Embedded rationale offers means for parametric transformation and exploration while possible outcomes conform to initially known material and construction constraints. After considering these approaches in relation to my previous work, I went back to the grid structures designed previously and found that some of them were pre-rationalized and some were post-rationalized. This observation in itself, however, turns out to be a post-rationalization and I began questioning if this distinction is of any operative value at the outset of a project. Can it inform a designer before there are ideas? Is any of the three more worthwhile investigating than the others? Before the application of a new idea, can it be known to which of the three approaches the idea will eventually turn out to correspond?

2.8. TEST INVOLVING TWO-DIMENSIONAL LATTICES

As co-rationalization or embedded rationale had so far not received much research attention, I decided to take a closer look at it. Following Whitehead's (2005) description of how embedded rationale was utilized in the rationalization of the Sage Music Centre façade (Foster and Partners), the approach taken was to constrain parametric variation ranges to a limited set of allowed points. As a test, this was implemented in two dimensions only, using Surface Evolver (Brakke 1992) as an engine to perform the parametric transformations. The outcome is reported in section 2.5 in Fischer (2007a). The two-dimensional test with 100 polygons was successful in terms of reducing the number of resulting strut lengths and node angles as well as in terms of achieving visual irregularity. Layering behind the resulting 2D grid a rotated copy of itself and connecting the two grids with a set of cross-beams resulted in a flat wall resembling liquid foam, which I now believe is the most successful solution to the Beijing problem so far. Turning this approach into a co-rationalizing tool I programmed a cursor based tool to assemble Kelvin cells in 3D space and to assign pressure parameters as in the 2D test. Surface Evolver, which triangulates and smoothes external surfaces of three-dimensional structures, did not yield the expected rationalization. Hence, I replaced Evolver with a small algorithm of my own, which involves no smoothing of the exterior surface. The result was once more a generic tool without project application.

2.9. TSUNAMI MEMORIAL DESIGN COMPETITION

Aiming to apply the co-rationalization approach in an applied context, the 3D tool was then applied in a project for the Tsunami Memorial Design Competition in Thailand in late 2005 together with the architects PTW and ARUP (Sydney) engineers. In this project, a sequence of foam-like pavilions was distributed along a path on the site extending into the sea. The tool was made available to the principal designer for application. However, it was operated only by myself, the toolmaker, according to agreements reached in (personal and email) conversations. During the design process, needs emerged for supporting other types of foam, alternative skinning representations and alternative data exchange facilities. The latter two of these were accomplished, while a fundamental re-programming of the space grid topology proved too challenging within the available time frame. The competition entry developed from this project did not win a prize. The winning entry of the first stage, however, also features an irregular space grid. The competition judges recommended that the space grid structure needs "more clarity." If this was addressed at the level of fabrication and construction economics, it would imply the necessity of a geometry rationalization strategy. The further development of the winning entry, though, still does not seem to address the issue of geometry rationalization. Its success indicates that attention to geometry rationalization is not necessarily seen as being of key relevance in the evaluation of a design proposal. This corresponds to the common pattern of relegating rationalization efforts beyond proposal stages.

2.10. POSTGRADUATE WORKSHOP WITH GENERALIZED 3D TOOL

Following the Tsunami Memorial Design Competition, the space grid design tool was extended to make it more generally applicable and suitable for use by others. I have implemented support for the design of three different foam topologies and improved data exchange facilities to other 3D modeling packages. The user interface was extended for greater clarity and overall reliability was improved in order to allow others to use the tool for their design purposes. The tool was then applied in a postgraduate design workshop (Fischer and Herr 2007). The designers chose their tools according to their needs and preferences and did not necessarily comply when the use of a tool was prescribed. Observations at the workshop showed that the toolmaker's perception of a tool's functional principles does not necessarily reflect the tool user's perception and intentions. Designers will likely re-appropriate tools and find their own uses for tools, ways of combining tools and interpretations of output generated with the tools.

3. Theory: Second-Order Cybernetics

The description of design as "the human capacity to shape and make our environment in ways without precedent in nature, to serve our needs and give meaning to our lives" (Heskett 2002, p. 7) is consistent with the theory of homeostasis, which states that living organisms *control* their external environments so as to stabilize their internal environments. Similarly, Glanville (1997) describes goal-seeking behavior as aiming for stability in varying circumstances. This positions the study of (toolmaking for) design in the domain of cybernetics, the theory of communication, feedback and control as presented by Wiener (1961). As an essential feedback and control system, Wiener (ibid. pp. 96-97) explains the function of a thermostat controlling a heater to stabilize the temperature of a room within certain boundaries. Below a certain temperature, the thermostat switches the heater on, above a certain temperature the thermostat switches the heater off. Either side of the control loop have identical numbers of states. Both can be "on" or "off" and the two side's states are mapped onto one of the other side's states. This leaves no ambiguity in the system. While the thermostat is often held to be controlling and the heater to be controlled, second-order cybernetician Glanville (2000) points out that the heater and the warmth it produces control the thermostat just as much. The relationship is circular and control resides between both sides. Any directionality (such as perceptions of intention or purpose) is attributed by an observer. The latter is not independent of the observed and must be considered part of it (Foerster 2003, pp. 283 ff.). By regarding something observable as stable or as instable, the observer places him/herself outside or inside of the control loop respectively (see appendix of Glanville 1997). Glanville (1996) points out that different observers necessarily observe differently but are nevertheless able to communicate as if dealing with the same observed thing. Glanville (1996) also notes that, as receiving a message is not the same as understanding it, the transmission of a message is not the transmission of the meaning. Meaning is constructed from the transmission by the receiver. Building on Pask's Conversation Theory (see Scott 2001), Glanville models novelty generation in design on the control loop, placing interacting designers at one or both ends of it. This also applies to one designer assuming both positions in different roles. With humans being capable of expressing and responding to vastly more than just two states, the conversation between designers involves ambiguity. In contrast to the control loop between thermostat and heater, design communication thus generates uncertainty and ambiguity, which is essential in making new meaning and in designing (see Glanville 2000). Glanville describes exchange loops, depending on whether they involve ambiguity or not as either "restricting" or "out of control." Accordingly, Glanville (1992) distinguishes types of computer support for designing as either (restricting) "tools" or (out of control) "media."

4. Reflection

The study took directions and direction changes I did initially not anticipate. My understanding of the design process, as well as of Glanville's description of designing as a goal-seeking behavior, has changed. Initially, I conceived of design as the uncovering of hidden set goals. Now I see the goals of design, and the path to those goals as unknowable and moving during a given design process. At the outset, I expected the study to develop in a directed, straight-forward manner. Had I had a glimpse of its eventual trajectory early on, I would have found it erratic and confused. Now, I look back at a path that, in terms of issues tackled, took numerous unanticipated turns. However, in terms of what I learned and how it will affect my approach to future projects, the path of the study appears, in retrospect, linear and directed. My ideas about design shaped the study, but the results and insights gained during the study also shaped my ideas about design in a learning process of feedback. The following points summarize the mutual relevance of the outlined study and second-order cybernetics in my view.

4.1. CONVERSATION AND NOVELTY GENERATION

During the study, I began looking at the outcomes of designing (including tools for designing) as articulations within conversations. Similarly to other kinds of articulations, such as those in language or music, there was little point in articulating design ideas without a receiver willing to pay attention. Making design tools for no applied design problem is not much different from making them for no particular user. The design process can be seen as a conversation with another designer or oneself. For this conversation to be effective in articulating design, both parties must be able and willing to listen to what is articulated, to possibly change their viewpoints, then to articulate something back to affect the other's thinking and so forth.

4.2. INSIDE-OUT AND OUTSIDE-IN VIEWS

Involvement in a design conversation entails acknowledging that the participants' ideas of the object of the conversation change during the conversation. Design project and designers change mutually. Taking the stance that the observed does not change, one takes an outside perspective, thus depriving oneself from a chance to change. Aiming to make tools for others, I repeatedly tried to position myself as controlling, assuming the other end not to change and to be willing to simply follow along the path I chose. But in doing so, I ignored that mutual changing permits and generates the ideas and knowledge which constitute designing. The postgraduate workshop showed that creating something new using a tool does not depend on accepting the tool for what it was intended to perform but on the receiver's ability to re-appropriate it.

4.3. MAKING MEANING

I also misconceived the nature of what can be exchanged in a conversation and the conditions under which the receiving end must operate. As articulations cannot contain meaning, it is up to the receiver to make meaning from them. This meaning will be different from the sender's and only thus can it have value with respect to designing. Therefore, there is on the one hand little point in controlling meaning when aiming to generate novelty. On the other hand, this shows the importance of the receiver in conversations. It is due to this side that design is an epistemological process.

4.4. ANALOG AND DIGITAL KNOWLEDGE

Receiving requires perceiving, and all perception is, at its basic level, analog. Oscillations in the air resulting in the perception of sound, changes in brightness and hue resulting in the perception of images and other sensuous stimulations are essentially continuous. Many of our articulations, however, can be perceived as discontinuous at some levels. Words, phrases, objects and other representations are used in discontinuous ways. In these cases words, phrases and objects are used as symbols in generally arbitrary, preconceived and effectively non-negotiable codes. Design seems to be an activity that takes place on the edge between the two kinds of representation, transforming continuous into discontinuous representations. Accordingly, knowledge has been described as existing in "analog" and in "digital" forms (Downton 2003, p. 65-66). This pertains to far more than the way data is entered, stored, manipulated and represented in computers. The tighter a code is controlled and the more its receivers are restricted in its interpretation, the greater is the control that the sender can achieve. The less it is controlled, the greater is the variety that can be achieved when communicating. The difference between analog and digital representations is appositely represented in Goel's (1995) distinction between a seismograph readout (analog) and a telephone number (digital). Wilden (1972, pp. 166-167) describes the activity of "mapping discontinuity onto continuity" as an "epistemological necessity." In the toolmaking study the variance of continuous representation and the control of coded representation became apparent in issues of mathematical precision and scale, the impossibility of hybrids between defined grid topologies, and in the context of words used to represent differentiated meanings to allow clear communication. The words also made it difficult to move away from what they represented.

Communication for the Tsunami competition initially made strong use of (perceived analog) visual material but eventually words like “bubble” and “façade” were used in coded (digital) ways that outsiders would not immediately understand.

4.5. ANALOGIES AND DISTINCTIONS

In coding of originally continuous and ambiguous perceptions, two elementary cognitive operations seem particularly important. One is the drawing of distinctions as described by Spencer-Brown (1997) and modified by Glanville (2002) and Varela, which can be characterized by the statement “this is different from that”. The other is the drawing of analogies as described by Lakoff and Johnson (1980), which can be characterized by the statement “this is like that.” A typical way of drawing analogies is by using metaphors, as it occurred many times in the toolmaking study. This has worked well as a means to inspire and to explain as in the case of PTW’s foam metaphor for the Beijing project. It has, however, not worked in the case of the cellular development metaphor and design. A metaphor is not the same as the phenomenon it refers to. It has no means to attain what is attained by what the metaphor refers to. Knowing developmental principles does not necessarily allow the imitation of natural processes of cellular form finding. Distinctions allow definitions and codes and are essential for control in communication. The tighter distinctions are controlled, the less ambiguous communication can become. The resulting restriction is detrimental to design when variety is reduced but can be helpful when clear communication is needed.

4.6. PRE AND POST RATIONALIZATION

Coded knowledge of something can exist before the event of communication or can emerge only after the event of communication. I found it hard to adhere to the two respective concepts of pre and post rationalization while designing but I found it easy to apply the concepts to what I did in retrospect. The idea of co-rationalization suggests the possibility of rationalization “as-one-goes.” Trying to do so, I was not able to support rationalization in this sense with the tools made in the study. Rather, I managed to support a combination of pre and post rationalization, for which the term “embedded rationale” seems quite appropriate. Examining digital (“notational”) and analog (“non-notational”) representations, Goel (1995, p. 166) refers to an intermediate third form of exchange, which he calls “discursive”. These point to what Glanville (1996) describes as meta-conversation: exchange that aims at making sure similar understandings are constructed on both sides. This type of communication controls the encoding of knowledge at the edge between the analog and the digital "as-one-goes."

4.7. SUPPORTING KNOWLEDGE GENERATION

Relinquishing control in communication is a necessity for making knowledge and hence for designing. Both require coding of uncoded knowledge, which is a co-rationalizing process that would be difficult to code in advance and thus to implement in software. Coding requires the drawing of analogies and distinctions. These cannot be drawn for others. It is the responsibility of the receiver to make meaning. Restriction of communication is practiced by senders who do not understand or who are not interested in novelty (and knowledge) generation. Aiming to support others in these activities, designers of tools for designing are well advised to relate their work to actual projects, to draw on Glanville's (1992) notion of design media or both. In contrast to my earlier plans, I no longer wish to support designers with design tools for projects in which I am not involved, making decisions for those whose responsibilities it is to do so. Instead, I want to share how the attempt to do so has changed me. Others who are perceptive to what I present here might agree that CAAD research needs to consider technology as a facilitator of two-way exchanges and thus exercise sensitivity towards those who are to be supported by it.

Acknowledgements

I gratefully acknowledge the feedback and support from my colleagues at the School of Design at HKPU and at SIAL at RMIT University, in particular Ranulph Glanville, my supervisors Mark Burry and John Frazer as well as Timothy Jachna.

References

Baber, C: 2003, *Cognition and Tool Use*, Taylor and Francis, London.

Bosse, C: 2004, Schwimmsporthalle für d. Olymp. Spiele 2008, Peking, *Archplus* **168**: 33–35.

Brakke, K: 1992, The Surface Evolver, *Experimental Mathematics* **1**(2): 141–165.

Downton, P: 2003, *Design Research*, RMIT University Press, Melbourne.

Goodman, CS and Coughlin, BC: 2000, The evolution of evo-devo biology, *Proceedings of the National Academy of Sciences* **97**(9): 4424–4425.

Fischer, T, Fischer, T and Ceccato, C: 2002, Distributed agents for morphologic and behavioral expression in cellular design systems, *in* G Proctor (ed), *Proc. ACADIA 2002*, Pomona, pp. 113–123.

Fischer, T: 2002, Computation-universal voxel automata as material for generative design education, *in* C Soddu (ed), *Generative Art 2002 Conference Proceedings*, Generative Design Lab, DIAP, Polytechnico Di Milano University, Italy, pp. 10.1–10.11.

Fischer, T, Burry, M and Frazer, J: 2003a, Triangulation of generative form for parametric design and rapid prototyping, *in* W Dokonal and U Hirschberg (eds), *eCAADe 2003 Proceedings*, Graz University of Technology, Austria, pp. 441–447.

Fischer, T, Burry, M and Frazer, J: 2003b, How to plant a subway system, *in* ML Chiu et al. (eds), *CAAD Futures 2005*, Kluwer Academic Publishers, Dordrecht, pp. 403–412.

Fischer, T and Fischer, T: 2003a, Parametric voxel geometry control for digital morphogenesis, in *Proceedings of the 19th European Workshop on Computational Geometry*, Institute of Computer Science I, University of Bonn, pp. 35–40.

Fischer, T and Fischer, T: 2003b, Toolmaking for digital morphogenesis, *in* G Proctor and W Jabi (eds), *International Journal of Design Computing*, Vol. 6.

Fischer, T: 2005, Generation of apparently irregular truss structures, *in* B Martens and A Brown (eds), *CAAD Futures 2005*, Springer Dordrecht, pp. 229–238.

Fischer, T: 2007a, Rationalizing bubble trusses for batch production, *Automation in Construction* **16**(1): 45–53.

Fischer, T and Herr, CM: 2007c, The designer as toolbreaker? Probing tool use in applied generative design, *CAADRIA 2007*, forthcoming.

Frazer, J: 1995, *An evolutionary architecture*, Architectural Association, London.

Frazer, J: 1974, Reptiles, *Architectural Design* **4**, pp. 231–240.

Foerster, H von: 2003, *Understanding Understanding, Essays on Cybernetics and Cognition*, Springer, New York.

Glanville, R: 1992, CAD abusing computing, *in* E Mortola et al. (eds), *CAAD Instruction: The New Teaching of an Architect? eCAADe Proceedings*, Barcelona, pp. 213–224.

Glanville, R: 1996, Communication without coding: Cybernetics, meaning and language (How language, becoming a system, betrays itself), *Modern Language Notes* **111**(3): 441–462.

Glanville, R: 1997, A ship without a rudder, *in* R Glanville and G de Zeeuw (eds), *Problems of Excavating Cybernetics and Systems*, BKS+, Southsea.

Glanville, R: 2000, The value of being unmanageable: Variety and Creativity in CyberSpace, *in* H Eichmann et al. (eds), *Netzwerke*, Falter Verlag, Vienna, pp. 303–321.

Glanville, R: 2002, Francisco Varela (1946–2001): A working memory, *Cybernetics and Human Knowing* **9**(2): 67–76.

Goel, V: 1995, *Sketches of Thought*, MIT Press, Cambridge.

Goodman, CS and Coughlin, BC: 2000, The evolution of evo-devo biology, *Proceedings of the National Academy of Sciences* **97**(9): 4424–4425.

Heskett, J: 2002, *Toothpicks and Logos. Design in Everyday Life*, Oxford University Press, Oxford.

Kolarevic, B (ed): 2003, *Architecture in the Digital Age*, Spon Press, London.

Lakoff, G and Johnson, M: 1980, *Metaphors We Live By*, University of Chicago Press, Chicago.

Scott, B: 2001, Gordon Pask's conversation theory: A domain independent constructivist model of human knowing. *Foundations of Science* **6**: 343–360.

Spencer-Brown, G: 1997, *Laws of Form – Gesetze der Form*, Bohmeier, Lübeck.

Thompson, DAW: 1992, *On Growth and Form*, Dover Publications, New York.

Weaire, D and Phelan, R: 1994, A Counterexample to Kelvin's Conjecture on Minimal Surfaces. *Philosophical Magazine Letters* **69**: 107–110.

Whitehead, H: 2005: *Pre-, co- and post-rationalization*. Personal email correspondence.

Wiener, N: 1961, *Cybernetics or Control and Communication in the Animal and the Machine*, MIT Press, New York.

Wilden, A: 1980, *System and Structure,* Tavistock Publications, New York.

Yim, M, Lamping J, Mao, E and Chase JG: 1997, *Rhombic dodecahedron shape for self-assembling robots*, Xerox Parc SPL TechReport P971077.

CONTACT AUTHOR'S E-MAIL ADDRESS

Chan, CS	cschan@iastate.edu
Chen, Y	yvchen@sfu.ca
Chen, ZR	Ru.zero@gmail.com
Collo, M	matcollo@yahoo.es
Diniz, N	n.diniz@ucl.ac.uk
Duarte, JP	jduarte07@gmail.com
Grasl, T	thomas.grasl@gatech.edu
Herr, CM	ydnac@graduate.hku.hk
Hirschberg, U	hirschberg@tugraz.at
Holzer, E	dominik.holzer@rmit.edu.au
Huang, CC	scottie.c.c.huang@gmail.com
Iordanova, I	ivanka.iordanova@umontreal.ca
Kaga, A	kaga_atsuko@env.eng.osaka-u.ac.jp
Kiang, TB	akitanbk@nus.edu.sg
Koutamanis, A	a.koutamanis@tudelft.nl
Lai, I-C	ihcheng@ms32.hinet.net
Lertlakkhanakul, J	jumphon@yonsei.ac.kr
Mahalingam, G	Ganapathy.Mahalingam@ndsu.edu
Maher, ML	m.maher@arch.usyd.edu.au
Marques, D	dmarques@sfu.ca
Mitchell, J	JohnMI@fbe.unsw.edu.au
Moloney, J	jmoloney@unimelb.edu.au
Moum, A	anita.moum@ntnu.no
Özkar, M	ozkar@metu.edu.tr
Peng, W	wei.peng@csiro.au
Penttilä, H	hannu.penttila@hut.fi
Pickersgill, S	sean.pickersgill@unisa.edu.au
Prousalidou, E	e.prousalidou@uclmail.net

Rosenman, MA	m.rosenman@arch.usyd.edu.au
Ryu, J	jaehoryu@enveng.titech.ac.jp
Schnabel, MA	marcaurel@usyd.edu.au
Seichter, H	hartmut.seichter@canterbury.ac.nz
Smith, G	g_smith@arch.usyd.edu.au
Stavrić, M	mstavric@tugraz.at
Sun, C	apolloc@online.sh.cn
Thomas Fischer	sdtom@polyu.edu.hk
Tsai, HC	tomtsai@mail.nhu.edu.tw
Vande Moere, A	andrew@arch.usyd.edu.au
Wang, X	x.wang@arch.usyd.edu.au
Whiting, E	ewhiting@mit.edu
Yan, W	wyan@archmail.tamu.edu
Zedlacher, S	zedlacher@tugraz.at

AUTHOR INDEX

MIX
Papier aus verantwortungsvollen Quellen
Paper from responsible sources
FSC® C105338

If you have any concerns about our products,
you can contact us on
ProductSafety@springernature.com

In case Publisher is established outside the EU,
the EU authorized representative is:
Springer Nature Customer Service Center GmbH
Europaplatz 3, 69115 Heidelberg, Germany

Printed by Libri Plureos GmbH
in Hamburg, Germany